FOR REFERENCE

ENCYCLOPEDIA OF AMERICAN INDIAN LITERATURE

ENCYCLOPEDIA OF AMERICAN INDIAN LITERATURE

Jennifer McClinton-Temple
Alan Velie

Facts On File
An imprint of Infobase Publishing

Encyclopedia of American Indian Literature

Facts On File, Inc.
An imprint of Infobase Publishing
132 West 31st Street
New York NY 10001

ISBN-10: 0-8160-5656-0
ISBN-13: 978-0-8160-5656-9

Library of Congress Cataloging-in-Publication Data
McClinton-Temple, Jennifer
   Encyclopedia of American Indian literature / Jennifer McClinton-Temple, Alan Velie.
      p. cm.
   Includes bibliographical references (p.) and index.
   ISBN 0-8160-5656-0 (acid-free paper)
   1. American literature—Indian authors—Encyclopedias. 2. Indians in literature—Encyclopedias. 3. Indians of North America—Intellectual life—Encyclopedias. I. McClinton-Temple, Jennifer. II. Title.
   PS153.152E53 2007
   810.9'89703—dc22   2006023762

Facts On File books are available at special discounts when purchased in bulk quantities for businesses, associations, institutions, or sales promotions. Please call our Special Sales Department in New York at (212) 967-8800 or (800) 322-8755.

You can find Facts On File on the World Wide Web at http://www.factsonfile.com

Text design by Rachel L. Berlin
Cover design by Takeshi Takahashi

Printed in the United States of America

VB FOF 10 9 8 7 6 5 4 3 2 1

This book is printed on acid-free paper.

TABLE OF CONTENTS

Introduction   vi

A to Z Entries   1

Appendixes   415

Selected Bibliography of Works
by American Indian Authors   417

Bibliography of Secondary
Sources   435

Contributors   437

Index   447

INTRODUCTION

North American Indians had a rich literature at the time of first contact with Europeans. The principal genres of traditional literature were songs, the equivalent of European lyric poems, which were often put to music before 1700, and tales, which were very similar to European short narratives. Indians continue to employ these forms today, especially in tribal settings, but Indians who are professional authors in North America utilize the same genres as writers of other ethnic groups, that is, fiction (the novel and short story), poetry, drama, and various forms of nonfiction.

The first American Indian to publish a literary work in English was Samson Occom (Mohegan, 1723–92), who wrote *A Sermon Preached at the Execution of Moses Paul, an Indian* in 1772. Occom later published a collection of hymns that included several of his own works. Other early Indian writers of note were Yellow Bird (Cherokee, 1827–67), Sarah Winnemucca (Paiute, 1844–91), and Alexander Posey (Creek, 1873–1908).

Yellow Bird, also known as John Rollin Ridge, published the first novel by an Indian, *The Life and Adventures of Joaquin Murieta, the Celebrated California Bandit*, in 1854. Yellow Bird later published a volume of poems, establishing a precedent of Indian writers proficient in more than one genre.

Few American writers of other ethnic groups have achieved excellence in both prose and verse, but quite a few Indian writers (e.g., Scott Momaday, James Welch, Louise Erdrich, and Sherman Alexie) have done so.

Sarah Winnemucca was a memoirist and historian whose *Life among the Piutes* is a classic. Winnemucca was the first Indian woman to achieve literary recognition. Alexander Posey was a poet and humorist. His verse was generally considered mediocre, but his "Fus Fixico Letters" are appreciated as excellent examples of political satire. They inspired the work of a later Indian satirist, Will Rogers (Cherokee, 1879–1935). Many Americans familiar with Will Rogers think of him as a cowboy rather than an Indian. He was, in fact, both, starting his career as an entertainer under the stage name "The Cherokee Kid."

In the first half of the 20th century, the major Indian writers were Charles Eastman (Sioux, 1858–1939), John Joseph Mathews (Osage, 1894–1979), and D'Arcy McNickle (Cree, Flathead, 1904–77). Eastman lived the life of a Plains Indian until age 15, when his father put him in school. Eastman eventually graduated from Dartmouth and ultimately became a physician. He was active in early pan-Indian movements in the United

States and had a good deal of influence as a public intellectual, rubbing elbows with the likes of Matthew Arnold, Longfellow, Emerson, and Teddy Roosevelt. Eastman reworked traditional Sioux tales for white audiences, cleaning up the racier ones to make them appropriate for children.

John Joseph Mathews's writings were often a surprise to readers of his time, who generally viewed Indians as hapless, impoverished victims. At the turn of the 20th century the Osage had large land holdings in eastern Oklahoma, and when they struck oil there, they became some of the wealthiest people in the state. Mathews attended the University of Oklahoma, where he played football and belonged to a fraternity. After a stint as a pilot in World War I, Mathews turned down a Rhodes Scholarship as too restrictive and paid his own way at Oxford to get a second B.A. Mathews's novel *Sundown* (1934) tells of an Osage, Challenge Windzer, who also attends Oklahoma University and faces many of the same situations Mathews had, though Chal copes far less successfully.

D'Arcy McNickle's work represents the high-water mark of Indian literary achievement before the American Indian Literary Renaissance that began in the late 1960s. His most highly regarded novel is *The Surrounded* (1936), a story of the encroachment of Euro-American culture on the Indians living on the Flathead Reservation in northern Montana. The novel has the mood and power of a Greek tragedy.

The 1960s, a decade of dramatic cultural and political upheaval in the United States, ushered in a renaissance in American Indian culture that embraced literature, painting, philosophy, and, to an extent, music. This renewal was accompanied by the establishment of Native American studies programs in universities around the country and, somewhat later, an economic renaissance for some tribes, based partly on gaming and partly on economic development.

Indian literature was affected most of all. Before 1968, Indians had published nine novels in the United States. Today the number is approaching 300. This difference is reflected not only in quantity of works but in their quality. As good as McNickle and Mathews were, they were not among the top American novelists of their time. N. Scott Momaday and Louise Erdrich are in that select circle: *House Made of Dawn* and *Love Medicine* are undoubtedly among the best half-dozen novels of the second half of the 20th century.

The renaissance in Native American culture began almost concurrently with the publication of Momaday's *House Made of Dawn* and *The Way to Rainy Mountain*. *Rainy Mountain* is a highly poetic memoir and brief history of the Kiowa. *House,* a novel of an Indian veteran's inability to adjust to life on the reservation after World War II, won the Pulitzer Prize in fiction in 1969. Momaday, who gained recognition as a poet before he turned to fiction, originally planned *House* as a series of poems. Momaday's celebrity served as a spur and inspiration to other Indian writers, especially James Welch (Blackfeet, 1940–2003), Leslie Marmon Silko (Laguna, 1948–   ), and Gerald Vizenor (Chippewa, 1934–   ).

Indian writers have a particularly strong influence on one another. Momaday's *House Made of Dawn* features an Indian veteran of World War II who has trouble readjusting to civilian life when he returns to his New Mexico pueblo. Silko's *Ceremony* also focuses on a World War II veteran returning to a New Mexico pueblo, but Silko develops a new literary genre—Momaday calls it a "telling"—to treat the subject. Silko's telling combines the techniques of the modern novel with the subject matter of traditional Laguna legends. Her characters are contemporary avatars of Laguna mythic figures. Momaday borrowed the form of the telling for his next novel, *The Ancient Child* (1989), the story of an Indian artist who turns into a bear. Momaday uses a Kiowa legend as the basis of his novel, but he was also alludes to Gerald Vizenor's hero, Proude Cedarfair, who turns into a bear in *Darkness in Saint Louis Bearheart* (1978), later revised and retitled as *Bearheart: The Heirship Chronicles*. Louise Erdrich pays homage to both Vizenor and Momaday when her heroine Fleur turns into a bear in *The Bingo Palace* (1994).

James Welch wrote principally about the Blackfeet of his native Montana. As did Momaday, Welch published poetry before he turned to fiction, although his first collection of poems, *Riding the Earth Boy 40* (1975), came out a year after his first novel, *Winter in the Blood.* The story of a nameless Blackfeet layabout, *Winter in the Blood* is a comic masterpiece. Students often criticize Indian novels for centering on characters who are footloose, feckless, oversexed, and underemployed—characters like the hero of *Winter* or, for that matter, *House Made of Dawn, Ceremony,* or other novels of the early years of the American Indian Literary Renaissance. One reason for exploring this sort of stereotypical character is that in their first few novels, Indian writers were concerned to show Indians who are authentic—that is, distinctive in their tribal identity, and lack of assimilation into the greater society. And, as ethnicity tends to be viewed stereotypically, it is those characters who leave the strongest impression.

A second influence on characters portrayed in novels by American Indian writers is the archetype of the trickster. The trickster is ubiquitous as an archetype among Indian tribes. Taking the form of man, such as Sendeh among the Kiowa or Napi of the Blackfeet, or an animal, such as Coyote in the Southwest, the trickster plays tricks; is the victim of tricks; has insatiable appetites, especially for sex; and is a law unto himself. Trickster is so central a figure in tribal mythology that it is inevitable that Indian writers would incorporate aspects of him into their fiction. And, if a protagonist is a trickster he is far more likely to be chatting up a woman in a bar than working away at his desk.

Welch went on to write about middle-class Indians, particularly in *The Indian Lawyer,* where the hero, Sylvester Yellow Calf, rises from poverty to become a successful corporate lawyer who eventually runs for a House seat. Momaday's second novel also has a middle-class protagonist, Locke Setman, a Kiowa painter who exhibits his work in galleries in San Francisco, New York, and Paris. Today middle-class Indians are common in fiction, but this is partially a function of the fact that the 1990s saw considerable wealth generated in Indian country.

Leslie Silko was another of the early renaissance writers to win critical acclaim. Her book *Ceremony* led her to receive the highly prestigious MacArthur Award, the so-called genius grant. Both *Ceremony* and *The Almanac of the Dead,* her second novel, excoriate Euro-American society for stealing and desecrating Indian homelands and brutalizing their inhabitants.

The last of the major authors of the first generation of the Native American literary renaissance, Gerald Vizenor, is the most prolific. At last count he had published eight volumes of poetry (most of them haiku), 10 novels, and nine works of nonfiction, and he had written and produced a film. Vizenor is Trickster as contemporary literary figure—"Coyote with a word processor"is the way the Cherokee novelist Tom King puts it. Vizenor's first work, *Darkness in Saint Louis Bearheart,* is a surrealistic look at America after it literally runs out of gas, and the government begins confiscating wooded land on reservations. To escape a group of Indian tricksters and clowns the hero, Proude Cedarfair, sets off on a trip across America, fighting off enemies like Cecil Staples, an avatar of the Evil Gambler of tribal myth, and the fast food fascists of the Ponca City, Oklahoma, Witch Hunt Restaurant. Cedarfair finally escapes the perils of this (the third) world by magically ascending into the fourth world through a vision window in a New Mexican pueblo.

Louise Erdrich begins the second generation of the American Indian literary renaissance. Like Momaday and many others, she was a poet initially, later focusing on fiction. For the most part, her novels are an extended saga of a Chippewa reservation she calls Little No Horse. Loosely based on the reservation where her maternal grandfather was chief, Turtle Mountain, in north-central North Dakota, Little No Horse has become like a character over the course of six Erdrich novels. *Love Medicine,* the first and best regarded of the series, was published in 1984. It covers a period from the mid-1930s to the mid-1980s. Erdrich later extends the saga backward into the 19th century and forward into the mid-1990s, detailing the fate of scores of characters. She begins with the last days of the traditional way of life (including a surrealistic account of the death of the last herd of buffalo on the reservation), continues through the difficult days after the Dawes Act cost the Chippewa much of their land and tuberculosis almost wiped them out, through their misery during the depression, the grinding poverty that lasted until the 1990s, when gaming and a measure of business development lifted most of the survivors into the middle class. The Little No Horse series, presumably still a work in progress, now numbers seven volumes. In addition, Erdrich has published two other novels, two volumes of verse, and several children's stories.

The latest of the Indian literary stars is Sherman Alexie (Spokane/Coeur d'Alene, 1966–   ). Alexie, like many writers, began as a poet but turned to fiction. His earlier works, *The Lone Ranger and Tonto Fistfight in Heaven* (1993) and *Reservation Blues* (1995), take place on the reservation in Welpinit, Washington, a bleak settlement of Housing and Urban Development (HUD) houses where the underemployed Spokane try to scratch out a living. In his later collections of short stories, *The Toughest Indian in the World* (2000) and *Ten Little Indians* (2003), the protagonists are computer programmers, businesspeople, government officials—tribal yuppies from Seattle who are more at home in Starbucks than on the reservation they or their parents left.

There has always been an Indian middle class in America, but it was very small until the Indian economic revival of the 1980s and 1990s finally drew money into Indian country. Contemporary Indian fiction has chronicled the fortunes of the Indians as they trade the miseries of poverty on the reservation for the anxieties of the urban business world.

Indian fiction is the mainstay of the literary aspect of the American Indian renaissance, but poetry is important as well, and not only the poetry of Indian novelists. There are many important American Indian poets who are not primarily novelists, enough so that any selection seems arbitrary, but the leading Indian poets today are probably Simon Ortiz (Acoma, 1941–   ) and Joy Harjo (Muscogee Creek, 1951–   ).

Ortiz writes intensely political poetry, presenting a running critique of American history, primarily focusing on Indian-white relations. His short poems are history lessons from the underside of the American experience, filled with references to Cotton Mather, Colonel John Chivington, Kit Carson, and Black Kettle as well as faceless veterans from 20th-century wars. Ortiz's verse is sharp, but not bitter; ultimately he strikes a hopeful tone. Despite the grim events of the 19th century, Ortiz does not think of whites as the other: He very much considers himself an American. As he puts it in an epigraph to *from Sand Creek* (1981):

> *This America*
> *has been a burden*
> *of steel and mad*
> *death,*
> *but look now,*
> *there are flowers*
> *and new grass*
> *and a spring wind*
> *rising*
> *from Sand Creek.*

Joy Harjo studied painting and theater before she became a poet. Her collections of verse, especially *The Woman Who Fell from the Sky* and *She Had Some Horses,* have established her as one of the leading poets in the United States. In the early 1990s, she formed the band Poetic Justice and began reciting her poems to a backdrop of tribal-jazz-reggae rhythms. Harjo also plays saxophone with the sextet.

Harjo's most striking poems blend crystal-clear conversational diction with surrealistic imagery, for example, in "Nautilaus":

> *This is how I cut myself open—*
> *with half a pint of whiskey, then*
> *There's enough dream to fall through*
> *To pure bone and shell*
> *Where ocean has carved out*
> *warm sea animals,*
> *and has driven the night*
> *dark and in me*
> *like a labyrinth of knives.*

In drama Hanay Geiogamah (Kiowa, 1945–   ) was an early renaissance figure, producing his best-known play, *Body Indian,* in 1972 in New York City. The play incorporates the blackest of black humor in treating the sad condition of a disabled alcoholic named Bobby Lee. Bobby has saved money for rehabilitation, but when he passes out (repeatedly), his friends steal his money, and when that is gone, they pawn his artificial leg. White viewers generally react with horror; Indian audiences find grim humor in the situation.

The troupe Geiogamah founded, Native American Theatre Ensemble (NATE), took *Body Indian* on a nationwide tour, playing at the Smithsonian and a number of western states, including Geiogamah's native Oklahoma.

The other fine playwright of the American Indian literary renaissance is the Canadian Tomson Highway (Cree, 1951–   ). Born in a tent in the middle of a snowbank in northeast Saskatchewan, an area so remote it makes Alexie's Welpinit look like Chicago, Highway made it to the University of Manitoba, then moved to London to study to be a concert pianist. Eventually he received a degree in English, and after working for a number of years in Indian social and cultural programs, he started writing plays. His first work, *The Rez Sisters,* won an award as best new play in the 1986–87 Toronto theater season. *Sisters* is a frank and very funny look at the life of seven women on a Canadian reserve who try to better their lives socially and economically, through bingo. The play became a great success as it toured Canada and was selected as one of two plays to represent Canada in the Edinburgh International Festival. Thomson followed *Sisters* with a play about seven men on a reserve, *Dry Lips Oughta Move to Kapuskasing,* and a musical, *Rose.*

Although it would be almost a century before Indians were producing their own films, Indians have been involved in filmmaking since Pathé Frères hired James Young Deer (James Younger Johnson, Winnebago, c. 1880–1946) and his wife, Princess Red Wing (Lillian St. Cyr, Winnebago, 1883–1974), to give authenticity to their westerns. Young Deer produced and directed *White Fawn's Devotion* and *Cheyenne Brave* in 1911. As time went on, white actors such as Sal Mineo and Tony Curtis began playing Indians, and it was not until the 1970s that Indian actors regained some importance in Hollywood, primarily as actors, when Sherman Alexie's *Smoke Signals* (1997), a film written, directed, and acted by Indians, achieved commercial and critical success.

It is difficult to do justice to American Indian literary renaissance nonfiction here, but it is important to mention a few things. In the area of autobiography, Charles Eastman, Scott Momaday, and Gerald Vizenor have produced important works, and both of the latter men have written numerous essays. However, the major nonfiction writer of the period is Vine Deloria (Sioux, 1933–2005). Deloria's work is impossible to categorize but for political-theological-satirical polemic there are few like him. Deloria's first shot across America's bow was *Custer Died for Your Sins* (1969), a manifesto challenging whites to abandon their stereotypical ideas of Indians. Over the years, Deloria has taken on what he sees as flawed white concepts of religion (*God Is Red,* 1973) and science (*Red Earth, White Lies,* 1995). While some of his ideas are hard to accept—his skepticism about evolution, for instance—Deloria is a master of argumentation and an endlessly fascinating writer.

In short, today Indian literature is flourishing in many genres. Some see it as the most vibrant of America's many ethnic literatures; others view it as a separate anglophone literature. Clearly the Indians of North America are currently producing some of the most lyrical and powerful works in the world.

ABOUT THIS BOOK

Developing a strong, coherent list of entries for this text was a difficult task. What makes literature worthy of discussion? What qualifies a work or list of works to be included in a reference volume such as this? These questions are important for any reference work, but when dealing with works that address American Indian literature, answering them becomes quite complex.

First, there are few templates to follow. Until recently, American Indian literature has been considered only as a footnote to the broader category of American literature. There are few reference works with the scope of this project to use as models for what might be included here. Next, controversies lurk within the question of what does or does not qualify as American Indian literature. For instance, should authors whose status as Indians has been generally viewed as suspect be included here? And what of authors whose status as Indian is unquestionable but whose works seldom, if ever, address issues that we might think of as "Indian," or even contain characters who identify as Indian? As the writer Thomas King has noted, there is no single category that will encompass "full-bloods raised in cities, half-bloods raised on farms, quarter-bloods raised on reservations, Indians adopted and raised by white families . . ." (x). In the end, we decided that authors whose works have made a mark on the tradition of Native literature, whether that mark is positive or not, should be included. Individual entries on such controversial figures and texts address these issues.

Next, geography poses a problem. The contiguous 48 states are obviously what most people think of when imagining where "American Indian literature" might be written. Beyond that, however, questions arise. For instance, Alaska and Hawaii both have a vivid and complex tradition of Native literature. Native Alaskans, however, possess several cultural similarities to Americans Indians in the Pacific Northwest and have always been included in the legal definition of Native Americans. Thus, including the tribes of Alaska in this volume was never really a question. Native Hawaiians, on the other hand, belong to a Polynesian culture and have only recently, in July 2005, been declared to have the same rights, such as sovereignty and rights governing the use and ownership of sacred artifacts and places, as others who have long been considered American Indians. A sophisticated discussion of Hawaiian literature, was, we felt, beyond the scope of this encyclopedia.

Last, there is the question of our neighboring countries, Canada and Mexico. Many works such as this one do not stray outside the boundaries of the United States in their coverage. For us, this made sense in terms of our southern border. Reporting on Mexican literature, and the indigenous cultures of Mexico, requires an expertise that, while it might sometimes overlap with the field of Native American literature, as it surely does among the Navajo, Hopi, and Pueblo tribes of the Southwest to name a few, is nowhere near a perfect fit. That discussion, we feel, would be better left to the editors of Facts On File's encyclopedia of Hispanic American literature. Canada, however, is not so easily dealt with. The indigenous people of Canada, known as First Nations peoples in their home country, have much in common with the indigenous people of the lower 48 states and Alaska. In fact, many tribes, such as the Chippewa (also known as the Ojibwe or the Anishinabe), the Cree, and the Sioux (Nakota, Dakota, Lakota), have ancestral homes on both sides of the border. Remembering that that border is an artificial marker, drawn by European governments without regard to the people living there before it was drawn, is an essential point in the conversation regarding the relationship between Native Americans and First Nations peoples. In addition, there are too many similarities in the cultures, histories, languages, and social problems of these groups to draw that artificial line once more. We include in this volume, therefore, a great number of First Nations authors and their works as well as a long entry on First Nations literature.

Issues of time and longevity exerted pressure on us as well. In most literary reference books, more weight is given to works that have stood the test of time and to authors who have a large and influential body of work. While that remains true here, mitigating factors play a role too. For instance, we include entries on several novels written in the past 10 years, texts that in many cases are the authors' first or second novels. American Indian literature is a field that is expanding, changing, and creating itself as we speak. Being as up to date as possible is more important in this field than in other fields that might have accepted and well-established foundations. Nonetheless, we have also made every effort to include entries on all important Native writers and all the Native works that are commonly taught in high schools and colleges.

Finally, this volume was not an easy one to name. From several possibilities we ultimately choose *Encyclopedia of American Indian Literature.* This was not a simple decision. Indian authors themselves are torn on the matter of what this literature, and these people, should be called. Gerald Vizenor, for instance, says, "The name *Indian* is a convenient word, to be sure, but it is an invented name that does not come from any native language, and does not describe or contain any aspects of traditional tribal experience and literature" (1). Jace Weaver, on the other hand, points out that both *Indian* and *Native American* are instantly contradictory, as the first seems to point to people from India and the second to anyone born in the United States; therefore, he uses the terms interchangeably. Russell Means, activist and founding member of the American Indian Movement, says flatly, "I abhor the term Native American." Means chooses *American Indian* because he "knows its origins" (Means 2). Finally, a 1995 survey by the U.S. Census Bureau showed that the majority of American Indians prefer that term to *Native American,* and the most recent addition to the Mall in Washington, D.C., the National Museum of the American Indian, reflects this preference. However, within the entries themselves, which were written by various scholars in the field, different terms are used to refer to the authors, the tribes in which they originate, and the people about whom they write. Given the responses, quoted from Vizenor and Means, it would seem arrogant to ignore what individual scholars might

prefer. Many of the contributors to this encyclopedia are American Indians themselves, so the terms they use matter to them as well. Many of the entries use tribally specific adjectives, referring to an author as Cherokee or Navajo and avoiding the more general choice altogether. Other terms, such as *indigenous, aboriginal,* and *Native* are used by contributors as well, generally to invoke a sense of origin that might be applied in a more universal way than either *American Indian* or *Native American.* All of these words imply a kind of unsurpassable connection to place: the first inhabitants, brought from nowhere, always here. In addition, in the entries that discuss Canadian authors and their texts, contributors use the preferred term, *First Nations,* as well as tribally specific descriptors.

BIBLIOGRAPHY

King, Thomas. *All My Relations: An Anthology of Contemporary Canadian Native Fiction.* Toronto: McClelland, 1990.

Means, Russell. "I Am an American Indian, Not a Native American." Available online. URL: http://www.peaknet.net/~aardvark/means.html. Accessed on August 15, 2005.

Vizenor, Gerald. Introduction. *Native American Literature: A Brief Introduction and Anthology.* New York: HarperCollins, 1995.

Weaver, Jace. *That the People Might Live. Native American Literature and Native American Community.* New York: Oxford, 1997.

Alan R. Velie and Jennifer McClinton-Temple

A to Z
Entries

꧁꧂

Absence of Angels, The   W. S. Penn (1994)

The title of W. S. Penn's first novel, *The Absence of Angels,* has particular significance to the narrative itself. First, the Absence of Angels is the spirit world that the young protagonist, Alley (Albert) Hummingbird, communicates with throughout the novel. Second, this place, the Absence of Angels, is an antidote to the streets of Los Angeles. Penn's title suggests, then, a form of personal growth that accompanies the character's spiritual and physical abandonment of the inappropriately named city, which is covered by a blinding "smog that hid Los Angeles from the light of the sun" (51).

A rather atypical bildungsroman, or coming-of-age story, the plot concerns Alley's attempt to understand his Indian heritage, first as a boy and later as a teenager and young adult. Little guidance in reaching any such understanding is provided by his father, who is the son of "two-half breeds" (30). Turning away from his Nez Perce and Hopi ancestry, Alley's father has long since left the reservation, married a white woman, and taken up employment in the petroleum industry. If his father proves an inadequate source of guidance, neither can Alley's white mother help him understand his tribal heritage. Instead, she tells him and his sisters "stories of Indians raping white women" and later, during her mental instability, converses with household appliances more often than she does with her family (11).

Unmoored within this rather dysfunctional family, the young Alley oscillates between Los Angeles—later Palo Alto—and the reservation. The reservation, Chosposi Mesa, is home to his Indian grandfather, Billy Hummingbird.

The old man is the only figure in Alley's life who constantly offers instruction or whose presence seems to give clarity to his grandson's understanding of an otherwise confusing world. It is his grandfather's presence that keeps Alley alive when he is jaundiced and starved of oxygen at birth. Billy arrives from Chosposi and leads Death, another recurring figure in the novel, back to the reservation. Having cheated Death at birth, Alley has a life that is a series of trials and tribulations. Through his relationships with Rachel, an Indian girl from Chosposi; Allison DeForest, an Anglo from L.A.; and his one true love, his fellow college student Sara, Alley begins to understand his place in the world and his own MIXED-BLOOD identity. Ultimately—at the novel's end—the grandfather, Billy Hummingbird, passes to the spiritual world known as the Absence of Angels. This passing gives Alley a new level of comprehension of his own place and presence in the world. Finally, able to "close [his] eyes and listen to [his grandfather's] voice coming out of the Absence of Angels," Alley understands his mixed heritage and has "discovered a landscape" within (29, 268).

Bibliography

Penn, W. S. *The Absence of Angels.* 1994. Norman: University of Oklahoma Press, 1995.

Review of *The Absence of Angels. Publisher's* Weekly, 10 January 1994.

Sherwin, Elisabeth. "William Penn Is Not an Imagined Native American Stereotype." Available online. URL: http://www.dcn.davis.ca.us/go/gizmo/1998/penn.html. Accessed in August 15, 2005.

Padraig Kirwan

Adams, Howard   (1921–2001)

Dr. Howard Adams was both an academic and a Métis activist. Of Cree, English, and French ancestry, Adams was born in 1921 in the Métis community of St. Louis, Saskatchewan, where he struggled with poverty and the discrimination experienced by the Métis. But he excelled in academic subjects, receiving a Ph.D. in history from Berkeley in the turbulent early 1960s. Inspired by the Red Power movement of the late 1960s, he founded the Saskatchewan Native Action Committee in 1968 and the Vancouver Métis Association in 1987. He taught at the University of Saskatchewan and the University of California.

In his two books, *Prison of Grass: Canada from a Native Point of View* (1975) and *Tortured People: The Politics of Colonization* (1995), Adams mixes the personal and the polemic to address the colonization of aboriginal peoples from a Marxist perspective. He describes how his community was outraged that he called himself a *half-breed,* a derogatory term for the Métis that some Métis have reclaimed as a source of pride. Adams realized that as colonized people, aboriginal people must release their pain and anger to be able to discuss colonization objectively. Adams starts both his books with his own struggles to overcome internalized racism before turning to the larger issues of colonization.

Adams was never afraid of being outspoken. He advocated a nationalist policy for aboriginal people, believing that they should band together to fight common oppression. However, he also believed that revolutionary change for aboriginal people should occur at the local level and that they should forge alliances across class lines with the labor movement and other working-class struggles. In Adams's view, state sponsored aboriginal agencies such as band councils, the Assembly of First Nations, and the Métis National Council are tools of oppression that aboriginal people use against themselves. As he writes in *Tortured People,* "Neo-colonialism allows a corrupt class of Aboriginals to profit at the expense of the majority. In the end, the state succeeds in crushing the Aboriginal movement for self-determination by dispersing and disorganizing the Native population" (131). However, although an academic, Adams never considered himself to be a "collaborator" with the state, a position he never fully addresses in his writings.

Adams did find some hope in aboriginal literature. He cited books like MARIA CAMPBELL's autobiography *Halfbreed* (1973) and JEANNETTE ARMSTRONG's novel *Slash* (1985) as examples of decolonization. But he viewed POW wows and similar cultural gatherings as "cultural imperialism" that sets aboriginal people in the past and does not include a political component. Adams also saw hope in international indigenous movements like the Zapatistas in Mexico and in awareness in young people of the dangers of globalization.

Bibliography

Adams, Howard. *Prison of Grass: Canada from a Native Perspective.* Saskatoon, Canada: Fifth House, 1975.

———. *Tortured People: The Politics of Colonization.* Penticton, Canada: Theytus, 1995.

Purich, Donald. *The Métis.* Toronto: Lorimer, 1988.

Simons, Deborah. "Howard Adams, Métis Activist and Marxist." *Studies in Political Economy* (summer 2002). Available online. URL: http://archives.econ.utah.edu/archives/marxism/2002w25/msg00051.htm. Accessed in August 15, 2005.

June Schudler

(Ado)ration   Diane Glancy (1999)

The poetry collection *(Ado)ration* reflects DIANE GLANCY's commitment to her Cherokee heritage, Christianity, and the possibilities of postmodern writing techniques. Glancy's poetry, with its darkly humorous wordplay and misspellings, emphasizes the miscommunications between Western and Native sensibilities and ultimately reveals the unfolding relationship of Native and Christian spiritualities.

(Ado)ration opens by presenting the encounter of Native and Christian spiritualities as a clash between two systems. The more autobiographical middle portion of the collection depicts private sorrows, family moments, and visits to national parks. Eventually historical, personal, and spiritual encounters merge, and by the conclusion of *(Ado)ration* a new and syncretic form of spirituality is created and the transformative power of faith is reaffirmed.

To address the ongoing process of religious, national, and personal transformations, Glancy adopts the imagery of journeys, for example: a road trip across the plains; Jesus as a punk kid riding a Harley; conquistadores on horses; a mind being pushed along a road; the tracking of footprints; and Jesus giving a sermon from a rocking boat. In "Ledger Book Drawing" Glancy describes an old drawing in which an Indian is depicted riding sidesaddle because the Native artist did not know how to draw a leg on the other side of the horse. The two-dimensional drawing is linked to a recurring religious and metaphysical query in *(Ado)ration*: how the visible relates to the invisible. In "Well You Push Your Mind along the Road," the tribal religious perspective, which Glancy frequently presents as engaged with the tangible and the material, confronts its antithesis—an intangible eclipse that is called God—and this collision creates a new being: "You lift your voice and say *praise to you nothing* and nothing begins to hear," "then nothing becomes something," until finally "there's / A confrontation of wills / a split in understanding / that penetrates to the very nature of being" (20). This phenomenological creation of being is called "a migration" between the self and the other.

In keeping with its exploration of the clash and intermingling of religious systems, *(Ado)ration* acknowledges Native American anger at the colonizer but it also recognizes the desirability of certain European artistic and spiritual ideas. The epigraph and the opening poem establish this emotional framework. The epigraph quotes the Old Testament

tale of Jacob and Esau, which from an American Indian point of view, is a skinwalker tale of trickery: Rebekkah fixes venison stew for her husband and teaches her favored son to wear animal skins in order to change his identity. The first poem, "You Know Them by Their Stealing," alludes to the epigraph while acknowledging that some things that the Europeans introduced, such as goats and ragtime bands, are not so easily dismissed. The closing poem, "Stolen Blessing," refers to the epigraph, but now the speaker glories in the continual struggle and exchange—"a head-on / *inclision* of faith"—and the strength of the new spirituality that is achieved through this struggle (59).

See also SPIRITUALITY.

Bibliography

Glancy, Diane. *(Ado) ration.* Tucson, Ariz.: Chax Press, 1999.

Donelle Ruwe

After and Before the Lightning   Simon J. Ortiz (1974)

The harsh and inescapable force of the South Dakota winter is the principal concern of SIMON ORTIZ's *After and Before the Lightning,* a book of poems that stems from Ortiz's experiences with the Lakota Sioux on the Rosebud Reservation, where he taught at Sinte Gleska College during the winter of 1985–86. In the poems, Ortiz seeks to chart his position in time and within the universe. The poems map the reservation in relation to the United States, to the North American continent, and to the universe. Throughout the book, Ortiz repeatedly drives the stretch of Highway 18 between Mission and Okreek; the poems themselves search for a larger meaning in such seemingly ordinary journeys and events.

The book's title refers to the season Ortiz takes as his subject; the thunderstorms of autumn and spring mark the beginning and the end of winter. Some, but not all, of the poems are dated: Ortiz records a period from November 16 to March 21. In total, the book includes nearly 200 prose and verse entries in this "diary" of life during winter.

The poems in *After and Before the Lightning* range from the anecdotal and conversational to the visionary. Ortiz includes prayers and dream poems with his depictions of mundane activities during winter. He divides the book into four sections: "The Landscape: Prairie, Time, and Galaxy," "Common Trials: Every Day," "Buffalo Dawn Coming," and "Near and Evident Signs of Spring." The titles of the sections announce some of the book's most prominent subjects and themes and reflect Ortiz's desire to write about the ordinary and particular as well as the cosmic.

Despite the length and viciousness of winter, one of the last poems in the book, "Our Eagerness Blooms," is cautiously hopeful. It expresses a certainty that spring will in fact return, even though the signs of the change of the seasons appear slowly in the Dakotas. Such a poem stands in stark contrast to "Coping," for example, one of the many poems in the book that portray the psychological difficulty of surviving the freezing temperatures of winter. In "Coping," Ortiz describes the severity of the wind and notes that its ferocity is not lessened by his knowledge that the wind is coming. Comparing these two poems illustrates one of the central tensions in *After and Before the Lightning*: Ortiz records both the stark beauty and the grim hardships of the South Dakota winter, finding comfort in the cold even as he looks forward to the smell of the spring.

Bibliography

Bruchac, Joseph. "The Story Never Ends: An Interview with Simon Ortiz." In *Survival This Way: Interviews with American Indian Poets,* edited by Joseph Bruchac, 211–29. Tucson: University of Arizona Press, 1987.

Silko, Leslie Marmon. "Language and Literature from a Pueblo Indian Perspective." In *English Literature: Opening Up the Canon,* edited by Leslie A. Fiedler and Houston A. Baker, Jr., 54–72. Baltimore: Johns Hopkins University Press, 1981.

Wiget, Andrew. *Simon Ortiz.* Boise, Idaho: Boise State University Press, 1986.

Nicholas Bradley

Akiwenzie-Damm, Kateri   (1965–   )

The mixed-blood Anishinabe (Ojibwa) writer Kateri Akiwenzie-Damm was born in Toronto, Canada, in 1965. Akiwenzie-Damm received an M.A. in English literature from the University of Ottawa in 1996. She manages Kegedonce Press, the mandate of which is to publish the works of indigenous authors both nationally and internationally, including Akiwenzie-Damm's *My Heart Is a Stray Bullet* (1993). She is also the author of *bloodriver woman* and is anthologized in *An Anthology of Canadian Native Literature in English* (1998) and *The Colour of Resistance: A Contemporary Collection of Writing by Aboriginal Women,* among other publications.

As Akiwenzie-Damm is of Anishinabe, Polish, Potawatomi, and English descent, identity is a major concern in her work. In "mixed blood: notes from a split personality," Akiwenzie-Damm explores the alienation aboriginal students feel in postsecondary settings. She has "an out of body experience," feeling "part of my spirit / swirling around my head" (*heart* 23). The nonaboriginal part of Akiwenzie-Damm, however, "concentrates wildly / all power / in this pen" (23). She calms herself by remembering her grandparents' hands reuniting the disparate part of Akiwenzie-Damm: "stitch together with strong threads / and I will be like patchwork: fragmented but whole" (24).

Identity is also explored in "Indian enough," which examines the prejudice she encounters from both aboriginal and nonaboriginal people. Akiwenzie-Damm has "seen the disappointed looks / at my fair skin shining . . . not even a feather . . . to redeem me" (*heart* 20). Aboriginal people are just as fixated on Akiwenzie-Damm's mixed heritage, as a woman elder tells Akiwenzie-Damm that she "is 'not a very good Indian' / because I can't speak Ojibwa" (21). However, by using the colonizers' term *Indian* for First Nations/aboriginal/Native American people, as well as *Ojibwa,* a term of unknown origin that is applied to the Anishinabe, Akiwenzie-Damm highlights how aboriginal people have internalized the colonizers' ways of thinking.

Erotica is another important theme in Akiwenzie-Damm's writing, so much so that she edited the anthology *Without Reservation: Indigenous Erotica* (2003). The poem "desire" illustrates how Akiwenzie-Damm "longed for images and stories of love between our people" (*Without* x). The three-stanza poem chronicles how Akiwenzie-Damm wants to have an unattainable lover "inside me / I want to be / inside you," a dissolving of bodily boundaries. Akiwenzie-Damm bluntly states her desire, "I want to shake the earth / with you"(*heart* 43). Akiwenzie-Damm asserts, "Indigenous erotica is political. . . . For better or for worse, because of the societies surrounding us, it is, like everything we do, political" (*(Ad)dressing* 143).

Bibliography

Akiwenzie-Damm, Kateri. *My Heart Is a Stray Bullet.* Wiarton, Canada: Kegedonce, 1993.

Goldie, Terry, and Daniel David Moses, eds. *An Anthology of Canadian Native Literature in English.* Don Mills, Canada: Oxford University Press, 1998.

"kateri-akiwenzie-damm." Available online. URL: www.hanksville.org/storytellers/damm. Accessed on August 15, 2005.

Martin, Tony. "Fierce Aboriginal Vibe." Guerrilla: Ottawa Culture at Ground Level. Available online. URL: http://www.getguerilla.ca/content/kateri/index.html. Accessed on August 15, 2005.

June Schudler

alcoholism

Alcohol consumption was initiated among Indians when European colonists, intent on acquiring furs, skins, and slaves from the natives, determined that liquor, primarily rum produced on the sugar plantations of the West Indies, was one of their most valuable assets with which to trade. This trade developed along with colonialism, moving from New England and the Chesapeake to the Ohio and Mississippi River valleys. By the end of the colonial period Europeans and Indians were trafficking kegs of rum, legally and illegally, deep into Indian country (Mancall 30–31). This legacy of trade turned into a legacy of consumption, with the abuse of alcohol, then and now, exacerbating the problems of displacement, POVERTY, disease, and loss of culture.

Scholars do not have an easy answer for why Indian communities have historically been so devastated by alcohol. Although a popular misconception holds that Indians metabolize alcohol at a slower rate than people of other ethnicities, and thus have a higher sensitivity to it, clinical studies have shown this not to be the case. In fact, medical science has found no identifiable genetic trait that would in any way effect the use or abuse of alcohol by Indians. However, one cannot deny the staggering effect of alcohol on Indians, as witnessed by the following statistics from the Indian Health Service:

> Indians are three and half times more likely than other Americans to die from cirrhosis of the liver, a benchmark of addiction. They are also four times more likely to die from accidents, and three times more likely to die from homicide and suicide, in all of which alcohol is usually present. Between 5 percent and 25 percent of Indian babies may be born mentally and physically damaged by fetal alcohol syndrome, compared to less than one fifth of 1 percent in the general population. . . . Alcohol also takes an immeasurable toll in chronic disability, lost earning capacity, unemployment, emotional pain, family disruption, and child abuse. (Bordewich 248)

This list of sad and shattering consequences has inevitably led many Indian writers to address alcoholism in their work. CEREMONY, HOUSE MADE OF DAWN, WINTER IN THE BLOOD, and LOVE MEDICINE, among other texts, introduced the topic of the alienated Indian destroyed by liquor. JAMES WELCH, LOUISE ERDRICH, LESLIE MARMON SILKO, and N. SCOTT MOMADAY deal with the issue of alcohol and alcohol abuse in many of their novels; they express a true concern about the situation of their tribes that is due to alcoholism and propose the return to the ancient ceremonies and traditions to cure tribal members addicted to liquor and restore their link with the Earth.

For instance, in *House Made of Dawn*, Abel's alcoholism makes him react violently to tribal ways: "For him (Abel) alcohol is no tranquilizer, but a fire that feeds his sullen, speechless rage until he explodes in a violence that results in his near-fatal beating by the culebra policeman Martinez" (Allen 139–40). He will die understanding tribal ways but unable to deal with the role they play in his MIXED-BLOOD life. In *Ceremony*, Tayo suffers posttraumatic stress disorder as a consequence of the death of his cousin and the horrors of war and finds consolation in drinking. But Tayo's problems with alcohol started long before discovering his legacy and feeling tribal rejection in a pattern started by his mother, a Laguna woman who, in mating with a white man, lost her soul and life. Death found her alone, drunk, and without shelter.

In *Love Medicine* a drunken June Morrissey, having separated herself from her family on the reservation, walks off into a snowstorm and dies, only to haunt her former husband and fellow alcoholic, Gordie, who is crazed with grief and guilt. Driving drunk on the reservation, he hits a deer, throws it into the back seat, then manages to convince himself that it is June herself and that he is responsible for her death. The abuse of alcohol has the potential to destroy the families in *Love Medicine*; in fact, June's funeral preparation, during which pies are smashed on the floor by the (drunken) son of Gordie and June, symbolizes the break of the family unity. Most of Erdrich's novels address the issue of alcohol abuse, but it is in *Love Medicine* that the whole question of drinking acquires the utmost importance since many chapters deal with conflicts that result from some character's drunkenness: Henry Lamartine drowns in his car after drinking with Lyman Lamartine, Gordie loses control of himself and his life in his mother's kitchen, and June perishes, buried in snow.

In addition to that of the authors mentioned, SHERMAN ALEXIE's fiction frequently deals with issues surrounding alcohol and alcohol abuse. *RESERVATION BLUES* deals with fetal alcohol syndrome in the protagonist: "His mother's drinking had done obvious damage to Michael in the womb. He had those vaguely Asian eyes and the flat face that alcohol babies always had on reservations. But he'd grown large and muscular despite the alcohol's effects" (39). *THE LONE RANGER AND TONTO FISTFIGHT IN HEAVEN* and *THE TOUGHEST INDIAN IN THE WORLD* both incorporate characters who have been raised in alcoholic households and engage in various methods of coping with that fact. Alexie is careful to demonstrate in his fiction the danger of stereotypes, however; he writes with irony and uses satire to force the reader to question assumptions, in this case assumptions about the stereotypical "drunken Indian." All of Alexie's Indians are not drunk, but they are not all sober either, and they cannot all be saved by a return to tradition. His is a complex Indian world, but he never shies away from handling the reality of alcoholism.

Finally, one of the most famous books written about Indians and alcoholism is MICHAEL DORRIS's *The Broken Cord*, a work of nonfiction. It is a journalistic account of the problems of raising his adopted son, Abel, a victim of fetal alcohol syndrome. Dorris's book portrayed the dangers of combining pregnancy and alcohol in stark relief for Indians as well as for people of other ethnicities, as it is both informative and heartbreaking.

To be sure, alcoholism is a sensitive, difficult topic, and not all Indian authors agree on how (or even whether) it should be treated. The words of JOY HARJO, however, illuminate the danger of the problem itself: "Alcoholism is an epidemic in native people, and I write about it. I was criticized for bringing it up, because some people want to present a certain image of themselves. But again, it comes back to what I was saying: part of the process of healing is to address what is evil" (140).

Bibliography

Alexie, Sherman. *The Lone Ranger and Tonto Fistfight in Heaven.* 1993. Reprint, New York: HarperPerennial, 1994.

———. *Reservation Blues.* New York: Warner Books, 1996.

———. *The Toughest Indian in the World.* New York: Atlantic Monthly Press, 2000.

Bordewich, Fergus M. *Killing the White Man's Indian: Reinventing Native Americans at the End of the Twentieth Century.* New York: Anchor, 1997.

Dorris, Michael. *The Broken Cord.* New York: Harper Collins, 1990.

Erdrich, Louise. *Love Medicine.* New and expanded ed. New York: HarperPerennial, 1984.

Harjo, Joy. "A Laughter of Absolute Sanity: Interview with Angels Carabi." In *The Spiral of Memory: Interviews,* edited by Laura Coltelli, 133–42. Ann Arbor: University of Michigan Press, 1996.

Mancall, Peter. *Deadly Medicine: Indians and Alcohol in Early America.* Ithaca, N.Y.: Cornell University Press, 1995.

Momaday, N. Scott. *House Made of Dawn.* New York: Harper & Row, 1968.

Silko, Leslie Marmon. *Ceremony.* New York: Penguin, 1977.

Imelda Martín-Junquera

Alexie, Sherman   (1966–   )

On October 7, 1966, Sherman Alexie was born in Wellpinit, Washington, on the Spokane Indian Reservation. His father, Sherman, Sr., is Coeur d'Alene and his mother, Lillian, is Spokane. Sherman Sr.'s interest in reading sparked his son's passion for the power of language; Alexie characterizes himself as a voracious reader. After graduating from Reardan High School, off reservation, Alexie initially attended Gonzaga University before graduating in 1991 from Washington State University in Pullman with a degree in American studies. Today Alexie lives in Seattle with his wife, Diane, and his two sons. Alexie's formative experiences—as a child of alcoholics in the context of the harsh economic realities of rural RESERVATION LIFE—are focal points in his early fiction and poetry. More recently, his attention has turned to the experiences of urban Indian people living in a multiethnic context, in situations in which identities and cultural loyalties are questioned because of class standing or romantic and sexual relationships.

During college he faced his own ALCOHOLISM, gave up drinking, and has remained sober since he was 23. Switching from his initial plans to go into medicine, Alexie found his calling in poetry writing workshops and was especially encouraged by his professor Alex Kuo, who first exposed him to poetry by contemporary Native writers such as SIMON ORTIZ, LESLIE MARMON SILKO, JOY HARJO, JAMES WELCH, and ADRIAN LOUIS, whom he now includes alongside Walt Whitman and Emily Dickinson as his most important influences.

His first books of poetry, *The BUSINESS OF FANCYDANCING* and *I Would Steal Horses,* were published in 1992 and laid the foundation for future successes. In 1993 his first collection of short stories, *The LONE RANGER AND TONTO FISTFIGHT IN HEAVEN,* was awarded a PEN/Hemingway Award for Best First Book of Fiction. He went on to be named one of Granta's best young American novelists and received the Before Columbus Foundation's American Book Award for his first novel, *RESERVATION BLUES,* published in 1995. His short fiction has often been published in *The New Yorker* and has been selected for inclusion in both the annual O. Henry Award collections and the Best American Short Story collections. Beyond the typical literary readership, Alexie has fostered a public fan base with public speaking engagements that impart a typical poetry reading format with doses of politically charged commentary and stand-up-style routines. Such platforms have cast him as a public spokesperson for Native America, such as his participation in President Clinton's summit on race in 1998. When asked by CBS in 2001 about his rapid ascent in the literary world, he noted that he always knew it was possible: "I thought I had that combination of skills which was very conducive to being successful in the United States in the earliest 21st century. I write well enough. I'm funny. I'm good in front of the camera" (*Sixty Minutes*).

Alexie's self-description outlines some of the unique aspects of his writing and his public performances as a writer-speaker that have set him apart from other Native American writers. Alexie's refreshingly inventive style conveys to readers his characters' suffering and anguish, but also the enduring power of humor and imagination. His most well-known character, Thomas Builds-the-Fire, from *The Lone Ranger, Reservation Blues,* and the film *SMOKE SIGNALS,* illustrates the power of storytelling to connect the past, present, and future; to reinvent traditional forms; and to infuse tragedy with a dose of laughter and a refusal to submit to traumatizing forces. The scholar Jane Hafen (Taos Pueblo) notes that she enjoys Alexie's writings because "they make me laugh. In the face of dismal reservation life, urban crisis of self, community, and identity, he can make me laugh, often by inverting imagery and turning inside jokes. He helps make the pain bearable" (84).

Alexie reached his largest audiences via the 1998 film *Smoke Signals,* directed by Chris Eyre (Cheyenne/Arapaho) and adapted by Alexie himself from several short stories, including "What It Means to Say Phoenix, Arizona." *Smoke Signals* follows the journey of Victor Joseph and Thomas Builds-the-Fire on their trip to recover the ashes of Victor's deceased father, from whom he was estranged. Their journey is also metaphorical, as their shared experiences lead to discoveries for both about their abilities to forgive, understand, and transcend the legacies bestowed on them by their parents, but more specifically their fathers. When the two return to their home, to the reservation and tribal homeland their fathers had left behind, Victor returns his father's ashes to the river where salmon return to mate and die. In the final scene of the movie, the ashes mix with the rising mists of the rapids and his father's spirit leaps like the salmon; we hear Thomas speaking in a voice-over: "Do we forgive our fathers for leaving us too often or forever when we were little? . . . If we forgive our fathers what is left?" (scene 151). Viewers are left to consider whether they can any longer afford to live in the shadow of terrible legacies or should instead consider taking the risks required to forge new futures and identities from the raw materials of empathy and forgiveness.

Alexie's character Thomas Builds-the-Fire is known for his abilities to tell stories, but Alexie himself has bristled when he is described as a storyteller, connecting the characterization to stereotypes forced upon Native writers. Alexie is quite aware that he is writing in the face of such assumptions: "It's that whole 'corn pollen, four directions, Mother Earth, Father Sky Indian thing where everybody starts speaking slowly, and their vocabulary shrinks down until they sound like Dick and Jane. And it's all about politics. So I try to write about everyday Indians, the kind of Indian I am who is just as influenced by the Brady Bunch as I am by my tribal traditions, who spends as much time going to the movies as I do going to ceremonies" (*Sixty Minutes II*). Nonetheless, Alexie is aware that he will always be labeled an "Indian writer," no matter what his focus may be. Instead of worrying about limits imposed from without, Alexie parodies such preconceptions or self-fashionings in poems such as "How to Write the Great American Indian Novel," through his character Jack Wilson in the novel *Indian Killer,* or in his essay/memoir, "The Unauthorized Autobiography of Me." In later works such as "Search Engine" from *Ten Little Indians* and his film *The Business of Fancydancing,* Alexie continues to question the expectations placed on indigenous writers. Although his views have shifted over his career, he has stated on more than one occasion that he is moved to explore certain subjects not just because they produce insight into the experience of Native American people but because they lead to a deeper understanding of aspects of himself or his thoughts at a particular moment. In an interview in 1999 Alexie noted, "There's always a huge difference between public persona and private person. In my art I try to keep that as narrow as possible. I try to write about that kind of Indian I am, the kind of person I am and not the kind of person or Indian I wish I was. . . . It's the difference between writing with imagination about an imaginary world and writing with imagination about a real world. I try to write with imagination about a real world" (Torrez).

In most of his writing Alexie reshapes readers' attitudes about Native peoples, in particular notions that are based on stereotypes and misinformation. While Alexie's characters and subject matter are most often rooted in the realities of life on the Spokane or Coeur d'Alene Reservation, his attitude is pantribal. For example, his repeated references to Crazy Horse, to the GHOST DANCE, to Sand Creek, or to WOUNDED KNEE, to name several examples, develop associations and assert a shared history among Native peoples across space and time. While Alexie notes the responsibility he has to other Native Americans, and to the building of a better, less factionalized America, he is not interested in making his readers feel comfortable or complacent. If anything, he works to frustrate complacency. His series of poems "The Alcoholic Love Poems" from FIRST INDIAN ON THE MOON are just one example of how his writing confronts readers without pretense. Readers see the poet trying to come to terms with his own family legacies, with his own personal demons, with internal conflicts not easily resolved.

In "Shoes" from his book OLD SHIRTS AND NEW SKINS he asks, "How do you explain the survival of all of us who were never meant to survive?" (90). In other contexts, Alexie has offered a personal answer to this rhetorical question. For example, in "Imagining the Reservation" from *The Lone Ranger and Tonto Fistfight in Heaven,* Alexie writes, "Survival = Anger × Imagination. Imagination is the only weapon on the reservation" (150). Anger is a likely reaction to deep economic, social, and political inequities, but it is a self-destructive force if left to fester. If mediated through the creative process of poetry making, anger can be transformed into survival.

Bibliography

Alexie, Sherman. *The Business of Fancydancing.* Brooklyn: Hanging Loose Press, 1992.
———. *First Indian on the Moon.* Brooklyn: Hanging Loose Press, 1993.
———. *Indian Killer.* New York: Atlantic Monthly Press, 1996.
———. *I Would Steal Horses.* Niagara Falls, N.Y.: Slipstream Press, 1992.
———. *The Lone Ranger and Tonto Fistfight in Heaven.* New York: Atlantic Monthly Press, 1993.
———. *Old Shirts and New Skins.* Los Angeles: American Indian Studies Center, 1993.
———. *Reservation Blues.* New York: Atlantic Monthly Press, 1995.
———. *Smoke Signals.* New York: Hyperion Press, 1998.
———. *The Summer of Black Widows.* Brooklyn: Hanging Loose Press, 1996.
———. *Ten Little Indians.* New York: Atlantic Monthly Press, 2003.
———. *The Toughest Indian in the World.* New York: Atlantic Monthly Press, 2000.
Bird, Gloria. "The Exaggeration of Despair in Sherman Alexie's *Reservation Blues.*" *Wicazo Sa Review* 11, no. 2 (1995): 47–52.
Cox, James. "Muting White Noise: The Subversion of Popular Culture Narratives of Conquest in Sherman Alexie's Fiction." *Studies in American Indian Literatures* 9, no. 4 (winter 1997): 52–70.
Evans, Stephen F. "Open Containers": Sherman Alexie's Drunken Indians." *American Indian Quarterly* 25, no. 1 (winter 2001): 46–72.
Hafen, P. Jane. "Rock and Roll, Redskins, and Blues in Sherman Alexie's Work." *Studies in American Indian Literatures* 9, no. 4 (winter 1997): 71–78.
Hollrah, Patrice. "Sherman Alexie's Challenge to the Academy's Teaching of Native American Literature, Non-Native Writers, and Critics." *SAIL* 13, no. 2–3 (summer–fall 2001): 23–35.
Newton, John. "Sherman Alexie's Autoethnography." *Contemporary Literature* 42, no. 2 (summer 2001): 413–428.
Sixty Minutes II. "The Toughest Indian in the World." Available online. URL: http://www.cbsnews.com/stories/2001/01/19/60II. Accessed on August 15, 2005.
Torrez, Juliette. "Juliette Torrez Goes Long Distance with Sherman Alexie." *Vice & Verse* (August 31, 1999). Available online. URL: http://poetry.about.com/li...true&COB=home&terms=alexie&PM=113_300. Accessed on August 15, 2005.

Jeff Berglund

Allen, Paula Gunn   (1939–   )

Paula Marie Francis was born in Albuquerque, New Mexico, to Elias Lee and Ethel Haines Gottlieb Francis on October 24, 1939. Raised in Cubero, New Mexico, a Spanish-Mexican land grant village abutting the Laguna and Acoma Pueblo reservations and the Cibola National Forest, Allen was the third of five children. She refers to herself as a "multicultural event," recalling her Laguna/Sioux/Scottish-American ancestry from her mother and her Lebanese-American heritage from her father. These influences account for her ability to bridge perspectives and offer understandings across cultures, religions, and worldviews.

For most of her schooling Allen attended a Sister of Charity boarding school in Albuquerque, graduating in 1957. She received a bachelor's degree in English (1966) and a M.F.A. in creative writing (1968) from the University of Oregon. In 1975 she received her doctorate in American studies with an emphasis on Native American literature from the University of New Mexico. However, Allen's personal and professional life was often difficult. She had three marriages and five children before realizing that she was lesbian. She had difficulties with editors and professors who wanted her to fit conventional Western literary standards and to disregard her Native American aesthetics.

Allen is the author of numerous volumes of poetry. Because of her multicultural background, Allen can draw upon varying poetic rhythms and structures that emanate from such sources as country-western music, Pueblo corn dances, Catholic masses, Mozart, Italian opera, and Arabic chanting. Allen became interested in writing in high school when she discovered Gertrude Stein, whom she read extensively and tried to copy. Other influences were American writers such as William Carlos Williams, Robert Creeley, Charles Olson, Allen Ginsberg, Denise Levertov, Adrienne Rich, Patricia Clark Smith, and E. A. Mares. It was not until she was finishing up her M.F.A. in Oregon that she had any exposure to Native American writers. When she was feeling isolated and suicidal, Allen says, the presence of a Santee Sioux friend and the discovery of N. SCOTT MOMADAY's HOUSE MADE OF DAWN were what helped her to continue.

In addition to being a poet and novelist, Allen is recognized as a major scholar, literary critic, and teacher of Native American literature. Among her teaching positions are those at San Francisco State University, the University of New Mexico, and the University of California at Berkeley and at Los Angeles. Allen's 1983 *Studies in American Indian Literature: Critical Essays and Course Designs* has an extensive bibliography to aid in teaching Native American literatures. *The SACRED HOOP: RECOVERING THE FEMININE IN AMERICAN INDIAN TRADITIONS*, 1986, exhibits Allen's belief in the power of the oral tradition embodied in contemporary Native American literature to effect healing, survival, and continuance.

Allen was awarded a National Endowment for the Arts writing fellowship in 1978, and she received a postdoctoral fellowship grant from the Ford Foundation-National Research Council in 1984. She is an activist involved with such movements as those related to antinuclear and antiwar, gay and lesbian, as well as feminist, issues. She won an honorable mention from the National Book Award Before Columbus Foundation for her 1982 book of poetry *SHADOW COUNTRY*. Allen uses the theme of shadows—the not dark and not light—to bridge her experience of mixed heritage as she attempts to respond to the world in its variety.

She won an American Book Award in 1990 for *SPIDER WOMAN'S GRANDDAUGHTERS: TRADITIONAL TALES AND CONTEMPORARY WRITINGS BY NATIVE AMERICAN WOMEN,* an attempt to add stories by and/or about Native women to literature collections. She also won the 1990 Native Prize for Literature. In her 1991 *Grandmother of the Light: A Medicine Woman's Sourcebook* Allen expands her interest in the ritual experience of women as exhibited in the traditional stories. More recently she has extended her interest in Native American writing by publishing collections of Native writing: *VOICE OF THE TURTLE: AMERICAN INDIAN LITERATURE 1900–1970* (1994) and *SONG OF THE TURTLE: AMERICAN LITERATURE 1974–1994* (1996).

Allen writes from the perspective of a Laguna Pueblo woman from a culture in which the women are held in high respect. The descent is matrilineal—women owned the houses and the primary deities are female. Major themes of Allen's work are delineation and restoration of this woman-centered culture. Her work abounds in the mythic dimensions of women's relationship to the sacred, as well as the struggles of contemporary Native American women, many of whom have lost the respect formerly accorded to them because of the incursion of Euro-American culture. This tragedy is the subject of her 1983 novel *The Woman Who Owned the Shadows*. Besides loss of respect, her main character must sort out the various influences of having a mixed ancestry in order to reclaim a Native American woman's spiritual tradition. Through her poetry, novel, essays, collections of stories, and activism Allen has made a major contribution to Native Amcrican literary studies, women's studies, gay and lesbian studies, and American literature.

Bibliography

Allen, Paula Gunn. *The Sacred Hoop: Recovering the Feminine in American Indian Traditions*. Boston: Beacon Press, 1986.

———. *The Woman Who Owned the Shadows*. San Francisco: Spinsters/Aunt Lute Books, 1983.

———. *Shadow Country*. Los Angeles: University of California Indian Studies Center, 1982.

Hanson, Elizabeth J. *Paula Gunn Allen*. Western Writers Series. Boise, Idaho: Boise State University Press, 1990.

Keating, Ana Louise. *Women Reading Women Writing: Self-Invention in Paula Gunn Allen, Gloria Anzaldua and Audre Lorde*. Philadelphia: Temple University Press, 1996.

Van Dyke, Annette. "The Journey Back to Female Roots: A Laguna Pueblo Model." In *Lesbian Texts and Contexts*, edited by Karla Jay and Joanne Glasgow, 339–354. New York: New York University Press, 1990.

Annette Van Dyke

All My Relations: An Anthology of Contemporary Canadian Native Fiction   Thomas King, ed. (1990)

As Thomas King states in the introduction of *All My Relations,* we currently do not have a definition to construct a Native body of literature; nor do we even have "a process for determining who is a Native writer and who is not" (x). The importance of this collection docs not lie in determining either of these definitions, but rather in contributing to the overall scope of Native writing in such a way as to move toward a "critical mass" (x) where patterns can emerge.

In an essay published the same year as this collection, King outlines some patterns to begin theorizing Native writing. This paper, entitled "Godzilla vs. Post-Colonial," is King's reaction to the assumptions contained in the current theoretical labels themselves: "the full complement of terms—pre-colonial, colonial, and post-colonial—reeks of unabashed ethnocentrism and well-meaning dismissal, and they point to a deep-seated assumption that is at the heart of most well-intentioned studies of Native literatures" (11). He instead proposes the terms *tribal, interfusional, polemical,* and *associational* (12). In essence, *tribal* are those works that are directed at a specific community and are not readily accessible to those outside that community; *interfusional* are works that use both the written and oral traditions; *polemical* are works that look at Native versus non-Native culture and often find non-Native values inferior; finally, *associational* are works that do not fit readily into the aforementioned categories but are still centered on a Native community, in order to reinforce community values without taking refuge in the clichés of either "the glamour and/or horror of Native life" (14).

Since these categories are developed by the editor himself, it is constructive to look at how the stories collected in *All My Relations* may fit into, or render problematic, this model. Out of the four, there will not be any true examples of tribal text, since by definition the stories collected here are shared with both pan-Native and non-Native readers.

A wonderful example of oral literature in a written format—pure interfusional—is the work of Harry Robinson, here represented by "An Okanagan Indian Becomes a Captive Circus Showpiece in England." Although Robinson told this story in English and it was transcribed in the same, King points out that "the patterns, metaphors, structures, as well as the themes and characters come primarily from oral literature" ("Godzilla" 13). The rhythm and repetition, the meandering and recursion of spoken language, are readily seen in such passages as

And the road gang,
they building a road.
And they call it McCurdy place.
And after that, they call it,
I forget the new man that lived there.
Anyway, McCurdy place,
that's the first man that lived there. (7)

There are quite a number of other stories combining oral style with writing. Out of these, most are concerned with characters outside the realist tradition. Coyote plays a prominent part, with all of the "trickiness" that entails, in Jeannette Armstrong's "This Is a Story," Peter Blue Cloud's "Weaver Spider's Web," and King's "The One about Coyote Going West." Other stories use different characters arising from the oral tradition, such as the title character in Bruce King's "Hookto: The Evil Entity," or the guardian of the coulees, Sam, who protects the community from a wolverine masquerading as an old woman in Shirley Bruised Head's "An Afternoon in Bright Sunlight." J. B. Joe's "Cement Woman" similarly introduces us to a figure harnessing traditional powers, although from a distinctly female point of view.

The story that fits most easily into the category of polemical is Richard G. Green's "The Last Raven," which is the first-person narrative of a Mohawk boy who moves from one form of alienation to another. The story begins in Sunday School, where he is shunned by a girl because he is Native; he then moves with some friends to play a pinball machine nicknamed "The Chief," where "the caricature of an Indian in Sioux headdress swings his tomahawk and dances" (157); he stops off at his parents' house, where his older sister speaks Mohawk only in order to aggravate him; finally he goes to slaughter "a flock of crows [that] has been gathering on the edge of town menacing people for several days" (158). Here his two (presumably white) friends massacre the flock: Although the birds are not "drunk" as first thought, they are nevertheless helpless since they are too full to fly. The narrator does not wish to participate in the destruction, but his friends insist, and so with the last shell he destroys the last raven just as it takes flight. Thus he completes his renunciation, and so when his friend creates a headdress from the largest feathers, he can only state that "a feeling of sardonic ridicule blossoms inside me, but humility pacifies the notion" (163).

The last category, the associational, reveals the vibrancy of Native family and community. King points out that this "is not an idea that is often pursued by non-Native writers who prefer to imagine their Indians as solitary figures poised on the brink of extinction" ("Introduction" xiv). The excerpts from Tomson Highway's *The Rez Sisters* and Jovette Marchessault's *Mother of the Grass,* as well as Emma Lee Warrior's "Compatriots," Basil Johnston's "Summer Holidays in Spanish," Ruby Slipperjack's "Coal Oil, Crayons and Schoolbooks," Barry Milliken's "Run," and Daniel David Moses's "King of the Raft" all fit the associational.

There are two stories here that ultimately resist these categories. Beth Brant's "Turtle Gal" tells of an urban Native girl who is taken in by an old black man when her mother dies; this event spurs a fascinating monologic text that functions as a dialogue between the experiences of blacks and Indians. Jordan Wheeler's "The Seventh Wave" tells of a Cree man feeling his age as he negotiates a relationship with a younger woman, which ultimately fails, and an attempt at surfing, which ultimately succeeds. Perhaps in these stories we have yet another beginning, an as-yet vestigial way to negotiate what it means to write Native.

See also First Nations literature.

Bibliography

Davidson, Arnold E., Walton, Priscilla L., and Andrews, Jennifer. *Border Crossings: Thomas King's Cultural Inversions.* Toronto: University of Toronto Press, 2003.

King, Thomas, ed. *All My Relations.* Toronto: McClelland & Stewart, 1990.

———. "Godzilla vs. Post-Colonial." *World Literature Written in English* 30, no. 2 (1990): 10–16.

———. *The Truth about Stories: A Native Narrative.* Toronto: Anansi, 2003.

Derek Irwin

Almanac of the Dead   Leslie Marmon Silko (1991)

At the core of SILKO's novel is an ancient almanac full of prophesies encoded in an archaic script that foretell the arrival of the Europeans in the Americas and their eventual disappearance. The novel holds out the promise that all lands in the Americas will in time revert to the indigenous peoples through an uprising, up from the south, that will occur both spontaneously and inevitably. Simultaneously European society in the Americas will fall from the weight of its own corruption, making way for the return of the original inhabitants.

With an extensive cast of characters Silko portrays the corruption of white society. Drug dealers, arms dealers, assassins, kidnappers, illegal traffickers in body parts, and a judge obsessed with bestiality are just a few of the corrupt folk who populate the novel, giving evidence that those of European descent living in the Americas have lost touch with their land and their cultural origins. But not all corruption resides north of the border. Characters obsessed with class and wealth as well as some overly zealous Marxist revolutionaries cause problems to the south. Even those of indigenous descent risk self-destruction if they have lost their ancestral connections. Menardo, for example, a wealthy businessman, suffers from feelings of inferiority because of his mestizo heritage (mixed Indian and Spanish blood). Menardo's shame over his Indian heritage leads directly to his downfall, whereas his Indian driver, Tacho, becomes one of those destined to lead the uprising.

In between north and south there is the borderland typified by a ranch near Tucson, Arizona. The ranch belongs to Zeta, one of two elderly Mexican/Indian twins who are the keepers and translators of the almanac in contemporary times. Zeta engages in smuggling and arms dealing, but her illegal activities are a rebellion against the European culture, a revenge for what was once taken away from her people. Her sister, Lecha, is psychic.

Both Zeta and Lecha work at translating the almanac, and Lecha hires a young white woman, Seese, as her secretary. Seese, a drug addict, seeks Lecha's help to find her kidnapped baby. Also at the ranch is Sterling, an Indian man who has been banished from his pueblo because he allowed a Hollywood movie crew to see his tribe's sacred snake statue. Seese and Sterling play out the fall of European civilization and the return of the Indians to their homelands in microcosm. Seese ends up without hope, learning she will never find her kidnapped baby. Sterling, however, returns home and finds that the sacred snake has reappeared. At the end Sterling looks contentedly southward, the direction from which the uprising is approaching, and anticipates the long-awaited return of the indigenous people.

See also MIXED-BLOOD.

Bibliography

Harder, Bernie. "The Power of Borders in Native American Literature: Leslie Marmon Silko's *Almanac of the Dead.*" *American Indian Culture and Research Journal* 24, no. 4 (2000): 95–106.

Holly E. Martin

American Indian children's literature

The image of the Native American, in war paint and war bonnet, has been a compelling image since the so-called discovery of America in the 15th century. The proliferation of books for children that either directly represent Native peoples and lifeways or employ "Indian" figures in their narratives attests to the fact that playing "Indian"—or of course playing at fighting Indians—has ever been a perennial favorite of childhood imaginative play. What is fast becoming just as widespread, and far more intellectually compelling, is the criticism of the kinds of stereotypes such games, images, and representations create, disseminate, and maintain.

In American Indian children's literature, as in the wider field of American Indian literature, the debate turns on notions of authenticity and accuracy: Who tells the stories, how are they told, and whom are they told for, are all key questions, embedded in complex political and ideological arguments. Sharon Creech, author of the Newberry Medal–winning *Walk Two Moons,* has been held up by Michelle Pagni Stewart as an excellent example of a non-Native creator of a culturally sensitive work that accurately reflects, among other things, the narrative techniques of American Indian storytelling. The white authors Scott O'Dell (*Island of the Blue Dolphin*) and Jean Craighead George (*Julie of the Wolves*) are similarly lauded by Stewart and others for sensitive advocacy of Native cultures and beliefs (Stewart 179–186).

In stark contrast texts such as Lynne Reid Banks's *The Indian in the Cupboard* feeds on stereotypes, maintaining, as MICHAEL DORRIS has pointed out, the idea of the Indian as under the ownership of the child and fostering negative portrayals of Indians as war-hungry and savage; or Ann Rinaldi's *My Heart Is on the Ground: The Diary of Nannie Little Rose, a Sioux Girl. Carlisle Indian School, Pennsylvania, 1880,* which has drawn vehement criticism from a number of Native American scholars and writers for its inaccuracies and abuses of sensitive areas and issues. Finally the notorious (and notoriously popular) *The Education of Little Tree* by "Forrest" Carter sets a benchmark for controversial speculation over the provenance of both the author and the text (Hirschfelder vii–ix).

As steadily greater emphasis is placed on multiculturalism and cultural understanding in the classroom, such issues become all the more important, and thinking about and studying American Indian children's literature become not merely a matter of reading and learning about America's first peoples, but of engaging with the modes of analysis that expose stereotypical attitudes, as well as learning and teaching strategies for combating them. There is clearly no better place to start than by turning to children's books written *by* Indian authors.

American Indian children's literature covers a wide range of authors and tribal orientation and the full span of age ranges, from picture books such as the Anishinabe writer LOUISE ERDRICH's *Grandmother's Pigeon,* through bilingual readers such as the Creek author Susannah Factor's *Maskoke Unvkuce Cokv Enhvteceskv (Muskogee first story book)* (illustrated by Chester Scott), to book for fourth- to seventh-grade readers such as JOSEPH BRUCHAC's *Skeleton Man* and *The Gathering Tree* by the First Nations Canadian writer LARRY LOYIE, to books recommended for older children, such as

Joseph Bruchac's poetry book *No Borders,* David Wallace Adams's *Education for Extinction: American Indians and the Boarding School Experience, 1875–1928,* and LINDA HOGAN's *POWER.*

In all of these instances these writers emphasize Native experience, often subverting those common stereotypes that many see as detrimental. For instance the Pulitzer Prize–winning novelist and poet N. SCOTT MOMADAY's 1999 text *Circle of Wonder* describes Jemez Pueblo participation in the Catholic mass and is seen by the critic Jim Charles, for instance, as an example of contemporary Indian experience that accentuates *both* the traditional and adaptive aspects of Jemez Pueblo life. Leaving the village procession after midnight Mass on Christmas Eve, Tolo, a mute boy, follows an apparition of his deceased grandfather to a bonfire in the foothills of the mountain. Teaching about inclusivity and harmony, as well as continuity between the traditional and the adapted Jemez Pueblo culture, the book climaxes with Tolo's realization that he is part of all creation and can find his voice again. Just as Erdrich's own drawings illustrate her first full-length children's novel, *The Birchbark House, Circle of Wonder* is illustrated with Momaday's own watercolors, drawn, as the stories are, from memories of his own childhood.

Language acquisition is of course one key factor of children's literature. In American Indian children's literature this has a double spur, in that a number of writers also try to introduce their readers to linguistic patterns—and in some cases, languages—that differ from those of the "mainstream" culture. This ranges from the pedagogic—Susanah Factor's second- and third-grade readers in the Creek language, for instance—to the didactic, such as Erdrich's *The Birchbark House,* which includes a number of Ojibwe words and a glossary at the back of the book. Alongside Factor's readers bilingual picture books for pre–school age children and up are not uncommon, engaging young Native readers, in particular, in cultural and community heritage through language: See, for example, BETH CUTHAND's *TheLITTLEDUCK/SIKHIPIS,* Lenore Keeshig-Tobias's *Emma and the Trees/Emma minwaah mtigooh,* and Deanna Himango's *Boozhoo, Come Play with Us,* which includes photographs of Fond

Du Lac children at play, taken by Rocky Wilkinson. A number of small and large presses that publish bilingual books and board books, such as Kiva and Clear Light, Cherokee Publications, Willowisp, and Press Pacifica, attest to the interest in, and popularity of, this kind of publication, which explicitly promotes both verbal and written language, while implicitly promoting self-esteem, tolerance, and social interaction (Capshaw Smith and Higgonnet 217–224).

The didactic aspect of this type of work is clear and manifests itself not only in language, but also in direct teaching of traditional customs and values. Kristina Heath's board book *Mama's Little One,* for instance, teaches Mohican values and customs such as greeting the morning. Similarly traditional stories retold in picture books, such as Donna Joe's *Salmon Boy: A Legend of the Sechelt People,* teach those values and customs with which oral stories traditionally engage. Older children, meanwhile, are taught aspects of individual cultures, as well as the more complex relationships between cultures, the inaccuracies and abuses of history and historiography, and the trials and tribulations of growing up Native in America through such texts as Cynthia Leitich Smith's *Rain Is Not My Indian Name,* Joseph Bruchac's *The Heart of a Chief,* ELLA DELORIA's *WATERLILY,* or MARIA CAMPBELL's *HALFBREED.*

The majority of these texts are both about teaching Native children about their heritage and the pride they can feel in their culture and its continuation and about exposing non-Native children, regardless of their backgrounds, to unfamiliar cultures, thus countering stereotypes and misrepresentations and encouraging understanding. Authors often appeal to both the culturally specific and the universal, as in Michael Dorris's *Sees behind Trees,* wherein the complexities of the passage from adolescence to adulthood are met head on by a precolonial American Indian boy. Cheryl Savageau's *Muskrat Will Be Swimming,* meanwhile, deals with such conflicts as being and feeling an outsider and such universal needs as the loving care, support, and guidance of one's elders, all within a context that stresses the importance of story and ritual for Native peoples. Engaging with

the wider issues of multiculturalism, VIRGINIA DRIVING HAWK SNEVE has stressed on occasion the joys and dilemmas of raising bicultural children (her husband is third-generation Norwegian), describing texts such as *The Trickster and the Troll* as "Sioux-wegian." These texts, as does American Indian literature in general, clearly explore such issues as identity, tradition, the importance of orality and language, culture and community continuity, history, tolerance and diversity, family, the environment, and nature, to name but a few key themes.

Bibliography

Adams, David Wallace. *Education for Extinction: American Indians and the Boarding School Experience, 1875–1928.* Lawrence: University Press of Kansas, 1995.

Banks, Lynne Reid. *The Indian in the Cupboard.* Garden City, N.Y.: Doubleday, 1981.

Bruchac, Joseph. *Skeleton Man.* New York: HarperCollins, 2001.

———. *No Borders.* Duluth, Minn.: Holy Cow! Press, 1999.

———. *The Heart of a Chief.* New York: Dial, 1998.

Campbell, Maria. *Halfbreed.* Lincoln: University of Nebraska Press, 1973.

Capshaw Smith, Katharine, and Margaret R. Higgonnet. "Bilingual Books for Children: An Interview with Nicolás Kanellos, Director of Piñata Press." *MELUS* 27, no. 2 (summer 2002): 217–224.

Carter, Asa Forrest. *The Education of Little Tree.* Albuquerque: University of New Mexico Press, 2001.

Craighead George, Jean. *Julie of the Wolves.* New York: Harper Trophy, 1972.

Creech, Sharon. *Walk Two Moons.* New York: Harper Trophy, 1994.

Cuthand, Beth. *The Little Duck/Sikhipis.* Vancouver: Theytus Books, 1998.

Deloria, Ella. *Waterlily.* Lincoln: University of Nebraska Press, 1988.

Dorris, Michael. *Sees behind Trees.* New York: Hyperion, 1992.

Driving Hawk Sneve, Virginia. *The Trickster and the Troll.* Lincoln: University of Nebraska Press, 1997.

Erdrich, Louise. *Grandmother's Pigeon.* New York: Hyperion, 1996.

———. *The Birchbark House.* New York: Hyperion, 1999.

Factor, Susannah. *Maskoke Unvkuce Cokv Enhvteceskv* (Muskogee first story book). Washington, D.C.: U.S. Office of Education, 1978.

Heath, Kristina. *Mama's Little One.* Gresham, Wis.: Muh-he-con-neew Press, 1998.

Himango, Deanna. *Boozhoo, Come Play with Us.* Fond Du Lac, Wis.: Fond Du Lac Head Start Program, 2002.

Hirschfelder, Arlene, ed. *American Indian Stereotypes in the World of Children: A Reader and Bibliography.* Metuchen, N.J.: Scarecrow Press, 1982.

Hogan, Linda. *Power.* New York: W. W. Norton, 1998.

Joe, Donna. *Salmon Boy: A Legend of the Sechelt People.* Vancouver: Nightwood Editions, 2001.

Keeshig-Tobias, Lenore. *Emma and the Trees/Emma minwaah mtigooh.* Toronto: Sister Vision, 1995.

Loyie, Larry. *The Gathering Tree.* Vancouver: Theytus Books, 2005.

Momaday, N. Scott. *Circle of Wonder.* Santa Fe, N.Mex.: Clear Light, 1994.

O'Dell, Scott. *Island of the Blue Dolphins.* New York: Houghton Mifflin, 1960.

Rinaldi, Ann. *My Heart Is on the Ground: The Diary of Nannie Little Rose, a Sioux Girl: Carlisle Indian School, Pennsylvania, 1880.* New York: Scholastic, 1998.

Savageau, Cheryl. *Muskrat Will Be Swimming.* Flagstaff, Ariz.: Northland, 1996.

Smith, Cynthia Leitch. *Rain Is Not My Indian Name.* New York: HarperCollins, 2001.

Stewart, Michelle Pagni. "Judging Authors by the Color of Their Skin? Quality Native American Children's Literature." *MELUS* 27, no. 2 (summer 2002): 179–196.

David Stirrup

American Indian drama

In its broadest sense American Indian drama can range from ceremonial-ritual events from the traditional past such as the Bear Ceremonials of the Chippewa; to the *Trail of Tears* drama, a pantribal production designed for tourists and the tribe by the Cherokee Nation in Tahlequah, Oklahoma; to contemporary plays like *BODY INDIAN* by HANAY GEIOGAMAH and *The Woman Who Was a Red Deer Dressed for the Deer Dance* by DIANE GLANCY, to mention only two of the over 100 published plays by American Indians (Vassar 5).

Drama or theater has always been a part of American Indian cultures. The modern Native playwright William Yellow Robe (Blackfoot) sees "a very theatrical tradition in Native American culture" (Interview 5). From the aforementioned Bear Ceremonials of the Chippewa to the Cherokee Booger Dance, the Pawnee Hoka dance, and the Navajo Chants, many tribes had dramatic events that were integral to their traditional cultures. Several of these events simply had theatrical elements to them, such as an adult Hopi dressing in costume and exiting a kiva onto the pueblo square, or an Oglala Sioux shaman enacting a ritual before his tribe. Other rituals actually employed what might be thought of as scripts, such as the Horse Dance enacted by Black Elk and his tribe in *BLACK ELK SPEAKS,* in which the ceremony was carefully planned prior to the ritual: Roles were cast, movements were specified or "blocked," and lines were rehearsed. The line between where these ceremonials stopped and modern playwriting begins is shaky.

Modern Indian theater, such that would be familiar to a contemporary audience, is relatively recent. This form of drama is different from the traditional theatrical gatherings of old in that it features plays by and about Indians in sets, theater buildings, or outdoor theaters. LYNN RIGGS, a Cherokee from Claremore, Oklahoma, was the first well-known Indian playwright. Whereas his first few plays were mostly about the white settlers in the area and their interaction with Native peoples after the Oklahoma land runs, his 1932 play *The Cherokee Night* was completely focused on Native themes. In six individual scenes focused on disparate characters, Riggs illustrates the difficulty for the MIXED-BLOOD offspring falling upon the trails of the Cherokee diaspora. Characters have failed to meet their expectations and lost their way in the absence of traditional culture (much as Riggs himself did). The play's final statement, that a beating drum "is like a fevered and aching disquiet at the pit of the world," is fitting, for it illustrates the difficulties of a Native playwright in the thirties. Riggs's greatest success was with his play GREEN GROW THE LILACS, which went on to become the Rodgers and Hammerstein musical *Oklahoma!* Nominated for a Pulitzer Prize, this play portrays the complicated social state of turn-of-the-20th-century Oklahoma, where Riggs grew up.

Following upon Riggs's success, Arthur Junaluska and Jay Silverheels were able to mount some productions with Native themes in the mid-1950s and 1960s, but none of these productions was retained in script or amounted to anything other than an off-off-Broadway production. Silverheels, who had played the Lone Ranger's Tonto, was able to start the Indian Actors' Guild in Los Angeles and get Indian actors some positions, but without mounting many meaningful productions.

It would not be until the early 1970s that Indian drama would see its true contemporary "birth." On the night of October 25, 1972, at the off-off Broadway La Mama Experimental Theater Club, Geiogamah launched the contemporary era of Indian drama with his play *Body Indian.* With his production company, Native American Theatre Ensemble (NATE), Geiogamah would go on to become the foremost Native American playwright in the seventies. The group spawned a number of theater companies, including Red Earth Performing Arts in Seattle, Washington, and Navajoland Outdoor Theater in Window Rock, Arizona. While Geiogamah's experiment was unable to sustain itself, it was a necessary and productive first step in the creation of a Native American theater. With *Body Indian* and two other plays, *FOGHORN,* and *49,* Geiogamah would be the first American Indian to publish a collection of plays.

Since then other Indian playwrights, including, William Yellow Robe, Bruce King, and Spiderwoman Theater have formed theatrical groups with varying success. King has written a number of plays but few have been published. William Yellow Robe has written and published a number of successful plays and continues working in the area. Spiderwoman Theater, of New York City, which comprises the Colorado and Miguel sisters with Lisa Mayo and Murielle Borst, has mounted many successful productions, mostly at the American Indian Community House in New York City.

However, by far the most successful Native or indigenous theater on the continent is coming out of Canada. In the late 1980s TOMSON HIGHWAY presented *THE REZ SISTERS* (1986) and *DRY LIPS OUGHTA MOVE TO KAMPUSKASING* (1988) to sold-out theaters in Canada's Broadway in Toronto. Other Canadian playwrights, both men and women, including Drew Hayden Taylor and Monique Mojica, have also met with greater commercial success than their American counterparts.

Another interesting arena of Native drama are plays that are written but never published. The Five Civilized Tribes Museum in Muskogee, Oklahoma, hosts a literature contest in three categories each year, one of which is for drama. Since the contest's inception in the early 1970s hundreds of plays have been submitted and a few have eventually been performed or published. This is only one such example, for the number of tribes assures that similar contests exist but are unknown beyond the local level.

It is the lack of knowledge and interest in Native American drama that is its major enemy. It has been said that the only true Native American literary genre is the tribal newspaper, because it is the only literature written and read solely by Indian people. Perhaps because the theatrical productions are often written, acted, and produced by Indians, drama can offer a fresh and new perspective on issues that cannot be called to full public view in novels, essays, or poems. As Geiogamah has written very clearly, "Neither the novel nor polemic has proved effective as means to inspire and stir up dialogue among Indians themselves. This leaves the theater to accomplish the task" (380).

See also GORDON, ROXY; SEVENTH GENERATION: AN ANTHOLOGY OF NATIVE AMERICAN PLAYS.

Bibliography

Aponte, Mimi Gisolfi. "Introduction." *Seventh Generation: An Anthology of Native American Plays,* edited by Mimi D'Aponte, ix–xxiii. New York: Theatre Communications Group, 1998.

Bigsby, C. W. E. "American Indian Theatre." In *A Critical Introduction to Twentieth-Century American Drama.* Vol. 3, *Beyond Broadway,* 365–374. Cambridge: Cambridge University Press, 1992.

Darby, Jaye, and Hanay Geiogamah, eds. *American Indian Theater in Performance: A Reader.* Los Angeles: UCLA American Indian Studies Center, 2000.

Huntsman, Jeffrey. "Native American Theatre." In *Ethnic Theater in the United States.* edited by Maxine Schwartz, 355–385. Westport, Conn.: Greenwood Press, 1983.

Heath, Sally Ann. "The Development of Native American Theater Companies in the United States." Thesis, University of Colorado, 1994.

"Indian Theatre in the United States—1991: An Assessment." *Canadian Theatre Review* 68 (fall 1991): 12–14.

Jenkins, Linda Carol Walsh, and Ed Wapp, Jr. "Native American Performance." *Drama Review* 20 (1976): 5–13.

Stories of Our Way: An Anthology of Native American Indian Plays, edited by Hanay Geiogamah and Jaye Darby. Los Angeles: UCLA American Indian Studies Center, 1999.

Vassar, Andrew. 2002. Hanay Geiogamah, Kiowa-Delaware playwright: A critical biography. Ph.D. diss., University of Arkansas.

Andrew Vassar

American Indian film

Throughout Hollywood history there have been thousands of films that are about American Indians or include Native characters. Usually these depictions of Native peoples can be placed into two categories: "red devil" or "noble savage." The red devils are Indians who stand as impediments to "progress" and resist the settlement of the American West. The noble savages are characters who befriend and serve the white characters. Noble savages are often seen as childlike, yet possessing mystical powers. However, comparatively little attention has been paid to films (often written and directed by American Indians) that portray Indians as complex characters rather than as convenient villains or dupes.

The popular negative images of Native peoples persistent still in the 21st century have their roots in the 19th century. James Fenimore Cooper's *Leatherstocking Tales* clearly establishes the red devil/noble savage dichotomy and the "last of" motif, that Native cultures no longer exist. His works also presented 19th-century audiences with the Indian-as-Sidekick device, which later became popularized by *The Lone Ranger and Tonto* films and series. We also see the Indian sidekick role reprised in the critically acclaimed film *Dances with Wolves* (1990). Fenimore Cooper's work also reflects negative views of miscegenation, as characters who engage in interracial relationships must die. Other forms of entertainment media in the 19th century responsible for the creation and exploitation of such negative stereotypes are Buffalo Bill's Wild West Shows, Indian dramas, and the mass production of dime novels.

Since the civil rights movement in the 1970s, American Indians have become more involved in acting and filmmaking. Among contemporary Indian actors who have been acknowledged for their achievements are Chief Dan George (Salish), Geraldine Keams (Navajo), Will Sampson (Creek), Graham Greene (Oneida), Tantoo Cardinal (Cree), Sheila Tousey (Menominee), Michael Horse (Apache/Zuni), Wes Studi (Cherokee), John Trudell (Santee Sioux), Elaine Miles (Umatilla), Gary Farmer (Mohawk), Irene Bedard (Inupiat Eskimo/Cree), Adam Beach (Saulteaux), Evan Adams (Coast Salish), and Michelle St. John (Cree).

Many Native people have been involved with acting in films since the beginning of Hollywood, but rarely have they been behind the lens. Over the last 50 years Native peoples have been taking a more active role to combat the stereotypical images produced by mainstream Hollywood films, which often show Indians living only in the 19th century and existing as savages with no culture, language, or real spiritual base. Among the contemporary Native directors are Beverly Singer (Santa Clara Pueblo), Victor Masayesva, Jr. (Hopi), Bob Hicks (Creek/Seminole), Melanie Printup Hope (Tuscarora), Sandra Osawa (Makah), Phil Lucas (Choctaw), Arlene Bowman (Navajo), Randy Redroad

(Cherokee), Chris Eyre (Cheyenne/Arapaho), Valerie Red Horse (Cherokee/Sioux), and SHERMAN ALEXIE (Spokane/Coeur d'Alene).

Most notably, in 1997 Miramax picked up the independent film SMOKE SIGNALS, written, acted, and directed by Native peoples. This marked the first time that a Native production had made it to mass distribution. The screenplay, written by Sherman Alexie, was based on his collection of stories THE LONE RANGER AND TONTO FISTFIGHT IN HEAVEN. The film, originally titled *This Is What It Means to Say Phoenix, Arizona,* was directed by Chris Eyre and stars Evan Adams, Adam Beach, Irene Bedard, Gary Farmer, and Tantoo Cardinal. The film is about Victor Joseph, a young man who must travel from the Coeur d'Alene reservation in Idaho to a trailer park outside Phoenix, Arizona, in order to collect his recently deceased father, Arnold. Throughout the film Victor must confront his anger at his father's past transgressions and attempt to resurrect his relationship with his father. Along the way he is aided by his companion Thomas Builds-the-Fire and his father's friend Suzy Song. The film is important because it offers a contemporary story of Native peoples and consciously tears down the stereotypical Hollywood Indian. One source of HUMOR in the film occurs when a number of stock stereotypes are addressed and then swiftly dismantled, such as the noble savage, the Plains warrior, the Indian-as-sidekick, and the "last of" motif.

Not long after the release of *Smoke Signals,* the director Randy Redroad's feature film *The Doe Boy* (2001) was released. It also offers a contemporary story of a young man, Hunter Kirk, who is only one of two Indian people in Oklahoma who suffer from hemophilia. His condition establishes a metaphor for his MIXED-BLOOD heritage. The film, which takes place in 1984 and is set in the Cherokee Nation of Oklahoma, has been praised for its subtle storytelling. Also on the heels of *Smoke Signals* Valerie Red Horse's film *Naturally Native* was released in 1998. Red Horse wrote, directed, produced, and starred in this film about three Indian sisters who try to start up their own line of beauty products. The sisters were raised in a white foster family, and they each deal with their own individual struggle for identity. The film also raises issues about the treatment of Native people in corporate America and about tribal GAMING, which is not surprising since the film was entirely funded by the Mashantucket Pequot Tribal Nation of Connecticut. All of these feature-length films have received a lot of attention and acclaim, and they give hope that someday films such as Masayesva's *Imagining Indians* (1992), Bowman's *Navajo Talking Picture* (1986), Singer's *One Mind, Body, and Spirit* (1993), and Osawa's *Pepper's Powwow* (1995) will become as widely appreciated and as readily available as *Smoke Signals.*

Besides the Mashantucket Pequot, many tribal nations have sponsored the production of film and video projects such as the Chickasaw Nation Cultural Center, Choctaw Video Production, Creek Nation Video, Ojibway & Cree Cultural Center, Suqumish Museum, and Ute Indian Tribe Audio Visual Department. There are also many film festivals that focus on Indian films and videos such as the Native American Film and Video Festival (New York), American Indian Film Festival & Video Exhibition (California), Two Rivers Native Film and Video Festival (Minnesota), American Indian Film and Video Competition (Oklahoma), First Nations Film and Video Festival of Chicago (Illinois), Heard Museum Indigenous Film Festival (Arizona), Native American Film and Television Alliance Film Fest (California), and Native Cinema Showcase (New Mexico). The Sundance Film Festival (Utah) and the Santa Fe Film Festival (New Mexico) also feature categories that highlight the works of Native filmmakers.

It is the hope of many audiences, Native and non-Native, that films and videos that honestly depict Native peoples' experiences will no longer be the exception but the rule.

Bibliography
Berkhofer, Robert F. *The White Man's Indian: Images of the American Indian from Columbus to the Present.* New York: Vintage, 1978.

Kilpatrick, Jacquelyn. *Celluloid Indians: Native Americans and Film.* Lincoln: University of Nebraska Press, 1999.

Leuthold, Steven. *Indigenous Aesthetics: Native Art and Identity.* Austin: University of Texas Press, 1998.

Rollins, Peter C., and John O'Connor, eds. *Hollywood's Indian: The Portrayal of Native Americans in Film.* Lexington: University of Kentucky Press, 2003.

Singer, Beverly R. *Wiping the War Paint off the Lens: Native American Film and Video.* Minneapolis: University of Minnesota Press, 2001.

Smith, Andrew Brodie. *Shooting Cowboys and Indians: Silent Western Films, American Culture, and the Birth of Hollywood.* Boulder: University of Colorado Press, 2003.

Meredith James

American Indian languages

When Christopher Columbus arrived in 1492, North America contained a vast number of indigenous languages within its borders. Some scholars suggest a minimum of 500 languages in North America; others suggest that there must have been at least 1,000 (Cutler 23). Currently there are approximately 300 languages still spoken. Many of these languages have had extensive linguistic scholarship; many others are just now being studied. Early linguistic scholarship amounts to accumulated narratives, ethnographies of the language, grammatical and morphological analyses, and accompanying dictionaries.

Tremendous linguistic diversity reigned on this continent before European contact. In 1976 Mary Haas, commenting on the prehistory of American Indian languages, reported, "We have truly begun to discover the New World, a world of wealth of linguistic variety beyond our most extravagant expectations" (43). Those who appreciate language must concur with her notion that this was a land of linguistic extravagance (and, for the time being, still is).

As with the number of languages, there are also various views on the number of language families in North America. Early scholars suggested there were many linguistic families. Franz Boas, an early leader in the field of American Indian language study, proposed 55 different families (82–83). J. W. Powell, a colleague of Boas, suggested 58 different families (121). Some current scholars prefer to be minimalists, such as Joseph Greenberg, who categorizes the languages into only three families: (1) Eskimo/Aleut; (2) Na-Dene, which includes the Northwest Coast and Athapaskan; and (3) Amerind, which includes all others in North, Central, and South America (38). The Scholars Charles Frederick Voeglin and Florence Marie Voeglin assign approximately eight different linguistic categorizations on their map produced by the American Ethnological Society. However, whether there are only three Native North American linguistic families or 58, or some number between, the multiplicity of languages within those families is undeniable.

Among the first Europeans to contact Native cultures were MISSIONARIES who recorded and translated the stories, songs, and histories of the tribes they had been serving. Publications of these texts usually had a very small readership, and still do, but the influence of the text collection remains today. Many of the missionaries endeavored to translate the Bible (in portions or completely) into the tribal languages of the people with whom they worked. John Elliot secured one of the first translations in Algonquian. This is commonly known as the "Massachusetts Bible," which appeared in Boston in 1633. More than 200 years would pass before the next translation appeared in Cree. The work of these missionaries reveals the importance of language in the context of culture; unfortunately these missionaries did not reflect the majority opinion of later influences, but their contribution to translating the Bible and hymns into American Indian languages remains as an important body of work. It was soon after the Cree translation that American Indian languages would receive attention from academia. Largely because of the notion that Indian languages were vanishing, efforts to record and salvage the languages in America became a priority for linguists.

The latter part of the 19th century culminated in a concerted effort to document American Indian languages. The work that Franz Boas pioneered, *The Handbook of American Indian*

Languages, is a prime example of the early scholarship of the late 19th and early 20th centuries. Boas and his protégés provided works of various tribes, including the Fox, Haida, Hupa, Kwakuitl, Tlingit, Sioux, and Tsimshian. Each effort included a synopsis of the language concerning its phonemic inventory, morphology, and syntax. Each language analysis was usually accompanied by a story or two with interlinear translation and a free translation and a small section of vocabulary. It is from these efforts and ensuing texts that the academic community begins to see the complexity of Native American languages.

Currently the state of Native American languages among Native American communities reflects varied situations for the survival of their languages. The Diné (Navajo) have over 130,000 native speakers of their language, with many children learning it as a first language. Even so, there is concern, because some children are learning to speak English first and some elders feel their language is now endangered as well. Other communities, such as the Haida, are not able to boast such numbers, with only 5,400 members in their tribe. With fewer than 10 percent of the Haida population fluent in Haida, the number decreases each year with the loss of elders who speak the language.

Fear of language loss is a global issue throughout the world. Motivated by this fear, there is a growing concern among American Indian communities and scholars to implement efforts at preserving Native languages. Much research has confirmed the positive aspects of language renewal efforts in North America: Brandt (235) suggests that using the ancestral language improves academic performance. Kroskrity suggests, "Rethinking some of the norms of educational policy and practice" (99) in order to improve the educational situation of American Indians. He indicates that "research along such lines will provide Native American communities both with a means of controlling their linguistic resources and with a basis for appropriate educational reforms" (109). Many other linguists and scholars also confirm that local community involvement concerning Native languages and educational matters is crucial.

Present research points to an undeniable conclusion that maintaining the ancestral language is extremely important. With much of the current language renewal effort relegated to the local schools, understanding different participation styles of Native students provides insight and implications for ancestral language pedagogy.

Compared to the number of Indian authors writing today, the number who incorporate the languages of their tribes in their work is relatively small. Luci Tapahonso is an important example of a well-known writer who publishes in both English and her tribal language, Diné. Because she often writes her poetry in Diné and then translates it into English, it retains a lyrical structure that "sounds" distinctly Navajo. Laura Tohe, another Navajo writer, is fluent in both languages as well. Her poem "Our Tongues Slapped in Silence" documents the pain of being forbidden to speak her native language at boarding school. Nora Marks Dauenhauer is another poet who writes in both English and in her tribal language, Tlingit. She has written several nonfiction books on the language and even includes untranslated poems in her book *The Droning Shaman.*

The playwright Tomson Highway incorporates Cree in his play *The Rez Sisters,* adding one more dimension to the disparate elements at play in the lives of the play's characters. It is especially significant when playwrights such as Highway write in their tribal languages, because doing so gives audiences the chance to hear these little spoken languages.

For those who can speak the ancestral language, its presence nurtures intimacy with the author, as well as a tie with oral tradition. The ancestral language creates bonds closely tied to a particular speech community. The fact that the ancestral language is not the language of wider communication furthers intimacy because of the small community of ancestral language speakers, in some cases a very small circle of speakers. The small community shares the intimacy, a tightly knit community speaking a language that few outsiders recognize or understand. Through putting that language in written form and in a text surrounded by English, the intimacy of the understanding community extends to those who endeavor to grasp its presence.

The situation of many Native languages is at a crucial stage. Goddard, editor of the language volume of the *Handbook of the North American Indian,* suggests that approximately 209 Native North American languages are still being spoken, "perhaps roughly half the number that existed five hundred years earlier." He writes, "Nearly 80 percent of the extant native languages of North America were no longer spoken by children and were facing effective extinction within a single lifetime, or, in most cases, much sooner" (3). Explicit in Goddard's observation is that children need to learn their ancestral language as a first language in order to maintain the linguistic heritage. While there is still tremendous linguistic diversity among Native American communities, the warning is important because in only one generation a language can be lost.

See also HOBSON, GEARY; *HOME PLACES;* JOHNSTON, BASIL; *THE LITTLE DUCK,* YOUNG BEAR, RAY.

Bibliography

Boas, Franz. "Introduction." *Handbook of American Indian Languages.* Smithsonian Institution, Bureau of American Ethnology Bulletin 40. Washington, D.C., 1911, 1–83.

Brandt, E. "Applied Linguistic Anthropology and Language Renewal." *Human Organization* 47 (1988): 103–112.

Cutler, Charles L. *O Brave New Words! Native American Loanwords in Current English.* Norman: University of Oklahoma Press, 1994.

Goddard, Ives. "Introduction." In *Language: Handbook of the North American Indian,* 17, edited by Ives Goddard. Washington D.C.: Smithsonian, 1996.

Greenberg, Joseph. *Language in the Americas.* Stanford, Calif.: Stanford University Press, 1987.

Haas, Mary. "American Indian Linguistic Prehistory." In *Native Languages of the Americas,* edited by Thomas A. Sebeok 2 vols., 23–58. New York & London: Plenum Press, 1976.

Leap, W. "Applied Linguistics and American Indian Language Renewal: Introductory Comments." *Human Organization* 47 (1988): 283–291.

Ortiz, Simon. "Simon Ortiz." *In Poetics and Politics: A Series of Readings by Native American Writers.* Tucson: University of Arizona Press, 1992.

Powell, J. W. "Indian Linguistic Families of America North of Mexico." In *American Indian Languages,* edited by Preston Holder. Lincoln: University of Nebraska Press, 1966.

Sapir, Edward. "Central and North American Languages." In *Encyclopaedia Britannica.* 14th ed., Vol. 5. New York: Encyclopaedia Brittanica, 138–141.

Swanton, J. R. "Haida." *Handbook of American Indian Languages.* Smithsonian Institution, Bulletin of the Bureau of American Ethnology 40, Washington, D.C.: 1911, 205–282.

Voeglin, C. F., and Voeglin, F. M. *Map of North American Indian Languages.* Seattle: University of Washington Press, 1966.

Frederick White

American Indian Literary Renaissance

A period of renaissance, a French word meaning "rebirth," during which American Indian writers have been recognized for their contributions to literature. The term was first used (as "Native American Renaissance") by the literary scholar Kenneth Lincoln in his 1983 book of the same name. In 1968 N. SCOTT MOMADAY (Kiowa) published *HOUSE MADE OF DAWN,* a novel in which the main character, Abel, desperately searches for identity and fights for survival as a Native American male in contemporary American society. After trying to fit into American mainstream society and failing miserably, Abel finally finds his identity by reconnecting himself to the myths, legends, tales, and rituals, not only of his tribal people, the Navajo, traditionally referred to as the Diné, but also of other Native peoples such as the Kiowa. In doing so, Abel finds a way to heal from both the alienation and the ALCOHOLISM that torment him. When Momaday's book won the Pulitzer Prize in 1969, the renaissance began, and American Indian authors and their writing were suddenly popular with a larger mainstream American audience. The popularity of Native American stories was "reborn" within the larger American literary community.

Many other writers contributed to this rebirth that N. Scott Momaday, often referred to as the Father of Native American Literature, initiated with the publication of his novel. Several novelists, short story writers, and poets began writing and publishing: LESLIE MARMON SILKO, JAMES WELCH, LOUISE ERDRICH, JOY HARJO, LUCI TAPAHONSO, SIMON ORTIZ, ELIZABETH COOK-LYNN, and GEARY HOBSON, to name just a few. These writers have contributed literary works that focus on their people and their cultures from which a whole new area of literary study has emerged.

The American Indian Literary Renaissance is truly a rebirth, not a beginning, of a literary tradition. American Indians established that tradition long before 1969. For example, stories are evident throughout the Southwest in ancient towns and cities that were located in places like Chaco Canyon and Mesa Verde. This written tradition appears in the form of rock art called petroglyphs, or carvings or inscriptions. Important dates, beliefs, or events were recorded through a variety of these symbols and pictures. In many instances petroglyphs clustered together in an area, such as a mountain or mesa, in a way became a book, an informally published manuscript that generations of people wrote.

Another type of written tradition appears in the artwork Native Americans created. For example, the Lakota decorated teepees with artistic pictures that told stories of important events and historical events. Stories were also woven into Diné woolen blankets, and totem poles of the northwestern tribes told stories of old adventures and ancestors. In all these forms of written traditions the author is unimportant—the stories belong to the people.

Storytelling, which was and is very important to Indian cultures across America, is yet another part of the rich literary history. Storytelling is a type of literature that is spoken not written and is often referred to as an oral tradition. Within many Native American societies storytellers remember stories that record the important events and religious beliefs that shape the people's culture. They are, in essence, the books and libraries of their people. These storytellers, who hold extremely important

positions within their societies, tell these stories to interested audiences, usually during the long winter nights. Unlike stories in written texts, these stories are fluid, changing; storytellers remember the essence of the stories, or the main points, a duty of great importance, but each storyteller is allowed to change the details of these stories with each telling. In contrast to the authors within written traditions who own the words they wrote in their books, storytellers never think of stories as their own; they are merely the tellers of stories that belong to the people. Within this type of literature are mythical or sacred stories highlighting religious beliefs, legendary stories about historical figures or events, or instructional tales about imaginary figures usually for children. Many of these stories continue to influence contemporary Native American authors, and these myths, legends, and tales from the oral tradition often appear in the published texts in the Native American Literary Renaissance.

When European adventurers, such as the Spanish, Dutch, English, and French, sailed to the American shores, they often had books with them. Indians, who were influenced by this technology of the printed word Europeans took to the Americas, began writing. The result was another type of literary or written text that appeared within American Indian societies. Often, however, Americans of European descent did not always recognize these texts as important forms of American literature. Nevertheless, these early Indian writers influenced later writers, and some of their contributions are artistic creations in their own right. One of the earliest texts was written by SAMSON OCCOM, a Mohegan and Methodist missionary, who became the first published Native American author with his "SERMON PREACHED AT THE EXECUTION OF MOSES PAUL" in 1772. This sermon was very popular and widely read. In 1809, Sequoyah, a Cherokee man who was fascinated by the European alphabet, began inventing 85 characters that represented all the consonant-vowel combinations, or syllables, in the Cherokee language. Others wrote histories and autobiographies. For example, William Warren (Ojibway) wrote *The History of the Ojibway Nation* in 1885; ZITKALA-ŠA (Dakota) published three autobiographical stories in *The Atlantic Monthly* in

1900; and LUTHER STANDING BEAR (Dakota) contributed MY PEOPLE, THE SIOUX in 1928.

The American Indian Literary Renaissance is a period in which Indian writers were recognized for beautifully written literary texts. However, it is only a period of rebirth, or recognition, for these Indian writers. Contemporary poets, short story writers, and novelists owe much of their popularity and their success not only to the publishers who noted the literary significance of their works but also to those earlier Indian writers and storytellers who told stories on rocks, in artwork, in oral stories, and in written works. Nevertheless, these contemporary Indians contribute a plethora of new stories about Indian cultures across America, stories steeped in history and rich in tradition. (See the *Internet Public Library: Native American Authors*, http://www.ipl.org/div/natam, for a listing of numerous Indian authors, both those included in the renaissance and those who preceded them.)

Bibliography

Krupat, Arnold. *The Voice in the Margin: Native American Literature and the Canon.* Berkeley: University of California Press, 1989.

Lincoln, Kenneth. *Native American Renaissance.* Berkeley: University of California Press, 1983.

Owens, Louis. *Other Destinies: Understanding the American Indian Novel.* Norman: University of Oklahoma Press, 1992.

Velie, Alan R. *The Lightning Within: An Anthology of Contemporary American Indian Fiction.* Lincoln: University of Nebraska Press, 1991.

Wiget, Andrew. *Native American Literature.* Boston: G. K. Hall, 1985.

Jami L. Huntsinger

American Indian Movement

Frequently referred to as the "Red Power Movement," the American Indian Movement (AIM) began in 1968 as a means to address issues of police brutality against Native Americans. In 1969 AIM members joined with the Indians of All Tribes in occupying Alcatraz Island in protest of the living conditions on reservations. After their 1973 siege of WOUNDED KNEE the movement's activities nearly halted as leaders were embroiled in legal battles. Leaders such as Dennis Banks and Russell Means went on trial for their involvement at Wounded Knee, while Leonard Peltier was convicted of the 1975 murder of two Federal Bureau of Investigation (FBI) agents. Despite these setbacks, AIM remains politically active, participating in the movement to free Leonard Peltier and to end racism in sports.

Several works of literature deal with AIM. Russell Means's autobiography *Where White Men Fear to Tread* (1995) details his involvement in the leadership of AIM. The first two parts of Means's book explain the many forces in his childhood and young adult life that led him to militancy and the American Indian Movement. Means's activities with AIM and the courtroom trials he endured because of his affiliation compose the third part. In the fourth part of the book Means discusses his life after AIM, including his film career. Another prominent figure, Leonard Peltier, also recounts his involvement with AIM, as well as his subsequent incarceration, in his *Prison Writings: My Life Is My Sundance* (1999). Peltier constructs his narrative as a mixture of journal entries and poetry, calling for readers to take action, to deliver his message.

GERALD VIZENOR and LOUISE ERDRICH have incorporated AIM in their novels. In Vizenor's BEARHEART: *The Heirship Chronicles* (1990), the title character shatters a young AIM member's assumptions about tribal culture in his opening monologue. In Erdrich's LOVE MEDICINE (1993) Lyman Lamartine mentions in passing that his mother, Lulu, is involved with AIM. Another vignette in Erdrich's novel notes that King, an unethical character, informed on an AIM member.

While few works of fiction focus on AIM, JOY HARJO's poem "For Anna Mae Pictou Aquash, Whose Spirit is Present Here and in the Dappled Stars (for we remember the story and must tell it again so we may all live)" (1990) directly addresses the life and death of the AIM activist. Aquash was murdered and her body dumped in 1975. FBI medical examiners attributed her death to exposure. Aquash's family requested an independent autopsy, which concluded that a gunshot wound to the base of the skull killed her. Harjo's poem urges the reader to remember Aquash's vibrancy and beauty in life, as well as her violent death.

Bibliography

American Indian Movement Grand Governing Council. Available online. URL: http://www.aimovement.org. Accessed on August 15, 2005.

Matthiessen, Peter. *In the Spirit of Crazy Horse.* New York: Viking, 1991.

Smith, Paul Chaat, and Robert Allan Warrior. *Like a Hurricane: The Indian Movement from Alcatraz to Wounded Knee.* New York: New Press, 1996.

Robin Gray Nicks

American Indian novel

The American Indian novel is the most widely read and most studied genre of American Indian literature. Beginning with JOHN ROLLIN RIDGE's *THE LIFE AND ADVENTURES OF JOAQUIN MURIETA, THE CELEBRATED CALIFORNIA BANDIT,* in 1854, which, as did most novels of the 19th century, employed a traditional, chronological narrative, the genre has grown to encompass daring postmodern narrative techniques, comic situations, and complex characters who embody tradition and modernity at the same time. Ridge, also known as Cheesquatalawny and Yellow Bird, published his novel, based on the life of the legendary Mexican-American Californian bandit Joaquín Murieta, in 1854 and the University of Oklahoma Press reissued it in 1955. In the novel Murieta's attempt at gold mining is disrupted by the state's Foreign Miner's Tax Law of 1850, which made it virtually impossible for Latin Americans to mine in the state. He is beaten and forced to leave the state and decides to settle with his wife in Sonora. When he is pushed out again, he becomes a professional monte dealer. Almost immediately, he is falsely accused, with his half brother, of stealing horses. His half brother is hanged without judge or jury, and it is this event that spurs Murieta's bloody bandit life.

Some might question why Ridge chose the Mexican-American bandit as the subject of his only novel. Some critics have speculated that Ridge used Murieta's life to represent the racist and violent treatment Indians suffered as a result of U.S. Indian policy. Ridge constantly reminds the reader that Murieta was driven to his bloody outlaw life despite the fact that he consistently tried to live peacefully.

The second Indian-authored novel, and the first by a woman, is *WYNEMA: A CHILD OF THE FOREST* by Sophia Alice Callahan. It was originally published by H. E. Smith & Co., of Chicago in 1891 but remained relatively unknown until 1955, when Carolyn Thomas Foreman came across it while doing research on Callahan's father, Samuel Callahan. The novel was reprinted in 1997 by the University of Nebraska Press. It is a story about the lifelong relationship of the title character, Wynema Harjo, and Genevieve Weir, a Methodist teacher. It discusses issues such as the DAWES ACT of 1887, Christianity and Indians, and women's suffrage.

Despite its merit as being the first novel by an Indian woman, *Wynema* has engendered criticism. Some scholars have pointed out that because of the different perspectives within the narration, the story is seldom told from a Native one. Indian characters, other than Wynema, are sporadically placed throughout the text, and even Wynema's voice is often dominated by Genevieve. Some critics have even taken issue with the inaccuracies of the Callahan's historical events, such as the introduction of Christianity to the Creek people and some misrepresentations of Creek culture. Some have suggested that the novel is not so much about Wynema as Genevieve's confronting her misconceptions of Creek culture.

Another notable Indian novelist is MOURNING DOVE (Hum-Ishu-Ma, Cristal Quintasket Mcleod Galler), who wrote *COGEWEA, THE HALF-BLOOD: A Depiction of the Great Montana Cattle Range,* published in 1927. Intended as a romantic western, the book focuses on life on the fictional H-B Ranch (some critics speculate the *H-B* stands for *Half-Blood*) in Montana. Although there are numerous characters who symbolize different aspects of MIXED-BLOOD social, economic, and political issues, the narrative focuses on the protagonist, Cogewea, who is half-Okanoga and half-white.

In 1934, the Osage writer JOHN JOSEPH MATHEWS published his novel *SUNDOWN.* The plot follows the life of Challenge Windzer, a mixed-blood Osage. Chal's birth occurs at a critical point in Osage history, a transition between the old into the new. With *Sundown* Mathews articulates the overall feeling of Osage country during the 1920s and 1930s. Chal found himself between two conflicting factions among the Osage: the traditionalists—those who opposed the encroaching western expansion—and the progressives—those who felt ASSIMILATION would only benefit the Osage. Chal never sways completely to one side or the other. He is both critical of and open to both stances throughout the novel.

Sundown has not received critical attention equal to D'ARCY MCNICKLE's *The SURROUNDED*, published in 1936. McNickle is arguably the most influential and important American Indian writer of the first half of the 20th century. *The Surrounded* begins with Archilde Leon, half-Salish and half-Spanish, returning to the Flathead reservation in Montana with aspirations to return to Portland, Oregon. In the beginning he finds himself in conflict with almost every social and cultural reality on the reservation. He has trouble negotiating his relationships with his parents, his father's outside status, his mother's loyalty to traditional ways, and the missionary school he attended, which his nephews are being forced to attend. Although bleak, the ending does represent Archilde's return to his tribal community. The "homing" plot would set a paradigm that would carry into contemporary Indian novels.

The year 1968 proved a watershed year for the American Indian novel. It was in this year that Kenneth Lincoln coined the phrase *Native American Renaissance* to describe the surge in popularity and volume of works produced by contemporary Native writers that began with the Kiowa and Cherokee author N. SCOTT MOMADAY's *HOUSE MADE OF DAWN*. In addition to *House Made of Dawn*, four other novels by American Indian writers have received an extensive critical attention, JAMES WELCH's *WINTER IN THE BLOOD*, LESLIE MARMON SILKO's *CEREMONY*, GERALD VIZENOR's *DARKNESS IN SAINT LOUIS BEARHEART*, and LOUISE ERDRICH's *LOVE MEDICINE*.

N. Scott Momaday's best-known novel, *House Made of Dawn*, won the Pulitzer Prize in 1969. The novel's protagonist, Abel, is a young World War II veteran from Jemez Pueblo who struggles to reconcile his existence in two different worlds. Beginning in Jemez Pueblo, the novel takes a nonlinear approach that chronicles Abel's personal journey from alienation to reconciliation as he finds his place in his home community upon his return from the war. Abel moves to Los Angeles after he is convicted of killing another Pueblo man and proves incapable of functioning in the white world as well. Abel eventually returns to Jemez, where he is reintegrated into the community through healing ceremonies.

James Welch is a Blackfeet and Gros Ventre author from Montana who won the Lifetime Achievement Award for Literature in 1997. His most famous novel, *Winter in the Blood*, is a surreal glimpse into the life of a Blackfeet man who remains unnamed throughout the story. *Winter in the Blood* (1974) is an Indian coming-of-age story that presents the development of the narrator's Indian identity in a harsh, yet comic manner.

Leslie Marmon Silko, Laguna Pueblo, is most well known for her novel *Ceremony* (1977), which tells the story of a Laguna mixed blood, Tayo. Tayo returns home after World War II and is plagued by imbalance that manifests itself in alcoholism and other self-destructive behavior until he begins to heal by achieving a deeper understanding of traditional Laguna ways of life. The novel weaves traditional stories from the Laguna Pueblo people into Tayo's personal story, creating a healing ceremony in and of itself. This novel is most often compared to Momaday's *House Made of Dawn* because of its modernist style and plot line.

Gerald Vizenor, a White Earth Chippewa from Minnesota, has published a large volume of work that spans various genres and themes. Vizenor's novels often take a poststructuralist approach to Indian identity through the use of wordplay. Vizenor has coined several neologisms such as *postindian survivance* and *terminal creeds*, which defy static notions of identity construction. Vizenor is most well known for his use of the TRICKSTER FIGURE motif to deconstruct imposed notions of Indianness upon contemporary American Indian people. *Darkness in Saint Louis Bearheart: The*

Heirship Chronicles (1978) is a picaresque novel about the encounters of a family of tricksters and the pilgrims who accompany them to various places in America during a time of crisis due to an oil shortage. These tricksters seek healing through their journeys where they meet mythic characters taken mainly from Chippewa oral traditions.

Louise Erdrich, Turtle Mountain Chippewa, constructs an entire community of characters based on her home reservation in North Dakota in a series of novels that begins with *Love Medicine,* published in 1984. *Love Medicine* introduces the reader to a number of characters in the Kashpaw and Morrissey families, examining the lives of several generations, ultimately showing how individual stories are inextricably tied to communal existence.

The Spokane and Coeur d'Alene tribal member SHERMAN ALEXIE, from Washington, addresses Indian issues. from a contemporary standpoint and relies heavily on pop culture references directed primarily toward a younger audience. His novel *RESERVATION BLUES* (1995) narrates the adventures of an Indian blues band from the Spokane Indian reservation. *INDIAN KILLER* (1996) is about the racial tensions that surface in Seattle when a serial killer begins to murder and scalp white men.

THOMAS KING is a Cherokee author whose main subject matter is Canadian First Nations people as he lives and teaches in Ontario and has been a longtime Canadian resident. His novel *GREEN GRASS, RUNNING WATER* tells the story of four escaped American Indian mental hospital patients whose previous escapes coincide with seemingly unrelated catastrophes in history. The escapees find themselves on a Blackfeet reserve in Canada, and the novel tells of their interactions with one family on that reserve.

ELIZABETH COOK-LYNN, Crow Creek Sioux tribal member, has written one novel, *From the River's Edge* (1991), which developed into a larger work entitled *Aurelia: A Crow Creek Trilogy* (1999). *Aurelia* recounts the stories of a Sioux family over several generations and their struggle to retain land against destructive federal government policies and simultaneously captures Sioux cultural nuances and subtleties through characterization.

Other Indian novelists include the Meskwaki writer RAY YOUNGBEAR, who wrote *BLACK EAGLE CHILD: THE FACEPAINT NARRATIVES* (1996), which is a fusion of autobiography and fiction that offers the story of the narrator while constructing a Meskwaki history that integrates oral tradition and pop culture. LINDA HOGAN, Chickasaw, authored *SOLAR STORMS* (1995) and *POWER* (1998); her most well-known novel is *MEAN SPIRIT* (1990), which tells of the choices that an Osage family must make between white and Indian worlds during the Osage oil boom. A *PIPE FOR FEBRUARY* (2002) by the Osage author CHARLES RED CORN is a historical novel that depicts the life of the Osage during the oil boom in the early 20th century. The Cherokee author Betty Louise Bell wrote *FACES IN THE MOON* (1995), which addresses the struggles that Cherokee women face over a period of three generations.

As can be noted from the publication dates of the novels discussed, the American Indian novel has virtually exploded in the past two decades New promising writers appear on the scene every year. At the heart of any good novel is a good story, and the storytelling traditions held sacred in tribal communities make this genre an especially good fit for American Indian authors.

Bibliography

Lincoln, Kenneth. *Native American Renaissance.* 2nd rev. ed. Los Angeles: University of California Press, 1985.

Rainwater, Catherine. *Dreams of Fiery Stars: The Transformation of Native American Fiction.* Philadelphia: University of Pennsylvania Press, 1998.

Velie, Alan R. *Four American Indian Literary Masters: N. Scott Momaday, James Welch, Leslie Marmon Silko, and Gerald Vizenor.* Norman: University of Oklahoma Press, 1982.

Veronica Pipestem, John Sexton, and Jennifer McClinton-Temple

American Indian poetry

While the genre of poetry holds a place of great significance within the larger dynamic of American

Indian literature, what is and has been historically considered American Indian poetry continues to be a point of debate. As early as the 1600s Indian songs and oral performances were referred to in European narratives as "poetry." In *Historie of Travell into Virginia Britania* (1612), William Strachey provides a literary introduction to the text of a Powhatan song citing the "homely rhymes" and the "amorous dittyes in their language." However, the songs and oral stories of the Powhatan and other Indian tribes were not intended for literary interpretation. Recording the songs and stories as poetry removed from them the specific ceremonies, activities, and beliefs originally associated with them. In addition, transcribing oral performances as poetry led to the blurring of the line between two separate cultural forms: oral performance and crafted poetry.

Before the American Indian Literary Renaissance in the late 1960s, most of what was identified as American Indian poetry was actually oral stories and songs recorded in verse as poetry by missionaries, ethnographers, and anthropologists who were inclined to define Native artistic forms in relation to their own cultures. Collections of and translations of oral narratives, such as Natalie Curtis's *The Indians' Book* (1907), Mabel Washborne Anderson's "Nowita, the Sweet Singer" (1908), George W. Cronyn's *The Path on the Rainbow* (1918), Mary Austin's *The American Rhythm* (1932), Margot Astrov's *The Winged Serpent* (1946), and A. Grove Day's *The Sky Clears* (1951) primarily present translations and ethnographers' selections, not original American Indian poetry.

American Indian poetry does locate its roots in the oral tradition. The principles informing the oral tradition, such as the belief in the power of language to organize experience, to effect change, and to heal, greatly influence the ways in which Indian writers conceptualize language and craft poetry. While the oral tradition informs a poet's relationship with language and rhythm and shapes his or her poetry in a fundamental way, oral narratives transcribed in verse as poetry should not be read as consciously crafted Indian poetry. No evidence suggests that Native people expected their oral stories and songs to be recorded or analyzed as literature.

The beginning of a written American Indian poetic tradition can be traced to the 1800s. Among the first poets to find her way into print was Jane Johnston Schoolcraft. In the early 1820s her poems appeared in *The Literary Voyager,* a magazine founded by her husband, the ethnographer Henry Rowe Schoolcraft. Though her poems are heavily influenced by her European education, "Otagamiad" and "Invocation to My Maternal Grandfather on Hearing His Descent from Chippewa Ancestors Misrepresented" draw upon her Ojibwe heritage.

The African-American/Montauk poet Olivia Ward Bush-Banks published *Original Poems* in 1899 and *Driftwood* in 1914; however, with the exception of "Morning on Shinnecock," most of Bush's poetry focuses not on her Montauk heritage but on her African-American heritage.

In the early 1900s the Lakota writer ZITKALA-ŠA (Gertude Simmons Bonnin) published several poems in *American Indian Magazine.* Unlike that of her predecessors, Zitkala-Ša's writing focused almost exclusively on Indian issues. In "The Indian's Awakening" (1916) Zitkala-Ša writes, "I've lost my long hair; my eagle plumes too. / From you my own people, I've gone astray. / A wanderer now, with no where to stay" (17–19). Zitkala-Ša's poetry often explores the feelings of trauma, alienation, and self-questioning brought on by experiences with Indian BOARDING SCHOOL and ASSIMILATION and relocation policies.

Though a few Indian poets did publish before the mid-1960s for the most part Indian voices were either completely silenced or transcribed by non-Natives. In her essay "The 19th Century Native American Poets" (1980) LINDA HOGAN suggests that the federal government's efforts to "escalate assimilation altered and limited the possibilities of literature being written by Native American poets." Not until N. SCOTT MOMADAY received the Pulitzer Prize for *HOUSE MADE OF DAWN* in 1969 did the long silencing of Indian writers end.

Though it was a novel of Momaday's that garnered mainstream awareness of Indian literary production, interestingly, most accomplished Indian novelists began their careers as poets, and many of them, including Momaday, LESLIE MARMON SILKO, Linda Hogan, and SHERMAN ALEXIE, have said that they imagine themselves first as poets and second as writers of fiction.

After mainstream recognition of *House Made of Dawn,* the movement Kenneth Lincoln dubbed the *Native American Renaissance* gained momentum. In the early 1970s an unprecedented number of poets began to publish their works: Besmilr Brigham's *Heaved from the Earth,* LANCE HENSON's *Keeper of Arrows,* SIMON ORTIZ's *NAKED IN THE WIND,* and JAMES WELCH's *RIDING THE EARTHBOY 40* in 1971; PAULA GUNN ALLEN's *Blind Lion,* N. SCOTT MOMADAY's *ANGLE OF GEESE,* Wendy ROSE's *HOPI ROADRUNNER DANCING,* and Leslie Marmon Silko's *LAGUNA WOMAN* in 1974; *The LAST SONG* by JOY HARJO and *Conversations from the Nightmare* by CAROL LEE SANCHEZ in 1975; Gladys Cardiff's *To Frighten a Storm* and Marnie Walsh's *A Taste of the Knife* in 1976; ELIZABETH COOK-LYNN's *The Badger Said This,* MAURICE KENNY's *North: Poems of Home,* ADRIAN LOUIS's *Muted War Drums,* and NILA NORTHSUN's *DIET PEPSI AND NACHO CHEESE* in 1977; Linda Hogan's *Calling Myself Home* in 1978; and the list goes on.

The materialization of so many poets during the 1970s signaled the emergence of an American Indian poetic tradition. The existence of a generation of living, writing poets meant that Indian poetry could, for the first time, be defined and analyzed not only in relation to Euro-American culture but also on its own terms. Furthermore, it meant that later generations of poets such as Sherman Alexie, KIMBERLY BLAESER, CHRYSTOS, Tiffany Midge, Cheryl Savageau, LUCI TAPAHONSO, and LAURA TOHE would have Indian literary predecessors.

Although Indian poets hail from heterogeneous tribes from regions across the United States, their works often share common characteristics. Among them is a concern for the ways in which thriving Native cultures are studied and discussed as though the tribes are no longer existent. Poets such as CARTER REVARD, Chrystos, and Wendy Rose attack those who either profit from a history of Indian genocide or perpetuate stereotypes of Indians. In "Winter Count" from *Dream On* (1991)

Chrystos writes, "We are the butt of jokes, the gimmicks for ad campaigns / romanticized into oblivion. So carefully obscured / that many think we are all dead" (18–20). Similarly, Rose, becoming aware of how the bones of Indians are priced and sold, wonders in "Three Thousand Dollar Death Song" from *LOST COPPER* (1980), "How one century / turns our dead into specimens, our history / into dust, our survivors into clowns" (33–35).

American Indian history and the contemporary exploitation of Indian culture prompt poets to focus on the theme of survival. Though the need to preserve tribal traditions in order to ensure personal and tribal survival is evident in much Indian poetry, poets approach the theme in a multitude of ways. Joy Harjo often writes poems in which a reconnection to a mythic, transformational presence provides hope for survival in the present moment. In "Song for the Deer and Myself to Return On" from *IN MAD LOVE AND WAR* (1990), the speaker sings an old Creek song and deer appear in her city apartment. "Now," the speaker explains, "the deer and I are trying to figure out a song / to get them back, to get us all back" (11–12). By reconnecting to her Creek heritage, the speaker hopes to be able to return either physically or psychically to her Native home.

Simon Ortiz also treats the theme of survival in his poetry. In "A San Diego Poem: January–February 1973" from *A GOOD JOURNEY* (1977), he writes, "[m]ountains and canyons and plants / grow." He concludes, "'We shall survive this way'" (96–97, 105). Ortiz finds a map for survival in the regenerative powers of the natural world.

Many poets depict human survival as intimately interconnected with and interdependent with the survival of the natural environment. In her poem "Desert" from *Seeing Through the Sun* (1985), Linda Hogan erases distinctions between the human body and the earth as she tells her daughter that the earth "wills itself out of our skin. / The red sky ends at our feet / and the earth begins at our heads" (28–30). As in Hogan's work, in the poetry of Momaday, Indian attitudes of reciprocity with nature are emphasized. Characters in his poems define their existence in terms of landscape.

Not all Indian poets have an innate relationship to their natural landscapes. Many are from urban environments and struggle to rehistoricize place. In poems like "New Orleans," "Crossing the Border," and "Anchorage," Joy Harjo's speaker travels to ancestral homelands and to historical sites of triumph and loss. As new landscapes are explored and the stories of the lands learned, the way in which the speaker connects to place is transformed.

The environment, however, is not always transformed in a positive way. In *Laguna Woman* (1974) Leslie Silko exposes the exploitation and negative transformation of the natural world. In "Toe'osh: A Laguna Coyote Story" she describes the "Trans-Western pipeline vice president," who came to "discuss right-of-way" (45–46). Silko juxtaposes a description of the "vice president" with a depiction of greedy Toe'osh stealing picnic food. The developer does not have a reciprocal relationship with the land; he exploits it avariciously.

In "That Place Where Ghosts of Salmon Jump" from Sherman Alexie's *The SUMMER OF BLACK WIDOWS* (1996), the poet expresses disbelief in man's ability to disconnect from and to ignore the nurturing potential of the natural world. He asks whether "concrete ever equals love" (19). White men, he explains "sometimes forget to love their own mothers / so how could they love this river which gave birth / to a thousand lifetimes of salmon?" (20–22). The loss of the salmon leaves the speaker searching for a new way to imagine the natural world.

Reimagining the natural world, the human beings' place in the world, and the effects of the past on the present and the future is characteristic of American Indian poetry. Many poets set out to reclaim their histories. In "Pocahontas" and "The One Who Skins Cats" from *SKIN AND BONES: POEMS 1979–87* (1991), Paula Gunn Allen revises history by giving voice to those who have been historically silenced. In both poems Allen allows the women to respond to distorted accounts of their experiences. In "The One Who Skins Cats," for example, Sacagawea resists appropriation by constantly redefining herself. She says, "I am Slave Woman, Lost Woman, Grass Woman, Bird Woman. / I am Wind Water Woman and White Water Woman, and I come / and go as I please" (25–27). Indian poets often return to their histories in order to challenge the dominant narrative that has for so long controlled the images of Native Americans.

Reclaiming their stories, histories, and images proves to be a difficult process. Because not all poets have access to their tribal tongues and because those who do live primarily in an English-speaking world, the poets must find new ways to write and to imagine themselves into being. Through their adoption of poetry, Indian writers have created a poetic tradition built on history and imagination, magic and loss, provocative language and an acute awareness of the loss of language. Not only have they created an American Indian poetic tradition, but they have also permanently redefined and expanded the American literary scene.

See also AMERICAN INDIAN LITERARY RENAISSANCE.

Bibliography

Bruchac, Joseph. *Survival This Way: Interviews with American Indian Poets.* Tucson: Sun Tracks and University of Arizona Press, 1987.

Fast, Robin Riley. *The Heart as a Drum: Continuance and Resistance in American Indian Poetry.* Ann Arbor: University of Michigan Press, 1999.

Lincoln, Kenneth. *Sing with the Heart of a Bear: Fusions of Native and American Poetry, 1890–1999.* Berkeley and Los Angeles: University of California Press, 2000.

Wilson, Norma C. *The Nature of Native American Poetry.* Albuquerque: University of New Mexico Press, 2001.

Amanda Bass Cagle

American Indian Religions
See SPIRITUALITY.

American Indian Stories   Zitkala-Ša (1901)
American Indian Stories is a collection of pieces, both fiction and nonfiction, by the early Sioux

writer, teacher, and activist ZITKALA-ŠA. Many of the pieces were first published in the magazines *Harper's* and *Atlantic Monthly* in 1900 and 1901. Zitkala-Ša's work is especially important because it is unmediated by others, by translators, editors, or ghostwriters. It is one of our only glimpses of 19th-century Indian life through the eyes of a woman. The three essays that begin the text, "Impressions of an Indian Girlhood," "School Days of an Indian Girl," and "An Indian Teacher among Indians," are the most widely read. They offer a plain, unsentimental view not only of the author's unspoiled childhood on the plains, but also of the heart-wrenching torment of being taken, even voluntarily, as was the case with her, from that life and being schooled in the ASSIMILATIONist methods of the U.S. government.

In the first story, "Impressions of an Indian Girlhood," we see the elements that made Zitkala-Ša's childhood idyllic. She spends her days with her beloved mother, living simply and happily among the people of their clan. They eat well, live in a wigwam, and as a child, she feels secure, loved, and carefree. In chapter 2, she gives us a detailed account of how her mother passes on to her the intricate art of beadwork, and how she works to become more proficient at it. During this section of the text, however, there are hints of the problems ahead. She mentions how the "paleface" made her mother cry and how she observed the gradual changes to her mother's home: the buffalo skin of the wigwam that was exchanged for the "whiteman's canvas," the clumsy "home of logs" in which her mother eventually lives. She tells, finally, the story of the red apples. When she is eight years old, she feels the temptation to go with the whites to the East, as her brother had gone before her and her friend is going now. In describing this yearning, however, significantly she uses Christian imagery, the famous symbol of temptation, the apple. She says, "I had never seen apple trees. I had never tasted more than a dozen red apples in my life; and when I heard of the orchards of the East, I was eager to roam among them" (42). Readers of the time, both Indian and non-Indian, would certainly have seen this symbol as a foreboding sign.

Indeed, when she is taken to the BOARDING SCHOOL, she immediately longs to go back to her mother, aunt, and brother. She rebels against the trappings of this white education: the tight dresses, the short hair, the seemingly arbitrary punishments. But she learns; not only does she learn academically, but she learns how to rebel within the white system. Once told to mash the turnips for supper, she takes out her rage by mashing them to a pulpy mess and accidentally breaking the jar. She feels triumphant, however, because she has simultaneously done what she was told to do and rebelled. Throughout this section, entitled "School Days of an Indian Girl," perhaps the most widely anthologized portion of the text, we see that as she gradually learns how to navigate the system of white education and moves away from her Sioux roots, she learns to hate the system and yearns to go back to those roots.

When one of her classmates dies at the school, the sick child talks incoherently of Jesus Christ, infuriating Zitkala-Ša. She says, "I blamed the hard-working, well-meaning, ignorant woman who was inculcating in hearts her superstitious ideas" (67). But later, she says, "Though I was sullen in all my little troubles, as soon as I felt better I was ready again to smile upon the cruel woman" (67). This duality, or the ability to feel a part of the white world and to despise it at the same time, runs throughout much of the text. When she wins a prestigious state oratory contest and the crowd refers to her as a "squaw," her reaction is not to deflate, but rather to harden and become more determined to show the whites what she can do.

In the final autobiographical essay, "An Indian Teacher among the Indians," Zitkala-Ša devotes much space to describing the sense of hopelessness and difficulty an educated Indian had working with the government. In general, assimilation was the goal, but once assimilated, Indians would never be accepted into society as full-fledged members. She ends this section with a bleak statement, noting that few of the whites who congratulate themselves for their charity to the Indian stop to ask whether "real life or long-lasting death lies beneath this semblance of civilization" (99).

The remainder of *American Indian Stories* consists of fictional accounts that dramatize many of the themes of her nonfiction. Most notable is the story "The Soft-hearted Sioux," in which a young Sioux brave leaves his home to be educated and when he returns, faces the tragedy that he no longer fits into either world. He accidentally kills his father and ultimately is put to death by the white man for his crime. This story effectively demonstrates Zitkala-Ša's question, Is "civilization" a path to life, or a path to certain death?

Bibliography

Cutter, Martha. "Zitkala-Ša's Autobiographical Writings: The Problems of a Canonical Search for Language and Identity." *MELUS* 19, no. 1 (1994).

Ancient Acid Flashes Back   Adrian C. Louis (2000)

In his 10th book of poetry *Ancient Acid Flashes Back,* ADRIAN C. LOUIS explores the complexities of a "half-breed" Indian, Naatsi, trying to survive on the margins of Indian country and dominant American society with his characteristic blend of biting humor, anger, and tenacity. Unlike much of Louis's work, the bulk of these poems take place away from the reservation, in 1960s Haight Ashbury (a neighborhood in San Francisco that was the center of the counterculture movement), which Louis refers to as a "living borderlands / of American life—a homeland for outsiders" (2–4). Louis's portrait of Haight Ashbury reveals that outsider status results from a variety of cultural backgrounds and experiences and is in fact endemic to life in the United States for anyone who objects to its defining myths and foreign policies.

While many American Indians are fighting in Vietnam, Naatsi avoids the war and blocks out the realization that "the true religion / of man is killing his fellow man" (3–4). Sex and drugs anesthetize Naatsi to the realities of war and what he sees as the grim state of existence as an outsider within the United States. The fantasy world of lysergic acid diethylamide (LSD) allows him to imagine America's "sweet possibilities," but they are only drug-induced hallucinations.

The book reads as layers of flashbacks within flashbacks. Naatsi writes as a middle-aged man, returned to his homeland, surrounded by dying trees and engulfed in a wave of bitterly nostalgic memories of the 1960s. He thinks of "the general incompetence & aimlessness / of this lost nation" (7–8), haunted by the feeling that the hippie movement failed. Through their "shallow & indulgent escapism" they "tried to tame the manic, / anal-retentive beast that America was, / but they only wounded & maddened it" (12–14). As much as this wistful reflection suggests a belated hope for social change, the young Naatsi, in Washington, D.C., during a Vietnam War protest, betrays the political despair that defines his older self: "Maybe the revolution has started / but Naatsi no longer cares" (17–18). Now in 1971 Naatsi sees the movement as dying, and even in its peak moment of social activism, a vain hope. He sees the future as "mind-dead & televised, / grim, greedy & goofy" (19–20). It seems his forecast is accurate, given the book's depiction of the older Naatsi, numbed by bad television, without the motivation to reach for the remote control and change the channel.

Bibliography

Brown, Ruoff, and A. LaVonne. *American Indian Literatures: An Introduction, Bibliographic Review, and Selected Bibliography.* New York: Modern Language Association, 1990.

Louis, Adrian. "Adrian-C-Louis.com." Available online. URL: http://www.adrian-c-louis.com/testsite/index2.htm. Accessed on August 15, 2005.

———. *Ancient Acid Flashes Back.* Reno: University of Nevada Press, 2000.

Owens, Louis. *Mixedblood Messages: Literature, Film, Family, Place.* Norman: University of Oklahoma Press, 1998.

Roppolo, Kimberly. "Upcoming: Entry on Adrian Louis." In *Encyclopedia of American Indian History,* edited by Barry Pritzker and Bruce Johansen. Santa Barbara: ABC-CLIO, 2006.

Tereza Szeghi

Ancient Child, The   N. Scott Momaday
(1989)

This novel is a combination of Kiowa legend, Wild West history, and mystic powers. The novel is divided into four books. The individual sections of each book vary greatly in their structure and length. The reader needs to pay special attention to the way each section is narrated since the perspective moves among different characters. Momaday begins with a prologue briefly telling of Tsoai, the Kiowa legend of a boy who became a bear and chased his seven sisters into the sky, where they became stars. He also provides a list of nine major characters, including the Bear, who is described as the mythological manifestation of the wilderness.

The main male character is Locke Setman, who is known as Set. After being orphaned as a child, he was raised in a Catholic school for Native American children, the Peter and Paul Home, which echoes the unforgiving Indian BOARDING SCHOOLS children were forced into by the U.S. government. The nuns created a long list of things the children could not do. But Set still had the wanderlust and would travel paths that literally were forbidden. His free spirit found an expression in his art, which became his vocation.

The main female character is Grey. We first see her very early in the book as a young girl with the frail but wise Kope'mah, the ancient medicine woman. When Set gets word that Kope'mah, his grandmother, is dying, he travels to his family's home. There he enters the more traditional Kiowa world of Grey. She takes over for the grandmother as a guide and protector to her people. Set is drawn immediately to her and Grey realizes she has seen Set in a vision.

Many historical Old West characters fly in and out of the story. Most famous of them are Billy the Kid, or Henry McCarty as Momaday calls him, and Pat Garrett. The legends of both sides in the Old West are alive, but Grey also fights against history. In a very graphic scene Grey circumcises a stereotypical white, Dwight Dicks. He believes Grey is there to satisfy his wants, but she captures him and he is handled as a piece of livestock. Afterward, as she bathes in the river, it is said the voice of her late grandmother is shimmering on the water's surface.

Set falls madly in love with Grey, with the freedom he has as artist, and with the ancient story of the Bear. Set and Grey begin travel into the high country of the Southwest to find the truth of her visions and the truth of his identity as man or bear. As the story ends, he is transformed to complete the cycle begun by Tsoai.

Bibliography

Schubnell, Mathias. *Conversations with N. Scott Momaday.* Jackson: University Press of Mississippi, 1997.

Michael Young

Angle of Geese and Other Poems
N. Scott Momaday (1974)

N. SCOTT MOMADAY had been writing poetry since his college days at the University of New Mexico, and this volume incorporates many of his earlier efforts. Momaday admired the poetry of Hart Crane as an undergraduate, and early poems like "Los Alamos" reflect Crane's influence. Under the tutelage of Yvor Winters at Stanford University Momaday developed an ability to provide clear, precise details and images in his verse.

As a graduate student at Stanford, Momaday absorbed the influence of an eclectic group of poets including Emily Dickinson, Wallace Stevens, Paul Valéry, Charles Baudelaire, and Frederick Goddard Tuckerman, the subject of Momaday's Ph.D. dissertation. What these poets had in common, at least in the eyes of Momaday and Winters, was the practice of establishing a conceptual theme, but then giving it meaning with concrete, sensory images.

The title poem, "Angle of Geese," shows how Momaday employs sensory experience as an integral part of the message, not just as ornament. In the first part of the poem Momaday relates his reactions to the funeral of a friend's child: "How shall we adorn / Recognition with our speech? / Now the dead firstborn / Will lag in the wake of words." *Wake* refers to the trail of water behind a boat, but also to the gathering one has to celebrate the life and mourn the loss of a dead person. Momaday broaches a favorite theme: the power and limitations of language.

The second part of the poem relates an incident that occurred in Momaday's youth. On a hunting trip he had shot a goose and held it as it died. He had told the story in a column in the *Santa Fe New Mexican* and included a fictionalized version of the story in *HOUSE MADE OF DAWN*. The incident brought home to Momaday the reality of death, and he was impressed with the calm demeanor of the goose in the face of it.

In an effort to force language to express emotions that defy its resources, Momaday employs the trope of catachresis, twisting words out of their normal usage: In the phrase "pale angle of time and eternity" Momaday describes the formation of the geese, and "wide of time" is the way he describes the goose's awareness that it is leaving life on Earth.

Momaday also includes some very different types of poems in *Angle of Geese,* poems in what one might call his "Navajo style." For seven years when he was a young child Momaday lived among the Navajo on the Dine, as they call their lands. He often heard Navajo songs, which make use of parallelism, repetition, and accretion for poetic effect. "The Delight Song of Tsoai-talee" from *Angle* clearly appropriates Navajo tropes and rhythms: "I am a feather in the bright sky . . . / I am the farthest star / I am the cold of the dawn" (1–3). "Tsoai-talee" is Momaday's Kiowa name. It means "Rock Tree Boy," a reference to Devils Tower, a monolith in northeastern Wyoming sacred to the Kiowa. The poem is about Momaday's recognition of his [place in the cosmos, to] the earth, the gods, all that is beautiful.

Bibliography

Momaday, N. Scott. *Angle of Geese and Other Poems.* Boston: D. R. Godine, 1974.

Aniyunwiya/Real Human Beings: An Anthology of Contemporary Cherokee Prose Joseph Bruchac (1995)

In the brief introduction volume JOSEPH BRUCHAC— not a Cherokee himself, but of Abenaki ancestry—

tells readers: "Few Native peoples have had more written about them and in the long run, been less understood than the people most Americans call 'Cherokee'" (2). He points out that *Ani-yun-wiya,* meaning "real human beings," is what the Cherokee originally called themselves, and this is how they continue to see themselves, regardless of the mispronunciation and the countless stereotypes.

In this volume Bruchac brings together 35 stories or excerpts of prose by 23 contemporary Native authors; only 10 of these works had been published. This work includes a bibliography of works and detailed author information on Carrol Arnett/Gogisgi, Rilla Askew, Marilou Awiakta, Betty Louise Bell, Charles Brashear, E. K. Caldwell, ROBERT J. CONLEY, Karen Coody Cooper, Robert Gish, DIANE GLANCY, Rayna Green, CATRON GRIEVES, Raven Hail, GEARY HOBSON, Cynthia Kasee, Wilma Mankiller, Ron Rogers, Ralph Salisbury, Jean Starr, Winn Starr, Glen Twist, Eddie Webb, and Ron Welburn.

Bruchac says that all of those writers "claim Cherokee ancestry as a defining point in their artistic vision" (2) and whether a reader selects an excerpt from a memoir, such as the one written by the Cherokee chief Wilma Mankiller, or a retelling of an ancient tale, by a "newcomer" such as Eddie Webb, the reader is sure to see the great "variety and complexity of voices," which "though they stem from one particular Native people," are "emblematic of the vitality and the range of experiences" of "contemporary American Indian lives" (3).

The entire collection is made up of individual works that would stand alone, but explored together they demonstrate a greater depth of spirit. One line in particular from the anthology may strike a cord with Native readers, "There's power in the blood," from an old song the author grew up hearing in the Appalachian Mountains, in Marilou Awiakta's "Red Clay: When Awi Usdi Walked Among Us." There *is* power in the blood, and it is evident throughout the collection. The prose is heartbreaking, enlightening, empowering, and hopeful. This collection is an excellent resource for anyone who wants to read high-quality contemporary Cherokee prose.

Geraldine Cannon Becker

Antelope Wife, The   Louise Erdrich (1998)

LOUISE ERDRICH's sixth novel moves beyond the boundaries of her earlier works, transporting the reader away from familiar settings and characters. The novel introduces a new group of urban Chippewa people living in Minneapolis. Strong thematic echoes link *The Antelope Wife* with Erdrich's more connected works: It continues her exploration of memory, loss, and obsessive love. The novel has an ambitious, overarching sweep, spanning several generations of three families. Erdrich steeps her narrative in Ojibwe history, interweaving layers of myth with a suspenseful present-day narrative.

The novel tells the story of the Roys, the Shawanos, and the Whiteheart Beads, whose lives intersect to create a complex genealogical history. As a descendant of all three lineages, Cally Roy, one of the novel's narrators, senses that such has a duty to "understand and to report" this history (220). Drawing from the family myth of twins competing for prized whiteheart beads, she seeks the beads of her relative, Sweetheart Calico. The act of beading becomes an extended metaphor in the novel for the process of unraveling history and continuing its design through storytelling. As Klaus Shawano, a key character, notes, this is a continuous, collaborative process: "My beadwork is made by relatives and friends whose tales branch off in an ever more complicated set of barriers" (27).

Sweetheart Calico is Klaus's lover and the "antelope wife" of the title. When the Ojibwa settled on the plains the antelope people entered their mythology as elusive beings that move between two worlds, changing their form. When Sweetheart Calico joins the Shawano family as a woman she continually longs for the freedom of the plains. Before she returns home she passes on to Cally the beads that represent a potential connection between them, suggesting that the pattern of history will survive. She enters the tradition of Erdrich's female characters who wander between two worlds, forging connections.

Readers familiar with Erdrich will recognize her signature narrative techniques. The novel's episodic structure moves swiftly from past to present, requiring the reader to make imaginative leaps backward and forward in time. A large cast of narrators includes Almost Soup, a witty dog who observes events with a touch of Indian survivalist humor.

Although *The Antelope Wife* celebrates continuity and survival, at the end of the book Erdrich questions the process fulfilled by Cally. Framing the narrative is a first-person storyteller who concludes by asking whether such patterns of history truly exist: "Did these occurrences have a paradigm in the settlement of the old scores and betrayals that went back in time? Or are we working out the minor details of a strictly random pattern? . . . Who are you and who am I, the beader or the bit of colored glass sewn into the fabric of this earth?" (240).

Bibliography

Erdrich, Louise. *The Antelope Wife.* London: Flamingo-Collins, 2002.

Jacobs, Connie A. *The Novels of Louise Erdrich: Stories of Her People.* American Indian Studies 11. New York: Lang, 2001.

Stookey, Lorena L. *Louise Erdrich: A Critical Companion.* Critical Companions to Popular Contemporary Writers. Westport, Conn.: Greenwood, 1999.

Rachel Lister

anthropology and Native Americans

Since the 19th century Native American peoples have been primary subjects of interest in North American anthropology. This interest has been a mixed blessing in the eyes of many Native scholars. While many anthropologists have been staunch advocates for Indian rights, anthropology has also been recognized as an instrument of imperialism, a branch of the colonial administration that subjugates indigenous peoples. For most of relevant history anthropologists lived among Natives, irrespective of Native choices in the matter.

The "imperialist" attitude of early anthropologists is implicit in the work of the American Bureau of Ethnology during the late 19th century. The bureau's mandate to record Native languages, customs, and beliefs was not directed toward the protection of Native ways of life, but toward the ASSIMILATION of a supposedly savage and barbarous race in the American melting pot. Government anthropologists observed traditional practices of elders, while federal policy forced younger generations to abandon Native languages, customs, and beliefs. Some information collected by anthropologists proved valuable to later generations of Indians, when a more relaxed federal policy allowed them to practice their rituals and speak the languages of their great-grandparents. But for Native Americans to study old anthropological texts to gain knowledge of their culture is ironic, considering the texts were a product of the same federal policy that stripped the tribes of this knowledge.

In 1911 the Seneca Arthur Parker cofounded the Society of American Indians, a major pan-Indian organization, and in 1935 he became the first president of the Society for American Archaeology (SAA), a major organization of professional anthropologists. Parker's vision of anthropology, in his words, was "as an intermediary not only between the Indians of today and their past history, but between the Indian and the white man of today" (Thomas 181).

But not all anthropologists have been as successful as Parker at mediating between the world of traditional natives and a mostly white audience of anthropological scholarship. Zuni Pueblo in present-day New Mexico is an example of a community betrayed by the anthropologists it hosted. Frank Cushing was a 19th-century anthropologist, a white man adopted by the Zuni. In their midst he developed the now standard anthropological field methods of participant observation. A government ethnologist and a Zuni war chief, he was fluent in Zuni language and ceremony. He published detailed accounts of secret Zuni rituals and manufactured a sacred Zuni mask for display in the Smithsonian. He never expected his Zuni friends to learn of his betrayal, but they did soon after his death in 1901 (76).

As a result of such betrayals many tribes became more secretive and refused access to anthro-pologists, at which point anthropologists used deception in order to gain access. The anthropologist Ruth Bunzel lived at Zuni for five years in the late 1920s, ostensibly as a student of Zuni pottery craft. Having secretly taken field notes, she later published descriptions of the ceremonies she had attended. The result of such subterfuge was a strong movement by the mid-20th century to exclude whites from authentic Indian ceremonies. Some 20th-century anthropological literature is of dubious quality, because anthropologists were themselves deceived by Native American informants who desired to keep their secrets.

In this context the "rebel" anthropologist Frank Waters, son of a mixed-race Cheyenne father and a white mother, wrote his classic novel *The Man Who Killed the Deer* (1942), on the subject of Pueblo life and ceremonialism. He presented it to the Pueblo council for review, writing that their "approbation meant more . . . than all the reviews" (Waters 375).

VINE DELORIA, JR.'s classic *CUSTER DIED FOR YOUR SINS* (1969) contains a chapter entitled "Anthropologists and Other Friends," which adequately sums up Indian resentment of anthropologists. In a litany of criticisms of the profession, he claims that Native peoples are treated as objects, that anthropologists do not recognize contemporary Indians as authentic (because, for example, they do not still hunt buffalo), and that anthropologists consume tribal resources but do not contribute to tribal well-being. The new generation of anthropologists, exposed to Deloria's work, transformed the discipline. Most contemporary anthropologists are more sensitive to Native concerns as a direct result of Deloria's critique (Grobsmith 36). Support of anthropologists was instrumental in the passage of the Native American Graves Protection and Repatriation Act (NAGPRA) in 1990, mandating the return of Indian remains held by scientists. Subsequent conflicts between Natives and scientists have divided the anthropological community over their responsibility to Natives.

Deloria remains one of the staunchest critics of traditional anthropology. After the passage of NAGPRA Deloria criticized the Society of American Archaeology in the pages of its own journal, *American Antiquity.*

> Some representatives of the SAA feel that their final efforts of support [for NAGPRA] should ... mask what were some dreadfully arrogant attitudes earlier in the struggle. (1992 595)

Further, he wrote that the reconciliation of Indians and scientists would require more than a few "civil conversations." He nonetheless suggested that archaeology could benefit Natives, if practiced under the direction of Native leaders.

The views of N. SCOTT MOMADAY contrast with those of Deloria on this subject. As Deloria does, he acknowledges abuses by anthropologists and archaeologists, most grievously "the theft of the sacred" and the "violation of burial sites and the confiscation of human remains" (206–207). Unlike Deloria, he does not oppose scientific conclusions or suggest that Native input is required to ensure their soundness. Momaday argues that Deloria and others "assume unreasonable attitudes," in refusing to believe "hard evidence" gathered by anthropologists. Momaday states, "Reason is on the side of science" (207). What constitutes the ideal relationship between anthropologists and Native Americans will likely continue to divide the communities involved. There is no consensus among anthropologists or Native American authors.

Bibliography

Deloria, Vine, Jr. *Custer Died for Your Sins.* New York: Macmillan, 1969.
———. "Indians, Archaeologists and the Future." *American Antiquity* 57, no. 4 (1992): 595–598.
Grobsmith, Elizabeth. "Growing Up on Deloria: The Impact of His Work on a New Generation of Anthropologists." In *Indians and Anthropologists: Vine Deloria Jr. and the Critique of Anthropology,* edited by T. Biolsi and L. J. Zimmerman, 35–49. Tucson: University of Arizona Press, 1997.
Momaday, N. Scott. "Science, Tradition, and the Future." In *The Epic of Evolution: Science and Religion in Dialogue,* edited by James B. Miller, 206–208. Upper Saddle River, N.J.: Pearson Prentice Hall, 2004.
Thomas, David Hurst. *Skull Wars: Kennewick Man, Archaeology, and the Battle for Native American Identity.* New York: Basic Books, 2000.
Waters, Frank. *Masked Gods: Navaho and Pueblo Ceremonialism.* Athens, Ohio: Swallow Press, 1950, 1970.
———. *The Man Who Killed the Deer: A Novel of Pueblo Indian Life.* Athens, Ohio: Swallow Press, 1942, 1970.

Joe Wilson

Apess, William   (1798–1839)

The Pequot author, historian, preacher, and activist William Apess was born in Colrain, Massachusetts, on January 31, 1798, to mixed-race parents William and Candace Apes (Apess changed the spelling of his surname in adulthood). Apess's family moved to Colcester, Connecticut, shortly after his birth and lived there for approximately three years. When William and Candace separated, they left Apess and his siblings in the custody of the maternal grandparents, who treated the young boy harshly. After a particularly severe beating Apess was taken from his grandparents and made a ward of the town. Starting at the age of four or five, he was bound out to a neighbor and subsequently was indentured to a string of guardians.

Regularly attending Methodist meetings, Apess experienced a religious conversion in March 1813. Later that year he and another indentured boy ran away and joined the militia, in which he served until 1815. Apess wandered in Canada for a few years before returning to New England. He married Mary Wood in 1821. After his baptism in 1818 he decided to preach. When the Methodist Episcopal Church refused to ordain him, Apess turned to the more inclusive Protestant Methodist Church, and he served as an itinerate preacher both before and after his ordination in 1829. From the late 1820s through the 1830s he wrote in a variety of genres promoting Native American rights and the Christian faith. According to a newspaper account, Apess died in 1839 of apoplexy (not alcoholism, as suggested in recent treatments). He was survived by his second wife, Elizabeth, and several children.

Apess's *A Son of the Forest,* the first autobiography written and published by a Native American, appeared in 1829 and in a revised edition in 1831. Its format closely follows that of the conversion narrative, chronicling the author's progression from orphan to preacher. Apess shared his life story again in *The Experiences of Five Christian Indians of the Pequot Tribe* (1833) along with the conversion narratives of Mary Apess, Hannah Caleb, Sally George, and Anne Wampy. Apess's *The Increase of the Kingdom of Christ: A Sermon* (1831)—published with the appendix *The Indians: The Ten Lost Tribes*—and *Eulogy on King Philip* (1836) give us an idea of the power of Apess's oratory. In *Indian Nullification of the Unconstitutional Laws of Massachusetts Relative to the Marshpee [sic] Tribe; or, the Pretended Riot Explained* (1835), Apess chronicles the Mashpee Revolt of 1833–34, when the Native American residents of Mashpee, Massachusetts, with the aid of Apess, challenged the commonwealth's management of their land and funds and called for self-government.

All of Apess's works are marked by their vigorous challenge to racism and the historical oppression of Native Americans. In particular he considers how racist terms like *savage* obscure long-standing injustices. In *A Son of the Forest,* for example, he rejects the term *Indians* as "a slur upon an oppressed and scattered nation," preferring instead *"Natives"* (10). Further, he notes the irony that whites do not act as the "civilized people" they claim to be (33). Apess asserts that children, white and Native alike, learn a partial and damaging history of race relations, recalling how, as a young child, he ran from a group of dark-skinned women in the forest because he assumed they were Indians and feared they would take him captive.

Appended to *Experiences of Five Christian Indians,* "An Indian's Looking-Glass for the White Man" contains Apess's most striking attack on racism and injustice. As he does throughout his writings, he argues that racism contradicts Christian precepts, for God made all of humanity in his image. In fact, he notes, Jesus Christ and the apostles, as Sephardic Jews, were people of color.

Apess further rejects racist justifications for the oppression of minorities by "not talking about skin but about principles" (156). The "black inconsistency" of whites' treatment of Native Americans and other people of color, Apess declares, "is ten times blacker than any skin that you will find in the universe" (157). The essay, then, serves as a mirror for white readers, who, rather than focus on the skin color of others, should instead gaze upon the moral darkness of their own racial prejudice.

In his final publication, *Eulogy on King Philip* (which he delivered in Boston twice in January 1836), Apess rewrites American history by replacing the leaders of the revolution with a new American hero: the Wampanoag leader King Philip, or Metacom, who led a coalition of New England Native Americans against English colonists from 1675 to 1676, when he was killed by colonial forces. (Interestingly enough, in *A Son of the Forest* Apess claims to be descended from the Wampanoag leader, but he does not mention this in the *Eulogy.*) Apess names this murdered rebel "the greatest man that ever lived upon the American shores" (290). Anticipating Frederick Douglass's "What to the Slave is the Fourth of July?" Apess also asserts that Native Americans consider December 22 (the anniversary of the landing at Plymouth Rock) and July 4 days of mourning rather than celebration. Thus he alters the typical patriotic address of the period to reveal the hypocrisy at the heart of the democracy's history and society.

Bibliography

Apess, William. *On Our Own Ground: The Complete Writings of William Apess, a Pequot,* edited by Barry O'Connell. Amherst: University of Massachusetts Press, 1992.

Konkle, Maureen. "William Apess, Racial Difference, and Native History." In *Writing Indian Nations: Native Intellectuals and the Politics of Historiography, 1827–1863,* 97–159. Chapel Hill: University of North Carolina Press, 2004.

O'Connell, Barry. "Introduction." In *On Our Own Ground: The Complete Writings of William Apess, a Pequot,* edited by Barry O'Connell, xiii–lxxvii. Amherst: University of Massachusetts Press, 1992.

Sayre, Gordon M. "Defying Assimilation, Confound-
ing Authenticity: The Case of William Apess." *a/b:
Auto/Biography Studies* 11, no. 1 (spring 1996):
1–18.

Laura L. Mielke

Armstrong, Jeannette C.   (1948–   )

Jeannette Christine Armstrong was born in 1948 on
the Penticton Indian Reserve in British Columbia.
She is a fluent speaker of the Okanagan language
and has studied traditional teachings under the direction of Okanagan elders. Her formal education
includes a diploma of fine arts from Okanagan College and bachelor of fine arts degree granted in 1978
by the University of Victoria. In 2000 Armstrong
received an honorary doctorate of letters from St.
Thomas University.

An environmental activist, creative writer of both
fiction and poetry, visual artist, and literary critic,
Armstrong began her writing career at an early age
with the publication of a poem about John F. Kennedy in a local newspaper. Influenced by the literary
career of the Okanagan novelist MOURNING DOVE,
her mother's great-aunt, and the storytelling traditions of the Okanagan people, Armstrong counts the
works of E. PAULINE JOHNSON, Harry Robinson, and
George Ryga as important indigenous literary influences. Her writing is also deeply political through its
examination of the effects of cultural imperialism
and the everyday consequences of cultural intoler-
ance that manifests itself through cultural exclusion
and disrespect for difference. In her first novel written for adolescent readers, Armstrong explores the
early life of two girls growing up in the Okanogan
Valley prior to the arrival of non-Native people.
SLASH, her second novel, which followed *Enwhisteekwa: Walk in Water,* documents the coming-of-age
story of Tommy Kelasket, a young Okanagan Indian who is torn between his attraction for the "Red
Protest" movement of the 1960s and the traditional
teachings of the Okanagan elders. The story of Tommy's attempts to understand racial prejudice reflects
Armstrong's ongoing commitment to promoting
literature as a vehicle for fostering indigenous education and alternative conceptions of Native history

and identity so as to eradicate misconceptions and
cultural prejudice toward indigenous peoples. Armstrong's role as executive director of the En'owkin International School of Writing, an Okanagan cultural
and educational institution dedicated to the practice
of traditional knowledge systems, and her environmental activism to foster education that leads to sus-
tainable patterns of living have received international
recognition. She has served as a consultant to the
Centre for Ecoliteracy, the Omega Institute, and the
Centre for Creative Change and World Institute for
Humanities, in addition to participating as an international observer to the Continental Coordinating
Commission of Indigenous Peoples and Organizations. In recognition of her artistic achievement, she
has received the Mungo Martin Award, the Helen
Pitt Memorial Award, and the Vancouver Founda-
tion Graduate Award. In 2003 she was awarded the
Buffett Award for Indigenous Leadership.

Bibliography
Armstrong, Jeanette C. *Enwhisteekwa: Walk in Water.*
Penticton, Canada: Okanagan Indian Curriculum
Project, 1982.
———. *Looking at the Words of Our People: First Na-
tions Analysis of Literature.* Penticton, Canada:
Theytus Books, 1993.
———. *Native Poetry in Canada: A Contemporary An-
thology.* Peterborough, Canada: Broadview Press,
2001.
———. *Slash.* Penticton, Canada: Theytus Books,
1985.
Isernhagen, Hartwig. *Momaday, Vizenor, Armstrong:
Conversations on American Indian Writing.* Nor-
man: University of Oklahoma Press, 1999.
Petrone, Penny. *Native Literature in Canada: From Oral
Tradition to the Present.* Toronto: Oxford University
Press, 1990.

Cheryl Suzack

Arnett, Carroll   (Gogisgi) (1927–1997)

Carroll Arnett was born in Oklahoma City in 1927.
He was the grandson of Tennessee Ellen Belew
(Ballou), a Cherokee woman from North Carolina.
He attended Oklahoma University for one semester

in 1945, then enlisted in the U.S. Marine Corps and served in 1946–47. After his military service ended, Arnett attended Oklahoma City University in 1947, then transferred to Beloit College, where he earned his B.A. magna cum laude in 1951. In the spring of 1952 Arnett returned to Oklahoma University for graduate studies, then transferred to the University of Texas, where he received his M.A. Arnett taught at Knox College, Stephens College, and Nassón College before being hired in 1970 to help build a graduate writing program at Central Michigan University (CMU). Arnett was still teaching at CMU at the time of his death in 1997.

Arnett wrote under both his birth name and his Cherokee name, Gogisgi (Smoke), which he relates was given to him by his grandmother, Tennie, in a dream ("Ayanvdadisdi" 21). He served his tribe as a Deer Clan Chief of the Overhill Band of the Cherokee Nation. He served the greater Native American community through his activism and the Native American writing community through his mentorship of early-career writers.

Arnett received a National Endowment for the Arts Fellowship in Creative Writing in 1974. He has published 14 books of poetry, beginning with *Then*. The most recent are *Spells* and *Night Perimeter: New and Selected Poems 1958–1990*. The Native literary critic GEARY HOBSON notes that the four signature characteristics of Arnett's poetry are "the understatement, the irony, the brevity, and humor" (Hobson 45). He often explores the theme of respect, juxtaposed against its Gogisgian opposite, wastefulness. For Gogisgi respect is always the antidote to wastefulness. This selection, from one of Gogisgi's best known poems, "The Old Man Said," is representative of Arnett's style: "It is only done with / those who waste. / They are not wasted. / they are thrown away."

Carroll Arnett's poetry and his life were infused with wisdom and respect. He was, above all, a teacher, an elder brother. He left for our instruction a poetry that continues to inspire respect and delight.

Bibliography

Arnett, Carroll. *"Avanvdadisdi: I Remember."* In *Here First: Autobiographical Essays by Native American Writers*, edited by Arnold Krupat and Brian Swann. New York: Modern Library, 2000.

———. *Night Perimeter: New and Selected Poems 1958–1990*. Greenfield Center, N.Y.: Greenfield Review Press, 1991.

———. "The Old Man Said." In *South Line: Poems*. New Rochelle, N.Y.: Elizabeth Press, 1979.

Spells. Blue Creek, Ohio: Bloody Twin Press, 1995.

Hobson, Geary. "Carroll Arnett." *Nimrod: Oklahoma Indian Markings*. 32, no. 2 (1989): 44–49.

Jeanetta Calhoun

Arrow over the Door, The   Joseph Bruchac (1998)

The Arrow over the Door is a volume of historical fiction, a narrative based upon a true event, the tale of the "Easton Meeting." This is the story of two communities (a scouting party made up primarily of Abenaki American Indians and a small community of Quakers meeting in prayer) who meet during the Revolutionary War and find friendship.

With this short piece JOSEPH BRUCHAC is retelling the true story that illustrates not only the similarities between disparate cultures, but the way their very differences can unite them both and lead toward greater understanding. Utilizing an alternating first-person narrative form, the story switches back and forth between the young Abenaki Stands Straight and the young Quaker Samuel Russell. Samuel Russell finds himself at odds with his Quaker upbringing. In a time of war he feels anger and frustration with the world and dreams of lashing out at those who would threaten his family. Stands Straight is a young tracker who is fighting on the side of the British during the Revolutionary War. During a scouting expedition of the "Bostoniak," Stands Straight draws upon the wisdom of his elders and a growing sense of maturity to see beyond stereotype and rumor. Samuel Russell is fighting a battle between his love for his family and the ways he is most familiar with, and a desire to protect these treasures at any cost. The violence he is beginning to feel an affinity for is alien to Quaker tradition and causes him great emotional distress. These two boys, young adults to their individual cultures in the sense of the term, find a sense of brotherhood when they encounter each other at the Quaker meetinghouse. Readers can see through their differences their true similarities and perhaps then understand the underlying similarities among all peoples.

Bibliography

Bruchac, Joseph. *The Arrow over the Door.* New York: Puffin Books, 1998.

Owens, Lewis. *Other Destinies: Understanding the American Indian Novel.* Norman: University of Oklahoma Press, 1994.

Scarberry-Garcia, Susan. *Landmarks of Healing: A Study of* House Made of Dawn. Albuquerque: University of New Mexico Press, 1990.

Slapin, Beverly, and Doris Seale, eds. *Through Indian Eyes: The Native Experience in Books for Children.* Berkeley, Calif.: Oyate, 2003.

Weaver, Jace. *That the People Might Live: Native American Literatures and Native American Community.* New York: Oxford University Press, 1997.

Solomon Davidoff

assimilation

The process by which an ethnic group abandons its culture to adopt that of a larger, dominant group is called assimilation. It was the title of the official policy of the United States to encourage the assimilation of American Indians from 1870 to 1934 (the "Assimilation period"), and again from the 1940s to the 1960s. During the Assimilation period, Indian reservations were divided into individual properties (DAWES ACT, 1887) to foster individualism as opposed to tribalism, and American Indian children were taken out of the reservations to attend special BOARDING SCHOOLS that would "civilize" them. They had to wear uniforms, have short hair, convert to Christianity, eat no traditional foods, speak only English, and use new names. In the 1950s assimilation was again encouraged with incentives for the Indians to move to big cities.

Even if assimilation is no longer the official policy, it still affects American Indians. First, they bear the consequences of the past policy. Second, some decide to live off the reservations and try to assimilate themselves. Third, the mixed ancestry of many Indians makes assimilation both inevitable and impossible for them.

Assimilation in American Indian literature appeared first in narratives, often autobiographical, written between the 1850s and the 1930s. American Indian writers told their personal, real assimilation stories. In 1883 *Among the Piutes; Their Wrongs and Claims* by SARAH WINNEMUCCA recounts her experience as an intermediary between her tribe and the government, describing assimilation practices and Indian resistance. Other major works include Francis LaFlesche's *The Middle Five* (1900), LUTHER STANDING BEAR's *My People the Sioux* (1928), and CHARLES EASTMAN's *From the Deep Woods to Civilization* (1916), in which the authors describe their childhoods in boarding schools. Standing Bear sold his reservation allotment, toured with Buffalo Bill's Wild West Show, and obtained American citizenship; as a result his autobiographical work is an essential piece of literature on assimilation.

Major works of fiction appeared in the 1930s, such as JOHN JOSEPH MATHEWS's *SUNDOWN* (1934), which depicts the conflict within an American Indian family between a traditional mother and a father in favor of assimilation. The main character of the novel, their son, Chal, rejects Indian culture but finds little comfort in the white world.

The AMERICAN INDIAN LITERARY RENAISSANCE, starting in the late 1960s, produced many works dealing with various negative forms of assimilation: boarding schools or female sterilization, specific to Indian assimilation policies, but also partial assimilation, due to enrollment in the U.S Army, a MIXED-BLOOD identity, or modern RESERVATION LIFE. Tragic novels show mixed-bloods trying to integrate into American society failing because they can neither deny nor enjoy their Indian heritage. This is the case of JAMES WELCH's main characters in such novels as *WINTER IN THE BLOOD* (1974), *The DEATH OF JIM LONEY* (1987), and *The HEARTSONG OF CHARGING ELK* (2001).

The trauma caused by assimilation in the U.S. Army during World War II leads the main character of N. Scott Momaday's *House Made of Dawn* (1968), Abel, to lose touch with his Native side and flirt with insanity, alcoholism, and violence. Louise Erdrich underscores the power of Christian conversion in *Love Medicine* (1984, 1993), in which Marie's personality is shaped in a convent by her constant physical and psychological fight against a white nun, Sister Leopolda. The convent's dominant location at the top of a hill makes it a pervading symbol of assimilation throughout the novel.

The necessity of partial assimilation has developed since the 1970s, particularly through the ironic tones of Gerald Vizenor's, nila northSun's, and Sherman Alexie's works. They appeal to the American literary and academic scene, because of their postmodern techniques, which happen to coincide with Indian traditions of trickster figure tales and oral storytelling: a playful attitude toward hardships, language, and storytelling, as well as narrative structures that do not follow the traditional Western patterns of chronology and conflict resolution. Their books offer epitomes of a culture of semiassimilation. They reveal the danger but also the power of an appropriation of the white culture instead of assimilation, as in Alexie's short story "The Only Traffic Signal on the Reservation Doesn't Flash Red Anymore," which discusses "reservation basketball heroes" (45). The title of northSun's chapbook of poems *diet pepsi & nacho cheese* (1977) also testifies to this ironic turn. It involves appropriating the stereotypes of the Indian created by the whites, to debunk these stereotypes, but also to deal with them and what may be true in them, so that a healthier contemporary Indian identity may emerge.

Bibliography

Alexie, Sherman. "The Only Traffic Signal on the Reservation Doesn't Flash Red Anymore." In *The Lone Ranger and Tonto Fistfight in Heaven.* New York: HarperPerennial, 1994.

Eastman, Charles Alexander. *From the Deep Woods to Civilization: Chapters in the Autobiography of an Indian.* 1916. Reprint. Lincoln: University of Nebraska Press, 1977.

Erdrich, Louise. *Love Medicine.* New and expanded ed. New York: HarperPerennial, 1993.

Hopkins Winnemucca, Sarah. *Among the Piutes: Their Wrongs and Claims,* edited by Mrs. Horace Mann. 1883. Reprint, Reno: University of Nevada Press, 1994.

LaFlesche, Francis. *The Middle Five: Indian Schoolboys of the Omaha Tribe.* 1900. Reprint. Madison: University of Wisconsin Press, 1963.

Mathews, John Joseph. *Sundown.* 1934. Reprint, Norman: University of Oklahoma Press, 1988.

Momaday, N. Scott. *House Made of Dawn.* New York: Harper, 1968.

northSun, Nila. *Diet Pepsi and Nacho Cheese.* Fallon, Nev.: Duck Down Press, 1977.

Senier, Siobhan. *Voices of American Indian Assimilation and Resistance: Helen Hunt Jackson, Sarah Winnemucca, and Victoria Howard.* Norman: University of Oklahoma Press, 2003.

Shaper, Dan. "A Brief History of Education for Native Americans" and "Native American Images." *Native Americans in Education* (10 August 2002). Available online. URL: http://tc.unl.edu/cci861/webpages/dshafer/dshafer5.html; http://tc.unl.edu/cci861/webpages/dshafer/dshafer6.html. Accessed on August 15, 2005.

Standing Bear, Luther. *My Indian Boyhood.* 1931. Reprint, Lincoln: University of Nebraska Press, 1988.

———. *My People, the Sioux.* 1928. Reprint, Lincoln: University of Nebraska Press, 1975.

Welch, James. *The Death of Jim Loney.* 1979. Reprint, New York: Penguin, 1987.

———. *The Heartsong of Charging Elk.* New York: Anchor, 2001.

———. *Winter in the Blood.* New York: Penguin, 1992.

Claire Gallou

Atanarjuat/The Fast Runner   Zacharias Kunuk (2001)

Atanarjuat/The Fast Runner, directed by Zacharias Kunuk, is the first feature length aboriginal language Canadian film. Among other awards, *The Fast Runner* won the Camera d'or as best first feature film at the 2001 Cannes Film Festival and has been seen by audiences around the world. The film was shot entirely in digital video using local actors and materials in the Canadian Arctic near Igloolik, and it should be noted that the transfer to 35 millimeter in theatrical release is a radically different viewing experience from the VHS and DVD versions, which present video in its full force, rendering immediacy and an intimate, documentary quality. A relatively inexpensive medium, digital video is also less cumbersome to use in remote locations than traditional film stock, and its visual quality enhances the vast flatness of the arctic horizon.

The story of *Atanarjuat* is based on an ancient Inuit legend of a mysterious shaman (Tungjuat) who incites conflict between two families in a small clan. Atanarjuat and his brother, Amaqjuat, have been raised to reclaim the honor of their father and their family's good name. Atanarjuat falls in love with Atuat, a kind and beautiful young woman who has been promised by her father to Atanarjuat's rival, Oki. Oki bets his right to Atuat in a fight with Atanarjuat and is thus forced by the community to give her up when Atanarjuat wins. Atanarjuat and his new wife set up camp with Amaqjuat and his wife at water's edge, and all seems well. One afternoon, Atanarjuat returns in his kayak to the campsite, cutting through the sun as it dazzles on the quiet surface of the water. In an image that subverts the famous (and to some, racist) disembarkment of another arctic hunter from his kayak in Robert Flaherty's NANOOK OF THE NORTH, Atanarjuat steps out of his boat and greets his smiling pregnant wife, bearing a fat seal.

This domestic idyll soon ends, when Atanarjuat takes Puja, the devious sister of his rival Oki, as a second wife to help with domestic duties while Atuat is pregnant. After having wreaked havoc in the family into which she has married, Puja invents a story to provoke Oki's revenge on Atanarjuat, and Atanarjuat's brother is killed in the ambush. Atanarjuat makes a dramatic escape by outrunning his pursuers across miles of treacherous ice floes, until he finally collapses from exhaustion and is taken in by a sympathetic family, who sense

his goodness (and turn out to be relatives). They nurse him back to health, and when he returns to his clan to reclaim his rightful place, he stages a final showdown with his rival. In a remarkable departure from the traditional myth (in which Atanarjuat kills Oki), however, the Atanarjuat of Kunuk's film strikes the decisive blow beside Oki's head, announcing that the cycle of violence must stop. The matriarch of the clan banishes Oki, his cohorts, and his sister, Puja, instead, thus breaking the shaman's evil spell over the families.

Anne Kern

Aurelia: A Crow Creek Trilogy
Elizabeth Cook-Lynn (2000)

Comprising three interlinked texts—*From the River's Edge, Circle of Dancers,* and *In the Presence of River Gods*—ELIZABETH COOK-LYNN's trilogy *Aurelia* examines Dakota Sioux senses of *tiospaye* or community, dealing with specific themes and issues throughout. These themes, "tradition, language, mythology, and politics," are all readily evident in *Aurelia* (43).

The trilogy opens in 1967 with the story of John Tatekeya's 40 stolen cattle and the flooding of the Dakota homelands after the damming of the Mni Sosa (Missouri) River. Cook-Lynn employs the theft of the cattle and the loss of the land as a metaphor for the many injustices suffered by the Dakota people at the hands of white ranchers and federal agents. Tatekeya, "a tall man in his early sixties," laments the loss of moral values evident in the federal government's justice system, the false testimony given against him by a tribal member, and his own extramarital affair with Aurelia, a woman much younger than he is.

This examination of tribal values continues during the next two books, the action of which is specifically concerned with Aurelia and her journey to become "a storyteller and a witness" of the tribe's history (133). In *Circle of Dancers* Aurelia has ended her affair with Tatekeya and fallen in love with the young man who once testified against him, Jason Big Pipe. Although never married, they have a child, Blue. By the opening lines of *In The*

Presence of River Gods their relationship is nearing its end, and Aurelia is steadily beginning "to accept her role as witness, recorder of memory, and carrier of culture" (Rozelle 205).

The three works that make up *Aurelia* incorporate various historical and cultural events that have shaped Native American communities over the last two centuries: broken treaties, governmental relocation of Native Americans, the foundation of the AMERICAN INDIAN MOVEMENT, the siege of WOUNDED KNEE in 1973, and the 1980s legal case in which the U.S. Supreme Court awarded damages to the Sioux for the loss of the Black Hills. These stories, and Elizabeth Cook-Lynn's interweaving of them, result in *Aurelia*'s being not only a truly important work of tribal writing, but also a sourcebook for those who wish to understand indigenous sovereignty and examine historical events and race relations in the United States. As such, *Aurelia: A Crow Creek Trilogy* reaffirms Elizabeth Cook-Lynn's status as a frank and vehement defender of Dakota culture, tradition, and rights.

Bibliography

Cook-Lynn, Elizabeth. *Aurelia: A Crow Creek Trilogy.* Boulder: University of Colorado Press, 1999.

———. *Anti-Indianism in Modern America: A Voice from Tatekeya's Earth.* Urbana: University of Illinois Press, 2001.

Stripes, James. "'We Think in Terms of What Is Fair': Justice versus 'Just Compensation' in Elizabeth Cook-Lynn's *From the River's Edge.*" *Wicaso Sa* 12, no. 1 (spring 1997): 165–187.

Rozelle, Page. "The Teller and the Tale History and the Oral Tradition in Elizabeth Cook-Lynn's *Aurelia: A Crow Creek Trilogy.*" *American Indian Quarterly* 25, no. 2 (spring 2001): 203–215.

Padraig Kirwan

Aztecas del Norte. The Chicanos of Aztlán Jack Forbes (1973)

Written by the Native American studies scholar Jack Forbes, this volume revolves around the history of Mexican people in the Southwest. The author's refreshing analysis offers a "decolonized" Native American perspective on the social and cultural impact that the Aztecs had on the development of the U.S. nation and territory. As he explains in the introduction, the contacts among Iberian, American, and Mexican traits led to a colorful blend "with the Mexican influence dominant in everyday affairs." In fact, the ancient Nahua past is still a strong component of today's Mexican and Mexican-American identity: Along with the intellectual heritage and worldviews, the societal and family structures left by the ancestors have survived throughout centuries of colonialism and migration.

The book moves from an in-depth account of Mexican religion and traditional ways of living to the history of Mexican migration to the north with a heavy emphasis on the economic and the cultural changes that the Spanish invasion and the Treaty of Guadalupe-Hidalgo (1848) brought about. Each chapter presents extended passages from several sources that range from newspaper articles, historical and sociological essays, to indigenous oral tradition and poetry: "O youths, here there are skilled men in the flowers of shields, / in the flowers of the pendant eagle plumes, / the yellow flowers which they grasp" (87). The author gives detailed information on the diverse, ever-changing socioeconomic situation of Mexican communities in Texas, New Mexico, and California from the end of the 19th century: Not only did U.S. Assimilation policies aim at destroying the tribal lives of North American indigenous populations but they also demeaned Mexican culture in the Southwest. Twentieth-century Anglo imperialism, prejudice, and "anti-Mexicanism" were to welcome the new immigrants, who were not met with equal opportunities, adequate education programs, and political representation. The author also explains how—according to the area and to the period of time under examination—Mexican and Mexican-American identities soon became confused, stereotyped, and defined in opposition to the Anglo one: "Anglo-American writers such as Zane Grey, helped to keep alive and spread a derogatory stereotype of Mexicans by frequently referring to 'greasers' who were 'treacherous' and 'cruel.'" Given this, not even the term *mestizo*—as the essay "The Mestizo Concept: A Product of European Imperialism" argues—does justice to the complexities and to the Native component of Mexican-American identity. In fact, Forbes goes on to show that it is yet another label that U.S. scholarly tradition erroneously applies to Mexican-Chicano people.

However, far from falling victims of class, racial discrimination, and forced "Americanization" processes, generations of Mexicans have been able to organize and to reclaim their rights to self-determination. The book's concluding chapters specifically focus on contemporary Mexican-American activism and on the development of grassroots movements that went hand in hand with the growing awareness of Native and Latino consciousness and with the rediscovered, native homeland of Aztlán, or the American Southwest.

Bibliography

Anaya, Rudolfo A.-Lomelí, Francisco A., eds. *Aztlán; Essays on the Chicano Homeland*. Albuquerque, N. Mex.: Academia/El Norte, 1989.

León-Portilla, Miguel. *Aztec Thought and Culture*. Norman: University of Oklahoma Press, 1963.

Weber, David. *The Spanish Frontier in North America*. New Haven, Conn., and London: Yale University Press, 1992.

Dina Fachin

B

Bad Medicine Ron Querry (1998)

Bad Medicine portrays life on a reservation through the eyes of both outsiders and insiders. Dr. Push Foster, a Choctaw from Oklahoma, finds himself seeking advice among the Navajo and Hopi people when his modern medical knowledge fails him. RON QUERRY shows how contemporary and traditional medicines try to combine to fight the mysterious disease that seems to be targeting only the Navajo.

The prologue begins with a brief history of the area, particularly Massacre Cave and "Two Fell Off," where many women and children were killed while Spanish troops invaded. The first fatalities occurred when a Navajo woman attacked a Spanish soldier and threw both of them off the cliff. Querry's descriptions of the vast landscape and the communities within the reservation illuminate what is unfamiliar territory for most readers.

Dr. Push Foster is new to the area, and just 45 minutes into his first day it is clear that something terrible has entered the Navajo reservation. A young seemingly healthy woman has just died of an illness that is similar to the hantavirus. Soon more and more healthy people are dying of the same illness. Foster and his friends Sonny Brokeshoulder and Leslie Blair ask for help from outside sources, but as long as the disease is contained on the reservation no help will arrive. The three must seek answers within the Native American community. They soon find out that the disease might have a darker origin. There are several other puzzling circumstances such as the recurring appearance of a young woman, badly injured and crying, and the recent discovery of a stone tablet that belongs to the Hopi. Someone is practicing bad medicine among the Navajo.

Modern medicine cannot cure this disease and Dr. Foster finds himself in unknown territory, literally and figuratively. Foster considers himself intelligent in matters relating to Choctaw culture, but he has never encountered firsthand the traditions with which he is having contact on the reservation. As his friend Sonny does, Foster finds himself searching for his place within two cultures. While Sonny acts as a gateway to the Navajo culture, Foster must learn to trust in the traditions and not solely on science. Foster finds himself head to head with matters he had only heard about secondhand.

As with *The DEATH OF BERNADETTE LEFTHAND* (1993), *Bad Medicine* leaves hints as to what is the real cause of the problem. Clifford Lomaquaptewa, an important man among the Hopi, tells Dr. Foster, "Everything's connected. . . . The Earth and everything that lives on it has just nearly got to be working together or else something is bound to start to die off. And it seems like this time it's people" (145). Nothing happens by chance, and it is up to Dr. Push Foster to figure out the connections.

See also RESERVATION LIFE.

Bibliography

Querry, Ron. *Bad Medicine.* New York: Bantam Books, 1998.

Schwarz, Maureen Trudell, and Louis Lamphere. *Navajo Lifeways: Contemporary Issues, Ancient Knowledge.* Norman: University of Oklahoma Press, 2001.

Rikki Noel Williams

Baptism of Desire   Louise Erdrich (1989)

In *Baptism of Desire,* her second collection of poetry, LOUISE ERDRICH examines the intersections of her Chippewa traditions, Roman Catholic religion, and human sexuality. The progress of missionaries through Native American territory brought about a collision of worldviews that, when they merged, did so uneasily. The title of this work suggests the convergence of the spiritual and the carnal. The phrase *baptism of desire* refers to a disputed Catholic theory that holds that baptism is not necessary for salvation. The word of *desire* also suggests physical attraction. Erdrich deals with the merging of religious and sexual desire throughout her works, but rarely as specifically as she does in this text.

The tension between the two desires comes to a head in "The Sacraments," a seven-part poem based on the seven sacraments of the Catholic faith. In this poem Erdrich describes each sacrament through domestic imagery, simultaneously elevating desire to the same level as religious fervor. Matrimony correlates to a sexual joining, and penance to apologizing after a domestic squabble. Erdrich unites the two types of desires in the fifth section: "God, I was not meant to be the isolate / cry in this body. / I was meant to have your tongue in my mouth" (1–3). Erdrich envisions spiritual and erotic longing as inextricably linked and sees the fulfillment of each desire as related to that of the other. She closes her section on the last rites with some sexual imagery and then connects the cessation of heartbeats to the entrance of heaven, finalizing the link between the body and the spirit (20).

While exploring the relationship between these two types of desire, she never travels far from her Chippewa background. The fourth section of *Baptism of Desire* continues the story of Potchikoo, which Erdrich began in *Jacklight.* Potchikoo dies and is kept out of heaven because his name is connected to one word in the Book of Life: *Indian.* Erdrich populates her fictional worlds with characters who appropriate aspects of Christianity without ever letting go of their traditional heritage. Potchikoo stands as a symbol of the outcome of this bipolarity—he is banned from the European Christian heaven, unsatisfied in "Indian heaven," and frightened of the commerciality of the "hell for white people" (52–53). Spiritually and emotionally alone, Potchikoo unsuccessfully (and painfully) seeks refuge in sex. Amid the confusion of the afterlife, his widow finally vanquishes an evil twin by using the name of the Catholic "Holy Mother of God," joining Christian and Chippewa tradition in an unsteady union.

The pieces in this collection are concerned with a longing for personal and spiritual union as well as with the dangers of pursuing such satisfaction. In *Baptism of Desire* Erdrich reveals that the difficulty lies not only in fulfilling these types of desire, but also in understanding their synthesis.

Bibliography

Earnshaw, Doris. Review of *Baptism of Desire. World Literature Today* 64 (1990): 645.

Erdrich, Louise. *Baptism of Desire.* New York: Harper and Row, 1989.

Norris, Kathleen. Review of *Baptism of Desire. Library Journal* 114 (1989): 128.

Justin Cober-Lake

Barnes, Jim (1933–)

Jim Barnes was born in Summerfield, Oklahoma, on December 22, 1933, to Bessie Vernon and Austin Oscar, ranchers. He is of Choctaw and Welsh descent. He earned his B.A. from Southeastern Oklahoma State University in 1964 and Ph.D. from the

University of Arkansas in 1970. He married Carolyn Turpin in 1973. He was awarded a National Endowment for the Arts fellowship in 1978 and won a translation prize from the Translation Center at Columbia University in 1980 for his work on Dagmar Nick's *Summons and Sign: Poems.* He has twice received the Rockefeller Foundation Bellagio Fellowship and has worked throughout Europe. He was writer in residence and professor of comparative literature at Truman State University (formerly Northeast Missouri State University) until his retirement in 2003. He taught Native American literature, American literature, French, and creative writing. Along with his teaching duties, he was the editor of the *Chariton Review.*

Barnes has published hundreds of poems in dozens of collections. Running throughout his first major collection, *The American Book of the Dead* (1982), are themes related to the land and to the loss and preservation of indigenous cultures. Similar themes appear in *La Plata Cantata* (1989) and *The Sawdust War* (1992), which won the Oklahoma Book Award. Thus, although he does not consider himself a Native American poet, many critics find a strong relationship between his work and the concerns of other Indian writers.

In addition to his poetry, Barnes is the author of an autobiography, *On Native Ground: Memoirs and Impressions* (1997), for which he won an American Book Award. In this book he traces his life from rural Oklahoma to his time spent studying in Europe and on to his work in translation and comparative literature. Barnes emerges from his autobiography as a man who is concerned with the inevitable slipping away of the past, even as he forges into the future. This concern with the loss of the past is enacted time and again on both the local and global scenes throughout much of Barnes's work.

Bibliography

American Indian Literatures: An Introduction, Bibliographic Review, and Selected Bibliography. New York: MLA, 1990.

Barnes, Jim. *The American Book of the Dead: Poems.* Urbana: University of Illinois Press, 1982.

———. *La Plata Cantata: Poems.* West Lafayette, Ind.: Purdue University Press, 1989.

———. *On Native Ground: Memoirs and Impressions.* Norman: University of Oklahoma Press, 1997.

———. *The Sawdust War.* Urbana: University of Illinois Press, 1992.

Brian Johnson

Bearheart: The Heirship Chronicles Gerald Vizenor (1990)

Originally published as *The Darkness in St Louis Bearheart* (1978), GERALD VIZENOR's first novel challenges Native American stereotypes. The book is deliberately provocative, containing images that are shockingly violent and sexually explicit. Yet the novel is also deeply traditional, drawing on the TRICKSTER FIGURE of various tribal religions, from Naanabozho of the Anishinabe to the "sacred clowns" (kachinas) of the Pueblos.

The book begins with a raid on the offices of the Bureau of Indian Affairs by radicals in the AMERICAN INDIAN MOVEMENT. One of the raiders, a young woman dressed in chicken feathers and other plastic "Indian" accessories, discovers the MIXED-BLOOD shaman narrator Bearheart in the depths of the building, where he has been writing the novel *Bearheart: The Heirship Chronicles.* This eight-page opening section introduces the conflict to be played out through the rest of the book, with a strong contrast between the healing humor used by Bearheart and his assailant's pose as a kitschy Native American warrior.

Bearheart's novel, as with many trickster stories, takes the form of a quest. Driven from the cedar grove that has been his family's home for generations, Fourth Proude Cedarfair and his wife, Rosina Cedarfair, travel through the ruins of a collapsed American civilization to reach the "window to the fourth world." The racial and environmental politics of this are quite clear: It is "whitemen treekillers" who have destroyed the world and the Native heroes who must escape the disaster these white men have created.

Along the way they collect a group of fellow "pilgrims" undertaking the journey for their own complicated reasons and with their help overcome many obstacles placed in their path by the forces of evil. Pilgrims are a very diverse group, including a giant transsexual, a bishop, a tiny blonde Sundancer, and a sexually voracious clown.

The most important chapter for reading Vizenor's message is "Terminal Creeds at Orion." Here the pilgrims enter a community made up of "the descendants of famous hunters." After a meal Belladonna WinterCatcher gives a speech on "tribal values," filled with statements about Indians as being peaceful, shy of physical contact, and "connected to mother earth," which are mercilessly picked apart by the hunters as mere stereotypes. Before poisoning Belladonna, one hunter tells her, "Indians are an invention. . . . The rest of the world invented the Indian."

The pilgrims' diversity and the death of Belladonna are significant clues to Vizenor's main aim in the novel, which is to break down the concept of "indian-ness." Vizenor shows that the conventional definition, which he calls a "terminal creed," is a burden on present-day Indians, who are expected to act according to codes created from white myths. Instead *Bearheart* draws on ancient traditions to open up the range of possibilities for the NATIVE AMERICAN INDIAN NOVEL.

Bibliography

Vizenor. Gerald. *Wordarrows: Indians and Whites in the New Fur Trade.* Minneapolis: University of Minnesota Press, 1978.
———. *Manifest Manners: Postindian Warriors of Survivance.* Hanover, N.H.: Wesleyan University Press, 1994.

James Mackay

Beet Queen, The Louise Erdrich (1986)

The Beet Queen covers a 40-year span, from 1932 to 1972. In contrast to the other novels in the Little No Horse series (*The BINGO PALACE, FOUR SOULS, The LAST REPORT ON THE MIRACLES AT LITTLE NO HORSE, LOVE MEDICINE, TALES OF BURNING LOVE, TRACKS,*), most of the major characters in *The Beet Queen* are white rather than Chippewa. The novel treats seven characters from the other Little No Horse books: June Kashpaw is mentioned but never seen; Fleur Pillager, Sister Leopolda, and Eli and Russell Kashpaw have cameo roles; and Dot Adare, the eponymous Beet Queen, and her mother, Celestine James, are major figures.

Most of the action in *The Beet Queen* takes place in a town LOUISE ERDRICH calls "Argus." Fleur Pillager, Lulu Lamartine's mother, who does not appear as a character in the original version of *Love Medicine,* has lost her land (the subject of the next novel, *Tracks*) and is supporting herself by peddling goods from a cart she pushes down the railroad tracks. Karl Adare, a white teenager, upset by a homosexual experience he has in a boxcar, jumps off the train and breaks his legs. Fleur finds Karl and takes him to the reservation to heal him. Karl describes their long walk to the reservation, ending with a description of the women. He says, "The women who came out . . . wore house dresses and had their hair cut, curled and bound in flimsy nets. They were not like Fleur, but all the same they were Indians and spoke in a flowing language to each other" (54).

Most important of the Indians is Wallacette Darlene "Dot" Adare, the love child of Celestine James and Karl Adare. Celestine is Puyat on her mother's side, and so Dot is related distantly to Sister Leopolda (born Pauline Puyat). Dot is a difficult child from birth. She "was never meant to be a baby," her aunt Mary Adare says (180). Her first word is *MORE* (181). When young Dot is playing with other little girls and boys Mary thinks of her as a hawk among sparrows (183).

Dot remains rebellious throughout her teenage years, and in an attempt to please her and defuse her anger, Wallace Pfef, Dot's father's lover, who takes an avuncular interest in the girl, rigs the Argus Beet Queen election so that Dot will win. Dot is first delighted at being selected queen of the Beet Festival but is furious when she finds out that the election was fixed. The novel ends with Dot's reconciliation with her estranged mother. A remarkable note about the character of Dot is that Erdrich had written most of *The Beet Queen* before she realized that Wallacette Darlene Adare was the Dot who marries Gerry Nanapush in *Love*

Medicine. This fact highlights Erdrich's unique method of writing and narrating. Her characters, both within and between novels, are always inter-related, even if those connections do not surface until after the book has been written.

Bibliography

Chavkin, Allan, ed. *The Chippewa Landscape of Louise Erdrich.* Tuscaloosa: University of Alabama Press, 1999.

Erdrich, Louise. *The Beet Queen.* New York: Holt, 1986.

Bent Box Lee Maracle (2000)

LEE MARACLE is a prolific aboriginal writer and influential social and political activist; *Bent Box* (2000) is her first volume of poetry. It is a collection of 68 free verse narrative style poems, divided into four parts: "Deep Regret," "Turbulent Storm," "Bent Box," and "Warm Wind." Traditionally bent boxes were found in longhouses and contained precious cargo, possibly even the meaning of life, according to some Salish people. This title, as does much of Maracle's writing, provokes the reader to participate with the text. Any specific meaning for this poetic bent box is elusive and shifting; *Bent Box* does, however, tease the reader with promises of women's wisdom, if she/he is willing to reject preconceived notions and learn from what the poems offer.

In the first section, "Deep Regrets," Maracle evokes what it is like to be Native in contemporary Canada. These poems explore the dark side of life, and death. The effects of alcohol are addressed in "Paralysis" and "Carry Her Away." These two poems, respectively, illustrate a symbolic stopping of life and a literal death of cirrhosis of the liver. "Sister" addresses the fragmentation of Native families caused by an intentionally unnamed entity that could be the BOARDING SCHOOL system or any other social organization that has historically destroyed Native families. "Performing" and "Actress (Nilak Butler)" emphasize what it means to live as a Native woman in a white society that forces women to conform to ideals, values, and behavior that are not their own—to *act* rather than

to *be.* In other poems Maracle presents the self-destruction of the Native community when the rage they feel for white society has no outlet and frustrations with white Canada are expressed as self-hatred and domestic and community violence. In "Autumn Rose" she writes, "If the state won't kill us, then, we will have to kill ourselves" (15). These poems are melancholic and any beauty in them is a tragic beauty.

"Turbulent Storm" speaks to colonial oppression and the fight for freedom and equality in a global context. As in her collection of short stories SOJOURNER'S TRUTH AND OTHER STORIES (1990), Lee Maracle explores the commonalities between the Aboriginal struggle for empowerment and the struggles of other tyrannized peoples worldwide, from El Salvador, to Nicaragua, to Chile, to Palestine, to Mandela's South Africa, to historical and contemporary North America. These poems illustrate struggles and wars, both personal and communal.

The third section," Bent Box," explores a number of themes often revealed in the titles of the poems: "Bent Box (Racist I)," "Bent Box (Sensuality)," "Bent Box" "(Youth)," and so on. The definitions of the bent box hinted at in these poems toy with the reader, never revealing the specifics of the bent box: its location in time and space or its meaning. Perhaps, as Maracle's feminist Raven does, her bent box plays with the reader, forcing him/her to contemplate the slippery context of meaning: something that changes with world-views, time, place, age, class, ethnicity, gender, politics, and so forth.

The fourth section of the collection, "Warm Wind," is about inheriting and bequeathing woman's legacy. "My Box of Letters" is the first childhood poem that Lee Maracle's mother ever saved. The first part of the poem was written on December 23, 1959. It explores her struggle to tame language. Specifically it is about being forced "to take the box of beastly letters," which were not her friends (96). The 26 she refers to are clearly the letters of the alphabet, both English and French, of which she was only one. In 1991 Maracle added two final stanzas, which reveal that with persistence she has been able "to make them [the letters] behave" (97). This poem and other suggestively autobiographical poems such as "Mama" and "To My Children" evoke Maracle's mother, her, and her children as part of a much larger nation, both past and future. Maracle's clearly autobiographical poems are juxtaposed with biographical poems such as "Ka Nata" and poems about unnamed women; the relationship between individual womanhood and collective womanhood is blurred, as the poems become the legacy of Native women passed on by the "Warm Wind."

Bent Box reinforces individual experience as part of the collective experience of Native women, bound by their common oppression in a patriarchal class system that denies them. While many of the poems are solemn and tragic, the poetry in the last section contemplates continuity, legacy, and hope for the future. Maracle ends the collection by acknowledging the strength of women's power, past and future: "Amazing women with sure feet, endless energy and a great vision of community, *Migwech* to each and every one of you" (128).

Bibliography

Maracle, Lee. *Bent Box*. Penticton, Canada: Theytus Books, 2000.

Sheena Wilson

Bernard, Gertrude   (Anahareo) (1906– 1986)

Born in Mattawa, Canada, Gertrude Bernard was raised largely by her grandmother, Mary. Her description of herself as having had Mohawk and Ojibwe ancestry has been inconclusively challenged in recent years. This may, however, be guilt by association, via her marriage to the celebrated Native impostor Grey Owl (in reality an Englishman named Archie Belaney): Certainly there seems little doubt that she believed herself to be Native American.

Although Bernard took a self-deprecating delight in recalling the many mistakes she made as a novice trapper on her first month-long trip with Belaney, she was clearly an unusually courageous and resourceful young person. There were not many other 19-year-old women on the traplines in the depths of the Canadian winter, living with a virtual stranger (she had met Archie only weeks beforehand) and dreaming of making enough money to open her own dance hall in a gold rush town. Grey Owl found her independence attractive, and the two were married in a traditional Ojibwe ceremony. It was at around this time that he gave her the nickname "Anahareo" derived from a 19th-century Mohawk chief, Naharrenou, supposedly Bernard's great-great-grandfather.

In March 1928 the sight of a lynx that had chewed off its own paw in an attempt to escape a snare convinced her to abandon the cruelties of the fur trade. Adopting two orphaned beaver kittens, she gradually convinced her husband that they should try to arrest the dramatic fall in the Canadian beaver population. Belaney began to write stories of the wild under his assumed persona as an "Indian chief," while Anahareo took up gold prospecting; the joint profits were used to start Canada's first wildlife sanctuary.

Belaney quickly achieved fame, making a fortune from writing and speaking, most of which was put into the conservation movement Anahareo had started. The couple had a daughter, but they were soon afterward divorced. In 1938 Grey Owl died, and the lifelong hoax he had perpetrated became a scandal discussed in outraged headlines around the world. His wife claimed until her dying day to have been ignorant of the deception and insisted on continuing to be known by the name he had created for her.

Shortly after her first husband's death Anahareo married the Swedish count Eric Moltke, with whom she was to have two children. She published two autobiographical accounts, *My Life with Grey Owl* (1941) and the best-selling *Devil in Deerskins* (1972), both entertaining versions of her famous marriage, if very obviously sanitized. She continued to campaign vociferously for conservationist and animal rights causes and, in recognition of her life's work, was awarded the Order of Canada by Governor-General Shreyer in 1983.

Bibliography

Bernard, Gertrude. *Devil in Deerskins: My Life with Grey Owl.* Toronto: New Press, 1972.

Smith, Donald B. *From the Land of Shadows: The Making of Grey Owl.* Toronto: HarperCollins 1991.

James Mackay

Billy Jack (1971)

The extraordinarily successful countercultural 1971 film *Billy Jack* starred Tom Laughlin as the eponymous half-breed former Green Beret who, in the film's infamous tagline, "protects children and other living things," in particular the director (Delores Taylor) and students at an Arizona school for runaways. Made for less than $800,000 largely outside the studio system and marketed and distributed in unorthodox fashion, it has grossed to date close to $100 million.

Laughlin (who directed the film under a pseudonym) and Taylor (his wife) modestly called their work "the greatest youth culture picture of our times," and indeed it panders directly to that demographic. "I can't help believing," writes Danny Peary, "that (whatever the Laughlins' politics) this picture was specifically designed to financially exploit the youth market. *That* is why it gives them everything it wants. There is a 'do-your-own-thing' mentality that dominates the film, as well as continuous praise for youthful idealism and independence" (29). Looking sometimes like a home movie, *Billy Jack* is a weird, often pretentious and preachy amalgam of 1960s clichés, completely unaware of its own glaring contradictions. At least 20 minutes of its 112-minute running time is spent in role-playing activities carried on at the Freedom School. Another 10 minutes offers real-time coverage of an incoherent city-hall meeting. A film that fully engages the issue of pacifism, *Billy Jack* is never so alive as when its hero is kicking one-dimensional bigots in the face and depicting a rape scene that is truly disturbing.

At its heart, of course, is Billy Jack, a Vietnam War veteran hapkido karate expert with a slow-to-rile but nevertheless violent temper, able to take on 20 attackers at once but devoted to recovering his soul through the pursuit (at least) of nonviolence and the full embrace of Native American beliefs and rituals. (The film credits Rolling Thunder of the Shoshone Nation for assistance with the "Indian Snake Ceremony," in which Billy engages, and Andy Vidovich of the Paiute Nation for his assistance with the "Wovoka Friendship Dance," in which he leads the students of the school.) With the spirit of Wovoka, one of the leaders of the Ghost Dance movement of the late 19th century, still working through him, he even offers the assembled throng his own blasphemous Sermon on the Mount: "The Indian tradition is now what the young people of the world are looking for. The young whites know there is a supernatural world and a great spirit, and they try to reach the great spirit. They try by drugs. They are made to do this because their religions no longer believe in the other world. Heaven is not out there. The other world is here. The great spirit, the messiah, the Christ, are here."

Billy Jack spawned two sequels: *The Trial of Billy Jack* (1974) and *Billy Jack Goes to Washington* (1977).

Bibliography

Peary, Danny. "*Billy Jack.*" In *Cult Movies: The Classics, the Sleepers, the Weird, and the Wonderful,* 28–32. New York: Delta, 1981.

David Lavery

Bingo Palace, The Louise Erdrich (1994)

This novel is part of the Little No Horse series, which also includes *The Beet Queen, Four Souls, The Last Report on the Miracles at Little No Horse, Love Medicine, Tales of Burning Love,* and *Tracks.* Much of the action in *The Bingo Palace* takes place in a gaming facility, which Lyman Lamartine has made into a thriving concern. A large Quonset hut on the highway, "it comes at you across the flat dim land like a Disney setup, like a circus show, a spaceship, a constellation that's collapsed," as Lipsha Morrissey describes it (41). The novel continues the adventures of Fleur Pillager,

June Morrissey (actually, her ghost), Gerry Nanapush, Lipsha Morrissey, and Lyman Lamartine. Zelda Kashpaw, who had only a cameo role in *Love Medicine* and did not appear at all in the other novels, is a major character, as is Shawnee Ray Toose, who makes her first appearance in the series. Fleur Pillager returns to the reservation in a Pierce Arrow, a little boy in tow. She wins back her land in a poker game with the former Indian agent.

Here we also get the back story that explains why June is suicidal: As a teenager she had been raped by her mother's boyfriend. June chiefly appears in the book as a ghost, giving Lipsha the luck to win a good deal of money and a luxury minivan at bingo.

The chief action of the novel concerns the rivalry between Lyman the entrepreneur and Lipsha the loafer. One major source of friction is Shawnee Ray Toose, who has had a child with Lyman (at least he is the leading candidate) but is sufficiently attracted to Lipsha to have an affair with him. Shawnee Ray is an attractive, intelligent, and gifted young woman, who is saving for college.

It turns out in *Bingo Palace* that Lipsha is not as dim as he seemed at first. The man who cannot tell the Philippines from the Philistines in *Love Medicine* gets high scores on his American College Test (ACT) exams in *Bingo Palace*. Lipsha does not go to college, however, and cannot seem to keep a decent job. In fact, "There was nowhere the boy could fit. He was not . . . one of us" (9). Shawnee Ray recognizes Lipsha's limitations sufficiently to refuse to marry him, though she cannot resist him physically. Despite the animosity between Lipsha and Lyman, which culminates in a food fight at the Dairy Queen, Lipsha works for Lyman, who extracts a measure of revenge by swindling him out of the bingo winnings Lipsha gives him to invest.

The novel climaxes in a highly exciting car chase in a blizzard. Gerry Nanapush, who has escaped from prison, calls his son, Lipsha, to help him evade the police. They steal a car, which unfortunately has a baby in it, and head off into the snow, the father of the child hanging on to the trunk for a while before falling off. As they drive, June's ghost appears driving a car beside them, and Gerry follows her off the highway and across the fields. Gerry climbs into June's car, abandoning Lipsha and the baby. What happens to that pair is ambiguous, but in the last chapter Fleur sets out across frozen Machimanito Lake for the island where Moses Pillager had lived. There she apparently turns into a bear—an homage to Scott Momaday's *The Ancient Child*—and starts down the road of death, taking the place of "the boy out there," ostensibly Lipsha.

See also GAMING.

Bibliography

Erdrich, Louise. *The Bingo Palace.* New York: HarperCollins, 1984.

Morace, Robert A. "From Sacred Hoops to *Bingo Palaces*: Louise Erdrich's Carnivalesque Fiction." In *The Chippewa Landscape of Louise Erdrich,* edited by Allan Chavkin. Tuscaloosa: University of Alabama Press, 1999.

Bird, Gloria   (1951–   )

Bird is a member of the Spokane Tribe of Washington State. A poet, essayist, and fiction writer, she is also contributing editor of the interdisciplinary journal of Native American studies *Wicazo Sa Review* and a founding member of the Northwest Native American Writers Association. After earning an M.A. in English at the University of Arizona, Bird taught literature and creative writing at the Institute of American Indian Arts in Santa Fe. She has conducted numerous writing workshops and has served as a contributing editor for *Indian Arts Magazine.* Presently she works for the Spokane Tribe in Wellpinit, Washington, and teaches at Salish-Kootenai College, an institution providing postsecondary education for Native Americans. She received the Diane Decorah First Book Award for her collection of poems *Full Moon on the Reservation* (1993) and has edited with Joy Harjo RE-INVENTING THE ENEMY'S LANGUAGE: *Contemporary Native Women's Writings of North America* (1997).

Influenced by African-American feminist writers, Bird "began writing criticism that attempted to *read* Native American literatures as a product of colonization" ("Autobiography" 69). In her criticism and fiction she explores a paradox: whether expression "is an act of liberation or the illusion of liberation" (*River* 18). Ultimately she defends language's ability to affect reality. For example, in the poem "Beginning" Bird describes writing as a catalyst for healing—"a beginning, identifying submerged pain" (*River* 9). In the essay "Breaking the Silence: Writing as 'Witness'" she describes writing as a political force: "At its liberating best writing is a political act. Through writing we can rewrite history, and we can mobilize our future" (30).

Self-effacing and critically aware, Bird is careful to establish a context for her writing, emphasizing how it records one woman's experiences and challenges "Indian" stereotypes exploited both outside and within the Native writing community. For Bird her story, the subject of her works, is a means of processing experience, a tool for her primary audience: Native people.

Bibliography

Bird, Gloria. *The River of History.* Portland, Oreg.: Trask House Books, 1997.

———. *Full Moon on the Reservation.* Greenfield Center, N.Y.: Greenfield Review Press, 1993.

Blankenship, Bethany. "Gloria Bird." In *Native American Women: A Biographical Dictionary,* edited by Gretchen M. Bataille and Laurie Lisa, 34–35. New York: Routledge, 2001.

Harjo, Joy, and Gloria Bird, eds. "Introduction" and "In Chimayo." In *Reinventing the Enemy's Language: Contemporary Native Women's Writings of North America,* 19–31; 39–41. New York: Norton, 1997.

Blake G. Hobby

Black Eagle Child: The Facepaint Narratives   Ray A. Young Bear (1992)

A mixture of free verse poetry and prose, *Black Eagle Child: The Facepaint Narratives* is typically cited as the first novel by RAY A. YOUNG BEAR. As do other Native novelists, such as LESLIE MARMON SILKO, N. SCOTT MOMADAY, and SHERMAN ALEXIE, Young Bear lets his roots as a poet shine through in the structure and lyrical quality of his prose. Part autobiography and part fiction, the novel is set in the fictional Black Eagle Child settlement, modeled after the Mesquakie settlement in Iowa in which Young Bear is an enrolled resident. Much of the text revolves around Edgar Bearchild, the text's narrator and Young Bear's alter ego, and his attempts to maneuver between tribal traditions and beliefs and the often seductive, but nonetheless alienating, white world.

Young Bear opens his novel with a striking pairing: a Thanksgiving party at the settlement's elementary school that Edgar refers to as "another attempt to duplicate another man's observance" and a Star-Medicine ceremony conducted by Ted's grandfather (2). Long ago the Facepaints, Edgar notes, were originally "Painters of Magic and Protective Symbols for the soldier clans and their subdivisions" (85). His own family, the Bearchilds, "were deemed opportunistic and unwise" and "clung to the heels of leaders"; eventually the Bearchild patriarch would "unknowingly accept education on behalf of the tribe," thus setting into motion the tribe's slow demise (86). By the time Edgar attends his first Star-Medicine ceremony as a guest of Ted, bicycles "represented self-improvement in school and society," and generations of "internalized agony led us to hurt or seriously injure one another for no reason other than sheer disgust in being Indians" (5; 8).

The most obvious example of such violence occurs in "Brook Grassleggings Episode," in which Edgar and Ted encounter the Hi-Na, or Hyena family, at the fairgrounds. The roots of the family's violence may be attributed to their Enrolled But in Name Only (EBNO) status, as well as to their mother's promiscuity and duplicity, which have made the family unwelcome in the settlement. Before the Hyena boys can attack, Ted drives away, covering the family in mud and rocks and causing a bat to propel itself into the face of Patty Jo, the matriarch, and the stomach of her pregnant daughter, who promptly has a miscarriage (103).

In "Black Eagle Child Quarterly" the story of Claude Youthman is the centerpiece. Claude is imprisoned for several years for "deadly assault with a 'round-shaped projectile'"—a cantaloupe thrown at a man he thought had sexually insulted his wife (223). During his time in prison Claude acquires a degree in art history and endeavors to learn the English language so that the language barrier that quite literally resulted in his imprisonment will no longer be an issue. When he returns to the settlement, he becomes an art instructor at the elementary school and along with another teacher, Lorna Bearcap, pens the "Weeping Willow Manifesto," which argues for "an immediate return to the Old Ways beginning from the bottom up" to combat corrupt tribal leadership and the many problems plaguing the people of the settlement (238).

Young Bear's writing teems with the spiritual and mysterious, the material and the ordinary. His use of pairings—the Bearchilds and Facepaints, Native knowledge and white education, tradition and ASSIMILATION, hope and despair, love and hatred—and the intricate ways in which those pairs intersect powerfully evoke for the reader the complexity of the Native American experience. In the "Afterword" to the novel Young Bear notes that Edgar's journey of self (and tribal) discovery through poetry reveals that "concrete answers, like windfish, are elusive" (257). Instead, Edgar, and his creator, write in order to "finish out the whizzing star's cataclysmic course, to be . . . the 'Fred Astaire of words'" (257).

Bibliography

Stone, Albert E. "Foreword." In *Black Eagle Child: The Facepaint Narratives.* Iowa City: University of Iowa Press, 1992.

Young Bear, Ray A. "Afterword." In *Black Eagle Child: The Facepaint Narratives.* Iowa City: University of Iowa Press, 1992.

———. *Black Eagle Child: The Facepaint Narratives.* Iowa City: University of Iowa Press, 1992.

Erika Hoagland

Black Elk   (1863–1950)

Born to a Lakota holy man and his wife in December 1863, Black Elk experienced both the battle of Little Bighorn and the WOUNDED KNEE Massacre. *Black Elk Speaks,* the narrative of his life told in 1931

to John G. Neihardt (poet laureate of Nebraska), ultimately became one of the most influential and widely read works of American Indian literature.

Following in his father's footsteps, Black Elk, whose name in Lakota is *Hehaka Sapa,* was himself a Lakota holy man (or *Wichasha Wakan*). As a young teenager he witnessed the battle of Little Bighorn and later, when the Sioux were forced onto reservations, joined Buffalo Bill's Wild West Show, with which he traveled around the United States and Europe. In 1889 he returned to the Pine Ridge Reservation and soon became a supporter of the GHOST DANCE religion. In 1890 he was wounded in the Wounded Knee Massacre. In 1892 he married his first wife, Katie War Bonnett, and in 1904 he was baptized a Catholic by a Jesuit priest, taking the first name of Nicholas. He remarried, to Anna Brings White, in 1905 and subsequently became active in promoting the Catholic religion to the Lakota.

In the summer of 1930 John Neihardt, who was researching the Ghost Dance, contacted Black Elk. Through a series of conversations Black Elk related both his history and his "Great Vision" to Neihardt. Black Elk spoke in Lakota; his son, Ben, translated; and Neihardt's daughter, Enid, took shorthand. Neihardt then crafted *Black Elk Speaks* from this transcript. The vision, powerful both in the world it evokes and the spirituality to which it is indebted, is the most widely reference part of the text.

Black Elk's great vision, which he had at the age of nine, is detailed in chapter 3 of the text. He sees horses, 12 black, 12 white, 12 sorrel, and 12 buckskin, each representing one of the four directions: west, north, east, and south. He also meets six grandfathers, again from the west, north, east, and south, and also from the sky and from the Earth. The horses proceed to give Black Elk gifts, including "a cup of water to make live the greening day, and also the bow and arrow to destroy" (30). Most importantly, they give him "the sacred stick and [his] nation's hoop, and the yellow day" and they tell him, "In the center of the hoop you shall set the stick and make it grow into a shielding tree, and bloom" (31).

Later in his life Black Elk will understand that he must "perform," or reenact what he saw in his vision. He says, in chapter 18, "A man who has a vision is not able to use the power of it until after he has performed the vision on earth for the people to see" (204). When he does perform the "Horse Dance" portion of his vision, he sees the tasks involved as a way of giving power to the Lakota people, that they may survive and grow in the face of hardship.

Although *Black Elk Speaks* is most well known for its description of Black Elk's visions, a great deal of personal and Indian history is detailed in the text as well. Black Elk describes his recollections of Little Bighorn and his time touring with Buffalo Bill. He relates, in a moving passage, the Wounded Knee Massacre. And finally, he tells of conversion to Christianity (although this is not rendered in much detail). It is this last point, Black Elk's relationship to Christianity, that has generated a great deal of the controversy surrounding Black Elk and *Black Elk Speaks*. Some scholars see Black Elk's career as a Catholic catechist to be a sham and argue that he was only pretending to have been converted. Others see him as a devout Christian and argue that the image presented by Neihardt in the text was too "Lakota" in its spirituality. Still others see problems with both of these views, arguing that Black Elk was not a devoted Christian *and* that Neihardt portrayed him inaccurately, despite the fact that Neihardt's text, if anything, obscures Black Elk's Christianity.

Since 1970, when the text was rediscovered by American readers thanks to Neihardt's appearance on the *Dick Cavett Show*, controversies such as this one have raged. Many people have centered on Neihardt's role as a shaper of Black Elk's words. For many readers in the counterculture of the early 1970s the mythical "Vanishing Indian" was an attractive image of a purer, more natural time, and Neihardt's Black Elk certainly fueled this image. Neihardt did seem to view Black Elk as a tragic figure, a remnant of a bygone era for which we should all mourn. While the losses undergone by Indians in the years since European contact are undoubtedly tragic, many scholars take exception to the way *Black Elk Speaks* places Indians only in the past and only in a culture that is foreign, fundamentally different from 20th-century America. It is difficult to deny that Neihardt, in what was

most likely an attempt to share an extraordinary person with the world, simplified him unnecessarily, and thus added to the perception that Indians are singular, are homogeneous, and, in general, do not exist anymore.

While never generating the readership or controversy of *Black Elk Speaks,* two other texts provide further insight into Black Elk and his many-faceted life. *The Sacred Pipe: Black Elk's Account of the Seven Rites of the Oglala Sioux* (1953), as told to Joseph Epes Brown, is a description of sacred Lakota ceremonies that serves to enrich our picture of Black Elk. *The Sixth Grandfather: Black Elk's Teachings Given to John G. Neihardt* (1984) edited by Raymond J. Demalle, reproduces the transcripts of Black Elk's conversations with John Neihardt, and many consider this a better, more complete view of the Lakota holy man.

Bibliography

Brown, Joseph Epes. *The Sacred Pipe: Black Elk's Account of the Seven Rites of the Oglala Sioux.* Norman: University of Oklahoma Press, 1989.

Demaille, Raymond J. *The Sixth Grandfather: Black Elk's Teachings Given to John G. Neihardt.* Lincoln: University of Nebraska Press, 1984.

Holler, Clyde. *The Black Elk Reader.* Syracuse, N.Y.: Syracuse University Press, 2000.

Neihardt, John G. *Black Elk Speaks: Being the Life Story of a Holy Man of the Oglala Sioux.* Lincoln: University of Nebraska Press, 1988.

Rice, Julian. *Black Elk's Story: Distinguishing Its Lakota Purpose.* Las Cruces: University of New Mexico Press, 1994.

Steltenkamp, Michael F. *Black Elk: Holy Man of the Oglala.* Norman: University of Oklahoma Press, 1993.

Jennifer McClinton-Temple

Blaeser, Kimberly M.   (1955–   )

Kimberly Blaeser, who is Anishinabe and German descent, was born in Billings, Montana, and raised on the White Earth Reservation in northern Minnesota. She is the daughter of Anthony and Marlene Blaeser and has been married to Leonard

Wardzala since 1985. They have one child, Gavin. She received her B.A. from the College of St. Benedict in St. Joseph, Minnesota, and her M.A. and Ph.D. from the University of Notre Dame. She is currently professor of English and comparative literature at the University of Wisconsin at Milwaukee. Blaeser has received the North American Native Authors First Book Award (1993) and the Wordcraft Circle Storyteller of the Year Award (1999). Her major works include *Trailing You* (1993), *Gerald Vizenor: Writing in the Oral Tradition* (1996), and *Absentee Indians and Other Poems* (2002). She is also the editor of *Stories Migrating Home: A Collection of Anishinaabe Prose* (1999).

Blaeser has received acclaim for her willingness to acknowledge the difficult way the outside world and the Native world connect to one another. Her poems seem natural and unforced whether they invoke an urban setting or life on a reservation. One especially striking image from *Trailing You* demonstrates how she lives in these two worlds at the same time. She writes of her jewelry—she wears turquoise and silver, traditional Indian jewelry, on one arm, and diamonds, gold, and a stylish watch on the other.

Blaeser's poems also have a strong sense of history and the way in which history never "ends" but just becomes part of the never-ending past. One has a sense, when reading her work, of a continuous stream, rather than a sharply demarcated past, present, and future. For instance, in "Family Tree" each stanza represents a different member of her family and as these stanzas are arranged in a nonsequential manner on the page, the effect given is one of continuity and community, rather than hierarchy. In addition, by ending the poem with the simple "All my relations" she drives home the point that they all, whatever their ethnicities, or the different roles they occupy, played a part in creating who she is.

Blaeser has also received acclaim for her scholarly work, especially *Gerald Vizenor: Writing in the Oral Tradition*. This important work, about her fellow writer from the White Earth Reservation, is a detailed analysis of GERALD VIZENOR's many writings, one that is often cited and relied upon heavily by students of Vizenor. The work grew out of her dissertation and includes numerous interviews with the writer. The critic ROBERT ALLEN WARRIOR notes that Blaeser accomplishes the difficult task of finding an overall theme in the dense and often difficult body of Vizenor's work. He says, "What Blaeser finds as she reads across three decades of Vizenor's work is a consistent commitment to overturning entrenched images of Native people."

Bibliography

Warrior, Robert Alan. "Review of *Gerald Vizenor: Writing in the Oral Tradition*." *World Literature Today* (winter 1998): 181.

"Kimberly Blaeser." Voices from the Gaps. Available online. URL: http://voices.cla.umn.edu/vg/Bios/entries/blaeser_Kimberly.html. Accessed on August 15, 2005.

Blue Cloud, Peter   (Aroniawenrate) (1935–   )

Peter Blue Cloud, also known as Aroniawenrate, was born Peter Williams on June 10, 1935, in Kahnawake, Quebec. He is a Turtle Clan Mohawk who was raised on the Caughnauaga Reservation. He is the father of three three children, Meyokeeskow, Arion, and Kaherno, and in addition to being a nationally recognized poet, has worked as an ironworker, a logger, a carpenter, and a woodcutter.

The noted American poet Gary Snyder says, in the preface to Blue Cloud's collected poems, *Clans of Many Nations,* that while most of Blue Cloud's poetry sits "squarely in the mode of twentieth-century American poetry," he has "lived through territories most poets haven't dreamed of " (xx). He dedicates his work not to any tribe, but to "all people" and works to show connections across time and across cultures.

In his long poem "White Corn Sister" the many different voices connect to one another as through in a conversation. The speakers, some of whom are simply referred to as "first speaker" and "second speaker" while others get more descriptive titles such as "medicine man" and "clan woman," all talk of continuity and circles. They speak of the children who form the nucleus of the smallest unit, the family, and they speak of the largest unit, the nation, and beyond that, the world. "The man" says, "We are a family, within a clan, a tribe, a nation / We are born a nation" (20).

Some of the speakers also explore the duality of nature and of humanity, acknowledging that both good and evil reside in the world. The "medicine man" says, "We are born twins of good and evil / in one body" (22). He struggles with this concept, initially attempting to hide from the negative, but ultimately understanding that along with the good, it too belongs to him.

The poem is framed by the image of corn, or seeds, being dropped from the mouth of Crow, who is "offspring and brother to Raven." The corn represents the Indian people of the poem, "a nation scattered." However, as Raven often represents a TRICKSTER FIGURE, the ultimate symbol of good and evil in the same body, perhaps Blue Cloud is asking the reader not to see only the negative in this scattering of "corn." At the end of the poem the people have joined to support the old and the young sit by their grandmother so that "she may know / a nation lives" (33).

Blue Cloud often writes of traditional subjects: the sweat lodge, sweet corn, Raven, and Bear. However, he consistently addresses modern Indian concerns as well, never failing to note how difficult it is to blend the two ways of living.

Jennifer McClinton-Temple

Blue Dawn, Red Earth   Clifford E. Trafzer, ed. (1996)

This collection by Clifford Trafzer offers 30 stories by 30 different authors. The subtitle, *New Native American Storytellers,* reflects the fact that some stories are by less well-known authors, and the book design by Jennifer Ann Daddio is beautiful, with a great variety of illustrations.

A brief foreword to Trafzer's introduction states it is "an imaginative story about tribal librarian Agnes Yellowknee, a fictional character and composite of people [he has] known and respected" (4); thus the introduction itself stands as a story in its own right. In this respect Trafzer follows a con-

temporary current that aims at felling the barriers between fiction and criticism.

Among authors is the Canadian Georges E. Sioui (Wyandot), originally from Quebec, whose "Belated Letter to Christopher Columbus" has been written at a time when the Indian Nation of America has just been recognized by the World Assembly of Nations, and on the occasion of the 500th anniversary of Columbus's landing in the "New World." His letter is actually two: The first, an ironic and positive reply to the great "discoverer's" wish to be present at the nation's inaugural session at the World Assembly; the second, addressed to the prime minister of India in a brotherly manner, a request that East Indians give their name over to Indians of the West, to "correct an act which still needs to be repaired" (375). Sioui's utopian stance reminds one of MARTIN CRUZ SMITH's harsher *The Indians Won,* but his HUMOR here is definitely rooted in a deep belief in peace and goodwill the world over.

In an altogether different tone GERALD VIZENOR's "*Oshkiwiinag*: Heartlines on the Trickster Express" is a perfect introduction to the author's world and style: Lexical creations, such as *acudenturist, exodontist, federal exclave, pose of dominance;* the ever-present TRICKSTER FIGURE; as well as a mixture of seriousness and hilarious situations, are easily accessible in the context of the short story. *Oshkiwiinag* is the name of the crystal trickster that impregnates a company of Girl Scouts and the nurse Cozie Browne (also known as Sour in the morning, and Burn at night) in Camp Widikin, built on stolen tribal land. Cozie's uncle, Gesture Browne, works as a tribal acudentist on a moving "trickster train," for "motion is autonomous, . . . natural reason and memories are motion, and motion can never be stolen. Bones and blankets are stolen; motion is a natural sovereignty" (246). In spite of the banker Cameron Williams's wish to repay the healing of his dental abscess by sending Gesture to dental school, the exodontist refuses the offer; the banker feels uncomfortable and insists:

"Would you consider a scholarship to study at the university?" asked the banker. . . .

"Why the university?"

"Say, to study literature," said the banker.

"I already do that," said Gesture.

"Anthropology, then."

"Anthropology studies me."

"You have a point there," said the banker.

"Natural reason is the point." (244–45)

Bibliography

Smith, Martin Cruz. *The Indians Won.* New York: Nordon, 1970.

Trafzer, Clifford E., ed. *Earth Song, Sky Spirit: Short Stories of the Native American Experience.* New York: Doubleday Dell, 1992.

Simone Pellerin

Blue Horses Rush In: Poems and Stories   Luci Tapahonso (1997)

Blue Horses Rush In is a seminal collection of poetry that reflects upon the power of stories and storytelling and the functionality of the "oral text." In her preface LUCI TAPAHONSO reiterates that the lives of Navajo people have always depended on language; her community has a great love for stories. Her collection, she purports, aims to "convey the setting for an oral text" and through this means enables her "and other Navajos to sojourn mentally and emotionally to our home, Dinétah" (xiv). For Tapahonso her poetry *is* song, calling upon her people's oral tradition and creating what she calls a "dance in one's imagination" (Bruchac 279). Her poetry, then, is an extension of her place as a Navajo women.

In order to study Tapahonso's work, one must take into consideration the complex integration of belief systems of the poet's tribal background. For example, her signature poem, "Blue Horses Rush In," mirrors Navajo worldview on many levels, as it draws upon Navajo traditions, landscape, language, and belief systems. The poem begins with a birth of a baby, the mother laboring and the "father's eyes wet with gratitude" (103). However, in the middle of the poem the literal moment of the birth opens into a creation story grounded in Navajo tradition. The speaker says, "This baby arrived amid a herd of horses, / horses of different colors" (103), and it is after this that the speaker describes the four directions from which the horses arrive.

The Navajo's homeland is called the four-corners area, so the four directions are significant and sacred as they are depicted in the poem by not only color, but time of day and the phases of life; all of this, of course, constitutes the complementary and cyclical pattern of Navajo worldview. "White horses from the east" (103) represent birth and dawn; "Blue horses enter from the south" (104) signifying childhood and midday; "Yellow horses rush in" (104) from the west, symbolizing adulthood and dusk; finally, completing the circle, "Black horses came from the north" (104), indicating death and night. Implicit in this, indeed, is the cycle returning to morning and to birth, and thus, a balance is continually maintained. The physical birthing of the baby becomes harmonious with the spiritual and epistemological understandings within Navajo oral traditions.

The poem, as do many of Tapahonso's pieces in *Blue Horses Rush In,* carries rhythms of an "oral text" that are incantatory and meditative. For Tapahonso creative expression is song and prayer that stems from her deeply rooted connection to her homeland and culture.

Bibliography

Bruchac, Joseph. *Survival This Way: Interviews with American Indian Poets.* Tucson: University of Arizona Press, 1987.

Tapahonso, Luci. *Blue Horses Rush In: Poems and Stories.* Tucson: University of Arizona Press, 1998.

Molly McGlennan

boarding schools

Off-reservation federal Indian boarding schools trace their origins to the army officer Richard Henry Pratt's "educational experiment" on a group of Native prisoners at Ft. Marion, Florida, in 1875. Pratt determined to assimilate his Cheyenne, Arapaho, Kiowa, Comanche, and Caddo prisoners into European-American culture through an educational program focused on literacy in English, Christianization, and vocational preparation for farming Allotment land. Gathering federal and private support, in 1879 Pratt founded the Carlisle Indian Industrial School in Pennsylvania, which served as the prototype for a system of off-reservation boarding schools developed in the late 19th and early 20th centuries. Carlisle collected together children from many different tribes, who were forbidden to speak Native languages, wear traditional clothing, or practice ancestral religions. The students were kept away from home and families for years at a time. Pratt's stated goal was to "kill the Indian to save the man," or exterminate tribal sovereignty and culture through the isolation and programmatic cultural transformation of Indian children. While Carlisle closed its doors in 1918 and Indian policy began to shift with the 1928 Meriam Report, boarding schools continued to be a significant component of Indian education through World War II.

Despite the antitribal goals of the BOARDING SCHOOLS, student response was far more complex than the educators intended, as many students found ways to maintain or adapt tribal and pan-Indian cultural practices within the institution. The cultural negotiations students undertook have been the frequent subject of American Indian writers. The vast majority of autobiographical writings by Native people through the mid-1900s include narratives about the authors' time at school. The Yankton Dakota writer ZITKALA-ŠA's essays, in particular, demonstrate the way she used her boarding school education as an advocate on behalf of Native people and communities. In "School Days of an Indian Girl" (1900) she explains that learning to speak English was not a marker of her ASSIMILATION but instead enabled her to "[assert] the rebellion within me" (61). D'ARCY MCNICKLE's novel *The Sur-rounded* (1936), in contrast, is a bleak look at the difficult life of Archilde Leon, who returned to his tribal community after years away at school. Indigo, the protagonist of LESLIE MARMON SILKO's *GARDENS IN THE DUNES* (1999), is a boarding school runaway taken in by a white couple who attempt to educate her in the ways of Victorian culture. Everything Indigo experiences in her travels, however, reinforces and validates the tribal education she received from her grandmother. She maintains her tribal identity, and tribal land, through a rooted hybridity.

The boarding schools have influenced American Indian literary form as well. Representations of the school experience constitute a shared repertoire of literary forms including renaming stories, stories of linguistic rebellion, and letters home, which are themselves hybrids of tribal and European-American literary forms and contribute to a distinctive, pantribal American Indian literary tradition.

Bibliography

Adams, David Wallace. *Education for Extinction: American Indians and the Boarding School Experience.* Lawrence: University Press of Kansas, 1995.

Archuleta, Margaret, Brenda Child, and K. Tsianina Lomawaima, eds. *Away from Home: American Indian Boarding School Experiences.* Phoenix: Heard Museum, 2000.

Child, Brenda. *Boarding School Seasons.* Lincoln: University of Nebraska Press, 1998.

Katanski, Amelia. *Learning to Write "Indian": The Boarding School Experience and American Indian Literature.* Norman: University of Oklahoma Press, 2005.

Spack, Ruth. *America's Second Tongue: American Indian Education and the Ownership of English.* Lincoln: University of Nebraska Press, 2002.

Amelia V. Katanski

Body Indian: A Play in Five Scenes   Hanay Geiogamah (1980)

In *Body Indian*, first produced in 1972 and published in 1980, HANAY GEIOGAMAH illustrates the warring forces of self-destruction and survival instinct that he sees in the American Indian (Geiogamah's preferred term). Taking place in a small impoverished apartment outside the Oklahoma reservations, this play is a microcosm of the life of the American Indians as they strive to survive and cope with their world and their weaknesses. On the surface *Body Indian* can easily be interpreted as a simple commentary on the Indians' long-running battle with ALCOHOLISM, but at its core lies a defiant Indian spirit refusing to give up on survival.

At the center of the play is Bobby Lee, an alcoholic Indian in his 30s who lost a leg years ago after passing out drunk on the train tracks. These tracks are projected at times behind the actors to serve as a metaphor not only for Bobby Lee's demons but also for the guilt his friends and relatives feel as a result of their mistreatment of Bobby. He fights to escape his own alcoholism, and he talks of plans to enter a treatment facility with the money he received from leasing his share of the reservation to a farmer. He is thwarted by his friends, quickly falling under their influence and drinking although well aware of the dangers, as the party conversation moves back and forth from the need for money to the need for alcohol. When Bobby drinks, he always passes out, and then his friends immediately steal his money. This scenario repeats four times in the play; when they try to find his money a fifth time, he has none. They instead steal his leg so they can pawn it for alcohol, knowing that Bobby will figure out a way to get it back. The play ends with Bobby Lee's reliving the accident that took his leg, realizing that his prosthetic had been taken from him while he slept.

Geiogamah ends each scene by projecting slides of train tracks at different angles and in quick sequences behind the stage while the sound of a train whistle echoes off stage, an exclamation point to the recurring cycle of causes and effects in the preceding scenes. Otherwise, the play comprises only the interactions of the characters with each other and through these interactions develops a network of virtue and vice, camaraderie and codependence.

Bibliography

Huntsman, Jeffrey. *New Native American Drama: Three Plays by Hanay Geiogamah.* Norman: University of Oklahoma Press, 1980.

Lincoln, Kenneth. "Indi'ns Playing Indians." *MELUS* 16, no. 3 (fall 1989–fall 1990): 91–98.

———. "Appendix C: Interview with Hanay Geiogamah." In *Indi'n Humor: Bicultural Play in Native America,* 326–377. New York: Oxford University Press, 1993.

Angela Courtney

Bone Dance: New and Selected Poems, 1965–1993   Wendy Rose (1994)

WENDY ROSE's *Bone Dance: New and Selected Poems, 1965–1993,* is not only a collection of poetry about survival but also one that comes full circle in Rose's quest for identity. As her introduction states, she now lives in close proximity to her known ancestors. Interestingly, while the text is set up according to selections that follow publication dates, the pieces chosen in each section reveal Rose's struggle to find her place in this world and her personal resolution to her lifelong quest.

Selections from her first book, *HOPI ROADRUNNER DANCING,* reflect her personal struggle with her divided ethnicity, her concern about the destructive powers of the colonizers, her consciousness of the resilience of Native peoples, and her realization not only that life is more than this earthly existence but also that there is another side of the story of conquest that needs to be told.

The second and third sections focus on poems from *LONG DIVISION: A TRIBAL HISTORY* and *LOST COPPER,* respectively. Each section condemns the colonizers' use of Native Americans for profit, be it from their bones, their artifacts, their spirituality, or their land. Rose rails at the colonizers, spilling her outrage at their callous treatment of Native Americans as commodity, and she underscores the importance of the spiritual connection of Native peoples to the land, something the colonizers have never understood.

The next two sections, "What Happened When the Hopi Hit New York" and "What the Mohawk Made the Hopi Say," reveal Rose's sensitivity to the past; in her travel poetry from California to New York she is acutely conscious of the ghosts of Native voices and the price they paid in the conquest of the land. She feels the haunting presence of Native peoples in New Orleans, Vermont, Connecticut, Alaska, New Hampshire—and gives power to their ghostly voices with her poems.

Section six is taken from *The HALFBREED CHRONICLES,* which are poems that give voice to all of those unable to speak on their own behalf, and section seven, *GOING TO WAR WITH ALL MY RELATIONS,* acknowledges Rose's multiethnic past, highlights the colonizer as a defiler and profit taker, and gives voice not only to Native ghosts but also to the injustice they suffered. Selections from *Now Poof She Is Gone,* highlighting the cruelty of the colonizers and linking the silencing of women's voices in literature to the way "colonial power seeks to silence the natives" (xviii), end the book.

Over the years Rose has learned one's place is determined by one's self-acceptance. By providing voice to any victims who suffer under the boot of oppressors, Rose not only finds her place but also realizes her importance to all who cannot speak for themselves.

Bibliography

Rose, Wendy. *Bone Dance: New and Selected Poems, 1965–1993.* Tucson: University of Arizona Press, 1994.

———. "Introduction." In *Bone Dance: New and Selected Poems, 1965–1993.* Tucson: University of Arizona Press, 1994.

Patti Diamond

Bone Game　Louis Owens　(1994)

Bone Game, the third of five novels written by Louis Owens, continues the saga of Cole McCurtain begun in *The Sharpest Sight* (1992). Although a sequel, *Bone Game* stands as an independent text whose meaning is enriched by knowledge of its antecedent. When readers meet Cole McCurtain, a MIXED-BLOOD Choctaw professor of Native American studies, he has recently relocated to the University of California, Santa Cruz, from Albuquerque and the University of New Mexico. This setting becomes a character in its own right, offering Owens a means of critiquing contemporary New Age attitudes about indigenous people, academic desires and limitations within the field of Indian studies, and, significantly, the haunting legacy of the bloody colonial history of Spanish missions in California.

McCurtain's initial experience in Santa Cruz in 1993 coincides with a series of gruesome murders in the Monterrey Bay area, which sets the region on edge. This third-person narrative, significantly focused on Cole, becomes both a murder-mystery thriller and a spiritual mystery simultaneously.

Readers discover how the spirit world gives voice to ignored past injustices and is mistaken as a cause of the ongoing episodes of violence. Cole dreams about Venancio Asisara and later learns this is the name of the Indian man charged with the murder in 1812 of Padre Andrés Quintana, a missionary to the Ohlone who was cruel and inhumane. Cole's dreams lead readers to wonder, for example, whether the current murders are continuations of Asisara's quest for justice. Readers are given glimpses of the action from the perspective of several unidentified entities who may be spirit incarnations, such as Asisara, or who may be human murderers.

While the spirit-Gambler, the real entity who appears to McCurtain and others and is engaged in the Bone Game, may initially appear to be mixed up with the current spate of murders, in the end, it is clear that his appearance in a variety of forms—as a painted figure, as a bear, and as Cole's brother, Attis—is partially a *response* to the current violence and its connection to century-old violence committed by non-Indians against indigenous people, the land, and the world generally, a world considered out of balance. Uncle Luther, for example, believes the Gambler has returned to gamble for his world, to set it right again. The plot twists leave readers wondering until the end about the identity of the contemporary murderer, though early hints that point to several Anglo students of McCurtain's, in particular, his graduate assistant, Robert, offer readers insight about the novel's conclusion. These plot developments offer critical readers rich material for analysis of Owen's representation of the New Age continuum, which includes the arena of academia and nonindigenous misappropriation and misapprehension of indigenous worldviews and knowledge.

The most memorable character in the novel may be Alex Yazzie, an embodiment of Gerald Vizenor's notion of a TRICKSTER FIGURE, a cross-dressing Navajo anthropologist who resists definitions, preferring instead "infinitions." Yazzie is a balanced character, sure of his traditions and his contemporary role in the world, who serves as a guide for Cole and others in the novel, offering at times comic relief and a sense of hope and transformative love in a rather dark narrative.

For McCurtain the journey to discover the truth is highly personal: It forces him to come to terms with his brother's death, which was unresolved in *The Sharpest Sight*; it makes him closer to his daughter, Abby, and leads to his sobriety; and it deepens his connection to his spiritual resources, his relatives, including Uncle Luther and his grandmother figure, Onatima, who travel west from Mississippi to be with him because of the urgency of his situation and who eventually inspire him to return to his home in New Mexico at the novel's conclusion.

Bibliography

Kilpatrick, Jacquelyn, ed. *Louis Owens: Literary Reflections on His Life and Work.* Norman: University of Oklahoma Press, 2004.

LaLonde, Chris. *Grave Concerns Trickster Turns.* Norman: University of Oklahoma Press, 2002.

Owens, Louis. *Bone Game.* Norman: University of Oklahoma Press, 1994.

Venuto, Rochelle. "*Bone Game*'s Terminal Plots and Healing Stories." *Studies in American Indian Literature* 10, no. 2 (1998): 23–41.

Jeff Berglund

Book of Medicines, The Linda Hogan (1993)

LINDA HOGAN's *The Book of Medicines* elaborates on several of the themes present in her earlier poetry as well as in her fiction and nonfiction prose. Some of these poems, however, are a bit more elliptical than her earlier work, and the collection is itself particularly coherent. Most striking about the poems in *The Book of Medicines* is the identification they make between humans and other animals—not simply through personification, but by manipulation of images such that distinctions between humans and other animals disappear. Rather than asserting that humans should respond to animals as relatives, the speaker simply assumes that belief and writes from that perspective. As in much AMERICAN INDIAN POETRY, the concerns of these poems are, therefore, mythic and universal rather than particularly autobiographical.

Among the most memorable poems in the collection is "The History of Red," which serves as a prologue. Although for most readers of Hogan's work, *red* will carry connotations of race, the first reference to red in the poem occurs several lines in, when blood "rose up" in "human clay." This blood is immediately transformed into the blood of bison, blood humans used to paint images of bison on cave walls. Images evocative of blood continue in the next stanza, in which a child is born, inevitably drawing blood from its mother. Then the focus of images shifts to earth, red earth, the clay from which humans are made, according to the previous stanza. Only after this link between literal blood and literal red earth has been established does the poem shift to abstract connotations of the color. Red becomes the variety of fear that provokes violence; even here, however, in the most abstract moment of the poem, Hogan again links the animal to the human by describing the knife with its claw handle. The body's blood becomes a wound, and the wound is healed through medicine's desire to understand the mystery of that body. The birth canal alluded to is linguistically linked to war, a "ditch of human blood" a soldier crawls through in exchange for his life. Near the end of the poem Hogan relies on images of fire to describe the life force within us. The poem, finally, celebrates the speaker's desire for life, the force capable of calling forth such desire.

The rest of the collection can be understood in terms of the speaker's yearning toward life. Whether Hogan describes whale, bear, buffalo, or some other creature, she dares to celebrate each life, even as she may also mourn the passing of that life. Her call to her readers is to consciousness of our place in creation.

Bibliography

Cook, Barbara J., ed. *From the Center of Tradition: Critical Perspectives on Linda Hogan.* Boulder: University Press of Colorado, 2003.

Rader, Dean, and Janice Gould, eds. *Speak to Me Words: Essays on Contemporary American Indian Poetry.* Tucson: University of Arizona Press, 2003.

Lynn Domina

Boy Who Lived with the Bears and Other Iroquois Stories, The Joseph Bruchac (1995)

JOSEPH BRUCHAC's *The Boy Who Lived with the Bears* is a collection of several traditional Iroquois stories. The stories reflect the gamut of traditional oral storytelling forms: from myths and legends to TRICKSTER FIGURE tales and lesson stories. In this respect it is similar to other collections of Iroquois stories (such as Arthur C. Parker's *Skunny Wundy* [1994, for which Bruchac wrote the foreword] or John Bierhorst's *The Naked Bear: Folktales of the Iroquois* [1987]) and collections of other tribal stories (such as Charles and ELAINE EASTMAN's *Wigwam Evenings: Sioux Folk Tales Retold* [1909]). All such collections share common purposes: to maintain and communicate aspects of their respective cultures, to foster intercultural relations, and to preserve oral traditions.

To accomplish these goals, most collections seek to create a reading experience that mirrors the experience of listening to the tales within their oral traditions. For example, they set their stories so that the storyteller appears as a character within the story speaking directly to the audience, usually other characters within the story; usually readers are not addressed directly at all. Bruchac invokes this tradition through his use of traditional Iroquois phrases at the beginning and end of each story. Such promotion of traditional perspectives also manifests itself literally and figuratively in Murv Jacob's illustrations, which combine characters and settings within a framework rearticulating traditional elements.

Bruchac extends such frameworks when he contextualizes these tales and their traditions in his introduction. There he recounts the forms and functions of traditional storytelling among the Iroquois. In doing so he defines these stories not as cultural oddities, but as integral parts of Iroquois culture. For example, he explains how traditionally stories function as teaching tools as well as disciplinary measures, replacing lectures and corporal punishment. Stories, then, function as devices to maintain order, as in the title story, which reveals the centrality of community and compassion for all members of the Iroquois nation, regardless of

their actions. It also reveals the inherent power of traditional life ways to overcome life's problems, as demonstrated by the way the boy's adherence to Iroquois principles leads him to heal his uncle's mental illness and familial dysfunction. Moreover, this story reveals the interrelation between human and nonhuman worlds when the boy, his uncle, and the bears all become members of the same family.

Bruchac maintains these stories for new generations to hear and appreciate. Through such careful crafting of form and content, Bruchac continues Iroquois traditional storytelling and provides audiences with new opportunities to learn about those traditions and Iroquois culture in general.

Bibliography

Bierhorst, John. *The Naked Bear: Folktales of the Iroquois.* New York: William Morrow, 1987.

Bruchac, Joseph. *The Boy Who Lived with the Bears, and Other Iroquois Stories.* New York: HarperCollins, 1995.

Eastman, Charles A. (Ohiyesa), and Elaine Goodale Eastman. *Wigwam Evenings: Sioux Folk Tales Retold.* Lincoln and London: University of Nebraska Press, 1990.

Parker, Arthur C. *Skunny Wundy: Seneca Indian Tales.* Syracuse, N.Y.: Syracuse University Press, 1994.

Clay Smith

Brant, Beth (1941–)

Beth Brant (Degonwadonti) is a Bay of Quinte Mohawk born in Detroit, in 1941. Her paternal grandparents left the Tyendinaga Mohawk Reservation in Ontario for Detroit, where her parents, Joseph and Hazel (of Irish and Scottish descent), met and were married. After ending an abusive marriage to an alcoholic, Brant struck out on her own with her three daughters, Kim, Jennifer, and Jill. She embraced her indentity as a lesbian at the age of 33 and began writing at 40. Her longtime partner is Denise Drosz.

Brant is the winner of two Michigan Council for the Arts Creative Writing Awards (1984, 1986) and the recipient of a Literature Fellowship from the National Endowment for the Arts (1991). Her major works are MOHAWK TRAIL (1985) and FOOD AND SPIRITS (1991), both collections of poetry and fiction, and WRITING AS WITNESS (1994), a collection of essays. She is also the editor of A GATHERING OF SPIRIT: A COLLECTION BY NORTH AMERICAN INDIAN WOMEN (1984). Her writing is honest, sometimes brutally so, and she refuses to shrink from any of her identities, Mohawk, woman, lesbian, mother, grandmother, First Nations, writer. She embraces this multiplicity and asks her readers to challenge stereotypes, racism, and gender roles along with her.

Brant's work tends to center around explorations of identity, the primary touchstones for her being a Mohawk, a person of color in a white world, a woman, and a lesbian. With Brant's insistence on multiplicity, it is important to note that those are in no particular order. Her story of how she came to writing late in life highlights her identity as an indigenous person. She and her partner, Denise, were driving one day when an eagle swooped down to meet them. She says: "We looked into each other's eyes. I was marked by him. . . . We looked into each other for minutes, maybe hours, maybe a thousand years. I had received a message, a gift. When I got home I began to write" (*Writing* 25).

Brant's keen observations of racism, both overt and subtle, run throughout her work. She is especially troubled by the appropriation of Native culture. She does not shun non-Indians, but rather wants to see more appreciation for the reality and the history of Indian culture. She says: "We do not object to non-Natives praying *with* us (if invited). We object to the theft of our prayers that have no psychic meaning to them" (34).

In addition to dealing with issues of race and culture, Brant often addresses gender and the specific issues Native women and Native lesbians face. In fact, in the story "This Is History" in *Food and Spirits* she rewrites the Mohawk creation story as a love story between two women, Sky Woman and First Woman, effectively linking her two major themes of Mohawk culture and gender. She makes a similar move in *Mohawk Trail* where she engages traditional TRICKSTER FIGURE stories, but her trickster is a woman.

Brant might be called by some a confrontational writer, but the battles she chooses to fight are crucial to the survival of her people. She forces readers to alter their preconceived notions of Native peoples and homosexuality, insisting on equality and respect for the many different identities human beings assume.

Bibliography

Cullum, Linda. "Survival's Song: Beth Brant and the Power of the Word." *MELUS* 24, no. 3 (fall 1999): 129–140.

Breath Tracks Jeannette Armstrong (1991)

Breath Tracks, JEANETTE ARMSTRONG's only book of poetry, addresses the gap between oral and written culture, a gap that might also be read as a gap between indigenous and nonindigenous culture. The collection is divided into four sections: "From the Landscape of Grandmother," "History Lesson," "Fire Madness," and "Wind Woman."

Much of Armstrong's writing is political or engages the politics of and the struggle for Canadian indigenous self-government, and the poems in *Breath Tracks* continue this project by creating an awareness of the issues, albeit on a more immediately emotional level than her fiction, as they are experienced by the First Nations people of North America. The section entitled "History Lesson" features the poem "First People," a piece that incorporates the oral history of the people into poetic structure. This poem celebrates the creation of the world, which is depicted here as a ceremony of light, fire, water, the seasons, silence, and air. Most importantly, it depicts the role of humans on Earth as one that is humble, and one that is contingent on a trust that "passes hand to hand / downward / toward tomorrow" (27). This statement, and its discussion of the relationship between humans and their environment, echoes what is generally held to be the basis for the conflict between traditional and nontraditional Native Americans, a theme that figures prominently in Armstrong's other literary works, most notably her novel *Slash*. This is an important observation as the indigenous struggle for SOVEREIGNTY is generally depicted as an Native/non-Native struggle, a view that would tend to oversimplify the complex process of decolonization.

A more overtly political piece is the mournful poem "History Lesson," within which colonization, during which Europeans gave gifts, "Small pox, Seagrams," and more importantly destruction, is depicted: "Somewhere among the remains / of skinless animals / is the termination / to a long journey" (29). This poem is an expression of the grief over the origins of the destruction of Native culture.

Issues of how humans relate to the environment also figure prominently in *Breath Tracks,* for example in "Winds." This poem also experiments with the arrangement and placement of words on the page, so that the reading forces multiple rereadings. In this poem harmony among the various natural elements and landscape and the person witnessing this act of nature is emphasized by the arrangement, which further serves to stress the necessity of humanity within nature. No line or set of words is given prominence over any other.

Bibliography

Armstrong, Jeannette. *Breath Tracks.* Vancouver: Williams-Wallace/Theytus Books, 1991.
———. "Land Speaking." In *Speaking for the Generations: Native Writers on Writing*, edited by Simon J. Ortiz, 175–194. Tucson: University of Arizona Press, 1998.
Isernhagen, Hartwig. *Momaday, Vizenor, Armstrong: Conversations with Native American Writers.* Norman: University of Oklahoma Press, 1999.

Jolene Armstrong

Breeze Swept Through, A   Luci Tapahonso (1987)

This collection of poetry, written by LUCI TAPAHONSO (Diné, or Navajo), was published in 1987. Including both traditional beliefs and contemporary images of life on the reservation, this collection creates a complex but accurate picture of Navajo culture today. For example, the structure of the book itself represents the traditional. In the collection she divides her poetry into four sections: "A Breeze Swept Through," "A Spring Poem," "Back Then, Sweetheart," and "There Is Nothing Quite Like This." In doing so, Tapahonso pays tribute to the sacredness of the number 4, important because it represents the four seasons or the four directions. However, the nontraditional is also present. Within these sections she includes poems that contain issues and problems of contemporary life. She easily mixes past with present, traditional with nontraditional.

Many of the poems in this collection address Tapahonso's children as well as express her yearning for her family "back home." Prominently placed within the poems are references to Tapahonso's daughters as well as other relatives and ancestors. For example, many of the poems include her children. In the title poem, "A Breeze Swept Through," she writes about the birth of her daughters, Lori Tazbah and Misty Dawn. Children again appear in "Seasonal Woman," but this time Tapahonso highlights the mother's role, writing, "She soothes her daughters gently / her hair falling down around her face / as she bends down, murmuring comfort." Many of her poems, such as "Yes, It Was My Grandmother," connect her to a larger family and represent Tapahonso's strong ties to them. In all these poems the power and strength of Diné women are integral to preserving the culture and heritage. Tapahonso uses the imagery to relate the importance of passing to one's children cultural knowledge, which is necessary for the culture to flourish and to remain vital and powerful.

Culture is also a recurring theme within the poems. Tapahonso delightfully mixes images of sacred clouds, desert landscapes, and fertile corn with Pepsi cans, cowboy boots, and fast cars. With these contrasting images she portrays a community shaped by a respect for both traditional and nontraditional ways. "Sheepherder Blues," for example, portrays a woman who drinks, fights, and travels, only to return home to be a sheepherder, a traditional profession for Diné. "Raisin Eyes," one of Tapahonso's most popular poems, creates a tension between the life of rodeoing and cowboys and the need to return home to the land and the culture. Through these contrasts she makes extremely powerful social and political comments about life on the reservation.

Tapahonso's style is also distinct. Speaking Diné as her primary language and English as her secondary, Tapahonso creates poetry that contains a strong sense of language and a heightened sense of usage. Within her poems are songs, memories, and histories of the land and her people. She weaves contemporary themes with Diné storytelling traditions, emphasizing for her readers the past, present, and future. Using primarily the present tense, her voice illustrates Diné sense of self, community, and humor. Her prose is straightforward, and her poems read as carefully crafted stories.

Jami Huntsinger

Bruchac, Joseph   (1942–   )

Born October 16, 1942, of Abenaki descent as well as Slavic and English, Bruchac was raised in Greenfield Center, New York, by his maternal grandparents, Marion Dunham Bowman and Jesse Bowman. His grandmother was educated as a lawyer at Albany Law School. Though she did not practice law, she enjoyed and had many books and shared her enthusiasm for reading with Joseph. He especially enjoyed reading children's classics that featured animals. The couple ran a small general store in Greenfield Center, which is at the foothills of the Adirondack Mountains, and Joseph helped out there as a boy, ringing up purchases on the cash register or washing cars or car windows for customers.

Joseph's grandfather was of Abenaki descent, but he did not tell Joseph the stories the writer would seek out later in life. Instead from him Joseph learned how to respect the woods by walking quietly there and how to fish. His grandfather was very kind and disciplined Joseph by speaking with him about any problems rather than spanking him. This was how his grandfather had been raised as well. Jesse Bowman could barely read or write.

Stories and writing became an early part of Joseph's life. During the fall and winter months Joseph enjoyed sitting by the woodstove and listening to the stories and tall tales told by the local farmers and lumberjacks. One of these storytellers was Lawrence Older. In school Joseph showed his writing promise early. In second grade he wrote poems to his teacher. One day she read one of them aloud to the class, a jealous classmate beat up Joseph after school. Though he always thought he would become a writer, Joseph did not start exploring his Native American roots through stories until many years later.

Bruchac received a B.A. from Cornell University, an M.A. in literature and creative writing from Syracuse University, and a Ph.D. in comparative literature from the Union Institute of Ohio. He worked as an educator for many years, including eight years as the director of a Skidmore College program inside a maximum security prison.

When Bruchac married his wife, Carol, and they had their two sons, James and Jesse, he became interested in learning more about the Abenaki stories of his ancestors. The result has been a life's work of recovering and retelling stories not only of the Abenaki but also of Native cultures across the United States. His prolific work began with his first publication of stories in 1975 and has risen to over 70 books for children and adults, including the anthology *Songs from This Earth on Turtle's Back, Breaking Silence,* the autobiography *Bowman's Store,* over 500 poems, stories, and articles in periodicals such as *American Poetry Review, National Geographic, Smithsonian, Aboriginal Voices,* and *Cricket;* and hundreds of storytelling events and programs. Bruchac's accolades include an American Book Award (for *Songs from This Earth*) and the Lifetime Achievement Award from the Native Writers Circle of the Americas. The author continues to live and work in the same house in Greenwich Center where he was raised and is an especially important voice for Native Americans among young people.

Bibliography

Ricker, Meredith. "A *MELUS* Interview: Joseph Bruchac." *MELUS* 21, no. 3 (fall 1996): 159–178.

Connie Ann Kirk

Business of Fancydancing, The
Sherman Alexie (1992)

SHERMAN ALEXIE's first book, a collection of stories and poems entitled *The Business of Fancydancing,* established him not only as a talented Native American writer, but as a major contemporary literary figure. Drawing from his childhood on the Spokane Indian Reservation in Wellpinit, Washington, Alexie's book, a loosely strung set of stories and poems, concentrates primarily on the realities of reservation life and its boundaries in the eastern side of the state, a cultural focus that many critics view as a remedy to mainstream ignorance of life on a reservation. The collection provides painfully honest glimpses of life from Wellpinit and its memorable ambience of basketball tourneys, POW wows, Housing and Urban Development (HUD) housing, and commodity foods. Throughout *The Business of Fancydancing* Alexie's clever wit and insightful observations give rise to enduring characters such as Thomas Builds-the-Fire and Lester Falls-Apart, who continue to surface in his later work. His writing tackles many facets of citizenship and selfhood, as evidenced in the poem "13/16," in which identity is figured by "blood, reservation mathematics, fractions" or by "enrollment number, last name first, first name last." The book also navigates through the "politics of time, distance, geography," as in the short story "Special Delivery." *The Business of Fancydancing* truly provides an alternative view of life in the United States, which Alexie clearly affirms in "Powwow" as he asks, "Did you ever get the feeling / when speaking to a white American / that you needed closed captions?"

Bibliography

Etter, Carrie. "Dialectic to Dialogics: Negotiating Bicultural Heritage in Sherman Alexie's Sonnets." In *Telling the Stories: Essays on American Indian Literatures and Cultures,* edited by Elizabeth Nelson Hoffman, 143–151. New York: Peter Lang, 2001.

Fast, Robin Riley. *The Heart as a Drum: Continuance and Resistance in American Indian Poetry.* Ann Arbor: University of Michigan Press, 1999.

Vickers, Scott B. *Native American Identities: From Stereotype to Archetype in Art and Literature.* Albuquerque: University of New Mexico Press, 1998.

Petra Ofloff

Business of Fancydancing, The (2002)

Unlike the film *SMOKE SIGNALS* (1998), which SHERMAN ALEXIE also wrote, the film *Fancydancing* is not a conventional narrative. Here, in his directorial debut, Alexie takes an experimental and poetic approach to the complexities of identity and ethnicity. There are flashbacks, achronic sequences, intertitles of the protagonist's writing, and interludes of various characters dancing or making music. The film's protagonist, Seymour Polatkin, is a successful poet, and the poems he reads are Alexie's own. "Influences," from *FIRST INDIAN ON THE MOON* (1993), is employed to stress that "this is about the stories." There is a great deal of pain and anger, and even a meditation on laughter, in this film, in which one of the problems of identity concerns ownership of stories.

The central characters—Seymour, Aristotle Joseph, Agnes Roth, and Mouse—grew up on the Spokane Indian Reservation in Washington. Seymour and Aristotle go away to university, but Aristotle drops out and returns home; Seymour graduates but stays away. Agnes, who had never met the others before university, graduates and goes home to teach. Mouse never leaves and records everything from high school graduation day to the end of his life on video, believing that life is a tape that plays over and over. Mouse has complained that Seymour's poems are stolen from his life, that they are his stories. Throughout the movie it becomes more and more difficult to know where one person's story stops and another's begins. All of the events that Seymour tells in his poems are indeed his, but he has given himself the central role, putting Seymour where Mouse and Aristotle were.

One of the techniques Alexie uses to great effect is the tendency to obscure faces. When Seymour is reflected in a mirror, the angle is such that his face is fragmented along the bevel in the glass. The blurred lines of identity are nowhere more vivid than when Seymour is sitting in a circle at an Alcoholics Anonymous (AA) meeting, reading a poem, when suddenly the speaker is Aristotle. We cannot extract influences, and Alexie has written this idea into the script in everything from his characters' names, to the to-be-or-not-to-be chant, to Seymour's unimaginative cry, "The reserve won't let me go." When Seymour meets his partner in a gay bar, there is fancydancing among the leathered patrons. It is a moment when Alexie makes visual the concurrent forces of identity at work in his character. Nowhere is it more powerfully illustrated than after Mouse's funeral, when Seymour walks up to the car and comes face to face with himself sitting behind the wheel and after a moment of speechless eye contact, drives away and leaves himself standing there.

Bibliography

Curiel, Jonathan. "*Fancydancing* Doesn't Sidestep Indian Issues," *San Francisco Chronicle,* 30 August 2002, D5.

Gage, Julienne. "Which Tribe?" *Sojourners* 31, no. 5 (September–October 2002): 54.

Harvey, Dennis, and Joe Leydon. Review of *The Business of Fancydancing, Variety* 28, January 2002, 33.

A. Mary Murphy

California tribal literature

Like the indigenous peoples who have populated the ecologically diverse region of California, the literature of California's Natives is of an extremely diverse nature. Tribes, such as the Cahuilla, Gabrielino, Chumash Tipai-Ipai, and Ohlone, of the arid inland have drawn on a mythology and storytelling tradition quite similar to those of southwestern peoples. The characters who appear frequently in their tales are Coyote, Raven, Hawk, Snake, and Rabbit. The coastal tribes, Costanoan, Miwok, Pomo (also inland), and Luiseno, include these characters in their stories but also tell of Dolphin, Whale, Seal, and Shark. Tribes of the north, Yuki, Wintun, the WHupa (or Hoopa), Karok, Achomawi, Yurok, also honor salmon, bear, and wood fowl in their stories.

In the late 19th and early 20th centuries, white ethnographers began to record the oral traditions of indigenous Californians, but in the 1970s not only did Native peoples step up to record the memories of their elders before tradition and regional knowledge faded away for all time, but a new crop of writers began to log the history of the many tribes of the region, record Native knowledge of the flora and fauna, preserve the language and customs of their peoples, and write about late 20th-century Indian life, as city dwellers, as modern people, and as nonwhites in a highly anti-Native society.

Among non-Native authors who have focused on Indian stories are Gerald Haslam and Scott O'Dell. Haslam has written numerous books, including retellings of Indian myths, drawing from his knowledge of the Great Central Valley of California. O'Dell's Newberry Medal–awarded *Island of Blue Dolphins* fictionalized the true story of a native American woman who lived alone but for her dog on San Nicolas Island for 20 years. GREG SARRIS, a Miwok, has written several critically acclaimed novels of Native life in the Sonoma region. Other authors of mixed Indian heritage from other regions in North America have elected to live in larger cities in California, prompting the growth of unofficial communities of writers concerned with Indian affairs. Among these are the poets Kim Shuck and Kimberly TallBear, the novelist-scholar PAULA GUNN ALLEN, the poet-essayist CAROLYN DUNN, and the poet-novelist Elizabeth Treadwell Jackson.

Bibliography

Allen, Paula Gunn. *Hozho: Walking in Beauty, Native American Stories of Inspiration, Humor, and Life.* Los Angeles: Lowell House, 2001.

Dunn, Carolyn. *Outfoxing Coyote.* San Pedro, Calif.: That Painted Horse Press, 2000.

Haslam, Gerald. *Constant Coyote: California Stories.* Reno: University of Nevada Press, 1990.

———. *The Man Who Cultivated Fire and Other Stories.* Santa Barbara, Calif.: Capra Press, 1987.

Margolin, Malcolm. *The Way We Lived: California Indian Stories, Songs and Reminiscences.* Berkeley, Calif.: Heyday Books, 1993.

Milliken, Randall. *A Time of Little Choice: The Disintegration of Tribal Culture in the San Francisco Bay Area, 1769–1810.* Menlo Park, Calif.: Ballena Press Publishers' Services, 1995.

O'Dell, Scott, *Island of the Blue Dolphins.* Boston: Houghton Mifflin, 1960.

Sarris, Greg. *Watermelon Nights.* New York: Hyperion, 1998.

Michelle LaFrance

Campbell, Maria   (1940–   )

Maria Campbell was born June Stifle in Park Valley, Saskatchewan, Canada, in April 1940. She is a Canadian of mixed Métis, Scottish, and French descent. Campbell has written several children's stories based on folklore and history, plays, and her autobiography, *Halfbreed* (1973). Her writing works to uphold and maintain the traditions of which she is a part, and she is an important voice not only for Native issues, but also for the strong females she portrays. Campbell has won the National Aboriginal Achievement Award, the Chalmers Award for Best New Play, and the Dora Mavor Moore Award for playwriting. In 2004 she won the Canada Council for the Arts Molson Prize.

Campbell is best known for *Halfbreed*, which recounts her childhood, the death of her mother, the breakup of her early marriage (she was married at the age of 15), and her firsthand experience with prostitution and drug and alcohol abuse. But *Halfbreed* also provides an emotional and at times heartbreaking narrative of life for Canadian Métis women in general and describes the racism and sexism that attend Métis existence. With Linda Griffiths, Campbell wrote *Jessica*, a play that dramatizes many of the events from *Halfbreed*. In the play the actors portray human characters as well as animal spirits, and the interaction between the human and spirit worlds is at the fore.

Campbell is also well known for writing plays and children's literature, in which she focuses on Native legends and folklore. In *Little Badger and the Fire Spirit* (1977) and *People of the Buffalo: How the Plains Indians Lived* (1976) Campbell blends legend, history, and folklore. In 1985 Campbell edited *Achimoona*, an anthology of fiction by young Native authors. Campbell also wrote the play *Flight*, the first all-Native production in Canada. She has written several other plays and, from 1985 until 1997, ran a film and production company that produced documentaries and the 1991 Native television series *My Partners, My People.*

The Road Allowance People, published in 1995, is based on factual events surrounding the forced migration of the Canadian Métis in 1948. Many die and once their journey is over, they realize that they have been lied to and that no new home has been provided for them. In this as well as her other writings Campbell brings to light the triumphs and tragedies of indigenous Canadians.

Bibliography

Bataille, Gretchen M., and Kathleen Mullen Sands. *American Indian Women: Telling Their Lives,* 113–126. Lincoln: University of Nebraska Press, 1984.

Campbell, Maria *Stories of the Road Allowance People.* Penticton, Canada: Theytus Books, 1995.

———. *Little Badger and the Fire Spirit.* Toronto: McClelland and Stewart, 1977.

———. *People of the Buffalo: How the Plains Indians Lived.* Vancouver: J. J. Douglas, 1976.

———. *Halfbreed.* New York: Saturday Review Press, 1973.

Contemporary Authors: New Revision Series. Vol. 54, 74–76. Detroit: Gale, 1997.

Contemporary Challenges: Conversations with Canadian Native Authors, edited by Hartmut Lutz, 41–65. Victoria, Canada: Fifth House, 1991.

Petrone, Penny. *Native Literature in Canada: From the Oral Tradition to the Present,* 113–137. Oxford: Oxford University Press, 1990.

Brian Johnson

Cannon Between My Knees, A   Paula Gunn Allen   (1981)

In *A Cannon Between My Knees,* a short collection of poetry published in 1981, Paula Gunn Allen explores the intersections between modern feminism and Native American culture, celebrating the beauty and power of Native American femininity.

Furthermore, with evocative imagery and experimental style she reveals that the cultural healing she envisions for her community must begin with the strength that lies naturally within womanhood.

In several of the poems in this collection Allen discusses the nature of Native American womanhood as being too complex for words. "The Beautiful Woman Who Sings," for example, begins with the assertion that a beautiful Laguna woman is not the same as a beautiful woman in Los Angeles. Throughout this poem Allen goes on to list the characteristics of Laguna women in a fragmented manner. She says they are "large," "smiling," "serious," and "self-contained." By placing periods and spaces between the frequently contradictory items in her list, Allen physically separates the characteristics that she names and suggests the unspeakable distances between the words available for her use. In the final lines of the poem Allen explains the joy that Laguna women produce as they perform the tasks of everyday domestic life. Many of the tasks Allen lists suggest renewal or rebirth, demonstrating the potential healing power inherent in Native American women.

In her poetry from *A Cannon Between My Knees* Allen also frequently utilizes images of mythic figures to lend power and strength to her vision of contemporary Native American womanhood. For instance, in the four-part "Suicid/ing(ed) Indian Woman," Allen's longest work, she evokes images of the corn woman Iyetiko. She compares Native American women to Iyetiko in that they are often "broken" and "unhappy." She goes on, however, to propose a path for women to escape the toxic influences in their lives. She suggests a solution in "division." In this poem Allen resolves that Native American women must separate themselves from the male "law" that "put women out of the center" and return to the woman-centered culture of the corn woman.

Throughout most of the poetry in this collection Allen calls her fellow Native American women to action. The last poem, "Thusness Before the War," for example, uses descriptions of the beauty of nature and the power of womanhood simultaneously in a way that empowers the female

spirit and readies it for an ensuing struggle. Her opening line, "Tall noon sun" (1), an image of the transition between morning and afternoon, implies that change is inevitable. With the following lines, "Geese, grass, wind. Tone of bells. / Mission out back. Streams, clear and cold. / Remembering simplicity (a cannon between my knees)" (8–10), Allen calls her fellow Native American women to use their natural beauty, strength, and power to restore their culture and communities to health and happiness.

Bibliography
Allen, Paula Gunn. *A Cannon Between My Knees.* New York: Strawberry Press, 1981.

Andrea Powell

Ceremony   Leslie Marmon Silko (1977)
In *The Cry for Myth* Rollo May asserts that every individual "*must* seek myth if he or she is to remain sane." Unrelated to the past, unconnected with the future, we hang "as if in mid-air." In LESLIE MARMON SILKO's partly autobiographical novel *Ceremony,* Tayo is stripped of his myths; he seeks meaning for the flood of violent emotions and images: the jungle rain, a sea of voices, the Japanese soldiers, and scorched civilians. Living at the margins even of his own culture—he is half white and half Native American—he has lost connection with his mythology. Only when he completes Old Betonie's ceremony of healing can Tayo appropriate myth to free him from the grasp of the "witchery." Silko employs what could be called an ecofeminist approach. In doing this, she uses several key female characters to help her male protagonist reject the stereotypical male world of dominance and destruction in favor of the traditional female world of community, connections to people, and connection to the land.

Born in Albuquerque, New Mexico, in 1948, Silko crossed several borders herself. As the daughter of a MIXED-BLOOD marriage Silko explores issues of shifting identity in much of her work. Learning the folklore of the Laguna people from her great-grandmother and her great-aunt, Susie, Silko, as did Tayo, internalized the traditions of her culture, claiming that storytelling provides "a whole way of seeing yourself," of putting yourself into a larger context (Crutchins 273).

With *Ceremony,* her first novel, her reputation as one of the most important writers of her generation and heritage was established. This novel has received more critical acclaim than her others, even though some of the later works demonstrate a more controlled maturity as a writer. A winner of several grants awards whose work is taught pervasively in literature classes and who is continually the subject of critical studies, Silko has secured a place in literary history as a voice of the disenfranchised and as a champion of ecoethnic concerns. In a letter to James Wright Silko said that in *Ceremony* it was as if "the land was telling the stories in the novel" (2).

At the beginning of *Ceremony* Tayo has returned from the war in the Pacific psychically dysfunctional, full of doubts, fears, and guilt—over the death of his cousin/brother Rock and the loss of Uncle Josiah's Mexican cattle. Tayo also suffers from his sense of cultural marginality; his aunt, having taken him in after the death of his outcast mother, never lets him forget that he is inferior to her son, Rocky. Tayo's companions—Leroy, Harley, and Pinkie, also war veterans—have resorted to alcoholic brawling in response to their war memories, and Tayo finds himself too often joining them. Tayo's mental sickness causes physical illness. The drought that Tayo believes he has prayed on his land matches the spiritual drought plaguing him; all Tayo can do is to vomit and lie in bed for days, totally physically and emotionally impotent.

Tayo's problem might be called a crisis of myth; he has lost touch with the patterns of existence and has become isolated and alienated. Early in life, however, he had listened to the wise ones and believed in the power of the stories until taken away by the white schoolteacher. Tayo then begins to doubt the efficacy of the old stories, especially when they fail him by allowing the deaths of Rocky and Josiah and a cloudless, dry period for the people.

To contextualize Tayo's story, Silko places 26 myth vignettes throughout the novel. By juxtaposing Tayo's search for meaning in his life beside the old stories of the Laguna people, Silko universalizes his psychic struggle, using Thought-Woman to begin the storytelling. Just as later in the myth/poems Silko will explain the creation of white people and the problems for the Indians, she accounts here for everything else that will occur in the novel: "You don't have anything if you don't have the stories" (2). These myths/poems/stories help to transform Tayo's attitude and lead him to healing, along with the intervention of three women: first, his grandmother, who recognizes the need to seek tribal wisdom; second, the medicine man Betonie's hazel-eyed grandmother, who had preserved the stories; and third, "the woman," Ts'eh, whose resurrecting love restores Tayo to life. Tayo finally realizes that his "sickness was only part of something larger, and his cure would be found only in something great and inclusive of everything" (125–126). With Betonie's help and the community of women, he begins to understand that he cannot entirely blame the white people for his sickness, which seems to symbolize all the evil in the world: "'Nothing is that simple . . . you don't write off all the white people, just like you don't trust all the Indians'" (128).

Silko then inserts in the novel one of the longest of the myth/poems, which explains the creation of white people by Indians, a common element in Native American mythology. It tells of white-skinned people who emerged from caves across the ocean, who grew away from the earth, who see everything around them as just objects, and destroy the landscape. These white people colonized America, and the storyteller presents an apocalyptic vision of the end of human civilization that foreshadows the atomic bomb. When Tayo discovers the site where the bomb was tested and exploded, Tayo's life and the stories he had learned all merge. In this epiphany Silko combines Tayo's very individual struggle with the global struggle for humanity to avoid annihilation. Once Tayo rejects the "witchery," he experiences true healing: all the stories join in a unified vision. Tayo realizes finally that "the pattern of the ceremony" is completed, and he cries in relief at "finally seeing the pattern, the way all the stories fit together. . . . He was not crazy; he had never been crazy. He had only seen and heard that world as it always was: no boundaries, only transitions through all distances and time" (246).

Bibliography

Crutchins, Dennis. "Leslie Marmon Silko." In *Dictionary of Literary Biography.* Detroit: Thomson/Gale, 2004.

Hokanson, Robert O'Brien. "Crossing Cultural Boundaries with Leslie Marmon Silko's *Ceremony.*" In *Rethinking American Literature,* edited by Lil Brannon and Brenda M. Greene, 115–127. Urbana, Ill.: National Council of Teachers of English, 1997.

Shapiro, Colleen. "Silko's Ceremony." *Explicator* 61, no. 3 (winter 2003): 117–119.

Peacock, John. "Un-Writing Empire by Writing Oral Tradition: Leslie Marmon Silko's *Ceremony.*" In *(Un) Writing Empire,* edited by Theo D'haen, 295–308. Amsterdam, Netherlands: Rodopi, 1998.

Kim Martin Long

Chrystos (1946–)

Chrystos was born in San Francisco, California, on November 7, 1946. Of MIXED-BLOOD heritage, she identifies more with her father, who is of Menominee ancestry, than with her mother, who is of northern European descent. Growing up in a city surrounded by racial and ethnic diversity instead of on a reservation, Chrystos is a self-identified "Urban Indian." Her poetry, often political and angry, explores the effects of colonialism, racism, and genocide as they affect the lives of Native people. This is highlighted in a 2002 interview in which Chrystos claims: "One of the things I find really difficult is how racism is presented as a black-white issue. It erases the whole issue of genocide. . . . The eradication of native people is still a core issue for me" (*The Gully*). Her first collection of poetry, *NOT VANISHING* (1988), puts these issues at the forefront and they have remained a major theme in all of her writing.

A self-educated writer and artist who designs the covers of her own books, Chrystos describes herself as "a Native American Lesbian poet and activist" (*Voices from the Gap*). Along with poems that challenge racism and the stereotypes about Native people, Chrystos's writing addresses issues of class, gender, and sexuality. Though Chrystos may be more known for her angry, political poems, which draw attention to "society's victims" and oppression, Barbara Dale May suggests that her erotic poems in *Not Vanishing* are the most elegant and thoughtful in the collection. In 1994 Chrystos won the Audre Lorde International Poetry Competition, and she won the Sappho Award of Distinction in 1995. Her poetry has appeared in *This Bridge Called My Back: Writings by Radical Women of Color* (1981) and *Living the Spirit: A Gay American Indian Anthology* (1988). She has been living on Bainbridge Island, Washington, since 1980.

Bibliography

Chrystos. *Not Vanishing.* Vancouver: Press Gang, 1988.

Hall, Lynda. "Her Howl inside Us." In *Canadian Literature.* Vancouver: University of British Columbia, 1996.

May, Barbara Dale. "Chrystos (1946–)." In *Contemporary Lesbian Writers of the United States: A Bio-Bibliographical Critical Sourcebook,* edited by Sandra Pollack and Denise Knight, 118–122. Westport, Conn.: Greenwood, 1993.

Murphy, Patrick D. "Voicing Another Nature." In *A Dialogue of Voices: Feminist Literary Theory and Bakhtin,* edited by Karen Hohne and Helen Wussow, 118–121. Minneapolis: University of Minnesota Press, 1994.

Stephanie Gustafson

Claiming Breath Diane Glancy (1992)

Claiming Breath DIANE GLANCY's eighth book, won the 1991 North American Indian Prose Award. Building on Glancy's mixed Cherokee, German, and English ancestry, one of the book's central themes is the negotiation of her diverse cultural and religious heritages in the process of creating a viable ethnic identity.

As do many Native American authors of mixed descent, Glancy uses her narrative *I* as a bridge between conflicting cultures. On the first page the text in the center of the page is shaped like a capital *I*; splitting the page, it introduces the reader to Glancy's fragmented identity as a writer: "I often write about being in the middle ground between two cultures, not fully a part of either. I write with a split voice, often experimenting with the language until the parts equal some sort of a whole" (xiii). These first lines of the book function as a programmatic announcement; subsequently Glancy defies literary boundaries by mixing poetry and prose, journal writing and storytelling, and Native American and Anglo-Christian themes. She finds her voice in what she calls "non-boundaried non-fenced open-prairied words" (4).

Claiming Breath chronicles a year Glancy spent mainly on the road, supporting her family by driving throughout Oklahoma and Arkansas to teach poetry in schools. Therefore, *Claiming Breath* can be seen as a road or quest narrative. Both physical and spiritual travel are significant in Glancy's work, from *Traveling On* (1980) to the short-story collection *The Voice That Was in Travel* (1999). In *Claiming Breath* traveling the American highways serves as an act of claiming cultural and physical space for Glancy's mixed identity as a Cherokee, an American, and a woman and mother. Her claim to space becomes a claim to breathe, to speak and write in order to create actuality (a belief that is a common theme throughout Native American literature).

By her migrations Glancy also invokes the collective historical trauma of her Cherokee forebears, the Trail of Tears of 1838–39. In many ways she transforms this traumatic experience by rewriting movement as empowering and poetic. Her "words make the trail" anew, and her poetry is a "prayer-ee for [her] territory"; "in travel," the narrator states, "in the act of migration, is the POEM" (28).

Glancy's narrative *I* struggles with her experience of being separated and divorced, of being a mother and a daughter, who within one year loses her own mother and sees her children move out. At times Glancy reflects the influence of both her generation's homebound mothers and its fathers and husbands at the center of the family. Yet by what she calls "SHEdonism," Glancy recovers "the enjoyment of oneself as a woman" (51–52) who has learned independence.

Bibliography

Glancy, Diane. *Claiming Breath.* Lincoln: University of Nebraska Press, 1992.

Alexandra Ganser

Clements, Susan   (1950–   )

Susan Clements was born in 1950 in Livingston Manor, New York, and is recognized as a member of the Seneca Nation. She is descended from the Blackfeet, Mohawk, and Seneca tribes and also has English, Irish, Swiss, Austrian, and Czech ancestors. Clements started writing as a child and has always felt a deep connection to the Native American community and its issues, which she incorporates into her poetry and essays. Her multiple tribal roots have also shaped her writing and have influenced her themes of "mixed" Native Americans versus "whole" Native Americans and the governmental certification policy of requiring Native Americans to identify with a tribe.

Clements attended Binghamton University of the State University of New York (SUNY) and earned her B.A. in 1980 and M.A. in 1982. After graduation, she then turned her attention to getting her work published. Her writing was quickly accepted and has been published in several journals and anthologies, including *Mid-American Review; North Dakota Quarterly; Akwe:kon, a Journal of Indigenous Issues;* and *Unsettling America: An Anthology of Contemporary Multicultural Poetry.* Her audience readily notes her adept skill of depicting the environment of Native Americans and the exploration of their struggles with assimilation, myths, stereotypes, and high percentages of suicide and unemployment.

In addition to writing poetry, Clements has produced acclaimed essays. In particular, literary critics lauded her essay "Five Arrows," which appears in the compilation entitled *American Mixed Race: The Culture of Microdiversity.* The essay gives Clements's personal account of her family's diverse heritage and their ethnic identification, her discovery of racism, her confrontation of psychological traumas affecting Native Americans, and her rediscovery of the physical abuse Native Americans face. Her overall message is to unite people beyond the definition of "blood" and to educate other cultures about Native Americans.

Clements has also written two books of poetry. Her first complication, *The Broken Hoop,* engages in poems of her family and upbringing. Her second collection, *In the Moon When the Deer Lose Their Horns,* explores these same themes and expands Clements's lucid style. During the same time *In the Moon When the Deer Lose Their Horns* was published, Clements received the New York State Foundation for the Arts Poetry Fellowship in 1993. This award and other honors have pushed Clements to great popularity and give numerous public readings. She currently lives in Binghamton, New York.

Bibliography

Clements, Susan. "Five Arrows." In *American Mixed Race: The Culture of Microdiversity,* edited by Naomi Zack, 3–11. Lanham, Md.: Rowman & Littlefield, 1995.

———. *In the Moon When Deer Lose Their Horns.* Midland Park, N.J.: Chantry Press, 1993.

———. *The Broken Hoop.* Marvin, S. Dak.: The Blue Cloud Quarterly, 1988.

Gillan, Maria Mazziotti, and Jennifer Gillan, eds. *Unsettling America: An Anthology of Contemporary Multicultural Poetry.* New York: Viking Press, 1994.

Trout, Lawana, ed. *Native American Literature: An Anthology.* Lincolnwood, Ill.: NTC/Contemporary, 1998.

Weingarten, Roger, and Richard M. Higgerson, eds. *Poets of the New Century.* Boston: David R. Godine, 2001.

Dorsia Smith

Close to Home　Gail Tremblay　(1981)

"Talking to the Grandfathers," Tremblay's section of this three-poet volume, is the first published collection of her poetry. It affords particular insight into Native poetics because of Tremblay's explorations of the connections among breath, spirit, power, and song. Moreover, her poetry demonstrates the virtues of hybridity—these poems are shaped by both her Native American heritage and, as her former mentor, John Haislip, points out, "the long heritage of English lyric poetry" (78).

The collection has four parts: the first group of traditional poems about tribal themes, a section of love poems ("Love Wakes New Worlds"), a series of darker poems entitled "The Dark Dance," and final poems, "A Few More Words of a Kind," which include "Poem in Praise of Marianne Moore."

Tremblay's first poem functions as a paradigm for the entire collection. "Returning to the Old Religion" is a reworking of a Cherokee song for the success of a hunter but also mirrors her poetics. Thus, the first section, "Search for a Guardian Spirit," entails the hunter's [poet's] baring himself to the elements until "Breath becomes my only answer" (1ine 29). In the next section, "The Hunt," the hunter must watch, wait, and pray until dawn. "The Dance" shows the hunter learning to dance around the deer he has killed until he is able to "begin / To sing" (3.11–12). (The rhythms of dance mark all of Tremblay's lyrics.) In "The Song" the hunter sings his kinship with the Bear. Then, in "Talking to the Grandfathers," the hunter recalls the ceremonies he undertook before ever embarking upon the hunt and ends by acknowledging the magical presence of the spirit world. Finally, the poem concludes with its understanding of how the "people" continue to survive: they "still / Breathe the hard north winds / and shape the world / With their tongues" (5. 21–23).

Tremblay's poems have a visionary, often ecstatic quality as they portray rhythms of nature empowering human deeds and imagination. One of the best examples is "Listening to the Dawn," Tremblay's contribution to the Native American genre of dawn poems. She documents how dawn's intensely cascading energies enable humans to "leap on a whirling sphere / and ride the earth" (26–28).

The Native American scholar Kenneth Lincoln has suggested that Native poetics has the potential for transforming literature in general: "Blending the genius of migrant and indigenous cultures . . . could lead readers . . . into a genuine new loam and literary ground" (164). Tremblay's ability to blend cultures and poetic forms speaks to her membership among those poets who may be able to accomplish such a goal.

Bibliography

Anderson, Nina Duval, Roy Scheele, and Gail Tremblay. *Close to Home.* Omaha: Creative Writing Program, University of Nebraska at Omaha, 1981.

Haislip, John. Introduction. "Talking to the Grandfathers," by Gail Tremblay. In *Close to Home,* by Nina Duval Anderson, Roy Scheele, and Gail Tremblay. Omaha: Creative Writing Program, University of Nebraska at Omaha, 1981.

Lincoln, Kenneth. "Native Poetics." *Modern Fiction Studies* 45, no. 1 (1999): 146–184.

Susan Bowers

Closets of Heaven, The   Diane Glancy (1999)

After quoting the biblical story of how Saint Peter restored a faithful seamstress back to life (Acts 9:36–43), DIANE GLANCY proceeds to tell her version of the story in this novel. The story is told in four sections or chapters, from the viewpoint of Dorcas of Joppa, the seamstress who was also known as Tabitha. Written using many short single lines and a conversational tone, the text gives the readers the impression that Dorcas is speaking directly to them.

The first section is about Dorcas's life before she became ill. She has a very quiet and humble life, but her thoughts are full of the news from Jerusalem of the new religion. She is already a believer and retells many of the stories of the evangelists, even discussing Saul, the hunter of Christians, who later becomes Paul the apostle. Glancy frequently quotes more sections of the Acts within Dorcas's monologue. During the last few pages she becomes ill and gives in to death, as if she is drowning.

The second section is the story of Dorcas's death and journey to heaven. The imagery of water taking her, as if she is gently floating away, continues. Joppa is a coastal town where there are many fishermen. As a symbol of herself, her faith, and God, the seamstress begins to dream of her needle. As she gets closer to heaven itself, God addresses her by her other name, Tabitha. Before she can see all that is in heaven, though, she feels someone calling her back to the living.

Saint Peter resurrects her in the third section. Initially she is angry with him for taking her away from such beauty and peace, but she remains polite and deferential. Her reaction to returning to life is calm, but what her friends and family, even Peter, do not seem to understand is that she is disappointed at having to leave immortal bliss. She did not ask Peter to resurrect her, but she knows his intentions were good. It is an interesting and very human element Glancy adds to the story that is ignored in the Scriptures. It is hard to be happy even on a beautiful day when she has glimpsed heaven.

Her life after the miracle of her resurrection forms the fourth and longest section. Dorcas resumes her life, returns to her vocation of sewing, and is embarrassed by the attention the miracle attracts to her. In time she remembers the trauma of her illness and feels separated from the people around her. She knows a language of heaven, metaphorically, that no one else understands.

Michael Young

Cogewea, the Half-Blood   Mourning Dove (1927)

One of the first novels written by a Native American female, *Cogewea* depicts the cultural turbulence of the settlement and ASSIMILATION periods. Set in the Flathead region of Montana, its plot follows the half-white and half-Indian Cogewea as she struggles with her cultural identities, chooses between suitors, and combats prejudice and confining roles. Genres also clash in the novel, with the melodrama and regional dialects of the western romance juxtaposed with Native American lore and texts, including authentic Salishan oral narratives. Its voice is further complicated by changes and additions made by MOURNING DOVE's white male editor. The result is a hybrid text that reflects the MIXED-BLOOD experience in its complex interweavings, an experience central to Mourning Dove herself as a partially assimilated writer attempting to negotiate dual cultures, who may have been of mixed blood herself. As the first fiction that organically incorporates elements of Native American culture, *Cogewea* has been called the first truly bicultural novel and is an important precursor to the AMERICAN INDIAN LITERARY RENAISSANCE, as well as a valuable record of the period from a Native American perspective.

From her position as "the socially ostracized of two races," the strong-willed and impetuous Cogewea is secure enough to confront prejudice by entering (and winning) both the "ladies" and the "squaws" horse races at the Fourth of July celebration, but culturally ambivalent enough doggedly to prefer the attentions of the false white easterner Alfred Densmore to those of Jim LaGrinder, the ranch foreman who is also a half-blood. Her full-blood grandmother, Stemteema, the embodiment of the traditional ways suppressed by government Assimilation policies, strives to pass on Native American forms of wisdom to Cogewea through cautionary oral narratives. Her recounting of the tale of Green-Blanket Feet, for example, foretells Cogewea's betrayal by Densmore, a message she initially denies. *Cogewea* rejects the standard tragic ending for the half-blood, however, and the work concludes with Cogewea and Jim's marrying and gaining a surprising inheritance.

Mourning Dove completed a first draft of *Cogewea* in 1912, writing in the face of many personal and financial hardships and hoping to critique and dispel stereotypes of Native Americans common in the dime novels she had read. In 1914 she met L. V. McWhorter, an amateur ethnologist and advocate for Native American interests who became her collaborator, friend, and ally in publishing the text. Mourning Dove and McWhorter initially worked together on revisions, as McWhorter edited the work and added anthropological notes and literary headings to chapters. Unsuccessful initially at publishing the novel, McWhorter continued working on *Cogewea*, adding stilted, rhetorical diatribes against white injustices to Native Americans. When it was eventually published in 1927, Mourning Dove saw McWhorter's additions for the first time. While well intentioned, the changes disheartened Mourning Dove, prompting her to write to McWhorter that she felt *Cogewea* was now "some one else's book and not mine." The novel raises crucial issues on the reading of collaborative texts; this uneasy relationship must be addressed by any reader and continues to be explicated in scholarship on *Cogewea*.

Cogewea received scant notice on publication and remained little known until revived interest in Native American and women's writings prompted its reprint in 1981. Now seen as a crucial link in the evolution of Native American literature, *Cogewea* also stands as a testament to Mourning Dove's resolve to find voice and status as a Native American woman writer, adapting language and genre from the dominant culture to transmit Native American culture and refashion the storyteller role.

Bibliography

Bernardin, Susan. "Mixed Messages: Authority and Authorship in Mourning Dove's *Cogewea, the Half-Blood: A Depiction of the Great Montana Cattle Range.*" *American Literature* 67 (1995): 487–509.

Krupat, Arnold. "From 'Half-blood' to 'Mixedblood': *Cogewea* and the 'Discourse of Indian Blood.'" In *Red Matters: Native American Studies,* 76–97. Philadelphia: University of Pennsylvania Press, 2002.

Sue Barker

Completing the Circle   Virginia Driving Hawk Sneve (1995)

In *Completing the Circle* VIRGINIA DRIVING HAWK SNEVE's focus is on the often neglected role of women in shaping history. Her book provides an in-depth perspective of a Lakota/Dakota woman's daily life prior to contact with Euro-Americans and how the postcontact period, particularly the forcible removal from Minnesota, impacted the lives of her relatives who lived through it, marking this work as an important contribution to the genre. Sneve's book not only reveals some popular cultural misconceptions of an Indian woman's role in her native society but also highlights the essential role the female plays in binding the Native society together, both before and after contact with white society. Moreover, Sneve allows readers to experience the effects of government deception on a personalized level as she retells history through the eyes of her relatives who lived with the broken promises that placed them in a situation of desperation. Sneve reveals how the food supplies promised in the treaty rarely got past St. Paul in transit—and what little food did arrive at the agencies was often spoiled; in fact, according to her great-grandmother, Hannah Frazier's, account, "'They were starving in Minnesota'" (54). Sneve points out that her great-grandmother's story is "a sad, bitter tale told from the point of view of the Santee, not found in the history books [Sneve] studied in college" (55).

Choosing to resist starvation, the Sioux fought back, the army was called in, and the Sioux were exiled from their native Minnesota and sent to South Dakota. Over 1,700 people were taken prisoner; Sneve's great-grandparents were among them. Sneve's writing highlights the fact that *only* women, children, and old men were taken as prisoners to Fort Snelling because the men of fighting age were awaiting trial in Mankato. She depicts the horror of the boat ride to Fort Snelling with standing-room-only conditions and reveals the devastation upon arrival: It was too late in the year to plant crops, there was no adequate clothing, and the people had to dress in burlap bags and wrap bags around their legs to stay warm. The few men who were able asked for permission to hunt, but the agent denied them. That first winter, over 300 people died. Sneve's book shows how this forced removal impacted the role of the Dakota woman: The "women labored so that their children and older relatives would survive" by cutting wood and selling it to the white settlers. The women also "dug trenches for the army and root cellars for the farmers" (59). In addition to taking jobs cooking and cleaning for the soldiers, some even turned to prostitution to pay for food. Written accounts like Sneve's are not only a stark revelation of the aftereffects of conquest that no other historical accounts have matched but also a tribute to the resilient, restorative female spirit.

Bibliography

Sneve, Virginia Driving Hawk. *Completing the Circle.* Lincoln: University of Nebraska Press, 1995.

Patti Dimond

Conley, Robert J.   (1940–   )

The Cherokee author Robert J. Conley was born in 1940 in Cushing, Oklahoma. He graduated from high school in Wichita Falls, Texas, and served in the Marine Corps Reserve from 1958 to 1964. At Midwestern University he received a baccalaureate degree in theater in 1966 and a master's degree in English in 1968. For the next decade he was an English instructor at many schools, including Eastern Montana College, where he was coordinator of Indian culture. In 1977–78 he served as assistant programs director for the Cherokee Nation of Oklahoma and was affiliated with the program in Native American studies at Bacone College in Muskogee, Oklahoma. From 1979 to 1990 he was a member of the English Department at Morningside College in Sioux City, Iowa, where he directed Indian studies. Since 1990 he has worked full-time as a novelist.

In the 1970s and early 1980s Conley first established himself as a poet, publishing two collections and editing several anthologies before he turned his energies primarily to fiction. The author of several short story collections and over 40 novels, Conley is perhaps best known for his Real People series, in which he has sought to re-create the history of the Cherokee people from about 1500 to the present. For instance, *War Woman* (1997) is set in the late 1500s and treats the life of a Cherokee woman named Whirlwind. Gifted with some preternatural powers, she earns the title "War Woman" for her leadership in the ongoing conflict against the Spanish, but she eventually marries a Spaniard and is instrumental in building a substantial trade relationship between the Cherokee Nation and the Spanish colonies in Florida. Set some 200 years later in the late 1700s, *Cherokee Dragon* (2000) focuses on Dragging Canoe, the last Cherokee war chief, who had some sustained success against the incursions of Anglo-American settlers.

Conley's better known nonseries novels have included *Mountain Windsong* (1992), *Crazy Snake* (1994), and *Brass* (1999). *Mountain Windsong* treats the forced relocation along the TRAIL OF TEARS of the Cherokee people and the other FIRE CIVILIZED TRIBES from their southeastern homelands to the "Indian country" of Oklahoma. *Crazy Snake* is a fictional biography of a Creek chief who fought against other relocated Indians, the Confederate army, and the U.S. government to preserve what remained of the Creek Nation in Oklahoma. In *Brass* Conley uses Cherokee legends about a demon that can assume any convenient shape as the basis for a contemporary horror tale with multicultural dimensions.

The winner of three Spur Awards and the recipient of a variety of other literary honors, Conley has sought to transform the popular western, which typically has served to popularize the historical and cultural imperative of the Anglo-American subjugation of Native Americans, into a medium for reconstructing Native American history and culture.

Bibliography

Brill de Ramirez, Susan B. "Walking with the Land: Simon J. Ortiz, Robert J. Conley, and Velma Wallis." *South Dakota Review* 38 (spring 2000): 59–82.

Bruchac, Joseph. "A More Realistic Picture: An Interview with Robert Conley." *Wooster Review* 8 (spring 1988): 106–114.

Conley, Robert J. *Ned Christie's War.* New York: M. Evans, 1990.

———. *Mountain Windsong: A Novel of the Trail of Tears.* Norman: University of Oklahoma Press, 1992.

———. *Crazy Snake.* New York: Pocket, 1994.

———. *The Dark Island.* New York: Doubleday, 1995.

———. *War Woman: A Novel of the Real People.* New York: St. Martin's, 1997.

Martin Kich

Cook-Lynn, Elizabeth   (1930–   )

The author of poems, short stories, novels, essays, and journal articles, Elizabeth Cook-Lynn has established herself as one of the major critical scholars and literary writers publishing in Native American studies today. Cook-Lynn, a descendant of the Dakota tribal leader Bowed Head, was born Elizabeth Irving on November 17, 1930, on the Crow Creek Agency in South Dakota. While she was an avid reader as a child, she found nothing in her reading that reflected her experiences as a Native American. Instead, she realized that much of what she read reflected a world from which she was excluded or, worse, in which she was a *"persona non grata."* The anger that resulted from this realization motivated her to write; she now considers that "an act of defiance born of the need to survive . . . an act of courage . . . an act that defies oppression" (Cook-Lynn, "You May Consider" 57–58). As such, her writing consistently protests against the myriad injustices done to her people, including the misrepresentations and exclusions of Native Americans in dominant culture.

As a young woman interested in reading and writing Elizabeth Irving pursued bachelor's degrees in English and journalism at South Dakota State University. Shortly after graduation in 1952 she married a fellow student, Melvin Cook; over the next two decades she worked as a high school teacher and as a journalist and raised four children. (Her 1970 divorce from Cook, and her remarriage to Clyde J. Lynn in 1975, resulted in her adoption of the surname Cook-Lynn.) In 1971 she earned a master's degree from the University of South Dakota and began an academic career teaching English and Indian studies at Eastern Washington University.

Cook-Lynn's literary writing received national recognition when *Then Badger Said This,* a collection of short stories, legends, poems, and songs rooted in her Sioux heritage, was published in 1977. In a second book of poetry, *Seek the House of Relatives* (1983), Cook-Lynn continues her thematic portrayal of the exploitation and mistreatment of Native peoples. Her collection of short stories THE POWER OF HORSES (1990) explores the struggle for survival of a variety of Native protagonists, many of whom suffer from past traumas and injustices. Cook-Lynn attacks the corruption of the American court system in her novel *From the River's Edge* (1991), the story of a Crow Creek Sioux man, John Tatekeya, whose efforts to bring a cattle thief to justice result instead in the ruin of his own life. The novel both exposes the corruption of the U.S. legal system and explores the moral and psychic effects of legally sanctioned discrimination on the main character. *From the River's Edge* was republished in 1999 as part of a trilogy, AURELIA; the two other novellas of the trilogy, *Circle of Dancers* and *In the Presence of River Gods,* continue the story of John Tatekeya's lover, Aurelia. Other recent literary publications include a full-length book of poetry, *I REMEMBER THE FALLEN TREES* (1998).

Cook-Lynn's fiction and poetry generally focus on past and present-day issues of great importance to the survival of her people and their culture. Her writing reflects her belief that the writer/artist should be a responsible social critic; in other words, the Native American writer must, in her view, write literature that reflects the historical context of the oppression and suffering that his or her people have endured at the hands of the U.S. government.

Her role as a social and literary critic has been articulated through a number of journal articles, particularly in *Wicazo Sa* [Red Pencil] *Review,* which she cofounded, as well as through several nonfiction publications: *Why I Can't Read Wallace Stenger and Other Essays* (1996), THE POLITICS OF HALLOWED GROUND: *Wounded Knee and the Struggle for Indian Sovereignty* (1999; coauthored by the tribal judge Mario Gonzalez), and *Anti-Indianism in Modern America* (2001). In these works Cook-Lynn addresses matters of political import, such as the defense of tribal water rights along the Missouri River, as well of issues related to the production and publication of Native American literature. In particular Cook-Lynn takes to task other contemporary Native writers, censuring them because in their work "they reflect little or no defense of treaty-protected reservation land bases and homelands to the indigenes, nor do they suggest

a responsibility of art as an ethical endeavor or the artist as responsible social critic" ("American Indian Intellectualism and the New Indian Story" 126).

In 1990 Cook-Lynn was awarded professor emeritus status at Eastern Washington University; in their emeritus description of her, colleagues wrote that she "was one of Indian Studies' secondary founders and also, in many ways, its conscience." Although she has since retired from her academic post, she continues to write and lecture, ever the powerful and outspoken "conscience" of Native American studies.

Bibliography

Cook-Lynn, Elizabeth. "American Indian Intellectualism and the New Indian Story." In *Natives and Academics: Researching and Writing about American Indians,* edited by Devon A. Mihesuah, 111–138. Lincoln: University of Nebraska Press, 1998.

———. "As a Dakotah Woman." In *Survival This Way: Interviews with American Indian Poets,* edited by Joseph Bruchac, 57–71. Tucson: University of Arizona Press, 1987.

———. *From the River's Edge.* New York: Arcade, 1991.

———. *I Remember the Fallen Trees: New and Selected Poems.* Cheney: Eastern Washington University Press, 1998.

———. *The Politics of Hallowed Ground: Wounded Knee and the Struggle for Indian Sovereignty* (with Mario Gonzalez). Urbana: University of Illinois Press, 1999.

———. *The Power of Horses and Other Stories.* New York: Arcade-Little, Brown, 1990.

———. *Why I Can't Read Wallace Stegner and Other Essays: A Tribal Voice.* Madison: University of Wisconsin Press, 1996.

———. "You May Consider Speaking About Your Art . . ." In *I Tell You Now: Autobiographical Essays by Native American Writers,* edited by Brian Swann and Arnold Krupat, 55–63. Lincoln: University of Nebraska Press, 1987.

Roemer, Kenneth, ed. *Dictionary of Literary Biography: Native American Writers of the United States.* Vol. 175. Washington, D.C.: Gale Research, 1997.

Kristen Girard

Crazy Dave   Basil Johnston   (1999)

BASIL JOHNSTON's explicitly political and intimately familial memoir opens with an introduction that positions his Uncle Dave as representative "of the place and situation of the North American Indian in Canadian society" (11). But this is also framed as a cultural lesson, in that the first chapter opens with Johnston's grandmother calling's him: "Grandson! Listen! I'll tell you what my grandmother told me" (17). The book becomes an application of the importance in aboriginal culture of telling and retelling stories, in order both to preserve tradition and to change it.

General history regarding European contact and conquest narrows to Johnston's ancestors' journey as refugees from their traditional home in Wisconsin, and then narrows further to reservation life. Johnston's angry, bitter tone surfaces regularly in the book. Along the way he cites the Treaty of 1854, through which "the Saugeen-Nawaush peoples became dependents, wards of the Crown" (24), in order to prepare the reader for the metaphorical treatment of "Crazy" Dave, who had Down's syndrome. The community figures who recommended placing Dave in an institution also were outsiders, the Indian agent, the priest, the doctor; no one close to Dave ever considered it.

Rosa, Dave's mother and Johnston's grandmother, devotes herself to her youngest child, but it is his brothers who help him become part of the world. Rosa protects and shelters, but the brothers tire of their caregiver responsibilities and see Dave as more capable than Rosa is able to perceive. The most uplifting parts of the book are those in which Stanley toilet-trains Dave, John teaches him to chop wood, and Walter teaches him names and signs. He learns to play hide and seek and horseshoes, to smoke and to dance, and to swear. Because of his brothers, Dave learns to be productive, to communicate, and to move more freely about the world of which he wants to be part. Chopping wood leads to an income and a little independence.

Dave's speech is difficult for everyone to understand, but there is no mistaking his frustration or anger when he exclaims, "Cheewi Cwise!" or "sudla-bitch," as he frequently does. One of Dave's stories was included in Johnston's earlier book *MOOSE MEAT AND WILD RICE* (1978), but in a far milder version. In *Crazy Dave* the amusing anecdote "Good Thing We Know Them People" becomes a brutal story, wherein Dave arrives in town during World War II and is mistakenly identified as Japanese, beaten, arrested, beaten again, and the ordeal is prolonged even further by bureaucratic red tape. The implied lesson and rebuke of this book are that the seemingly unteachable Dave is different from, but not less than, the majority around him.

Bibliography

Andrews, Jennifer. "Making Associations." *Canadian Literature* 168 (spring 2001): 151–152.
Challen, Paul. "Life on the Rez," *Toronto Star*, 10 September 2000, E15.

A. Mary Murphy

Crown of Columbus, The   Louise Erdrich and Michael Dorris   (1991)

In 1988 two of the most prominent Native American writers circulated a five-page outline for a book on Christopher Columbus to be completed before the 500th anniversary of his voyage to America, in 1992. HarperCollins won the rights to publish what became *The Crown of Columbus* for $1.5 million, a record advance for Native American authors. The novel, a mix of history, romance, detective story, and poetry, was published in 1991. It spent seven weeks on the *New York Times*'s bestseller list and remains one of the most widely read works of Native American literature.

By 1991 LOUISE ERDRICH and MICHAEL DORRIS were two of the most respected Native American authors and scholars in the country. Married in 1981, Erdrich and Dorris had published several books. Erdrich, a member of the Chippewa, was well known for her novels (*LOVE MEDICINE*, 1984; *The BEET QUEEN*, 1986) and poetry (*JACKLIGHT*, 1984), while Dorris, descended from the Modoc, had achieved praise for his novel (*A YELLOW RAFT IN BLUE WATER*, 1987) and nonfiction (*The Broken Cord*, 1989). By 1988 the authors wanted to explore the possibilities of collaborative writing that alternated points of view. In *The Crown of Columbus* four voices vie for the reader's attention: Vivian Twostar, Roger Williams, Nash Twostar, and Christopher Columbus.

The central characters of *The Crown of Columbus,* Vivian Twostar and Roger Williams, are professors at Dartmouth College. The authors' knowledge of academic politics and this particular campus make the first half of the novel, situated at Dartmouth, particularly rich. (Erdrich received her B.A. there in 1976, and Dorris had been teaching at the college since 1972.) In the novel Vivian Ernestine Begay Manion Twostar identifies herself as "Coeur d'Alene-Navajo-Irish-Hispanic-Sioux-by-marriage" (11). She is the only Native American professor on campus and not yet tenured. Roger Williams, ironically named after the colonial minister, friend of the Narragansett, founder of Rhode Island, and author of *Key into the Languages of America* (c. 1603–83), is from a cultured and wealthy New England family. A tenured academic star, he has been profiled by *People* magazine. He is writing an epic poem from the perspective of Columbus entitled "Diary of a Lost Man." Vivian has been strong-armed into writing a fluff piece about the explorer from the Native American perspective for the alumni magazine to pad her curriculum vitae before her tenure review.

Their professional competition is complicated by the fact that they ended an affair after Vivian became pregnant. She is already the mother of 16-year-old Nash, a troubled but intelligent youth. She ended their relationship in the belief that Roger would not accept the demands of fatherhood. Soon after their daughter, Violet's, birth, Vivian contacts the indicted and self-exiled American businessman Henry Cobb to inform him that she has found an item in the library's archive that his family donated almost two hundred years earlier. Several generations of the family had lobbied to have the unnamed item returned in a series of vitriolic letters. Cobb invites Vivian to his Bahamian retreat on Eleuthera in hopes of discovering a fabled treasure. She takes a semireconciled Roger, as well as Nash. The second half of the novel reads as more of a thriller. The financially desperate Cobb eventually tries to kill Roger and Vivian.

They survive; he is arrested; and Vivian, the representative of the exploited and forgotten Native peoples, solves the riddle of the crown of Columbus. The recovered diary of Columbus and a circle of shells inscribed with Hebrew lead her to the lost crown of Columbus, the crown of thorns given to the island chief by Columbus as Ferdinand and Isabella's representative in recognition of the Native people's SOVEREIGNTY.

Critical reception of the novel has been ambivalent. The earliest reviews recognized the influence of A. S. Byatt's *Possession* (1990) in its use of male and female narrators, the alternation between contemporary and historical settings, and the inclusion of a lengthy original poem. The *Independent*'s Ian Thomson credited the influence of Umberto Eco's "bibliographic detective story" *The Name of the Rose* on the novel. And the critic for *The Washington Post,* Nina King, judged the novels to be inferior to other Columbus novels (Alejo Carpentier's *The Harp and the Shadow,* 1979; Carlos Fuentes's *Christopher Unborn,* 1987; and Abel Posse's *The Dogs of Paradise,* 1987).

Longer works of scholarship by Thomas Matchie, Jamil Khader, and Susan Farrell have been more balanced. Matchie's short essay explores the novel's themes of pursuit and discovery and being lost and found. Khader's more theoretical analysis posits that the novel puts forth a "serious postcolonial engagement with the allegedly monolithic imperial politics of identity" (81–82). Farrell persuasively challenges critics who judge the novel harshly by calling upon them to recognize and dismantle their limiting expectations for Native American literature. These critics expect the mythic and tragic and castigate Erdrich and Dorris for going outside these narrow boundaries. Farrell argues, "Although critics have praised the postmodern techniques in contemporary literature—carnivalization, a pastiche or collage style, the blurring of the line between high and low culture, self-referentiality—they criticize Erdrich and Dorris for using such devices" in *The Crown of Columbus* (123).

The Crown of Columbus is a boundary-breaking novel. Erdrich and Dorris mix multiple genres and successfully utilize several postmodern techniques in a highly entertaining work. The authors published another joint work in 1991, *Route Two and Back,* and Dorris returned to the time of first contact with a 1992 young adult novel, *Morning Girl.* Dorris suffered from long-term depression and committed suicide in 1997 after the couple's 1996 separation. Erdrich has continued to publish remarkable novels and poetry, including *The Antelope Wife* in 1998 and *The Birchbark House* in 2002.

Bibliography

Erdrich, Louise, and Michael Dorris. *The Crown of Columbus.* New York: HarperCollins, 1991.

Farrell, Susan. "Colonizing *Columbus:* Dorris and Erdrich's Postmodern Novel." *Critique* 40, no. 2 (winter 1999): 121–136.

Khader, Jamil. "Postcolonial Nativeness: Nomadism, Cultural Memory, and the Politics of Identity in Louise Erdrich's and Michael Dorris's *The Crown of Columbus.*" *Ariel* 28, no. 2 (April 1997): 81–101.

Matchie, Thomas. "Exploring the Meaning of Discovery in *The Crown of Columbus.*" *North Dakota Quarterly* 59, no. 4 (spring 1991): 243–250.

Ann Beebe

Custer Died for Your Sins Vine Deloria, Jr. (1969)

In a new preface written for its 20th-anniversary edition, VINE DELORIA, JR., neatly divided the AMERICAN INDIAN MOVEMENT into the years before *Custer Died for Your Sins* and the years after. Because of literary and political activism, the "Indian world" changed substantially after Deloria's immensely readable argument. With satire and sympathy for both the urban and the tribal Native American, Deloria dissects every interference of white activism and jurisprudence. It is a testament to Deloria's skill that he can transition from government agencies to missionaries to Native American humor to the incompetence of tribal leadership in the span of 300 pages. The message, to both genocidal generals and eager evangelicals, is both intel-lectual and accessible. Rather than allowing white intellectuals, anthropologists, and scholars to act as surrogates for him, Deloria uses his singular, satiric voice to give voice to Indians who have been silenced by white interference and ventriloquism. Borrowing the words of Alex Chasing Hawk, who asked Congress for a "leave-us-alone law," Deloria demands a leave-us-alone cultural policy from the dominant culture (27). Such a policy would allow the settling of tribal conflict by tribal government and unravel the white society's attempt to freeze Indians at the moment of conquest, somewhere in the 19th century. The leave-us-alone policy at once separates itself from the appropriation of Indian culture by white liberals and allies itself with black nationalism, a kinship Deloria expresses in "The Red and the Black," the eighth chapter of *Custer Died for Your Sins.* Rather than accepting the beginning of Euro-American history as the end of Native American history, Deloria insists that the American Indian Movement can provide a new beginning. Anti-Indianism remains a powerful force in both Left and Right opposition to the renewal of tribal treaties; its continued dominance charges Deloria's polemic with the possibility of reenergizing the "dormant if not comatose" American Indian Movement (x).

Bibliography

Bordewich, Fergus M. *Killing the White Man's Indian: Reinventing Native Americans at the End of the Twentieth Century.* New York: Anchor Books, 1997.

Deloria, Vine, Jr. "Indian Studies: The Orphan of Academia." *Wizaco Sa Review* 2, no. 2 (1986): 1–7.

Sheraw, C. Darrel. "The Satiric Impulse in Vine Deloria's *Custer Died for Your Sins.*" *Studies in Contemporary Satire: A Creative and Critical Journal* 16 (1989): 33–43.

Warrior, Robert Allen. "'Temporary Visibility': Deloria on Sovereignty and AIM." *Genre: Forms of Discourse and Culture* 25, no. 4 (winter 1993): 365–375.

Jennifer Lightweis

Cuthand, Beth (1949–)

Beth Cuthand was born in 1949, is of Cree descent, and grew up in Saskatchewan and Alberta. She worked as a journalist for 16 years and taught at the Saskatchewan Indian Federated College, University of Regina. She also received a graduate degree in creative writing at the University of Arizona and has been involved with indigenous and academic studies at the Nicola Valley Institute of Technology in Merritt, British Columbia. Her poems and short stories have been included in numerous magazines and anthologies, including *An Anthology of Canadian Native Literature in English* (2nd ed.) (1997) and *Native Poetry in Canada: A Contemporary Anthology* (2001). In addition, she has coedited various publications, such as *Gatherings: The En'Owkin Journal of First North American Peoples* (1994) and *Reinventing the Enemy's Language: Contemporary Native Women's Writing of North America* (1997). She has also written children's literature, including the book *The Little Duck/Sikihpsis* (1999), which provides a text in both English and Cree.

Cuthand has published two books of poetry: *Horse Dance to Emerald Mountain* (1987), which is dedicated to her mother and sisters and is "a poem for peace," and *Voices in the Waterfall* (1989), which includes *Horse Dance to Emerald Mountain*. In the preface of *Voices* JEANNETTE ARMSTRONG writes to Cuthand: "Your poetry moves music in the blood, the words cutting through, exposing a stark truth" (10). JOY HARJO makes reference to the depth of Cuthand's poetry: "When I get lost in this crazy world and want to remember who I am as a Native woman in this sometimes confusing configuration of times and places I pick up Beth Cuthand's poetry of heart and soul" (*Voices,* back cover). Cuthand's work contains rich imagery, reveals an intimate relationship with nature, and examines with keen insight various aspects of existence in this world. For example, in her poem "This Knowledge" she writes of an elder who teaches a younger person that knowledge can be obtained "in the whisper of a butterfly's wings" and in "the rustling of the grasses blown by the winds" (*Voices,* 21). In "His Bundle" she juxtaposes the new with the old describing "old stars in new time," "new ways of seeing old things," "new clothes made of old stars," and "old sounds in new time" (*Voices,* 23). This poem, with various references to nature such as "living Earth," "desert flowers," and "rainbows," reveals the adaptability of a particular wise man.

Bibliography

Armstrong, Jeannette, and Lally Grauer, eds. *Native Poetry in Canada: A Contemporary Anthology.* Peterborough, Canada: Broadview, 2001.

Cuthand, Beth. *Horse Dance to Emerald Mountain.* Vancouver: Lazara, 1987.

———. *Voices in the Waterfall.* New ed. Penticton, Canada: Theytus, 1992.

"Beth Cuthand." Native American Authors Project. Available online. URL: http://www.ipl.org.ar/cgi/ref/native/browse.pl/A231. Accessed on January 12, 2004.

Moses, Daniel David, and Terry Goldie, eds. *An Anthology of Canadian Native Literature in English.* 2d ed. Toronto: Oxford University Press, 1998.

Sue Barker

Dance Me Outside   Dir. Bruce McDonald (1994)

Dance Me Outside is a Canadian film that resists relying on stereotypical expectations in a portrayal of Native peoples. This film is significant considering that most films about Native Americans or First Nations peoples are confined to stories from the 19th century. In the 1990s there was a trend to update Native peoples' roles in film and television, most notably CBC's *North of 60*, CBS's *Northern Exposure,* and Chris Eyre's film of SHERMAN ALEXIE'S *SMOKE SIGNALS. Dance Me Outside* provides roles that defy the usual stereotypes found in American westerns of the stoic Indian who speaks broken English and has visions of eagles. The film is about two young Anishinabe men, Silas Crow and Frank Fencepost, who are looking for direction in their lives. More specifically, they want to become mechanics. In order to get into the trade school, they have to write autobiographical essays, but they cannot think of anything interesting about their lives on the reserve. Their lack of determination delays their plans for the future. However, before much time passes, events that unfold force them to mature and become active members in their community.

The film focuses on the daily lives of the young people on the reserve and their dreams and aspirations. The story hinges on the murder of Little Margaret, a friend of Silas and Frank. The friends seek justice for her murder throughout the film, but the subplot of Silas's sister's pregnancy allows for light-hearted moments. Silas's sister realizes that her white husband cannot make her pregnant, and she must ask an old boyfriend to help. The most memorable scene in the film is the "secret private Indian name" ceremony that Silas and Frank use as a diversion to prevent Silas's sister's husband from knowing that his wife has gone to be with her friend. Her husband, Robert, is the subject of much ridicule during the ceremony, yet it is apparent that the family likes him and in the end respects him. This particular scene is significant for two main reasons. First, the white man is literally rendered impotent, and second, the white man is not in control of the story or the ceremony and is shown to have little knowledge of Native culture. This is important because it challenges the roles white people play in films about Native peoples such as *Dances with Wolves* (1990) or *Last of the Mohicans* (1992), which allow them to have control of the action of the story and to have complete access to Native culture. In *Dance Me Outside,* based on the stories by the non-Native author W. P. Kinsella, Native people control their stories.

This film also offers another twist in which the audience realizes that the women on the reserve control the men's lives. This is evident as Silas's girlfriend, Sadie, avenges Little Margaret's murder and saves Silas from life in prison. Because of her actions, Silas is able to finish his story for trade school and begin to pursue his dreams.

Bibliography

McGovern, Celeste. "From Noble Savage to Urban Hipster," *Alberta Report/Newsmagazine*, 27 March 1995.

Meredith James

Dancing Teepees: Poems of American Indian Youth   Virginia Driving Hawk Sneve (1989)

As implied by the title of her anthology, *Dancing Teepees* (1989), VIRGINIA DRIVING HAWK SNEVE creates a poetic structure that is uniquely supported by expressions of Native American identity from numerous sources. In doing so, Sneve causes this structure to dance around such diversity in a complex rhythm that unifies and underscores values central to Native American cultures. This image of a teepee circle containing a continuous and interconnected lifestyle informs every aspect of this book, as seen by the ways that her anthology chronicles the ways various poets have characterized the all-encompassing hoop of life, from birth/dawn (Sneve's own "Tble" 11) to death/evening (the Navaho "Farewell, My Younger Brother" 24), and all aspects of life in between. As these examples indicate, she draws on a wide range of western tribal works (from the Makahan "My Little Son" 15, to the Osage "I Rise, I Rise" 29). She also draws on a wide range of works written over the past two centuries, such as BLACK ELK's "The Life of a Man Is a Circle" and her own works. In doing so, Sneve does not simply collapse tribal distinctions or temporal periods to promote a pan-Indian identity. Instead, Sneve lovingly demonstrates the universality and timelessness of Native American values that stress the celebration of life, community, and cooperation.

Bibliography

Sneve, Virginia Driving Hawk. *Dancing Teepees: Poems of American Indian Youth.* New York: Holiday House, 1989.

Clay Smith

Dark River   Louis Owens (1998)

Grounded in the TRICKSTER FIGURE stories of Native oral tradition, LOUIS OWENS's last novel figures importantly in the tradition of contemporary Native satire. *Dark River* asks what it means to be Indian in the era of casino capitalism and citizen militias. Through the MIXED-BLOOD Choctaw ranger Jake Nashoba, who still sees himself as a tribal outsider after 20 years on the fictional Black Mountain Apache Reservation, Owens explores issues of racial essentialism and hybridity, tribal survival, and the continuing struggle for cultural integrity in the face of the American legacy of Indian killing: literary, cinematic, and historical. At its deepest level the novel considers how story constructs reality.

The three elders who guide the fictional Black Mountain tribe demonstrate remarkable adaptability in the face of cultural difference. Their lives bear witness to Shorty Luke's assertion that "change is traditional too." For these elders race is the greatest fiction of all. Mrs. John Edwards once married a fire-and-brimstone preacher and made him a member of the tribe, while Avrum Goldberg has transformed himself from resident Jewish anthropologist to Apache traditional, authentic from the breechclout he wears to the wickiup in which he lives. A master story thief and retired actor, Shorty was the only Indian cast as an Indian in the glory days of the Hollywood cowboy. From behind the scenes, he exposes all the creaky machinery of Indian representation.

Each of the elders enacts a traditional mythic Apache role in Owens's novel, offering important lessons on the relationship between individual and community, which traditionally includes not only living beings but spiritual beings. Jake Nashoba, or Lone Ranger, a Vietnam hero with unhealed psychic wounds, has forged connections with the natural world at the expense of human connections. The tribal chairman, Xavier Two-Bears, with a Harvard M.B.A., cannot see beyond the human community. He is central to *Dark River*'s exploration of capitalism, personal greed, communal good, and the ethics of profit making.

When the novel's twin plots converge, Jake finds the Dark River canyon, his passion and his sanity, full of wannabes, wannabe Indians who have paid for "authentic" vision quests and wannabe warriors who have paid for simulated combat training. Choosing the role of loner hero in a live-fire war game, Jake dies as so many Apache have in their historic encounters with white citizen militias, but he does not die alone. Shorty Luke enters the long death dream that makes Jake, at last, a tribal insider with his own role as a mythic hero in a revised version of Apache origin history. *Dark River*'s ending affirms that the larger tribal story will continue despite changes.

Bibliography

Bernardin, Susan. "Moving in Place: *Dark River* and the 'New' Indian Novel." In *Louis Owens: Literary Reflections on His Life and Work,* edited by Jacquelyn Kilpatrick, 103–118. Norman: University of Oklahoma Press, 2004.

Ronnow, Gretchen. "Secularizing Mythological Space in Louis Owens's *Dark River*." In *Louis Owens: Literary Reflections on His Life and Work,* edited by Jacquelyn Kilpatrick, 139–153. Norman: University of Oklahoma Press, 2004.

Linda Lizut Helstern

Dauenhauer, Nora Marks   (1927–   )

Born in Juneau, Alaska, in 1927, Nora Marks had a childhood divided between time spent aboard her family's fishing boat near Juneau and Hoonah and seasonal subsistence camps near Icy Straits, Glacier Bay, and Cape Spencer, all in southeast Alaska. Until she attended public schools at the age of eight she only spoke and understood her native Tlingit language. After raising the four children of her first marriage, she earned a general equivalency diploma (GED) and pursued higher education. She married Richard Dauenhauer on November 28, 1973. Before receiving her B.A. in anthropology from Alaska Methodist University in 1976, she served at the Alaska Native Language Center at the University of Alaska-Fairbanks as the Tlingit language researcher. She published her first book, *Beginning Tlingit,* a guide to studying and teaching the language, in 1976.

Throughout the 1980s she, along with her husband, Richard, Alaska's poet laureate (1981–85), collaborated on several projects, including *Because We Cherish You: Sealaska Elders Speak to the Future* (1981); *Alaska Native Writers, Storytellers, and Orators* (1986); and *Haa Shuká, Our Ancestors Speak* (1987). Her most important work was *Haa Shuka, Our Ancestors: Tlingit Oral Narratives* (1987). Besides its innovative bilingual approach and assumption of multiple audiences, its masterful transcription was invaluable for anthropologists and linguists studying the Tlingit and other northwestern Native cultures. In addition to the grammatical translating from Tlingit to English, Dauenhauer's transformation of oral traditions into written form was extraordinary; she preserved the spoken language's vigor and emphasis. Dauenhauer's grounding in Tlingit and English lent the text incisive vision and a robust narrative. Her sensitivity as a scholar who crossed cultures effortlessly in representing Tlingit traditions served as a model for new scholarship in the fields of anthropology and linguistics. The Dauenhauers received acknowledgment for the excellence and multicultural diversity of their writing when *Haa Tuwunaagu Yis, for Healing Our Spirit: Tlingit Oratory* (1990), edited by the couple, won an American Book Award in 1991.

Noted for her translations of the English poems of Basho, e.e. cummings, and Gary Snyder into Tlingit, Dauenhauer writes poetry as well. *Droning Shaman* (1988), her first volume of poetry, exemplified her connection with the natural world and displayed her facility with Tlingit and English.

Life Woven with Song (2000) again translates the oral tradition to written form. Here she records cultural memories of the Tlingit relationship with salmon and returns to themes of the land explored in her earlier work. As in the work of many other Native American writers, Dauenhauer experiments with form in a style that endows her work with fluidity and gracefulness. Her work has appeared in many collections, most recently *First Fish First People: Salmon Tales of the North Pacific Rim* (2000).

Bibliography

Dauenhauer, Nora Marks. *Haa Shuká, Our Ancestors: Tlingit Oral Narratives.* Seattle: University of Washington Press, 1987.

Lerner, Andrea. "Nora Marks Dauenhauer." *Native American Women: A Biographical Dictionary,* 73–47. New York: Garland, 1993.

Peterson, Andrew. "Preserving a Language." Available online. URL: http://www.coh.arizona.edu/english/poetics/dauenhauer/dauenhauer_weekly.htm. Accessed on August 15, 2005.

Rebecca Tolley-Stokes

Dawes Act, the

The Dawes Act of 1887, also known as the General Allotment Act, authorized the president of the United States to survey Indian tribal land and divide the arable area into allotments for individual Indians. This act, which purported to protect Indians and their right to land, had disastrous and still-felt consequences for the majority of tribes and individual Indians.

The need for land that followed the Civil War (1860–65) was tremendous, as a result of a steadily growing population and the approximately 4 million slaves freed by the war. The vast majority of unsettled, arable lands were either in the Indian Territory or on Indian reservations. Adding to the pressure of the growing population, several humanitarian groups, concerned with Indian rights, were pushing the federal government to dissolve the reservation system. Indian activists such as SARAH WINNEMUCCA and ZITKALA-ŠA believed that the reservation system was a hindrance to self-sufficiency and was bad for Indians in the long term.

The Dawes Act, upon its passing, was seen as a solution that would provide much-needed land for settlers as well as protect Indian rights. Its major points were that each Indian head of household would receive 160 acres, each single person over 18 and each orphan under 18 would receive 80 acres, and each single person under 18 would receive 40 acres. Each family was to choose its own allotment within four years, and the land would be held in trust for 25 years, when the title would belong to the allotment holder or heirs. After the title was transferred, the allotment holder would become a full citizen of the United States.

While the goals behind the Dawes Act may have seemed altruistic, in reality some 60 million acres of land were opened to settlement by non-Indians. In addition, abuses of the act were widespread. In 1928 the congressionally commissioned Meriam Report documented fraud and misappropriation of land that resulted in illegally depriving Indians of their considerable land rights. The Indian Reorganization Act of 1934 officially ended Allotment, but the damage could not be undone.

Several Native American authors address the legacy of the Dawes Act. *TRACKS* by LOUISE ERDRICH dramatizes the effect of Allotment on the Chippewa, effects that include starvation and the loss of language, land, and culture. JOHN JOSEPH MATHEWS's *SUNDOWN* powerfully demonstrates the corruption and dubious motives of those who administered the act among the Osage in Oklahoma. D'ARCY MCNICKLE's *The Surrounded,* set among the Salish 20 years after the enactment of Dawes, depicts the deplorable conditions it has wrought.

See also *BLACK ELK SPEAKS; FACES IN THE MOON;* POSEY, ALEXANDER.

Bibliography

Otis, D. S. *The Dawes Act and the Allotment of Indian Lands.* Norman: University of Oklahoma Press, 1973.

Jennifer McClinton Temple

Dawnland   Joseph Bruchac (1993)

Early in his career JOSEPH BRUCHAC established himself as a central voice in Native American literature by editing one of the most influential anthologies of Native American poetry, *SONGS FROM THIS EARTH ON TURTLE'S BACK* (1983). Subsequently he has turned most of his talents to children's literature as he (re)presents the oral traditions and tales from Abenaki, Iroquois, and other Eastern Woodland tribes. Through his efforts he has gained widespread recognition as one of the preeminent authors of AMERICAN INDIAN CHILDREN's

LITERATURE. He continues to produce several works a year, most in children's literature.

Dawnland (1993) represents yet another facet of Joseph Bruchac's multitalented artistry. In the briefest summary it is an adult novel about prehistoric Native America that focuses primarily on Abenaki traditions and culture. However, such a summary does not begin to appreciate the subtlety and complexity of Bruchac's artistry in crafting this novel. These finer aspects appear on virtually every page as Bruchac interweaves mythology, history, and psychology into a story that underscores the centrality and necessity of redemption. At times this novel appears to border on the fantastic as it resurrects One-Eye and his tribe of Stone Giants and his prehistoric killer bear (The Hunter), but such elements flow seamlessly with other elements of Native American spirituality such as the interventions by human healers such as Bear Talker and Sweetgrass Woman and by supernatural beings such as the Thunder Beings. What binds these apparently disparate and fantastic elements together is Bruchac's insistence on the power and potential of redemption.

As Bruchac explains in his foreword, this theme is a traditional aspect of Native American identity.

> There is also a strong tradition of redemption among native peoples. Rather than a fixed and permanent condition, "evil" in a human being is often seen as a twisting of the mind. Every person contains both the "good mind" and the confusion of the mind that is called "bad" or "evil" in the English language. Even monsters can be redeemed when their hearts are melted by the warmth of a fire. Thus, reforming your enemies rather than killing them is a more desirable solution in many traditional tales. (xiii)

Bruchac illustrates this theme primarily through Weasel Tail's fall and redemption by Young Hunter. In a powerful scene he has Young Hunter heal and restore Weasel Tail to himself and to the tribe, thereby empowering Weasel Tail (now renamed Holds the Stone) to help heal the rift caused by the Stone Giants.

Bruchac also invokes this theme of redemption through other characters. One of his most powerful examples occurs when he uses the traditional tale of the hunter who respects his dogs, who in turn sacrifice themselves for him. He presents this tale as part of his novel, then represents it through the actions of Young Hunter and his dogs Pabetciman, Danowa, and Agwesis as "the Battle of the Hunter." But rather than simply retelling this tale in the context of his novel, Bruchac modifies it by intersecting Weasel Tail's redemption as part of this tale. In doing so, he also demonstrates the interconnection of all of these elements and the possibility that results from such community. These elements also demonstrate Bruchac's remarkable ability to translate traditional values to contemporary audiences.

Bibliography
Bruchac, Joseph. *Dawnland*. Golden, Colo.: Fulcrum, 1993.

Clay Smith

Dead Voices: Natural Agonies in the New World Gerald Vizenor (1992)

Dead Voices, one of GERALD VIZENOR's lesser-known novels, draws together the author's interest in retelling classic Anishinabe tales (in this case the earthdiver and creation tales and those of the TRICKSTER FIGURE Nanabozho), showing modern Native people within urban settings, and fighting against stereotypical notions of Indian identity. *Dead Voices* is divided into 11 chapters that describe the interactions between Bagese, a crossblood trickster and resurrection shaman, and Laundry, a MIXED-BLOOD professor so nicknamed because he smells like soap to Bagese. These two characters share the novel's narration.

Seven of the chapters detail the events that occur while Bagese takes part in a wanaki game, which KIMBERLY M. BLAESER points out is a "fictional adaptation of an Ojibway dish game" (192).

The narrator explains, "Chance is an invitation to animal voices in a tribal world, and the word 'wanaki' means to live somewhere in peace, a chance at peace" (17). Each of these cards portrays an animal: bear, beaver, squirrel, crow, flea, praying mantis, and the trickster, which can transform players into other animals, or even into humans (17). Bagese explains to Laundry, "The players must use the plural pronoun *we* to share in the stories and become the creatures on the cards" (17). That is, as the narrator assumes the form of the animals and figures on the cards, she or he becomes those animals. Vizenor recasts this game of chance, which is played in varying versions across North America (often with seven dice, colored balls, carved figures, etc., tossed in a dish), to create and reinforce a sense of community with the other creatures (human and nonhuman) with whom we live. This game of chance also relates to Vizenor's emphasis on chance in life. Chance symbolizes being open to experiences, ideas, and events that we have not planned for, embracing the haphazard nature of the world.

Laundry also relates Vizenor's concept of chance to Bagese, stating that she "would never be considered traditional, or even an urban pretender who treasured the romantic revisions of the tribal past. She was closer to stones, trickster stories, and tribal chance than the tragedies of a vanishing race" (6). The narrator conflates the terms *traditional* and *urban pretender,* to show that both are falsified constructions of "Indian-ness." Vizenor uses the term *post-Indian* to describe Native people like Bagese: people who refuse to accept the false images of Indians that have been constructed by non-Indians (and reinforced by many Native people) since the moment of European contact. Vizenor calls those stereotypical images "dead voices"; they are dead because they do not grow, change, evolve, or accept chance.

Bibliography

Blaeser, Kimberly M. *Gerald Vizenor: Writing in the Oral Tradition.* Norman: University of Oklahoma Press, 1996.

John Gamber

Death at Rainy Mountain   Mardi Oakley Medawar   (1996)

MARDI OAKLEY MEDAWAR's *Death at Rainy Mountain* is the first of a series of detective stories, which provide an illuminating portrayal of both western frontier politics and Kiowa society as it uncovers the mystery surrounding the brutal murder of a Kiowa warrior. Set in 1866, the novel begins at Rainy Mountain, where Kiowa bands have gathered for the funeral of their chief, Little Bluff. While the bands' chiefs campaign for candidacy to lead the Kiowa Nation, the renowned Cheyenne Robber is accused of murdering Coyote Walking, one of the suitors of his beloved, White Otter. Under the threat of an impending civil war among the various Kiowa factions, the sage Skywalker enlists Tay-bodal, a gifted Kiowa healer not affiliated with any of the bands, to find out the truth about the suspicious death and clear the Cheyenne Robber's name.

Tay-bodal's status as a loner and outsider not only grants him unrestricted access to the opposing bands while he investigates the murder, but also places him in a position from which he can objectively critique the politics of the nation. From the beginning Tay-bodal alerts the reader to the importance of politics to the novel by framing his narration of Little Bluff's funeral with a commentary on the bands' divisive posturing for political power:

> What I could not understand, what I found truly astonishing was that the men were so excited, so eager to proclaim themselves enemies to their own brothers. . . . Their utter selfishness boggled the mind. They were rushing to be on what they believed was the *winning side.* There was no concern for anything else. Power was what they sought. . . . The future of the Nation did not seem to matter. I have to believe that they simply did not comprehend that this side-taking business would eventually lead to brother killing brother. (22)

By criticizing the "side-taking business" of the Kiowa, Tay-bodal highlights the importance of tribal unity to the future of the Kiowa Nation, which has already been drawn into the white settlers' civil war between the "Gray Jackets" and "Blue Jackets" (3). The Civil War serves as a backdrop to the rising tensions among the Kiowa bands, and threat of a similar war among his people compels Tay-bodal to defuse the conflict by identifying who really killed Coyote Walking.

Sidestepping the speculation and accusations that intensify the tension among the bands, Tay-bodal analytically investigates the facts of Coyote Walking's murder. While proving the Cheyenne Robber's innocence, Tay-bodal falls in love with one of his relatives, the widow Crying Wind. Although Tay-bodal does not become politically powerful as a result of successfully solving the murder mystery, he does find his place within Kiowa society as Crying Wind's husband and member of the band of her cousin, White Bear. At the close of the novel Tay-bodal suggests that he has received his just reward. "Being bound to someone you intensely love, someone you trust and love back," he explains, "is man's only true freedom" (262). "Everything else," he says, "most especially power, is fleeting" (262).

Bibliography

Medawar, Mardi Oakley. *Death at Rainy Mountain.* New York: St. Martin's Press, 1996.

Lauren A. Rule

Death of Bernadette Lefthand, The Ron Querry (1993)

The Death of Bernadette Lefthand is a chilling account of the tragedy that befalls a beautiful young woman and her family. RON QUERRY depicts the lives of a people who live in a modern world but hold to the traditional beliefs and wisdom of their ancestors. As the story is told by a young Jicarilla Apache/Pueblo and a former New York model, he effortlessly switches between the two systems of beliefs.

The novel begins with the news of Bernadette's death. Gracie Lefthand and Starr Stubbs retell the events that lead to Anderson George's apparent killing of his wife. Bernadette appeared to have everything. She was married to a good-looking Navajo bronc rider and had a new baby. She even had a good job cleaning Starr Stubbs's house. Everyone loved Bernadette, including Emmett Take Horse.

Bernadette had rejected Emmett's affection because she was seeing Anderson. Oddly enough, Anderson and Emmett became closer and closer. Throughout the story Gracie tells of strange occurrences and overall bad luck that seem to follow Bernadette and Anderson. Coincidentally Emmett is always around when something bad happens.

Through Gracie Ron Querry explains the customs and traditions of the Jicarilla Apache, Pueblo, and Navajo. Recognizing the strong beliefs of these tribes regarding death and evil is important to understanding how Querry generates the plot. Bad experiences and sickness can easily be dismissed as bad luck or coincidence; however, it is obvious to the Native people that everything happens as a result of a person's actions or interactions with the environment. Starr Stubbs represents the modern opinion of these beliefs, saying, "I can't understand how it is that otherwise intelligent and literate people living in this country and in this day and age can hold such beliefs" (184). Starr reads to try to understand these "Indian ideas" (183) but finds that her own cultural identity does not let her completely internalize these beliefs. Because the story is told in hindsight, the reader can see how all of the characters and circumstances actually led to Bernadette's death.

Details that seem minor at the time they are happening hold important evidence that something evil was indeed present. Animals, particularly dogs, are considered a good judge of character. Could it be a coincidence that Chaco, Anderson's dog, always grew uneasy around Emmett Take Horse? Chaco became very protective of Bernadette before she died. He refused to leave her side on her last night alive, and that steadfastness also resulted in his death. Gracie never understood why Chaco did not like Emmett because the dog liked everyone.

Ron Querry's *The Death of Bernadette Lefthand* is an excellent example of the differences in cultural beliefs even among different tribes. While

Starr and Gracie try to find a logical explanation for the death of their loved one, Querry leaves hints for the reader that something beyond what is tangible may be involved.

Bibliography

Querry, Ron. *The Death of Bernadette Lefthand.* Santa Fe, N. Mex.: Red Crane Books, 1993.

Rikki Noel Williams

Death of Jim Loney, The   James Welch (1979)

Similar in style and content to WINTER IN THE BLOOD (1974), JAMES WELCH's second novel is a considerably darker look at the small communities surrounding the Fort Belknap Reservation in Montana, although glimpses of hope and recovery are visible. The novel begins with Jim Loney's attending a Harlem high school football game in which the final play is a botched extra-point attempt that ends with the kicker's lying motionless on the ground as time expires. Loney's role in the novel is revealed to be hauntingly similar. As the kicker wears one white and one black shoe, Loney has an emotional paralysis that involves his biracial identity, which distorts his sense of time and prevents him from synthesizing his past into a coherent present, thereby negating his future. As his name implies, Loney is both alone and lonely; his name is a barrier that mirrors the slow drift of his life. Son of a white father (Ike) and a Gros Ventre mother (Electra), Loney longs to be either Indian or white, believing a single racial identity to be "nicer than being a half-breed" (Welch 1979, 14).

Loney also longs for a female presence in his life but is deeply distrustful of women, fearful of being abandoned. However, by withholding his emotions Loney ensures that his relationships will not achieve sustained intimacy, ultimately contributing to his isolation. Even so, his relationships with women hold promise, especially those with his sister, Kate, and girlfriend, Rhea; indeed, Welch bridges a crucial gap through Rhea and Loney's relationship. Rhea, a white woman, finds Loney to be an attractive and sensitive partner, a romantic dynamic Welch revisits in *The INDIAN LAWYER* and *The HEARTSONG OF CHARGING ELK*. Indeed, the critic Sidner Larson sees Welch's "pairing of Loney and Rhea together as a declaration of differences contrary to the stereotype of the 'raping Indian male' and of the mediating power of women who choose interracial relationships" (Larson 110).

Loney's relations with men, particularly in sports, demonstrate his uneasy participation in masculine traditions. Welch narrates Loney's experience with flawed white role models in flashbacks, including his father and the priest Brother Gerard, who teaches him basketball. And yet Loney and his classmates win the 1958 Class B basketball championship, the most significant community triumph of Harlem's downtrodden history. As Welch's modeling of his friend Myron Pretty Weasel's basketball fame on his Crow namesake suggests, the sport offers masculine achievement in the absence of a contemporary warrior culture. Fittingly, the novel's climax occurs in another male setting, a hunting trip. Welch uses the illicit pursuit of the sacred bear to underscore Loney and Pretty Weasel's estrangement from the communal and spiritual significance of hunting. The resulting "accident" stands as a reminder that their deaths are partially due to this separation.

See also RESERVATION LIFE.

Bibliography

Larson, Sidner. *Captured in the Middle: Tradition and Experience in Contemporary Native American Writing.* Seattle: University of Washington Press, 2000.

Owens, Louis. *Mixedblood Messages: Literature, Film, Family Place.* Norman: University of Oklahoma Press, 1998.

Scott Palmer

Deloria, Ella Cara   (1889–1971)

Ella Cara Deloria was born on January 31, 1889, on the Yankton Reservation in South Dakota. Her father, Phillip Deloria, was an Episcopal priest on the Standing Rock Agency serving a Teton Sioux congregation, and her mother was Mary Sully

Bordeaux. Young Ella was deeply influenced by the Christian faith and by her heritage as a traditional Dakota Sioux. She spoke the Dakota language in her home as a child. Deloria attended college at Oberlin College and at Columbia University Teachers College, where she received her degree in 1915. She had a successful career early as a teacher at schools in South Dakota and Kansas.

One of Deloria's greatest contributions to Native studies began in the late 1920s when she was asked to collaborate with the American anthropologist Franz Boas in collecting and translating Dakota Sioux ethnological material. In 1932 she published *Dakota Texts,* a collection of Sioux traditional stories that are still today a landmark of Dakota culture. She coauthored *Dakota Grammar* with Boas in 1941 and in 1944 published *Speaking of Indians.* Her work was also published in a number of scholarly journals of Dakota language and folklore in the 1940s. Deloria's firsthand knowledge of the Dakota language and her anthropological training suited her uniquely for the task of translating and explaining Dakota culture to scholars. Julian Rice in "Why the Lakota Still Have Their Own: Ella Deloria's *Dakota Texts*" argues that Ms. Deloria's collecting of these stories "renewed the spirit of Lakota values and Lakota symbolic expression" (205).

For modern readers Ella Cara Deloria is more widely known as the author of a novel, WATERLILY, which was completed by late 1944, but not published until 1988. Though her scientific work was highly respected, it seems apparent that a novel written by a Native American woman was not marketable in the early half of the 20th century but would have to wait for a modern renaissance of Native American writers to be discovered.

Part of the reason Deloria's novel did not attract the attention of publishers in its day was that it passed by cultural stereotypes of Indians common in popular fiction of the 1940s and presented the lives of Sioux families in realistic and recognizable terms. Another collection of Deloria's folklore, *Buffalo People,* was published by the University of New Mexico Press in 1994.

Bibliography

Deloria, Ella Cara. *Buffalo People.* 1994. Albuquerque: University of New Mexico Press, 1994.

———. *Waterlily.* 1988. Lincoln: University of Nebraska Press, 1988.

Picotte, Agnes. Biographical Sketch of the Author in *Waterlily,* 229–231. Lincoln: University of Nebraska Press, 1988.

Rice, Julian. *Ella Deloria's Iron Hawk.* Albuquerque: University of New Mexico Press, 1993.

———. "Why the Lakota Still Have Their Own: Ella Deloria's *Dakota Texts.*" *Western American Literature* 19, no. 3 (November 1984): 205–217.

Sligh, Gary Lee. *A Study of Native American Women Novelists: Sophia Alice Callahan, Mourning Dove, and Ella Cara Deloria.* Lewiston, N.Y.: Edwin Mellen Press, 2003.

Gary Sligh

Deloria, Vine (Victor), Jr. (1933–2005)

Author of numerous books and essays; professor of history, religion, law, political science, and Indian policy; legal activist for Indian rights and tribal recognition; and governmental adviser on multiple Indian issues, Vine Deloria, Jr., has been recognized as one of the leading advocates for Indian interests in his generation. Born Victor Deloria on March 26, 1933, to Vine and Barbara (Eastbuin) Deloria, of the Pine Ridge Indian Reservation, Martin, South Dakota, he originated from a distinguished Yankton Sioux family of priests, poets, authors, scholars, and activists. He is an enrolled member of the Standing Rock Sioux Tribe. His paternal great-grandfather was a Yankton medicine man; his grandfather was a respected Yankton chief and missionary (who converted to Christianity in the late 19th century) on the Standing Rock Reservation. Deloria's father followed in missionary work in South Dakota, devoting 37 years of his life to Episcopal ministry. ELLA DELORIA, Deloria Jr's paternal aunt, trained in anthropology under Franz Boas, publishing several notable books on Native language and tribal customs.

At the age of 21 Deloria entered the U.S. Marine Corps Reserve, serving for two years. He completed his degree at Iowa State University in 1958. That same year he married Barbara Jeanne Nystrom. The couple's three children are Philip, Daniel, and Jeanne Ann. In 1963 Deloria completed a master of theology degree at Lutheran School of Theology, Rock Island, Illinois. Originally he had intended to follow his father and grandfather by entering into Christian ministry but soon realized that practicing law would allow him to make a greater difference in Indian life. In 1970 he received a juris doctor from the University of Colorado. He died on November 13, 2005, in Tucson, Arizona.

Deloria's resume of service to Indian causes is exhaustive. During his tenure as the executive director of the National Congress of American Indians (NCAI) in Washington, D.C. (from 1964 to 1967), Deloria remade the organization into a powerful representative of Indian tribes. In the years following he worked with the United Scholarship Service toward the provision of scholarships and financial aid for Indian students in traditionally white school systems; he was a member of the Board of Inquiry on Hunger and Malnutrition in the U.S.A. and the National Office for the Rights of the Indigent. Deloria helped found the Institute for the Development of Indian Law in Washington, D.C., and was a ready participant in the Council on Indian Affairs and the Indian Rights Association.

Deloria's best-selling books CUSTER DIED FOR YOUR SINS (1969) and We Talk, You Listen (1970) gained him his first national attention. These first texts were alternately applauded and criticized for their humorous upbraiding of whites who romanticize Indian culture at the expense of real change for Indians living in POVERTY. Deloria's later writings—historical documentation of tribal culture, tradition, and struggle for SOVEREIGNTY, as well as essays on Indian affairs, edited collections, documentaries, interviews, and reports—frequently focus on the need for an Indian cultural nationalism and empowerment through legal and political action. His frequent theme is the necessity for Indian tribes to regain sacred lands purloined during years of deceptive and systematic government practices.

Deloria's public persona was at once provocative and thoughtful. His appearance on the *Dick Cavett Show* in 1971, for instance, became a platform for uncovering the brutality of federal agents in the arrest of 62 Indians in a federal raid on Puyallup fishermen during a dispute over treaty rights. Photos collected by Deloria exposed the truth that the threatening action agents had claimed precipitated their violent action against the fishing encampment was in reality a woman's making her daughter breakfast. Similarly, Deloria appeared in 1974 as an expert witness at the trials of 65 Oglala Sioux arrested after the AMERICAN INDIAN MOVEMENT (AIM) standoff against federal agents at the original site of the WOUNDED KNEE Massacre. Deloria and John Thorne crafted a defense that documented historical treaty rights for occupants of the Pine Ridge Reservation and argued motives for the stand as a civil protest against the Indian Reorganization Act—a bill purportedly drafted to restore self-government to tribes, which instead fostered corruption in internal tribal business. Deloria later wrote *Behind the Trail of Broken Treaties*, an account of the events leading to the Wounded Knee siege of 1973 that argued vociferously for the reestablishment of formal treaty negotiations between tribes and the U.S. government. These formalities, Deloria argues in this book, were crucial for the independence the United States promised.

Deloria's academic career was also quite distinguished. He began as a lecturer at Western Washington University in 1970 and joined the faculty of the University of California at Los Angeles in 1972. After a brief hiatus chairing the Institute for the Development of Indian Law, he accepted a professorship at the University of Arizona in Tucson, where he taught classes in law and philosophy from 1978 to 1990. From 1979 to 1982 he served as director of the graduate program in American Indian policy studies at the same institution. In 1990 he moved to the University of Colorado, Boulder, teaching law, history, political science, and religious studies at the Center for Studies in Ethnicity and Race in America.

Deloria's list of awards and honors for his writing and in recognition of his service to Indians is a testament to the importance of his work in calling Indian issues to mainstream attention. His book *Custer Died for Your Sins: An Indian Mani-*

festo (1969) was honored with the Anisfield-Wolf Award in 1970. He received the Indian Achievement Award from Indian Council Fire in 1972, Lifetime Achievement Award in 1969 from the Mountains and Plains Booksellers Association and Native Writers of America, Wordcraft Circle Writer of the Year Award in 1999, and Spirit of Excellence Award from the American Bar Association in 2001. *Indian Country Today* extended him the American Indian Visionary Award in 2005.

Most recently Deloria gained attention by refusing an honorary doctorate from the University of Colorado, citing his disappointment over the administration's response to questionable recruitment practices in the athletics program. In 2004 he publicly criticized Disney's fictionalization of the life of Frank Hopkins in the movie *Hidalgo*, starring Viggo Mortensen. In contrast to Disney and Mortensen's publicity for the film, Deloria debunked the claim that Hopkins was of Native American ancestry.

Bibliography

Carman, Diane. "Scholar: CU 'Honor' No Compliment," *Denver Post*, 25 May 2004.

Deloria, Vine Jr. "Across the Spectrum: Recent Literature on American Indians" (*Focus on American Indian Studies*). *The Social Science Journal* 34 (October 1997): 549–556.

———. *Custer Died for Your Sins: An Indian Manifesto.* New York: Macmillan, 1969.

———. *We Talk, You Listen: New Tribes, New Turf.* New York: Macmillan, 1970.

———. *God Is Red.* New York: Grosset, 1973.

———. *Behind the Trail of Broken Treaties: An Indian Declaration of Independence.* New York: Delacorte, 1974.

———. *Indians of the Pacific Northwest: From the Coming of the White Man to the Present Day.* New York: Doubleday, 1977.

———. *The Metaphysics of Modern Existence.* New York: Harper, 1979.

———. *Red Earth, White Lies: Native Americans and the Myth of Scientific Fact.* New York: Scribner, 1995.

———. *For This Land: Writings on Religion in America.* New York: Routledge, 1998.

"Editor's Report: Salute to Vine Deloria Jr.: American Indian Visionary." *Indian Country Today,* 1 January 2005.

Gridley Marian E., Contemporary American Indian Leaders. New York: Dodd Mead, 1972.

Kerr, James R. Review of *American Indians, American Justice, The Annals of the American Academy of Political and Social Science* 476 (November 1984): 186–187.

Warrior, Robert Allen. *Tribal Secrets: Recovering American Indian Intellectual Traditions.* Minneapolis: University of Minnesota Press, 1994.

Wiltz, Teresa. "A Man of Many Parts," *Washington Post,* 4 March 2004.

Michelle LaFrance

Doe Boy, The   (2001)

A coming-of-age film that follows a young man of mixed racial background as he attempts to understand his world, his culture, and his place in it, the award-winning *The Doe Boy* captures the frustration and confusion found with the search for identity between adolescence and adulthood, with the added complexities of race and illness.

The film opens with a glimpse into the childhood of the hemophiliac Hunter Kirk, who tries to live a normal life with a doting Indian mother, Maggie, and a detached white father, Hank. Allowed by his mother to accompany his father on a hunting trip, the young boy accidentally shoots a doe, an error that garners him the unfortunate nickname. It follows him into his young adult years, when the older Hunter is frustrated with life and still searching. His grandfather, Marvin Fishinghawk, is able to educate him in Indian history and lore and hands down to him the craft of flute making. Because of his MIXED-BLOOD heritage, Hunter continues to have unanswered questions about himself, and an unrewarding relationship with his heavy-drinker father offers no help.

Hunter's hemophilia and mixed blood relegate him to the role of an outsider, as a child unable to play as other children do and as a man unable to fight and hunt with reckless abandon. Hemophilia is considered a disease of the white race, and his tainted blood not only removes him from many activities but also creates a divide between him and his father, by default blamed for the affliction. Not until he moves out of his parents' house is he able to work through both his mixed heritage and his disease. Having dealt with the ghosts of childhood, the film ends as Hunter looks toward his own uncertain future, one with a girlfriend, the responsibility of carrying on his grandfather's art, and the looming specter of the acquired immunodeficiency syndrome (AIDS) virus, which killed the only other Native American hemophiliac in Oklahoma.

The Doe Boy won Perrier's Bubbling Under Award for First-Time Filmmakers at the Taos Talking Picture Festival in 2001, the American Indian Movie Award for best film, and the Sundance/ NHK International Filmmakers Award at the 2000 Sundance Film Festival.

See also MIXED-BLOOD.

Bibliography

Murg, Wilhelm. "The Doe Boy—Wellspring Media." *Native American Times,* 1 February 2003, p. 2A.

Norrell, Brenda. "Randy Redroad Captures First-Time Filmmaker Award at Taos." *Indian Country Today,* 25 April 2001, p. B1.

Rector, Leta. "Boy of Woe: A Film Review of *Doe Boy.*" *Native American Times,* 15 December 2001, p. 8.

Angela Courtney

Dorris, Michael   (1945–1997)

Born on January 30, 1945, in Louisville, Kentucky, Michael Dorris was part Modoc, and the Native American element of his mixed ancestry would become a driving force in his scholarly and literary work. Dorris received a bachelor's degree from Georgetown University in 1967 and completed a master's degree at Yale in 1970.

After teaching briefly at the University of the Redlands and Franconia College, he joined the Anthropology Department at Dartmouth College in 1972; he rose through the academic ranks from his initial appointment as an instructor to a full professorship in 1979. Dorris taught full-time at Dartmouth until 1988, serving as the chair of the Native American studies program from 1979 to 1985. From 1988 until his death by suicide in 1997, he remained an adjunct faculty member at Dartmouth while directing most of his energies toward his literary work.

In 1981 Dorris married the novelist LOUISE ERDRICH, and the photogenic couple achieved an extraliterary celebrity rare among "serious" authors. Moreover, although they coauthored only the novel *The CROWN OF COLUMBUS* (1991), they made no secret of their extensive input in each other's work. Ironically *The Crown of Columbus,* which combined an academic romance with a postcolonial reappraisal of the European discovery of America, may have received the most mixed reviews of any of Dorris's and Erdrich's books.

Given that all of Dorris's nonacademic books were published in the last decade of his life, the formal range of his literary work is quite extraordinary. Dorris's first novel, *A YELLOW RAFT ON BLUE WATER* (1987), is a multigenerational family saga set in Montana.

Dorris's next book was a dramatic change of pace. Much praised for both its writing and its social import, *The BROKEN CHORD* (1989) is a memoir of Dorris and Erdrich's attempts to come to grips with the extended effects of fetal alcohol syndrome on their adopted son. The son, Reynold Abel Dorris, would die in 1991, at age 23, of injuries he sustained when he was struck by an automobile.

In his last major book, Dorris would return to the family he treated in his first novel. *CLOUD CHAMBER* (1997) is not a prequel or a sequel to *A Yellow Raft on Blue Water* but, instead, provides a sort of parallel story, focusing this time on the women on the Irish-American side of the family.

Dorris also wrote several very well-received novels for children, cementing his reputation as a child advocate. So, although his 1996 separation from Erdrich seemed to contradict the public perception of their marriage, the news that Dorris was under investigation for child abuse was truly shocking. When Dorris subsequently committed suicide in April 1997, the conflicting accounts of the tensions in his marriage and family life made it clear that whatever the truth might have been, the image that the media had cultivated had missed much of that truth.

Bibliography

Cowart, David. "'The Rhythm of Three Strands': Cultural Braiding in Dorris's *A Yellow Raft in Blue Water.*" *Studies in American Indian Literatures* 8 (spring 1996): 1–12.

Dorris, Michael. *The Broken Cord: A Family's On-going Struggle with Fetal Alcohol Syndrome.* New York: Harper, 1989.

———, *Cloud Chamber.* New York: Scribner, 1997.

———. *A Yellow Raft in Blue Water.* New York: Holt, 1987.

———, and Louise Erdrich. *The Crown of Columbus.* New York: HarperCollins, 1991.

Matchie, Thomas. "Posttribal Sunshine in Michael Dorris's *Cloud Chamber.*" *North Dakota Quarterly* 66 (summer 1999): 33–41.

Martin Kich

Droning Shaman, The   Nora Marks Dauenhauer (1988)

Although she was already widely anthologized, *The Droning Shaman* is NORA MARKS DAUENHAUER's first published collection. Almost all the poems in this collection reflect, in some way, Dauenhauer's native Alaska. The text is deeply concerned with constructing a sense of place, not just visually, but linguistically, culturally, and spiritually. Peppered with Tlingit words throughout, and including a section at the end of some of Dauenhauer's favorite poems translated into Tlingit, this unique book provides a deep, textured picture of Native Alaskan culture.

The first section consists of six short poems, none more than five lines long. The first poem explains the title of the collection: The Bering Sea (*Alux* in Eastern Aleut) is the Droning Shaman. The fact that she calls it a shaman implies that it is wise, and the droning can be heard as a comforting, consistent sound, always in the background. The rest of the poems in this section each play a part in creating a portrait of the place about which Dauenhauer writes. She writes of the seals, the beach, and the sea and demonstrates the vital importance to the area of this constant maritime presence.

In part 2, Dauenhauer gets a bit more playful. Her piece "How to Make Good Baked Salmon from the River" explains in detail how to prepare the fish, in both the traditional way and the modern way. For instance, she says, "INGREDIENTS / Bar-b-q sticks of alder wood. / In this case, the oven will do" (8–10) and "Have some cool water from the stream with the salmon / In this case / water from the faucet will do" (113–116). Throughout the poem Dauenhauer switches back and forth like this, always taking care to remind the reader that even when using the modern method, the salmon is still good, and still a gift.

In part 3 several of the poems give way to a bitterness not seen elsewhere in the collection. In "Genocide" the speaker describes an "over-fed English girl" picketing the Eskimo Whaling Commission. Roughly halfway through the collection, this poem is well placed. By this point in the text the reader has such a good sense of the sacredness of the sea and its inhabitants to the Alaskan Natives that for such person to be protesting on behalf of the whales does seem absurd.

One of the most interesting aspects of this volume, and of Dauenhauer's work in general, is her use of the Tlingit language. In part 6 she states at the outset that readers from outside the culture may have a difficult time with the poems included here, all of which are about grandchildren. She says, "Much of the imagery relies on the meaning of the Tlingit names," which she translates to make them "more accessible to the general reader." For instance, in the gloss to the poem "Shnalnáa at Bat" she tells us the name means "Is carrying himself in pieces, with the pieces all together" (79). This knowledge adds much meaning to the line "Get it together, baby!" (1). The final section of the text contains poems Dauenhauer admires, from e.e. cummings, the Chinese poet Setcho, and the Japanese poet Matsuo Basho, translated into Tlingit. As this language is so little known to general readers, poems presented entirely in this format are interesting and give texture and depth to the portrait of Alaska presented here.

Drowning in Fire Craig S. Womack (2001)

Drowning in Fire, CRAIG WOMACK's powerful first novel, is both the coming-of-age and coming-out story of Josh Henneha, a Muskogee Creek Indian who grows up in rural Oklahoma and must learn to face both his homosexuality and his place within the Creek community. Josh is accompanied on this journey by his great-aunt Lucy, who must face her own history of abuse, and his adolescent crush Jimmy, who must come to terms with his own homosexuality and the racism he faces on a daily basis as a black Creek. By interweaving the perspectives of these three characters, Womack's novel demonstrates the power of love, family, and community to overcome the loneliness and exclusion the characters face.

As a young adolescent Josh is aware that he is different from other boys. Weak and effeminate, Josh flees the unbearable scrutiny of his peers by escaping into his mind, where he is able to fly above and observe the world without having to be a part of it. It is from this world that Josh first sends mental messages of desire to Jimmy. In most ways the athletic and popular Jimmy is the complete opposite of Josh, but when Jimmy unexpectedly returns his affections, Josh is overwhelmed by thoughts of confusion and shame stemming from his inability to negotiate his sexuality with his religious upbringing. Josh's confusion and reticence lead to a rupture in his relationship with Jimmy that lasts for nearly 15 years.

As adults both Josh and Jimmy come to terms with their sexuality in different ways. While Josh initially avoids facing his identity at all, Jimmy unsuccessfully searches for love in the bars of Tulsa, only to return to his hometown with nothing but emotional and physical scars. Josh and Jimmy are eventually united again by Aunt Lucy's legacy of family and community. Through Aunt Lucy Josh learns the story of Tarbie and Seborn, two Creek men who lived together during Lucy's childhood. In their story Josh is able to see parallels to his own relationship with Jimmy and gains the following realization:

I'd never considered the possibility that the world might be crooked, and I might be okay.

That might have been the reason I had to leave it so often, the meaning of my flights. I had to dream a little to get a proper perspective on things, from my place just above the earth. (184)

In *RED ON RED*, his book of literary theory, Womack argues, "To exist as a nation, the community needs a perception of nationhood, that is stories . . . that help them imagine who they are as a people, how they came to be, and what cultural values they wish to preserve" (26). Lucy's stories help Josh and Jimmy imagine not only who they are as Creek people but also how their relationship can coincide with their personal and cultural values.

Bibliography

Womack, Craig S. *Drowning in Fire*. Tucson: University of Arizona Press, 2001.

———. *Red on Red: Native American Literary Separatism*. Minneapolis: University of Minnesota Press, 1999.

Malinda Williams

Dry Lips Oughta Move to Kapuskasing Tomson Highway

In *Dry Lips Oughta Move to Kapuskasing* TOMSON HIGHWAY explores the often "violent juxtaposition [of] the cultural and spiritual values of Native and non-Native Canadians" (Nothof 34). Highway focuses such violent juxtaposition in the play's seven male characters' responses to the formation of an Indian women's hockey team on their Wasaychigan Hill reserve. While Pierre's sense of the scandal inherent in the "Wasy" women's assertion that "'ain't nobody on the face of this earth's gonna tell us women's got no business playin' hockey'" (29) is mitigated by the fact that they chose him as their referee, Big Joey asserts that this is "Wounded Knee Three! Women's version" (63). Big Joey's statement initially seems positive, given WOUNDED KNEE's history as an enduring symbol of Native resistance to white cultural dominance. However, Big Joey ultimately reveals that he associates the Native women hockey players with the white Federal Bureau of Investigation (FBI) agents who crushed the 1973 Wounded Knee protests, not with the Native men who participated in these protests. Forced to explain why he allows Dickie Bird to assault Patsy Pegahmagahbow sexually, Big Joey exclaims, "Because they—our own women—took the . . . power away from us faster than the FBI ever did" (120).

Alan Filewood argues that this scene, but also *Dry Lips* as a whole, forces the "Wasy" men to "confront their political impotence" (364). Big Joey's rage at the female hockey players, Dickie Bird's violence against Patsy, and other characters' more subdued discomfort with the women's hockey playing point to the real and much larger conflict lurking beneath the surface: the conflict between Natives who adhere to their culture's traditional faith (Simon in particular) and those who adopt the dominant culture's Christianity (Spooky). These two characters dramatize the poles of this cultural divide; they argue vehemently about the desirability of having the reserve's "only surviving medicine woman and mid-wife" (88) deliver Spooky's pregnant wife's baby:

SPOOKY:
Rosie Kakapetum? No way some witch is gonna come and put her witchy little fingers on my baby boy.
SIMON:
Rosie Kakapetum's no witch, Spooky Lacroix. (88)

In response to Big Joey's outburst but also to his own prejudices, particularly against Wasaychigan Hill's midwife, Spooky ultimately admits, however, that the women in Native culture have "always had" the power (120). The problem being worked out in *Dry Lips* then is not that women have always had power but that the infiltration of Christianity's masculine monotheism into Native culture has corroded Native men's ability to relate to women, to the mystical, and therefore also to themselves. Simon, formerly so sure of his traditional beliefs, is led by Dickie Bird's violence on his fiancée to question the TRICKSTER FIGURE Nanabush in the most fundamental way: "God! You're a man. You're a woman. You're a man? You're a woman?" (112).

Dry Lips Oughta Move to Kapuskasing explores the painful intersections of gender division, religious conflict, and cultural disempowerment, but it does so in a way that is rife with the potential for healing. The sinister and tragic events constituting most of the play are in the end revealed to have all been part of Zachary's dream. Dream visions in Native American cultures are typically understood as providing wisdom and insight into particular difficulties; here the issues so darkly played out in Zachary's dream are offset by his peaceful and loving interaction with his wife and daughter after he wakes up: *The last thing we see is this beautiful naked Indian man lifting this naked baby Indian girl up in the air, his wife sitting beside them watching and laughing"* (130).

Bibliography

Filewood, Alan. "Receiving Aboriginality: Tomson Highway and the Crisis of Cultural Authenticity." *Theatre Journal* 46 (1994): 363–373.

Highway, Tomson. *Dry Lips Oughta Move to Kapuskasing.* Saskatoon: Fifth House, 1989.

Nothof, Anne. "Cultural Collision and Magical Transformation: The Plays of Tomson Highway." *Studies in Canadian Literature* 20, no. 2 (1995): 34–43.

Colleen Shea

E

Eagle Nation, An   Carter Revard (1993)

Winner of the 1994 Oklahoma Book Award, *An Eagle Nation* is CARTER REVARD's third published collection of poetry and follows his works *Ponca War Dancers* (1980) and *Cowboys and Indians, Christmas Shopping* (1992). The title is an allusion to the Osage Nation's reverence for the ancestral eagles, which play an important role in tribal ceremonies and story. Comprising three sections— "An Eagle Nation," "Homework at Oxford," and "Sea-Changes"—Revard's collection reflects the richness and diversity not only of the author's poetic images and prose stories, but also, and perhaps more importantly, the poet's life as an Osage gourd dancer and scholar of medieval literature.

Ellen Arnold lays emphasis on that diversity, underlining the "unique and complex ways Carter Revard negotiates multiple cultural experiences" (i). These "multiple experiences" are central to Carter's life and poetry. As a consequence *An Eagle Nation* contains sections that chronicle Revard's time in Oxford at Merton College ("A Giveaway Special"), alongside poems that aim toward bringing about an understanding of Osage territory and culture as they exist within contemporary America ("Starring America"). The result is a far-sighted and engaging collection of poetry that forces the reader to consider not only modern tribal contexts, but also the wealth of cultural understanding made possible through poetry.

The poem bearing the title of the collection itself, "An Eagle Nation," illustrates these aspects of Revard's work. Written in blank verse, or unrhymed iambic pentameter, this poem relates a simple family visit to the Oklahoma City Zoo, and a pow wow. Opening with a remembrance of "this little Ponca woman," the piece is primarily concerned with Aunt Jewell and her grandchildren. Revard is careful to include images of past and present, detailing for the reader his aunt's use of language and meaning, whether "Ponca or English, sacred or / profane" (31). During a conversation with a bald eagle at the zoo the old woman says "good things," and the poet explains that he knows the eagle—the tribes' sacred being—will "pass them on" (33). The poem becomes a meditation on Osage heritage and a symbol of the mediation that occurs not only between different generations of Osage peoples, but also between different cultures and the different worlds that surround us: our world and the spirit world.

In telling such stories through poetry, Revard has established a humorous, multilayered web of images that is as concerned with the poetic forms of Middle English verse ("What the Eagle Fan Says") as it is with the ironies and horrors of America's colonial history ("Parading with the V.F.W."). *An Eagle Nation* succeeds in offering the most stirring of images gently but always forces the reader to remember this is a story born of Osage experiences—experiences that are as wide and eclectic as the poet's own interests and abilities.

Bibliography

Revard, Carter. *An Eagle Nation.* Norman: University of Oklahoma Press, 1993.

Studies in American Indian Literatures 15, no. 1 (spring 2003). Special Issue in Honor of Carter Revard.

Padraig Kirwan

Earthdivers: Tribal Narratives on Mixed Descent   Gerald Vizenor (1981)

As mythic TRICKSTER FIGURES question everything, play tricks on everyone, and can take any animal shape, *Earthdivers,* GERALD VIZENOR's first collection of short stories, destabilizes readers while entertaining them. This style, Vizenor's trademark, puts the reader in a position as unstable as that of MIXED-BLOOD Indians, who have both white and American Indian ancestors and are thus caught between two cultures. The 12 stories in *Earthdivers* parallel this imbalance with a mix of real facts and fiction, humor and tragedy, satire and lyric, journalistic reporting and surreal fantasy.

In between cultures mixed-bloods must create their own identities, the way earthdivers created the earth in northern American Indian myths. Earthdivers dove deep into the ocean to find the dirt that would serve to make earth. In Vizenor's stories mixed-blood Indians must metaphorically dive and find the raw material to establish their identity. As the compassionate trickster in the Chippewa version of the myth asked animals to dive for him, mixed-blood earthdivers can use white people. The metaphorical dirt they take to the surface can then be equal rights or government funds. Vizenor's stories show how this difficult metaphorical earthdiving succeeds or fails.

The five sections of the book identify the earthdivers, "Earthdivers in Higher Education" or "Earthdivers at the Indian Center," and each begins with an illustration. The collection mixes traditions: Written in English, it sometimes mimes oral storytelling. It is partly autobiographical, as the character of Clement Beaulieu, a mixed-blood scholar and teacher, stands for Vizenor.

In the first story, "The Chair of Tears," Beaulieu tells his conference audience about Captain Shammer, chair of the Department of American Indian Studies, who transformed the department as a trickster would have. A metaphorical earthdiver, Shammer dove quite far to find solutions, deciding to pay faculty and students according to the darkness of their skin and auctioning off the department (although picking the winner himself) to a group that would make it the Department of Undecided Studies. These decisions may seem absurd, shockingly racist, or morally unacceptable, but they also offer comic caricatures, and the paradox reveals real issues to the reader.

The book portrays many kinds of earthdiving. In "Natural Tilts" the "little people," elflike mythical creatures, mention Martin Bear Charme, "founder of the Landfill Meditation Reservation," who made a fortune by filling reservation wetlands with solid waste and organizing fancy seminars like "refuse meditation" on the site (91). In "the Sociodowser" Father Bearald One plays tricks on mixed-blood Indians who dive for government help but then abuse it shamelessly. The characters' names offer funny, fitting labels, but they also denounce the inadequacy of English. Martin Bear Charme, Touch Tone, Fine Print, and others, reappear in later works by Vizenor.

Bibliography

Blaeser, Kimberley M. *Gerald Vizenor: Writing in the Oral Tradition.* Norman: University of Oklahoma Press, 1996.

Vizenor, Gerald. *Earthdivers.* Minneapolis: University of Minnesota Press, 1981.

———. *Landfill Meditations: Crossblood Stories.* Middletown, Conn.: Wesleyan University Press, 1991.

Claire Gallou

Earth Power Coming   Simon Ortiz (1983)

The title of this collection of stories is taken from *WIND FROM AN ENEMY SKY,* by D'ARCY MCNICKLE

(1978), an extract of which serves as an epigraph to the book, thus asserting the continuity in Native American literature Simon Ortiz wishes to stress. He says, "There have always been those words which evoked meaning and the meaning's magical wonder" (vii). Thirty authors are represented here, with 39 short stories, mainly grounded in the oral tradition, ranging "from stark realism to surrealism" (viii).

CARTER REVARD's "Report to the Nation: Claiming Europe" starts as an inverted story of the conquest of America, a light, humorous pastiche, in the matter-of-fact manner of the 16th- and 17th-century explorers, though it takes place in the 20th century: "The Europeans kill each other pretty casually, as if by natural instinct, not caring whether they blow up women, kids or horses, and next day display the mutilated corpses on front pages or television screens" (167). But midway into the story, the narrator, Special Agent Wazhazhe No. 2,230, realizes that the elders believe they should be more civilized than the Europeans and thus forget "the military side of things."

Jack Forbes's "Only Approved Indians Can Play: Made in USA" is a parable, about an all-Indian basketball tournament in which the various players bicker about who is really entitled to be in the teams and end up with excluding all the Papago, Tarahumara, and Yaqui, Bureau of Indian Affairs (BIA) enrollment cards, until the Great Lakes team is declared winner by default. The last word in the story is that of a white BIA official, who wipes the tears from his eyes and says to his companion: "God Bless America. I think we've won." (263) The moral is unequivocal: Indians should not internalize the rules set by the whites, for these are made for their own profit.

"Waterbugs" by PETER BLUE CLOUD is a brief story about storytelling featuring the TRICKSTER FIGURE Coyote, Fox Young Man, and Flicker. Coyote tells Fox Young Man that waterbugs, being full of gas, "just fart themselves in circles all day long" (189). At first Fox Young Man does not believe Coyote, but as soon as Coyote has left for lunch, he puts one ear under the water and plugs his other one with a paw, trying to hear the waterbugs farting all around him. Coyote spies him, and when he meets Flicker, he tells him to ask Fox Young Man about waterbugs:

> "What?" said Flicker. "Coyote, what are you talking about?"
> "Me?" answered Coyote, "Oh, I'm just letting you know how stories are born. That's all."

Bibliography
McNickle, D'Arcy. *Wind from an Enemy Sky.* Albuquerque: University of New Mexico Press, 1988.

Simone Pellerin

Earth Song, Sky Spirit   Clifford E. Trafzer (1992)

Earth Song, Sky Spirit was awarded the Pen Oakland Literary Award for fiction. What is so remarkable about this first collection by CLIFFORD TRAFZER is that most of the texts are original, written for this volume—a few are excerpts from novels (as is the case for those by MICHAEL DORRIS, LOUISE ERDRICH, LESLIE MARMON SILKO, PAULA GUNN ALLEN, and JAMES WELCH). The subtitle of the book, *Short Stories of the Contemporary Native American Experience,* aptly expresses what makes the collection a coherent whole. All major contemporary Native American fiction writers are present here, as well as slightly less well-known writers.

Bracketed in elements of personal recollections of, and a dream about, Andrew George, an old Palouse medicine man, Trafzer's introduction is a short but effective history of Native American literature in the United States. Starting with the oral tradition and linking it to the first written novel by Elias Boudinot in 1823, *Poor Sarah,* it goes on, through the 19th and 20th centuries, down to our contemporaries. Trafzer identifies characteristic features of the Native tradition (i.e., weaving characters and plot in such a way as to introduce the history, religions, traditions, culture, and stories of their peoples) and states that contemporary writers, "consciously or unconsciously" (6), use the same technique to reflect "the community of the person." He also describes such stories as having "multidimensional characters" and lacking "absolute conclusions."

These texts deal with important issues—identity; the importance of family; the relations within the extended family; the role of the community, the power of women, of language, of voice; teachings about life—that are central to the Native American experience. The volume also explores such commonly recurring themes and topics as BOARDING SCHOOLS, the oral tradition, past and present as a continuum, the sense of place, RESERVATION LIFE, ALCOHOLISM, child abuse, but also ghosts, spirits, and dreams; HUMOR; and of course the continuance of cultural identity. As Trafzer puts it, "The events described occur throughout contemporary society, demonstrating that Native Americans are part of the world today and not quaint remnants of a 'vanishing race'" (19).

An excellent example is KIMBERLY BLAESER's "From Aboard the Night Train," which paints the author's experiences of traveling at night, dreaming, having nightmares, and undergoing a very intense feeling of seeing life going by, through the train window. At the end of the story, she is at the end of one of her trips; she reads on a fellow traveler's newspaper about the Russian cosmonaut who had been in orbit for 16 months, while the Union of Soviet Socialist Republics (USSR) dissolved, and who is eventually returned to Earth. She reaches home, "thinking about that poor cosmonaut coming back to find his whole world changed, to find himself a man without a country—at least without the country he left behind." When she sees him on television, emerging from his capsule, she notices his knees buckle when he tries to stand: "I know they said it was because he hadn't been able to exercise for such a long time, but I wonder if his weak-kneed feeling might not have more to do with what he saw out the window of the space station and how the world was happening without him" (36).

Bibliography

Trafzer, Clifford E., ed. *Blue Dawn, Red Earth: New Native American Storytellers.* New York: Doubleday Dell, 1996.

Simone Pellerin

Eastman, Charles Alexander (Ohiyesa) (1858–1939)

On the title pages of his books the man many have called the most prominent Indian of the early 20th century identified himself by both his English and his Dakota names—"Charles Alexander Eastman (Ohiyesa)." The decision to include both of his names, to juxtapose the English and Dakota languages as he claimed authorship of his books, indicates the complicated identity and profoundly bicultural life of this important author and intellectual. Eastman's choice also points toward the most persistent theme in his writing: finding balance and connection between Dakota and European-American cultures.

As a boy Ohiyesa received the education and upbringing of a traditional Santee boy from his paternal grandmother, Uncheedah, and his uncle, Mysterious Medicine. Ohiyesa grew up among his Wahpeton band of Dakota in Minnesota and later in exile in Manitoba, where they fled from contact with European-Americans when his father, Many Lightnings, and hundreds of other Dakota men were captured and sentenced to death after the 1862 Sioux Uprising.

In 1872 Ohiyesa's life changed when Many Lightnings returned to the Wahpeton, revealing to his shocked relatives that he had escaped death when he and most of the condemned Dakota were pardoned. Many Lightnings had converted to Christianity, named himself Jacob Eastman, and moved to a settlement of Christian Dakota at Flandreau, South Dakota. The boy and his grandmother moved to live with his father at Flandreau, where Ohiyesa took the name Charles and began a lengthy education in European-American ways that culminated in a medical degree from Boston University in 1890. Charles made sense of the vast changes in his life by focusing on the continuities between Santee and European-American cultures. In *Indian Boyhood* (1902), the first of two autobiographies he would author, Charles recounts his father's explanation of the parallel between Western education and Dakota ways: "'The way of knowledge,' [my father] continued, 'is like our old way in hunting. You begin with a mere trail—a footprint. If you follow that faithfully, it may lead you to a clearer trail—a track—a road. Later on there will be many tracks, crossing and diverging one from the other. Then you must be careful, for success lies in the choice of the right road" (29).

After completing his education, Eastman held several positions with the Bureau of Indian Affairs—most notably as a physician and as the translator of more than 25,000 Sioux names into English. Charles later worked for the Young Men's Christian Association (YMCA), performed on the lecture circuit, and (along with his wife, Elaine Goodale Eastman, a white educator and poet) owned and ran a summer camp. He was a founding member and an officer of the Society of American Indians, a pan-Indian reform organization. The degree to which his wife, Elaine, served as his editor and collaborator is not entirely known, but with her encouragement and at least some editorial assistance, Eastman published 11 books and numerous articles. In 1923, after 32 years of marriage, Eastman and Elaine separated. Charles never again published a book after their separation, but he continued to be an active speaker and representative of Indian people. In his later years he returned to the woods, mostly living in a cabin along the Canadian coast of Lake Huron. In 1939 he died in Detroit, home of his son, Ohiyesa II.

As his father predicted, Eastman's experiences as a college-educated Dakota man did result in a life lived at the intersection of many paths. Even the form of his writing blends Dakota storytelling conventions with European-American narrative style to emphasize the multiple cultural and literary traditions from which he drew and to which he contributed. It was difficult to communicate hybrid identity during Eastman's era, in which U.S. government policy shifted from the removal and extermination of Indian people to Assimilation—a policy that devalued and discouraged the continuation of tribal cultures, languages, and religious beliefs. Nevertheless, Eastman struggled to carve out a space for his own multifaceted identity and voice. Because they explore these complex issues, Eastman's two autobiographies are his most frequently studied texts today. For example, in his second autobiography, *From the Deep Woods to Civilization* (1916), Eastman tells of his discovery, during his first assignment for the Bureau of Indian Affairs as a "white doctor" on the Pine Ridge Reservation in 1890, that it could be traumatic and dangerous to be affiliated with both white and Dakota cultures. Barely a month after his arrival (and three days after his engagement to Elaine) the U.S. Army slaughtered approximately 300 Lakota men, women, and children who were participating in the Ghost Dance along Wounded Knee Creek. Eastman doctored the few surviving victims of the Wounded Knee Massacre, bearing witness to the atrocity. Eastman's reflection, "All this was a severe ordeal for one who had so lately put all his faith in the Christian love and lofty ideals of the white man," indicates both his adherence to white culture and his denunciation of white treatment of Native people, to whom he also maintains allegiance (114). Ironically, Eastman felt, and he makes this a central point of *From the Deep Woods*, that his Indian upbringing prepared him to follow the path of the white man and pursue a career in medicine. He referred to it as his "warpath," and since he had been raised to be a warrior, he felt suited to the task.

Eastman negotiated the tension between his Christian faith and Western education and his Dakota values and kinship in his philosophical books as well. In *The Soul of the Indian* (1911) Eastman most fully presses his critique of European-American culture. According to Eastman, the Dakota and other tribes held spiritual beliefs that are closer to the ideal of Christianity than the actions of many white American Christians, whose materialism and lack of spiritual awareness fail to live up to their faith. He asserts, "It is my personal belief, after thirty-five years' experience of it, that there is no such thing as 'Christian civilization.' I believe that Christianity and modern civilization are opposed and irreconcilable, and that the spirit of Christianity and of our ancient religion is essentially the same" (24). He notes in this text that in his culture spiritual training was primarily provided by the women, who taught children to respect nature, to respect other human beings, and to pray often: all important tenets of Christianity. He believed that Christianity had strayed too far from its roots and that it had become too competitive and materialistic, flaws he did not see in the Native religion.

While assimilationists and MISSIONARIES had long set Christianity and civilization in opposition to Native religions and savagery to justify the eradication of Indian cultures, Eastman throws these categories into question. In doing so, he complicates the simple path of assimilation that his title *From the Deep Woods to Civilization* would seem to lay out for him, valuing Indian cultures as superior to so-called civilization. At the end of that autobiography he states: "I am an Indian; and while I have learned much from civilization, for which I am grateful, I have never lost my Indian sense of right and justice. . . . Nevertheless, so long as I live, I am an American" (195). In the end Eastman took many paths rather than choosing a single "right" one, a survival strategy that some have criticized as vacillation or as complicity with assimilationists, even as it is praised by others as "the beginning of a rhetoric of survivance" (Powell 427). Eastman's multiplicity continues to challenge readers of his work to understand the variety of pressures and possibilities facing Indian intellectuals at the turn of the 20th century and to hear the complex stories they tell of creativity, persistence, accommodation, and survival.

Bibliography

Carlson, David J. "'Indian for a While': Charles Eastman's Indian Boyhood and the Discourse of Allotment." *American Indian Quarterly* 25, no. 4 (fall 2001): 604–625.

Eastman, Charles Alexander. *From the Deep Woods to Civilization: Chapters in the Autobiography of an Indian.* Lincoln: University of Nebraska Press, 1977.

———. *Indian Boyhood.* Lincoln: University of Nebraska Press, 1992.

———. *The Soul of the Indian: An Interpretation.* Lincoln: University of Nebraska Press, 1980.

Eastman, Elaine Goodale. *Sister to the Sioux: The Memoirs of Elaine Goodale Eastman, 1885–1891.* Lincoln: University of Nebraska Press, 2004.

Peterson, Erik. "'An Indian . . . An American': Ethnicity and Balance in Charles Eastman's *From the Deep Woods to Civilization.*" In *Early Native American Writing: New Critical Essays,* edited by Helen Jaskoski, 170–182. New York: Cambridge University Press, 1996.

Powell, Malea. "Rhetorics of Survivance: How American Indians Use Writing." *College Composition and Communication.* 53, no. 3 (February 2002): 396–434.

Wilson, Raymond. *Ohiyesa: Charles Eastman, Santee Sioux.* Urbana: University of Illinois Press, 1983.

Amelia V. Katanski

Eclipse Linda Hogan (1983)

Eclipse is organized into six sections that honor the four winds, Father Sky, and Mother Earth. The landscapes of Oklahoma, her tribal homeland, and Denver, Colorado, where LINDA HOGAN has put down "long taproots" (vi), are the settings for her poems. These landscapes, her adopted daughters and others in her community, and the fusion of Native American and global concerns form the heart of the poetry in this volume.

Many poems lament the loss of children, both their innocence and their lives, to war. The poems describe mothers, and often fathers as well, trying to protect their children with prayers, lighting of candles, and night watches. In "The Women Speaking" "Japanese women / light lanterns / the shape of children." The image is repeated in "The Women Are Grieving" and mothers "light fat candles their hands molded / in the hopeful shape of children / who are thin." Images of light and fire fill Hogan's poetry. "Black Hills Survival Gathering, 1981" glows with line after line of "fragile fire," "burning hills," "warm sun." The warmth of light is a metaphor for the warmly beating heart of the land and its people. In Hogan's poems children are described as "fiery creature furnaces," "bright children," with "strong arms" and vulnerable skin. They are ours to protect, Hogan reminds us again and again.

She also tries to tell the stories of those people to whom no one listens. Hogan wants to give voice to the fears and concerns of her own life, but also to those of people who have no voice or have been silenced as a result of their gender, race, or economic status. In "Houses" the reader is told that the only thing her people have is the desire to speak. In her essay "Hearing Voices" Hogan tells the story of a corn plant growing in the center of Chaco Canyon. The people of the canyon have long since disappeared, but the plant reseeds itself every year and "rises up to tell its story" (81).

Hogan calls mythology "the true language of inner life" (*Hearing Voices* 77); what she attempts to do in her poetry is to use the common language, that mythological collective voice that those who do not listen to the earth and the stories it tells never hear. She says, "I believe the divine, the magic, is here in the weeds at our feet, unacknowledged" (80). In *Eclipse* a father bathes his daughter in the early morning, yucca pods spill their seeds, a rabbit sleeps in his burrow. The mundane details of everyday life are invested with meaning that gives Hogan's poems the spiritual quality that characterizes much Native American poetry. There is no line between nature and human. People, animals, plants, and landscapes are equally valued. Her lovingly portrayed details of the land seek to forge a connection between the reader and the natural world. By doing so, Hogan seems to hope that the values learned will spread to the reader's relationships with the rest of humanity.

Bibliography

Hogan, Linda. "Hearing Voices." *The Writer on Her Work.* Vol. 2, *New Essays on New Territory.* New York: W. W. Norton, 1991.

Niatum, Duane. "Introduction." In *Harper's Anthology of 20th Century Native American Poetry,* edited by Duane Niatum, xiii–xxxii. San Francisco: Harper & Row, 1988.

Patricia Kennedy Bostian

Enwhisteetkwa—Walk in Water
Jeannette C. Armstrong (1982)

This first-person narrative, divided into four chapters, one for each season—beginning with winter—tells about a year in the life of a little girl named Enwhisteetkwa at the time the first whites entered the Okanagan country. As does Neekna and Chemai, it deals with traditional customs, life, and lore and is illustrated (illustrator's name unknown); it also features a glossary of 12 Okanagan names and words. A traditional song about frightful Ska-Loo-La, or Owl Woman (8), and a poem are nicely woven into the text proper. The story is written in a very simple manner and aims at instilling in children values of good behavior and respect.

The emphasis is on everyday work, with an Okanagan worldview, as illustrated in such sentences as "Night was coming soon because grandfather Sun was sliding down the last stretch of sky and pulling his shadow cloak over the land and sky" (11). But the general impression is more complex than just that of a land of plenty, of a harmonious world, with happy people laughing and rejoicing: The children may discover frustration when not allowed to sit up at night to watch the dances (13); the people may have to fight outsiders, whether other tribes (12) or white men (24). Those have very strange ways and behave rudely: They never respect the rules of the inhabitants of the country they are entering; the old ones are greatly troubled: "In fact it sounded like they wanted our people to do strange things" (24). In the summer the tribe has to go back to their winter living quarters, in Penticton, without fishing first, as usual, because the missionaries intend to build a place in their homeland to teach them new ways. Resistance builds up and after talks between the two parties, the whites are allowed to pass through and settle north of Penticton.

But from then on conditions keep changing: The Okanagan now use new products, guns, and some of them, such as the Similkameens, Chief Nicola and his niece, called Therese, even choose to follow the ways of the white men. The last sentences of the story stand out in ironical contrast to the impending disruption of their way of life: "I liked our food and how we lived. I hoped it would never change. It had been the most exciting year of all my life" (44).

Bibliography

Armstrong, Jeannette C. *Neekna and Chemai.* Penticton, Canada: Theytus Books, 1991.

———. *Breath Tracks.* Penticton, Canada: Theytus Books, 1991.

Simone Pellerin

Erdrich, Karen Louise (1954–)

Karen Louise Erdrich, one of the most talented novelists and poets of the AMERICAN INDIAN LITERARY RENAISSANCE, was born in 1954 in Little Falls, Minnesota, where her German paternal grandparents ran a butcher shop. Her mother, of Ojibwa and French descent, grew up on Turtle Mountain Indian Reservation, on the Canadian border in North Dakota. Erdrich's grandfather served as tribal chair of the Turtle Mountain Chippewa from 1953 to 1959. Erdrich grew up in Wahpeton, North Dakota, where both parents taught at the Wahpeton Indian School.

Erdrich's family encouraged her to avail herself of scholarships for Native Americans at Dartmouth University, and in 1972 she became part of the first coeducational class in Dartmouth's history. At Dartmouth her creative writing teachers encouraged her to publish her poetry, and in her junior year she was awarded an American Academy Poets Award.

Upon graduation from Dartmouth Erdrich returned to North Dakota, where she worked for the Poets in the Schools program, a nationwide organization whose goals are to expose children to the practices of working writers. Erdrich also worked during this time as a lifeguard, waitress, construction worker, and weeder in the beet fields. In 1978 Erdrich entered the Johns Hopkins University creative writing program. After she earned her M.A. she worked in Boston as editor of *The Circle,* a newspaper published by the Boston Indian Council.

In 1981 Erdrich took a position at Dartmouth as writer in residence, and shortly afterward she married MICHAEL DORRIS, a Modoc anthropologist who headed the Native American studies program, whom she had met as an undergraduate. Dorris took his three adopted children to the marriage, and the couple had three more.

In 1982 Erdrich won the Nelson Algren fiction competition with the story "The World's Greatest Fisherman." The story became the basis (and first chapter) of LOVE MEDICINE, her first novel, which she published in 1984. The novel won Erdrich the 1984 National Book Critics Award.

Love Medicine is the first of a series of novels based on a fictionalized version of the Turtle Mountain Reservation. She would ultimately name this reservation, and the series, Little No Horse. Subsequent books in the series include *The BEET QUEEN* (1986), *TRACKS* (1988), an expanded and revised *Love Medicine* (1993), *The BINGO PALACE* (1994), *TALES OF BURNING LOVE* (1996), *The LAST REPORT ON THE MIRACLES AT LITTLE NO HORSE* (2001), and *FOUR SOULS* (2004).

The Little No Horse saga begins in the late 19th century, when the Turtle Mountain Chippewa, a band of the Chippewa tribe who moved west from Minnesota and adopted the lifestyle of the PLAINS TRIBES, were still hunting buffalo. In one of the most dramatic scenes in *Last Report,* the book that contains both the earliest and latest chronological episodes of the Little No Horse saga, a vast herd of buffalo commit mass suicide because "they saw the end of things" (i.e., the traditional way of life they shared with the Indians) and did not choose to live any longer. In other early episodes the Chippewa suffered greatly from starvation, disease, the destruction of much of their culture, and the loss of their land through the DAWES ACT. In the latest episodes (*The Bingo Palace, Tales of Burning Love*) many of the characters have entered the middle class. The tribe had, through industrial development and GAMING, about which Erdrich is profoundly ambivalent, been able to pave reservation roads, improve housing, and generally better the quality of life of its members.

The Little No Horse saga is notable for the brilliant depictions of the characters who populate the novels. Fleur Pillager, the matriarch, survives being drowned twice and saves herself from starvation only to lose her land in *Tracks.* Fleur reappears in *The Bingo Palace* dressed in a white suit and driving a Pierce Arrow and wins her land back in a card game. At the end of *Bingo Palace* she apparently turns into a bear, ending her life as a human to save the life of her great-grandson. Fleur's character is a good example of the intricacy of Erdrich's characterizations over the course of this series of novels. Fleur is a mysterious, shadowy presence in *Love Medicine,* mentioned several times but appearing only once, to deliver Marie's baby. In *The Beet Queen* again our view of her is short, but tentalizing. In both of these early texts the other characters fear Fleur and the dark powers they believe she possesses. In *Tracks,* however, we finally get a complete picture of this rich character. We see what she has lived through and begin to understand that her only "powers" are cunning and determination. In *The Bingo Palace* she makes the mysterious return to the reservation and in 2004's *Four Souls* we learn where Fleur was and how she acquired that white suit and that fancy car. She left the reservation to extract revenge on John Mauser, the man who was responsible for taking her land. She married him, had his child, became an alcoholic, and finally returns to the place where she belongs.

Another unforgettable character is Fleur's daughter, Lulu Lamartine, the reservation siren, a female TRICKSTER FIGURE of prodigious sexual appetites, who retains her sexual attractiveness into her 80s. Her son, Gerry Nanapush, is another trickster (the name *Nanapush* is a variant of *Nanabozho,* the name of the Chippewa trickster), an escape artist who is an expert in breaking out of prison.

Perhaps the most memorable character is the fascinating if repulsive nun Sister Leopolda, who kills the father of her illegitimate child (believing he is the devil), pours boiling water into the ear of the daughter when she becomes a novice at the convent, and works heroically during the smallpox epidemic that follows World War I. She has such a reputation on the reservation that the church institutes an investigation to determine whether she should be canonized.

As the Little No Horse saga progresses, Erdrich uses more and more magical realism. This is a literary technique, often associated with South American literature, that combines supernatural elements, events that could not possible happen, with the gritty realism of everyday events, births,

deaths, poverty, illness. In addition to Fleur's return from the dead, and her metamorphosis into a bear, the ghosts of Nector Kashpaw and June Morrissey play prominent roles in the action of the novels. A number of critics, among them Amaryll Chandy, have argued that magical realism in South American novels can be attributed to two conflicting codes: the realistic code that is the heritage of the European worldview and the magical code that results from the Indian worldview. Erdrich's magical realism derives from the same tension between conflicting codes.

Manipulating the conventions of traditional narration is another trademark of Erdrich's fiction. In the Little No Horse saga the stories jump around quite a bit chronologically, even within a single book. In addition, the books in this series employ many different narrators, and occasionally the same event is related more than once by multiple different narrators. These strategies encourage the reader to question the stability of such categories as time, truth, narration, and reliability.

Although the novels are rich with political commentary, the core around which they all revolve is the importance of family. More specifically, the novels explore the ways in which the female characters continue to sustain their families against the considerable odds of poverty, infidelity, and alcoholism. The matriarchs of the two main families, Marie Kashpaw and Lulu Lamartine, spend much of their lives competing for the love of the same man, Marie's husband, Russell Kashpaw. Although this competition often reduces them to less than dignified encounters, both women manage to raise children and grandchildren, take care of (and manipulate) the men around them, and sustain life on the reservation.

Erdrich has also written novels about subjects other than Little No Horse Reservation: *The AN-TELOPE WIFE* (1998) is about Indians living in Minneapolis, and *The Master Butcher's Singing Club* (2003) is about Germans much like Erdrich's paternal forebears. Erdrich and Dorris collaborated on *The CROWN OF COLUMBUS* (1991) about academic life at Dartmouth and a hunt for a mysterious treasure in the Caribbean. Her most recent novel, *The Painted Drum* (2005), weaves three different tales surrounding a found artifact, an Ojibwa drum (made from the bones of Fleur's older sister).

Although known principally for her novels, Erdrich is a respected poet and short story writer. Her awards include the Pushcart Prize in Poetry and the O. Henry Prize for short fiction. Her first book of poetry, JACKLIGHT, appeared in 1984, and her second, BAPTISM OF DESIRE in 1989.

Erdrich examines many of the same themes in her poetry that she does in her fiction: issues of identity, particularly among MIXED-BLOOD individuals; the painful nature of love; and the use of myth in literature. In *Jacklight* her poetic voice is cynical, conversational, and very direct, but as in her novels, realism often has a surrealistic dimension. For instance, "Rugaroo," a portrait of an alcoholic relative, begins with very concrete, specific details and quickly moves into the surreal, describing the man's arms falling off like branches and being thrown into a ditch.

In her second collection, *The Baptism of Desire*, Erdrich turns her attention to religion, a subject that becomes increasingly important in her novels, especially *Last Report*. Erdrich was raised a Catholic, and although in her adult life she ceased to be a communicant, she remained a "cultural Catholic," fascinated with the religion. In *Baptism* Erdrich has poems on the Virgin Mary, Mary Magdalene, St. Teresa, and St. Clare, the disciple of St. Francis. Her most interesting and controversial poems are about Jesus, however, especially the poem about St. Thomas, the doubter, who was reputed in the apocryphal Acts of Thomas to be Christ's twin. Erdrich's Thomas fakes stigmata to become the figure the church makes into Jesus, which she claims was then "sold" to the world.

Erdrich has also written a memoir, *The Blue Jay's Dance* (1995), depicting relationships between mother and child, and two children's books, *Grandmother's Pigeon* (1996) and *The Birchbark House* (1999).

Several of her stories appear in the Best American Short Stories series. Other achievements include a Guggenheim Fellowship, the Western Literary Association Award, and the Returning the Gift Lifetime Achievement Award.

Erdrich's life has not been without tragedies. Her oldest child and only son died when hit by an automobile. In 1996 she and Dorris separated; a year later Dorris committed suicide. Erdrich has returned to the Great Plains, where she resides in Minneapolis and runs a bookstore with her three youngest children.

Bibliography

Beidler, Peter G. A *Reader's Guide to the Novels of Louise Erdrich.* Columbia: University of Missouri Press, 1999.

Erdrich, Karen Louise. *The Antelope Wife.* New York: HarperFlamingo, 1998.

———. *The Beet Queen.* New York: Holt, 1986.

———. *The Bingo Palace.* New York: HarperCollins, 1994.

———. *The Last Report on the Miracles at Little No Horse.* New York: HarperCollins, 2001.

———. *Love Medicine.* New York: HarperPerennial, 1993.

———. *Tales of Burning Love.* New York: HarperCollins, 1996.

———. *Tracks.* New York: Henry Holt, 1998.

Jacobs, Connie A. *The Novels of Louise Erdrich: Stories of Her People.* New York: Peter Lang, 2001.

Faces in the Moon Betty Louise Bell (1994)

Bell's praised first novel depicts a complex, realistic Native female identity that addresses the complexity of a MIXED-BLOOD ancestry and demonstrates the political nature of Native writing.

The adult protagonist Lucie Evers remembers how she "was raised on the voices of women. Indian women" (4), with whom, she continuously asserts, one should not trifle. Three generations of Cherokee and mixed-blood women are depicted: Lucie's great-aunt, Lizzie, fosters her as a child and teaches her the stories of her past: Lucie places her ancestors in historical events such as the TRAIL OF TEARS and the Allotment times of the DAWES ACT, and she learns the story of the legendary Comanche rebel Quanah Parker, and about her grandmother, Hellen, whose devotion to her daughters cannot help Gracie (Momma) and Rozella (Auney) escape a life of abusive white men, poverty, and drinking. Gracie rejects her Indian heritage, bleaches and perms her hair in order to look more white, and overlooks the sexual and psychological abuse of her daughter Lucie by her boyfriend. When she abandons Lucie to Lizzie's care, however, she is actually saving the girl from continuing her own painful life by allowing her to reconnect to her tribal past.

Lucie hates her mother for her betrayal and for what she has become, except when she is telling her stories. She also has to come to terms with her need to run away from her past and the pull of the storytellers' kitchen table. This complex relationship to her mother and past determines Lucie's main adult choices: She marries and divorces a Jewish man, and she finally becomes a professor of English literature in California. It is when her mother is dying and Lucie returns home and reads Gracie's attempt to write the story of her life for her that she ultimately understands and forgives her. Lucie then finds her place in a lineage of Native women who are watching her from the Moon and who embody her memory and future: "I am centuries of Indian women" (192).

Far from becoming a nostalgic search for her past, however, Lucie's reconnection to Indianness and womanhood through the Moon is expressed as an affirmation of transformed continuance. At the end of the novel she confronts the white librarian at the Oklahoma Historical Society, who claims he has the power to tell her who she is, and threatens his control of history. Because Western words will not tell the truth about her, she will resort to her ancestors' hunger to talk and transform their powerful stories into written text. When she tells the librarian, "I am your worst nightmare: I am an Indian with a pen" (192), she is embodying the political implications of contemporary Native writing and their redefinition of their own identity.

Bibliography

Hilden, Patricia Penn. *"Faces in the Moon." American Indian Culture and Research Journal* 18, no. 3 (1994): 295–298.

Maddox, Lucy. "The Indian Writer: America's Worst Nightmare?" *Anglo-Saxónica* 2, nos. 10–11 (1999): 377–393.

Silvia Martínez Falquina

Fight Back: For the Sake of the People For the Sake of the Land   Simon Ortiz (1980)

A poet, fiction writer, and essayist from Acoma Pueblo, New Mexico, SIMON ORTIZ celebrates and gives voice to the oral tradition of indigenous storytelling as the basis of his people's existence.

The poems collected in *Fight Back: For the Sake of the People For the Sake of the Land* revolve around the interdependency between the land and Acoma Pueblo people: Ortiz looks at how centuries of European and American imperialism deeply altered that relationship, yet at the same time he depicts his people as a strong and assertive one in the fight against ASSIMILATION and cultural loss.

"Fight Back" is the phrase that best exemplifies Ortiz's poetics: In fact, over and over again in his work he advocates the appropriation of the colonizer's language in the struggle for his own people's land and historical truth. The uniqueness of his style—ranging from the use of Native words to colloquial and traditional storytelling speech—consolidates the central idea of a language that emerges from the earth and that shapes human experience in unison with the rhythms of nature, hence, the consistent presence in these lines of "all-important items" such as seeds and corn, whose symbolic meanings invite a return to traditional and spiritual ways of knowing. The collection is scattered with images of labor force exploitation and of capitalist abuse of the natural environment: The poem "We Have Been Told Many Things but We Know This to Be True" offers a clear example. Here the inextricable connection between the land and the people is sealed by the verb *to work*: Its reiteration gives the poem an extraordinary sense of dynamism that is fostered, in its turn, by the speaker's implacable desire to receive life and give it back to the land. These lines also emphasize the historical significance of human labor for indigenous people: As Ortiz states, today's unification of factory workers, miners, and farmers across different ethnic groups is nothing but the continuation of a "legacy of resistance" inaugurated by the Pueblo Revolt of 1680. In the long concluding piece "No more Sacrifices" written both in verse and in prose, Ortiz denounces, very sharply, the violation of human rights and the deaths that decades of "Western progress"—railroad development and uranium mining—have been disseminating across New Mexico.

Bibliography

Ortiz, Simon J. *Fightin': New and Collected Stories.* Chicago: Thunder's Mouth, 1983.

———. ed. *Speaking for the Generations. Native Writers on Writing.* Tucson: University of Arizona Press, 1998.

———. *Telling and Showing Her: The Earth, the Land.* Buffalo, N.Y.: Just Buffalo Literary Center, 1995.

———, and Rudolfo Anaya, eds. *A Ceremony of Brotherhood (1680–1980).* Albuquerque, N. Mex.: Academia, 1981.

Dina Fachin

First Indian on the Moon   Sherman Alexie (1993)

Appearing early in SHERMAN ALEXIE's publishing career, *First Indian on the Moon* is poetry, predominantly prose poetry, arranged under thematically connected headings. Each subsection opens with an epigram selected from the writing of a minority author: Lucille Clifton, LINDA HOGAN, Lorna Dee Cervantes, Donna Brook, and JOY HARJO. These narrative poems have a rhetorical edge that does not forsake artfulness. *First Indian on the Moon* is poetic, not prosaic, with a careful attention to form that is lively and experimental, and never structurally pedantic.

For example, in "Occupational Hazards" the seventh stanza departs from the tercet of the other stanzas and instead appears with line breaks indicated by a back-slash, as the quoted lines of a poem appear in expository prose, and in this way the stanza appears as prose but maintains the rhythm of separate lines. This same convention is employed in "Billy Jack." Some of the poems, such as "Reservation Mathematics," move between prose and poetry presentation on the page, making them even more difficult to define by genre. The sequences in "House(fires)" and "Collect Calls" are linked vignettes created by repeating the ending of one movement as the beginning of the next. In these ways Alexie demonstrates his command of the formal characteristics of poetry, not binding himself to them, but rather incorporating them in innovative ways with a freshness of image.

The other significant repetitions in the book are its six anchors: Crazy Horse, alcohol, Lester FallsApart, fire, fancydancing, and old blankets. They are characters in the overarching story being told, acknowledging the past and its continued existence. Alexie's strategies are by turns poignant, ironic, humorous, and angry. The poems depend on the richness and range of his fully developed voice, which does not resort to maudlin emotion or strident, shrill polemic, or stale, stereotypical images. Many of the poems add an aboriginal twist to dominant cultural perceptions, as in "Year of the Indian" and its meditations on New Year's Day, Groundhog Day, St. Patrick's Day, and Veteran's Day, among others.

Alexie frequently readdresses assumptions and interpretations and regularly makes sure his readers cannot forget the social conditions under which American Indians (his preferred term) live. This is done through diction that includes "commodity cheese" and the Housing and Urban Development "HUD house." These poems strike a balanced posture by speaking of both love and treaties, and even of love treaties, so that the varied tones and subjects do not become tiresome. The collection's first poem, "Influences," remarks three times, "This is not about sadness. This is about the stories" (9–10), and near the end of the book, in "Captivity," Alexie reveals that "the best weapons are the stories" (99). Sadness cannot change anything, but stories can.

Bibliography

Alexie, Sherman. *First Indian on the Moon.* Brooklyn: Hanging Loose Press, 1993.

Brill de Ramirez, Susan Berry. *Contemporary American Indian Literatures and the Oral Tradition.* Tucson: University of Arizona Press, 1999.

McFarland, Ron. "'Another Kind of Violence': Sherman Alexie's Poems." *American Indian Quarterly* 21, no. 2 (spring 1997): 251–264.

A. Mary Murphy

First Nations literature

Any discussion of First Nations literature should open with two important questions: What is First Nations? And what is literature? The Canadian government has implemented the term *First Nations* to recognize the presence of the original people of the land before European visitations and subsequent colonization. The term *literature* suggests a written tradition not found among First Nations communities until after they had learned English or French and become literate. Immediately this definition runs the risk of ignoring oral narratives that existed previously. As with the literature of the indigenous people of the United States, simply defining the terms can prove difficult.

First Nations literature that precedes European contact was generally not written and survives only in translation. Normally referred to as oral literature, these texts represent precontact life and lore. Often it was only text that interested most translators and the identity of the speaker or owner of the song was never recorded; rather, just a simple tribal affiliation was noted. Thus, within traditional song, anthologies normally include such titles as "My breath" and "Magic words" attributed to the Inuit; or the "Fragments of a Song" and "Song for Medicine Hunting" attributed even more generally to "Southern First Nations." The translators often provided the title for the text and the typical tribal attribution for the text rather than any individual name.

The boundaries between orality and literature will fuse as we proceed to the next phase and the issue of First Nations identity becomes prominent.

Identity has been problematic for First Nations from the very first contact experience and has remained an essential concern. Depictions of early contact represent images that are still common among Canadians and the rest of the world. From early artistic depictions and literary descriptions of First Nations peoples, conflicting images begin to flood the colonial and European minds, often unflattering to First Nations communities. By the time they could address those depictions Canada and the rest of the world had already ensconced the false images. Even the First Nations peoples would succumb to erroneous imagery that perpetuates misrepresentation of their communities. The subsequent literary impact was an inability to discern authentic First Nations voices from voices that conform to the popular images of First Nations people. Thus, identity and confusion about identity become dominant themes for early First Nations writers. The texts that emerge from contact signal an important transition, as a First Nations person is assimilated to the colonial culture.

Early First Nations authors wrote intentionally trying to voice a sense of identity that was not akin to the popular versions promulgated by Euro-Canadian artists and authors. It is very important to see that First Nations people see themselves in the context of their own community. Joseph Brant, a Mohawk man, tried to express this notion of community when writing to Captain Green about the land he and his tribe were promised, but never received. Brant's letter, written in 1798, is one of the earliest First Nations texts written in English. It addresses concerns that later First Nations authors would echo, including resistance, fair treatment, respect, hunting and fishing rights, land stewardship, formal education, relationship with the newly formed governments, and the issue of identity. While all of these are important, the issue of identity would become a primary concern for all the subsequent First Nations authors.

Kah-ge-ga-gah-bowh, also known as George Copway, was an Ojibwe man who instantiates the conversion to Christianity and an eclectic ASSIMILATION to the early Canadian culture. His father, a medicine man and one of the chiefs of the Rice Lake Indian Village, adopted the Christian faith.

Copway converted to Christianity at the age of 12 and studied at Ebenezer Methodist Seminary in Jacksonville, Illinois. His accomplishments include translating part of the Bible into Ojibwe and writing his autobiography in 1847.

Copway's autobiography reveals much about his identity, his love for his people, and his concern for their well-being. One of the most important aspects of identity is language, and Copway's introduction to his autobiography reveals self-consciousness about writing in English about himself because English is not his first language. Not only is language a concern, but so is ethnicity. He begins by acknowledging, "The Christian will no doubt feel for my people, when he hears the story of one brought from that unfortunate race called the Indians" (17). Copway then recalls the life he lived before his conversion and how his new perspective has allowed him to be a voice to his people for God and a liaison for them to the encroaching colonialists. He writes with passion about his identity in Christ and does not discount the truth when colonial inconsistencies contradict the message of the gospel. He simply challenges the colonialists to live as they believe and treat the Indians with respect in all matters pertaining to their lives, including their land, hunting and fishing rights, their education, and ultimately, their continued survival. He warns the reader of impending judgment from God because of their treatment of the First Nations communities: "to save the Indians, and consolidate, and perpetuate peace between them and us, and by doing so, ward off the terrible retribution which must sooner or later, unless it be averted, fall upon this nation" (25).

Another representative voice of the contact phase is that of Nah-nee-bah-wee-quay, or Catherine Soneegoh Sutton. Her name means "upright woman' in Ojibway, and her life reveals similarities to Copway's; she is educated away from her home and then returns after her education. She was a tireless advocate for her tribe and their rights to the land, for citizenship, and especially for identity. Two issues that she confronts in her letter response to an 1864 editorial in *The Leader* are identity and the right to exist. The editorial lamented the condition of reserves and portrayed the First Nations people as monkeys. Nah-nee-bah-wee-quay's response reveals penetrating intellect as she observes characteristics of monkeys and then retorts, "The same trait stands out prominently in his natural disposition and character . . . an entire lack of humanity" and concludes that the editor exhibits more traits of the monkeys than the Indians do (26). She then argues the regardless of the condition of the reserve, the Indians have a right to exist, and a right to the titles of their land and should be paid fairly for their land. She also notes that the deplorable conditions of the reserve are also found in the colonial settlements and if the editor were to be consistent, the settlers should also be banished as well. What is most evident concerning this emerging literature is the feature of resistance, of not allowing colonization to annihilate rights, being, and culture of First Nations communities. Resistance becomes a dominant theme in subsequent First Nations writing.

As the transition to the postcontact period ensues, a focus on culture and history dominates the literature with accounts of narratives and history; subsequently the First Nations authors begin to explore the realm of creative literature. Early in this period writers are still focused on the issue of identity, the relationship of their people to their land, the issue of harmony, the role of oral discourse in their community, the transmission of these aspects to their children, and more strongly focused resistance. Challenges to Christianity's claim of truth begin and some authors reject the church and maintain allegiance to the traditional ways.

Observing traditions then becomes very problematic because during this phase the Canadian government with the aid of various church denominations abducts many children from their homes and communities in order to educate them in government BOARDING SCHOOLS. The ultimate goal is assimilation to Canadian culture, annihilating First Nations culture. With the advent of residential schools the government ruthlessly implemented methodical cultural reprogramming that targeted every aspect of First Nations culture.

This educational practice began with the stated goal of civilizing the First Nations. As the 20th century began, the efforts to civilize these students invariably included the elimination of every aspect of First Nations community life that the children had known. They had to endure a resocialization process that included a harsh transition from an informal mode of learning to a formal mode. The students had to learn and speak English and only English, or swift punishment resulted. One devastating result of this education was that the students no longer felt part of the First Nations community and because of their ethnicity could never be part of mainstream Canada. They no longer spoke their language, and they did not know their history. Thus, being purely traditional could never be possible again, though many First Nations authors tried to recover from this cultural upheaval. This loss included language, oral history, cultural practices, and even of traditional names. MARIA CAMPBELL addresses these issues thoroughly and emotionally in her autobiography, *Halfbreed* (1973). An anomaly at the time, a book about Natives by a Native, this text helped to break down some of the doors to mainstream publishing as it effectively traced the racism and sexism Campbell had encountered as a Native in Canada. Campbell focuses on the plight of the "half-breeds"—in Canada known as Métis. She describes them as being forced to the margins of society, denied both the rights of First Nations Indians under the Indian Act and the entry into white society that would treat them as full-fledged Canadians. This work is noted as the first text by a contemporary Native woman that openly discusses the oppression they all felt.

Another important nonfiction writer is BASIL JOHNSTON, whose work tends to focus on the intersections between Native language and English (he is fluent in both English and Anishnabe), as well as the importance of mythology and SPIRITUALITY in the Ojibway community. Johnston writes in a variety of genres and mediums and is a crucial resource for understanding the traditional ways of his tribe. Although his work is clearly tribally specific, one can apply the theory of honoring the indigenous in a way that is pan-Indian.

A flowering of significant First Nations novels began in the 1980s, shortly after the AMERICAN IN-

DIAN LITERARY RENAISSANCE in the United States. Beatrice Culleton's (later Mosionier) *In Search of April Raintree* (1983) remains a crucial text because of the way in which it examines the problem of First Nations children in the foster care system. It was based loosely on Culleton's own experiences and was widely read across Canada.

More well-known outside Canada are novelists such as JEANNETTE ARMSTRONG, RUBY SLIPPERJACK-FARRELL, and THOMAS KING. Although King was born in the United States, be moved to Canada in 1980 and sets much of his work there. He is also the editor of an important anthology of First Nations literature, *ALL MY RELATIONS*.

First Nations literature—precontact, contact, and postcontact—includes aspects of strong cultural ties to identification, land, survival, and resistance. Within the communities' struggle for survival there is a strong desire for tradition, especially esteem for oral traditions. The problem of vanishing First Nations languages exacerbates the current lament in the literature as linguistic skill directly impacts the identity conflict. Thus, in First Nations literature the authors resist colonialism and negotiate identity within their communities while fusing the two traditions of oral culture and literature into orature.

Bibliography

Armstrong, Jeannette. *Looking at the Words of Our People: First Nations Analysis of Literature.* Penticton, Canada: Theytus, 1993.

Hulan, Renee. *Native North America.* Toronto: ECW Press, 1999.

Moses, Daniel David, and Terry Goldie, eds. *An Anthology of Canadian Native Literature in English.* Don Mills, Canada: Oxford University Press, 1992.

Frederick White
Jennifer McClinton-Temple

Five Civilized Tribes

The Five Civilized Tribes were a loose federation of Indian nations consisting of the Cherokee, Chickasaw, Choctaw, Creek, and Seminole, occupying lands once belonging to the Osage and Quapaw. The term was invented by European Americans to refer to this group of Indian nations.

The federation was established in 1859, after the forced removal of the five nations from their ancestral homelands in the Southeast to the Indian Territory in what is today Oklahoma (1838–60). The term *Five Civilized Tribes* has been in use ever since. As late as 1971 the Bureau of Indian Affairs developed regulations incorporating the term "Five Civilized Tribes," and the City of Muskogee still maintains the Five Civilized Tribes Museum in what once was the home and office of the superintendent of the Indian agency assigned to the federation.

Civilized refers to a tactic employed by the five nations in their fight against removal, which involved the adaptation and incorporation of aspects of white culture in tribal society. A small part of the cultural work done by these adaptations was meant to persuade the United States that the so-called civilization policy begun by the Washington administration had done its intended work, that is, that the five nations were already "civilized" by the standards of the early republic, and forced removal from ancestral lands was, hence, unnecessary. For instance, prior to REMOVAL the Cherokee Nation developed a writing system, adopted a constitution modeled after that of the United States, adopted standardized laws, established a court system, began plantation-style farming, and were in the process of building a capital city (New Echota). Despite undeniable evidence of the supposed success of the civilization policy, the five nations were still removed. The label *civilized* is, thus, a product of these early adaptations of aspects of American culture, which continued after removal as each nation established centralized government, a system of laws, a public school system, and so forth.

Though the term *Five-Civilized Tribes* has been legitimized in federal policy—there are even a series of congressional laws, such as the Five Civilized Tribes Citizenship Act (1901), that bear the name—the imposed label has been less formally accepted by the members of the Indian nations included, and some insist that merging onetime enemies under this label was a means of colonialization and control. There are and have been, however, many exceptions. For instance, the Creek Nation donated the land for the federation's Union Indian Agency because it saw the centralization of the various national governments as advantageous.

The descendants of these forcibly removed tribes have been prolific in their contributions to Indian literature. ALEXANDER POSEY, born in Indian Territory in 1873, celebrated his Creek tribe's past in his poems, while gaining national acclaim for the Fus Fixico letters, which satirized life in Indian Territory. Contemporary authors such as LINDA HOGAN, DIANE GLANCY, and JOY HARJO all reflect their heritage as members of this confederation of tribes, frequently addressing issues of displacement and destructive federal policy, issues central to the legacy of the Civilized Tribes.

See also SOUTHEASTERN TRIBAL LITERATURE; GOVERNMENT AGENCIES.

Bibliography

Cotterill, R. S. *The Southern Indians: The Story of the Civilized Tribes before Removal.* New York: Textbook, 2003.

Steve Brandon

Flutie   Diane Glancy (1998)

In this novel DIANE GLANCY gives her young female character a voice that overcomes the silence derived from colonial and patriarchal domination. Through this voice contemporary Native American literature and identity are shown to be compounds of Native and Western influences, a recognition that leads to survival and wholeness.

Flutie lives in Vini, a small town in western Oklahoma offering scarce opportunities. Her own family is an example of poverty and violence, upon which she blames her frustrating inability to talk to anybody outside her closest circle: She chokes, silenced by an ocean that threatens to drown her and make her disappear (22–23), an image that reflects the process that makes Native Americans invisible. Her inarticulateness stems from her lack of stories to relate to the land; her father, to whom she resorts in search for a link with her heritage as a Cherokee—a people displaced from Georgia to Oklahoma during Andrew Jackson's presidency—tells her that there are no stories left, that he had to drop them for they could not tell about his loss (14). Flutie, however, strives to listen to the "tongues of the land" (47) and, through them, to her ancestors speaking the old language (17).

In her search for a language Flutie identifies with the Greek mythological story of Philomela, whose sister's husband rapes her and cuts her tongue off. Afterward she weaves a tapestry to reveal the crime and escapes transformed into a bird, an animal to which Flutie is constantly related in her quest for freedom. In combination with this Western mythological association, Flutie is also depicted as a deer, a portrayal that moves her close to the Native side of her heritage and the Oklahoma landscape. The syncretism of Flutie's characterization is reflected on her hybrid visions, such as the spirit being who reflects her dual heritage and is reminiscent of MIXED-BLOOD Kateri Tekakwitha, whose image is reproduced on the book cover.

Flutie looks for a firm connection to place that combines both the Native and the Western vision: She listens to the voicings of the land of her ancestors and she will study geology to acquire a scientific way of knowing. Before she can overcome her inability to talk, however, she needs to strengthen her sense of belonging. This she achieves during a sweat lodge ceremony when her elders and helpers show her their support, and she finds a place in sisterhood with the dispossessed of the world. She then decides she will go to college and then go home to teach other people how to talk, so her voice returns to her community. A fragmented and silenced mixed-blood woman whose tongue has been symbolically cut off, Flutie learns to link that tongue to land and community, weaving both Native and Western stories and influences and becoming an active subject in the telling of her own story.

Bibliography

Fitz, Brewster E. "Philomela on the Plains: Remarks on Mixedblood Intertextual Metaphor in Diane Glancy's *Flutie*." *Studies in American Indian Literatures* 11, no. 2 (1999): 79–87.

Silvia Martínez Falquina

Foghorn   Hanay Geiogamah (1980)

This satirical and disconnected parade of stereotypes was produced in 1973 and published in 1980. *Foghorn,* a riotous commentary on the treatment of the American Indian (GEIOGAMAH's terminology), embraces a Brechtian epic approach to this history, as [it creates an alienating distance that clarifies] the truth of five centuries of American Indian's fighting for their identity under the control of European settlers. The play, named for the foghorns around Alcatraz Island, moves jarringly through history by using a series of recognizable and overblown characters in disconnected scenes. The characters include a nun who is holding the Yellow Pages in place of a Bible, accompanied by an altar boy holding a cross covered in paper money; a schoolteacher who insults her Indian students until they converge upon her in a show of mob violence; Pocahontas, who giggles with her friends about the color and fleeting virility of Captain John Smith; participants in the 1969–71 occupation of Alcatraz Island; the first lady of the United States, Ladybird Johnson, as she reappropriates reservation land for a national park; and the Lone Ranger plotting Tonto's death moments before Tonto slits the Lone Ranger's throat. Each scene represents a different epoch in the legacy of the American Indian and reverses the traditional interpretation of history. The audience sees conventional American history from the point of view of the American Indians as they are moved from their land, converted at the hands of Christian MISSIONARIES, taught to speak English by settlers, and finally arrested at the 1973 siege of WOUNDED KNEE.

In addition to the text, the play is a combination of media, sound, and motion. Typical of Geiogamah's works, it includes precise stage directions for actors' motions and guidelines for music, song, and sound that accompany each scene. The scenes are connected with sounds of drilling and images of earth being drilled. Geiogamah explains in his introductory note that the play is best performed with an emphasis on the slapstick and comedic, assured that this approach will allow the serious and tragic to emerge with greater force. The play represents the eternal spirit of the American Indian, first forced from their land by settlers, finally arrested at Wounded Knee. All the while, there remains a group solidarity of spirit.

Bibliography

Huntsman, Jeffrey. *New Native American Drama: Three Plays by Hanay Geiogamah.* Norman: University of Oklahoma Press, 1980.

Lincoln, Kenneth. "Indi'ns Playing Indians." *MELUS* 16, no. 3 (fall 1989–90): 91–98.

———. "Appendix C: Interview with Hanay Geiogamah." In *Indi'n Humor: Bicultural Play in Native America,* 326–377. New York: Oxford University Press, 1993.

Angela Courtney

Food and Spirits   Beth Brant (1991)

BETH BRANT's short-story collection *Food and Spirits* affirms two-spirit perspectives in many American Indian cultures, in which homosexuals have long held unique roles in their communities. Brant, who is Mohawk, explains that as a Native lesbian, she is motivated to write by her power to use language to give wholeness to her community, creating beautiful offerings in the spirit of American Indian giveaway traditions. According to Tara Prince-Hughes in this restorative spirit Brant and other gay Native writers emphasize the abilities and responsibilities of two-spirit characters to contribute to their societies in traditional ways, offering alternatives to Western understandings of homosexuals' social roles (10). In *Food and Spirits* characters face adversity because of their gender identities but nonetheless serve their communities in significant capacities, fulfilling roles as creators, seers, and guardians.

The collection begins with "This Is History," which initiates Brant's characterization of the power of feminine creativity. The narrative recounts Mother Turtle's creation of the Earth and of Sky Woman, the world's first inhabitant. In contrast to the biblical creation story, Brant portrays Turtle's creative persona as distinctly female, and bestows upon Sky Woman the responsibility of naming all creatures and of giving birth to the first human, First Woman. First Woman becomes Sky

Woman's lover and companion, and together they create music, pray, and observe the cycles of nature. Ultimately, after Sky Woman dies, the moon informs First Woman that she will give birth to the Twin Sons and that she is to instruct the sons to honor their Mother. The tale ends as First Woman is waiting "for the beings who would change her world" (26). The story thereby offers a portrait of femininity and female love that is creative and life-affirming and of masculinity that is a source of some harm.

Brant's introductory story is the foundation for later selections in *Food and Spirits,* which present characters who are wounded psychologically and sometimes physically but who achieve healing power through feminine traits. From Violet, the protagonist of "Wild Turkeys," who through communing with women at a diner is able to articulate her pain resulting from her husband's abuse; to James William of "Turtle Gal," who adopts a needy nine-year-old and becomes a foster father to her with the assistance of his dead lover, Brant's characters honor Sky Woman, whose legacy is an alternative to the male-dominated society that surrounds them.

Bibliography

Brant, Beth. "Giveaway: Native Lesbian Writers." *Signs: Journal of Women in Culture and Society* 18, no. 4 (summer 1993): 944–947.

Cullum, Linda. "Survival's Song: Beth Brant and the Power of the Word." *MELUS* 24, no. 3 (fall 1993): 129–140.

Prince-Hughes, Tara. "Contemporary Two-Spirit Identity in the Fiction of Paula Gunn Allen and Beth Brant." *Studies in American Indian Literatures* 10, no. 4 (winter 1998): 9–31.

Lindsey Smith

Fools Crow   James Welch (1986)

Published in 1986, *Fools Crow* is considered by many scholars and critics to be JAMES WELCH's greatest achievement. Set in 1869–70 in the Two Medicine Territory of northern Montana, the novel follows the life and maturing of Fools Crow, a member of the Lone Eater band of Blackfeet Indians. However, the novel is more than a mere bildungsroman; it also mourns the loss of the Great Plains Indian peoples.

Born White Man's Dog, Fools Crow leads an unremarkable life in his youth. Son of Rides-at-the-Door, a leader of the Pikuni people and honored warrior, Fools Crow does not become a significant member of his tribe until his success on a horse-stealing party against the Crow. This party is led by Yellow Kidney, one of the tribe's most respected leaders. Before this party Fast Horse, a friend of Fools Crow and son of Boss Ribs, a heavy-singer-for-the-sick and keeper of the Beaver Medicine bundle, has a vision of Cold Maker. In this vision Fast Horse learns that in order to protect the safety of the party, he must visit a particular spring and move a rock for Cold Maker, as a sign of his faith. His failure in performing this task leads to the party's loss of Yellow Kidney, who is captured, is tortured, and eventually returns to the Pikuni camp crippled and unable to care for his family.

Fools Crow—so renamed for a later episode when he is thought to be a Crow in the heat of battle—marries Red Paint, Yellow Kidney's daughter, and takes over the responsibility of providing for the family. This is one of the two changes in Fools Crow's life that lead to his maturity and earn him the respect of his tribe. After participating in the Sun Dance, a painful ritual involving dancing around a pole while flesh is torn off by straps attached from the pole to the body, Fools Crow is given a vision of Wolverine, his spirit animal, whose song gives him strength and whose guidance will help him to live his life as a man of the tribe.

However, despite his original desires, Fools Crow does not become a warrior. Instead, he apprentices himself to Mik-api, an aging medicine man. Over the course of his apprenticeship, and through the main body of the novel, Fools Crow becomes a healer for his people, healing both the physical wounds suffered by his tribe as well as the emotional wounds accumulated as the tribe (and all the Blackfeet tribes) increasingly are subjugated by the Napikwans (their word for the white people spreading west). In a development both historically accurate as well as symbolic, the Blackfeet tribes, including the Pikuni, fall ill with small-pox—the white-scabs—a disease introduced by the Napikwans. Smallpox decimates the Blackfeet, forcing hardships on a people already suffering a loss of game, an inability to provide as well as in past years, and the encroachment of a people bent on taking away their lands and ending their way of life.

This new way of life is best seen in the person of Fast Horse, who left the Pikuni after his humiliation when Yellow Kidney was captured. Living away from his people and following the renegade Owl Child, Fast Horse increasingly drops his tribal ways in favor of white ways. He takes to spending time at white forts, drinking white man's whiskey, and loses his spiritual connection to his people and the land. Acting as both tribal healer and friend, Fools Crow sets out to take Fast Horse back, to restore him to his tribal ways, to ease the pain of his aging father, and to heal the sickness—both real and symbolic—of which his tribe suffers.

In perhaps the most vividly detailed and symbolically rich section of the novel, Fools Crow is shown a vision by Feather Woman, a spiritual being he has sought out for help for his people. In this vision Fools Crow is shown a congregation of the many tribes during a Sun Dance ceremony, the Hard Topknots, Never Laughs, Grease Melters, Many Chiefs, as well as his own Lone Eaters. The white-scabs disease has ravaged the tribes in this vision and is followed by the entrance of the Napikwans into tribal lands and the disappearance of the blackhorns (bison), the economic basis of Pikuni culture. At the end of the vision Fools Crow is shown a picture of the reservation that will eventually occupy his homeland, and the Pikuni children being raised on it, dressed as Napikwans and happily playing their games.

By the close of the novel Fools Crow's wife is pregnant, his tribe prepares for a great feast, and the blackhorns are returning to provide food and economic security to the tribe. However, despite this hopeful ending, the imminent decimation is at hand with the Massacre of the Marias in 1870.

In his novel describing the last days of the Pikuni, Welch provides for his readers a detailed account of the cultural, religious, and economic lifestyle of Blackfeet people. *Fools Crow* is a powerful lamentation for a culture whose life was forever changed by the close of the 19th century.

Bibliography

Ballard, Charles G. "The Question of Survival in *Fools Crow*." *North Dakota Quarterly* 59, no. 4 (spring 1991): 251–259.

McFarland, Ron, ed. *James Welch.* Lewiston, N.Y.: Confluence, 1986.

Velie, Alan. "The Indian Historical Novel." *Genre* 25, no. 4 (winter 1992): 391–406.

James J. Donahue

49   Hanay Geiogamah (1980)

Named for a casual social gathering of young American Indians that involves singing, dancing, and drinking, usually after a more official or ceremonial event such as a POW WOW, *49* creates an eternal community to represent the spirit of the intertribal Indian community. The play was produced in 1975 and published in 1980. At its most basic level the play is a series of vignettes that constitute the events of the midnight to dawn revels of the 49, but HANAY GEIOGAMAH adds to the festivities an omnipresent spiritual voice and the unseen though frequently heard off-stage voice of police authority. The Night Walker, the tribal spiritual leader who transcends time, ties together the past, present, and future as he moves freely among the eras. He worries for the future of the young people. Their frivolous, dangerous, and divisive actions at the 49 concern him, and he doubts that the youth will have the strength to maintain the solidarity needed to hold together the community. As the 49 continues the thoughts and actions of the police are announced on their radios as they try throughout the play to surround the large group of partygoers and put an end to the revelry. The play ends as those who attended the 49 join arms and move outward, warding off the encroaching authorities and acting as one in a show of force against the still unseen police. This final action assures the Night Walker that the young people indeed respect and maintain the values and beliefs of the past. This gesture represents the eternal spirit inherent in the American Indian community, and as long as the spirit of solidarity is intact so, too, is the community.

The setting for this play requires little, demanding that the actors create the space with their actions and calling upon the audience to use their collective imagination. In the place of Geiogamah's usual exploitation of visual projections and aural stimuli, he instead uses the Night Walker to create the sense of eternal community. This play subordinates the external societal forces that denigrate the Indian communities—forces that cross tribal boundaries and belittle the entire race—and it emphasizes the power and strength the American Indian possesses when as a group they share a common goal.

Bibliography

Huntsman, Jeffrey. *New Native American Drama: Three Plays by Hanay Geiogamah.* Norman: University of Oklahoma Press, 1980.

Lincoln, Kenneth. "Indi'ns Playing Indians." *MELUS* 16, no. 3 (fall 1989–90): 91–98.

———. "Appendix C: Interview with Hanay Geiogamah," In *Indi'n Humor: Bicultural Play in Native America,* 326–377. New York: Oxford University Press, 1993.

Angela Courtney

Four Souls   Louise Erdrich (2004)

Four Souls, LOUISE ERDRICH's seventh novel chronicling the lives of the inhabitants of the Little No Horse Reservation in North Dakota, is a tale of revenge gone wrong. Fleur Pillager, one of Erdrich's most interesting characters, has left the reservation for the city, carrying the bones of her parents, to seek revenge on the white man who took her land. This story is a continuation of Fleur's life as described in *TRACKS,* in which the drama of Fleur's loss of land is described in detail. Revenge does not play out quite as Fleur has planned, however. She does, after a fashion, get her land back in the end, but at the expense of her Ojibwe identity.

Fleur's plan is to go to the city and kill John James Mauser (grandfather of Jack Mauser from *TALES OF BURNING LOVE*), the rich man who spent his youth marrying and discarding young Ojibwe women for their allotments under the DAWES ACT. She takes a job in his household as a laundress, ultimately becomes his wife, bears a child by him, and becomes an alcoholic. When she finally returns to the reservation, there is no trace of the woman she was, and her son is developmentally disabled, perhaps autistic (Erdrich is careful not to name the boy's disability using modern terms, but her descriptions sound a great deal like what we know as autism today). Margaret Kashpaw (Rushes Bear), who has been like a surrogate mother to Fleur, forces her to the island in the middle of Machimonoto Lake, in a sense to smoke out the poison of the city. She does return to her old self, but the damage she has done to her children, including Lulu, whom she abandoned at a BOARDING SCHOOL, is irreversible.

Fleur's revenge plan is not the only one that goes wrong in *Four Souls*. The old man Nanapush, who is clearly one of Erdrich's favorite characters, is obsessed with another old man, Shesheeb, half brother to Pauline Puyat (from *Tracks, LOVE MEDICINE, The BEET QUEEN, Tales of Burning Love,* and *The LAST REPORT OF THE MIRACLES AT LITTLE NO HORSE*). Shesheeb is Nanapush's longtime rival, whom he has tried to kill many times. In *Four Souls* he tries again, rigging a snare that will hang Shesheeb. Unfortunately Margaret is caught in the snare and is almost killed. About both revenge attempts Nanapush says, "Do you know what I'm telling you is a reflection of errors? There was Fleur's vengeance, which you'll see has an outcome unpredicted," and "my vengeance, which led down paths of perfect foolishness but which, at each juncture, seemed logical and sane" (204).

What makes the two failed plots worth the effort, however, is the way Margaret takes over the narrative at the end of the text. She begins to narrate her own chapters, transforms Fleur to her old self, and retains her love for Nanapush. In doing so, Margaret ends both stories by highlighting the values of love, trust, and family and by shunning the need for revenge, a lesson Erdrich clearly believes is crucial in the Indian community.

Jennifer McClinton-Temple

from Sand Creek   Simon Ortiz (1981)

In *from Sand Creek,* a book-length sequence of untitled short poems accompanied by prose fragments, SIMON ORTIZ attempts to document a massacre of Southern Cheyenne and Arapaho by the U.S. cavalry in 1864 and the effects of this historical event on Native people in the author's time. One of Ortiz's most explicitly political books, *from Sand Creek* won the 1981 Pushcart Prize for poetry published by a small press. The short, spare poems are marked by their short lines and emphasis on fragmentation. The prose segments—usually just one or two sentences—appear on the left-hand pages and typically explain or provide a context for the poems on the facing pages. Although the poems form a rough narrative and are linked by their setting and theme, they are frequently enigmatic and highly personal.

As an introductory note to the book explains, on November 19, 1864, the Colorado Volunteers and Fort Lyons troops—more than 700 men, led by Colonel John Chivington— attacked a camp of about 600 Southern Cheyenne and Arapaho at Sand Creek, in southwestern Colorado. Even though the native camp flew a flag indicating that they were at peace with the United States, the troops killed 133 Natives, including 105 women and children. The note concludes by observing that by the middle of 1865, the Cheyenne and Arapaho had been driven out of Colorado Territory.

Throughout *from Sand Creek* Ortiz calls attention to the selective historical memory and the willful ignorance that permit such events to be forgotten. One of the first poems in the book commands the reader, "Remember Sand Creek" and compares the 1864 massacre in Colorado to the massacre of Vietnamese civilians by U.S. soldiers at My Lai in 1968; neither event, the poem contends, commands much attention in the American imagination. The poem's exhortation, moreover, serves as a statement of purpose for *from Sand Creek* as a whole: Ortiz urges his readers to remember Sand Creek and to understand the cultural and historical forces that allow such atrocities to take place.

Ortiz is not solely concerned with historical fact, however; he also depicts his own experiences in southwestern Colorado. The book is primarily set in the Veterans Administration (VA) hospital in Fort Lyons, once the headquarters of Chivington's troops; Ortiz received treatment for alcoholism at this hospital in the 1970s, surrounded by veterans of the wars in Korea and Vietnam. Fellow patients—Toby, Billy, W., Nez, and others—appear repeatedly as characters in the book. These men are inhabitants of a contemporary world marked by alcoholism, gambling, illness, dereliction, and nuclear waste. Although Ortiz at times notes a camaraderie among the patients in the hospital—the men watch movies together and experience shared emotional responses to the films—the prevailing tone is one of deep unhappiness, both inside and outside the hospital. This landscape is also haunted by ghosts: Figures such as Black Kettle, a Cheyenne elder, lurk in the shadows.

In many of the poems Ortiz decries the history of American expansion westward, lamenting both its cultural and its ecological effects. He calls attention to the American appetite for raw materials— namely, wood, water, and minerals—and to the resultant environmental destruction. The railroad serves as a prominent symbol of the intrusion of the United States into western North America; the disappearance of the buffalo is one indicator of the railroad's effect. The first poem in the book deems America a burden but also announces the presence of "a spring wind / rising / from Sand Creek." In the rest of the collection Ortiz similarly alternates between a fierce critique of American history and politics and a fervent hope for a future of compassion and reconciliation. Ortiz is particularly critical of what he perceives as the self-righteousness and arrogance of the American drive into the West. The American refusal to admit any humility before the land, he asserts, has destroyed the wilderness and alienated people from their surroundings. In Ortiz's poems, then, present-day farmers are forced off their land and the country is dotted with ghost towns. In particular, Ortiz blames American Puritanism for turning hard-working immigrants into members of the political and social establishment, such as senators, bishops, MISSIONARIES, and heads of corporations.

Yet *from Sand Creek* calls for a "spiritual revolution," after which the country can be healed. As the book progresses, Ortiz develops his pivotal idea that a healthy anger will change the present state of affairs. This anger, he claims in one of the poems, will bring down the fortresslike walls of the Veterans Administration (VA) hospital in which he is trapped. Ortiz claims always to have loved America, and indeed the book concludes by referring to the dream of a better future rising "in this heart / which is our America." The present world that Ortiz depicts is, in many senses, a wasteland characterized by personal, environmental, and cultural loss. Yet despite the horrors of the past that Ortiz recalls and the bleakness of the present he experiences and describes, *from Sand Creek* concludes on a note of hopefulness, invoking a dream of love, knowledge, and compassion.

Bibliography

Bruchac, Joseph. "The Story Never Ends: An Interview with Simon Ortiz." In *Survival This Way: Interviews with American Indian Poets,* edited by Joseph Bruchac, 211–229. Tucson: University of Arizona Press, 1987.

Fast, Robin Riley. "'It Is Ours to Know': Simon J. Ortiz's *From Sand Creek.*" *Studies in American Indian Literatures* 12, no. 3 (2000): 52–63.

Purdy, John, and Blake Hausman. "A Conversation with Simon Ortiz." *Studies in American Indian Literatures* 12, no. 4 (2000): 1–14.

Silko, Leslie Marmon. "Language and Literature from a Pueblo Indian Perspective." In *English Literature: Opening Up the Canon,* edited by Leslie A. Fiedler and Houston A. Baker, Jr., 54–72. Baltimore: Johns Hopkins University Press, 1981.

Wiget, Andrew. *Simon Ortiz.* Boise, Idaho: Boise State University, 1986.

Nicholas Bradley

From Spirit to Matter Carol Lee Sanchez (1997)

From Spirit to Matter is a selection of the poetry by CAROL LEE SANCHEZ spanning the years 1969–96. Sanchez, or "Message Bringer Woman," is a New Mexico Native with a multicultural heritage that consists primarily of Laguna Pueblo and Lebanese-American ancestry. In addition to her work as a poet, Sanchez is a multicultural consultant, visual artist, teacher, and community activist.

Sanchez's work reflects her multicultural heritage. Within the poem "tribal chant" Sanchez describes and emphasizes her cultural heritage by effectively mixing the Spanish and English languages: "yo soy índia / pero no soy" (i am Indian / but i am not) (8–9).

The title, *From Spirit to Matter,* originated in the idea that all thought originates in spirit. Sanchez feels that the thoughts that build her poems are "a gift from spirit" and are subsequently transformed into matter when printed. The poems in "From Spirit to Matter" represent a diverse collection of Sanchez's work. She states that this collection characterizes the numerous stages of her personal and social consciousness. Such lifelong diversity is reflected in her poetry, which often traverses multidimensional themes of wonder, sarcasm, tragedy, change, belief, frustration, and place.

The section "Whistle Stops" was created from the images generated during her work as coordinator for the California Poets in Schools Program, a position that took her throughout the state. In this section each poem is titled for the particular California city or region it represents. In the poem "san francisco" Sanchez remarks that we must all decide who we are, who "lies trapped upon the page / unnamed / unspecified" (11–12). Identity, as Sanchez sees it, is a difficult question, as "so many lives seep through / my bones" (25–26).

Sanchez is particularly interested in the power of symbols. She writes, "Symbols release energy / move from mind to matter" (8–9). She further illustrates the origin of symbols in the poem "symbols." She writes that in the past humans recognized "nature's random paintings / as recorded reflections of / familiar things" (12–13). Her concluding poem, entitled "From Spirit to Matter," describes how the creation of the symbolic, or "matter," occurs: "beyond january sunsets / through golden doors of mercy" (1–2). She further illustrates that "within our fantasies of selves / god stuff swirled as invisible thought waiting to be born" (19–20).

This collection of poetry is the result of Sanchez's looking "underneath pale green rainbows" to find and impart her messages, which move from spirit to matter, through her, to us.

Bibliography

Sanchez, Carol Lee. *Excerpts from a Mountain Climber's Handbook.* San Francisco: Taurean Horn Press, 1985.

———. *From Spirit to Matter.* San Francisco: Taurean Horn Press, 1997.

———. *Message Bringer Woman.* San Francisco: Taurean Horn Press, 1977.

Aaron Denham

From the River's Edge   Elizabeth Cook-Lynn   (1990)

ELIZABETH COOK-LYNN's novella *From the River's Edge* represents a strong statement in defense of the SOVEREIGNTY of Native Americans. Since its message is overtly political, the novella has often been criticized. Some scholars consider the plot, and the trial in particular, a simple literary device that allows Cook-Lynn to comment upon and denounce the U.S. government's unjust and illegal actions toward her people.

The river the title refers to is the Missouri, which was dammed in order to provide electricity and running water to South Dakota. Indeed, while the plot revolves around the trial, the issue that dominates the background of the novella is the construction of the federally funded hydropower dam that caused the flooding of thousands of acres of tribal land belonging to the Crow Creek Agency. The land was illegally confiscated because it was protected by TREATIES signed by two sovereign nations, the U.S. federal government and the Sioux Nation.

The setting of the novella is therefore geographically and historically defined by the building of the Oahe Dam and reveals how place and history are inextricably intertwined with the Dakotan people who live in the area. The flooding destroyed plants, trees, and animals, making it impossible for traditional people to gather the medicine plants and practice the old ways. Hospitals, churches, and other buildings were destroyed as well, thus disrupting the lives of entire communities.

The illegal confiscation of tribal land finds a perfect reflection in the injustice of the trial itself, "an ongoing and consistent fraud, set up to make all of those concerned believe that justice in Indian Country was real" (*River's* 25). At the end of the trial the white defendant is found guilty of stealing Tatekeya's cattle but is free to walk out after paying his bail. Moreover, the stolen cows are never returned to Tatekeya. Both the construction of the dam and the trial prove that there is no justice for the Sioux Nation. And from destruction, suffering, and impotence arises the bitter awareness that "the wretchedness inflicted upon human beings by other human beings was inseparable from the violation of the earth" (138).

Bibliography

Rozelle, Page. "The Teller and the Tale: History and the Oral Tradition in Elizabeth Cook-Lynn's *Aurelia: A Crow Creek Trilogy.*" *American Indian Quarterly* 25, no. 2 (spring 2001): 203–215.

Stripes, James. "'We Think in Terms of What Is Fair': Justice versus 'Just Compensation' in Elizabeth Cook-Lynn's *From the River's Edge.*" *Wicazo Sa Review* 12, no. 1 (spring 1997): 165–187.

Cecelia Ragaini

Fuller Man   Diane Glancy   (1999)

DIANE GLANCY's novel *Fuller Man* sympathetically explores the inner conflicts of a born-again Christian. Although Glancy makes no explicit mention of a Native American or racially mixed ethnic heritage, relying instead on imagery and implication, she does continue to explore her familiar themes of Christianity and journey in this book.

Fuller Man is about the Williges family, three children, their parents, and their parents' siblings. Told from the perspective of the middle child, Hadley, the story focuses on the conflicting messages and outright conflict between their Christian mother and her sister, Aunt Mary, and their father and his brother, Farley.

Hadley, seeking to live in both worlds, goes to college and lands a job at the newspaper where her uncle and father work. She also marries and accepts the traditional role of wife and mother, giving up the freedom enjoyed by her traveling photographer uncle. As her responsibilities as homemaker increase and her freedom to pursue a career diminishes, Hadley calls on her faith (particularly, her faith in the saving power of a personal relationship with Jesus Christ, the "Fuller Man" of the novel) for the strength to maintain her family life.

At the same time Hadley's faith is challenged by Aunt Mary's death. The family discovers a re-creation of the Old Testament temple in Aunt Mary's attic, with an altar, the remains of sacrifices, and a journal of undelivered sermons. Hadley admits to her minister, "They made the gospel bitter" (140), yet, through prayer, she is cured of her headaches and saved from her desire to desert her husband and children, sparing them the pain her parents' marriage caused her.

Told in poetic, episodic interludes, this novel relies heavily on repeated motifs. Particularly, the idea of fish and fishing plays throughout the book. Hadley's vehemently non-Christian uncle and father are both avid fishermen. When Hadley's uncle returns from a trip to Mexico—a trip Hadley refused to take with him because of family obligations—he has a fish piñata for Hadley's daughter, explaining, "There's another word for the fish still in the water." Hadley replies, ". . . But I'm willing to be a caught-fish on the string of the Fisherman, while you remain in the water. . . . I've been gathered from the waters—saved, Farley—and that Christ life in me is stronger than anything that could pull me back into the water" (150).

Resolution in this novel is achieved as Hadley, after Farley's death, recognizes the spiritual value of her uncle's work yet rededicates herself to Christ, who ". . . *has on a fish suit with scales that teeth cannot hurt*" (190).

See also SPIRITUALITY.

Bibliography

Glancy, Diane. *Fuller Man.* Wakefield, R.I.: Moyer Bell, 1999.

Jennifer Andrews. "A Conversation with Diane Glancy." *American Indian Quarterly* 26 (2002): 645–658.

Angela M. Williamson

gaming

In 1988 the U.S. Congress passed the Native American Gaming Regulatory Act, which allowed tribes to attempt to negotiate pacts with individual states in order to offer gambling. Since 1974, when the Florida Seminole opened a bingo parlor, the states had been confronted with how to regulate, if at all, gambling on the reservations. Because the reservations are subject to some state and federal control, Congress decided that any gambling that the state permitted, the tribes could offer on the reservations. Also, Congress legalized tribal-run bingo establishments in all states.

According to the Federal Bureau of Investigation (FBI) report *Indian Country Crime,* 12 percent of the total number of tribal casinos earn $9.425 billion of the $14.5-billion generated annually. The remaining 88 percent of tribal casinos account for the $5.075 billion remainder. States usually require a percentage of the casinos' profits for allowing these establishments to operate. Of the 562 federally recognized tribes, fewer than half, about 220, operate gaming facilities. The most lucrative gaming establishments include the Mystic Lake Complex in Prior Lake, Minnesota (Shakopee Mdewakanton Sioux); the Turning Stone Casino in Verona, New York (Oneida); and Foxwoods in Mashantucket, Connecticut (Mashantucket Pequot). The profits fund child care facilities, scholarships for education, welfare programs, and the purchasing of lands, including those originally occupied by the tribe. Additionally, the casinos provide tribal members with employment.

The Indian gaming movement is referred to as the "New Buffalo" movement, which signifies its potential for Native American prosperity. Larry Jay Martin's *Sounding Drum* (1999) presents the casino in this positive light. However, some Native Americans are cautious about this new means to salvation, believing it to be another trap for their people. Because many Native Americans became dependent upon government programs in the 1970s and then were devastated once they were cut, many believe gambling will meet the same results. As more and more tribes become dependent upon casinos for their prosperity, there is a concern that they will be plummeted into poverty again when the states elect to legalize gambling.

Many contemporary Native American authors explore the tribal controversies regarding gaming. In *Don't Think Twice* (1999) Wayne Johnson captures these struggles in a Chippewa tribe of northern Minnesota. He juxtaposes those members who elect to run a casino with those who desire to preserve the naturalness of the reservation. Similarly, Jean Hager's *Seven Black Stones* (1995) uses a particular Native American's opposition to the construction of a bingo parlor as a potential motive for murder. GERALD VIZENOR's postmodern novel *THE HEIRS OF COLUMBUS* (1991) also highlights a Chippewa casino, which is managed by Stone Columbus. The premise is based on the idea that Christopher Columbus fathered numerous Native Americans, and the action revolves around returning Columbus and Pocahontas's bones to their descendants. Other novels that explore the casino in conjunction with crime and mysterious murders include Kathleen Eagle's *What the Heart Knows* (1999) and Thomas Perry's *Shadow Woman* (1997).

Gaming is also the subject of Native American poetry and song. Lawrence T, a.k.a. The One Who Walks, composed "The New Native" (2002), a poem that celebrates Native American success with an inclusion of the casino as one way to realize empowerment. Alanson Skinner's *Songs of the Menomini Medicine Ceremony* (1925) contains pieces on gambling. Also, contemporary Native American bands, such as Jerry Alfred and the Medicine Beat of the Tuchone Nation, continue to address gambling in their songs. "Caribou Stick Gambling Song" (1996), "Beginner Gambling Song" (1996), "Stick Gambling Rock" (1999), "Minto Gambling Song" (1999), and "McQuestion Stick Gambling Song" (1997) have been recorded by this band alone. Kathryn Gabriel also quotes many gambling-related songs and poems as epigrams to her chapters in *The Gambler's Way,* including "Song of the Gambler during the Rolling Ring Game" and "Crow Hand Game Song."

It is interesting to note that even before tribes were able to capitalize on the profits from gaming, that is, before the Native American Gaming Regulatory Act was passed, a more general concept of gambling or of the gambler was linked to Native Americans. In much non-Native American literature, particularly short stories, a gambling Native American character is a common stereotype. Fitzherbert Leather's "Kooswap: A Tale of Red and White Civilization" (1901) centers around a drunken, gambling Nez Perce. Charles V. Brereton's 1920s series of short stories also perpetuates the gambling Native American stereotype. His main character, a Deep Valley Wylackie Native American named Casco Billy, falls victim to his own indulgence in gambling in two stories in particular: "Next Came Casco" (1921) and "Casco, the Goat Getter" (1922). Moreover, these stories illustrate how gambling and drinking were linked by non-

Native Americans writing Native American characters. Other short stories portray motivations for why Native Americans cheat whites: A Native American has been cheated in the past or finds a way to thwart the whites' attempts to cheat him. Frederic Remington's "Sun-down Leflare's Money" (1898) depicts a half-breed cheating white men in a poker game after he falls victim to their dishonesty. The story also shows how engaging in cheating may become cyclical, as the cheated individual becomes the cheater. In Frank Thunen's 1910 short story "The Burning at Bald Rock" a similar plot unfolds. A white man hears of a Digger burning, a ritual involving thinning the forest, and decides that if he can intoxicate the Native Americans, he will be able to beat them at the gambling that is part of their ritual. In the end the Native Americans win the spoils.

In addition to money, Native Americans bet with and for horses and women—in actuality and in the literature. For instance, in the Navajo myth of the Great Gambler the first of four gambling games begins with a bet for wives. "Sun-down Leflare's Money" results in the title character's possession of a livery stable. In "The Spotted Dog's Bride" (1910) by Anthony Wilder, Spotted Dog cannot convince his intended's father to give consent for their marriage; therefore, he engages her father in a poker game in which he is able to win her.

In a contemporary twist on the gambling Native American motif LOUISE ERDRICH's supernatural short story "Fleur" (1986) describes the incidents that befall a group of white men who attack the aptly named Chippewa Fleur Pillager. Before her entrance into these men's worlds, that is, Kozka's meats, a local butcher shop, she had already acquired a reputation as a sort of femme fatale in her own village. When she relocates to Kozka's, she works by day in the shop and insinuates herself into the men's poker games by night. For 30 days Fleur manages to win exactly one dollar every night. Her unwavering winnings begin to frustrate the other players. In an attempt to break her streak, one of the men, Lily, forces a high-stakes game. However, Fleur wins the pot, causing Lily and the other men to become enraged and attack her. The day after they assault Fleur, a storm hits the town. The entire town survives its destruction except Kozka's meats and the men who assaulted her. Erdrich incorporated "Fleur" in her novel TRACKS (1988). In 1994 she published *The BINGO PALACE,* in which she masterfully explores the good and bad aspects of gaming and its effect on RESERVATION LIFE and Indian identity.

Many Native American traditions include narratives and rituals that incorporate gambling. For instance, tribes addressed gambling and betting in such narratives as the Anishinabe's "Some People Call Him Waynahbozho," which centers on a bet of who can eat more, the title character or a giant. Other examples include Lynn Maranda's *Coast Salish Gambling Games* (1984), a compendium of customs, games, and religious rituals of this people in Canada. John Bierhorst's collection *Lightning Inside You and Other Native American Riddles* (1992) includes riddles and their connection to gambling. JIM NORTHRUP, an Anishinabe, records his personal impressions of this practice, as well as commentary on other contemporary issues, in *The Rez Road Follies* (1997). The book includes the chapter "Gambling and Other Follies."

One of the most significant collections to deal with this topic is Kathryn Gabriel's *The Gambler's Way* (1996). The work contains more than 100 gaming legends from tribes all across the Americas with an emphasis on the Southwest. Although Gabriel is not a Native American, she takes great care to preserve the Native American stories by resisting the urge to rewrite the narratives according to Western ideas of plot. As she notes, Native Americans portray gambling with more ambiguity. Rather than merely categorized as a vice or addiction, it is an integral part of tribal religions. Gambling is shown as the great equalizer, maintaining a balance, or cycle, of riches. It can be used as an alternative to war as well as a means to exchange and acquire goods.

Gabriel's collection includes the Navajo legend of the Great Gambler, Noqoìlpi. After winning many tribes' property, children, wives, and gamblers themselves, excepting the Diné, who merely observed the games, Noqoìlpi becomes too greedy. He offends the Sun by refusing to give him two precious shells. In turn the Sun devises a way to humble him. The Sun approaches a young Diné to act as his avenger. He reshapes the youth so that he looks identical to Noqoìlpi. With the aid of other gods, the young Indian and the Sun plot the best way (in proportion to his offense) in which to defeat the offender. In the end the Great Gambler is overthrown by his "look-alike," and the freedom of all those persons and materials he previously won results. Interestingly, the Great Gambler is not completely devastated for his offense. Rather, he pleads his case before another god, who pities him and gives him the means to prosperity, including making him the ruler of the Mexican people.

As both the reality and the literature reflect, gaming may provide the means to realize many positive conditions; however, it also possesses the potential for many negative outcomes, including drug trafficking, fraud, and corruption. In the 1995 article "The Economic and Social Implications of Native American Gaming: The Case of Minnesota" in the *American Indian Culture and Research Journal,* Don A. Cozzetto posits that one of the most troubling findings regarding gaming is that Native Americans appear to have a greater propensity to succumb to gambling addiction than non-Native Americans (126). However, conclusive studies remain to be conducted, and in the meantime the reservations are tapping into this relatively new revenue source in order to provide better services to their people.

See also POVERTY; SOUTHWESTERN TRIBAL LITERATURE.

Bibliography

Castillo, Susan, and Victor M. P. Da Rosa. *Native American Women in Literature and Culture.* Porto, Portugal: Fernando Pessoa University Press, 1997.

Cozzetto, Don A. "The Economic and Social Implications of Native American Gaming: The Case for Minnesota." *American Indian Culture and Research Journal* (winter 1995): 118–128.

Erdrich, Louise. *The Bingo Palace.* New York: HarperCollins, 1994.

Gabriel, Kathryn. *Gambler Way: Indian Gaming in Mythology, History and Archeology in North America.* Boulder, Colo.: Johnson Books, 1996.

Hockenberry, John. *A River Out of Eden.* New York: Doubleday, 2001.

Johansen, Bruce E., ed. *The Encyclopedia of Native American Economic History.* Westport, Conn.: Greenwood Press, 1999.

Johnson, Wayne. *Don't Think Twice.* New York: Harmony Books, 2000.

Mitchell, Kirk. *Cry Dance.* New York: Bantam Books, 1999.

Native American Gaming Regulatory Act. Pub. L. 100–497. 17 October 1988. Stat. 102.467. Available online. URL: http://www.nigc.gov/nigc/laws/igra/index.jsp. Accessed on August 15, 2005.

Pasquaretta, Paul. "Gambling against the House: Anglo and Indian Perspectives on Gambling in American Literature." *Mosaic* 34, no. 1 (2001): 137–152.

Vizenor, Gerald. *The Heirs of Columbus.* Hanover, N.H.: University Press of New England, 1991.

Amy C. Branam

Gansworth, Eric (1965–)

Eric Gansworth is a member of the Onondaga tribe who grew up on the Tuscarora reservation in western New York. He holds a B.A. and an M.A. from Buffalo State College and is currently associate professor of English and Lowery Writer in Residence at Canisius College in Buffalo, New York. Gansworth's major works are the novels *INDIAN SUMMERS* (1998), *Smoke Dancing* (2004), and *Mending Skins* (2005) and the collection of poems and paintings entitled *NICKEL ECLIPSE: IROQUOIS MOON* (2000).

Gansworth's first three literary works contain his own original paintings interspersed with the text, reflecting his beginnings in visual art, a field in which he has achieved great success; his work has appeared in shows and galleries throughout New York State, and one of his paintings appears on the cover of SHERMAN ALEXIE's *FIRST INDIAN ON THE MOON*. For Gansworth visual art is a kind of storytelling, and branching out into narrative affords him a way of continuing that story. For instance, *Nickel Eclipse* centers on the image of the Buffalo nickel, both as a visual image and in the

poetry. Using a symbol such as this allows him to combine the two art forms, providing a richer picture than he could with either one alone.

Gansworth's texts tend not to focus on the clash between cultures often present between Indians and the white culture in which they live, but rather to look to the inside. They tend, as in *Indian Summers,* to show the reader life on a reservation, what it is like within. Gansworth focuses on how Indians see themselves and their culture, not how others see them, and for that emphasis his is a valuable contribution to Indian literature.

Gardens in the Dunes Leslie Marmon Silko (1999)

In *Gardens in the Dunes* LESLIE MARMON SILKO weaves indigenous storytelling with the drama of the Victorian novel, an uncustomary technique in the works of Native American writers. Restorative power in the novel arises from the spiritual forces of nature, myth, and the feminine sacred. The GHOST DANCE, Gnostic and Celtic mysteries, Roman and Greek garden statuary, Sister Salt's baby, Indigo's homecoming, and the return of the rattlesnake's daughter to the dunes counteract the destructive powers of manifest destiny in relation to the earth and indigenous people. In addition to depicting Victorian era botanists' imperialist collecting, Silko emphasizes positive possibilities for cultural "cross-pollination."

Colonization of the American Southwest forces the last free members of the fictional Sand Lizard tribe—11-year-old Indigo; her sister, Salt; her mother; and Grandmother Fleet—from their homeland in the dunes near the Arizona-California border. The journey of these women reflects the history of the vanishing tribes in the late 19th and early 20th centuries who escaped the confinement of reservations but were nevertheless displaced by private speculators and the U.S. government. The family moves to Needles, California, where they subsist on food from the local dump and Indigo's mother's meager salary as a washerwoman. After the soldiers' raid of a local Ghost Dance ceremony, the women are separated. Grandmother Fleet and her granddaughters are reunited at the dunes, and their presence makes possible the gardens' literal regeneration, which symbolizes a broader renewal of indigenous culture and SOVEREIGNTY.

After a failed attempt to locate the girls' mother, the revival abruptly ends. Indigo is shipped to the historical Sherman Institute, while Sister Salt launders in a labor camp. When Indigo flees the oppressive boarding school, which is ruled by capitalist, materialistic, and Christian ideologies, she finds refuge with college-educated Hattie, wife of the zealous botanist Edward Palmer. A parrot and a domesticated Brazilian monkey befriend Indigo during her stay with the affluent Euro-American couple. Indigo finds solidarity with these animals, since they, as have the indigenous people and Edward's collections of plants, stones, and relics, have been displaced and are coddled as exotic oddities. Through the commonality of exploitation in the ensuing Victorian drama, Silko challenges the Christianized perspective of human superiority with the indigenous view of respect for all creation.

Indigo remains a consistent symbol of spiritual renewal as she collects seeds for the dunes' regeneration during her travels abroad with the Palmers. Hattie undergoes her own spiritual revitalization when she is introduced to her indigenous roots in England. Greed inhibits Edward's spiritual development, however, and he dies after a failed citron project in Corsica and meteor crater investment. The revival cycle continues as reunited Indigo and Sister Salt restore their homeland's gardens while Hattie joins Aunt Bronwyn in England to explore her Celtic spiritual connection to the land and its history. As is symbolically suggested by the opening context of the Ghost Dance revival, the female characters in *Gardens in the Dunes* reclaim their restorative power when the connections among the self, earth, and spirit are in harmony.

Bibliography

Isernhagen, Hartwig. "Of Deserts and Gardens: The Southwest in Literature and Art, 'Native' and 'White'—the example of Leslie Silko and Georgia O'Keeffe." In *Literature and the Visual Arts in 20th-Century America,* edited by Michele Bottalico, 173–187. Bari, Italy: Palomar eupalinos, 2003.

Silko, Leslie Marmon. *Gardens in the Dunes.* New York: Simon & Schuster, 1999.

Waldron, Karen E. "The Land as Consciousness: Ecological Being and the Movement of Words in the Works of Leslie Marmon Silko." In *Such News of the Land: U.S. Women Nature Writers,* edited by Thomas S. Edwards and Elizabeth A. De Wolfe, 178–203. Hanover, N.H., and London: University Press of New England, 2001.

Laura Jeselnick and Elizabeth McNeil

Gathering of Spirit: A Collection by North American Women, A Beth Brant (1984)

A Gathering of Spirit (1984) is a remarkable achievement for many reasons. Perhaps the most celebrated reason is that it was the first anthology created and edited entirely by Native American women. As such, it established feminism (first formalized by PAULA GUNN ALLEN in *The SACRED HOOP* [1986]) as central to Native American literary studies. It also facilitated subsequent anthologies by Native American women, including SPIDER WOMAN'S GRANDDAUGHTERS (1987, edited by Allen) and most recently REINVENTING THE ENEMY'S LANGUAGE (1997, edited by JOY HARJO and GLORIA BIRD).

In addition to its original position, this anthology is noteworthy for its remarkable content. It includes everything from traditional and avant-garde poetry, to autobiography and monologue, to drawings and photographs. This diversity reflects the variety and vitality of work by Native American women. *A Gathering* further reflects this diversity by including works from famous artists (such as ALLEN and MARY TALLMOUNTAIN) as well as lesser known artists (such as Merry Harris and Midnight Sun). Finally this democracy of form and content illustrates the diversity (tribal and individual) of the artists included in this anthology.

Despite its emphasis on diversity, this anthology voices a commonality. Most of its pieces radically challenge the basic categories that define Native American literature in terms of its respect for tribal traditions, nature, and/or negotiation of tribal and nontribal identity. For example, these viewpoints openly and defiantly confront the violence inflicted against Native peoples, especially women; to counter such violence, many of these works argue for the need to return to perspectives and ways centered in tribal traditions that honor women. In this respect this anthology differs markedly from other anthologies of Native American literature that had begun appearing at this time.

Finally, *A Gathering of Spirit* is remarkable because it represents the first of BETH BRANT's major works. She began writing in 1981, at the age of 41, after she had been visited by an eagle spirit. Immediately after this visit she began writing and being published, an equally remarkable event given that she was a high school dropout. Since then she has published numerous works and received significant awards for her writing (e.g., the National Endowment for the Arts and the Canada Council Award for Creative Writing). *A Gathering of Spirit* gained for Brant immediate recognition and helped propel her career as a writer and activist.

Bibliography

Allen, Paula Gunn. *The Sacred Hoop.* Boston: Beacon Press, 1986.

Brant, Beth. *A Gathering of Spirit: A Collection by North American Women.* Ithaca, N.Y.: Firebrand Books, 1989.

Harjo, Joy, and Gloria Bird, eds. *Reinventing the Enemy's Language: Contemporary Native Women's Writings of North America.* New York and London: W. W. Norton, 1997.

———. *Spider Woman's Granddaughters.* Boston: Beacon Press, 1989.

Clay Smith

Geiogamah, Hanay   (1945–   )

Hanay Geiogamah (pronounced Heh-NAY GIG-a/mawh) was born Henry Lane Geiogamah in Lawton, Oklahoma, on June 22, 1945, to Lola Mae and Claude Geiogamah, Sr., of Anadarko, Oklahoma. While it appears that his mother was of Lenni Lenape descent, his father is solely of Kiowa descent, and the tribe figures prominently in Geiogamah's plays. Growing up in Anadarko, a town shaped by being the confluence of many western tribes—"a phantasmagoria of existence" Geiogamah once called it (Vahlberg 15)—he started writing in high school, inspired by teachers and trips to the movies.

Although Geiogamah is considered the first widely known and successful Native American playwright, his initial career was that of a student journalist. After graduation from Anadarko High School he went on a journalism scholarship to the University of Oklahoma, where he was heavily involved with the student newspaper as theater critic and editor in chief, and even won a Hearst editorial contest. After leaving the university before earning his degree, he spent half a year in Washington, D.C., working for Americans before Columbus, followed by the Bureau of Indian Affairs. He then began an internship project under Senator Ted Kennedy in which he formed a theater group in late 1971 at La Mama Experimental Theater Club in New York City. After successful reviews, performances, and a tour of Indian country with his first play, *BODY INDIAN* (produced in 1972), Geiogamah devoted himself full-time to playwriting and directing his theater group at La Mama. Together the group produced a double-bill with Geiogamah as the principal author, *Coon Cons Coyote* (1973) and Geiogamah's own *FOGHORN*, after a trip to Berlin. The group moved back to Geiogamah's native Oklahoma, where they produced a final play, *49* (1975), then disbanded. Geiogamah's career afterward led him to a B.F.A. in theater at Indiana University. After an unsuccessful attempt at reviving a theater group in New York City in the early 1980s, he moved to Los Angeles for work in the entertainment industry; he eventually worked at University of California Los Angeles (UCLA) teaching both in the Department of Theater, Film, and Television and in the American Indian Studies Center, where he now teaches and continues to write and produce plays, films, documentaries, and dance programs for various television networks. Recently with the help of a Kellogg Foundation Grant he has embarked on a program to jump-start Native American theater through predominantly Native universities.

Geiogamah's individual accomplishment is that he is the first Native American to publish a volume of plays; his first three appeared in *New Native American Drama* (1980). Many of his other works, *Coon Cons Coyote, Grandma* (1984), and *Grandpa* (1984), have been published in *Stories of Our Way* (1999); others have seen neither publication nor staging, as the lack of a Native American theatrical infrastructure is an underlying difficulty for all Native American playwrights. In Geiogamah's case that lack has led to his undertaking varying genres of plays, from comedies to musicals, to sell seats and develop an audience.

If there is a continuing theme in Geiogamah's work, it is the survival, through HUMOR, of some component of Indian heritage beyond the circumstances of the play. For instance, *Body Indian* concerns overcoming the hypocrisy of one's Indian "friends" and surviving amid the historical nightmare of modern Native America. In five scenes the Indian everyman Bobby Lee endures continually being rolled by his alcoholic buddies for money; eventually those Indian "friends" take the prosthetic leg he has used since he lost his leg to a train. Some historical blame is placed on the paternalism of Anglo society: Bobby has had to go home to have a blood relative sign for him to begin his alcohol treatment. The final message of the play, as Bobby relives the loss of his leg years before, clarifies that Indians are in a historical nightmare that they must triumph over on their own individually and without the treachery of their comrades. In its first performances Geiogamah was astonished that Indians laughed all the way through—until the end.

The subject of *Foghorn*, a Brechtian-type play with varied historical scenes that range from a dull Lone Ranger and a sharp Tonto to a romantic Captain John Smith and a vengeful Pocahontas, is an exorcism of historical atrocities such as WOUNDED KNEE. The final line, "I am NOT GUILTY," [expresses fault with the finger-pointing of the dominant society.] Appearing just before it, *Coon Cons Coyote* (1973), an adaptation of a Nez Perce tribal TRICKSTER FIGURE story that has been restaged for children's theater, makes a statement that tribal stories of Indian tricksters are just as stageworthy as Aesop's fables or the "Great Race."

Geiogamah's dramaturgical triumph in both form and subject matter was *49*, set in his native Oklahoma during the post–POW wow party known by that title. The play connects the past of a circa 1880s tribal leader giving his final instructions to Native youth to alternating scenes revealing the result in the modern age: the drunken revelry of the 49 that is the one remaining activity that defines young Indians as Indians. The play moves at a pace not unlike that of a tribal celebration or pow wow, with police dispatches creating the only dramatic tension. The emphasis here is on cultural survival, even if that culture, like the 49, is not pure. The 49ers may not know the songs of their tribe (one youngster cannot sing them), but they are aware of their Indianness to the point that they are willing to stand up to the police officers who surround them at the end of the play.

Geiogamah's other plays focus on survival through humor. In the comedy *Landsale* (1984) an old Kiowa grandmother tricks her family into accepting her plan of moving out onto their ancestral lands to save them from foreclosure. At times the play borders on vaudeville-style humor, as Annie feigns illness with her sister by her side as they trick the tribal commissioner into helping their family.

War Dancer (1977), and its more musical *War Dancers* (1981–82), place on stage the most widely known Indian performance art, the pow wow. Although the plays were not well received, they led to Geiogamah's production of American Indian Dance Theater, a compendium of pow wow dances that has made at least two successful traveling runs, including appearances on PBS's *Great Performances*.

However, the twin one-acts *Grandma* (1984) and *Grandpa* (1984) reveal Geiogamah's talent: his ability to depict Indians naturalistically through action and dialect. For instance, Grandma, in preparation for a tribal giveaway for her granddaughter, says, "Heck, we oughta start planning on sending Indians out to the moon, and to those places even farther on out. They'd probably like Indians pretty good out there. Hah" (323).

For Geiogamah Native theater is about humor and survival. As he wrote in a 1991 "Assessment" of Native American theater, "Neither the novel nor the polemic has proved effective as a means to stir up dialogue among Indians themselves. This leaves the theater to accomplish the task" (380).

Bibliography

Lincoln, Kenneth. "Indi'ns Playing Indians." In *Ind'in Humor: Bilcultural Play in Indian America,* 162–170. New York: Oxford University Press, 1989.

New Native American Drama: Three Plays, edited by Jeffrey Huntsman. Norman: University of Oklahoma Press, 1980.

Pinazzi, Annamaria. "The Theater of Hanay Geiogamah." In *American Indian Theater in Performance: A Reader,* edited by Jaye Darby and Hanay Geiogamah. 175–194. Los Angeles: UCLA American Indian Studies Center, 2000.

Stories of Our Way: An Anthology of Native American Indian Plays. Edited by Hanay Geiogamah and Jaye Darby. Los Angeles: UCLA American Indian Studies Center, 1999.

Andrew Vassar

gender

Traditional gender roles in Native American cultures varied somewhat from nation to nation; most commonly men were warriors and protectors and women were keepers of the home and the community. Food gathering was shared, as men hunted and women farmed. The roles of men and women within each tribal community were complementary and in some aspects shared, including the spiritual.

The western tradition has tended to stereotype all Native Americans. The images many of these stereotypes evoke range from the "good Indian" to the "bad Indian" and everything in between, including gender representations, more often than not either blurring or subverting reality. Since early Native American literature was strictly oral, many misrepresentations were unchallenged until fairly recently. Many modern Native American writers have chosen to become voices of their culture in two major ways. First, they have contributed significantly to the body of Native American literature as writers of nonfiction, fiction, prose, and drama; these include

such notables as LOUISE ERDRICH and LESLIE MARMON SILKO. Second, a number of modern Native American writers such as PAULA GUNN ALLEN also serve as literary and cultural critics, offering analysis of alternative views of gender roles and gender representations in modern works by and about Native Americans as well as interpretations of traditional Native American literature.

Bibliography

Allen, Paula Gunn. *The Sacred Hoop: Recovering the Feminine in American Indian Traditions.* Boston: Beacon Press, 1986.

Bataille, Gretchen, ed. *Native American Women: A Biographical Dictionary.* New York: Garland, 1993.

Brown, Kathleen M. "The Anglo-Algonquin Gender Frontier." *American Indians,* edited by Nancy Shoemaker, 48–62. Blackwell Readers in American Social and Cultural History Ser. 2. Malden, Mass.: Blackwell, 2001.

Carr, Helen. *Inventing the American Primitive: Politics, Gender, and the Representation of Native American Literary Traditions, 1789–1936.* New York: New York University Press, 1996.

Champagne, Duane, ed. *Contemporary Native American Cultural Issues.* Contemporary Native American Communities Ser. 3. Walnut Creek, Calif.: AltaMira Press, 1999.

Dearborn, Mary V. *Pocahontas's Daughters: Gender and Ethnicity in American Culture.* New York: Oxford University Press, 1986.

Hewitt, Nancy A., ed. *A Companion to American Women's History.* Malden, Mass.: Blackwell, 2002.

Hoffman Nelson, Elizabeth, and Malcolm A. Nelson. *Telling the Stories: Essays on American Indian Literatures and Cultures.* American Indian Studies Ser. 7. New York: Peter Lang, 2001.

Irwin, Mary Ann, and James F. Brooks, eds. *Women and Gender in the American West.* Albuquerque: University of New Mexico Press, 2004.

Jacobs, Sue-Ellen, Wesley Thomas, and Sabine Lang, eds. *Two-Spirit People: Native American Gender Identity, Sexuality, and Spirituality.* Urbana: University of Illinois Press, 1997.

Lang, Sabine. *Men as Women, Women as Men: Changing Gender in Native American Cultures.* Austin: University of Texas Press, 1998.

Matsumoto, Valerie J., and Blake Allmendinger, eds. *Over the Edge: Remapping the American West.* Berkeley: University of California Press, 1999.

Milner, Clyde A., II. *A New Significance: Re-envisioning the History of the American West.* New York: Oxford University Press, 1996.

Roscoe, Will. *Changing Ones: Third and Fourth Genders in Native North America.* New York: St. Martin's, 1998.

Woodsum, Jo Ann. "Gender and Sexuality in Native American Societies: A Bibliography." *The American Indian Quarterly* 19, no. 4 (1995): 527–553.

Beth Maxfield

Ghost Dance

By the last decade of the 19th century the quality of life for most American Indians had become deplorable. Crowded onto reservations with little arable land, many tribes faced starvation, along with the corruption of the GOVERNMENT AGENCIES and the ongoing attempts of Christian MISSIONARIES to convert them. It was into this ripe atmosphere that Wovoka, a member of the Paiute tribe, introduced the Ghost Dance. The dance itself was different from other traditional dances, in that it was slower; included the participation of men, women, and children; and had no accompanying drumming or other instrumentation. There were Ghost Dance songs to be performed during the dance, and a performance could last four to five days.

More important than the dance itself, however, was the accompanying message, sometimes referred to as the Ghost Dance religion. In general Wovoka claimed that he had been shown, in a dream or in a vision, a future in which whites would disappear from the earth by either supernatural means or by natural disaster, and only Indians and their resurrected dead would remain. Given the difficult climate in which Indians found themselves in the 1890s, this message was quite attractive. It meant a return to traditional customs; a rejection of the white culture and its trappings, especially weapons, technology, and alcohol; and hope for the future of all Indians.

Ghost Dances were held throughout the West and the central plains, ultimately gaining enough popularity to worry the U.S. government. In December 1890 Sitting Bull, a respected Lakota leader and medicine man, held a Ghost Dance that was to be well attended. Before the dance began, however, his arrest was ordered. Gunfire was exchanged by the Ghost Dancers and the police, and Sitting Bull was killed. Shortly thereafter his followers were rounded up and massacred by the U.S. military at WOUNDED KNEE Creek. Many of those killed, including many women and children, were wearing the ghost shirts some tribes wore while practicing the dance.

Because the Ghost Dance movement poignantly evokes the despair and hunger for the past among the Indian population in the late 19th century, many writers have turned to it in their work. SHERMAN ALEXIE makes frequent references to the movement in an attempt to build unity among all contemporary Indians. In LESLIE MARMON SILKO's *GARDENS IN THE DUNES* the Ghost Dance is one of many elements used to counteract the destructive spirit of imperialism. Finally in *BILLY JACK* the title character invokes the spirit of Wovoka himself in his inspirational sermon delivered at the end of the film.

Bibliography

Hittman, Michael. *Wovoka and the Ghost Dance.* Lincoln: University of Nebraska Press, 1997.

Jennifer McClinton-Temple

Ghost Singer Anna Lee Walters (1988)

In *Ghost Singer* ANNA LEE WALTERS (Pawnee/Otoe) targets the Euro-American history of conquest and some of its disturbing aftermath that extends to our own day. Walters suggestively juxtaposes scenes of 19th-century Navajo facing murderous enslavers with the modern-day institutionalized collection of Native bodies and artifacts in the Smithsonian. A Native warrior spirit—angry about the collection, which contains medicine bundles, a necklace with dozens of human ears, a mummified child, a Navajo man's scalp—takes vengeance on oblivious researchers who do not understand what they are participating in. The macabre political novel raises questions about how mainstream American ignorance toward tribal traditions, religions, and possessions may be a form of neoconquest.

The novel's opening scene, which portrays the brutality of slave hunters who scalp an old medicine man, White Sheep, and steal his granddaughter, branches out to symbolize the colonial losses that also afflicted many other tribes. The Smithsonian collection represents a culmination of the unacknowledged legacies of violence against tribes. A Smithsonian employee who oversees the stolen items, Donald Evans, nonchalantly hangs the necklace of Native ears over his desk because, for him, they seem to be merely a gruesome curiosity, not a record of actual death and anguish. Through Jonnie Navaho, a descendant of White Sheep, the novel implies that Natives need to uncover the imperial past to deal with the present.

Jonnie Navaho's grandson, Willie Begay, while doing research in Washington, D.C., accidentally touches a scalp and becomes deathly ill. Willie feels implicated in U.S. corruption and betrayal and tells his grandfather that "representatives of the American government" supposedly on a mission to "make a peace treaty with the Navajos" killed and scalped "one of our most respected leaders, Narbona" (180). The scalp in the Smithsonian, which could be Narbona's or White Sheep's, signifies a white American will to destroy Natives and their cultures. The collection implies that white imperialists meant to possess, catalogue, and eliminate Natives. The loss and damage have not been atoned for, and insult and injury continue because living Natives have no control over the institution and its collection. The Smithsonian implicitly tries to prevent Natives from possessing their own histories and identities.

While many Americans would like to declare conquest to be a moot point, a vestige of a past that does not concern the present, Walters shows how an attitude of denial maintains a problematic status quo. Walters's novel taps into themes from the Native repatriation movement that started in the 1960s in order to indict those who objectified and exploited Natives and their culture; since the movement began, many tribes have been engaged in an uphill battle to reclaim possessions and artifacts from museums and private collections.

Bibliography

Graber, Dorothy J. "Anna Lee Walters's *Ghost Singer* Links Native Diasporas in Time and Space." *Wicazo Sa Review* (2000): 7–16.

Walters, Anna Lee. *Ghost Singer*. Flagstaff, Ariz.: Northland, 1988.

Roland Finger

Glancy, Diane   (1941–   )

Diane Hall Glancy was born March 18, 1941, in Kansas City, Missouri, to Lewis and Edith Hall. Of Cherokee and German descent she is an important voice for MIXED-BLOOD, nonreservation Indians. She grew up in Kansas City, with only occasional trips to Arkansas to visit her Cherokee grandmother. She describes herself as having a background of illiteracy; her father, a part Cherokee stockyard worker, had only an elementary school education, and her mother was the child of German-English farmers. Glancy was married to Dwane Glancy from 1964 to 1983 and is mother to David and Jennifer. She has taught Native literature and creative writing at Macalester College in St. Paul, Minnesota, since 1988.

Frequently honored, she has won the Five Civilized Tribes Playwriting Laureate Prize numerous times, an American Book Award in poetry, and a Sundance Screenwriting Fellowship. She has also been artist in residence for the Arts Council of Oklahoma and the 1998 Edlestein-Keller Minnesota Writer of Distinction at the University of Minnesota.

Glancy is accomplished in a variety of genres, having written novels such as PUSHING THE BEAR (1996) and FLUTIE (1998), plays such as those found in *American Gypsy* (2002), poetry in *The RELIEF OF AMERICA* (2000) and *The Shadow's Horse* (2003), essays in CLAIMING BREATH (1992) and *The Cold-and-Hunger Dance* (1998), and the short story collections FIRESTICKS (1993) and MONKEY SECRET (1995).

Glancy's work has been particularly important to mixed-blood Indians, a presence she identifies in herself as a "displaced part-Indian, part-white, mixed-message heritage" (WEST POLE 21). Her anthology, *Two Worlds Walking* (1994), gathers writers from a variety of mixed-race backgrounds. In this anthology writers strive to form an identity that integrates their various ethnic communities. Glancy's work editing this volume produced a significant resource for those who have difficulty identifying with only one ethnic group. This theme is repeated in subsequent texts, in which both Glancy and her characters struggle with a bicultural identity.

In *Flutie* Glancy pushes her reader to question the importance of ethnic community, clearly illustrating what Flutie lacks at the same time that she offers hope for Flutie's ability to gain a strong, ethnic-identified voice. In another novel, Edith, a "watered down" Pawnee in *The Mask Maker* (2002), is always on the road because of her work as an art instructor for the Arts Council of Oklahoma (46). Edith creates masks, a metaphor that takes different meanings through the course of the novel, one of which is ethnic identity: "Sometimes I don't even know I'm Indian. I don't know the Indian in myself. My heritage is a mask I wear" (90). As Edith begins to feel more comfortable with herself, she asserts that "the schools could get used to her. They could rewrite their history to include her Indian/part-Indian history" (137). These two novels illustrate the personal and emotional, and the growth of the female main character.

Glancy's work explores the difficulties of being a woman in contemporary society. Flutie struggles to speak as she tries to create a coherent sense of self. Rachel struggles to become an adult in *The ONLY PIECE OF FURNITURE IN THE HOUSE* (1996). Edith wrestles to develop self-respect after divorce in *The Mask Maker*. These searches eventually lead to hard-won resolutions that are characterized by a greater sense of belonging and self-respect. This trajectory is repeated in Glancy's more personal essays, in which she struggles with her own divorce and the difficulties of being a single parent. In particular *Claiming Breath* seems to have been written at a crucial time in Glancy's own personal development. In this collection Glancy's diarylike entries reveal her anger and her growth in moving beyond a painful marriage.

Glancy's work also illustrates hope for resolution for Native communities. In *Pushing the Bear* Glancy explores the TRAIL OF TEARS from a variety of perspectives both Indian and non-Indian. These characters illustrate the difficulties encountered during this forced removal, which split the Cherokee Nation. But the novel also illustrates the resilience of Native peoples, the ways that Indians have survived despite great hardships, violence, and pain. *Designs of the Night Sky* (2002) takes the Cherokee survival into the present, recording the story of Ada, a Tahlequah, Oklahoma, librarian, who bridges the gap between the past and the future.

Glancy not only writes in a variety of genres, she experiments with form. From the multiple perspectives in *Pushing the Bear* to the "broken drama or voice fragments" of the play *Jump Kiss* in *American Gypsy,* Glancy plays with ways life can be best translated into art (87). Her experimentation is self-conscious as articulated in the notes to the play *Lesser Wars*: The two characters represent men and women, or the dualities of one individual, or "possibly there's no character at all, only thought" (144). Ultimately she concludes that the play "explores the risk of relationship with the *other,* the risk of knowing self, and the risk of relationship with the structure of writing" (145). Similarly Glancy is a risk taker, whose fearless inventiveness is one of her defining characteristics as a writer.

Bibliography

Elias, Amy J. "Fragments that Rune Up the Shores: *Pushing the Bear,* Coyote Aesthetics, and Recovered History." *Modern Fiction Studies* 45 (1999): 185–211.

Fitz, Brewster. "Philomela on the Plains: Remarks on Mixedblood Intertextual Metaphor in Diane Glancy's *Flutie.*" *SAIL* 11 (1999): 79–87.

Glancy, Diane. *American Gypsy: Six Native American Plays.* Norman: University of Oklahoma Press, 2002.

———. *Claiming Breath.* Lincoln and London: University of Nebraska Press, 1992.

———. *Flutie*. Wakefield, R.I.: Moyer Bell, 1998.

———. *The Mask Maker*. Norman: University of Oklahoma Press, 2002.

———. *The West Pole*. Minneapolis and London: University of Minnesota Press, 1997.

———. *Pushing the Bear: A Novel of the Trail of Tears*. San Diego and New York: Harvest, 1996.

———. *The Relief of America*. Chicago: Tia Chucha, 2000.

Glancy, Diane, and C.W. Truesdale, eds. *Two Worlds Walking: Short Stories, Essay, and Poetry by Writers with Mixed Heritages*. New York: New Rivers, 1994.

Kathleen Godfrey

God Is Red: A Native View of Religion   Vine Deloria, Jr.   (1972, rev. 1994)

God Is Red is a classic in the field of Native American religions and SPIRITUALITY and a pioneering work in the study of sacred places. VINE DELORIA, JR., suggests that tribal religions possess authenticity rooted in the landscape, authenticity lacking in history-based Western religious institutions. Presenting a cogent expression of theology from an indigenous perspective, Deloria also deconstructs Western Christian concepts of the individual in relation to the land. The fractured state of American spirituality and the ongoing environmental crisis are, in Deloria's view, the result of a disconnection between Christianity and the earth. *God Is Red* heralds "the revival of Indian tribal religions at a time when the central value of Indian life—its land—is under incredible attack from all sides" (246). Deloria suggests an environmentalist ethic in tribal religions: "The lands wait for those who can discern their rhythms . . . and call for relief from the constant burden of exploitation" (292).

One of Vine Deloria's more controversial books, *God Is Red* is highly critical of both the Euro-American religious and academic establishments, pointing out the complicity of scholars and clergy in the maintenance of a biased historical record that is in perpetual conflict with indigenous values. Deloria's seminary training has given him insight into the Judeo-Christian worldview. His view of the concept of original sin is that it represents the alienation of humanity from both the creator and the creation by way of the expulsion of Adam and Eve from the Garden of Eden. Deloria suggests that tribal peoples are alienated from neither the creator nor the creation, and that consequently Native American religions are becoming stronger during a period of crisis in American spirituality. In general Native American and tribal religions do not place the constraints of history upon divinity and so do not restrict God "to a particular mode of operation and sequence of appearance" (266).

God Is Red is an analysis of "concepts of general religious interest" (76) and a comparative study of Christian and tribal religion. Deloria abandons Eurocentric assumptions typical of comparative studies of this kind, dethroning Western history in the process. This mode of writing makes this work significant outside the field of American Indian studies and arguably places *God Is Red* among the foundational books in postcolonial theory, alongside Edward Said's classic *Orientalism*.

As are many of Deloria's books, *God Is Red* is humorous in its critique of the sacred cows of white America. Sarcasm is second nature to Deloria, and no political camp or religious sect is spared his barbs. He indicates that just as conservative televangelist fund-raisers try to sell salvation to the highest bidder, so do liberal Christians appropriate watered-down versions of other religions in a vain effort to be tolerant and inclusive. Deloria is equally critical of both versions of contemporary Christianity: "We cannot reject the Christian religion piecemeal," he says; "the whole religion has been misdirected from its inception" (265). He says further that Christianity may survive only if it surrenders "its narrow interpretation of history" (266). *God Is Red* is not for the easily offended. There is validity in the criticism that Deloria's style is polemical and confrontational, but readers of any ideological persuasion who are secure in their own beliefs may find Deloria's observations illuminating.

The secular branch of Western history is complicit, in Deloria's eyes, because "Christian religion and the Western idea of history are inseparable and mutually self-supporting" (112). One way that history has buttressed Christian claims of ownership of North American lands is through support for the doctrine of "Discovery": the notion that "discovered" non-Christian lands are there for the taking by colonial powers. Deloria argues for a long history of pre-Columbian transoceanic contacts between the New and Old Worlds that invalidates European claims to discovery. Such views are at odds with the academic establishment, religious views aside. As a historian Deloria advocates not an end to historical studies, but a reformation of history from a non-Western vantage. This requires first and foremost a serious consideration of non-biblical ancient history.

Deloria's style often places the reader outside his or her comfort zone. Even a sympathetic reader may find some of Deloria's arguments straining credulity. Deloria vehemently defends the psychoanalyst Immanuel Velikovsky's radical suggestions that ancient myths derive largely from a series of global catastrophes. Scholars have a difficult time with this idea, and some argue that Deloria's defense of fringe scholarship is the main weakness of the book. But if one does not overstress the details, one sees the larger point: that fringe ideas are no less believable than history founded on biblical accounts. Velikovsky's ideas resonate with Deloria's because they suggest that ancient religions were inextricably linked to the rhythms of the earth, an idea in fundamental agreement with Native American religion.

Otherwise sympathetic religious scholars may be disappointed when Deloria conflates post-Augustinian (circa fifth-century) Western Christian theology with early Judeo-Christian theology. St. Augustine's view of humankind's "fall from Grace" as a historical event dominates Judeo-Christian thought today, but not as the only perspective. Jews do not subscribe to it, and neither did the Christians of ancient Asia and elsewhere outside the Roman sphere. Deloria asks, "Where did Westerners get their ideas of divine right of conquest, of manifest destiny, of themselves as the vanguards of true civilization, if not from Christianity?" (113). Indeed they did, but these and other abusive formulations of Christian doctrine appeared after the appropriation of Christianity as state religion by the vestiges of imperial Rome. This provides context for Deloria's observed contrast between Christianity, which emphasizes social control of populations, and Native American religions, which emphasize lived experience of communities through generations. Deloria brilliantly captures the negative impression that Christianity made upon tribal peoples. His insufficient knowledge of early Christian diversity to some extent, however, weakens his argument.

As Deloria puts it, "White America and Western industrial societies have not heard the call of either the land or the aboriginal peoples" (292). This book presents a direct challenge to white America's inherited religious doctrines, doctrines that allow the continued exploitation of the land and Native peoples.

Bibliography
Deloria, Vine, Jr. *Custer Died for Your Sins.* New York: Macmillan, 1969.
———. *God Is Red: A Native View of Religion.* Golden, Colo.: Fulcrum, 1994.
Said, Edward. *Orientalism.* New York: Pantheon, 1978.

Joe Wilson

Going for the Rain   Simon Ortiz   (1976)
Before becoming a writer, Simon Ortiz worked in uranium mines, attended college with an eye to becoming a chemist, and joined the army, yet, no matter what path he took, he always maintained an interest in writing. These early experiences provided him with material that became the subject of his poetry and short stories. When one reads Ortiz's early work, however, it is imperative that one be familiar with the political activism of the 1960s, because this period is important for understanding his early writing.

While *Going for the Rain,* Ortiz's first major publication, is not as overtly political as some of his later writing, it does celebrate traditional indigenous beliefs, a political-cultural stance that grew out of the Red Power Movement. Members of this movement engaged in political acts that drew national and international media attention. At the peak of American Indian activism, Ortiz's initial publication established him as a major writer at a time when non-Natives believed that Native American literature was nonexistent. The literary movement that coincided with this period, now referred to as the AMERICAN INDIAN LITERARY RENAISSANCE, began in 1968, when N. SCOTT MOMADAY's *HOUSE MADE OF DAWN* received the Pulitzer Prize. After this success, a host of Native American writer's works were published, critically recognized, and used in college classrooms. While this would seem to indicate a new beginning for Native American literature, Ortiz's poetry collection *Going for the Rain* illustrates that Native Americans have never stopped telling their stories; rather, a non-Native book-buying public finally started listening to and reading them.

Inspired by the Red Power Movement's ideology, Ortiz positions his poems against Western culture and values. *Going for the Rain*'s prologue clarifies the Acoma Pueblo belief in the importance of journeys for personal growth and development, and Ortiz invites us to follow his narrator on a journey to learn how he confronts life and transforms experience into lessons that lead to self-understanding. Each section incorporates an Acoma worldview that has shaped and influenced the narrator, with the most important influence sacred stories. The first poem, "The Creation, According to Coyote," portrays Coyote as a storyteller. Because Acoma sacred stories tell that Coyote was created before humans, Coyote is able to tell the People about their creation as well as their emergence into the world they now occupy: "You were born when you came / from that body, the earth; / your black head burst from granite" (5–7). Here one learns why the land figures largely in Ortiz's work and why his homeland remains a significant component of his identity—Coyote instructs him that the earth gave birth to his people. This poem illustrates a familial relationship between the Acoma and their homeland in which the earth is their mother. Several poems link land, childbirth, and Ortiz's children with the Acoma people's regeneration and ongoing relationship to their homeland, reinforcing the relationship between land and people. His children, nature, and

the landscape become reminders that Ortiz will recall as he prepares for the journey ahead when he "goes for the rain."

Going for the Rain contains four sections with titles that reflect different times and places in Ortiz's travels. In the first section, "Preparation," Ortiz prepares for a journey away from home. To ensure that he remembers where he started, he reflects on his past and recalls significant events in his life thus far. These memories will strengthen him when moments of weakness occur.

In "Leaving," the second section, Ortiz reminds us that for the Acoma people traveling is like praying. Just as praying forms a spiritual bond with a higher power, traveling will help the narrator "to recognize / the relationships [he] share[s] with everything" ("Many Farm Notes" 4–5) around him, even the cold and impersonal cityscapes that contrast with home, where there are "red and brown land, / sage, and when it rains, / it smells like piñon" ("Leaving America" 11–13).

In the third section, "Returning," Ortiz goes home, recognizing the interconnections among language, identity, and place, all of which are expressed in "A Story of How a Wall Stands." Ortiz's father uses metaphors of earth and stone to highlight the source of Acoma strength and unity: "Underneath what looks like loose stone, / there is stone woven together" (6–7). The lesson that Ortiz's father passes on is that the land remains the foundation that will hold the people together in the same way that mud made from the earth holds together the stones that form the wall.

In the final section, "The Rain Falls," Ortiz is strengthened in the knowledge that he knows where he belongs in the world. The speaker thinks that wherever in the world he has traveled, his vision of his home has always been with him. He says, "When loneliness / for myself has over come me, / the Mountain has occurred" (72–73). The mountain known as Kaweshtima to the Acoma, a feminine snow-capped peak renamed Mount Taylor in honor of Zachary Taylor, will always remain a strong female presence in Ortiz's mind. These images of the mountain nourish his soul and remind him where he belongs even when he is far from home.

Going for the Rain chronicles the journeys that the Acoma believe are necessary for life and for survival, and as on all journeys there is always a return home. Ortiz's poems illustrate his early journeys, which become part of the stories that chronicle Native peoples' survival in a world that had always believed in their impending demise, so Indians' survival became a political statement voiced in the 1960s. In his journeys Ortiz shares his victories and his defeats, his joys, and the sadness that visits all of us. By returning home, he tells us, "The cycle has been traveled; life has beauty and meaning and it will continue because life has no end."

Bibliography

Litz, A. Walton. "Simon J. Ortiz." In *The American Writers.* Supplement IV. Part 2, 497–514. New York: Charles Scribner's Sons, 1996.

Ortiz, Simon. *Going for the Rain.* New York: Harper & Row, 1976.

———. "The Language We Know." In *I Tell You Now: Autobiographical Essays by Native American Writers,* edited by Brian Swann and Arnold Krupat, 187–194. Lincoln: University of Nebraska Press, 1987.

Elizabeth Archuleta

Going to War with All My Relations: New and Selected Poems   Wendy Rose (1993)

Powerful and tightly knit, this collection uses the poet's personal, spiritual, and pacifist concerns for the political work of making culture and history. The titular "war" is the nonviolent movement against colonization and destruction. WENDY ROSE claims in her preface, that this war is "everyone's war": Reverence for life should be natural for everyone because all are indigenous to the earth and therefore related (vii). Women, whom Rose links to the earth, are central to the book, and while many poems celebrate the ongoing work of creation and rebirth, this process is held in tension with threats of dissolution and failures of memory and empathy.

Stylistically much of this work is deeply ironic, yet Rose maintains her much-praised lyricism. Typically the irony hinges on a final turn of phrase blur-ring the subject and object of critique. Ambiguity does not undermine the political power of the work, however, but emphasizes the importance of empathetic imagination to power relations. In "Notes on a Conspiracy," for example, an Indian skull on museum display concludes that the scientist who digs her up is perhaps less alive, for he cannot hear her humanity nor sense the loss of his own (11–13). Many other poems also visit sites of cultural appropriation to rehumanize the commodified lives and deaths of Native peoples. Rose challenges stereotypes and other failures of memory and imagination in two later poems directly addressed to her European ancestors, in several others pointed at academics, and in a few about international conflicts. Rose's critique is generally double-edged, for even when identifying with indigenous bones in "Excavation at Santa Barbara Mission," for instance, she also appears as the digging anthropologist, seduced by the romantic colonial narrative (6–8). Identifying with both subject and object, she invites readers to pass in and out through the voices of her poems, balancing empathy with responsibility.

At "war" with deathly colonialism is the life power of women—as healers, midwives, mothers, and earth itself. In "To the Vision Seekers, Remember This," the speaker chastises scientists searching outer space to recall that "it is women / all women, where you come from / Earth the one to remember" (32–34). The ambiguous turn in this final line is rich: Earth is both remembered source and remembering spirit, able to restore her children to wholeness and relation. The natural and cultural work of creation is also celebrated as a feminine task in "To Make History," which has a compelling metaphor for Rose's own poetry, "Backlit spider webs . . . / fragile and tough as morning"—mystical songs by which a whole world is woven (22–23).

Bibliography

Fast, Robin Riley. "Who Speaks, Who Listens? Questions of Community, Audience, and Language in Poems by Chrystos and Wendy Rose." *Other Sisterhoods: Literary Theory and U.S. Women of*

Color, edited by Sandra Kumamoto Stanley, 139–170. Urbana: University of Illinois Press, 1998.

Rose, Wendy. Going to War with All My Relations. Flagstaff, Ariz.: Northland, 1993.

Wiget, Andrew. "Blue Stones, Bones, and Troubled Silver: The Poetic Craft of Wendy Rose." *Studies in American Indian Literatures* 5, no. 2 (1993): 29–33. SAIL Homepage. Available online. URL: http://oncampus.richmond.edu/faculty/ASAIL/sail-hp.html. Accessed on August 15, 2005.

Sheila Hughes

Good Journey, A Simon Ortiz (1977)

Through its celebration of ritual, remembrance, renewal, and personal growth, SIMON ORTIZ's second published work, *A Good Journey,* contains themes familiar to readers of his first collection. As in GOING FOR THE RAIN, Ortiz demonstrates his commitment to preserving and celebrating Acoma culture and identity through storytelling. The interview excerpt that opens the book emphasizes the prominent role that stories have played and continue to play in Native American communities. When asked why and for whom he writes, Ortiz tells us he writes "because Indians always tell a story. . . . The only way to continue is to tell a story and there is no other way. Your children will not survive unless you tell something about them—how they were born, how they came to this certain place, how they continued" (1). In other words, for the Acoma storytelling has been synonymous with survival.

Because survival includes not only the sacred but also the seemingly ordinary and everyday, Ortiz claims that he can only write what he knows. He concedes: "I can only give substance / and form to places I am familiar with" (16–17). Therefore, despite his many travels, he cannot identify with artificial structures. Whether encapsulated in a plane, wandering the labyrinth of an airport, or lost in urban mazes, his cityscapes contrast with the living landscape he calls home.

Yet, at times even nature appears perplexing. In "Grand Canyon Christmas Eve 1969" the forest demands, "CAMP ONLY IN CAMPING AREAS / NO WOOD GATHERING" (98–99). In "A Designated National Park" a sign demands that Ortiz "buy a permit to get back home," the charge being "AUTHORIZED / BY THE LAND AND WATER CONSERVATION-FUND / ACT OF 1965" (11–15). Ironically these fees support land and water conservation in a place where American Indians had managed to preserve and protect both without imposing laws or fees.

Powerful figures preserve some lands while they exploit and develop others for material gain. In "Long House Valley Poem" Ortiz describes a landscape wounded by Peabody Coal, and he points to power lines that stretch over mountains "toward Phoenix, toward Denver, / toward Los Angeles, toward Las Vegas, / carrying our mother away" (24–26). He indicts corporations that have obscured the land with "railroads, electric lines, gaslines, highways, phone / companies and cable TV" (28–29). Although progress has scarred the land, his poem "Earth and Rain, The Plants & Sun" proclaims, "Again and again, / the earth is new again" (34–35).

Similarly, "Survival This Way" traces the physical space he calls home, because this landscape is storied with features that connote his people's continuance in spite of everything: "Survival, I know how this way. / This way, I know. / It rains" (1–3). The stories that make up *A Good Journey* provide hope that life will endure. For Ortiz storytelling is synonymous with survival, so he keeps on telling the stories.

Bibliography

Oandassan, William. "Simon Ortiz: The Poet and His Landscape." *Studies in American Indian Literature.* 2, no. 1 (1987): 26–37.

Ortiz, Simon. *A Good Journey.* Tucson: University of Arizona Press, 1984.

———. "The Language We Know." In *I Tell You Now: Autobiographical Essays by Native American Writers,* edited by Brian Swann and Arnold Krupat, 187–194. Lincoln: University of Nebraska Press, 1987.

Elizabeth Archuleta

Good Message of Handsome Lake, The   Joseph Bruchac (1979)

This volume, as does much of JOSEPH BRUCHAC's work, aims to educate readers by correcting unfair stereotypes of Native Americans. To those who perceive Indians as a dejected group, Bruchac offers these poems and translations from Handsome Lake, a Seneca prophet and seminal figure in early 19th-century Iroquois history. After the American Revolution the tribes of the Iroquois were discouraged by their betrayal at the hands of the revolutionaries. At this low period Bruchac notes in his introduction, the "fresh vision" of Handsome Lake, or Ganio-dai'yo, as he is known to his people, revitalized the tribes. Unlike that of the Paiute prophet Wovoka, whose GHOST DANCE ended with the massacre at WOUNDED KNEE, Handsome Lake's influence continues today. Bruchac asserts in the introduction, "His vision holds up many of the enlightened and humane teachings which were part of the life of his people long before the coming of the Europeans, teachings which have assisted people to find their way back to the sacred circle."

Much of Bruchac's work retains the flavor of oral narrative, repeating important details and points. Poems in "The Coming of the Good Message" record the rise of the prophet Ganio-dai'yo. As many of his people despaired of the destruction that the revolution wrought on their lands and traditions, Ganio-dai'yo sought solace in the white man's drink. As a result, "There was much that was bad then / among his people, cheated of their land, / weakened with drink" and fearful that the Creator's Messengers "had forgotten them forever" (9). An aged man presumed dead, but instead taken to the spirit world, Ganio-dai'yo received a warning: "The Creator is not pleased / to see your people drunk / and doing evil" (10). For the rest of his life Ganio-dai'yo travels among his people, offering ways to reconstruct the traditional center for their lives.

"Sections from the Gai'wiio of Handsome Lake" provide lessons for proper conduct in this world. In straightforward language they offer positive guidelines for parent-child relationships as well as rules for compassionate treatment of poor children, orphans, and the aged. Individual poems make clear the benefits of hospitality and the damages wrought by gossiping, boasting, and drinking. Ganio-dai'yo delivers some of his messages through vivid metaphors. Greed, for example, is a large seated woman who grasps "frantically / at all the things / within her reach" but can never stand, either in this life or "upon the heaven road" (34). Other sections detail proper treatment of the earth. In response to Iroquois fears that "the white race / will wipe you out," Ganio-dai'yo assures them, "The Creator will care / for his real people" (33).

In the last section of the work whites forecast the demise of the Iroquois, but the Good Message has assured their survival. For Bruchac this belief system, revived from precolonial days, carries an important message not just to American Indians, but to all human beings. His translations make this message accessible to a wide audience.

See also NORTHEASTERN TRIBAL LITERATURE.

Margaret O'Shaugnessey

Gordon, Roxy   (1945–2000)

A participant in the AMERICAN INDIAN MOVEMENT (AIM), Gordon is as noted for his work coproducing Wowapi Press with his wife, Judy, as for his own literary, songwriting, and visual art activities.

Gordon attended the University of Texas (UT) at Austin before moving to Fort Belknap Reservation, Montana. He entered the publishing field as editor of UT's student literary magazine and the Belknap Reservation's newsletter. His first book was the autobiography *Some Things I Did* (1971), which details Roxy and Judy's experiences working for Project VISTA, a health care outreach organization, in the late 1960s. In 1974 the couple published a short-lived country-western music journal, *Picking up the Tempo*. They next created Wowapi Press, which would publish 20 books and Compact discs (CDs) between 1985 and 2001. With Wowapi's publication of *Coyote Papers* (1985), he began a series of lucrative collaborations with LEANNE HOWE, first as her publisher and later as coauthor of three plays: *Big Pow Wow: A Time to Change* (1987), *Indian Radio Days* (1993), and *Indian Road Show* (1995).

Gordon's BREEDS (1984) is a collection of short stories, poems, drawings, and essays, including "Pilgrims." According to PAULA GUNN ALLEN, this regularly anthologized short story reverses the traditional wisdom that the foundation of American democracy lies in the English Pilgrim settlements, suggesting that the generosity of the Algonquian people, and the pilgrimages of the Native Americans, produced the true breeding ground of democratic principle (Allen 115).

Gordon also made five music recordings, most with the support of the musician/producer Wes McGee. His premature death left behind an elaborate estate of multimedia work, such as the album *Townes Asked Did Hank Williams Ever Write Anything as Good as Nothing* (2001), which is gradually being released. Ever the activist, he arranged for his memorial announcements to instruct that gifts be submitted to the defense fund of Leonard Peltier, a fellow AIM member who is currently serving two consecutive, and controversial, life sentences in Leavenworth Federal Prison.

Bibliography

Allen, Paula Gunn, ed. *Song of the Turtle: American Indian Literature 1974–1994.* New York: Ballantine Books, 1996.

D'Aponte, Mimi Gisolfi, ed. *Seventh Generation: An Anthology of Native American Plays.* New York: Theatre Communications Group, 1999.

Shoemaker, Nancy, ed. *Clearing a Path: Theorizing the Past in Native American Studies.* New York: Routledge, 2002.

Ben Fisler

Gould, Janice   (1949–)

Of Koyangk'auwi and Maidu descent, the writer, poet, and scholar Janice Gould was born in San Diego in 1949. Gould completed undergraduate and master's degrees at the University of California at Berkeley before eventually undertaking doctoral studies in the Department of English at the University of New Mexico (UNM). While a graduate student at UNM she was the recipient of several academic awards, including the prestigious Ford Dissertation Fellowship. Upon completion of her Ph.D. she held various teaching positions at the University of Santa Fe and the University of Northern Colorado. She is currently an assistant professor at Willamette University in Salem, Oregon, where she also holds the Hallie Ford Chair in Creative Writing.

Gould has been writing for over two decades and is the author of three poetry collections— *Alphabet, Earthquake Weather,* and *Beneath My Heart.* In 2003 she collaborated with Dean Rader in editing *Speak to Me Words: Essays on American Indian Poetry.* In addition, her writings have appeared in several academic and popular journals and anthologies. For her contributions to the field of English literature, Gould has been the beneficiary of grants from the National Endowment for the Arts and the Astraea Foundation.

Gould's scholarly and creative writing often attempt to negotiate the myriad cultural trajectories that lie at the interface of identity politics for a Native American lesbian. In *Earthquake Weather* this interface is amplified when she introspectively asks: "What's wrong with me? / Where do I belong? Why / am I here? Why can't I / hold on?" Here Gould clearly invokes those dilemmas associated with living in a heterosexist culture that privileges whiteness. Through her engagement with such issues Gould routinely utilizes her writing to express marginalization encountered by homosexuals and visible minorities. In conscientiously incorporating anecdotal experience in the purview of poetry and academic work, Janice Gould is a seminal figure in describing the contextual realities of Native American women who do not conform to, and thereby defy, the Western paradigm of compulsory heterosexuality.

Bibliography

Gould, Janice. *Beneath My Heart: Poetry.* Ithaca, N.Y.: Firebrand Books, 1990.

———. *Speak to Me Words: Essays on Contemporary American Poetry* (with Dean Rader). Tucson: University of Arizona Press, 2003.

Ajnesh Prasad

Gourd Dancer, The　N. Scott Momaday　(1976)

N. Scott Momaday's *The Gourd Dancer* includes all 18 of the poems from his chapbook *Angle of Geese and Other Poems* (1974), as well as two dozen new poems. Although it was the result of nearly 20 years of writing poetry, the book contains relatively few poems. Yet the collection, crucial in establishing Momaday's reputation as a poet, demonstrates the author's wide range of formal and thematic concerns.

The first poem in *The Gourd Dancer,* "Bear," is also the first poem in *Angle of Geese* and in *In the Presence of the Sun* (1992), a major collection of poetry and stories from throughout Momaday's career. "Bear" can be understood as one of Momaday's signature works; first published in the *New Mexico Quarterly,* it won an Academy of American Poets Prize in 1962. The poem takes as its subject an old bear that, though once maimed by a trap, persists in surving even as buzzards fly overhead. The bear is endangered yet stubbornly courageous. The poem's five unrhymed quatrains signal Momaday's interest in conventional poetic forms and reveal the stylistic influence of Yvor Winters, the poet and professor who supervised Momaday's studies at Stanford University. The syllabic verse and six quatrains of the complex "Angle of Geese" and the rhyming couplets of "Plainview: 1" similarly reveal Momaday's careful attention to poetic form.

The four poems in the Plainview series are formally very different from each other, but they are all set on the Oklahoma plains, in the traditional Kiowa territory. These poems and others in the collection address Momaday's Kiowa heritage. "The Gourd Dancer," for example, is dedicated to Mammedaty, Momaday's deceased grandfather. (Mammedaty also occupies a central role in Momaday's *The Way to Rainy Mountain* [1969].) The poem is composed of four sections, two verse and two prose: "The Omen," "The Dream," "The Dance," and "The Giveaway." Each of these sections is concerned with aspects of Kiowa ceremony and ancestral knowledge.

In contrast, the poems in the third section of *The Gourd Dancer,* such as "Krasnopresnens-kaya Station," draw on Momaday's experiences in the Soviet Union, where he taught a course in American literature at the University of Moscow in 1974. Momaday also makes reference in *The Gourd Dancer* to the Japanese painter Hokusai and the American painter Georgia O'Keeffe, demonstrating his interest in the visual arts. The book also includes ink drawings by Momaday himself. As much of Momaday's writing does, *The Gourd Dancer* reflects the author's interests in a wide range of subjects, themes, forms, and influences.

Bibliography

Bruchac, Joseph. "The Magic of Words: An Interview with N. Scott Momaday." In *Survival This Way: Interviews with American Indian Poets,* edited by Joseph Bruchac, 173–191. Tucson: University of Arizona Press, 1987.

Lundquist, Suzanne Evertsen. "N. Scott Momaday." In *Dictionary of Literary Biography.* Vol. 256. edited by Richard H. Cracroft, 203–218. Detroit: Gale, 2002.

Schubnell, Matthias. *Conversations with N. Scott Momaday.* Jackson: University Press of Mississippi, 1997.

———. *N. Scott Momaday: The Cultural and Literary Background.* Norman: University of Oklahoma Press, 1985.

Nicholas Bradley

government agencies

Perhaps no other ethnic group has had their lives so utterly dominated by U.S. government agencies as American Indians. Government agencies had dramatic and far-reaching effects over many aspects of Native lives, and equally of Native literature. The two government institutions that affected Native lives the most are the military and the Bureau of Indian Affairs (BIA), especially BIA-run boarding schools. Both put an enormous amount of effort into assimilating Natives into Anglo-American culture, seeking to "kill the Indian, save the man." Natives successfully resisted forced assimilation, but not without great pain and lasting devastation of Native cultures such as loss of language and culture and the horrors inherent to war. These struggles were both fought with and vividly illustrated through some of the finest works in Native literature.

Most early Native novelists were products of BIA boarding schools. Ironically their experiences often turned them into activists seeking to preserve and defend Native cultures. Dilemmas of whether or how much to assimilate and how or how much to hold on to traditional Native cultures were central to these novels. D'Arcy McNickle, Charles Eastman (Ohiyesa), and Zitkala-Ša, leaders in the premier Native activist group of the early 20th century, the Society of American Indians, decried the boarding school experience as alienating and destructive. In McNickle's *The Surrounded*, Archilde León's time in boarding school leaves him torn between white culture and the Salish heritage of a mother who is returning to her Native culture in her old age. Similar themes showed up in McNickle's short stories such as "The Hawk Is Hungry." Zitkala-Ša's criticism of the military discipline and Christian evangelizing in most BIA schools in a series of articles finally led to her being fired by the BIA. This did not deter her further criticisms in *American Indian Stories*. Eastman's autobiography *From the Deep Woods to Civilization* not only criticized the bigotry in boarding schools, but offered the wisdom of Native cultures as an alternative that whites should learn to understand.

The wave of emerging Native literature in the 1960s and 1970s was dominated by revolutionary works on Native military veterans. N. Scott Momaday's *House Made of Dawn* was a stunning depiction of the alienation and trauma caused by war and the particular hardships and ironies faced by Native veterans in particular. What both it and Leslie Marmon Silko's *Ceremony* shared was the use of the mixed-blood veteran experience to depict the alienation caused by the persistent ironies of serving a nation that fails to acknowledge sacrifice and a society that only temporarily accepts you. The characters of Abel, from *House*, and Tayo, from *Ceremony*, are mute and anguished, suffering until healed by a return to Native values and beliefs.

David Seals's film *Powwow Highway* put together two mismatched characters who often misunderstand each other, the burned-out militant activist and veteran Buddy Redbow and the comic misfit/philosopher Philbert Bono. Buddy is a very accurate picture of many Native veterans, seemingly hostile but well informed in why he has every right to be so. Adrian Louis's *Skins* has another pair of opposites, the brothers Rudy and Mogie Yellow Shirt, Mogie an alcoholic veteran who can only deal with life through humor and constant drinking.

Louise Erdrich and Louis Owens deal in part with the subject of Native draft resistance in their novels. In Erdrich's *Love Medicine* one of the novel's principal characters, Henry, Jr., is a veteran whose tragic death follows his taking home the violence of war and abusing women. Lipsha Morrissey tries to join the military, only wanting to gain the approval of the community and to avoid the draft, only to find he is exempt because of the "flaw" of his heart's loving too much. Owens's *The Sharpest Sting*, while on the surface a murder mystery, is more an exploration of the meaning of Native military service and the irony of seeking white approval through service coupled with denials of being Indian and wishing to be assimilated. Owens argues the Choctaw way of being a warrior has been warped by service to the U.S. military, from its original intent of being unafraid to die or sacrifice, to following orders to kill.

Phillip Red Eagle's *Red Earth: Two Novellas*, as do *House Made of Dawn* and *Ceremony*, deals with themes of surviving the pain of war through ceremonies. As Owens does, Red Eagle contends that Native (in this case, Lakota) warrior traditions were once about serving people, but the lack of honor in forcing soldiers to kill the people they kill in wartime leads to spiritual darkness. Mark St. Pierre's *Of Uncommon Birth: Dakota Sons in Vietnam* takes a similar approach. St. Pierre's work is historical fiction, based on the true story of the brothers Dale and Billy Jealous of Him. In common with other writers, St. Pierre focuses on the contradictions of serving in a war for an often hostile or bigoted society and the use of ceremony to heal veterans.

Running through all these works is a persistent argument that not only do government attempts at ASSIMILATION fail, the effort itself exposes the hypocrisy of the dominant society while wreaking havoc on the lives of those the effort allegedly helps. Cultural self-determination and struggle to escape the power of government agencies over Native lives remain persistent themes and demands of Native literature.

Bibliography

Bonnin, Gertrude. *American Indian Stories.* Washington, D.C.: Hayworth, 1921.

Eastman, Charles. *From the Deep Woods to Civilization.* Boston: Little, Brown, 1916.

Erdrich, Louise. *Love Medicine.* New York: Holt, Rinehart, & Winston, 1984.

Louis, Adrian. *Skins.* New York: Crown, 1995.

McNickle, Darcy. *The Surrounded.* Albuquerque: University of New Mexico Press, 1978.

Momaday, N. Scott. *House Made of Dawn.* New York: HarperCollins, 1968.

Owens, Louis. *The Sharpest Sting.* Norman: University of Oklahoma Press, 1995.

Red Eagle, Phillip. *Red Earth: Two Novellas.* Duluth, Minn.: Holy Cow Press, 1997.

Seals, David. *The Powwow Highway: A Novel.* New York: Orion Books, 1979.

Silko, Leslie Marmon. *Ceremony.* New York: Viking Penguin, 1977.

St. Pierre, Mark. *Of Uncommon Birth.* Norman: University of Oklahoma Press, 2004.

Al Carroll

Grand Avenue Greg Sarris (1994)

Subtitled *A Novel in Stories, Grand Avenue* is a collection of short stories with interlocking plots about a poverty-stricken multiethnic community—including Native Americans, African Americans, and Hispanics—in Santa Rosa, California. These stories portray the life of five generations of an extended Pomo family who struggle for survival. In this debut fictional work GREG SARRIS creates an assortment of characters who relate their frustration, despair, longing, and redemption with candor, humor, and irony. Critics have applauded the talent of the author, calling him an important part of the modern AMERICAN INDIAN LITERARY RENAISSANCE.

Grand Avenue consists of 10 stories, five of which have been previously published. "The Magic Pony," "Slaughterhouse," and "How I Got to Be Queen" are narrated by young adolescents whose growing pains are exacerbated by their dysfunctional families and crime-infested environment. In "The Magic Pony" a 14-year-old named Ruby Jones is obsessed with a disabled pony, which takes on uncanny powers in her imagination and serves as an escape from her deprived existence. Ruby returns in "Slaughterhouse" as the object of Frankie Silva's sexual desire, but to his great horror and dismay, the well-mannered virgin turns out to be the newest member of a prostitution ring. In "How I Got to Be Queen" teenage violence culminates in Alice's firing a shotgun to stop an attack on her sister, Justine.

Four stories are told from the perspectives of middle-aged narrators about life-changing events. In "The Progress of This Disease" Anna (daughter of Zelda Toms and wife of Albert Silva) faces the prospect of losing a 14-year-old daughter to cancer. "Joy Ride" is Albert's story about his temptation to have sex with a 16-year-old girl (Justine) and being reminded of Mollie (Justine's mother), the passion of his youth. In "The Indian Maid" Stella (another daughter of Zelda) is on the verge of leaving home to become a secretary in Tucson, Arizona. "Secret Letters" depicts Steven Pen's quest to claim his illegitimate son, whom he fathered unknowingly with his half sister, Pauline (a cousin of Anna).

"Waiting for the Green Frog" and "The Water Place" are both narrated by the magic healer Nellie Copaz (a cousin of Zelda). In the first story Nellie recalls her childhood experience of acquiring healing songs from a green frog. In the second story she teaches Alice the art of basket weaving, which signals the passing on of culture and tradition to the future generation. "Sam Toms's Last Song" depicts the protagonist's thwarted attempt to move in with Nellie. At 100, Sam Toms (Zelda's father) is the oldest surviving member of the clan.

A two-part miniseries of *Grand Avenue* was produced by Home Box Office (HBO) and first aired on June 30, 1996.

Bibliography

Bellafante, Ginia. "*Grand Avenue.*" *Time,* 1 July 1996, 65.

Bissley, Jackie. "*Grand Avenue.*" *Wind Speaker* 14, no. 8 (1996): 12–13.

Burnham, Michelle. "Pomo Basketweaving, Poison, and the Politics of Restoration in Greg Sarris's *Grand Avenue.*" *Studies in American Indian Literatures* 14, no. 4 (2002): 18–36.

Sanchez, Greg. "*Grand Avenue: A Novel in Stories.*" *World Literature Today* 70, no. 1 (1996): 219–220.

Wenxin Li

Grass Dancer, The   Susan Power   (1994)

In her novel *The Grass Dancer* the Standing Rock Sioux author SUSAN POWER fluidly blends history with stories of contemporary Dakota life in a narrative style reminiscent of LOUISE ERDRICH's. The earliest chapter of the novel, "1981," introduces the initial cast of characters: Pumpkin, an 18-year-old Menominee woman who transgresses gender norms by dancing the Grass Dance, a men's dance, as she travels the POW WOW circuit the summer before beginning college; Harley Wind Soldier, a young Dakota Grass dancer whose mother, Lydia, has not spoken since the deaths of her husband, Calvin, and his son, Duane, 17 years earlier; Charlene Thunder, a schoolmate of Harley's whose unrequited love for him is paralleled by the community's fear of her grandmother; Charlene's grandmother, Mercury (aka Anna) Thunder, who is called the "reservation witch," since she uses her inherited power for personal gain; and Mercury's foil, Herod Small War, a Yuwipi man, or spiritual adviser, who is the grandfather of Harley's best friend, Frank Pipe. Most of the remaining sections of *The Grass Dancer* spiral back toward an 1864 narrative of contact to explain the histories and subsequent motivations behind these characters and events.

Power's novel begins in the late 20th century; the intertwined narrative strands all lead back to the story of Charlene and Mercury Thunder's ancestress, Cuwignaka Duta, or Red Dress, a young Dakota woman who answers the call of a dream and travels with her brother to Fort Laramie in 1864. At the fort Red Dress becomes a conduit for Dakota spirits, who cause three soldiers to commit suicide before Red Dress is killed. Red Dress's ghost then follows her brother back to their camp, where Harley's ancestor, Ghost Horse, awaits their return. When Red Dress's body is taken back to camp, Ghost Horse keeps her spirit alive for a year in a traditional Sioux practice called Ghost keeping. However, Ghost Horse does not release Red Dress's spirit appropriately at the ceremony's conclusion. Thus, Red Dress is caught in the land and ongoing story of her Dakota people, where she becomes a repository of tribal and familial memory. As such, Red Dress is central to Harley's ultimate recovery in the vision quest that concludes the text.

Bibliography

Brogan, Jacqueline Vaught. "'Two Distinct Voices': The Revolutionary Call of Susan Power's *The Grass Dancer.*" *North Dakota Quarterly* 67, no. 2 (spring 2000): 109–125.

Susan Power. *Roofwalker.* Minneapolis: Milkweed Press, 2002.

Lisa Tatonetti

Green Grass, Running Water   Thomas King   (1993)

Green Grass, Running Water suggests that Native people can take control of their world by taking control of the stories told about them. The novel blends Native and Christian mythology, classics of Western literature, romances, movies, history, and contemporary realistic narratives, retelling many traditional Western stories from an indigenous point of view.

In the frame story an unnamed first-person narrator guides the TRICKSTER FIGURE Coyote, and the readers, through the overlapping narratives, but s/he is not necessarily reliable. *Green Grass, Running*

Water was written, in part, for an academic audience, and King's narrator leads academic readers into traps set especially for them. The text is littered with references to historical, literary, and cultural figures that invite an academic scavenger hunt. As well, the stories are linked through floating and water imagery, which, as Coyote says, "must mean something" (293). To an academic reader this imagery connects to the phrase *running water* in the title, which in turn refers to treaty language; many TREATIES were supposed to be valid as long as the rivers ran. American and Canadian authorities dammed the rivers and ignored treaty rights. The breaking of the dam at the end of the novel thus represents the reclaiming of rights by Native peoples. The narrator, however, dismisses Coyote's and the reader's attempts at academic decoding by saying that the water and floating imagery are simply "the way it happens in oral stories" (293). Coyote's lack of awareness illustrates the shortfalls of the Western critical tradition. Most academic tools do not take into account the oral traditions from which much Native literature springs.

The four sections of the novel are narrated by four traditional Native mythological figures: First Woman, Thought Woman, Changing Woman, and Old Woman. As each tells her story, she moves from Native stories to Christian and literary ones, and her identity shifts. In the Native tales each is female and central; in the Christian texts each is female, but relegated to a secondary position; in the literary texts each takes on a white male persona in order to resist the role of "Native sidekick." The new personas do not erase the identities that preceded them. The Lone Ranger, Robinson Crusoe (from Daniel Defoe's novel of the same name), Ishmael (from Herman Melville's *Moby-Dick*), and Hawkeye (from James Fenimore Cooper's *Last of the Mohicans*) are still Native women, but their new labels help them subvert the sexism and racism of the texts in which they find themselves. The women create their own stories, and thus their own worlds.

Interwoven with these mythic narratives are the realistic stories of the Blackfeet inhabitants of the town of Blossom on a single weekend during the Sundance. Flashbacks show how the characters' experiences and family histories have influenced them, and how other people's narratives have affected their lives. Alberta resists Western romantic traditions by dating both Lionel and Charlie, and by attempting to have a baby on her own. Eli resists the political, economic, and scientific narratives that have led to a dam's being built on the reservation. Lionel has allowed other people's medical, political, and economic discourses to govern him and, consequently, is not in control of his own life. When the Lone Ranger, Robinson Crusoe, Hawkeye, and Ishmael arrive in Blossom and attempt to fix Lionel's life, the mythic and realistic narratives merge.

The narrator asserts that "there are no truths . . . only stories" (326); stories provide meaning and order to the world. The novel begins with a creation myth, and in Hawkeye, Ishmael, Robinson Crusoe, and the Lone Ranger's stories, whoever is telling the story also creates the world. But creation is always plural and never complete. The four narrators see it as their function "to fix up the world" (104), but they recognize the danger of this project: Their earlier attempts led to a fire in Yellowstone, the eruption of Mount Saint Helens, and the stock market crash of 1929 (38). Coyote, on the other hand, believes in his own omniscience and omnipotence; he illustrates King's belief that, although human beings think they are "very smart, able to fix anything . . . In actual fact, human beings can destroy a lot easier than they can fix. They may do that yet" (Lutz 116). Industrialized society, with its Coyote-like confidence, is trying to create a paradise using modern technology, but in doing so, it unbalances the world, leading to destruction.

The ambiguous end of the novel illustrates the difficulty of fixing the world. The destruction of the dam frees the river, but the resulting flood kills Eli. Alberta becomes pregnant with Coyote's child; the union between a trickster who represents Native belief and a woman whose name (because it is also the name of a Canadian province) connects her to the land seems to offer a new beginning and a new world. The star that leads the characters to Blossom indicates the importance of the child. However, the Lone Ranger, Robinson Crusoe, Ishmael, and Hawkeye point out the ambiguity of this miraculous conception by implying that Coyote also impregnated Mary, the mother of Jesus Christ:

> *"But I was helpful, too," says Coyote.*
> *"That woman who wanted a baby. Now*
> *that was helpful."*
> *"Helpful!" said Robinson Crusoe. "You*
> *remember the last time you did that?"*
> *"I'm quite sure I was in Kamloops," says*
> *Coyote.*
> *"We haven't straightened out that mess*
> *yet,' said Hawkeye. (348)*

Not only does Coyote refuse to take responsibility for his offspring, but the Christian religion and its colonizing missionary impulse, which King criticizes in the novel, are also the result of his lust. Given this background, and Coyote's propensity for making mistakes, this second nativity is as likely to cause chaos as it is to engender a bright new future.

Bibliography

Davidson, Arnold E., et al. *Border Crossing: Thomas King's Cultural Inversions.* Toronto: University of Toronto Press, 2003.

Flick, Jane. "Reading Notes for Thomas King's *Green Grass, Running Water.*" *Canadian Literature* 161, no. 2 (1999): 140–172.

King, Thomas. *Green Grass, Running Water.* Toronto: HarperCollins, 1993.

Lutz, Hartmut. *Contemporary Challenges: Conversations with Canadian Native Authors.* Saskatoon: Fifth House, 1991.

Judith Leggatt

Green Grow the Lilacs Lynn Riggs (1931)

While in France on a Guggenheim Fellowship in 1928–29, LYNN RIGGS began his Pulitzer Prize–nominated play. The original 1931 production by the Theatre Guild starred Franchot Tone, Richard Hale, and June Walker, with Lee Strasberg in a supporting role. Still, the play is probably most famous as the source of Richard Rodgers and Oscar Hammerstein II's highly acclaimed 1943 breakthrough musical *Oklahoma!* Writing to the drama editor of the *New York Times,* Hammerstein praises Riggs's script, calling it "the wellspring of almost all that is good in *Oklahoma!* I kept many of the lines of the original play without making any changes in them at all for the simple reason that they could not be improved on—at any rate, not by me. . . . Lynn Riggs and *Green Grow the Lilacs* are the very soul of *Oklahoma!*" (Lynn Riggs Memorial).

Indeed, even before Rodgers and Hammerstein introduced audiences to such memorable songs as "Oh, What a Beautiful Mornin'" and "The Surrey with the Fringe on Top," music played a central role in telling the story of the rivals Curly McClain, a cowboy, and Jeeter Fry, a farmhand, each pursuing the affections of Laurey Williams. Throughout the play Curly, Laurey, Aunt Eller, Ado Annie, and other members of the ensemble sing folksongs and cowboy tunes that help establish setting, develop character, and comment on dramatic action. This gives the entire work a folksy, lyrical quality that invites audience rapport yet resists simplistic interpretation or categorization.

In his preface to the Samuel French edition of the play, Riggs explains his intent to "recapture in a kind of nostalgic glow . . . the great range of mood which characterized the old folk songs and ballads I used to hear in my Oklahoma childhood—their quaintness, their sadness, their robustness, their simplicity, their hearty or bawdy humors, their sentimentalities, their melodrama, their touching sweetness" (iii). True to the multifaceted qualities of the songs Riggs hoped to reflect, the plot and characters of *Green Grow the Lilacs* raise complex questions and embody paradoxes. The romantic hero Curly defends Laurey against unwelcome advances from others but also jokes that he'll tie her to the hitching post after they get married, lest another man run off with her while he's at work. Laurey herself possesses an ingénue's feminine sweetness and purity, as well as strong wit and intuition. At the same time, though, her daydreams reveal an unattractive materialism and acquisitive desire that may be read as a critique of colonialism. Stage directions indicate Jeeter has a "curious earth-colored face," but whether this appearance suggests something of his work in the fields, his ethnicity, or both, is unclear. He perpetrates antisocial behavior but also criticizes that society for belittling and ostracizing him.

In Indian Territory in 1900 "society" was undergoing significant changes, a dynamic influencing Riggs's play on several levels. While picking buttercups in a meadow, Laurey encounters a symbol of death and renewal: a snake eating its own tail. Characters question issues of nationality, criminality, and communal culture, some eagerly anticipating change and Oklahoma's admission to the Union, others hoping to preserve the status quo. Aunt Eller's advice for surviving hardships, appreciating goodness, and navigating life's drastic changes resonates as much today as in 1931: "You got to be hearty. You *got* to be" (76).

Bibliography

Kirle, Bruce. "Reconciliation, Resolution, and the Political Role of *Oklahoma!* in American Consciousness." *Theatre Journal* 55, no. 2 (2003): 251–274.

Riggs, Lynn. *Cherokee Night and Other Plays.* Norman: University of Oklahoma Press, 2003.

Julie K. Gonnering

Griever: An American Monkey King in China   Gerald Vizenor (1987)

Praised for the unique comparison between Chinese folk myth and Native American TRICKSTER FIGURE tales, *Griever: An American Monkey King in China* was awarded the Fiction Collective Prize in 1986 and later awarded the American Book Award in 1988. Similar to GERALD VIZENOR himself, Griever De Hocus, a MIXED-BLOOD tribal reservation teacher, takes a trip to teach in China. The story that follows is typical of a trickster narrative, full of pandemonium and humor. Cecilia Sims calls Griever the "trickiest of trickster[s]," and he is by turn a philosopher, trickster, man, teacher, clown, animal, and political protester. Though switching roles is an integral part of what makes a "trickster," Griever is unique in the parallel portrayal of Chinese cultural icons, most notably the Monkey King. The many roles of Griever alternate lest we take one too seriously, but he is not the only character in the book who has a multifaceted identity. Many of Vizenor's characters are already rewritten versions of characters from Wu Che'eng-en's *Monkey,* and in the novel their identities rapidly multiply as well. Take, for example, China, who is not only a friend from Griever's childhood reservation back home, but also the very country he addresses in his letters to her. In this way, with multiple roles for each character, identity becomes unstable and highly questionable throughout the book.

Vizenor uses Griever's story to set up cultural comparisons between Chinese culture and Native history, life, and religion. As political prisoners drive by on their way to execution, Griever remembers childhood stories about the government's pushing his own people onto a reservation. When he has religious discussions with Chinese philosophers, the two seemingly distinct sets of belief blur with their similarities. And throughout the whole text, Griever may be a trickster to Native American peoples, but to the Chinese he is the Monkey King.

On Griever's journey we meet a man who breaks stones with his hands, pigs that play basketball, a warrior clown, a rooster named Matteo Ricci (named after the European who "discovered" China, another trickster antic) who always knows the time of day, Chinese political figures, and "common" men and women whose lives are no different from those of the figures mentioned before them. Griever meets these people on his escapades and always takes each for what he is, man or beast: a kindred spirit. Vizenor writes that Griever is

> an old mind monkey. . . . With colored pens he thinks backward, stops time like a shaman. . . . The lines and curves in his pictures are dance, meditation moves, those silent gestures in an opera scene. . . . There is much more to this trickster than mere transcendence. . . . He

paints the comic resolutions back into tragic dances; he paints to find a patron, and he found one in the white cock with the feathered shanks. (84)

In this passage dance, an element vital to Native American identity, is compared to meditation moves and gestures from an opera, which is vital to Chinese culture. We learn much more about Griever as a figure here: Griever embodies a trickster because he can make comic resolution into tragic dances, can reverse a situation at will.

This is illustrated through the discovery of Matteo Ricci, the rooster that becomes Griever's companion after he is liberated. On one of his first outings from the university Griever creates a commotion in the marketplace by demanding the freedom of chickens. "Cutthroat"—the merchant selling the chickens—does not understand why Griever wants every chicken in the cage. Griever's behavior attracts a crowd, which views him as what he is: a clown. Yet while others are laughing, Griever's own laughter is strained. He takes this enterprise very seriously. Finally, after handing over all of his money, he succeeds in freeing the remaining chickens and takes Matteo Ricci home with him.

While this scene is preposterous, and while the crowd laughs at the woman who is hit with a chicken or Griever, who is dancing on the butcher's table, this moment foreshadows a scene much more serious later in the novel. In a very similar gesture Griever highjacks a truck taking political prisoners to be executed by acting as a clown and leading the soldiers to believe he is merely performing for the sake of the crowd. After escaping with the truck, Griever tells them they are free, and they respond, "No one is free." Many of the prisoners are recovered and shot on sight, while Griever's memory leaves us with the remaining prisoners waiting in the truck for the soldiers to find them. This scene becomes a serious commentary on Communist China.

His crazy behavior, while often funny, also has serious consequences in this political climate. In one such moment Griever replaces the music played every morning, "The East Is Red," with "Stars and Stripes Forever"—an act that could send him to jail or worse. In keeping with the ability to turn "comic resolutions into tragic dances," the last two scenes comment on the politics in China, turning a sober note into a beautiful scene: Griever, floating over China in an ultralight airplane, with a view of the countryside, where the "world of the peasants is very peaceful, like those brush strokes in an ink painting."

A novel that is both funny and serious, *Griever: An American Monkey King in China* is a unique effort in Native American literature. Vizenor's writing leads the reader to embrace Griever's philosophy that "this is a marvelous world of tricksters."

Bibliography
Krupat, Arnold. *The Turn to the Native: Studies in Criticism and Culture.* Lincoln: University of Nebraska Press, 1996.

Sims, Cecilia. "The Rebirth of Indian and Chinese Mythology in Gerald Vizenor's *Griever: An American Monkey King in China.*" In *Native American Writers,* edited by Harold Bloom. Philadelphia: Chelsea House, 1998.

Vizenor, Gerald. *Griever: An American Monkey King in China.* Minneapolis: University of Minnesota Press, 1987.

———. *Narrative Chance: Postmodern Discourses on Native American Indian Literatures.* Norman: University of Oklahoma Press, 1993.

Brianna R. Burke

Grieves, Catron   (1951–   )
Catron Grieves, of the Cherokee Nation of Oklahoma (born Brenda Catron, 1951), lived in a traditional settlement east of Tahlequah, until economic hardship forced her to leave high school and enter a trade school at the age of 17.

Grieves's poems and stories often function as Native translators or storytellers, with their multiple-voiced indigenous perspectives demonstrating her strong sense of place and heritage. Her poetry first appeared in 1978 in Oklahoma's small press journals. Many of these poems are compiled in

Yellow Silk and Other Poems (1987), her master's creative thesis in poetry, written for her M.A. in creative studies (1987). The first 50 poems were published as *Moonrising* under the name *Catron Grieves*. Her chapbook is *A Terrible Foe This Bear*.

Grieves writes from a feminist perspective about ground level, concrete experiences of Native Americans. JOY HARJO calls this approach "her rootedness," something not "trotted out for show" but true poetry. Grieves's mother—who also wrote poetry and taught her as a child about Karl Marx's theory—introduced her to the strange and contradictory problems of Cherokee Indian identities. "Indian Car" (1996) poignantly explores these difficulties. While traveling to a POW WOW across Iowa in this car, she and her companion talk "about becoming more like the people / at home," even though each has lost native fluency. The car is a moving home base, one that leaves her feeling dislocated but also able to rediscover her Indian identity. After all, it is a vehicle with "good transmission, bald tires, cracked windshield," "you probably know the type."

Grieves explores and examines the personal cost of Cherokee women's dislocation in poems that function for her as letters—letters written to ancestors past and yet to be. "You asked once for something really Native," she replies in "Connuche" (1997), and provides the detailed recipe in what Geary Hobson has noted as "a prose style that cleverly masks its surprising poetic rhythm," yet concludes she "must be a displaced poet" after imagining a white person's asking, "What makes you Indian?" in "This Poem Takes Its Place in Oklahoma" (1992). A sensitive scholar of the complex mix of culture and gender, Grieves writes poetry to strengthen and enrich the connections between Indian women.

Bibliography

Grieves, Catron. *Moonrising.* Oklahoma City: Red Dirt Press, 1987.

Lori Vermaas

Hale, Janet Campbell (1947–)

The youngest of four daughters, Janet Hale was born in Riverside, California, and lived on the Couer d'Alene Reservation in central Washington and the Yakama Reservation in northern Idaho. Her father was a full blood Coeur d'Alene and her mother was Kootenai/Cree/Irish. Her childhood was nomadic, as she moved with her mother to escape her alcoholic and abusive father. Hale's mother was also verbally abusive to Hale, causing the young girl to write, beginning at age nine, as refuge from the abuse and isolation. At 16, she moved to Santa Fe, New Mexico, to study at the Institute of American Indian Arts. There she met her first husband, whom she would divorce in 1965. They have a son together, Aaron Nicholas. Alone in San Francisco, without a high school diploma, Hale worked and received welfare assistance to survive. With her son at a government-funded day care center, she studied at City College of San Francisco, transferred to Berkeley after one year, finished her B.A. in rhetoric in 1974, and studied law for two years. At Berkeley she met her second husband, Stephen Dinsmore Hale, and they had a child together, Jennifer Elizabeth. She received her M.A. in English at University of California (UC) Davis in 1984.

Hale has taught at several locations including Iowa State University and at the University of California, Santa Cruz. She has won several accolades including the Vincent Price Poetry Award (1963), New York Poetry Day Award (1964), a McNickle Research Fellowship at the Newberry Library in Chicago (1984), a Pulitzer Prize nomination for *The Jailing of Cecelia Capture* (1985), the American Book Award for *Bloodlines: Odyssey of a Native Daughter* (1994), a National Endowment for the Arts Grant (1995), a Carnegie Authors Fund grant (1997), and a fellowship from Idaho Commission on the Arts (1998).

Hale's first poetry collection, *The Owl's Song* (1974), covers themes of racism and prejudice. The novel/autobiography *The Jailing of Cecelia Capture* (1985) continues those themes and also discusses class, single motherhood, welfare, abuse, and family. *Bloodlines: Odyssey of a Native Daughter* (1993), a collection of nonlinear tales, examines themes of family and abuse. Not only a writer, but a painter, Hale painted the cover for her short story collection *Women on the Run* (1999) and a mural at the Coeur d'Alene Tribal School. She is currently living on the Coeur d'Alene Reservation in Desmet, Idaho.

Bibliography

Hale, Frederick. *Janet Campbell Hale.* Boise, Idaho: Boise State University Press, 1996.

Hale, Janet Cambell. *Bloodlines: Odyssey of a Native Daughter.* New York: Random House, 1993.

————. *The Jailing of Cecelia Capture.* Albuquerque: University of New Mexico Press, 1985.

————. *The Owl's Song.* Garden City, N.Y.: Doubleday, 1974.

————. *Women on the Run.* Moscow, Idaho: University of Idaho Press, 1999.

Hale, Janet Campbell, and Karen Strom. "Janet Campbell Hale." Storytellers: Native American Authors Online. Available online. URL: http://www.hanksville.org/storytellers/jchale/. Accessed on August 15, 2005.

Holub, Maria-Theresia. "Janet Campbell Hale." Voices from the Gap: Women Writers of Color. Available online. URL: http://voices.cla.umn.edu/newsite/authors/HALEjanetcampbell.htm. Accessed on August 15, 2005.

Laura Madeline Wiseman

Halfbreed Chronicles and Other Poems, The   Wendy Rose (1985)

These poems transform the raw experience of a MIXED-BLOOD woman into powerful insight on questions of identity and relationship. Both personal and political in content and tone, they lament the isolation that often accompanies mixed identity and also use the condition of difference as a resource to sing healing.

The collection is composed of four sections—concentric circles rippling outward. "Part One: Sipapu" refers to the place where the Hopi ancestors emerged from earth. These poems express human identity as a relation to the earth, a mother of great power. In "Loo Wit" the sleeping volcano strikes back at machinery that "snarls and plows / great patches / of her skin," and WENDY ROSE celebrates her fiery eruption into song (24–26). Distinctively Hopi, poems like "What My Father Said" suggest that clan identity and history are spirits rooted in the earth (19–20). Part two steps from time immemorial into political history, recounting the pan-Indian struggle to reclaim what colonialism all but destroyed. "Wounded Knee: 1890–1973" memorializes the slaughter of the Sioux and identifies across history and tribe with the victims ("they shoot / at me / at all / my relations") (124–127). It then grants to them a vision

of their grandchildren—AMERICAN INDIAN MOVEMENT (AIM) activists protesting at the site—thus offering remembrance and rebirth. In "Naayawva Taawi" the Indians transform settlers' weapons "into charms" and grow strong on what ranchers discard: building nests and weaving the next generation from white refuse (37). "Dancing for the Whiteman" criticizes whites who desecrate pieces of Indian culture. By opening the poem "Yes, we are still doing it," though, Rose implicates herself and other artists in the process (1).

The most autobiographical, part three articulates the haunted isolation of a mixed-blood urban Indian. Images of ghosts, scars, and bones predominate. "Decide What to Do with Her" discusses a woman returned to her people after years among whites, a problematic survivor "nourished by her enemies," who must be reckoned with (17). In "If I Am Too Brown or Too White for You" the speaker is "garnet woman," the traditional red of the Indian, yet also irregular and unpredictable, frustrating and pleasing (1). Part four, "The Halfbreed Chronicles," reaches yet further, in the voices of "half-breeds" of other sorts: historical figures from other continents, branded outsiders, freaks, or unlikely survivors. "Truganinny," "Yuriko," "Kitty," and "Julia" articulate unimaginable pain in ways that nonetheless emphasize their humanity and invite empathy. Emerging and moving outward from Hopi territory, the poems in this collection attest to the power of the land in shaping spirit as well as to the social and political forces that threaten all life. In remembrance, lament, and stubborn imagination, Rose sings against destruction.

Bibliography
Hughes, Sheila Hassell. "Unraveling Ethnicity: The Construction and Dissolution of Identity in Wendy Rose's Poetics." *Studies in American Indian Literatures* 16, no. 2 (2004).

Rose, Wendy. *The Halfbreed Chronicles and Other Poems.* Los Angeles: West End Press, 1985.

Tongson-McCall, Karen. "The NetherWorld of Neither World: Hybridization in the Literature of Wendy Rose." *American Indian Culture and Research Journal* 20, no. 4 (1996): 1–40.

Sheila Hughes

Harjo, Joy   (1951–)

Joy Foster was born in Tulsa, Oklahoma, on May 9, 1951, to Wynema Baker and Allen W. Foster. She is a member of the Creek tribe and is also of Cherokee, French, and Irish descent. Descended from a long line of tribal leaders on her father's side, including Monahwee, leader of the Red Stick War against Andrew Jackson, she often incorporates in her poetry themes of Indian survival amid contemporary American life. In 1970 at the age of 19 with the blessings of her parents, Foster took the last name of her maternal grandmother, Naomi Harjo. As she often credits her great aunt, Lois Harjo, with teaching her about her Indian identity, this name change may have helped her to solidify her public link with this heritage.

Although primarily known as a poet, Harjo conceives of herself as a visual artist. She left Oklahoma at age 16 to attend the Institute of American Indian Arts in Santa Fe, New Mexico, originally studying painting. After attending a reading by the poet SIMON ORTIZ, she changed her major to poetry. At 17 she returned to Oklahoma to give birth to her son, Phil Dayn, walking four blocks while in labor to the Indian hospital in Talequah. Her daughter, Rainy Dawn, was born four years later in Albuquerque. For years Harjo supported herself and her children with a variety of jobs: waitress, service-station attendant, hospital janitor, nurse's assistant, dance teacher. She then went on to earn a B.A. in English from the University of New Mexico in 1976 and an M.F.A. in poetry from the University of Iowa's famed Iowa Writer's Workshop in 1978. Her subsequent teaching career included many positions, beginning with the Institute of American Indian Arts and ending with her current position with the American Indian Studies Program at the University of California at Los Angeles.

Harjo is an award-winning poet, who has won the Lifetime Achievement Award from the Native Writers Circle of the Americas, the Oklahoma Book Award in 1995 for *The WOMAN WHO FELL FROM THE SKY* and in 2003 for *How We Became Human: New and Selected Poems,* the William Carlos Williams Award from the Poetry Society of America and the American Book Award from the Before Colum-

bus Foundation for *IN MAD LOVE AND WAR* (1991), among other awards. She has published seven books of poetry and a work of prose and poetry to accompany Stephen Strom's photographs called *Secrets from the Center of the World* and coedited, with GLORIA BIRD, the anthology *REINVENTING THE ENEMY'S LANGUAGE: CONTEMPORARY NATIVE AMERICAN WOMEN'S WRITINGS OF NORTH AMERICA.*

In addition to Simon Ortiz, Harjo counts as her influences LESLIE MARMON SILKO, Flannery O'Connor, James Wright, Pablo Neruda, Meridel LeSueur, Galway Kinnell, Leo Romero, Audre Lorde, Louis Oliver, and June Jordan. Harjo has said, and this list reflects, that the "larger" community of black, Asian, and Chicano people has had an influence on her work. One of her most powerful poems, "Strange Fruit," takes its title from the song by Lewis Allan, most often associated with Billie Holiday. This poem tells the story of Jacqueline Peters, an African-American activist lynched by the Ku Klux Klan in Lafayette, California, in 1986. The speaker says, "I didn't do anything wrong. I did not steal from your mother. My brother did not take your wife" (23–25). The plain language Harjo uses here emphasizes the grotesque absurdity of racist hatred by enabling the reader to relate to the victim. At the same time she slowly, subtly builds the case against the mob, "hooded ghosts from hell," contrasted with the image of the victim, a mother, a wife, in heaven.

As we see from "Strange Fruit," Harjo does not limit her subject matter to her own heritage, but rather includes other tribal traditions, such as Navajo and Kiowa, and other ethnicities and strives to universalize the experiences about which her poetry speaks, at the same time retaining the referential specificity of her own Native traditions and concerns. For instance, in the poem "For Alva Benson, and For Those Who Have Learned to Speak," she writes of the cycle of life for a specific Navajo woman, beginning with her own birth: "And the ground spoke when she was born / Her mother heard it. In Navajo she answered / as she squatted down against the earth" (1–3). She moves on to this same child's giving birth herself, this time in the "Indian Hospital in Gallup" (7). Unlike her mother, she has been restrained, unable to commune with the earth during this powerful experience. She says, "She strained against the metal stirrups / and they tied her hands down" (9–15). Harjo's poem might seem to speak only of the experiences of the individual woman, because of the way she is named, and her tribe is named, and even the hospital in which she gives birth is named, but as the second half of the title forecasts, this poem is for "all who have learned to speak." The last stanza makes this clear; she says, "And we go on, keep giving birth and watch / ourselves die, over and over" (35–38). This universalizes the experience of the woman in the poem, making a larger reference to all who give birth and listen to the experience going on inside them and surrounding them. In this poem land is the source of life, and listening to the land enables women to speak themselves.

In "Alva Benson" Harjo also takes up the theme of modern society and its oppression of Native American domain. The women in that poem move from giving birth outside, in communion with the earth, to laboring in the confines of a cold, sterile concrete and metal hospital. Yet, in Harjo's world they can still hear the earth. She combines these worlds in other poems, such as "New Orleans." Here she roams the city, looking for "evidence / of other Creeks, for remnants of voices" (1–2). The poem speaks of tribal memory, claiming "there are voices buried in the Mississippi mud" (32). Harjo highlights the legacy of colonialism and oppression by placing her Creek ancestors along the banks of the Mississippi River in the south—near the ancestral home they were forced to leave upon REMOVAL to Oklahoma. The speaker mocks DeSoto's search for gold, saying, "The Creeks lived in earth towns, / not gold, / spun children, not gold" (51–54). The last stanza places DeSoto in the modern city of New Orleans, demonstrating that his destructive legacy is still evident.

What we see here, as in other poems by Harjo, is not a straight lament for the precolonial civilization, although the lament is certainly there. Instead, Harjo works again and again in her poetry to see Indians as they are in the present, the good and the bad, and to recognize not just the pain of a colonialist legacy, but the triumph of the modern Indian as well. She does not allow her DeSoto in

"New Orleans" to be the conquering hero; rather, he has become mad, and the spirit of the Indians he attempted to destroy remains so strong it can be felt beneath the earth centuries later.

This ability to portray ancient traditions in a modern light can perhaps best be seen in Harjo's poem "Deer Dancer." Here a young woman enters a cold, cheerless bar, where "nearly everyone had left," "except the hardcore," the "Indian ruins." Here Harjo portrays modern Indians bleakly, seeming to say that these regulars in a desolate bar are what is left of Indian civilization. But the dancer offers hope; she is interpreted as a promise for the future:

She was the myth slipped down through dreamtime. The promise of feast we all knew was coming. The deer who crossed through knots of a curse to find us. She was no slouch, and neither were we, watching. (52–54)

Harjo's deer dancer not only demonstrates the power left in the "Indian ruins," she restores that power even to those who watch her. As in other poems she presents modern Indian reality without despair; she balances the bad with the good and manages to depict individual experience in a universal way.

See also AMERICAN INDIAN POETRY; *The Last Song; A Map to the Next World; She Had Some Horses;* SOUTHEASTERN TRIBAL LITERATURE.

Bibliography

Coltelli, Laura. Ed. and Introduction. *The Spiral of Memory: Interviews with Joy Harjo.* Ann Arbor: University of Michigan Press, 1996.

Harjo, Joy. *How We Became Human: New and Selected Poems.* New York: Norton, 2002.

———. *In Mad Love and War.* Hanover, N.H.: Wesleyan University Press, 1990.

———. *The Last Song.* Las Cruces, N. Mex.: Puerto del Sol Press, 1975.

———. *A Map to the Next World.* New York: Norton, 2000.

———. *Secrets from the Center of the World,* (with Stephen Strom). Tucson: University of Arizona Press, 1989.

———. *She Had Some Horses.* New York and Chicago: Thunder's Mouth Press, 1983.

———. *What Moon Drove Me to This?* Berkeley, Calif.: Reed, Cannon, Johnson, 1979.

———. *The Woman Who Fell from the Sky.* New York: Norton, 1994.

Jaskowski, Helen. "A *MELUS* Interview: Joy Harjo." *MELUS* 16 (1989–90): 5–13.

McAdams, Janet. "Castings for a (New) New World: The Poetry of Joy Harjo." In *Women Poets of the Americas: Toward a Pan-American Gathering,* edited by Jacqueline Vaught Brogan and Cordelia Chávez Candelaria, 210–232. Notre Dame, Ind.: University of Notre Dame Press, 1999.

Harpoon of the Hunter   Markoosie
(Markoosie Patsang) (1970)

Harpoon of the Hunter is the first published Canadian Inuit novel and the first text to transmit aspects of oral Inuit storytelling to written literature. It was initially published in Inuktitut syllabics in serial form in the Inuit magazine *Inuttituut* and later translated into English by the author. The foreword, written by James H. McNeill, introduces the author within an Inuit context, the importance of Inuit storytelling in general, and of Markoosie's text in particular. The novel is illustrated by Germaine Arnaktauyok. *Harpoon of the Hunter* is inspired by traditional Inuit stories, as they existed before contact with Western civilization. It is set in the Arctic, an unforgiving environment in which the survival of the individual depends on the whole community and its ability to survive and provide for its members. Markoosie's novel also underscores how every individual is an invaluable part of the community and its survival in Inuit culture. The story focuses on 16-year-old Kamik, who hopes to become a great hunter as his father is but doubts that he is ready. When tragedy strikes his small Inuit settlement—a rabid polar bear has entered the settlement during the night and killed five dogs—Kamik is unable to act and feels ashamed. Leaving only two hunters behind to provide for the women and children, the rest of the hunters, including Kamik, set out to find the bear before it can do more damage. The hunt goes terribly wrong and all the men except Kamik are killed. Alone, Kamik struggles to survive and is able to use all the knowledge handed down to him from his father. He is forced to face the harsh weather and possible threats as well as depression, extreme fatigue, and suicidal thoughts.

Although the narrative focuses on Kamik's quest for survival, a subplot is developed parallel to the main story that emphasizes the importance of the community as well as the individual. Back in the settlement the women, faced with the possibility of not seeing their husbands again, sends the two remaining hunters to get help in the village across a perilous ice channel that never freezes. The two men manage to cross the channel and the villagers organize a search party, prepared to risk their lives to save the hunters.

Despite his efforts to survive, Kamik cannot prepare himself for the perils of the land. A bear attacks him and leaves him defenseless. At this point the two narratives merge, and the search party kills the bear and rescues Kamik. It is decided that the people remaining in the settlement should join the villagers where they will be safe and not have to worry about surviving after the loss of their hunters. The story seems to suggest a happy ending, but then tragedy strikes again as Kamik's mother and bride-to-be drown in the channel. These events prove too much for Kamik and he drifts out to sea and commits suicide.

Bibliography
Bovey, Seth. "Markoosie's *Harpoon of the Hunter*: A Story of Cultural Survival." *American Indian Quarterly* 15, no. 2 (1991): 217–223.

Joanna M. Daxell

Hawk Is Hungry and Other Stories, The   D'Arcy McNickle (1992)

D'ARCY MCNICKLE's novels, particularly *The SURROUNDED* (1936), are widely read and receive considerable critical scrutiny. His short stories, however, were not well known before the publication of *The Hawk Is Hungry and Other Stories.* The editor, Birgit Hans, collected 16 stories, 10 hitherto unpublished. These were taken from McNickle's manuscripts in the Newberry Library, Chicago. Many are fragmentary and/or incomplete—some reviewers complained that some should have remained in the archives.

Hans cannot date the stories precisely; they were written between 1927 and 1935. The stories are categorized into three sections, according to the environments in which they are set: "The Reservation," "Montana," and "The City." Only the first section deals directly with Indian issues. The "Montana" stories critique romantic fantasies about easy living in the West. In "The Hawk Is Hungry" a raptor's killing of two settlers' favorite hen symbolizes the toughness of rural living; the hysterical response to the fowl's death typifies easterners' failure to accept the realities of western agriculture. Other stories dwell on westerners' contempt for and suspicion of eastern "strangers." "The City" stories are cynical and unattractive, conveying a bitter distaste for the selfish bourgeoisie of New York and Paris. "The Reservation" stories are the collection's most satisfying, in part, simply because they are the most polished and complete—three were published in periodicals during McNickle's lifetime. Also, in mapping the gulf in culture and comprehension that exists between white and Indian worlds, the stories most clearly reflect McNickle's own anxieties about his MIXED-RACE heritage and subsequent identity crises.

"The Reservation" stories demonstrate—with indulgent compassion—white men's failures to understand Indian connectedness to their lands. In "Hard Riding" a reservation superintendent, Brinder Mather, fails to convince a tribal council to adopt white farming practices. Mather cannot understand that Indians have different conceptions of land and livestock ownership. "*En Roulant. . .*" lambasts reservation courts: The trial of an alleged rape case is botched farcically. In "Meat for God" the emasculation of a once-proud hunter is outlined: Now a formerly independent gatherer of nourishing game, old Sam Peël (an Indian-adopted Frenchman), cannot shoot for fear of the warden. When he does errantly kill a deer, the meat is wasted, lest the shooting be detected and punished. In "Train Time" a white agency man,

Major Miles, is markedly benevolent. Determined to help out young Eneas, an impoverished Indian orphan, Miles sends the boy off to school in Oregon, unaware of the permanent hurt that removing the child from his environment will cause. McNickle's anger at the incomprehension shown by well-meaning whites is balanced by his acceptance that the counterproductive policies are motivated by genuine goodwill. This compassion for whites typifies the "Reservation" stories and adds to the importance of *The Hawk Is Hungry* collection.

Bibliography

D'Arcy McNickle Papers, The Newberry Library, Chicago. Available online. URL: www.newberry.org/nl/collections/McNickle.html. Accessed on August 15, 2005.

Kevin DeOrnellas

Heartsong of Charging Elk, The   James Welch (2000)

The Heartsong of Charging Elk (2000), JAMES WELCH's final work, traces the life of Charging Elk, an Oglala Sioux whose adventures are loosely based on the life of Black Elk, as he experiences life on the western plains and in France, which represents the Western worldview rapidly encroaching on Native traditions on the plains. The novel explores the disparity between these two lifestyles, as well as the choices open to Native Americans at the end of the 19th century as the Plains Indians lose their independence.

This curtailing of freedom is presented to the reader in the prologue, where young Charging Elk witnesses Crazy Horse's surrender at the Red Cloud Agency, often regarded as the transition to reservation life for the Plains Indians. The narrative then moves between Charging Elk's present experiences in France and his past life at the Stronghold, an encampment set up by those who reject reservation life. Charging Elk's flashbacks to the Stronghold remind him of his past and the cultural traditions that are now lost to his people. Although these traditions are carried on by Buffalo

Bill's Wild West Show, they no longer tie Charging Elk to his cultural heritage. As the novel develops, these flashbacks become less frequent, as Charging Elk's desire to return to America abates and his assimilation into French culture strengthens.

Inadvertently abandoned by Buffalo Bill's Wild West Show after an injury, Charging Elk awakens in a French hospital. Throughout the rest of the novel he suffers through many trials, all of which result of his being a cultural outsider, unfamiliar with the language, customs, and worldview of France. He is arrested for vagabondage, sexually molested by a former business acquaintance, and subsequently found guilty of his murder. Because of the differences in worldview and understanding of the presence of evil (not to mention Charging Elk's decision to voice his defense in Lakota), he is jailed. When a new treaty with America forces France to recognize Sioux sovereignty, Charging Elk is freed. He works as a gardener, falls in love with his employer's daughter, and plans a family, and a life, in France.

At the close of the novel Charging Elk returns to Buffalo Bill's Wild West Show, this time as a spectator. He learns about his family and is offered the chance to return to America, a dream long since deferred. However, contrary to his earlier desire to return home, Charging Elk decides to stay in France with his pregnant wife, as well as with his new adoptive culture. This decision represents the choice to assimilate to Western culture, a choice being forced upon the Plains Indians. However, because Charging Elk retains his worldview—worshipping Wakan Tanka, dreaming in Lakota, and keeping Winter Count—the novel does not sound a note of lamentation for the plains culture. Rather, Welch's final novel sounds a more hopeful note, demonstrating that assimilation into Western culture does not necessarily mean a loss of traditional cultural values and ideals.

Bibliography

Black Elk. *Black Elk Speaks, as Told through John G. Neidhardt (Flaming Rainbow) by Nicholas Black Elk.* Lincoln: University of Nebraska Press, 2000.

Jim Donahue

Heat-Moon, William Least   (William Trosdon) (1939–)

William Trogdon was born on August 27, 1939, in Kansas City, Missouri. His literary pseudonym is an acknowledgment of the degree to which his Native American ancestry has informed his work. In 1961 he earned a baccalaureate degree in literary studies from the University of Missouri, and he completed a master's degree at the school the following year. Trogdon subsequently served for two years in the U.S. Navy, including a year of duty in the war zone aboard the USS *Lake Champlain.* After his discharge he joined the faculty of Stephens College in Columbia, Missouri, and resumed his literary studies at the University of Missouri, completing his doctoral work in 1973. Then he made the unusual decision to enroll in the University of Missouri's baccalaureate program in photojournalism and earned the degree in 1978. He would put this additional education to good use in all of his subsequent literary projects, but especially in the development of his first and still most well-known book, *Blue Highways: A Journey into America* (1982).

Trogdon followed the old highways that the interstate system had bypassed, driving his van in a complete circuit around the continental United States. Starting in the East, Trogdon logged about 13,000 miles in about three months of travel. Along the way he kept extensive journals about the places, people, and curiosities that he encountered, and he made audiotapes of his informal interviews with just about anyone who was willing to sit and talk. At the end of the trip he had a small mountain of raw material, which took almost four years to shape into *Blue Highways.* During this process he experienced a personal transformation, his development of a self-knowledge and of a confidence about his place in the world that are represented in his assumption of the name *William Least Heat-Moon.*

Blue Highways became a representative work in the definition of the "new" literary genre of creative nonfiction. Heat-Moon's two subsequent books have only added to his reputation as a careful craftsman who has an eye for the details that aggregate into "meaning" and an instinct for the moments in which the observer enters into the essence of the thing observed. In *PrairyErth* (1991) Heat-Moon explores the seemingly empty geographical center of the continental United States—the place that he had, in effect, circled in *Blue Highways.*

In his latest book, *River Horse: The Logbook of a Boat across America* (1999), Heat-Moon recounts his attempt to travel across the continental United States by water. Echoing the early explorers' obsession with finding the fabled "northwest passage" to the Pacific, Heat-Moon's quixotic quest is firmly grounded in his detailing of the many logistical difficulties that must be overcome in order to complete such a quest. It has become a cliché to say that a travel writer brings a landscape to life, but in *River Horse,* Heat-Moon conveys the muscular vitality of the American ground and of the water that runs through it.

Bibliography

Chisholm, Scott. "The Essential Hyphenated Heat-Moon." *Creative Nonfiction* 6 (1996): 61–72.

Heat-Moon, William Least. *Blue Highways: A Journey into America.* Boston: Little, Brown, 1982.

———. *PrairyErth.* Boston: Houghton Mifflin, 1991.

———. *River Horse: The Logbook of a Boat across America.* Boston: Houghton Mifflin, 1999.

Levin, Jonathan. "Coordinates and Connections: Self, Language, and World in Edward Abbey and William Least Heat-Moon." *Contemporary Literature* 41 (summer 2000): 214–251.

Weltzien, O. Alan. "A Topographic Map of Words: Parables of Cartography in William Least Heat-Moon's *Prairyerth.*" *Great Plains Quarterly* 19 (spring 1999): 107–122.

Martin Kich

Heirs of Columbus, The Gerald Vizenor (1991)

The Ojibwe author GERALD VIZENOR's *The Heirs of Columbus* is a comic, postmodern satire on Euro-American history, especially the "discovery" of America by the explorer Christopher Columbus.

Written and published in the year preceding the 500-year anniversary of Columbus's landing in North America, the novel imagines that the Italian explorer was descended from Mayan shamans and that he sired descendants in the New World by Samana, a native. The action of the novel concentrates on the lives of these "Heirs of Columbus"—a group of MIXED-BLOOD Ojibway Indians living in northern Minnesota near the headwaters of the Mississippi River. The situation of the novel allows Vizenor to question and mock European notions of history, law, culture, and assumed superiority. In addition, the novel plays with generic conventions, combining elements of biography, historical narrative, detective fiction, and fantasy.

The novel opens in northern Minnesota, where Stone Columbus, one of the Heirs of Columbus, is a radio talk show host. He also operates the floating Santa Maria Casino in international waters in Lake of the Woods on the American-Canadian border. The casino survives a legal challenge by the U.S. government, and the ship is granted SOVEREIGNTY; however, the casino sinks in a storm shortly afterward. The novel then introduces the other Heirs of Columbus, who "come together at the stone tavern each autumn to remember the best stories about their strain and estate" (4) and who share a genetic signature of "survivance" and "stories in the blood." The Heirs include Stone's parents, grandparents, wife, Felipa Flowers, and others. The third chapter retells the life of Christopher Columbus, combining historical and fictional elements, especially that Columbus is a descendent of Mayan shamans and Sephardic Jews, that he remembers the genetic "stories in his blood," that he is "touched with a vision to return to the New World" (34), and that he encounters Samana. Rather than rejecting Columbus (a source and symbol of pain for most Native Americans), Vizenor reverses his meaning: As a Mayan descendent, Columbus returns to the New World as a creator, not a destroyer (Blaeser 96).

The latter two-thirds of the novel focus on the repatriation of Native American remains and the founding of a new sovereign nation on Point Assinika, Washington. Told that the Brotherhood of American Explorers has sacred medicine pouches stolen from the Ojibway by Henry Rowe Schoolcraft, Felipa travels to New York to attempt to retrieve them. She meets Doric Miché, a wealthy descendant of Schoolcraft, who trades in tribal remains and ceremonial objects (48), and he offers to sell the pouches and the remains of Columbus (also stolen) to the Heirs for $1 million. With the help of a tribal shaman Felipa double-crosses Doric, steals the pouches, and remains in front of Doric and the surveillance cameras of the vault. Doric subpoenas Felipa and her friends to "answer questions about the shamanic repatriation of medicine pouches and human remains" (63). The long and whirlwind trial, dominated by a legal and moral debate over the ownership of sacred objects and stories, ends in favor of the Heirs.

Humiliated by Felipa and the Heirs, Doric sets a trap for Felipa. Offered the remains of Pocahontas (another controversial figure for Native Americans) for repatriation, Felipa travels to London and meets a rare book dealer who gives Felipa the location of the casket. While in London Felipa follows in the footsteps of Pocahontas. On the verge of possessing the remains, Felipa is murdered, but the crime remains unsolved.

Stone and the other Heirs, inspired by their previous sovereignty legal victory and the death of Felipa, decide to move closer to the mountains and the ocean. In a scene reminiscent of the Columbus story, the Heirs declare Point Assinika, Washington, a sovereign nation on October 12, 1992: "The Heirs of Columbus bear faith and witness that we have taken possession of this point in the name of our genes and the wild tricksters of liberties" (119). Using the money earned from his previous casino, Stone builds another casino and a genetics research facility, the latter used to "pursue genetic therapies and biogenetic research on survivance to heal the tribal world" (122). Using the remains of Columbus and the deoxyribonucleic acid (DNA) of the Heirs, the new nation's scientists isolate "the genetic code of tribal survivance and radiance, that native signature of seventeen mitochondrial genes that could reverse human mutations, nurture shamanic resurrection, heal wounded children, and incite parthenogenesis in separatist women" (132). The new nation is a comic utopia, which attracts thousands of people searching for bingo and heal-ing, especially thousands of "wounded children who would be humored, honored, and healed" (132).

The nation attracts the attention of federal and reservation authorities, but neither can stop the Heirs in their acts of liberation and healing. Stone aims to abolish the blood quantum measure of Native identity and make a "world tribal, a universal identity, and return to other values as measures of human worth" (162). The novel ends with Felipa's murder solved, Doric arrested for murder, and Pocahontas's remains returned. Vizenor's narrative sounds an optimistic note: After years of suffering caused by Euro-American conquest, Columbus provides the means for healing the world with HUMOR.

Bibliography

Blaeser, Kimberly M. *Gerald Vizenor: Writing in the Oral Tradition.* Norman: University of Oklahoma Press, 1996.

Blair, Elizabeth. "Whodunwhat? The Crime's the Mystery in Gerald Vizenor's *The Heirs of Columbus.*" In *Loosening the Seams: Interpretations of Gerald Vizenor,* edited by Robert A. Lee, 155–165. Bowling Green, Ohio: Popular, 2000.

Velie, Alan R. "The Indian Historical Novel." *Native American Perspectives on Literature and History,* edited by Alan R. Velie, 77–92. Norman: University of Oklahoma Press, 1995.

Vizenor, Gerald. *The Heirs of Columbus.* Hanover, N.H.: University Press of New England, 1991.

Troy Bassett

Henson, Lance (1944–)

Henson is a Cheyenne poet recognized internationally for his work published in both English and Cheyenne. He was born in Washington, D.C., but was raised in Calumet, Oklahoma, by his great-uncle and great-aunt, Bob and Bertha Cook. His bloodlines are Cheyenne, Oglala, and French. Growing up steeped in the traditional Southern Cheyenne culture, Henson is influenced in his work by the Cheyenne philosophy and tradition, which serve as dominant frameworks. A prolific writer, Henson has published more than 20 books, half of these in the United States. Henson's texts address injustice, not only in America but also in the modern world. In 1985 he addressed the European Free Alliance in the Netherlands as an official representative of the Southern Cheyenne Nation. He was also the official representative of the Southern Cheyenne Nation at the Indigenous People's Conference at the United Nations in 1988. In 1993 Henson represented the United States Information Service as featured lecturer in Singapore, Thailand, Papua New Guinea, and New Zealand. Henson served as an observer at the United Nations in Papua New Guinea from 1997 to 1999. In 1999 his project "Words from the Edge" assembled poets for a reading tour across Europe. As Norma C. Wilson writes in *The Nature of Native American Poetry,* "Henson conceives of his poetry as 'reflective of a globalized tribal vision'" (66). Henson is a member of the Cheyenne Dog Soldier Society, the Native American Church, and the Native American Indian Movement. In addition to the numerous poetic texts, Henson has coauthored two plays. He is also a traveling professor/lecturer for the newly formed Red Winds College, accredited by the University of Arizona in Tempe.

Henson's work is not for the faint of heart; he writes about truth and will strip away many misconceptions, for he is of the "conviction that the poet must condemn the crimes of American history" (Wilson 71). However, his stark perceptions of injustice are not limited to America; Henson condemns imperialism and highlights the destruction of colonialization around the world, for his writing reflects "a continuing cry against injustice, a cry that runs deep in the consciousness of nature and humanity everywhere" (Wilson 74). With the precision of a surgeon and the focused energy of a martial artist, Henson's exacting word choices, powerful imagery, and minimalist presentations are a force to move the soul, for Henson has not forgotten that language is sacred; language has power. Making no secret of the fact that he belongs to the Dog Soldier Society, whose warriors of long ago used to stake themselves to the ground by their sashes, indicat-ing their willingness to either die in battle or fight until the entire tribe was safe, Henson uses as his "sash" his pen. He stands ready to take on the injustices of the world and fight until either they are resolved or another warrior comes along to take up the battle.

Bibliography

Wilson, Norma C. *The Nature of Native American Poetry.* Albuquerque: University of New Mexico Press, 2001.

Patti DiMond

Highway, Tomson (1951–)

Since the premier of *The Rez Sisters* (1986) Tomson Highway has been one of Canada's most important dramatists. He is responsible for drawing mainstream attention to the field of Native Canadian drama and preparing the ground for such playwrights as Marie Clements and Drew Hayden Taylor.

Though he trained in both Canada and London as a concert pianist, Highway began working for various Native groups after finishing college. *The Rez Sisters* appeared while he was running the De-Ba-Jeh-Ma-Jig Theatre Group in Manitoulin, Ontario. After a local workshop performance, the play opened in Toronto to considerable success, winning the Dora Mavor Moore Award for best play and enjoying a sold-out national tour. A delicate balance of Native music, Cree language, European dramatic form, household chores, the game of bingo, and nonrealism, the play elevates everyday experiences of seven Native women to the level of poetry. *Rez Sisters* is the first play of a projected seven. The second Rez drama, *Dry Lips Oughta Move to Kapuskasing* (1989), parallels the first, depicting seven native men in order to expose the harshest consequences of white colonization. It won Highway the Dora Mavor Moore and Floyd Chalmers Canadian Play Awards.

In the 1990s Highway turned to fiction while preparing his third play in the cycle, a musical entitled *Rose* (2000). His popular novel *Kiss of the Fur Queen* (1998) is a semiautobiographical look at government conversion of Natives through the eyes of magical realism. He has also written a children's book trilogy, *Caribou Song* (2001), *Dragonfly Kites* (2002), and *Fox on the Ice* (2003).

Currently Highway is a faculty member of the University of Toronto. His first drama in 15 years, *The Laurier Memorial,* inspired by the initial meeting between whites and the indigenous nations of the Kamloops area, was performed during the 2004–05 seasons at Alberta Theatre Projects and the National Arts Centre. Highway was inducted into the Order of Canada, the country's highest lifetime achievement honor, in 1994. In 1999 *McLean Magazine* named him one of the most important figures in Canadian history.

Bibliography

Gilbert, Helen, ed. *Postcolonial Plays: An Anthology.* New York: Routledge, 2001.

Heath, Sally Ann. "The American Indian Community House." In *American Indian Theater in Performance. A Reader,* edited by Hanay Geiogamah and Jaye T. Darby. Los Angeles: University of California Press, 2000.

Highway, Tomson. *Comparing Mythologies.* Ottawa: University of Ottawa Press, 2003.

———. *Dry Lips Oughta Move to Kapuskasing.* Vancouver: Talonbooks, 1994.

———. *Johnny National, Super Hero.* Ottawa: Health Canada, 2001.

———. *Kiss of the Fur Queen.* Toronto: Doubleday Canada, 1998.

———. *The Rez Sisters: A Play in Two Acts.* Saskatoon: Fifth House, 1988.

———. *Rose.* Burnaby, Canada: Talonbooks, 2003.

King, Thomas. "Native Literature of Canada." In *Dictionary of Native American Literature,* edited by Andrew Wiget, 353–369. New York: Garland, 1994.

Taylor, Drew Hayden. "Alive and Well: Native Theatre in Canada." In *American Indian Theater in Performance: A Reader,* edited by Hanay Geiogamah and Jaye T. Darby. Los Angeles: University of California Press, 2000.

Ben Fisler

Hill, Roberta (Roberta Hill Whiteman) (1947–   )

Roberta Hill was born on February 17, 1947, to Eleanor Smith and Charles Alan Hill in Baraboo, Wisconsin. She is of MIXED-BLOOD parentage, having Choctaw, European, and Oneida ancestry.

Initially Hill pursued premedical studies at the University of Wisconsin. She then switched majors to creative writing and psychology and received her bachelor's degree in 1971. Realizing that her failure to become a doctor fueled her desire to write, Hill moved to Montana, where she earned an M.F.A. in creative writing at the University of Montana. She studied poetry with Richard Hugo and wrote about Native American traditions. Since receiving her M.F.A. she has taught at a wide variety of colleges and universities in the Midwest. In 1980 she married Ernest Whiteman, and they had three children. In 1993 she left her position at the University of Wisconsin to pursue doctoral work in American studies at the University of Minnesota. After completing her doctoral studies, Hill became a professor of English and American Indian studies at University of Wisconsin. She is currently working on a biography of her grandmother, Dr. L. Rosa-Minoka Hill.

Hill's poems first appeared in print in literary magazines and anthologies in the 1970s. In 1984, as Roberta Hill Whiteman, she published her best-known work, *Star Quilt.* Two poems, "Star Quilt" and "In the Longhouse, Oneida Museum," capture the history and traditions of Hill's Oneida roots and how her dispossession from these traditions left her with a fragmented identity. What marks both poems is her attention to detail, which gives her poems a spiritual force.

In "Star Quilt" the speaker's quilt reveals itself to be a map to her reunion with her traditions. Under the quilt she finds sanctuary from the loneliness of her life. "The quilt unfolds against sheets . . . it covers my cuts" (lines 3, 5). While the speaker feels safe under the star quilt, she feels lost "In the Longhouse, Oneida Museum." This poem describes how the loss of the tribal longhouse has fragmented the identity of the speaker.

For Hill as for other Native American writers, displacement from the ethnic, occupational, or cultural past has been a defining characteristic of identity. As a result Hill's poems arise from her experiences as a displaced person, seeking healing in her work. By internalizing this loss, Whiteman is able to produce poetry of great power and concrete images that allow readers to feel their own loss and find ways to overcome it.

Bibliography

Amrani, Norma Harwit. *American Indian Women Poets: Women between the Worlds.* New York: Vantage Press, 1993.

Bruchac, Joseph, ed. *Survival This Way: Interviews with American Indian Poets.* (Sun Tracks Books, No. 15). Tucson: University of Arizona Press, 1990.

Hill, Roberta. *Star Quilt: Poems.* Duluth, Minn.: Holy Cow! Press, 1984, 2001.

———. *Philadelphia Flowers.* Duluth, Minn.: Holy Cow! Press, 1996.

Sumeeta Patnaik

Hobson, Geary   (1941–   )

Born June 12, 1941, in Chicot County, Arkansas, Hobson (Cherokee/Arkansas Quapaw) spent his childhood learning fishing, hunting, trapping, and traditional tribal values. Hobson joined the U.S. Marines and from 1959 to 1965 served as a radioman and machine gunner in Southeast Asia during the early years of the VIETNAM WAR. He earned both a B.A. (1968) and an M.A. (1969) in English at Arizona State University and completed his Ph.D. in American studies (1986) at the University of New Mexico. Currently he is an associate professor of English at the University of Oklahoma, serves on several editorial advisory boards, and is project director for the Native Writers' Circle of the Americas.

In 1979 Hobson's anthology *The Remembered Earth,* includes contributions from over 70 Native American writers, poets, and artists, was published. It is considered an important contribution to the dissemination and study of Native American writing. It includes his own highly respected poem "Deer Hunting," which is composed of paired but contrasting "scenes" in which hunters have killed a deer. The first group demonstrates complete disregard for the taking of life, in contrast to the traditional respect practiced by the Cherokee hunters, who understand they have been given the deer for meat from the Great Spirit.

Hobson's writing is noteworthy for inclusion of traditional values that emphasize respectful relationships to others and to the land. He draws heavily upon tribal histories, tribal languages, genealogical research, and personal experiences for his inspiration. His novel *The Last of the Ofos* (2000) demonstrates these varied interests. Recently he has begun a series of short stories based on his experiences in the Vietnam conflict. He continues to do extensive research concerning southeastern tribes, the Arkansas Quapaw in particular.

He has had numerous poems, essays, reviews, and short stories published in a variety of journals and anthologies. The essay "On a Festival Called Returning the Gift," in *Returning the Gift* (1994), details the birth of the Native American Writers' Circle and the international festival that remains the largest gathering of Native American writers.

Hobson has received several awards, among them Wordcraft Circle's 1998 Mentor of the Year Award, the Presidential Professor Award for 1998–99 from the University of Oklahoma (the first American Indian faculty member to receive this award), and in 2003 the Lifetime Achievement Award from the Native Writers' Circle of the Americas.

Bibliography

Baird, David W. *The Quapaw Indians: A History of the Downstream People.* Norman: University of Oklahoma Press, 1980.

Bruchac, Joseph, ed. *Returning the Gift: Poetry and Prose from the First North American Native Writer's Festival.* Tucson: University of Arizona Press, 1994.

Hobson, Geary. *Deer Hunting and Other Poems.* New York: Strawberry Press with Points Riders Press, 1990.

———. *The Last of the Ofos.* Tucson: University of Arizona Press, 2000.

———. *The Remembered Earth: An Anthology of Contemporary Native American Literature.* Albuquerque: University of New Mexico Press, 1979.

Holm, Tom. *Strong Hearts, Wounded Souls: Native American Veterans of the Viet Nam War.* Austin: University of Texas Press, 1996.

Barbara Robins

Hogan, Linda (1947–)

Linda Hogan was born in Denver, Colorado, in 1947 to a white mother and a Chickasaw father. Part of a military family who moved often, Linda did not grow up in an Indian community. She spent much of her childhood in Oklahoma and Colorado. She earned an M.A. in English from the University of Colorado at Boulder in 1978, and she has taught at that institution as well as the University of Minnesota.

A poet, novelist, short story writer, playwright, essayist, and environmental activist, Linda Hogan is a prominent writer in contemporary Native American literature. She has published several collections of poems, including *The Book of Medicines* (1993), *Savings* (1988), *Seeing Through the Sun* (1985), and *Eclipse* (1983). Her novels include *Power* (1998), *Solar Storms* (1995), and *Mean Spirit* (1990). Hogan's work has been widely represented in anthologies of Native American literature, women's writings, multicultural literature, and contemporary American poetry.

Linda Hogan's prolific and powerful writing has been recognized by numerous awards, including a 2002 Wordcraft Circle Writer of the Year for *Woman Who Watches Over the World: A Native Memoir* (2001); a 1998 Lifetime Achievement Award from the Native Writers' Circle of the Americas; a 1994 Lannan Award for outstanding achievement in poetry; a 1993 Colorado Book Award for the poetry collection *The Book of Medicines,* and the same award in 1996 for the novel *Solar Storms.* Her novel *Mean Spirit* won the 1991 Oklahoma Book Award for fiction and made her one of three finalists for the Pulitzer Prize in 1990. Hogan has also received grants from the National Endowment for the Arts (NEA), the Guggenheim

Foundation, and the Minnesota Arts Board. In addition, she was an NEA poetry panel member for two years, and she is an activist for wildlife rehabilitation—not surprisingly, the environment occupies a central role in her work.

Linda Hogan's work generally deals with the quest for identity, traditional Native American culture and its relationship to the environment, the beauty and strength of women, humanity, and love.

Linda Hogan's MIXED-BLOOD heritage has informed the theme of identity in her work, for example, in her collection of poetry *Seeing Through the Sun* (1985) and in her novel *Solar Storms* (1995). About identity she has said, "I think the split between the two cultures in my life became a growing abyss and they were what I did to heal it; weave it back together. . . . You are Indian and could pass for white. Go to powwows and to the opera with equal ease. . . . One life does not fit neatly into the other always" (Bruchac 155). Hogan's poetry creates an imaginative landscape free of human bias and manipulation that allows her to merge her double identity. Instead of lingering in a no-man's-land, she maintains her cultural distinctiveness through a third way shaped by natural images.

The tension of dual identity is seen, for example, in "The Truth Is," a poem from the collection *Seeing Through the Sun:* "In my left pocket a Chickasaw hand / . . . / In my right pocket / a white hand /" (1, 3–4). These lines reflect her awareness of belonging to two cultures at the same time, but the speaker suggests that they are all hers—the white hand does not belong to a thief, meaning that she does not allow the white culture to dominate the Native American worldview. One senses, in fact, that overall she favors her Native American culture through her use of natural, primordial images, "those other things" that "a woman of two countries" can use to reclaim herself.

In the same vein Hogan's second novel, *Solar Storms* (1995), features a 17-year-old woman's quest for identity. Angela Jensen returns to her Native American community and to its simple life and natural elements (such as earth, clay, blood, bone, and skin). When her idyllic odyssey is ruined by a hydroelectric dam project, she also realizes that the ruins suffered by the environment are analogous to the devastation suffered by her own mother, who was abandoned when she was a child, was separated from her family, and was abused. In the course of the story Linda Hogan celebrates female beauty and strength, the beauty of the unspoiled environment, self-love, humanity, and love. Angela Jensen realizes that her quest for personal identity is closely tied to her Native American community and its natural milieu of land, water, colors, and other natural elements. As with Angela Jensen's coming of age, the voices in Linda Hogan's poetry and fiction ultimately find harmony in their inner life, self-love, community, humanity, and the environment.

Bibliography

Bruchac, Joseph. "Linda Hogan: Interview." In *Survival This Way: Interviews with American Indian Poets.* Tucson: Sun Tracks, University of Arizona Press, 1987.

Cook, Barbara, ed. *From the Center of Tradition: Critical Perspectives on Linda Hogan.* Boulder: University of Colorado Press, 2003.

Hogan, Linda. *The Book of Medicines.* Minneapolis: Coffee House Press, 1993.

———. *Calling Myself Home.* Greenfield Center, N.Y.: Greenfield Review Press, 1978.

———. *Eclipse.* Los Angeles: American Indian Studies Center, University of California, 1983.

———. *Mean Spirit.* New York: Atheneum, 1990.

———. *Solar Storms: A Novel.* New York: Scribner, 1995.

———. *Power.* New York: W. W. Norton, 1998.

———. *Red Clay: Poems and Stories.* Greenfield Center, N.Y.: Greenfield Review Press, 1994.

———. *Savings.* Minneapolis: Coffee House Press, 1988.

———. *Seeing Through the Sun.* Amherst: University of Massachusetts Press, 1985.

———. *Woman Who Watches Over the World: A Native Memoir.* New York: W. W. Norton, 2001.

St. Clair, Janet. "Fighting for Her Life: The Mixed Blood Woman's Insistence upon Selfhood." In *Native American Women Writers,* edited by Harold Bloom, 13–26. Philadelphia: Chelsea House, 1998.

———. "Uneasy Ethnocentrism: Recent Works of Allen, Silko, and Hogan." *Studies in American Indian Literatures* 6, no. 1 (1994): 83–98.

Aimable Twagilimana

Home Places: Contemporary Native American Writing from Sun Tracks   Ofelia Zepeda (1995)

The importance of *Home Places: Contemporary Native American Writing from Sun Tracks* can be found in the history of *Sun Tracks: An American Indian Literary Series,* which began in 1971 as a quarterly journal and then grew from a semiannual magazine, to an annual anthology, and finally to a literary series in 1982. Since its inception the Sun Tracks series has provided an outlet for young and emerging Native American writers, and *Home Places* collects together 19 of the storytellers, singers, and poets who have appeared in past volumes. To celebrate 25 years of Sun Tracks, OPHELIA ZEPEDA, the current series editor, and Larry Evers compiled in a multigenre collection several pieces of contemporary Native American writing. The home places to which the title alludes are the many locations that Native Americans call home and that form a central theme in their writing. *Home Places* is a culmination of Evers's and Zepeda's efforts to collect a representative sample of oral and written narratives about home to correct the common assumption that oral traditions are vanishing in the wake of writing.

Native American oral traditions' ongoing presence indicates the additional significance of Sun Tracks—its editors have been determined to publish bilingual Native-language texts. As an excuse for not publishing these works, mainstream presses point to Native-language publications' limited audience; however, Sun Tracks's success proves otherwise. As a result of the series's success, Zepeda has continued to solicit bilingual projects. Her goal is to recognize the importance of Native-language texts outside linguistics and anthropology departments by emphasizing the quality of Native American narratives.

Known equally for her work in linguistics and her bilingual poetry, Zepeda includes "Pulling Down the Clouds" in *Home Places* with portions written in her language, Tohono O'odham. She describes the importance of rain in the Southwest desert she calls home: "He contemplates the smell, what is that smell? / It is rain. / Rain somewhere out in the desert." (2–4) "Ta" by Nora Naranjo-Morse (Santa Clara Pueblo), which pays homage to her father's wisdom, is the only other bilingual poem included.

The poems and songs by George Blueeyes (Navajo), Daniel Lopez (Tohono O'odham), Felipe Molina (Yaqui), and Ralph Cameron (Maricopa) appear entirely in their Native languages with English translations. Other writers included are JOY HARJO (Creek), LANCE HENSON (Cheyenne), LINDA HOGAN (Choctaw), N. SCOTT MOMADAY (Kiowa), SIMON ORTIZ (Acoma Pueblo), CARTER REVARD (Osage), Refugio Savala (Yaqui), LUCI TAPAHONSO (Navajo), Georgiana Valoyce-Sanchez (Chumash/O'odham), Ramona Wilson (Colville Confederated Tribes), WENDY ROSE (Hopi/Miwok), Dan Hanna (Havasupai), and Elizabeth Woody (Warm Springs/Wasco/ Navajo).

Altogether this collection embodies the strength of Native Americans and their homelands as voiced by Ortiz: "Pretty soon, you can hear it, / coming far away / deep in the ground, deep down there coming." And Zepeda rightfully recognizes that this power can sometimes only be expressed in Native languages.

Bibliography

Cochran, Stuart. "The Ethnic Implications of Stories, Spirits, and the Land in Native American Pueblo and Aztlán Writing." *MELUS* 20, no. 2 (summer 1995): 69–91.

Rader, Dean "Luci Tapahonso and Simon Ortiz: Allegory, Symbol, Language, Poetry." *Southwestern American Literature* 22, no. 2 (spring 1997): 75–92.

Wilson, Michael. "Speaking of Home: The Idea of the Center in Some Contemporary American Indian Writing," *Wicazo Sa Review* 12, no. 1 (spring 1997): 129–148.

Elizabeth Archuleta

Honour the Sun Ruby Slipperjack-Farrell (1987)

Honour the Sun, RUBY SLIPPERJACK-FARRELL's first novel, is a coming-of-age story about a young Anishinabe girl in a small Native community in northern Ontario, Canada. The novel spans more than six years and follows the first-person narrator, Owl (her Christian name is never revealed in the text), from childhood to adolescence. Written from within an oral tradition, the narrative does not follow a linear structure; instead, it is presented as a series of often unrelated events in a matter-of-fact fashion nearly devoid of commentary. This narrative approach allows the reader to learn about the narrator and her world through observation, paying attention not only to what is said but also to the nonverbal language, or silences, permeating the narrative. These are aspects of traditional Native learning that also guide the protagonist's learning process as she matures. The first-person narrative lets the reader see the world through the narrator's eyes, but it is a limited perspective, as the reader sees only what the young girl sees and has to make sense of the world as it appears to the narrator. Scenes that have little meaning to the young girl and to the reader become significant as she matures and gains a different understanding of the world around her. For instance, the violence and ALCOHOLISM present in the Native community do not affect the narrator on a conscious level until she becomes aware of these problems.

As the narrative progresses, the reader learns to appreciate the gaps and silences as clues important to the understanding of the text. For instance, as the narrator matures, silence takes on different meanings. Early on it evokes the inattentiveness of a child but also safety and peace. Later it suggests misunderstanding and shyness. In school the children, who speak Ojibway at home, have to use English. Toward the end of the novel the silence becomes contemplative. The narrator is told by her mother to "listen to the silence" (187), in order to ward off the inner turmoil she is experiencing and to pay attention to the silence rather than the noise around her.

At the outset of the novel the reader gains an understanding of the importance of the land and nature to the narrative. Rather than serving as a backdrop, nature is an active participant, on an equal status with the rest of the characters in the novel. The narrator's descriptions of her surroundings make the land come alive. Like silence, nature is always there and its importance may be overlooked as a result.

Although *Honour the Sun* is the story in diary form of a young girl's passage from childhood to adulthood, it is also the story of an extended family and a community. The importance of the community in supporting its members and in teaching Native values is emphasized throughout the novel and plays a significant part in the narrator's development.

Bibliography

Hoy, Helen. *How Shall I Read These? Native Women Writers in Canada.* Toronto: University of Toronto Press, 2001.

Joanna M. Daxell

Hopi Roadrunner Dancing   Wendy Rose (1973)

WENDY ROSE's first collection of poetry is about a search for self-identity, a recurrent theme that places her work firmly in the genre of NATIVE AMERICAN POETRY. As Norma Wilson states in *The Nature of Native American Poetry,* "The assertion of her Hopi identity is at the heart of Rose's first book" (Wilson 100). Rose's MIXED-BLOOD mother rejected her own Indian heritage and was ashamed of her Indian daughter. In "New Born Woman, May 7, 1948," Rose reveals both the physical and the mental pain her birth caused her mother: "Dreams of my mother i shattered, i arrived, . . . i Indian" (9). In addition, Rose's father's people could not accept Rose because Hopi tribal identity is matrilineal. Finally searching out the man who is reported to be her father, Rose

is full of questions for him. In the piece "Oh Father," she ends the poem asking, "oh father, who am i?" (11). Though lack of capitalization and punctuation was a popular poetic convention of the era, the recurring lack of capitalization of *I* is only located in the poetry to, for, or about her parents in this book, highlighting Rose's feelings of being unimportant to them.

Growing up with feelings of alienation from both parents and from both cultures is demonstrated in the poem "For My People;" Rose writes, "I was myself blown / two leaves apart" (3), and again in the poem "We Mourn Our Mirrors," where Rose often finds herself "searching in debris for my past" (4). Rejected by both cultures, Rose searches for belonging; that search is only quelled when she joins other Native Americans. The poem "Oh My People I Remember" not only is a reflection upon the taking over of Alcatraz Island in the early 1970s, as a political statement that temporarily unified many misplaced Native Americans, but also demonstrates that when surrounded by other Natives, Rose feels a connection to Indian people; she writes, "You reached out to me. Forming a circle, a sacred Hoop, I felt / protected" (6). In poems about other Natives or the land Rose uses the capitalized *I,* indicating she feels an importance of self as she identifies with other Natives who are as marginalized or invisible to mainstream society as Rose is to her parents. In the poem "Grandfather Pipestone Soul," she writes, "I send this to you while home is a museum / and our loved ones zoo specimens—and KNOW / that I love you and hear you still!" (13). Rose closes this book with a poem echoing the same sentiment "Thanksgiving Poem, 1971" reveals: "and we surprise you now; still living, still growing, still borning, / still Indian!" (37). It is through her blood ties to other Indians that Rose finally finds a family to welcome her home.

Bibliography

Rose, Wendy. *Hopi Roadrunner Dancing.* Greenfield Center, N.Y.: Greenfield Press, 1973.
Wilson, Norma C. *The Nature of Native American Poetry.* Albuquerque: University of New Mexico Press, 2001.

Patti Dimond

Horse Dance to Emerald Mountain Beth Cuthand (1987)

BETH CUTHAND'S writing is mostly characterized by a strong activist streak, giving poems such as "She Ties Her Bandanna" a certain violence in tone and rhetoric (Harjo 549). *Horse Dance to Emerald Mountain* does not exemplify Cuthand's political activism as clearly; that characteristic might explain the lack of attention it has been given while most of her poems and other writings have been selected as part of large First Nations literary editions, *Native Poetry in Canada,* for instance (Harjo 392). Nevertheless, *Horse Dance to Emerald Mountain* "examines and reveals the rhythms and traditions of the People of the Plains" (GoodMinds. com).

The epic quality of this short (20 pages) prose poem following a horse dancer in her quest for identity must be acknowledged for its originality in form and its provocative content. Indeed, in seven episodes Cuthand reinvents both "The Spirit Stallion and The Origin of Horses," two traditional Cree myths. In doing so, she feminizes a text traditionally placing men at the center of the action and leads her reader metaphorically through the great northern Canadian plains, following the rhythm of the dancer in a form of trance.

The stanzas aim to reproduce the rhythm of the horse dancers: "heart beats / drum beats / hooves beat" (7–9). In addition, the choice of the Horse dance, as opposed to any other, is here pertinent as well. Indeed, contrary to the sun, the earth, or the Buffalo Dances, the Horse Dance never had an important status in the Cree mythology; that explains the rarity of its performance (Mandelbaum 63, 208–9). Furthermore, considering that the acquisition of the horse marks one of the first shifts in the Plains Indians cultures due to white influence, the choice of this dance as seminal catalyst in the poem shows Cuthand's awareness of how interwoven and complex Native identities become in the 21st century.

The omnipresence of the horse is Cuthand's way of reclaiming her Plains Cree heritage: In the same way that the horses emerge from the waters of a lake in both myths, the cultural identity of the narrator in Cuthand's poem is described as a birth.

Bibliography

Bloomfield, Leonard. *Sweet Grass Cree.* Ottawa: Fifth House, 1993.

Good Minds.com. Available online. URL: http://www.goodminds.com/books/Voices%20in%20the%20Waterfall%20%20new%20ed.html. Accessed on August 15, 2005.

Harjo, Joy, and Gloria Bird, eds. *Reinventing the Enemy's Language.* New York: W. W. Norton, 1997.

Hoeble, E. Adamson. *The Plains Indians.* Bloomington: Indiana University Press, 1977.

Mandelbaum, David G. *The Plains Cree.* Regina: Canadian Plains Research Center, 1978.

Anne Dotter

Hotline Healers: An Almost Browne Novel Gerald Vizenor (1997)

In *Hotline Healers* GERALD VIZENOR gleefully satirizes a range of targets, including religion, reservation politics, academics, racism, and late-night talk radio, through the mighty figure of Almost Browne, a MIXED-BLOOD TRICKSTER FIGURE about whom nothing is certain. Recounted by Almost's cousin, who accompanies him on most of his adventures but never tells us his own name, this novel, made up of interrelated short stories, focuses on Vizenor's usual themes—the contradictions faced by Native Americans in negotiating a modern world that assumes they are noble savages without renouncing their culture or playing the part of "Indian."

Almost's name demonstrates Vizenor's quirky and playful use of language, and there are many "almosts" in the book (e.g., the narrator almost never uses the word *I,* almost all the chapters are set around Almost's exploits), including Almost's own birth: His mother had almost reached the reservation before delivering him at the side of the road. The multiple occurrences of this word function to warn the reader not to read the book as a naturalistic sequence of events, but instead to look for hidden messages and jokes that reflect the Native American experience. For example, when Almost becomes a commencement speaker dressed as Peggy Lee, he reappropriates her song "Fever" as an ironic reminder of the diseases passed on by white settlers.

A feature of Vizenor's writing is his use of real people in fictitious contexts, and one of the novel's more surreal chapters, "Fifth Deal," depicts many well-known philosophers and professors of language and anthropology participating in a "*debwe* heart dance." *Debwe* is the Ojibwe word for "truth," and what becomes apparent as the respected academics swap identities and dance naked through the seminar rooms and corridors of the University of California is that real life does not conform to narrow academic interpretation. Vizenor's own professorial style owes much to literary theory, but he reverses his critical gaze from the objects of study and onto those doing the studying.

However, *Hotline Healers* is also a very funny book, with much of the HUMOR deriving from the extended Browne clan of tricksters, who appear in many of his novels. From Cozie Browne, who becomes pregnant by touching a crystal sculpture, to Gesture, who runs his own dental office from a railroad car, the Brownes serve as a defiant reminder that Native Americans are not defined merely by their shared traditions. Another source of great humor are the antics of the many mongrel reservation dogs, some of whom talk, whistle, and even establish their own driving schools. Mongrels are an obvious metaphor for mixed-bloods people, and their fantastic adventures here suggest Vizenor's thesis that mixed bloods, by belonging to two worlds simultaneously, have the ability to alter fixed perceptions.

Bibliography

Vizenor, Gerald. *Griever: An American Monkey King in China.* Minneapolis: University of Minnesota Press, 1987.
———. *The Trickster of Liberty: Tribal Heirs to a Wild Baronage.* Minneapolis: University of Minnesota Press, 1988.

James Mackay

House Made of Dawn   N. Scott Momaday (1968)

House Made of Dawn, the novel that began the AMERICAN INDIAN LITERARY RENAISSANCE, is N. SCOTT MOMADAY's masterpiece. He originally conceived the work as a series of poems, but under the tutelage of Wallace Stegner at Stanford, Momaday reconceived the work first as a set of stories, then as a novel. *House* is the story of Abel, an Indian from the Pueblo Momaday calls "Walatowa," a fictionalized version of Jemez Pueblo in New Mexico, where Momaday grew up. Abel returns from World War II a victim of what we would call today posttraumatic stress syndrome. He is unable to speak, even to his grandfather, Francisco, who raised him.

Abel, who is drunk when his grandfather picks him up on the return to the reservation, is based in part on a veteran Momaday knew at Jemez, but also in part on Ira Hayes, the Pima marine who raised the flag at Mt. Suribachi and was memorialized in the statue that became the symbol of the Marine Corps. Hayes could not adjust to civilian life and died drunk in a ditch on the reservation.

The Indian veteran who is a hero in war but cannot find a niche in civilian life when he returns to America has become an archetype. Abel's name (Momaday only gives him one) suggests the biblical victim, and many readers assume the Cain who lays him low to be white society. But readers should remember that in the Bible Cain is Abel's brother, and the characters in *House Made of Dawn* who cause Abel the most harm are indeed his fellow Indians. Furthermore, Abel's troubles begin even before his stint in the army. He is illegitimate and as a result has always been an outsider at Walatowa. The war has exacerbated his problems, but they started at his birth.

Abel's first tormentor is a 75-year-old Jemez albino named Juan Reyes Fragua. Fragua, whom Momaday calls "the white man," humiliates Abel at a Jemez ceremony. Fragua bothers Abel because he is an outsider at Walatowa, and clumsy in participating in the ceremony, which consists of pulling up a rooster that has been buried in the ground. Abel takes revenge by knifing Fragua. In the passage describing the murder Momaday uses language redolent of sex:

> Abel waited.... The white man raised his arms, as if to embrace him.... Abel heard the strange excitement of the white man's breath, and the quick, uneven blowing at his ear, and felt the blue shivering lips upon him, felt even the scales of his lips and the hot slippery point of the tongue, writhing (82).

Although on a literal level one Indian is killing another, on a symbolic level the white man is raping an Indian. After Abel spends eight years in jail for his crime, he participates in the government's relocation program, taking a job in Los Angeles. He befriends a Navajo named Benally and discovers that they are related; Abel's father had apparently been Navajo.

In Los Angeles Abel meets his second tormentor, the Reverend John Big Bluff Tosamah, a Kiowa Indian who bears a strong resemblance to Momaday. Both are large Kiowa men with strong, deep voices, and when Tosamah tells his story, it turns out to be the story of Momaday's own life, in the account Momaday gives in his memoir *The Way to Rainy Mountain* (1969).

Goaded by Tosamah into a drinking spree that costs him his job, Abel fights a corrupt Chicano policeman, who beats him so severely that Abel is hospitalized. Upon recovery he returns home to Walatowa, where for the first time in his life he is able to participate in a satisfactory fashion in tribal life. Abel buries his grandfather in the prescribed Walatowan fashion, then joins the race for good hunting and harvests, a ceremonial race that his grandfather had won. As he runs he sings the Navajo hymn that Benally had taught him, "House Made of Dawn." The ending signifies that Abel has come to terms with both sides of his heritage and made his peace with his world.

House Made of Dawn was an immediate success—it won the 1969 Pulitzer Prize—and has since become an American classic. The lyrical nature of Momaday's writing owes much to his training as a poet; many Indian novelists (e.g., James Welch,

Leslie Marman Silko, Gerald Vizenor, Louise Erdrich, and Sherman Alexie), Momaday was a poet before he became a novelist. A reader familiar with American modernism also hears echoes of William Faulkner and Ernest Hemingway in Momaday's prose. Hemingway is manifest in the passages of spare diction, and the use of hendiadys, simple clauses linked with *and*: "The feasting had begun, and there was a lull on the town." Faulkner's influence can be seen in the stream of consciousness passages and the use of the bear as a symbol of the wilderness.

But Momaday's novel is distinctly Indian as well. The Cherokee novelist and critic Louis Owens says: "What has matured with Momaday is not merely an undeniable facility with the techniques and tropes of modernism, but more significantly the profound awareness of conflicting epistemologies [Euro-American and Indian].... Momaday's novel represents more fully than any Native American novel before it the 'assertion of a different perspective' (92).

Bibliography

Momaday, N. Scott. *House Made of Dawn*. New York: Harper, 1968.

Owens, Lewis. *Other Destinies: Understanding the American Indian Novel*. Norman: University of Oklahoma Press, 1994.

Scarberry-Garcia, Susan. *Landmarks of Healing: A Study of* House Made of Dawn. Albuquerque: Univesity of New Mexico Press, 1990.

Howbah Indians   Simon Ortiz (1978)

This collection of short stories provides the distinctly Native American perspectives on place and peoples that typify Simon Ortiz's poetry and fiction. Deceptively simple in tone and plot, the stories raise fundamental questions about knowledge, justice, and tradition. All of them reflect Ortiz's belief that language carries both political and spiritual force.

Each story revolves around the friction created in cross-cultural encounters. Sometimes the encounters are humorous, as in "Men on the Moon," when an old man watches an Apollo Moon mission on his new television. His grandson's explanations of the astronauts' purpose make no sense. Why would men fly to the Moon, which harbors no life, to seek knowledge from rocks and dirt? The foolishness of "Mericanos" is, to the grandfather, amusing and bewildering.

Other stories highlight both the pain of cross-cultural encounters and the resilience of people living in oppressed circumstances. The female narrator of "Home Country" recalls being forced by poverty to leave home for a job at faraway Keams Canyon Indian Boarding School. Instead of dwelling on her husband's death in Okinawa or the war-wrought changes splintering the reservation, she remembers in great detail the moments before the bus arrived to take her away. Her distinctive dialect and fond memories of her cousin's blue sweater and her grandfather's silver dollar say that her heart has never left her home country. In the title story the narrator awakes with a memory of a huge sign emblazoned WELCOME HOWBAH INDIANS. When Eagle, a Korean War veteran, bought a gas station, he put up this sign, which means "Welcome ya'll Indians." The pride that the sign evoked among Indians and the good memories of Eagle's teaching the narrator to make sparks by skipping rocks on asphalt are more enduring that the depressing circumstances of Eagle's uninvestigated murder.

The final story, "Something's Going On," focuses on the psychic toll of cultural differences. Told from the perspective of nine-year-old Jimmo, the story re-creates the day that his father, a World War II veteran with an amputated leg, becomes a suspect in his boss's murder. Jimmo's tension and his mother's worry are palpable as the tribal governor translates police questions about the father's whereabouts. Unable to soften her husband's anger since he returned home, injured, from the war, Jimmo's mother fears the worst: "There has been something wrong, not only with him but with the way things are in this country—that is what hurts him." The father never appears in the story and the facts of the situation remain unresolved as Jimmo sets out to find and protect his father.

Although the effects of war, poverty, and prejudice exist at the margins of each story, Ortiz does not belabor them. Instead, he creates three-dimensional characters by highlighting the fortitude and dignity with which they face life.

Bibliography

Wiget, Andrew. *Simon Ortiz.* (Western Writers Series 74). Boise, Idaho: Boise State University Press, 1986.

Margaret O'Shaughnessey

Howe, LeAnne   (1951–   )

A prolific writer and member of Oklahoma's Choctaw Nation, LeAnne Howe centers novels, dramas, short stories, and essays on how broad historical events and family bonds contribute to the modern identity of the individual. Howe calls the process by which stories are created from this deep heritage and become the property of both past and future kin "Tribalography." She received an American Book Award from the Before Columbus Foundation and was named Wordcraft Circle Writer of the Year (both 2002) for her first novel, SHELL SHAKER (2001). The MacDowell Colony, Ragdale Foundation, and Atlantic Center for the Arts have granted Howe fellowships.

Howe was in her 30s, a divorced mother of two, before her writing career began. Noting a visible gap in Native literature, which idealized traditional Natives and early history and ignored urban Indians, she produced "Biodegradable Indians," harsh tales of the Native American population who frequent the streets and bars of Oklahoma City. The piece began her long collaboration with her fellow Choctaw writer ROXY GORDON. The pair had some success with their play *Big Pow Wow* (1987), produced at Sojourner Truth Theater in Fort Worth, Texas. In 1993 with help from the Iowa Arts Council their second play, *Indian Radio Days,* was presented at CSPS Theater in Cedar Rapids. This sprawling, satirical "radio play" about the sins, failures, and misunderstanding (both European-American and Native) throughout Native American history and culture, from the creation of the world to *Dances with Wolves,* was both staged and broadcast. It also produced the Wagon Burner

Theater Troop, a community of Native artists who combine political action and art and are dedicated to educating Natives and the world at large.

Presently, Howe teaches at the University of Minnesota. In November 2004 her documentary *Native Americans in the 21st Century,* which she wrote and narrated, aired on the Public Broadcasting System (PBS). Her writings appear in multiple anthologies, and she is the author/coauthor of five theater productions.

Bibliography

Howe, LeAnne. "My Mothers, My Uncles, Myself." In *Here First: Autobiographical Essays by Native American Writers,* edited by Arnold Krupat and Brian Swann, 23–30. New York: Modern Library, 2000.

———. *Shell Shaker.* San Francisco: Aunt Lute Books, 2001.

———. *A Stand Up Reader.* Dallas: Into View Press, 1987.

Shoemaker, Nancy, ed. *Clearing a Path: Theorizing the Past in Native American Studies.* New York: Routledge, 2002.

Ben Fisler

Hozho: Walking in Beauty: Native American Stories of Inspiration, Humor, and Life   Paula Gunn Allen and Carolyn Dunn Anderson, eds. (2001)

Hozho, the Navajo word for walking in beauty and title of this book, is a collection of 25 Native American authors telling stories with themes such as invisibility, survival, transcendence, sadness, playfulness, oral tradition, and humor/irony. Featured writers include both well-known and up and coming authors: John M. Oskison, CHARLES A. EASTMAN, Lorenzo Baca, D. Renville, Anna Lee Walters, CARTER REVARD, Vickie L. Sears, Suleiman Russel, Carolyn Dunn, Dawn Karima Pettigrew, Steve Russel, Karen Wallace, Raven Hail, Lynda Martinez Foley, M. L. Smoker, Emma Lee Warrior, Debra Earling, MARY RANDLE TALLMOUNTAIN, Antia Endrezze, Gary Robinson, S. Bruised Head, Irvin Morris, Larry Littlebird, and Vee F. Browne.

The introduction is by Mark Robert Waldman, the foreword by PAULA GUNN ALLEN, and the prequel by Johnny Rustywire.

This collection explores the process of residing in both Western and Native worlds of contemporary society as a Native American. "Bicenti" by Walters is a story of a woman named Maya who frighteningly witnesses a fracture in infinite time and space. Sears's short story, "Everything Works Together," incorporates themes of spirituality, animals, and nature. Many stories discuss the meaning of family. "Fishing" is a tale of two brothers and how one contends with loss and alcoholism. "Loaves and Fishes" describes a woman, Manna, who accidentally inherits a child and learns to survive in poverty. Wallace's piece "Alyssa's Father" deals directly with internalized racism, drug and alcohol abuse, masculinity, and fractured families. Other stories in *Hozho* incorporate mythological characters and magic. For example, "Night of Radishes," focusing primarily on marriage, women's sexuality, motherhood, and magic, tells of Manuela, a young newlywed, who seeks out a dark witch to punish her husband's promiscuity.

Bibliography

Allen, Paula Gunn. *The Sacred Hoop: Recovering the Feminine in American Indian Traditions.* Boston: Beacon Press, 1992.

Keating, Ana Louise. *Women Reading Women Writing: Self-Invention in Paula Gunn Allen, Gloria Anzaldua, and Audre Lorde.* Philadelphia: Temple University Press, 1996.

Laura Madeline Wiseman

humor

In the feature-length *SMOKE SIGNALS* several common stereotypes about Native Americans are presented comically, allowing the film ultimately to subvert them. In the film Victor (Adam Beach) teaches his friend Thomas (Evan Adams), who suffers from terminal Indian geekness, "how to be a real Indian" (Alexie 61–63). His several pointers include talking less and letting his braided hair down so that he looks like a warrior. In short, Victor knows and employs the conventions of identity politics:

> "You got to look mean," he tells Thomas, "or people won't respect you. White people will run all over you if you don't look mean. You got to look like you just got back from killing a buffalo."
>
> Thomas reminds him, "But our tribe never hunted buffalo. We were fishermen."
>
> This sets Victor off: "What? You want to look like you just came back from catching a fish? It ain't *Dances with Salmon,* you know? Man, you think a fisherman is tough? Thomas, you got to look like a warrior."

Victor and Thomas's exchange is revealing for both its use of Indian humor and its self-reflexive commentary on identity. Victor has learned that Indians are not meant to be funny. As cigar store Indians should, they are supposed to be stoic, hard. Humor suggests weakness, yet it is hard not to laugh at Victor's overzealous defense of the age-old stereotype of the "Noble Savage." Victor's idea of Indianness seems to be based on popular culture rather than his own tribal experience. Or, to be more specific, Victor's education has been provided by Hollywood representations of Native people (controlled primarily by Euro-Americans), such as John Ford's westerns or perhaps Kevin Costner's romantic epic *Dances with Wolves.* As much Indian humor does, the comedy of the scene works to undercut the stereotype. The film viewer can no longer believe in the validity of the stereotype without being on the wrong end of the joke.

In commentary on SHERMAN ALEXIE's *The LONE RANGER AND TONTO FISTFIGHT IN HEAVEN,* one critic says, Alexie "uses humor—or his characters use humor—to reveal injustice, protect self-esteem, heal wounds, and create bonds" (Coulombe 94). This statement might be applicable to the humor of most Native writers. Much Indian humor has a social function. In "Indian Humor" from *CUSTER DIED FOR YOUR SINS,* VINE DELORIA, JR., argues that Native humor has a number of vital social functions. For example, teasing was a method of social control. Deloria says, "Rather than embar-

rass members of the tribe publicly, people used to tease individuals they considered out of step with the consensus of tribal opinion. In this way egos were preserved and disputes within the tribe of a personal nature were held to a minimum" (147). According to Deloria, Native people often employ self-deprecating humor to "show that they were not trying to run roughshod over tribal desires" (147). This humor positions them to "highlight their true virtues and gain them a place of influence in tribal policy-making circles" (147). Sometimes humor has the ability to direct and perhaps even galvanize people. "Often," Deloria says, "people are awakened and brought to a militant edge through funny remarks" (147).

Humor has long played a central role in tribal life and the body of Native literature and art that represents tribal life. One important character in both traditional and so-called modern Native American storytelling is that of the TRICKSTER FIGURE. Depending upon his tribe of origin, he may appear as Coyote, Rabbit, Raven, or another. He is often a loner, a shape shifter; he conveniently ignores social convention; and he often possesses a voracious appetite for both food and sex. In "Living Sideways: Social Themes and Social Relationships in Native American Trickster Tales," Franchot Ballinger describes the very serious function of the comic trickster in this manner:

> As Trickster wends his way through human and non-human societies, we see, comically, how vulnerable community ideas, values and institutions are to the twistings and inversions of the ego-centered individual ensconced in that society.... Compelled by self, rather than by community as the Native American ideal would have it, Trickster pursues socially acceptable goals or values and manipulates, in the process violating, the social contract in some fashion. (21–22)

The tension between what is and is not acceptable usually results in comedy. The trickster is the proverbial bull in a china shop. In the Winnebago Trickster Cycle, for example, Trickster is challenged by a talking "laxative bulb": "He who chews me, he will defecate; he will defecate!" (128). Not to be outdone by a talking bulb, Trickster eats the bulb and, after a series of comic explosions that knock Trickster off his feet, he defecates so much that he has to climb a tree to escape the rising pile of excrement. His comic antics remind Trickster, as well as the audience, that he is no better than the next member of the tribe.

Many contemporary Native American writers, such as SIMON ORTIZ, JOY HARJO, CARTER REVARD, and SHERMAN ALEXIE, continue to employ the figure of trickster as a comic device. For example, in what is surely LOUISE ERDRICH's most widely read novel, *LOVE MEDICINE*, Gerry Nanapush possesses all the major characteristics of the traditional trickster. In fact, the Ojibwe trickster figure is often named *nanabush* or *nanabozho*. Gerry is described by his son, Lipsha, as a "famous politicking hero, dangerous armed criminal, judo expert, escape artist, charismatic member of the American Indian Movement, and smoker of many pipes of kinnikinnick in the most radical groups" (248). As the trickster cannot, Gerry Nanapush cannot be contained by the four walls of prison or home. His form and identity are "slippery," his character ever shifting. In the process of being surrounded by police officers, "his body lifted like a hot-air balloon filling suddenly. Behind him there was a wide, tall window. Gerry opened it and sent the screen into thin air with an elegant chorus-girl kick. Then he followed the screen, squeezing himself unbelievably through the frame like a fat rabbit disappearing down a hole" (169).

Few Native writers explore comic stereotypes as boldly and creatively as HANAY GEIOGAMAH, a Kiowa playwright. In *FOGHORN* Geiogamah, as many Native writers do, subverts the powerful myths of the dominant culture through comic retellings of their most popular stories about Native people. *Foghorn* uses 11 short episodes to sketch the story of Native and Euro-American contact in both history and popular culture. So, for example, the play contains a Euro-American teacher in one of the Indian BOARDING SCHOOLS, who is far more "savage" than the class of Indian children she is trying to "civilize" and a Tonto who, fed up with a racist and prima donna Lone Ranger, slits the throat of his

overbearing partner. The humor is generally over the top. Jeffrey Huntsman writes, "When Geiogamah presents a stereotype, as he does throughout *Foghorn*, it is to provide his audience an occasion to exorcise their own acceptance of the ancestral noble savage—dour, stoic, and dumb—or the contemporary welfare derelict—drunken, irresponsible, and shiftless. This purpose he accomplishes with unflagging good humor, classically exposing absurdity with teasing caricature" (xi).

In one scene a lovestruck Pocahontas returns from her first romantic encounter with Captain John Smith to give her "handmaidens" all the juicy details. She says, "And then he stood up and suddenly, and began to take off his clothes. He took off his boots, his shirt, his pants, all that he was wearing. He stood over me, his big, big, big body naked like one of the little children. There was so much hair on his body it made me a little afraid" (64). The punch-line is then given in the stage directions: "The handmaidens huddle closely with Pocahontas for the intimate details. . . . Pocahontas rises above them, lifts her arms in a manner to suggest an erect phallus. The handmaidens gasp. Then a kazoo whistle indicates that the erection falls quickly, and the handmaidens explode with laughter" (64–65). Pocahontas goes on to say, "He said to me, I love you dear Pocahontas. I promise you it won't happen next time, I promise, promise, promise" (65). Once again we see the power of Native humor. The mythic hero is revealed as just another white man with an erectile dysfunction.

Native humor is by no means bound by the printed word. It also finds voice in the stand-up comedy of Charlie Hill (Oneida), the performance art of James Luna (Luceno), and the feature films of Chris Eyre (Cheyenne/Arapaho). Contemporary Native art is fresh with visual puns and play. The work of Shelley Niro (Mohawk) is a good example of the vitality of Native art. Among her many projects is a series of photos "capturing that inner beauty of Native women on film" (Ryan 62). As Geiogamah and Alexie's work does, Niro's comedy disrupts a rigid identity constructed by the dominant culture, an identity that has been taken on by some Native people. Niro's work is a welcome corrective to those humour-less depictions of nubile princess, nurturing earth mother, sultry vixen, and servile squaw that have long been fixed in the popular imagination. Niro brings these fanciful notions of Native identity into sharp (and sometimes soft) focus to illuminate their deficiency. (Ryan 62)

In "500 Year Itch" a triptych with three Indian women (two of them Niro herself) comments on the "contrasting idealized notions of (White) femininity with familiar images of Native reality" (Ryan 77). In the first image Niro is dressed as Marilyn Monroe in the famous scene from the *Seven Year Itch* in which Marilyn's white dress fills with air, giving the viewer a thrill. Juxtaposed with Niro's Marilyn are two photos of Native women, one dressed for a social event and the other dressed in very plain around-the-house clothes. The Marilyn image is a wonderful parody of Marilyn's beauty. Niro fully embraces the role and, thus, subverts the power of Marilyn over women.

Regardless of the genre or form of a text, humor often plays a vital role in Native work. Very little is sacred. Bodily humor is prevalent, stereotypes disrupted. Ultimately humor has the power to teach and even help to shape the collective identity of the audience. Never underestimate the power of a good joke.

Bibliography

Alexie, Sherman. *Smoke Signals: A Screenplay.* New York: Hyperion, 1998.

Ballinger, Franchot. "Living Sideways: Social Themes and Social Relationships in Native American Trickster Tales." *American Indian Quarterly* 13, no. 1 (winter 1989): 14–30.

Coulombe, Joseph L. "The Approximate Size of His Favorite Humor: Sherman Alexie's Comic Connections and Disconnections in *The Lone Ranger and Tonto Fistfight in Heaven.*" *American Indian Quarterly* 26, no. 1 (winter 2002): 94–115.

Deloria, Jr., Vine. "Indian Humor." *Custer Died for Your Sins: An Indian Manifesto.* Norman: University of Oklahoma Press, 1988.

Erdrich, Louise. *Love Medicine.* New York: Bantam, 1989.

Geiogamah, Hanay. "Foghorn." *New Native American Drama: Three Plays by Hanay Geiogamah,* 46–82. Norman: University of Oklahoma Press, 1980.

Huntsman, Jeffrey. "Introduction." In *New Native American Drama: Three Plays by Hanay Geiogamah,* edited by Hanay Geiogamah, ix–xxiv. Norman: University of Oklahoma Press, 1980.

Lincoln, Kenneth. *Indi'n Humor: Bicultural Play in Native America.* Oxford: Oxford University Press, 1993.

Owens, Louis. *Other Destinies: Understanding the American Indian Novel.* Norman: University of Oklahoma Press, 1994.

Ryan, Allan J. *The Trickster Shift: Humour and Irony in Contemporary Native Art.* Vancouver: University of British Columbia, 1999.

"The Winnebago Trickster Cycle." *Norton Anthology of American Literature.* Vol. 1. 5th ed., edited by Nina Baym et al., 125–131. New York: Norton, 1998.

Brad Gambill

I

Indian Killer   Sherman Alexie (1996)

Indian Killer is SHERMAN ALEXIE's third novel and winner of the 1996 *New York Times* Notable Book and *People*: Best of Pages Awards. In the canon of American literature the novel is not easily categorized. It is a spellbinding story, a psychological thriller, and a work of political resistance that is a bracing exploration of identity, social architecture, racial hatred, and yearning. His ninth book, *Indian Killer* demonstrates Alexie's literary mastery and stylistic innovation; it is marked by the language of thoughts and dreams, magical realism, and a Whitmanesque exploration of words. In its invocation of mythological reality it may be compared to the work of such Native writers as LESLIE MARMON SILKO in *CEREMONY*, GERALD VIZENOR in *BEARHEART*, and others who interweave Indian spirituality into the grit of modern life. Neither readers nor characters can grasp, Alexie tells us in *Indian Killer*, "the difference between dreaming and reality. How one could easily become the other" (403). As an exploration of the impact of genocide and racism on the Native psyche, the entirely fictional *Indian Killer* stands in resistance along with such historical treatments as Dee Brown's nonfiction *Bury My Heart at Wounded Knee* (1973). As a treatment of the subject of the cultural relativism of modern life, *Indian Killer* compares well with JAMES WELCH's *WINTER IN THE BLOOD* and N. SCOTT MOMADAY's *HOUSE MADE OF DAWN*.

Through an innovative narrative technique of juxtaposed perspectives, *Indian Killer* is a kaleidoscope of levels of reality experienced by characters at all strata of society and at all degrees of racial purity and mix. It depicts the frustration of those who want a better society but cannot find reasonable means to make one. To that extent its subject matter resonates through the whole of Native American literature.

The protagonist, John Smith, is a 27-year-old Indian construction worker, adopted as an infant by a caring white Seattle couple. His tribal affiliation is unknown, even to him, though the Smiths had tried to expose him to generic Indian culture as he grew up. John is obsessed with a childhood figure, Father Duncan, a Spokane Indian Jesuit who one day "walked into the desert . . . and was never seen again" (16). To John's childhood question "Was Jesus an Indian?" Father Duncan responds, "he should have been" (15). John's mental pursuit of Duncan, who seems for a while to fuse both worlds, takes him to the end of his quest for himself. Metaphorically John stands for the estrangement from self and heritage that Anglo-European imperialism has inflicted upon Native America. Caught between cultures, John becomes increasingly disoriented and paranoid, moving between literal realities and the magical meaning he ascribes to them.

As the novel unfolds, there are several murders and a child abduction. A period of social upheaval follows in which whites and Indians turn on each other. As tension over the murders mounts, we meet the characters whose actions shape the novel and articulate some of the sociopolitical issues to which modern society is heir. One of these people is Marie, a college student who fiercely identifies with and is isolated from the Native community; she cannot speak her own language. She feeds the homeless and aggressively resists the pretensions of such Indian wannabes as a white university professor whose Native American literature course features the novel of a former Ku Klux Klansman. Her choices lead her into the tension of a constant pull between worlds.

In *Indian Killer* perspective is everything. Readers must look for truth, and sometimes Alexie's truth is brutal.

Bibliography

Alexie, Sherman. *Indian Killer.* New York: Atlantic Monthly Press, 1996.

McDonald, John Q. "The Thumbnail Book Reviews, *Indian Killer,* 31 May 1999." Available online. URL: http://sprg.ssl.berkeley.edu/~jmcd/book/revs/inki.html. Accessed on August 15, 2005.

Nicholls, Richard E. "Skin Games." *New York Times.* 24 November 1996.

Spillman, Robert. "Review of *Indian Killer* from Salon." Available online. URL: http://www.salon1999.com/sneaks/sneakpeeks961003.html. Accessed on August 15, 2005.

Ellen Rosenberg

Indian Lawyer, The   James Welch (1990)

JAMES WELCH's fourth novel, *The Indian Lawyer,* can be categorized as a mystery or thriller, but it is also the story of a successful Native American man struggling with his humanity. Other Native American authors have written in the mystery genre, such as LINDA HOGAN, LOUIS OWENS, and SHERMAN ALEXIE, and Welch's contribution is no less significant. Work by Native American authors in this genre is necessary, considering all of the mystery novels written about Native peoples by non-Native peoples, most notably Tony Hillerman.

Welch's novel is not only a mystery novel, but also a great contribution to the field of Native American literature because it examines the life of a successful Native person who is not stereotypically walking in two worlds, but rather a character who must make a moral decision that could ruin his career. The main character, Sylvester Yellow Calf, has opportunities that seem limitless from the outset. Despite his meager beginnings on the Blackfeet Reservation in Montana, Yellow Calf is a prominent lawyer who has potential for political success.

The setting of the novel switches back and forth from a Montana state prison to downtown Helena to reinforce the dilemma that Yellow Calf will find himself in at the end of the novel. Yellow Calf sits on the Montana state parole board and denies parole to the felonious accountant Jack Harwood. Unknown to Yellow Calf, Harwood hatches a plan that involves using his wife, Patti Ann, who will "accidentally" bump into Yellow Calf and then seduce him. Harwood's intention is to blackmail Yellow Calf in order to get parole. However, Patti Ann finds herself falling in love with Yellow Calf and does not want to hurt him or his career. While Harwood is putting his plan into motion, the head of Yellow Calf's law firm has political aspirations for Yellow Calf to run for Congress. As Yellow Calf realizes how his relationship with Patti Ann will hurt his career, he knows he can no longer run for Congress and will not be able to be the first Native American congressman to represent western Montana.

Yellow Calf returns to his reservation, where his alcoholic parents had abandoned him and where his career as a star basketball player began. While he is playing basketball alone, he has a flashback of his last game in the championship playoffs, in which he fouls out. This mistake causes the end of his basketball career. Looking back on his life, he realizes that all it takes is one mistake to end a career. The end of the novel gives promise that Yellow Calf will continue challenging himself and overcoming his personal weaknesses. The last lines of the novel show Yellow Calf's endless inner struggle: "He was going one on one against the only man who ever beat him" (349).

Bibliography

Bak, Hans. "The Realism of Difference: James Welch's *The Indian Lawyer.*" *Annales du Centre de Recherches sur l'Amérique Anglophone* 18 (1993): 187–201.

Donahue, Peter. "New Warriors, New Legends: Basketball in Three Native American Works of Fiction." *American Indian Culture and Research Journal* 21, no. 2 (1997): 43–60.

Welch, James. *The Indian Lawyer.* New York: Norton, 1990.

Meredith James

Indian School Days   Basil Johnston (1988)

BASIL JOHNSTON's *Indian School Days* is the first full-length autobiography devoted solely to the Native Residential School experience in Canada. Although numerous autobiographies, such as Jane Willis's *Geniesh* (1973), Anthony Apakark Thrasher's *Skid Row Eskimo* (1976), and RITA JOE's *Song of Rita Joe* (1996), contain a Residential School component, Johnston's alone limits itself entirely to Native encounters with this assimilative system—the Canadian equivalent of the Bureau of Indian Affairs (BIA) BOARDING SCHOOL system in the United States—jointly run by the federal government and the churches.

In 1939 at the age of 10, Johnston was relocated from his home on the Cape Crocker Reserve to St. Peter Claver's Indian Residential School in Spanish, Ontario, at the behest of "the Indian agent and the priest" (19). There Johnston experienced the Jesuit pedagogical structure, in which "the individual . . . [is] made to conform . . . [and] bend to the will of another" through "order, authority, discipline, . . . [and] regimentation" (43). *Indian School Days,* however, is far from a straightforward indictment of residential school policy. In fact, Johnston responds to the "inevitable question, 'Is there a place for residential schools in the educational system?'" with "a qualified yes" (12). Johnston's focus is not on the oppressive character of the system, but rather on the precocious and rebellious behavior of the students persisting within it, without whose "spirit . . . every day would have passed according to plan and schedule, and there would have been no story" (47). Adopting a colloquial and nostalgic tone rather than a critical or academic one, Johnston endeavors to recall "not the dark and dismal, but the incidents that brought a little cheer and relief to a bleak existence" (11).

Breaking with Western notions of autobiography as the development of an individual identity, *Indian School Days* is a communal story about the bonds forged among students living in exile from their tribal communities. The story Johnston relates is not his alone, but one that belongs to all of the school's "former inmates," some of whom, Johnston has stated, "suggested which stories were to be included" (Lutz 237). Because the narrative is developed from the raw materials of communal memory, Johnston is able to depict events and dialogue for which he was not personally present, assuming for the "autobiography" a quasi-omniscient, or all-knowing, narrative voice. For example, Johnston provides detailed discussions among three students who attempted a daring escape from the school by stolen boat after two of them had received severe physical punishments. This act of defiance marked a small victory for the remaining students, who that evening taunted their overseers in the darkened dormitory, "Betcha can't fin' 'em, Father!" (114). That night, Johnston declares, "We fell asleep feeling triumphant" (114). And although the students who escaped were eventually caught and returned to the school's oppressive environs, Johnston celebrates here and throughout *Indian School Days* the precious opportunities seized, through which the students became rebellious, active, and empowered—even joyous.

Bibliography

Johnston, Basil. *Indian School Days.* Norman: University of Oklahoma Press, 1988.

Lutz, Hartmut. *Contemporary Challenges: Conversations with Canadian Native Authors.* Saskatoon: Fifth House, 1991.

Rymhs, Deena. "A Residential School Memoir." *Canadian Literature* 178 (2003): 58–70.

Sam McKegney

Indian Singing in 20th Century America   Gail Tremblay (1990)

In an interview about her basket art, a woven mix of sweet grass and camera film, Gail Tremblay says she often uses film from old cowboy-and-Indian movies. The baskets are a way of reclaiming a heritage that was often misrepresented by the Hollywood film industry in which Native Americans were frequently ignored or, worse, portrayed as savages. Her poetry combines the same qualities as the baskets she creates. In her preface to *Indian Singing in 20th Century America* Tremblay acknowledges the traditions of the past that shape the poet's experience of the present.

Tremblay says her poems are based on old traditions even as they speak to the individual experiences of modern Native Americans, including her. Poems such as "Relocation" and "Urban Indians, Pioneer Square, Seattle" offer a glimpse into the worldview of the Indian, who knows that he is being looked at and judged by those who do not understand his Native ways and how they clash with the modern world. The pain of having to leave one's family to seek employment elsewhere is mitigated somewhat by the arrival of a gift of a hawk's claw in "Relocation." The delight felt by the recipients of the gift lessens the loneliness of living in a culture that finds no significance or joy in such an object.

In the book's title poem, "Indian Singing in 20th Century America," the same dislocation of experience occurs, and the Native speaker is aware that others are judging and misunderstanding her: "We dance in two worlds, / inevitable as seasons in one, / exotic curiosities in the other" (9–12). Tremblay's speakers live in the borderland between two worlds, where they are represented by others as curiosities, "exotic," whereas in their own culture they are as normal as the passing seasons.

A sense of isolation from others who do not understand or share the speaker's culture is evident in more than just the Anglo disregard of nature. The lack of understanding of other parts of Native culture is attacked in "Reflections on a Visit to the Burke Museum, University of Washington, Seattle" and "Coyote Hanging in a Museum Comes off the Wall." "Coyote" begins with the lines "After days of

blue-haired ladies commenting / on the odd slant of your eyes . . . After hearing, 'My, what big eyes you have' . . . Coyote gets lonely for brown women" (8–9). The total ignorance of Coyote and his place as a TRICKSTER FIGURE in Native American terms and the inevitable appropriation as Coyote as the wolf from a children's story anger the speaker.

A similar anger informs many of Tremblay's poems. "Reflections on a Visit" finds an Indian visitor to the museum appalled to find Native American artifacts housed with dinosaur bones as if to indicate that both were remnants of a world long gone when "grandsons still explain how we did this / in the old days" (3–6). *Indian Singing in 20th Century America* is not just about the anger of Native American dislocation, however. Many poems offer beautiful depictions of festivals, dances, and other traditions of Native American life. In many of them the reader is told to remember: *Sehiá-rak,* "remember it," is the underlying message of Tremblay's poems.

See also AMERICAN INDIAN FILM.

Bibliography

Fast, Robin Riley. "Borderland Voices in Contemporary Native American Poetry." *Contemporary Literature* 36, no. 3 (autumn 1995): 508–536.

P. K. Bostian

Indians' Summer   Nas'naga (1975)

The only novel by the Shawnee poet and artist NAS'NAGA (Roger Russell), *Indians' Summer* is unusual among Native American books in being set in the near-future. It is a rare example of a Native utopia: a vision of a world in which all historical injustices done to Native peoples are corrected.

On July 3, 1976, the day before the American bicentennial, a war council is convened in the Black Hills by Sioux traditionals, in the shadow of Mount Rushmore. The following day the president of the United States is interrupted halfway through his Independence Day address to be told that the Navajo, Hopi, Pueblo, Apache, Sioux, and Mohawk tribes have simultaneously declared independence from the United States; armed Natives have disabled the water and electricity supplies of several large cities in the United States and Canada; the ambassador of India has conveyed to the United Nations the declaration of independence of a new country, Anishinabe-waki (Land of the People); and, worst of all, the Sioux have taken control of several nuclear weapons aimed at the White House.

The action that follows, directed at educating both white and Native readers, is poised uneasily between all-out farce and a deadly serious recounting of the issues surrounding SOVEREIGNTY. *Indians' Summer* is intended for a young adult audience, and in consequence there are moments when a historically aware reader may find the passages devoted to explanation somewhat overlong.

The plot is perhaps too reliant on a combination of irony and idealism. The soldiers of the new Anishinabe-waki state are the best fighters in the United States because of their training for the Vietnam War. Virtually every "good" character turns out to have a percentage of Native blood. There are virtually no dissension among Natives and no sense of division between full- and MIXED-BLOODS people. Yet there are also darker moments—suicides, sudden outbursts of serious fighting—that serve to throw this into relief and make the tricksterish final twist all the more unexpected.

Nas'naga's text remains one of the fullest literal explorations of Indian separatism, and one of the few books to envision a pan-Indian state. Probably more likely to be read as a chronicle of Native politics in the mid-1970s than as a work of literature, *Indians' Summer* remains a surprisingly enjoyable antidote to many more formally accomplished works in the Native American canon.

See also TRICKSTER FIGURES.

James Mackay

Indian Summers Eric Gansworth (1998)

ERIC GANSWORTH's first novel reflects his own background as Onondaga and his childhood on the Tuscarora Indian reservation. Set primarily on a reservation and framed by death and generational passing at both the beginning and the end of the narrative, *Indian Summers* explores the identities, families, and home of its characters. Bordered at the beginning by the death of Sy "Bug" Jimison and at the end by that of Johnny Flatleaf, the work dramatizes Floyd Page's developing and changing identity as a member of the Eel Clan. It also depicts the return of Hank, Floyd's cousin, to the reservation and his difficult but eventually successful reintegration into the family and lifestyle he had left behind as a small child. Although the text uses a roughly linear and chronological narrative style as it moves from June to October 1992, it combines both first-person and third-person points of view in its depiction of Floyd, and it often uses flashbacks in order to give the reader additional information and tie together seemingly unrelated or distant moments in Floyd's life.

While Gansworth does occasionally describe contact between the reservation and outsiders—as in the chapter "Gazebos," when Floyd takes a white university professor home—his primary focus is on a vision of life on the reservation as seen from *within* the reservation. Indeed, the "outsider" most interesting to Gansworth is not any white man, but Hank, a Native American returning to his culture and history after a long separation. Hank must accept a very different lifestyle from the urban civilization he has been accustomed to, and he takes small steps toward acceptance of conceptions of time and personal property and stronger bonds of family and friendship.

For Floyd the months described in Gansworth's novel revolve around a healing journey. After an injury in a swimming accident in the dike—as the reservoir is familiarly known on the reservation—Floyd's memory and sense of place and time only finally heal when he begins to accompany his friend Jan to the Longhouse and helps Jan take Johnny Flatleaf back to the reservation to die. Floyd and Jan also engage in an understated but nonetheless genuine romance, and *Indian Summers* concludes with a suggestion of a cyclical pattern of life and death, leaving and returning to the reservation; Bug's death has been eased by his son, Hank's, return, and Johnny's death is mediated by Floyd's assumption of his own Eel identity.

The novel's title also contributes to its generally positive depiction of reservation life. In the most simplistic sense the novel does take place over one long summer—and, obviously, its characters are Native Americans or Indians. But in the meteorological sense in which the term *Indian summer* is most often used, the words imply an unseasonable period of warmth and pleasant weather in late autumn or fall. Similarly after Bug's death and a fierce storm in which Johnny Flatleaf dies, the main characters of *Indian Summers* have come to terms with themselves and with each other, and the novel ends with a warm vision of unity and friendship.

See also RESERVATION LIFE.

Bibliography

Gansworth, Eric. *Indian Summers.* East Lansing: Michigan State University Press, 1998.

Strom, Karen M., and Eric Gansworth. *Storytellers: Native American Authors Online.* Available online. URL: http://www.hanksville.org/storytellers/ericg/. Accessed on April 4, 2005.

Winter Elliott

Indian Time: A Novel of Western Oklahoma   Charles Penoi (1984)

Charles Penoi's *Indian Time* focuses on the story of Jake Hawkins, a young man of Kiowa and white descent. Stylistically the novel is lacking on several levels, such as the stilted dialogue and the confusing stream of consciousness episodes; however, Penoi captures the landscape of western Oklahoma and provides a road map, leading the reader through the small towns and exposing the peculiar, yet endearing, characteristics of the inhabitants of this region. Penoi also addresses important issues in the field of Native American literature such as characters' relationships to the land, MIXED-BLOOD identity, experience in BOARDING SCHOOLS, mineral rights, and discussions of Christian and American Indian SPIRITUALITY.

At the beginning of the novel Jake Hawkins graduates high school at the Riverside Indian School in Anadarko, Oklahoma. Jake is the son of a Kiowa preacher and a white mother from Kansas. His parents are depicted as loving, and

their relationship offers a portrayal of a functioning and nurturing interracial relationship, which is rarely portrayed in American literature. The novel deals with Jake's discovering his sexuality with the lover he sees in dreams, Mary Marie Tinker, whom he eventually finds. Jake's obsession with his "dream" woman leads him to Hominy, Oklahoma, where he finds Mary Marie waiting for him. This episode is interesting only because Mary Marie explains her Osage heritage and her acquisition of wealth through inheritance and oil money. Jake's time with the wild and flamboyant Mary Marie is interrupted by his father's heart attack, which sends him back home. His family moves to Kansas, yet Oklahoma calls Jake back.

Halfway through the novel Jake encounters his old school friend, Robert Gombi, and they embark on romantic adventures. The narrator comments on Jake's ambitions, "What he really wanted to do was meet some more Indian girls" (85). The rest of the novel is a confusing cavalcade of romantic episodes. At the American Indian Exhibition in Anadarko Jake meets Joy; he then quickly falls in love with and proposes to Beverly Ross.

An interesting subplot of the novel involves Jake's interaction with a shaman. Before Jake can marry Beverly, he has to be tested by the shaman Ku-ken-ish; Jake is asked to spend the night on Rattlesnake Mountain and take home a rattlesnake to prove his manhood. Ku-ken-ish accompanies Jake and is bitten by a rattlesnake. Jake tries to save him but cannot. After the Ross family and the community find out what happened, they do not want Jake to marry Beverly because he will cause bad luck.

The last chapter is rushed, and as in much of the novel, plot lines are dropped as quickly as they are introduced. Jake reflects on all the women he has encountered throughout the novel. He receives an unexpected phone call from Mary Marie and tells her that he might marry her after he finishes school, yet ultimately he chooses to marry Joy.

Aside from the rushed ending of the novel and other problems with style, Penoi's novel offers a realistic glimpse of small town life in western Oklahoma.

Bibliography

Penoi, Charles. *Indian Time: A Novel of Western Oklahoma.* Yukon, Okla.: Pueblo Publishing Press, 1984.

Penoi, Charles, and Mary Penoi. *No More Buffaloes.* Yukon, Okla.: Pueblo Publishing Press, 1981.

Meredith James

In Mad Love and War   Joy Harjo (1990)

The poems collected in JOY HARJO's second volume, *In Mad Love and War,* which has won an American Book Award and the Delmore Schwartz Memorial Award, include the nine poems from her first chapbook, entitled *The LAST SONG.* Harjo, a member of the Muskogee tribe originally from Oklahoma, has included these poems and expanded upon the themes already present in her early work. JOSEPH BRUCHAC has said that autobiography and nature writing are the same thing: that one cannot tell the story of oneself without telling the story of earth. Harjo takes this dictum to heart as she narrates the story of Native Americans while telling her own story.

In an interview with Bill Moyers, Harjo comments that she does not see time as linear: "For us [Native Americans], there is not just this world, there's also a layering of others" (*Spiral* 39). In the poems of *In Mad Love and War* there are timelessness and circularity. In "We Encounter Nat King Cole" the speaker walking home sees a rainbow, and "there were twin gods bending over to plant something like / themselves in the wet earth, a song / larger than all our cheap hopes" (51). The slipperiness of time as seen from a Native American perspective is evident in many of Harjo's poems. The past and the glory of its myths and legends, as well as the horrors of its Anglo oppression, are as current as today's rainbows. In a poem dedicated to the African-American poet June Jordan, Harjo experiences personal insights in the Egyptian Room of the Metropolitan Museum: Ancient Africa; stories of the Native American TRICKSTER FIGURES,

Rabbit and Coyote; and her own Oklahoma childhood are part of the same historical stream from which Harjo draws inspiration for her poetry.

Harjo plays saxophone with her band Poetic Justice, and references to the power of music, along with allusions to jazz musicians, appear frequently in *In Mad Love and War.* In "We Encounter Nat King Cole" the speaker knows that song has the ability to "invent / my lover of evening light" (2–3). The speaker of "Nine Below" gives her "heart's dogs . . . the sound of your blue saxophone to know you by" (5, 7). The jazz legend John Coltrane "knew love in the fluid shape / of a saxophone (8–9)," and Billie Holiday is urged to come home. But the music must be married to words to make a difference. "Chords to / other chords to other chords, if we're lucky, to melody" (10–11). In "Bird" the music is central; however, the poem ends with the speaker's saying, "Let me hear you / by any means: by horn, by fever, by night, even by some poem (15–16)."

Harjo acknowledges the power of poetry to convey the musical beat that coincides with the heartbeat: "ghosts of time in tilted hats are ushered / by our heartbeats into the living room" (7–8) ("We Encounter Nat King Cole"). Poetry and music have the power to transform the rational world into a spiritual one. In "Song for the Deer and Myself to Return On" the narrator seems skeptical about the power of song to call deer to hunters. She sings the "song Louis taught me: / a song to call the deer in Creek, when hunting, / and I am certainly hunting something as magic as deer" (3–5). She does not seem surprised, though, that "It works, of course, and deer came into this room / and wondered at finding themselves / in a house near downtown Denver" (7–9). The last lines find the speaker wondering how to get the deer, and all of us, back home.

The poetry of *In Mad Love and War* often addresses the desire for Native Americans to find their way home, even if that home is a spiritual one. Sometimes home can be found in a truck stop with friends eating pancakes ("Grace"), in a bar in the middle of winter ("Deer Dancer"), or driving through Tucson ("Javeleina"). The way home is often fraught with political oppression, though, and Harjo does not flinch from giving voice to those who have been silenced. A frequently anthologized poem, "For Anna Mae Pictou Aquash," tells the story of a young Micmac activist who was murdered, whose death authorities originally attributed to exposure. "Strange Fruit" graphically depicts the lynching of an African-American activist in the 1980s. And "The Real Revolution Is Love" is set in war-torn Nicaragua.

Harjo's poetry is often about transformations. The women of *In Mad Love and War* are often shape shifters, becoming mythological in their transformations. Woman becomes Death (57); she is "dark earth and round and full of names" (55); her body a chrysalis (32); she is "A myth slipped down through dreamtime" (6). "Transformations" is one such poem about mutability. Harjo insists that hatred can be turned into something else. The image of a dying old man changing into an old tree captures the grace of transforming hatred into love. Harjo ends the poem with the line "This is your hatred back. She loves you" (22). Not only is hatred described as a woman, but as one who loves her creator. The power of love as transformative moves through Harjo's poetry.

Harjo moves easily between the worlds of larger concerns of political oppression and racism and the personal one of relationships and friendships. History, tradition, and mythology all form a spiral of memory that tells the story of Native Americans and Harjo's own life.

Bibliography

Field, C. Renee. *Dictionary of Literary Biography.* Vol. 120, *American Poets since World War II, Third Series,* 114–119. Los Angeles: Gale Group, 1992.

Harjo, Joy. *In Mad Love and War.* Middleton, Conn.: Wesleyan University Press, 1990.

———. *The Spiral of Memory: Interviews,* edited by Laura Coltelli. Ann Arbor: University of Michigan Press, 1996.

Lang, Nancy. "'Twin Gods Bending Over': Joy Harjo and Poetic Memory." *MELUS* 18, no. 3 (fall 1993): 41–50.

Scarry, John. "Representing Real Worlds: The Evolving Poetry of Joy Harjo." *World Literature Today* 66, no. 2 (spring 1992): 286–291.

West, Kathleene. Review of *In Mad Love and War, Prairie Schooner* 66, no. 2 (summer 1992): 128–132.

P. K. Bostian

Interior Landscapes: Autobiographical Myths and Metaphors   Gerald Vizenor (1990)

GERALD VIZENOR is one of the most prolific contemporary Native authors, and his autobiography figures significantly in his work. This, Vizenor's formal "autobiography," functions less as a memoir than as a series of "imaginative histories" (263) or genre experiments. In contrast to N. SCOTT MOMADAY's *THE NAMES* and LESLIE MARMON SILKO's *STORY-TELLER,* which trace personal and tribal genealogies, Vizenor's autobiography involves "[c]hances, not causes" that provide for him "the best sense of the real" (Vizenor and Lee 57). Whereas traditional autobiography aims to articulate truths about identity, Vizenor's challenges these essentialist ends, claiming "my memories and interior landscapes are untamed" (263). Thus, as the title suggests, myth slides into life and life into metaphor, in what Vizenor calls a "visionary transmotion" (Vizenor and Lee 61).

Vizenor calls the book's 29 chapters "episodes of memory," which may be read as interconnected chapters in a life or as independent stories (Vizenor and Lee 58). "Families of the Crane" opens the book, intermingling tribal myth with stories of Vizenor's ancestral line. "June 1936: Measuring My Blood" deals with the violent murder of his biological father. The book chronicles other losses that plagued Vizenor's early life: his white mother's abandonment of him, growing up poor in Minneapolis, life in a series of sometimes violent foster homes, a surrogate father who died of injuries sustained from a fall down an elevator shaft, and his divided allegiances as a Cub Scout when he was forced to first confront Indian stereotypes.

As a journalist he investigates the suicide of Dane White and the murderer Thomas James White Hawk to explain his own life experience and the cultural schizophrenia felt by many contemporary Indians. His experiences traveling in Japan provide him with a sense of authenticity "closer to a tribal consciousness, than . . . the promises of missionaries and academic careers" (130). Vizenor's MIXED-BLOOD heritage prevents him from taking root in one place, however, and he leaves Japan because his "crossblood remembrance, lost tribal souls, uncertain identities, and wounded cranes in the poisoned cities, cause me the most miseries. I learned to remember these stories, and to honor impermanence," always remaining in motion, on the "run, run, run, run" (130). For Vizenor the mixed-blood experience offers a mythic and metaphorical means through which to foster "survival trickeries on the borders" (73); these border zones provide liberation from essentialized notions of identity and function as a possible means for Indian and, by extension, human survival in the contemporary world.

In this book's final chapter Vizenor argues the mixed-blood person exists between fixed points, as "a new metaphor, a transitive contradancer between communal tribal cultures and those material and urban pretensions that counter conservative traditions. The crossblood wavers in myths and autobiographies" (262–263). The book ends with eight ostensibly unrelated memories that underscore how autobiography is a construction that is never totally complete. If there are eight possible endings, Vizenor argues, countless others exist as well.

Bibliography

Vizenor, Gerald, and A. Robert Lee. *Postindian Conversations.* Lincoln: University of Nebraska Press, 1999.

Brian Gempp

In the Bear's House N. Scott Momaday (1999)

In the Bear's House is N. Scott Momaday's celebration of one of the most important themes in his life, the theme of the wilderness. That the book is nominally about Bear only serves to underscore Momaday's point that Bear is a symbol, a transparent and particular symbol that he refers to as a "template of the wilderness" (9).

The book is a collection of 40 paintings, 20 poems, two prose sections, and one extended dialogue between Yahweh and Urset (God and Bear). All of these texts are directly or indirectly focused on the subject of Bear, an animal of great spiritual importance to Momaday's Kiowa tribe, as well as to him personally. Momaday's Indian name is *Tsoai-talee,* or Kiowa "rock-tree boy." The "rock-tree" is Devils Tower in Wyoming, the famous stone tower that rises up out of the desert. In Kiowa mythology a boy turned into a bear at this site, and his seven sisters rose into the sky and became the stars that form the constellation known as the Big Dipper. Momaday relates this story both in the introduction to *In the Bear's House* and in one of the prose sections at the end. His novel *The ANCIENT CHILD* also revolves around the story of Tsoai-talee and his sisters.

The section "The Bear-God Dialogues" covers such topics as identity, prayer, dreams, time, and thought through the use of an imagined conversation between Yahweh (Great Mystery) and Urset (Bear). These dialogues blend Christian and Kiowa traditions in a way that is both plain-spoken and profound. For example, in the section "Prayer" Yahweh asks Urset what he heard him say that morning as he walked along the creek. Urset responds: "I said: 'The morning is crisp and bright. I expect something to define the air momentarily, perhaps the shrill cry of a rabbit or a wren. The water of Frijoles Creek runs southward through splinters of sunlight and patterns of shade'" (27). Yahweh explains to Urset that these simple observations were indeed prayer, blending the Christian concept of prayer with the Kiowa connection to the wilderness.

The poems of *In the Bear's House* evoke Bear's many sides and emotions: wonder, pain, fear, pride, ending with the liberation and fulfillment of death. The paintings, abstract and bold, serve to enhance the portrait of Bear delivered by the written parts of the text.

Bibliography

Momaday, N. Scott. *In the Bear's House.* New York: St. Martin's, 1999.

Jennifer-McClinton-Temple

In the Presence of the Sun   N. Scott Momaday (1992)

N. SCOTT MOMADAY's collected art forms, drawings, paintings, poems, and stories, are artifacts of cultural heritage. These art forms celebrate the shared traditions of Native American history but, more specifically, reflect the culture and the geography of the Great Plains region of the United States, influences that have shaped the artist's identity and work. In *In the Presence of the Sun* Momaday approaches these ancestral roots through the contemporary rhetoric of prose poetry, folktale, and musical forms, to examine the legends and customs of his Native American heritage. The subtle linking of universal themes and familiar sensory images evokes a meticulous sense of time and place, and a mythical wildness of the land and the formality of language create striking contrasts and harmonious images from Kiowa ritual and legend.

The artist moves between his tribal and white worlds, sketching and narrating the realities of each environment. Through Kiowa traditions, Wild West legends, and allusion to contemporary events, Momaday sets these worldviews alternately at right and odd angles. His words, images, and rhythms produce the poetry of a people who embrace the interconnectedness of the natural landscape and the human spirit. Momaday's work transforms tribal tradition and imagination into literary forms and words, which he views as sacred.

In the Presence of the Sun is a reflective collection of art that speaks with the voice of the Kiowa, representing 30 years of literary history, from 1961 through 1991. Critics note the influence of the American modernists William Faulkner and Ernest Hemingway, of Ivor Winters, and of Frederick Goddard Tuckerman, but Momaday credits home and culture as the primary catalysts for his work. Ordinary events assume extraordinary life in Momaday's memoirlike transformations of personal and imagined history. In the preface of *In the Presence of the Sun* Momaday emphasizes the close correlation between his written work and his artistic and cultural identity: "The poems and stories, the drawings here, express my spirit fairly, I believe. If you look closely into these pages, it is possible to catch a glimpse of me in my original being" (xx).

Bibliography

Gray, Kathryn Napier. "N. Scott Momaday." Literature Database Online. Available online. URL: www. LitEncyc.com. Accessed on August 15, 2005.

Lincoln, Kenneth. *Native American Renaissance.* Berkeley: University of California Press, 1985.

Momaday, N. Scott. *In the Presence of the Sun.* New York: St. Martin's, 1992.

Schubnell, Matthias, ed. *Conversations with N. Scott Momaday.* Jackson: University Press of Mississippi, 1997.

Stella Thompson

In the Time of the Present   Maurice Kenny (2000)

Within *In the Time of the Present* MAURICE KENNY, a Mohawk poet, essayist, and fiction writer, presents a diverse collection of poems that capture the power of and attachment to place, close friends, and old memories. Kenny's careful selection of words and their particular melodies is analogous to his description of the significant effort and delight garnered from picking blackberries.

In the Time of the Present is divided into three sections. The first, entitled "A View Backwards," provides a window into the past, offering distinct descriptions that frequently position the reader within the moment. The poem "Photograph: Carlisle Indian School (1879–1918)" describes the photo of a young boy that was taken during his attendance at the infamous boarding school. The photograph is one of numerous ones that Carlisle officials took depicting American Indian youth both before and after their "reformation." The primary intent of Carlisle was to shape the identity of American Indian youth. However, the school was a place of survival and loss, as residents were stripped of their language and culture. Unfamiliar clothing was worn, and "youthful warrior braids lay heaped / on the barber's floor" (20–21). Kenny describes the young boy as "nationless / non-descriptive in an army uniform" (7–8) and dressed in a "collar so tight that it proclaims a hanging" (13).

Within the second section, "Mostly in the Adirondacks," Kenny paints vistas "of spruce / white pine / cedar /" (2–5) and touches the dark and cool depths of water. These poems emphasize the connection to friends and his home around Saranac Lake. They affix readers in the moment, positioning them beside Kenny on early morning strolls past lilacs, enticing berries, and a sundrop: "sitting / among / daisies / and black-eyed susans" (5–8).

"The Note," a poem within the final section, "from out there . . . somewhere," describes the impact of the suicide of MICHAEL DORRIS, a controversial writer and scholar of American Indian studies. In his poem about Dorris, Kenny, referring to his own past, describes "the night I brought the knife / into the scalding waters of the bathtub" (53–54) and seems to sympathize with suicidal feelings in the pursuit of peace.

In the Time of the Present grounds readers in the here-and-now and often provides unique perceptual vantages. From historical events and personal experiences to oft-overlooked dandelions, Kenny captures and illustrates the essence and sense of place, the natural world, the "sound of purple," and the intersection of old roads cracked by time.

Bibliography

Kenny, Maurice. *In the Time of the Present.* East Lansing: Michigan State University Press, 2000.

———. *The Mama Poems.* Buffalo, N.Y.: White Pine Press, 1984.

———. *Tekonwatonti/Molly Brant (1735–1795: Poems of War).* New York: White Pine Press, 1992.

Aaron Denham

Invisible Musician, The   Ray A. Young Bear (1990)

RAY A. YOUNG BEAR, born and raised in the Meskwaki Indian Settlement, grew up speaking Meskwaki and did not learn English until he attended school. As a self-described collector of words, Young Bear began approaching the poetry of *The Invisible Musician* while attending Pomona College. His work is also significantly inspired by his grandmother, who taught him the Meskwaki language and cultural traditions; Robert Bly, who helped connect him with various editors; and his wife, Stella. Additionally the numerous references to Emily Dickinson in *The Invisible Musician* illustrate the diversity of influences behind his writing.

Young Bear's poetry is commonly described as offering dynamic, yet surreal or dream-based images. His poetry is dense, however, its meaning, once grasped, reveals a powerful voice worthy of the effort. *The Invisible Musician* sings a spectrum of poetry, from entwined, intricate, yet jarring descriptions of dreams and reality, to expressions of faith and the embodiment of power both past and present.

In "Wa ta se Na ka mo ni, Viet Nam Memorial" the invisible musician, "a lone frog, the same one / who probably announced / the premature spring floods" (4–6), cannot be presumed to be Young Bear, a traditional Meskwaki singer who did not fight in the VIETNAM WAR. Despite his hesitation and "guilt," Young Bear honors the veterans by adopting the respected collective voice of the invisible musician, who continues to sing throughout the book (McAdams).

Often ironically and without hesitation, Young Bear emphasizes that life is filled with contradictions. In "A Drive to Lone Ranger" he visits old man Bumblebee, who embodies such juxtapositions with "bilingual eloquence": "From communal weatherization / to peyote songs, regional and world / affairs," to an "obsession with technology" and knowledge of the supernatural, Bumblebee "has retained the ability to understand / traditional precepts and myths" (33–34).

A force in *The Invisible Musician* rests in Young Bear's arrangement and negotiation of disparate and often conflicting worldviews. Specifically, Young Bear constructs a notable representational bridge spanning "modern" and traditional ways. Perhaps these motifs are best symbolized by his often seamless incorporation of the Meskwaki language in several poems. However, we are reminded of the distance such an interpretive bridge must span by his inclusion of numerous Meskwaki songs presented adjacent to their English translations, translations that are unlikely to convey the totality of the songs' meaning and strength.

Bibliography

McAdams, Janet. "Book Reviews." *American Indian Quarterly* 18 (1994): 87–90.

Young Bear, Ray A. *Black Eagle Child: The Facepaint Narratives.* Iowa City: University of Iowa Press, 1992.

———. *The Invisible Musician.* Duluth, Minn.: Holy Cow! Press, 1990.

———. *The Rock Island Hiking Club.* Iowa City: University of Iowa Press, 2001.

———. *Winter of the Salamander: The Keeper of Importance.* San Francisco: Harper & Row, 1980.

Aaron Denham

I Remember the Fallen Trees: New and Selected Poems   Elizabeth Cook-Lynn (1998)

Born in 1930, ELIZABETH COOK-LYNN grew up along the Missouri River on the Crow Creek Agency in South Dakota. This area is among the poorest in the United States, but Cook-Lynn learned stories and culture from her ancestors and recounts fond childhood memories in her verse. However, that tone is not the norm. The loss of that textured life, to dams that put the richest tribal homelands underwater, informs this collection. Cook-Lynn does not simply regret or remember. She examines what to do next, how to retain those memories and keep Native American culture vibrant and the lands intact.

The central historical event in the collection is the government's building in the 1950s and 1960s a series of flood-control dams that ironically inundated and dislocated many tribal villages. Ft. Thompson, where Cook-Lynn was born, took in many refugees; to them, the backed-up river water is a visible reminder of arrogant white industrialized society, not only here, but also throughout Indian-white relations. Another reminder are the remains of those trees—the "fallen trees" of the title, dead gray limbs that jut above the dammed river.

The poems loosely follow the pattern of loss that the Crow Creek and other tribes faced with the inundation of their land by either water or "progress." In each section Cook-Lynn gathers myth, storytelling, personal memories, and historical facts to serve as building material for a hopeful plan for the future of Native Americans.

Cook-Lynn's personal history is fully on display, from pleasant memories of watching her uncles swim across the lazy river and sun themselves to the sadness of losing lovers. Mixed feelings about her academic pursuits are also visible, describing the professional politics and racism she endured while teaching, but also referring to herself as "Collaborator" for watching as "Persistent jets, unseen and ominous / as the thrill of the imagined Red Telephone / whisper in the river's gorge, lapping at the water's edge" (13–15). Modernity and tradition contrast, forcing reconciliation and revision, as in the poem "Tatekeya's Earth," in which hearing a beaver's splash leads to a traditional image of this builder animal contrasted with "those damn builders / whose turbid reservoirs could be heard / upstream for eight hundred miles" (3–5).

This blending is often evident, as the poet mixes references to European culture with her strong Native American voice. References to the Greek poet Homer and the mythological figures of Sisyphus and Orpheus appear, and Cook-Lynn uses French and Latin phrases and terms from Christian traditions.

But Cook-Lynn's central concern is Native American survival, especially the retention of spiritual and cultural traditions and concern for the land of her ancestors. The poems assert, sometimes angrily and bitterly, the need for reconciling loss with hope, relishing failures of white people, and celebrating resistance.

Bibliography

Cook-Lynn, Elizabeth. *I Remember the Fallen Trees: New and Selected Poems.* Cheney: Eastern Washington University Press, 1998.

John Nelson

Iron Woman Diane Glancy (1990)

DIANE GLANCY is one of the most prolific Native American poets to date, with 14 books of poetry published. *Iron Woman* is a pivotal collection that highlights Glancy's understanding of her mixed heritage. Glancy is of Euro-American and Cherokee descent and much of her poetry works to retrace these bloodlines. Although she was raised away from her Cherokee community—growing up in Missouri with a Cherokee/German father and an English/German mother—she is preoccupied in her writing with her Native heritage.

The collection *Iron Woman,* which earned her the Capricorn Poetry Prize, reflects Glancy's MIXED-BLOOD existence and divided identity. In the collection's epigraph, Glancy first asks why she even bothers with her Native American heritage: "What does it matter?" She answers by noting how she feels the "footsteps of the ancestors" in the air about her as she passes the sculpture *Iron Woman* each day. Thus, she proclaims: "So I dedicate this book to the 'visage,' if that's the right word, the 're mains' of a heritage I feel everyday."

In Glancy's signature poem, "Iron Woman," the speaker evokes an ambivalent yet complex identity that she attempts to define and ultimately honor: "I knew I came from a different place, / a story cut apart with scissors" (61). The speaker then proceeds to cite images of incomplete parts ("rust," "fog," "broken language," "iron welded," "mask," and "sewn teeth"), but as the poem progresses the speaker moves toward whole objects ("woman," "bird's nest"). A new persona emerges as the "I" and the "she" in the poem become indiscernible and offer each other strength: "Her voice rises in the trail of smoke / & mixes with mine in air" (61). The final lines, as they echo coalescence for the persona in the poem, illustrate Glancy's mixed identity: "It takes a while to speak with these two voices / as it takes a while to walk on two feet / each one going the other way" (61).

The collection also summons the spirit of her Native ancestors as the speaker muses on specific experiences, local landscapes, and painful memories. Poems such as "Red Moonwalking Woman," "Emigrant," "The Mission Ghost," "On Columbus Day," and "Palo Duro Canyon" reiterate the history of the colonization of Native Americans from a Native's point of view as they move the speaker's bloodlines closer to her heart. In this way Diane Glancy not only remembers her heritage through her poetry, but also creates the means to piece herself together through the motion her poems effect.

Bibliography

Glancy, Diane. *Iron Woman.* New York: New River's Press, 1990.
———. "Two Dresses." In *I Tell You Now: Autobiographical Essays by Native American Writers,* edited by Brain Swann and Arnold Krupat, 167–184. Lincoln: University of Nebraska Press, 1987.
———. *The West Pole.* Minneapolis: University of Minnesota Press, 1997.
Strom, Karen. "Native American Authors On-Line." Available online. URL: http://www.hanksville.org/storytellers/glancy/. Accessed on August 15, 2005.

Molly McGlennan

Jacklight   Louise Erdrich   (1984)

Though LOUISE ERDRICH is considered today primarily to be a writer of fiction, during her senior year at Dartmouth *Ms.* selected her poem "In the Midlands" for publication. Later retitled "Walking in the Breakdown Lane," the poem was included in *Jacklight,* her first published book. This poetry collection was written between 1977 and 1979, mainly while Erdrich was enrolled in the M.A. program in creative writing at Johns Hopkins University. Published in January 1984, *Jacklight* won the American Academy of Poet's Prize, establishing Erdrich as a new voice in American letters.

Critics often argue Erdrich's poetry suffers under the weight of her talents as a novelist. Soon after the publication of *Jacklight,* Erdrich began feeling "there was not enough room in a poem . . . to really tell the story" (Coltelli 23). *Jacklight* benefits, however, from her expansive narrative techniques, which test the limits of genre, culture, language, and identity.

The collection's 40 poems are organized in five sequences: "Jacklight," "Runaways," "Hunters," "The Butcher's Wife," and "Myths." Many of the poems deal with realistic and mythic subject matter, drawing simultaneously from the contemporary world and Chippewa myth. Erdrich's poetry juxtaposes these "two worlds and also hints at a natural unity which is broken yet hovering somewhere in the background" (Bruchac 95). This duality appears in poems like "Old Man Potchikoo" and "Whooping Cranes," the latter of which retells a Chippewa myth about a foundling discovered "in a ditch / sucking tea from a bottle"; (2–3) a contemporary Indian community raises the orphan, who eventually "grew / strange and secret among the others" (5–6). The poem ends with a return to myth when the orphan transforms into a crane and joins a flock formation as they "sailed over" head (10). Other poems depict marginalized female characters and offer a similar potential recuperation. In "Francine's Room" a prostitute confesses she is the town's infamous "minor attraction" (2), but she also identifies hope in explaining "What mending there is / occurs in small acts, / and after the fact of the damage" (5–7). Erdrich sees these examples of "symbolic transformation" as vital, especially for women, because they allow a means of challenging convention (Bruchac 101).

"Runaways" confronts themes that Erdrich returns to throughout her career: the effects of cultural hybridity (a condition felt when a culture is composed of elements from multiple cultures—a hybrid), colonization, and dispossession. "Indian Boarding School: The Runaways" focuses on those forcibly removed from their homes. For the dispossessed running away offers a potential return, "Home's the place we head for in our sleep. // The rails, old lacerations that we love // . . . Riding scars / you can't get lost. Home is the place they cross"

(16, 18–20). For the contemporary Indian home is a place just beyond reach—recollected in tribal histories but not in the present or future.

These poems evidence an intertextuality seen throughout Erdrich's work. "A Love Medicine" later appears as a short story and novel of the same name. *The Butcher's Wife* series investigates Erdrich's German-Catholic heritage, involving characters further developed in the novel *The BEET QUEEN* (1986) and in her second collection of poetry, *BAPTISM OF DESIRE* (1989).

Bibliography

Bruchac, Joseph. "Whatever Is Really Yours: An Interview with Louise Erdrich." In *Conversations with Louise Erdrich and Michael Dorris,* edited by Allan Chavkin and Nancy Feyl Chavkin, 100–110. Jackson: University Press of Mississippi, 1994.

Coltelli, Laura. "Louise Erdrich and Michael Dorris." *Conversations with Louise Erdrich and Michael Dorris,* edited by Allan Chavkin and Nancy Feyl Chavkin, 78–95. Jackson: University Press of Mississippi, 1994

Brian Gempp

Jailing of Cecelia Capture, The   Janet Campbell Hale (1985)

The Jailing of Cecelia Capture, JANET CAMPBELL HALE's second novel, though nominated for the Pulitzer Prize, has since fallen into relative obscurity. It is among the first novels to describe the urban Indian experience, making a great departure from the tradition of "reservation novels." The novel recounts the events of Cecelia Capture's 30th birthday, during which she has been arrested for drunk driving (and, as she later finds out, welfare fraud). In prison Cecelia recalls her childhood on the Coeur d'Alene Reservation in Idaho and her life in San Francisco from the 1960s to the 1980s. Much of the novel focuses on race and GENDER issues, alienation and detribalization, in addition to concerns about place and "home."

Cecelia remembers the reservation as a cold, isolated place. She is the youngest child of aging parents, Mary Theresa and Will Capture. Mary Theresa is a woman of mixed Irish and Native heritage whose internalized racism is projected onto Cecelia, whom she calls a "dirty little thing" (46). Will is an alcoholic who did not fulfill his father's wish for him to become a lawyer, one who could fight for the rights of his people.

Cecelia leaves home at the age of 16 and moves to San Francisco. She meets Bud Donahue, who becomes the father her oldest child, shortly before he ships off to Vietnam, where he dies in combat. An unwed teenage mother, Cecelia turns to welfare for survival. The other Indians she encounters in the city are there as a result of the Bureau of Indian Affairs' Relocation Program, designed to assimilate reservation Indians into urban areas, beginning in the 1950s. Cecelia describes them as "hopeless, displaced people" and "a band of outcasts" (112). She begins taking community college classes and is soon admitted to Berkeley.

In the "present" of the novel Cecelia Capture is a law student at Berkeley, a mother of two, and the wife of an English professor, Nathan, who lives in Washington State with the children. Cecelia has had a series of affairs, and her marriage is disintegrating. After her release from prison Cecelia is determined to commit suicide on Bud Donahue's grave. She recalls her experience in the occupation of Alcatraz Island (see AMERICAN INDIAN MOVEMENT), "Indians feeling effective," and decides to live (199).

The novel's stark realism and nontraditional "Indianness" have added to its critical neglect. Hale demonstrates how a Native subject can know multiple geographies, the reservation and the city. The novel is also clearly an articulation of feminist concerns. Cecelia Capture's experience of "captivity" extends beyond the confines of her jail cell. She is a captive of the welfare system and of an unhappy marriage. Hale's female protagonist learns the difficulties of being an Indian woman in contemporary society, of what it means to maintain an Indian identity in the urban space.

See also ASSIMILATION.

Bibliography

Hale, Frederick. *Janet Campbell Hale.* Western Writers Series 125. Boise, Idaho: Boise State University Press, 1996.

———. "The Perils of Native American Urbanization and Alcoholism in Janet Campbell Hale's *The Jailing of Cecelia Capture*." *Journal of American Studies of Turkey* 8 (1998): 51–63.

Hale, Janet Campbell. *The Jailing of Cecelia Capture.* Albuquerque: University of New Mexico Press, 1985.

Stromberg, Eric. "*The Jailing of Cecelia Capture* and the Rhetoric of Individualism." *MELUS* 28 no. 4 (2003): 101–123.

Laura Szanto

Joe, Rita (1932–)

Rita Joe began writing when she was nearly 40 years old. She says that poetry's success pleases her because it helps her people to believe they too can tell their stories. Joe was subjected to sexual abuse in foster care and physical abuse in her marriage, but she makes no time for recriminations. She uses "gentle persuasion," focuses on "the beauty in whatever place or circumstance she may be in," and maintains "an upbeat attitude about life" (Windspeaker 14). This attitude is demonstrated in the use of the word *song* in her titles and the use of her language, which serve to underscore the artistic purpose of Rita Joe.

Joe is Mi'kmaq, born Rita Bernard in Whycocomagh on Canada's Cape Breton Island, the youngest of seven children. She was raised in a series of foster homes after the deaths of both her parents by the time she was 10. Joe went to a residential school for four years, left when she was 16, married Frank Joe in 1954, and is the mother of 10, eight by birth and two by adoption. It was the steady barrage of negative depictions of and negative ideas about aboriginal people that prompted her to start writing. Her first manuscript won a Writers' Federation contest in 1974. She has become popularly known as the Poet Laureate of the Mi'kmaq and has edited two collections of Mi'kmaq literary art: *Kelusultiek* [We Speak] (1995), a collection of women's writing, and *The Mi'kmaq Anthology* (1997). Her own publications include four books of poetry: *Poems of Rita Joe* (1978), *Song of Eskasoni* (1988), *Lnu and Indians We're Called* (1991), and WE ARE THE DREAMERS (1999).

Rita Joe was made a member of the Order of Canada in 1990, was inducted into the Privy Council—a nonpartisan advisory group to the prime minister—in 1992, and received an honorary doctorate from Dalhousie University in Halifax, Nova Scotia, in 1993. She received another honorary doctorate from University College of Cape Breton in 1997, was awarded an Aboriginal Achievement Award in the same year, received a third honorary doctorate in 1998 from Mount Saint Vincent University in Halifax, and was awarded a fourth from St. Thomas University in Fredericton, New Brunswick, in 2001. Her autobiography, *Song of Rita Joe,* was published in 1996, and she is the subject of a short documentary, *Songs of Eskasoni* (1995). Her human touch is exemplified by her meeting with Queen Elizabeth II, at the Privy Council induction, when Joe spoke woman to woman, not awed by the ceremonious occasion, asking only, "How are your grandchildren?"

Bibliography

Pederson, Andy. "Rita Joe Film a Portrait of Natives' Way of Life," *Daily News,* 18 March 1995, p. 23.

"Rita Joe: Poet Conquers Hearts with Kindness." People of Honour, Windspeaker. *Aboriginal Multi-Media Society.* Available online. URL: www. ammsa.com. Accessed on June 28, 2004.

A. Mary Murphy

Johnson, Emily Pauline (1861–1913)

E. Pauline Johnson was a middle-class mixed-race (Mohawk and Irish) writer and performer. Born the second daughter of George Henry Martin Johnson and Emily Johnson in 1861, Emily Pauline Johnson later became known by her stage name, *Tekahionwake.* Though that name was one of her own choosing, *Tekahionwake* can also be considered a family name, since the reason Pauline chose it was that it was the name of her paternal grandfather, a renowned Mohawk chief.

Johnson was active during a period that may be considered one of the most oppressive for First Nations peoples in Canada. Shortly before she was born, Canadians had passed the "Indian Act." This act demanded that First Nations peoples relinquish their lands, language, and culture in exchange for British citizenship. As were many Natives of the time, Johnson was unwilling to renounce her Indian heritage. However, she could not inherit her father's Mohawk titles or wealth because such titles were matrilineal and, therefore, could not be passed from her father to her. Consequently much of her work, both as a writer and as a performer, was dedicated to her exploration of the issues she faced as a MIXED-BLOOD person, who was legally excluded from both Canadian and Mohawk societies but who still participated in both.

Rather early in her life Johnson discovered that she enjoyed reading and writing. Later she realized that she also liked to perform what she had written, so when other avenues of financial support closed to her, she supported herself and her ailing mother through her writings and performances. Among the most dominant influences on her work was her distant relative and one of her favorite writers, William Dean Howells. She was also influenced by the stories told to her by her Mohawk grandmother. Johnson was later known to recite these stories in the Mohawk language, sometimes rebuking her audience that "she had had to learn their language, the least they could do was hear hers" (Francis 30).

"A Cry from an Indian Wife" (1892), which addressed the first mixed-blood rebellion, in 1869–70, was one of her first performance pieces. "My Mother," from Johnson's *The Moccasin Maker* (1913), is perhaps her most important work, for it is an autobiographical sketch and family history, in which she addresses most powerfully her identity and heritage.

Bibliography

Francis, Daniel. *Imaginary Indian: The Image of the Indian in Canadian Culture.* Vancouver: Arsenal Pulp Press, 1992.

Johnson, Emily Pauline. *The Moccasin Maker.* Tucson: Arizona University Press, 1987.

Keller, Betty. *Pauline: A Biography of Pauline Johnson.* Vancouver: Douglas & McIntyre, 1981.

Strong-Boag, Veronica, and Carol Gearson. *Paddling Her Own Canoe: The Times and Texts of E. Pauline Johnson: Tekahionwake.* Toronto: University of Toronto Press, 2000.

Christie Firtha

Johnston, Basil (1929–)

Basil Johnston is an Anishinabe (Chippewa or Ojibwe) writer, storyteller, educator, translator, and scholar. Born on Parry Island Indian Reserves in Canada, Johnston attended elementary school at the Cape Croker Indian Reserve until the age of 10, after which he attended St. Peter Claver's Indian Residential School in Spanish, Ontario. In 1954 Johnston earned a B.A. with honors from Loyola College in Montreal. Johnston is fluent in both Anishinabe and English and writes in both languages. His novel *Indian School Days* (1988) is an account of his school years and deals with themes such as ASSIMILATION and cultural survival.

From 1955 through 1961 Johnston worked for the Toronto Board of Trade. In 1962 he received his secondary school teaching certificate from the Ontario College of Education and began teaching high school history. He then worked for the Royal Ontario Museum in the Ethnology Department, and for the next 25 years he devoted his energies to recording Ojibwe heritage and culture, especially language and mythology.

Johnston has published a number of books in both English and Ojibwe. His articles appear in newspapers, anthologies, and periodicals. Johnston writes about reserve life and documents traditional Ojibwe culture and its significance to the survival of North American Indians. His writings highlight the importance of language, mythology, and spirituality to the Ojibwe community as recurring themes. *CRAZY DAVE* (1999) recounts the struggles of a resourceful people faced with the threat of assimilation into white society. *The Mani-*

tous (1995) deals with spiritual tales, tribal teachings, and Native legends and attempts to explain the mysterious ways of the natural world. *MOOSE MEAT AND WILD RICE* (1978) are true stories about the differences in culture—the Ojibwe life and beliefs versus Western European attitudes. His books on Ojibwe heritage, tales, and ceremonies document the rituals and legends that are important to Ojibwe life. Johnston received the 2004 Aboriginal Achievement Award for Heritage and Spirituality.

In his essay "Bread before Books or Books before Bread," which appeared in *The Only Good Indian: Essays by Canadian Indians,* Johnston details events that contributed significantly to the decline of the Native American cultures. His understanding of the importance of the Anishinabe language to the Ojibwe culture is demonstrated by his work in recovering and preserving the language and heritage for present and future generations. He developed the *Ojibway Language Course Outline* and the *Ojibway Language Lexicon* in 1978 for the Ministry of Indian and Northern Affairs; together they help to recover and retain some of the lost language. Johnston produced audio programs in Anishinabe on cassette and compact disc (CD) as a way of communicating with and teaching an Anishinabe-speaking audience. He also wrote the script for the film *The Man, the Snake and the Fox* (1978), which is available from the National Film Board of Canada.

Billiography

Johnston, Basil. *Crazy Dave.* Toronto: Key Porter Books, 1999.

———. *Indian School Days.* Toronto: Key Porter Books, 1988.

———. *The Manitous: The Spiritual World of the Ojibway.* New York: HarperCollins, 1995.

———. *Moosemeat and Wild Rice.* Toronto: McClelland & Stewart, 1978.

Ryhms, Deena. "A Residential School Memoir: Basil Johnston's *Indian School Days.*" *Canadian Literature* 178 (autumn 2003): 58–70.

Sharon Morgan Lewis

Josanie's War   Karl H. Schlesier   (1998)

Josanie's War, volume 27 of the American Indian Literature and Critical Studies series, is the author Karl Schlesier's semifictionalized account of the last major Apache resistance to U.S. Indian Removal policies. History reveals that in May 1885 three Chokonen and two Chihenne Apache chiefs, along with approximately 100 members of their bands, escaped from the San Carlos Reservation in Arizona Territory. This final major revolt of the Southwestern Plains Indians culminated in a formal surrender to U.S. forces on March 27, 1886.

Told from the perspective of a courageous Apache warrior, *Josanie's War* is an eloquent defense of the historically maligned Chiricahua, whose reputation as bloodthirsty "human wolves" (88) has survived into the 21st century. The author's thorough knowledge of Apache customs and southwestern topography makes his version of the Chiricahua uprising compelling and the superior morality of his Indian characters highly credible.

Schlesier intersperses his plot with relevant historical documents and commentary that describe the same events from contrasting perspectives. Chihuahua, a Chokonen chief and Josanie's brother, explains the Indians' predicament:

> When we leave the reservation, the dead ground where they starve us and kill us, we have to fight our way out. Coming to these mountains, we have to fight our way in. They make us fight all the time.... They want us dead so our voices are silent in the earth. (22)

The plot begins two days after the escape, as the five refugee bands are discussing their next move. Four of the groups head to Mexico. Only Chihuahua and Josanie take an immediate stand despite the formidable odds. With the U.S. military in pursuit, Josanie escorts his Chokonen band to their native home in the Mogollon Mountains. The first enemy attack is repelled, but the second attack is devastating. Included among the captured are Josanie's sister-in-law, nephew, and son. Hopelessly outnumbered, Chihuahua leads the surviving women and children to Mexico while Josanie and a handful of men stay behind to rescue the captives.

Led by Josanie, the Chokonen warriors repeatedly risk their lives in unsuccessful attempts to free their *ndé* (their people). Josanie's military strategy works in the open field, but he lacks the forces to attack Fort Bowie and free the captives. Finally Josanie forsakes the rescue mission and rejoins his band in Mexico. Four of the refugee bands reunite and move deep into the rugged Sierra Madres hoping to settle permanently, but in January 1886 determined American forces locate the supposedly impenetrable hideout.

Faced with inevitable defeat, the remnant of Chokonen and Chihenne Apache negotiate with General Crook. Their historical fate is revealed in the novel's epilogue:

Undefeated in the field, the bands surrendered to be reunited with their families under a formal agreement that they would return to Arizona. In Florida prisons, later in an Alabama prison. . . , they were finally defeated by white people's diseases and by a cruel government that let them suffer. (290)

Although Schlesier's sympathies clearly lie with the Apache, the author does not support one group at the expense of another. His theme extends beyond an immediate historical event to examine the consequences of cultural paradigm shifts and the universal human response to territorial conflict.

Bibliography

Bricklebank, Peter. Review of *Josanie's War,* by Karl H. Schlesier. *The New York Times,* 15 November 1998, p. BR63.

Schlesier, Karl H. *Josanie's War: A Chiricahua Apache Novel.* American Indian Literature and Critical Studies Series. Norman: University of Oklahoma Press, 1998.

Karen Sloan

Keeping Slug Woman Alive Greg Sarris (1993)

In *Keeping Slug Woman Alive,* a collection of autobiographical, biographical, and critical essays, GREG SARRIS considers how the Pomo oral tradition can influence and complicate the way we should think and write about literature, art, and culture. A MIXED-BLOOD Kashaya Pomo/Coast Miwok/Filipino/Jewish/German/Irish scholar and writer, Sarris combines stories about himself with stories about Mabel McKay, a Pomo basketweaver and medicine woman. McKay has a reputation for befuddling most white interlocutors because she excels at turning conversations around and exposing and questioning expectations. In one scene that reveals McKay's style, she was "being interviewed as a native healer" "in a large auditorium," and a white student asked how she treated poison oak. Her disarming response was "Calamine lotion" (17), which revealed how her audience wanted to receive a tour of Native difference. Mabel makes her audience reconsider their expectations and why they hold them.

As Mabel does, Sarris wants to reveal how cultural discussions always harbor assumptions and motives. He wants scholars and students to figure out how to take their own experiences into consideration as they engage in cross-cultural verbal and literary exchanges. If this self-reflection can circumvent cultural barriers, it has a chance to open up exchanges and inquiries regarding premises and frames on which most people subconsciously rely.

Because Sarris wants people to relate to literary and cultural studies on a personal level—to break down bounds between personal narrative and scholarly argument—he forgoes the usual scholarly attempt at objectivity, which can be domineering as well as isolating. He asks his audience to find ways to connect their practical life experiences and beliefs with their studies in order to foster development: "How do scholars see beyond norms they use to frame experiences of others unless those frames are interrupted and exposed?" (29). Readers need to consider subjects and texts that make them uncomfortable—that are puzzling—because then they can possibly learn more about themselves, their own cultural assumptions, and the texts or cultures they study. Using Sarris's model means posing homespun questions and initiating down-to-earth dialogues that can jolt much standard academic discourse.

Sarris frankly reveals a lot about his own life—how years ago he abused drugs and assaulted innocent people. He grew up under a weight of illegitimacy, not knowing either his father or his mother, but his relatives gave him stories that eventually helped him to cope with his rage and hostility. Sarris describes how his father, Emilio, had similar problems: anger that led to alcoholism and violence. Many white men praised Emilio, as a fine high school athlete but thought that their daughters were too good to date a Filipino/Native American; as a result Emilio made it a habit to sleep with these "white daughters," some of whom he eventually abused. Sarris's approach to cultural studies would have pushed those white fathers to reconsider their assumptions and the damage they promoted.

Bibliography

Sarris, Greg. Keeping Slug Woman Alive: *A Holistic Approach to American Indian Texts.* Berkeley: University of California Press, 1993.

Roland Finger

Kenny, Maurice   (1929–   )

Maurice Kenny is a two-time Pulitzer Prize nominee and a two-time American Book Award recipient for his collections of poetry and essays. He was born August 16, 1929, to Andrew Anthony Kenny (Mohawk) and Doris Marie Parker Herrick Kenny Welch (Seneca) in Watertown, New York, a town in the foothills of the Adirondacks. When he was 12 years old, his mother separated from his father, and afterward Kenny spent time at his mother's new home in Bayonne, New Jersey; his father's home in Watertown; and his sister's home in St. Louis, Missouri. At the age of 23 he enrolled at Butler College in Indianapolis and four years later transferred to Saint Lawrence University, in Canton, New York—a university chosen in part so that he could be closer to his father's Akwesasne reservation. In 1957–58 Kenny studied under the poet Louise Bogan at New York University. Kenny has traveled extensively and has lived abroad in Mexico and the Virgin Islands.

Kenny's works often detail the predicaments of Native Americans caught between two worlds, especially the difficulties of forging Indian identity while inhabiting an urban environment. In other works Kenny is candid about his experiences as a gay Indian man. Kenny has also drawn inspiration from characters in Indian history, including ruminating on the life of significant historical figures such as the Mohawk military leader Tekonwatonti (also know as Molly Brant) and Isaac Jogues, a French Jesuit

missionary who drew the Iroquois into a confederacy for peace in the 1600s, is considered a martyr by the Catholic Church—because of his death at the hands of the Mohawk—and was canonized to sainthood in 1930.

Kenny was nominated for the Pulitzer Prize for *Blackrobe: Isaac Jogues* in 1982 and for *Between Two Rivers* in 1987. In 1984 *The Mama Poems* earned him the American Book Award. Kenny's other awards include the Bloomsbury Review Best Anthology award in 1983, a National Public Radio Award in 1984, the Cup Award from Signal in 1990, a fellowship from the New York State Council for the Arts in 1991, and a citation for achievement in the field of literature from St. Lawrence University.

In the 1970s Kenny served as editor for the influential journal *Contact II* and founded the Strawberry Press, an independent house dedicated to publishing the works of Indian authors. He has been on the faculty at the University of Victoria, British Columbia, and North Country Community College, Saranac Lake, New York. He served as a visiting professor at University of Oklahoma, Norman, and a visiting poet at Lehigh University. From 1989 to 1991 he was a board member of the public television station WCFE-TV. Kenny has also composed poetry for television and radio programs. He was a consulting editor for *New Voices from the Longhouse: An Anthology of Contemporary Iroquois Writing*, edited by JOSEPH BRUCHAC. He has contributed extensively to periodicals such as the *New York Times, Small Press Review, American Indian Quarterly, Saturday Review,* and *Beloit Poetry Journal.* In the summers of 1987 and 1988 he coordinated the Robert Louis Stevenson Annual Writers Conference. Since 1994 he has assisted the New York State Council for the Arts and the Educational Testing Service Arts Recognition and Talent Search in Princeton, New Jersey. He currently lives in Saranac, New York.

Bibliography

American Indian Culture and Research Journal 18, no. 1 (1994): 95–118.
Bruchac, Joseph, ed. *New Voices from the Longhouse: An Anthology of Contemporary Iroquois Writing.* Greenfield Center, N.Y.: Greenfield Review, 1989.

————, ed., *Survival This Way: Interviews with American Indian Poets.* Tucson: Sun Tracks and University of Arizona Press, 1987.

Castro, Michael. *Interpreting the Indian: Twentieth-Century Poets and the Native American.* Albuquerque: University of New Mexico Press, 1983.

Dictionary of Literary Biography. Vol. 175, *Native American Writers of the United States: A Bruccoli Clark Layman Book,* edited by Kenneth M. Roemer, 57–64. Arlington: University of Texas at Arlington, Gale Group, 1997.

Kenny, Maurice. *Between Two Rivers: Selected Poems.* Fredonia, N.Y.: White Pine Press, 1987.

————. *Blackrobe: Isaac Jogues.* Saranac Lake, N.Y.: Chauncey Press, 1987.

————. "Waiting at the Edge: Words toward a Life." In *I Tell You Now: Autobiographical Essays by Native American Writers,* edited by Brian Swann and Arnold Krupat, 37–54. Lincoln: University of Nebraska Press, 1987.

Michelle LaFrance

King, Thomas　(1943–)

Thomas King was born in Sacramento, California, in 1943. He is of Cherokee, Greek, and German descent and is best known for his writings that combine the culture and traditions of Native Americans with the style, politics, and culture of North America today. King grew up and went to school in Northern California and received a Ph.D. in English from the University of Utah. After graduation he became the chair of the American Indian Studies program at the University of Minnesota, where he remained until 1980, when he moved to Canada. There he works as a professor of creative writing and Native literature at the University of Guelph. His many years of teaching and writing Native American literature are enhanced by an understanding of other Native American writers, his editing of anthologies, and his work in film and radio.

Thomas King's poems, stories, and critical writings are widely published, and his first novel, *MEDICINE RIVER* (1990), became a television movie starring Grahame Greene and Tom Jackson. Also in 1990 he edited and introduced an anthology of contemporary Canadian Native American short stories, *ALL MY RELATIONS* (1990), which includes "The One about the Coyote Going West," later included in his collection of short stories *ONE GOOD STORY, THAT ONE,* published in the same year as his major novel *GREEN GRASS, RUNNING WATER* (1993). The story collection also included "Joe the Painter and the Deer Island Massacre," which was adapted for radio, as was his short story "Borders." A screenplay of "Borders" was also made and broadcast as part of the CBC television series *Four Directions,* for which King served as a story editor in 1993–94. His popular radio show *The Dead Dog Café Comedy Hour* aired for the Canadian Broadcasting Corporation (CBC) from 1996 to 2001. King has received numerous awards and honors for his work, including, in 2003, the Trillium Book Award for English Language Prose. In July 2004 King's contribution to Canadian culture was honored when he was made a member of the Order of Canada.

Medicine River, King's novel turned film, is a story about identity. Under Canadian law Will, whose full name is never revealed, is considered "stateless." The Indian Act, which determines Will's status and governs the life of many Canadian Indians, explains why Will, his brother, and his mother are prevented from living on the reserve. His mother, Rose Horse Capture, married a white man, and her legal status as an Indian could not be regained. A person of mixed race may remain an Indian only if the father is Indian so that, although Will thinks himself Indian, many of his relatives think otherwise. Will is characterized as Rose Horse Capture's son, while his white father remains nameless. Will wants to know his father, but the community provides little factual information. In keeping with oral tradition, they relate anecdotes and his mother tells stories, but no one names his father, and when his mother and brother return to Medicine River, Will finds work in Toronto. He returns to Medicine River after the death of his mother, not intending to remain, but is caught up in plans to make him the community photographer. There he discovers the connectedness he has been seeking.

Because he is a borderer himself, the question of borders, territorial and ideological, together with the importance of myth and the oral tradition are central to King's writings. His most recent novel, TRUTH AND BRIGHT WATER, is set directly on the 49th parallel, and as in *Medicine River,* we are uncertain of the protagonist's name. In the novel that illustrates this propensity best, *Green Grass, Running Water,* King demonstrates his capacity to be as comfortable in the Native American oral tradition as he is in the Western tradition. The book takes its form from Native American stories and its theme from numerous treaty betrayals, Western appropriation of territory, and subsequent loss. It chronicles the lives of five Blackfoot Indians in rural Alberta as they attempt to accommodate modern North America with Blackfoot traditions and ceremonies. At the heart of the story lies the prospect of borders, literary, cultural, and territorial. His short story "A Coyote Columbus Story" takes up a similar theme. It is a modern transformation of an ancient myth and itself a retelling of King's own children's story of the same name. In the adult version of the story some elements are changed, but by combining Coyote and Columbus in the same story, King alters our worldviews. Cultural centers become unfixed and borders less secure. Coyote, too, is a figure who travels between worlds. The children's version of the story begins with an assertion that it was Coyote who fixed up this world, but Coyote acts on impulse, as when he thinks Columbus into existence. When the adult story ends, some questions remain, such as "What happened to the Indians?" Christopher Columbus sold the Indians and became rich and famous, we are told. Coyote is pleased; he likes a happy ending.

Bibliography

Bright, William. *A Coyote Reader.* Berkeley, Los Angeles, and Oxford: University of California Press, 1993.

Davidson, Arnold, Priscilla Walton, and Jennifer Andrews. *Border Crossings: Thomas King's Cultural Inversions.* Toronto: University of Toronto Press, 2003.

King, Thomas. *All My Relations: An Anthology of Contemporary Canadian Native Fiction,* edited by Thomas King. Toronto: McClelland & Stewart, 1990.

———. *Green Grass, Running Water.* Boston: Houghton Mifflin, 1993.

———. *Medicine River.* Markham, Canada, and New York: Viking, 1990.

———. *One Good Story, That One: Stories by Thomas King.* Toronto: HarperPerennial, 1993.

Lutz, Hartmut, and Coomi S. Vevaina, eds. *Connections: Non Native Responses to Native Canadian Literature.* New Delhi: Creative Books, 2003.

Owens, Louis. *Other Destinies: Understanding the American Indian Novel.* Norman: University of Oklahoma Press, 1992.

Vizenor, Gerald. *The Heirs of Columbus.* Hanover, N.H.: Wesleyan University Press, 1994.

Jan Pilditch

Kiss of the Fur Queen Tomson Highway (1998)

TOMSON HIGHWAY's only novel to date, *Kiss of the Fur Queen,* is similar to his better-known plays in that it concerns the problems of cultural survival, the articulation of an aboriginal voice, and the reconciliation of identity with multiple cultural forces. More specifically this autobiographical novel anchors itself in a northern Manitoba setting and complicates the concrete reality of the story with Cree, Greek, and Christian myth.

When Abraham Okimasis wins the World Championship Dog Derby and receives his trophy from Miss Julie Pembrook, who has been crowned fur queen at the same Trappers' Festival, the kiss she bestows on his cheek serves symbolically as the kiss of cultures that is at the heart of Highway's novel. The story traces the lives of the brothers Jeremiah and Gabriel, both of whom endure the BOARDING SCHOOL experience, the younger of the two unable to survive the abuses he suffers there. The boys are an example of the generations of aboriginal children who were removed from their culture; forced into another, from which they could never extract themselves; and had varying degrees of success finding ways to reconcile the poles of their lives. As so often happens, the brothers end up in the city and one of them becomes lost there.

The brothers both have lives in art, one as a pianist, the other as a dancer. This parallels the paths of Highway and his own brother, dancer who died of acquired immunodeficiency syndrome (AIDS). Although the novel serves as a balm for Highway's grief over his brother's death, it is saved from sentimentality by humor. As Highway explains, "It's in the nature of the Cree language to be funny" (Morrow 12), and further that "at the very centre of that culture is a clown" (12). The novel's inherent humor and implicit myth making add depth to the story. The fur queen, who floats into the heavens in the first chapter and who is manifested in a variety of ways throughout the story, returns at the end wearing a fur cape to escort the dying Gabriel, and as they go, "the little white fox on the collar of the cape turned to Jeremiah. And winked" (30).

Bibliography

Morrow, Martin. "Cree Author Explores Dark Territory with Highway Humour," *Calgary Herald*, 15 October 1998, p. B12.

A. Mary Murphy

LaDuke, Winona (1959–)

Winona LaDuke was born in East Los Angeles in 1959 to the Anishinabe activist and later actor Vincent LaDuke and Betty Berstein from the South Bronx. After her parents divorced when LaDuke was five, she and mother relocated to Oregon, where she was raised. She attended Barnard College in New York City before attaining an economics degree from Harvard University in 1982 and holds a master's degree in rural development from Antioch College. She has also been a fellow at the Massachusetts Institute of Technology. Although half-Jewish on her mother's side, LaDuke strongly identifies with her Anishinabe inheritance through the Mississippi Band and has lived on the White Earth Reservation since 1981, when she moved to the community to become principal of the local school.

An enormously popular social activist and politically committed advocate for indigenous rights worldwide, LaDuke is also one of the most widely recognized spokespeople on behalf of indigenous environmental, political, and economic issues. She served as Ralph Nader's vice presidential candidate for the Green Party in the 1996 and 2000 elections, was chosen by *Time* magazine in 1994 as one of America's 50 most promising leaders age 40 and under, and was selected by *Ms.* magazine in 1997 as one of its women of the year. In 1988 she received a $20,000 award from Reebok in recognition for her human rights activism; she used the prize money to buy back nearly 1,000 acres of reservation land on White Earth (Cronin 10). She has been instrumental in forming community-based organizations, such as the White Earth Land Recovery Project and Anishinaabe Akeeng (The People's Land), to explore alternative mechanisms for recovering tribal lands after participating as a claimant in two court cases that exhausted all legal recourse available to the community (LaDuke 1999 3). LaDuke is also a cofounder of the Indigenous Women's Network, a nongovernmental organization that advocates a collective identity for all women as representatives of "Mothers of our Nations."

Although LaDuke defends her views on "the living wage, health care, [and] welfare reform" as "women's issues," she has failed to secure the support of mainstream feminist groups, particularly during the 2000 election in the United States, when she was accused by prominent women activists not only of discussing "motherhood" issues at the expense of a concern for "feminis[t]" ones, but also of dividing support for the Left by running on behalf of the Green Party and "taking votes away from the Democratic Party" (Rampell "Towards an Inaugural Pow-Wow"). While it is probably more accurate to describe LaDuke's commitments to mainstream feminist concerns as a form of "green feminism" in keeping with her support for the Green Party's core values on women's issues, her engagements with tribal history and gender representation in LAST STANDING WOMAN (1997) demonstrate a form of "feminist indigenism" that connects the erosion of intertribal historical ties with transformations to the status of women as a result of the disruption of power relations within the tribal community.

Aside from her important public activism on behalf of indigenous rights, LaDuke is best known as the author of *Last Standing Woman* (1997), a novel that explores seven generations of women as they struggle to maintain the integrity of community ties and intertribal relations, and for her nonfiction work *All Our Relations: Native Struggles for Land and Life* (1999), which explores eight distinctive Native land and environmental struggles taking place in North America, including in Hawaii.

Bibliography

Baumgardner, Jennifer. "Kitchen Table Candidate." *Ms.* 11, no. 3 (April–May 2001): 47–53.

Cronin, Mary Elizabeth. "Activist/Author Looks to the Future." *Seattle Times.* 23 April 1998, 10. Available online. URL: http://seattletimes.nwsource.com/news/lifestyles/html98/altduke_042398.html. Accessed July 16, 2002.

LaDuke, Winona. *All Our Relations: Native Struggles for Land and Life.* Cambridge, Mass.: South End Press, 1999.

Rampell, Ed. "Feminist Dream or Nightmare: The Green Party." *Women's International Net Magazine.* 11 June 2001. Available online. URL: http://winmagazine.org/issues/issue38/win38e.htm. Accessed on August 15, 2005.

———. "Towards an Inaugural Pow-Wow." *Women's International Net Magazine.* 8 June 2001. Available online. URL: http://www.winmagazine.org. Accessed on August 15, 2005.

Cheryl Susack

Laguna Woman   Leslie Marmon Silko (1973)

Laguna Woman is LESLIE MARMON SILKO's first published book. It is a collection of poems and drawings produced between 1972 and 1973, while she was teaching at a Navajo community college in Tsaile, Arizona. Many of the poems appeared in Silko's second publication, STORYTELLER, published in 1981. *Laguna Woman* earned the Chicago Review Poetry Award in 1974; however, the critical attention Silko's poetry attracted thereafter was not directly focused on *Laguna Woman,* but instead on *Storyteller,* thus placing the poetry in a broader narrative context.

Laguna Woman is composed of 18 poems and a comparable number of drawings rhetorically related. The semantic unity of these productions relies on many of the themes characteristic of Silko's work: family history and gossip, traditional storytelling, as well as the Laguna landscape. The omnipresence of the landscape, which pervades all her stories, is tantamount to the reiteration of Laguna cultural values and identity. The tension between the everyday events and the pervasive presence of traditional narratives runs throughout her prose poetry. *Laguna Woman* is about Native Americans' relation to the land, about their relation to animals, to stories, and with one another; it is also, to a lesser extent, about the European forces threatening the traditional ways of life.

The importance of the notion of relationship is expressed through a focus on hunting and sex, birth and death, as well as story and ceremony. Silko's elegant weaving of these relationships not only emerges from her storytelling qualities, mainly expressed by the blanks separating different verses (made to represent the silences of oral storytelling), but also through her choice of stanzas as format. In these relationships animals are not hierarchically under humans but partake in similar activities on an equal footing, in what the Laguna call the *hummah-hah stories.* Titles such as "When Sun Came to Riverwoman" or "Where Mountain-lion Lay Down with Deer" further exemplify the interconnectedness of the landscape in which the reader is invited to partake as well.

The 25 drawings scattered throughout *Laguna Woman* not only echo the poems near which they are placed, but emphasize certain aspects of these stories. The absence of title accompanying these drawings further implies their semantic belonging to the poems. The Native Americanized U.S. flag, for instance, functions as a loudspeaker for the last lines of the poem, telling the story of Toe'osh bumping into white people outside a bar "until they said / 'Excuse me' / And the way Simon meant it / was for 300 or maybe 400 years" (13–16). In a similar way a drawing representing what can be seen as both a sunflower and a womb accompanies the poem "Poem for Myself and Mei-Mei: Concerning Abortion." Although this poem tells the story of a journey, the sunflower reminds the reader that the issue of abortion is indeed central.

Anne Dotter

Landfill Meditations: Crossblood Stories Gerald Vizenor (1991)

Landfill Meditations: Crossblood Stories contains 14 short stories, almost all of which had been published previously; only "The Red Coin" is original. Within this collection the reader encounters a number of GERALD VIZENOR's recurring characters, Almost Browne, for example, from *HOTLINE HEAL-ERS* and *The HEIRS OF COLUMBUS* and Martin Bear Charme, who appears in *DEAD VOICES*. Vizenor's reuse of characters draws on Native story cycle traditions in which characters appear over and over, sometimes dying or being destroyed in one narrative only to return in the next. But his play with his characters' names (Father Father Mother, Pure Gumption, Almost Browne) also borrows from postmodern practices and is reminiscent of the 20th-century American Thomas Pynchon's novels in particular.

As does most of Vizenor's work, the stories in this collection deal primarily with crossblood (or MIXED-BLOOD) characters. The first story, "Almost Browne," begins: "Almost Browne was born on the White Earth Indian Reservation in Minnesota. Well, he was *almost* born there. . . . Almost, you see is a crossblood and he was born on the road; his father is tribal and his mother is blonde" (1). This passage speaks to Vizenor's emphasis on the hybrid and somewhat fluid makeup of identity. The character's name is the most obvious example; he is "almost" brown, nearly Indian. We learn that he is born in a car, on the road, near the White Earth Reservation (his birth certificate lists his place of birth as "Hatchback at White Earth"). All of these images speak to ideas of motion or proximity without a definite location or destination. So this character represents the opposite of what Vizenor calls "terminal creeds," concepts of identity that are fixed and can never move. Vizenor's characters are able to change, and their relationship to their Indian identities can evolve with them.

In "Ice Tricksters" Vizenor offers a definition of the TRICKSTER FIGURE: "The trickster is a character in stories, animal, or person, even a tree at times, who pretends the world can be stopped with words, and he frees the world in stories. . . . the trickster is almost a man and almost a woman, and almost a child, a clown . . . almost a free spirit" (24). The repetition of the word *almost* reinforces hybridity but also ties the cross-blood to the trickster, showing that the cross-blood allows for changes in the definition of what it means to be Native. This passage also places this story and collection within the framework of Vizenor's body of work. He focuses on the trickster, especially the Anishinabe figure Naanabozho, considering him to be the first cross-blood because he is born of the union of the sun and a young woman.

"Four Skin Documents" also relates the importance of descriptive names, tribal nicknames (Token White, Fast Food, Bad Mouth, and Uncle Secrets are examples from this story) that people carry with them but can change during the course of their lives. Vizenor emphasizes these nicknames in a number of his works as they represent the ways that people should always be willing to adapt to new circumstances; the changing of communally given names symbolizes those personal adaptations.

John Gamber

Last of the Ofos Geary Hobson (2000)

This short novel is about a man dedicated to a dying culture and language. Through his character Thomas Darko, GEARY HOBSON (Cherokee and Arkansas Quapaw) comments on a wide range of social issues including racism, identity, social class, the disenfranchisement of Native Americans that leaves families homeless within traditional tribal territories, and the economics of rural life in the first half of the 20th century.

Hobson skillfully blends Mosopelea or Ofo tribal history, Indian military history, and personal experiences, ranging from his rural Arkansas childhood to negotiation of the politics of an academic career, as sources for this novel. Hobson has stated, "The personal *is* political" to illustrate his belief that knowing family history creates a deeper understanding of societal issues at large. Tribal values and languages are especially important to Hobson, and his characters often speak in dialects that reflect rural/tribal sensibilities and the blended influences of tribal and European languages. As the novel's protagonist and narrator, Thomas Darko finds himself the last speaker of his native Ofo language and recounts his life's story to a tape recorder. His life begins in 1905 in rural Louisiana and spans nearly the entire 20th century as he travels America taking unusual jobs both legal and illegal, marrying, joining the marines, and eventually returning home. Through Darko's eyes, readers have a glimpse of an American history that is neither white nor black and strangely invisible. Several characters, including the outlaw duo Bonnie and Clyde, insist to Darko, "There ain't no more Indians around no more. Everybody knows that" (51). With his family gone, grief and loneliness become persistent themes; still, Darko does not become bitter and often pokes ironic humor at his situation. In the marines a military official tries to recruit Darko to be one of the famous World War II Code Talkers.

> "I wudn't positive, but I was real sure I was the only one left. Once again, the Lone-damn-Ranger. I ast the First Shirt, 'Who would I talk to?' And while he looked at me funny-like, I started laughing like a alligator." (80–81)

Darko does accept an offer to assist anthropologists in an Ofo language preservation project, a situation that recalls the real-life Ishi and raises concerns of academic appropriation of indigenous cultural history in the name of scholarship. Woven throughout this novel are the persistent reminders of Indians as participants in American history, and some well-known individuals such as Jim Thorpe and SIMON ORTIZ appear as characters. Darko may be the last speaker of Ofo, but his story convinces us he is not the last Indian in America.

Bibliography

Downs, Ernest C. "The Struggle of the Louisiana Tunica Indians for Recognition." In *Southern Indians since the Removal Era*, edited by Walter L. Williams, 72–89. Athens: University of Georgia Press, 1979.

Hobson, Geary. *Last of the Ofos.* Tucson: University of Arizona Press, 2000.

Hudson, Charles. *The Southeastern Indians.* Knoxville: University of Tennessee Press, 1994.

Kroeber, Thoedora. *Ishi in Two Worlds.* Berkeley and Los Angeles: University of California Press, 1967.

Nies, Judith. *Native American History: A Chronology of a Culture's Vast Achievements and Their Links to World Events.* New York: Ballantine, 1996.

Ortiz, Simon. *Woven Stone.* Tucson: University of Arizona Press, 1992.

Barbara K. Robins

Last Report of the Miracles at Little No Horse, The   Louise Erdrich (2002)

The sixth novel in LOUISE ERDRICH's complex Little No Horse series, *Last Report* is the story of Father Damien Modeste, whom readers met earlier in *TRACKS*. Father Damien, at the end of his life, writes the last in a long series of letters to the Vatican concerning the strange occurrences and possible sainthood of Sister Leopolda, who appears in many books in the series (in *LOVE MEDICINE*, *The BEET QUEEN*, and *TALES OF BURNING LOVE* as Leopolda and in *Tracks* as Pauline Puyat). One of the most interesting contributions of *Last Report* to the series is that readers finally learn how the transformation of Pauline into Sister Leopolda took place and why she was such a punishing, demented character. Although this novel centers on Father Modeste and his relationship with the Ojibwe, especially Nanapush, Lulu, and Mary Kashpaw, the contrast between his life and the life of Leopolda emerges as the most profound statement made here, a statement regarding the intersection of Native SPIRITUALITY and Catholicism and the effect of this intersection on Indian identity.

The novel plays throughout with notions of identity, for Father Damien himself is not really a priest, and, in fact, not really a man. Rather, he is Agnes Dewitt, a former nun, turned happy farm wife, turned victim of a bizarre kidnapping and robbery, and finally, turned Father Damien Modeste after she takes the identity of a dead priest. She conceals her gender from both the nuns and the Ojibwe, as she spends some 80 years working with the community on the reservation. Erdrich's narrator will switch back and forth, sometimes calling the character Agnes, sometimes Father Damien, depending on the situation. This character comes to question the solidity of many of the supposedly fundamental building blocks of identity: gender, religion, ethnicity. When she falls in love with Gregory, another priest who has been assigned to the mission, she ultimately requests that he be reassigned. He says to her, "Say it. . . . You are a *woman*," and she replies, "I am a priest" (216).

Father Jude Miller, who has been sent by the Vatican to investigate Leopolda's case for sainthood, is astounded by the way Father Damien accepts many of the old ways of the Ojibwa and does not feel it his duty to convert or to proselytize, but rather to comfort and befriend. In moving through her life with this attitude, Agnes becomes an integral part of the Indian community and, in fact, begins to perform what some might call miracles of her own. When she plays Chopin in the chapel, snakes rise up from the ground to listen: "Their heads were slightly raised off the floor and if they weren't actually listening to the notes, they were positively transfixed on the music" (220). She is also visited periodically by a talking black dog who claims to be the devil, there to claim Lulu's soul. Agnes bargains with the dog, saying she will go in Lulu's stead, but only at the end of her natural life. In the end, when Agnes does die, Father Jude has realized that it is not Leopolda whose life he should be in-

vestigating for evidence of sainthood, but rather Father Damien's.

In allowing this character to raise these questions, even implicitly, Erdrich gives the reader a portrait of humanity that resists standard black and white distinctions and rests in a shade of gray.

See also *The* BINGO PALACE; FOUR SOULS.

Bibliography

Wittmier, Melanie. "Erdrich's *The Last Report of the Miracles at Little No Horse*." *Explicator* 60, no. 4 (summer 2002): 241–243.

Last Song, The   Joy Harjo (1975)

In this chapbook of nine poems, JOY HARJO, of Muskogee (Creek) and Anglo heritage, demonstrates her ability to merge past and present in her poems, creating a nonlinear narrative environment in which to tell her stories. These stories are a blend of personal experience filtered through the eyes and voice of both legendary female Native American characters and 20th-century women.

The imagery that recurs throughout Harjo's poetry is already evident in her first published volume of poetry. Failed conversations and relationships and mythology play out against the landscape of Oklahoma, New Mexico, and Arizona. The fluidity of dreams and the hazy barriers between them and reality shade all of the poems in *The Last Song*. The poem "3 AM" is an example of Harjo's exploration of a theme seen frequently in Native American literature. To return home and reconnect to the spiritual worlds of one's ancestors is to return to oneself. In the poem two Native Americans find themselves in an Albuquerque airport at 3 A.M., trying to catch a flight to Oraibi, part of the Hopi Third Mesa settlements. The TWA attendant, with all her access to 20th-century technology, is not able to get them there. The poem ends with the speaker's saying that it is not too late to get back—both to themselves and to the Hopi village of their ancestors.

All of the poems in *The Last Song* appear in Harjo's 1979 collection *What Moon Drove Me to This?*

Bibliography

Scarry, John. "Representing Real Worlds: The Evolving Poetry of Joy Harjo." *World Literature Today* 66, no. 2 (spring 1992): 286–291.

Patricia Kennedy Bostian

Last Standing Woman   Winona LaDuke (1997)

In *Last Standing Woman* Winona LaDuke focuses on gender as in relates to Anishinabe culture. Set in the 19th century in the waning moments of Indian resistance to the U.S. government's treaty-making process and to settler incursions on Indian land, the novel begins with the story of Ishkwegaabawiikwe. She is an Anishinabe woman "drawn to the border" between Anishinabe and Dakota Territory and "drawn to battle" by the discord that surfaces in her abusive marriage when she has realized her mistake in marrying a man "at war" with everyone and everything. Isolated from her family and seeking to escape from the physical abuse of her spouse, Ishkwegaabawiikwe travels with her brother to the border zone that divides Anishinabe land from Dakota Territory and there witnesses the devastating effects of Little Crow's War with the United States (33). Confronted by the charred remains of the Dakota village, Ishkwegaabawiikwe searches for the Dakota woman whom she had observed and admired during a previous visit, and weary of the "battles between the Dakota and the *Anishinaabeg,* the battles between the Indians and the white men, [and] the war in her own lodge," she rescues the Dakota woman, "Situpiwin, Tailfeathers Woman," and claims her as her sister (34).

The central conflict in the novel illustrates LaDuke's concern to articulate a form of collective community identity through this friendship, which allows the social reconstruction of members' historically fractured lives. Indeed, many of the political sentiments expressed in the novel are also reflected in LaDuke's public statements about the relationship between activist engagements and ethical responsibility. In an interview with the *Seattle Times,* when asked how she felt about "white people who want to participate in native—land, environmental or social—justice causes," LaDuke replied, "'Do it because it's the right thing, . . . Don't do it because of guilt. Do it because it encourages your own humanity'" (Cronin).

The concluding events of the novel emphasize LaDuke's politics as they illustrate the return to the White Earth community of the bones of ancestors and their cultural belongings that resided for decades in the Smithsonian Institution in Washington, D.C. (270). Organized through the efforts of Elaine Mandamin and Danielle Wabun, who discover an "inventory of the people and belongings missing from the reservation through the years" (269), and with the aid of Alanis Nordstrom, who researches the "anthropologists and Indian agents' records for White Earth" to match "people [with] documents and sacred items," the community prepares for the return of "funerary objects, human remains, and objects of cultural patrimony" to be reburied on the land (271). The scene in which Moose Hanford's van breaks down while he is traveling from Washington to White Earth with the remains of "ancestors" from the Anishinabe community located in the back (274); his feelings of vulnerability when several people stop to assist him, including a police officer, who he worries might arrest him (276); and his buoyant response when he realizes that the people surrounding him have offered their help because they support the rights of American Indian peoples to repatriate their cultural artifacts (278) demonstrate the future moment of cooperation and understanding that LaDuke envisions between Indian and non-Indian peoples.

Bibliography

Cronin, Mary Elizabeth. "Activist/Author Looks to the Future." *Seattle Times.* 23 April 1998. Available online. URL: http://seattletimes.nwsource.com/news/lifestyles/html98/altduke_042398.html. Accessed on August 15, 2005.

Tsosie, Rebecca. "Privileging Claims to the Past: Ancient Human Remains and Contemporary Cultural Values." *Arizona State Law Journal* 31, no. 2 (summer 1999): 583–677.

Cheryl Susack

Life Is a Fatal Disease: Collected Poems 1962–1995 Paula Gunn Allen (1997)

Attributed to Pocahontas, the Native American princess who helped establish peace between the colonists and the Indians, the phrase that is the provocative title of the collection is immediately telling, since it is allied to a common thread in PAULA GUNN ALLEN's work of reconciling and mediating between diverse American subcultures.

In typical storytelling style Allen opts for a beginning, a middle, and an end, providing the reader with three sections to peruse: "Part I: The Warning," "Part II: Birth is 100% Fatal," and "Part III: Trinity." Although not chronologically ordered, the collection of 87 poems spans three decades and gives fascinating insight into Gunn Allen's development as a poet. From the melodrama of her early work "A Chloroformed Poem to Your Closed Eyes" to the faint cynicism of her later work "Teaching Poetry at Votech High, Sante Fe, the Week John Lennon Was Shot," this is very much a journey through time, and a journey through places. Those attracted by the nihilistic title will not be disappointed, since the overall mood is one of melancholy, hopelessness, and simmering resentment. In "Los Angeles" she writes that "the death culture swarms / over the land" (2–3), a reference to the hegemony of white America consumer society over Native culture. In the poem's parting shot she offers the following question and answer; "what will change / the inexorable dying we are facing?" (2–3). This theme of unremitting and consummate miserableness pervades the entire collection. In "The Dying," for instance, the narrator begins, "This Morning when I looked out / all the birds were dying" (11–12).

The fascinating poem "Dear World" is particularly representative of the collection's recurrent message that all half-breeds are condemned to a life sentence of illegitimacy, alienation, and interminable loneliness. Utilizing an undercurrent of macabre humor, the poem addresses the struggle a MIXED-BLOOD mother has with lupus, a "disease / of self-attack" (2–3), an unfortunate condition that renders the sufferer an eternal victim, such that when police arrive at the scene of a mugging, "they beat up on you / instead of on your attackers" (5–6). The narrator rationalizes the logic of such an affliction concluding that for a mixed-blood there is no alternative but victimization. "Being Indian and white," the narrator continues, "cancel each other out. / Leaving no one in the place" (7–9). Identity and the construction of race are themes that this collection repeatedly explores, always drawing the same conclusion summarized by Allen in *The* SACRED HOOP; "breeds are a bit of both worlds and the consciousness makes them seem alien to traditional Indians while making them feel alien among whites. Breeds commonly feel alien to themselves above all" (129).

Bibliography

Allen, Paula Gunn. *The Sacred Hoop: Recovering the Feminine in American Indian Traditions*. Boston: Beacon, 1986.

Anthony Patterson

Light People, The Gordon Henry (1994)

Winner of the 1995 American Book Award, Gordon Henry's multigenre first novel, grounded in Anishinabe language, stories, and rituals and the work of GERALD VIZENOR, explores what it means, at the personal and community levels, to recover tribal identity in a constantly changing world. Henry honors the depth of cultural loss at the heart of Native communities where the dominant culture was so harshly privileged for generations even as he suggests that trust in new visions may offer a more traditional approach to recovering tribal culture than any attempt to mimic the old ways.

Configuring a world that is at once mythic, historical, and contemporary, Henry tells the story of the education of the young Oskinaway at two key moments. Very early in life the boy learns that the mother who abandoned him will eventually return, though not in human form, to teach him healing and language. Trusting the process of change, however, is a TRICKSTER FIGURE lesson that takes a lifetime to learn. Only the wisest elders in this text fully master it. When the boy's sense of primal loss deepens to nightmare fear, his traditionalist grandparents seek the help of a tribal healer. Jake Seed agrees to try to locate Oskinaway's parents, but first the boy must have a greater understanding of his situation. Seed teaches in the traditional way, through story.

Henry uses drama; poetry, including linked haiku; and prose to create a complex chain of stories framed by the voice of Seed's apprentice, Arthur Boozhoo, whose name, because it is similar to that of the Anishinabe trickster Nanabozo, marks him as close kin to the tribal trickster. Beginning with Arthur's own story of losing his parents, his return to the reservation, and the vision of the irreverent little man that enabled him to become Seed's helper, the narrative chain circles the reservation, moving from one voice to another. Then quite unexpectedly, the order reverses itself to draw creative life out of each story of death. Oskinaway's story, another link in the chain, locates him as a member of this community even as he learns the history of his connections back to the very beginning.

Oskinaway ultimately decides to become a healer himself, a veterinarian, but only when he drops out of school does he learn the lesson that will make him a wise healer. For months he devotes himself exclusively to a crow with a broken wing, but when he finally envisions the bird in flight and translates his vision into a speech for the whole tribal community, even Oskinaway does not know what his words mean. The crow has one more lesson to teach: that departure carries with it the power to return.

Bibliography

Flys, Carmen. "Interview with Gordon Henry." *North Dakota Quarterly* 64, no. 4 (fall 1996): 167–179.

Salzer, Maureen. "Bones, Artifacts, and Ownership: Gordon Henry, Jr.'s *The Light People* and the Politics of Cultural Appropriation." *North Dakota Quarterly* 70, no. 1 (winter 2003): 38–51.

Linda Lizut Helstern

Little Duck, The/Sikihpsis   Beth Cuthand   (2003)

The Little Duck, titled *Sikihpsis* in Cree, not only provides a valuable lesson concerning the value of self, but also allows for what the American Library Association refers to as "multipurpose" use (11). Multipurpose usage of a text allows for learning lessons beyond those clearly defined within the storyline. The book allows its young adult readers to learn about Cree culture through the simple moral tale of a little mud duck, indicating to young readers the diversity within Native American cultures.

The Little Duck is the story of a small lonely mud duck who lives near a Cree camp. The duck watches the Cree every day and wishes he were like them. He admires their features, even as he disapproves of his own. He feels that if he looked more like the Cree, he would never be lonely again.

One day he sees the Cree men preparing their finery for a dance and thinks that if he joins in, he might be invited to live in their camp. And so he returns to the swamp to prepare dancing garb of his own, from the leaves, clay, shells, and salts of the swamp. When the little mud duck arrives at the village, although his quacking is not understood, a fine and polite Cree boy directs him to where the dancing will take place. People politely talk to him, but they do not understand each other. Sadly, when the dancing begins, the little duck is too slow and short to dance well with the others. Because of his failure at the dance, he returns to the swamp dejected and depressed. He then sees and hears other mud ducks and knows that there is joy in just being himself, and that he will never be lonely again.

All children's picture books are collaborations between the author and illustrator; *The Little Duck* displays the efforts of the author, BETH CUTHAND; the illustrator, Mary Longman; and the translator, Stan Cuthand. As in any picture book the illustrations play a large role. Here each set of facing pages contain one full-page illustration and one smaller one. The top half of the page with the smaller image tells the tale in English, the bottom in phonetic Cree. This arrangement allows the presentation of the Cree language to the larger non-Cree-reading population, and comparing the texts allows the reader to learn words and phrases in Cree. The illustrations by Longman provide accurate and illuminating presentations of Cree campsites and attire. Altogether the book creates an exceptional educational experience on many levels, presented as entertainment.

Bibliography

Cuthand, Beth. *The Little Duck / Sikihpsis.* Penticton, Canada: Theytus Books, 2003.

Lass-Woofin, Mary Jo, ed. *Books on American Indians and Eskimos: A Selection Guide for Children and Young Adults.* Chicago: ALA, 1978.

Slapin, Beverly, and Doris Seale, eds. *Through Indian Eyes: The Native Experience in Books for Children.* Berkeley, Calif.: Oyate, 2003.

Solomon Davidoff

Lone Dog's Winter Count Diane Glancy (1991)

Using a similar technique to that used in CLAIMING BREATH, DIANE GLANCY orders the poems in *Lone Dog's Winter Count* in a loosely chronological pattern. The cover of the volume shows the calendar of the Dakota Nation and includes a pictograph illustrating an event significant to the nation for every year from 1800 to 1871; the collection contains moments of significance for both Glancy and Native Americans in general.

In the notes Glancy includes, she discusses the history of winter counts (a winter count was a tribal storytelling device passed from one generation to another and marked with pictographs that recorded noteworthy events in tribal life) and explains what she sees as the significance of the spiraling pattern of pictographs of Lone Dog's winter calendar, created on a buffalo hide, and the way it shaped her poetry. The trophy for the hunter who fells a buffalo is the liver. Glancy speculates that the events recorded on the count spiral from the location of the liver. Her own interpretation of the spiral is that of the Milky Way and the shape of the universe: Either way she sees the spiral as rep-

resenting both a recording and an invocation of spiritual power.

In the manner of N. SCOTT MOMADAY's fusion of poetry and prose in the influential *The WAY TO RAINY MOUNTAIN,* Glancy's poems in *Lone Dog* are interspersed with prose sections. The selections in this volume are autobiographical in nature, tracing Glancy's journey of self-discovery as a woman of both Cherokee and Anglo descent. Poems such as "Here I Am Standing Beside Myself" explore the isolation that is inherent in one who has feet in more than one cultural world—the lack of total acceptance in either.

These autobiographical poems of Native American women exist to counteract PAULA GUNN ALLEN's assertion in SACRED HOOP that "Indian Women are non-existent." Typical of Native American autobiography, Glancy's autobiographical poetry is the act of giving voice not only to her individual self, but to her heritage as well—there cannot be one without the other. The power to create with words is seen in "And End to Drought": "Hold the AIR in your cupped hand, / say to the emptiness it is SOMETHING" (19–20). Like the life that has been silenced, the emptiness does not seem so is empty to the vessel that contains it.

Poems such as "The First Reader: Santee Training School, 1873" and the epigraphs to several sections of the collection force the reader to encounter the white man and the way he has impacted the lives of the Native Americans in negative ways. In "The First Reader" a young boy is forced to give up his native language—the images in the poem are of binding his hands and his tongue. The epigraphs from Cotton Mather and the treatises that justify colonization reinforce the image of the Anglo as both thief and silencer of the Native American.

Especially compelling is the inclusion of a passage from a Cherokee sketchbook, which shows how dependent the Native American was made on the beneficence of the Anglo community. Glancy's poetry, along with her prose and historical epigraphs, creates a winter count of her own, including events that are significant to her and her world—the world of a Cherokee of Anglo descent.

Bibliography

Abner, Julie LaMay. "Diane Glancy." In *Dictionary of Literary Biography. Vol. 175, Native American Writers of the United States,* 105–108. Detroit: Gale Group, 1997.

Andrews, Jennifer. "A Conversation with Diane Glancy." *The American Indian Quarterly* 26, no. 4 (fall 2002): 645–659.

Turner, Sarah E. "'Spider Woman's Granddaughter': Autobiographical Writings by Native American Women." *MELUS* 22, no. 4 (winter 1997): 109–132.

Welburn, Ron. "Review of *Lone Dog's Winter Count; Claiming Breath,*" *MELUS* 19, no. 4 (winter 1994): 138–140.

P. K. Bostian

Lone Ranger and Tonto Fistfight in Heaven, The   Sherman Alexie (1993)

The Lone Ranger and Tonto Fistfight in Heaven is a sophisticated collection of 22 interlinked stories that mix humor and frustration in their depiction of life inside and outside the Spokane Indian reservation. SHERMAN ALEXIE draws on postmodern narrative strategies to relate snapshot histories of characters such as Thomas-Builds-the-Fire (storyteller and outcast) and Victor, who also appear in the later novel *RESERVATION BLUES* (1995). The volume was Alexie's first collection of short stories and was a finalist for the PEN/Hemingway Award, while it also provided the basis for the film *SMOKE SIGNALS* (1998).

Alexie told Joel McNally that the eye-catching title came to him in a dream "where the Lone Ranger and Tonto got into a fistfight in heaven and the loser had to go to hell" (29–30), but it is interesting that, in spite of the racial conflict evoked by the title, the collection actually opens with a fistfight between two Indians. The opening story, "Every Little Hurricane," uses a tornado as a metaphor to describe a wave of bad feeling moving between Indians gathered at a New Year's Eve party. The conflict is stirred when two brothers begin fighting, but the dispute awakens pain and torment in other characters, who have "enough geography and history . . . to destroy the reservation and leave only random debris and broken furniture" (10–11). This opening story works as a kind of overture, providing an impressively compact distillation of the collection's major obsessions. Alcohol, basketball, dreams, and dancing all feature, and many characters who appear in later stories (Victor, Seymour, Lester FallsApart, James Many Horses) are introduced here. But the battle between the brothers also serves as a kind of preface for the fistfight (described in "This Is What It Means to Say Phoenix, Arizona" and recalled elsewhere in the collection) that takes place when an unprovoked Victor beats Thomas.

The motif of the false dawn is subtly incorporated in the temporal setting of "Every Little Hurricane," as the promise of a new year dissipates in fighting and the return of sour memories of the past. This motif recurs in several of the later stories, such as "The Only Traffic Signal on the Reservation Doesn't Flash Red Anymore." As the opening story is poised on the divide between years, so "The Only Traffic Signal" is split into two halves, divided by a year, that together show how the teenage sport prodigy Julius Windmaker squanders his athletic potential in alcoholism.

But while Alexie dramatizes tensions that exist among his Indians, the opposition that the title introduces, between the white world and the Indian, is also a frequent subject. This opposition provides the basis for the title story, which is composed of two intertwined narratives relating the narrator's late night encounter with the white employee of a 7-11, and the end of an affair with a white woman. Although neither of these narratives mentions the Lone Ranger or Tonto, memories of the tribal past interrupt both stories. The narrator's love affair is haunted by dreams, in which he is a minor war chief and his lover a missionary's wife. The couple are caught by the missionary, who kills the narrator, but his death provokes mass slaughter: "Whites killing Indians and Indians killing whites" (186). In the parallel story the 7-11 employee decides that the narrator's dark skin and long black hair are dangerous, and as the narrator begins to play on his fears the employee tries to placate him by giving him a Creamsicle free of charge, a token gesture that the story parallels with more sinister historical exchanges: *"We'll take Washington and Oregon, and you get six pine trees and a brand-new Chrysler Cordoba"* (183–184).

The structure of this story, joining two narratives and interspersing dream recollections with memories, is typical of this collection, as is the first-person viewpoint. Over the first 13 stories Alexie mixes first-person narratives with six stories narrated from a third-person perspective. This alternation gives way, however, in the last nine stories, which rely on first-person narrative. The predominance of the personal perspective may reflect that many of the characters in this collection draw on different elements of Alexie's personality ("all of my characters are me," Alexie told McNally [30]), but it is notable that the collection is also informed by the work of other writers. The collection begins with an invocation to earlier "Native writers," and although there are allusions to LOUIS OWENS Alexie also draws on the fundamental staples of mainstream postmodernism (the impact of television, the ubiquity of popular culture, and a narrative that relies on stories embedded within stories) and filters their light through a Native American lens to illuminate racial issues. The most important example here is Alexie's treatment of television. The collection ends with a family's watching television, and throughout the book televisions are described as broadcasting "white noise" (61, 160, 191): not just static, but implicitly the sound and viewpoint of white people. Faced with the homogenizing influence of broadcast culture, Alexie asks, "Does every Indian depend on Hollywood for a twentieth-century vision?" (151).

Against this vision Alexie posits the power of storytelling. Stories fill this book: stories told as apologies and dangerous truths and stories that can teach. It is, however, their imaginative power that matters most to Alexie, their assertion of imaginative freedom as a weapon against confinement. In a narrative, as Alexie observes in "A Good Story," there is "just enough to ensure survival" (141).

Bibliography

Alexie, Sherman. *The Lone Ranger and Tonto Fistfight in Heaven.* New York: Atlantic, 1993.

DeNuccio, Jerome. "Slow Dancing with Skeletons: Sherman Alexie's *The Lone Ranger and Tonto Fistfight in Heaven.*" *Critique* 44, no. 1 (2002): 86–96.

Dix, Andrew. "Escape Stories: Narratives and Native Americans in Sherman Alexie's *The Lone Ranger and Tonto Fistfight in Heaven.*" *Yearbook of English Studies* 31 (2001): 155–167.

McNally, Joel. "Profile: Sherman Alexie." *The Writer* (June 2001): 28–31.

Stephen Burn

Long Division: A Tribal History   Wendy Rose (1981)

The power of words is the focus of WENDY ROSE's second book of poetry, *Long Division: A Tribal History.* Divided into three sections, the book highlights the sacred capabilities of language that are often unnoticed. The first section reveals the potential of language to initiate change by giving voice to injustice; the second accentuates the ability of language to heal wounds of the soul; and the third section emphasizes the ability of language to comfort humans along our earthly journey. The poems move beyond the emotionally charged and self-centered poetry of her first book to the arena of social critique, and *Long Division: A Tribal History* demonstrates Rose's professional growth as a poet whose eye has now turned to a more global perspective.

The first section of this work, "Anger," focuses on Euro-American and Native American contact, which has been detrimental to the Native people and profitable for the conquerors. Her first poem, "Mission Bells," begins with two epigraphs that feature this sentiment. However, despite the attempts of the missions to assimilate Natives into mainstream culture through annihilation of Native culture, the Natives remain. Her second poem, "Long Division: A Tribal History," shows how the Native Americans have been used by the dominant culture as she writes, "It's our blood that gives you / those southwestern skies" (4–5). The final poem in this section, "Vanishing Point: Urban Indian," spotlights the present postcontact cultural ruin of many urban Indians as Rose condemns the dominant culture and pleads to her ancestors for help: "It is I who die / bearing cracked turquoise & making noise / so as to protect your fragile immortality" (18–20).

Section II, "Learning to Love," focuses on the ability of language to heal as Rose realizes that it is not only Native Americans who have suffered in this world, but also women and other minorities. The poems suggest that giving voice to suffering can be a way of reaching out to others to share the pain, to find support, and to begin to heal through acceptance and love.

The final section of the book is "Serenity." Here Rose stresses the magic of language to provide spiritual comfort for human beings, hoping to pass this message on to those who would hear. In "Hopi Overlay: Turquoise Words Going Home" she passes her poems to others whose form of communication is basic, oral, and innocent—children. In fact, her role as mother providing instruction to children is reiterated in the final poem, "Moon Metals: Inventing a New Daughter." Her "daughter"—poetry, emerging into the technological world "backwards"—forces perspective back to ancient tribal societies in which words were held in reverence and the magical force of words to implement change, to nurture recuperation, and to nourish the human spirit was understood by all.

See also ASSIMILATION.

Bibliography

Rose, Wendy. *Long Division: A Tribal History.* New York: Strawberry Press, 1981.

Patti Dimond

Louis, Adrian C.   (1946–   )

ADRIAN C. LOUIS is a poet, novelist, newspaper editor, and university lecturer. In his writing he employs an incisive blend of satire, fantasy, and grim realism, which is aided by a good eye for detail and ear for natural dialogue. The picture he presents of contemporary Native American life is often as humorous and compassionate as it is disturbing and provocative.

Louis was born in 1946 in Lovelock, Nevada, the eldest of 12 children. His mother was a registered nurse, and his father, whom he never met, was an army veteran. His parents were never married, and Louis was raised by his mother and grandparents on the small Lovelock Reservation. A MIXED-BLOOD Indian, he is a member of the Lovelock Paiute Tribe. Louis and his wife live off the reservation in Rushville, Nebraska.

Although Louis began his education at the University of Nevada in 1964, he was soon expelled and later received his undergraduate degree from Brown University in Providence, Rhode Island. It was also there that he earned his M.A. in creative writing.

Louis is a former journalist and has been the editor of several tribal newspapers, including *Indian Country Today* and *Lakota Times,* the largest Native newspaper in the United States. He is also a cofounder of the Native American Journalists Association.

From 1984 to 1998 Louis taught English and writing at Oglala Lakota College on the Pine Ridge Reservation of South Dakota. Since 1999 he has been a lecturer in the English Department at Southwest State University in Marshall, Minnesota.

Louis started writing poetry in junior high school, and his first poem was published in 1963. In 1974 his first collection of poetry, *The Indian Cheap Wine Seance,* followed. Since then he has published 12 more books of poems. Louis was elected to the Nevada Writers Hall of Fame in 1999 and has won literary awards and contests for the collections *Fire Water World* (1989) and ANCIENT ACID FLASHES BACK (2000). Other prominent collections include *Vortex of Indian Fevers* (1995), *Ceremonies of the Damned* (1997), and *Bone and Juice* (2001). Louis is also the author of two prose works: a collection of short stories, WILD INDIANS AND OTHER CREATURES (1996), and a novel, SKINS (1995). Both books were translated into French, and *Skins* was adapted for a feature film directed by Chris Eyre (released in 2002).

In his poetry Louis does not employ any traditional forms or conventions and usually resorts to free verse, as most contemporary Native poets do. Louis's creative work continues a tradition of scathing Native HUMOR that runs from ALEXANDER POSEY to THOMAS KING to SHERMAN ALEXIE. The latter author, in fact, considers Louis one of the major influences on his own writing.

Although much of his writing is autobiographical and the overall theme of his work is personal survival, Louis's books encompass themes characteristic of contemporary Native fiction in general: alcohol and drug abuse, POVERTY, racism, violence, urban Indians, exploitation of Indians, and search for one's identity. As do other ethnic poets, Louis needs to confront his inheritance of the colonial past and present—conquest, segregation, ASSIMILATION—and the current conditions arising from that inheritance. As a result a justifiable anger fills many of Louis's writings.

Louis's earlier collections of poetry (e.g., AMONG THE DOG EATERS, 1992) reveal his harsh political and social criticism of the hopelessness and meaninglessness of reservation life; of particular concern here is the issue of alcoholism (*Fire Water World*). In other collections, such as BLOOD THIRSTY SAVAGES (1994) and *Vortex of Indian Fevers,* the author mourns the loss of tribal tradition and expresses contempt for his people's and his own longing for the material rewards of the Euro-American way of life. In *Ancient Acid Flashes Back,* narrated in the third person, Louis addresses his experience in the drug "scene" in San Francisco in the late 1960s. In *Ceremonies of the Damned* and *Bone and Juice,* composed in a lyrical and sad tone, the poet laments the illness of his wife, who no longer recognizes him. The latest collection, *Evil Corn* (2004), written in prose, offers an account of Louis's hard life in the Midwest.

Louis's fiction continues addressing issues raised in his poetry, subverting a romantic notion of modern Native American life and presenting a satirical look at the ills of life on and around the Pine Ridge Reservation. To achieve a comic effect in his novel and short stories, Louis employs irony, grotesque, hyperbole, and scatological humor. A significant peculiarity of his writing are the extensive use and revision of traditional TRICKSTER FIGURE tales, which have created fiction in which Iktomi the Spider from *Skins* as well as Coyote, Bear, and Raven from *Wild Indians and Other Creatures* symbolize the enduring power of the In-

dian race and express Louis's cautious optimism for the future.

Bibliography

Berner, Robert L. *Defining American Indian Literature: One Nation Divisible.* Lewiston, N.Y.: Edwin Mellen, 1999.

Elkins, Andrew. *Another Place: An Ecocritical Study of Selected Western American Poets.* College Station: Texas A&M University Press, 2002.

Louis, Adrian C. *Ancient Acid Flashes Back.* Reno: University of Nevada Press, 2000.

———. *Among the Dog Eaters.* Albuquerque, N. Mex.: West End, 1992.

———. *Blood Thirsty Savages.* St. Louis: Time Being, 1994.

———. *Bone and Juice.* Evanston, Ill.: Northwestern University Press, 2001.

———. *Ceremonies of the Damned.* Reno: University of Nevada Press, 1997.

———. *Evil Corn.* Granite Falls, Minn.: Ellis, 2004.

———. *Fire Water World.* Albuquerque, N. Mex.: West End, 1989.

———. *The Indian Cheap Wine Seance.* Providence, R.I.: Gray Flannel, 1974.

———. *Skins.* New York: Crown/Random House, 1995.

———. *Wild Indians and Other Creatures.* Reno: University of Nevada Press, 1996.

Paul Russe

Love Medicine   Louise Erdrich (1984, 1993)

Love Medicine, one of the most widely read and studied works of Native American literature, was first published in 1984. In 1993 ERDRICH published a revised and expanded version of the text. It is this later text that is taken to be the definitive version. *Love Medicine,* more a collection of connected short stories than a novel, is the first installment in the series that would eventually form the Little No Horse saga. In its pages we are introduced to the families whom we will meet again and again in the course of the works that are set in and around the Turtle Mountain Chippewa reservation in North

Dakota. The Kashpaws and Lamartines dominate the action in *Love Medicine,* but we are also introduced to the Morrisseys, the Lazarres, the Pillagers, and the Adares, who will reappear in more depth in later novels.

More than any other work of Native American literature, *Love Medicine* has found a solid place in the broader canon of American literature. One or more of the stories from *Love Medicine* can be found in many anthologies of 20th-century literature. "The Red Convertible" and "Love Medicine" are the most widely anthologized.

The main characters of *Love Medicine* are from the generation of Indians who were born in the early part of the 20th century. They are too young to know what life was like for the Chippewa before the DAWES ACT and Allotment, but they are old enough to have learned many of the traditional ways from their elders. They are perpetually caught between the traditional and the modern: less seduced by the modern than their children, but more adapted to it than their parents. The three most prominent characters are Marie Lazarre Kashpaw; her husband, Nector Kashpaw; and her rival and his lover, Lulu Nanapush Lamartine.

Although these three anchor the text, it begins with the description of the death of Marie's niece, June Morrissey, who was raised in the Kashpaw home. After a strange sexual encounter with a virtual stranger, June moves off into the snow, walking home to the reservation, and is never seen alive again. This story, "The World's Greatest Fisherman," depicts June as a redemptive figure, uniting the many characters of Erdrich's Little No Horse world. June is (purportedly) the offspring of Lucille Lazarre and Napolean Morrissey, a union that ties together two MIXED-BLOOD families considered "trashy" by many others on the reservation. She is the former wife of Gordie Kashpaw, son of Marie and Nector, and she is the former lover of Gerry Nanapush, son of Lulu. She is the mother of King and Lipsha, the latter of whom will become the protagonist of Erdrich's *The BINGO PALACE.* Finally in *Love Medicine,* *The Bingo Palace,* and *TALES OF BURNING LOVE* her ghost will serve as a guiding influence to those she loves, in a few cases literally leading them to safety.

From this opening story *Love Medicine* immediately moves on to the story of Marie Kashpaw in one of the most dramatic and far-reaching episodes, "Saint Marie." In this episode we see Marie, young, unwanted, mistreated by her family, decide to enter the Sacred Heart Convent located on the reservation. She wants, she says, to prove herself: "Because I don't have that much Indian blood. And they never thought they'd have a girl from this reservation as a saint they'd have to kneel to. But they'd have me" (43). Marie wants to be loved and honored but at the same time believes that she does not deserve to be. In this state she allows the sadistic nun Leopolda to abuse her, scalding her with hot water and beating her with a poker. Leopolda (who is actually Marie's biological mother, as we will learn in *TRACKS*) tells Marie that she is saving her from the devil, or the Dark One, and repeatedly insists that the pain and misery through which she puts Marie are for her own good. One can read this chapter as a metaphor for the larger project of ASSIMILATION—that is, the destruction of Indian culture in favor of Western ways that are said to be better to Indians.

Lulu's story is related through several different chapters of *Love Medicine,* primarily "The Good Tears," "The Island," "Lulu's Boys," and "The Plunge of the Brave." Lulu is the daughter of the mysterious healer Fleur Pillager (one of the main characters in *Tracks* and other novels). She is attractive, flirtatious, and constantly struggling with being abandoned and unfulfilled. Her mother sends her away to a BOARDING SCHOOL early in life, and after she returns to the reservation, she is inexplicably rejected by Nector in favor of Marie. She goes on to have nine children by several different men, including one by Nector during their five-year affair. It is worth noting here that Lulu's character and the exploits in which she is involved highlight Erdrich's characteristic HUMOR even in the fact of sadness. For instance, when Lulu and Nector begin their affair, they do it amid the 17 pounds of melting commodity butter Nector is supposed to be passing out throughout the reservation.

In the two most widely anthologized stories in *Love Medicine,* "The Red Convertible" and the title story, the main characters are not from Lulu and

Marie's generation, but from their children's and grandchildren's. In "The Red Convertible" Lulu's son, Henry Lamartine, Jr., returns from the VIETNAM WAR a scarred man and ultimately drowns himself in the river. In "Love Medicine" Marie and Nector's adopted grandson, Lipsha, attempts to create a love medicine, a potion that will turn Nector's heart toward Marie again, now that they and Lulu are in the same senior citizen center. Lipsha, although he does have healing powers, is impatient and uses a frozen turkey heart from the grocery store, which kills Nector when he chokes on it. This scene, like many of Erdrich's, is both sad and funny at the same time.

Thanks to juxtapositions such as this, *Love Medicine* is a delightful, complex, moving story.

Its interwoven tales can be sometimes confusing, sometimes ambiguous, and sometimes hard to read. But because it tells the story of a generation of Indians whose lives were almost always confusing, ambiguous, and hard, this approach seems quite appropriate.

See also BEET QUEEN, THE; FOUR SOULS; LAST REPORT OF THE MIRACLES AT LITTLE NO HORSE, THE; TRACKS.

Bibliography

Beidler, Peter G., and Gay Burton. *A Guide to the Novels of Louise Erdrich.* Columbia: University of Missouri Press, 1999.

Hafen, Jane P. *Reading Louise Erdrich's* Love Medicine. Boise, Idaho: Boise State University Press, 2003.

Manifest Manners: Postindian Warriors of Survivance   Gerald Vizenor (1994)

Manifest Manners offers a way of understanding Native American culture in a postmodern world where what is reality and what is merely image have become virtually indistinguishable from one another. In the first chapter, "Postindian Warriors," GERALD VIZENOR cites René Magritte's painting *The Treachery of Images* (1929) to introduce the problem addressed throughout the book. Magritte's painting shows a pipe with the caption *"Ceci n'est pas une pipe,"* or "This is not a pipe." Rather, the painting reminds us, it is a picture of a pipe. Vizenor asserts a similar distinction. Pointing to the collective image of Indians in literature, history, and popular culture, he proposes, "This portrait is not an Indian" (18).

Inspired by the poststructuralist theory of Michel Foucault, Vizenor investigates the connection between power and knowledge. For Vizenor the "Indian" we know is a colonial invention reflecting and enforcing the relationship of white dominance and Indian submission. His term *manifest manners* describes representations of the Indian that perpetuate racist assumptions and cooperate with the political ideology of "manifest destiny," or the concept that European-American settlers were destined to move ever westward in their march across the North American continent. Vizenor writes, "Manifest manners are the simulations of domi-

nance; the notions and misnomers that are read as the authentic and sustained as representations of Native American Indians" (5–6). In Vizenor's view the confusion of image and reality constitutes a direct threat to Native American culture, as "simulations of dominance" obscure and silence authentic tribal consciousness. Manifest manners, Vizenor writes, "annihilate tribal names, languages, oral stories, and natural reason," replacing them with false or simulated names like the word *Indian* itself (10).

Vizenor's primary message in *Manifest Manners,* however, is that these simulations of dominance might be controverted with "simulations of survivance." Another term introduced by Vizenor *survivance* merges *survival* with *resistance,* transforming the image of the Indian from one of weakness to one of strength and endurance. The *postindian* represents the personification of survivance, the postmodern Indian who consciously manipulates false images in order to undermine them. Through the use of "trickster hermeneutics," a liberated, imaginative mode of interpretation that emphasizes the fluidity of forms, HUMOR, and the blend of traditional tribal knowledge with a postmodern cultural awareness, "postindian warriors," Vizenor writes, "are new indications of a narrative recreation, the simulations that overcome the manifest manners of dominance" (6).

In the first chapter Vizenor identifies contemporary Indian activists and writers such as Russell

Means, PAULA GUNN ALLEN, and Ed McGaa as the primary practitioners of this creative resistance. In his chapters "Double Others" and "Shadow Survivance" he considers CHARLES ALEXANDER EASTMAN, D'ARCY MCNICKLE, JOHN JOSEPH MATHEWS, N. SCOTT MOMADAY, and JAMES WELCH in this theoretical context. In later chapters, "Eternal Havens," "Ishi Obscura," and "Casino Coups," Vizenor himself works to undermine the simulations perpetuated by the myth of Columbus, modern anthropology, and the Indian GAMING business.

For readers unfamiliar with the jargon of postmodern theory, further complicated by Vizenor's own penchant for coining new words, *Manifest Manners* can be difficult to comprehend. The book represents an idiosyncratic style of criticism, associative rather than argumentative, frustrating in its abstruse terminology and its apparent lack of a coherent theme, but also appealing in its creative freedom. At times we suspect that Vizenor himself poses as the trickster, purposefully obscuring his meaning to confound our preconceived ideas about Native American literature and criticism.

Bibliography

Blaeser, Kimberly. *Gerald Vizenor: Writing in the Oral Tradition.* Norman: University of Oklahoma Press, 1996.

Churchill, Ward. Review of *Manifest Manners, American Indian Culture and Research Journal* 18, no. 3 (1994): 313–318.

Vizenor, Gerald. *Manifest Manners: Postindian Warriors of Survivance.* Hanover, N.H.: Wesleyan University Press, 1994.

Harry Brown

Man Who Loves Salmon, The   Sherman Alexie   (1998)

This is SHERMAN ALEXIE's eighth collection of poems. Unlike many of his works, it minimizes sharp irony and employs a more subtle, emotional tone. It contains 11 short poems, written mostly in unrhymed couplets and in the first person. They express intense love, loss, and hope and offer symbolic scenes of death and birth related to the life of American Indians in today's world.

A limited chapbook edition (750 copies), the books were presented artistically (sewn by hand, letterpressed, 100 copies bound in wooden boards), encouraging the reader's personal reflection. All poems feature salmon, a fundamental symbol for the Pacific Northwest tribes. Alexie belongs to two of them, the Coeur d'Alene and the Spokane. American Indians and salmon are intricately related in the book.

The first poem, "The Man Who Loves Salmon," relates the speaker's union with the last living salmon, which gives birth to a new generation. As it would in nature, the salmon in the poem dies after spawning, leaving the speaker alone to see the "finned children" swim in the river. As the endangered species (salmon) cannot survive in its original form and depends on the help, love, and genes of an outsider (the speaker), original tribal cultures may have to disappear and be integrated into new American Indian cultures by today's Indians. The poem conveys the pain of this loss when the lines of the poem, after growing steadily longer, are abruptly shortened: "I will hold their mother, my lover / broken / by birth" (1–3). Alexie provides the hopeful seed of a new culture by blending traditions. He creatively mixes sestina and tercet forms from Europe in "Salmon, Sea Lion, Ladder" and echoes Kafka's Austrian short story "The Hunger Artist" in "The Indigenous Hunger Artist." He also uses chanting effects from Native traditions, as in "Reunion": "I release the salmon / I release / I release my father and mother / I release" (1–4). Repetitions at the beginning of lines also point to African-American blues.

Some poems emphasize death, such as "At the Diabetic River." As salmon become extinct, the speaker's diabetic father, who represents the diseased Native heritage, becomes blind. Both salmon and father become mere ghosts. Other poems emphasize a new birth: In "Prophecy" the salmon have built mansions in the ocean and sent ambassadors to teach the Indians how to breathe under water. A new Indian culture is thus possible, although irony lurks: Who can learn to breathe under water, even with the best teachers? Perhaps with imagination, and art, it is possible.

Bibliography

Alexie, Sherman. *The Man Who Loves Salmon.* Boise, Idaho: Limberlost, 1998.

Kafka, Franz. "The Hunger Artist." In *Selected Short Stories of Franz Kafka.* New York: Modern Library, 1993.

"The Man Who Loves Salmon." Sherman Alexie.com. Available online. URL: http://www.fallsapart.com/lovessalmon.html. Accessed on August 15, 2005.

Claire Gallou

Map of Who We Are, The   Lawrence R. Smith   (1997)

The Map of Who We Are is the 24th volume of the American Indian Literature and Critical Studies series published by the University of Oklahoma. The novel is an epic tale of good and evil forces vying for control of the thousand-year-old "collective imagination" (281) that has shaped the American collective unconscious.

The primary setting is several major American cities of the near future, and the main plot is simple. Jerry Martinez, a Los Angeles auto detailer, is mysteriously motivated to organize a peaceful sit-in for the homeless, who flock to Laguna Niguel by the tens of thousands. Unknown to Martinez, his vision of social reform is energized by multiethnic and multicultural fifth-dimension "Travelers." The initial sit-in attracts nationwide attention and creates a groundswell movement that peaks at the Houston Astrodome when a huge explosion infuses everyone with a "spiritual diaspora" (308) that ushers in the "Great Millennial Shift" predicted in chapter 1. The story culminates in the birth of a mysteriously conceived and miraculously delivered child destined to lead "a world of Travelers, compassionate bodhisattvas" (308) into the next century.

Despite the simple plot the novel's narrative structure is highly complex. The author begins with the premise that history is composed of intricately interwoven, subjective accounts of reality. The narrative accordingly draws a nonlinear "map" encompassing major historical events from the Viking explorations to contemporary antiestablishment protests. These disparate topographies are preserved in the collective memory of Travelers psychically connected to the "Network"—an electrically charged "earth-sky grid" (3) "that holds everything together" (46) and instantly transports Travelers through time and space. The result, in the words of one reviewer, is that the narrative "jumps from one reality to another as fast as the sentences fly" (Glover and Hoffert 136).

Although a major thematic purpose of the book is to explode social categories, Native Americans are the most prominent among the special Travelers known as "memory heroes." John Walkingstick, a Cherokee medicine man, fathers the Millennial Shift; Walker Thompkins, an iconoclastic contemporary Lakota female, publicly promotes it; and Handsome Bear, an ancestral Chacoan Pueblan enervates it.

To illustrate the artifice of multiculturalism, Smith's ultimately coherent "map of who we [all] are" includes, among others, Eric the Red's daughter, a white Neanderthal living in Watts, a hairy ninth-century Chacoan Anasazi, a Chinese alchemist, and an African-American jazz musician.

Thematically the novel affirms the possibility of universal harmony by defying old paradigms and embracing "freestanding, independent stretches of time that could be used to make alternative endings to stories, to histories, until they all conjoin with the telling that brings the Great Millennial Shift" (Smith 48).

Bibliography

Glover, Charlotte L., and Barbara Hoffert. Review of *The Map of Who We Are,* by Lawrence R. Smith. *Library Journal* 122 (1997): 136.

Smith, Lawrence R. *The Map of Who We Are.* American Indian Literature and Critical Studies series 24. Norman: University of Oklahoma Press, 1997.

Karen Sloan

Maracle, Lee   (1950–   )

Lee Maracle, of the Sto:loh Nation, is of Salish and Cree descent; she was born in North Vancouver, British Columbia, Canada. Maracle—orator, writer, and activist—has been writing since her childhood; in 1975 she published her first book, *Bobbi Lee, Indian Rebel*, an autobiographical work. At that time she was one of very few Canadian aboriginal writers to have been published. She did not publish between 1975 and 1990 but has since become one of the most highly acclaimed and well-published Native Canadian writers.

A 13-year quiescence followed the publication of her first book; it ended with the 1988 publication of *I am Woman*. She was still an active writer and speaker during that period; however, she was hesitant about publication. In 1990 that attitude had clearly ended, and that year three of her books were printed: SOJOURNER'S TRUTH & OTHER STORIES, a new edition of *Bobbi Lee: Indian Rebel*, and *Telling It: Woman and Language Across Cultures,* of which she is a coeditor. Other fiction and nonfiction publications quickly followed: SUNDOGS (1992), *We Get Our Living Like Milk from the Land* (1993), RAVENSONG (1993), *I am Woman: A Native Perspective on Sociology and Feminism* (1996), BENT BOX (2000), *My Home As I Remember* (2000), *Will's Garden* (2002), and *Daughters Are Forever* (2002). Her work is also highly anthologized. In an interview published in 1994 she said, "One of the reasons I didn't publish for a long time between *Bobbi Lee* and *Sundogs* was that white people would be reading it. However, I just woke up one morning in 1988, really, and thought it was time Raven came out of the house. So, it doesn't bother me that white folks read it. I don't have this feeling that I'm writing to them as an audience, though" (Kelly 76). Lee Maracle is aware that white people read her work but claims she is unconcerned about whether they are able to overcome cultural barriers to access and understand her stories. She writes for a Native audience, and her attempts to alienate white readers are transparent throughout her stories.

More important to her than critical reception—which she conceives of as the domain of white academics—is her desire to continue a tradition of Native oral storytelling, which she does by combining Native storytelling techniques with the European written form. Maracle dedicates the 1990 publication of *Sojourner's Truth and Other Stories* to "all those Native people who find themselves staring at a blank white sheet and struggle to talk to it," making obvious her ambitions to be a contemporary storyteller for her community. The preface of that book, however, is inextricable from the stories that follow: It acknowledges the didactic role of the orator, and the stories must be read—listened to—within the context of that authorial message. If Maracle does not write the stories for a white audience, then she does write the preface with them in mind—along with any other reader who requires instruction on Native storytelling.

Entitled "You Become the Trickster," the preface is a short essay that outlines how to read and appreciate the text. Maracle provides the theoretical framework through which she wants her texts to be "heard," because while she seemingly identifies academics as non-Native, she works and writes within the very institutions she critiques and, as a theorist, endeavors to reclaim and contribute to the redefinition of *Native*. Lee Maracle has taught at a number of acclaimed universities and institutions including the University of Toronto, the University of Waterloo, and Western Washington University. She founded the En'owkin International School of Writing in Penticton, in her home province of British Columbia, and she is the traditional cultural director of the Centre of Indigenous Theatre in Toronto.

In addition to underlining the futility and falsity of the white man's attempts to define *Native*, specifically deriding white-academic assertions of authority, Lee Maracle has a number of other themes that run through her critical work, her prose, and her poetry: the institutional racism underpinning Canadian social, political, and economic power systems; the contemporary socioculturalscape, as adherent to European patriarchal values that undermine the necessity and potential for female empowerment; Native frustration and anger against whites and the unfavorable imbalance of power that is manifested in a variety of ways, including domestic violence; and a criticism of class hierarchies, to name a few. As a writer Maracle attempts to transform the tradition of Native oratory into written text. However, her writing also reflects her lifelong interests in history, politics, First Nations' self-government, community development, and feminism.

Just as Maracle's roles as writer, historian, and politician converge in her fiction and nonfiction, so do the oral and written storytelling forms. Maracle's writing advocates and aims to effect social change by provoking readers, forcing them to rethink their relationship to the Native world, whether they are white or Native. The breadth of her expertise is proportional to her influence, and her authorial reputation is comparable to that of EMILY PAULINE JOHNSON, MARIA CAMPBELL, and JEANETTE ARMSTRONG: iconic women in the tradition of aboriginal literature.

See also FIRST NATIONS LITERATURE.

Bibliography

Kelley, Jennifer. "Coming out of the House: A Conversation with Lee Maracle." *ARIEL: A Review of International English Literature* 25 (January 1994): 73–88.

Maracle, Lee. *Sojourner's Truth and Other Stories.* Vancouver: Press Gang, 1990.

Sheena Wilson

Mathews, John Joseph   (1894–1979)

John Joseph Mathews was born in Pawhuska, Oklahoma (then Indian Territory), on November 16, 1894. He was the son of a quarter Osage father, William, and a white mother, Eugenie. Although he grew up among full-bloods and spoke Osage (albeit not very well), he struggled with his MIXED-BLOOD identity as a young man. His lighter skin and the fact that he attended Pawhuska schools as opposed to reservation schools set him apart from other Indians he knew. In writing he referred to full-bloods as "they" and "them" and clearly held the opinion that he and they were not the same. Mathews attended the University of Oklahoma, graduating with a degree in geology in 1920. His course of study was broken up by his enlistment in the U.S. Army during World War I, when he served as a pilot in the 25th Squadron.

After finishing his undergraduate education, he was awarded a prestigious Rhodes Scholarship to study at Oxford in England. He turned down the scholarship but went to Oxford anyway, and earned a B.A. in natural science. He then moved on to Switzerland and the University of Geneva, where he studied international relations. He worked at various businesses in California; was married; fathered two children, Virginia and John; divorced; and ultimately returned in 1929 to Oklahoma, where his writing career began to take shape.

Mathew's first book, *Wah'Kon-Tah: The Osages and the White Man's Road* (1932), is an interesting history that blends the diaries of Laban J. Miles, the Quaker agent to the Osage in the 1920s and a friend of Mathews, with oral histories collected from full-bloods and others on the reservation. This book received widespread acclaim and readership, in part because it was chosen as a Book of the Month Club selection in November 1932.

Mathews's next book, the novel SUNDOWN, was not as widely read but is far more important to the field of literary studies. The main character, Challenge Windzer, is, at least to some degree, a fictional version of Mathews himself. He attends the University of Oklahoma, benefits from Osage oil royalties, and, most importantly, struggles as a mixed-blood lost between cultures. As this theme would become so prevalent in Indian literature, Mathews's novel is an important early engagement with the topic.

In addition to his career as a writer, Mathews became well known for his interest in education and Indian rights. He was appointed to the state board of education, was awarded a Guggenheim Fellowship to study education, was an eight-year member of the Osage Tribal Council, and led several delegations to Washington, D.C., to argue Osage rights. Two other books, *Taking to the Moon* (1945) and *The Osages: Children of the Middle Waters* (1961), did not receive wide notice during Mathews's life, but now, as oral history is being acknowledged as a more acceptable source of information, are generally acclaimed by historians and writers.

Bibliography

Bailey, Garrick. "John Joseph Mathews." *American Indian Intellectuals,* edited by Margot Liberty, 205–214. Saint Paul, Minn.: West, 1978.

Matrilineal Cycle   Mary TallMountain (1988)

That MARY TALLMOUNTAIN descends from a line of strong women is clear from her collection of poems dedicated to those women—*Matrilineal Cycle*. A collection of just 14 poems, the chapbook includes many of TallMountain's best-known poems: "Matmiya," "Song for My Mother," and "The Hands of Mary Joe."

TallMountain had a diverse cultural background. Her mother was Russian/Athabascan/Koyukon; her father was of Scots/Irish-American descent. In *Matrilineal Cycle* she writes about the Indian women in her family—her mother, Mary Joe, who died of tuberculosis; her grandmother, a strong personality who ran the family; and her aunt. "Matmiya" is about TallMountain's grandmother. *Matmiya* means "mountain," and in the poem the figure of her grandmother is that of a mountain growing from the earth: "I see you sitting / Implanted by roots / Coiled deep from your thighs" (1–3). In an interview with JOSEPH BRUCHAC TallMountain explains that although her grandmother was physically a thin and sharp woman, in her mind she thinks of her in the way she thinks of all Indian woman, as growing out of the earth in a lushly vegetative way—all curves and roundness as the earth is round: "I see your figure wrapped in skins / Curved into a mound of earth" (3–4).

TallMountain was adopted by a white family when she was very young in order to remove her from a tubercular environment. For many years she was angry with her mother for seemingly abandoning her. In TallMountain's poetry the image of her mother serves as both physical mother and spiritual presence. In "The Hands of Mary Joe," as well as "A Song for My Mother," her mother prepares King Salmon, a fish of mythic and spiritual proportions. In "Hands" Mary Joe is shown doing the things mothers do: preparing dinner, threading needles, cherishing a child. In the last lines of the poem her mother's hands "lie folded in her lap" (4) and "The hands of Mary Joe / Await / The approaching silence" (5–6).

In "A Song for My Mother" the relationship between mother and daughter is imagined more clearly as the mother passes on instructions on how to prepare the salmon: "Always do this with care, / you said" (1–2). The image of a young girl receiving instruction from her mother is made poignant since it never occurred for TallMountain. Living in the Anglo world with her adoptive parents, TallMountain felt the pain of belonging wholly to neither world. The poem concludes with the lines "So I went the alien ways / but held my life with you apart" (13–14). In poems from other collections the gulf between the Native SPIRITUALITY of her Athabascan ancestors and the Catholic spirituality in which she was raised, the "alien ways," is bridged. In *Matrilineal Cycle* the world of the Native women in TallMountain's life are central and the "otherworldliness" of a life experienced as a small child far away on the Yukon River in Alaska is foregrounded.

Bibliography

Bruchac, Joseph. "We Are the Inbetweens: An Interview with Mary TallMountain." *SAIL: Studies in American Indian Literature* 1, no. 1 (summer 1989): 13–21.

P. K. Bostian

McNickle, D'Arcy   (1904–1977)

Born on January 18, 1904, in St. Ignatius, Montana, William D'Arcy McNickle was a writer, historian, policy maker, educator, and Native American rights advocate whose contributions to modern Native American literature and history anticipate many of the concerns taken up by contemporary Native American writers. McNickle's early Salish upbringing and his predominantly Euro-American education, as well as his MIXED-BLOOD family history, provide a complex backdrop for his work. His novels and nonfiction critically examine the difficulty of communicating across racial and cultural barriers, the devastating effects of government policies on tribal societies, as well as the return of the Native to his tribal community—an early version of the "returning home" plot so characteristic of the early fiction of N. SCOTT MOMADAY and LESLIE MARMON SILKO. McNickle was a lifelong advocate of Native rights and offered an alternative to what were then considered the only two options for Native Americans—ASSIMILATION or extinction—by writing of Native life as persistent and changing.

McNickle's mother, Philomene Parenteau, was of half-Cree and half-French descent. Her family fled Canada in 1885 after her father's participation in the failed Riel Rebellion. The Parenteau, as were many other Métis, were adopted by their host tribe into the Salish and Kootenai Confederated Tribes, which afforded Philomene and her Anglo husband, William McNickle—son of Irish immigrants, a farmer and an industrial school arts teacher—the opportunity to take advantage of the DAWES ACT. After McNickle's parents divorced in 1914, McNickle's father was granted control over his children's land, and McNickle and his two sisters were sent to Chemawa, a federal Indian BOARDING SCHOOL in Oregon. Here the children had to speak English and were punished for displaying non-Anglo behavior.

In 1921 McNickle continued his Western education, enrolling at the University of Montana, where he studied literature and history. In 1925 McNickle left Montana for Oxford University in England. To finance the trip McNickle sold his allotment of tribal lands, distancing himself from his reservation roots both symbolically and literally. McNickle did not stay long at Oxford but instead traveled through Europe for several months. Upon his return to the United States in 1926 McNickle moved to New York City, where he married Joran Birkeland and attended classes at Columbia University. In the summer of 1931 he returned to Europe to study in Grenoble, France. McNickle never finished his university degree, but his work in applied anthropology was recognized with an honorary doctorate by the University of Colorado in 1966.

In 1935 McNickle joined the Federal Writers Project, and in 1936 he was hired by the Bureau of Indian Affairs (BIA) to work for Commissioner John Collier as administrative assistant and field representative. Collier's Indian New Deal programs, initiated as a result of the Indian Reorganization Act of 1934, which rejected Assimilationist policies of the previous years, greatly influenced McNickle's creative and political work, and it is during this period that he most significantly returns to an understanding of himself as Native American. He worked not only to counter public misconceptions of Native peoples, but also to educate tribal peoples about the challenges of living in a white-dominated country. McNickle wrote three novels; his best known, *The SURROUNDED,* was published in 1936, *RUNNER IN THE SUN* in 1954; *WIND FROM AN ENEMY SKY* was published posthumously in 1978. In addition to fiction McNickle wrote a number of ethnohistories, such as *They Came Here First* (1949) and *Indians and Other Americans: Two Ways of Life Meet* (1959), in which he wrote of white-Native relations and histories from a Native perspective, anticipating such historical rewritings as Welch's *Killing Custer* (1994). McNickle left the BIA in 1952, became director of American Indian Development, Inc., and traveled often to remote reservations as an adviser. From 1966 to 1971 he was chair of anthropology at the University of Saskatchewan, and from 1972 to 1977 program director for the Center for the History of the American Indian at the Newberry Library in Chicago (which was later renamed in McNickle's honor). After divorcing Joran in 1938, McNickle married twice more and had two daughters. On October 18, 1977, he died of a heart attack in his home in Albuquerque, New Mexico.

McNickle's first novel, *The Surrounded,* is the story of a young mixed-blood man who, after returning to the Flathead Reservation, struggles to achieve a tentative sense of belonging within his native culture. His difficulty communicating with his white father mirrors on a personal level the ways in which the tribe's political and social structures have been destroyed, thus foregrounding a prominent theme in McNickle's work: that of the importance of community over individual when striving for the survival and renewal of the tribe. Change, McNickle argues here, can only occur from within the tribe, a vision of tribalism he develops more strongly in his third novel, *The Wind from an Enemy Sky.* This last novel proposes a necessary compromise between finding individual identity within tribal community, accepting some of the whites' ways, and realizing that those changes strengthen the tribe rather than weaken it. The juvenile novel *Runner in the Sun* is set 4,000 years ago in the antiquity of the Southwest and maps a history of the region that shows not the origin of one culture but the connectedness of different Native cultures to the same landscape. In all three novels McNickle draws on his understanding of Native histories but also on the storytelling tradition he remembered from his early childhood. Even though McNickle wrote often about the devastating effects of government policies on Native life and culture, his work articulates a vision of the perseverance of Native American life, seeking compromise between different ways of living and knowing.

Bibliography

McNickle, D'Arcy. *Indians and Other Americans: Two Ways of Life Meet* (With Harold E. Fey). New York: Harper, 1959.

———. *Runner in the Sun: A Story of Indian Maize.* New York: Holt, Rinehart & Winston, 1954.

———. *The Surrounded.* New York: Dodd, Mead, 1936.

———. *They Came Here First: The Epic of the American Indian.* Philadelphia: Lippincott, 1949.

———. *Wind from an Enemy Sky.* San Francisco: Harper & Row, 1978.

Parker, Dorothy R. *Singing an Indian Song: A Biography of D'Arcy McNickle.* Lincoln: University of Nebraska Press, 1992.

Purdy, John Lloyd, ed. *The Legacy of D'Arcy McNickle: Writer, Historian, Activist.* Norman: University of Oklahoma Press, 1996.

Andrea Opitz

Mean Spirit   Linda Hogan (1990)

LINDA HOGAN's *Mean Spirit* is an excellent vehicle for the discussion of political issues pertaining to the exploitation and destruction of Native American lands and lives. It is a fine example of the power of Native American imagination to critique the kinds of colonial powers (oil company owners, the U.S. government, and the law) that have promoted and still promote the overexploitation of certain geographical areas—in the case of *Mean Spirit,* the drilling and burning of Osage land in Oklahoma for oil. The fictitious events of *Mean Spirit* rely on a true historical trauma: the localized genocide that took place in the 1920s in Oklahoma after oil was discovered on Indian Territory. Hogan produces here a new version of history and asks readers to bear witness to a deadly reality. The characters in the novel are the victims of, and thus witnesses to, a traumatic disturbance of land and life. Some of the Osage men and women try to resist traumatic change through seclusion: The Hill Indians were "a peaceful group who had gone away from the changing world some sixty years earlier, in the 1860s. Their survival depended on returning to a simpler way of life" (5). Others resist it by trying to find equilibrium between the modern, exploitative world of non-Indians and the traditional way of their people: Belle, Moses, and Letitia Graycloud as well as Michael Horse, Stace Redhawk, and Lionel Tall belong to that category.

These characters strive to retain spiritual harmony and work for the reestablishment of justice on Osage territory. Others have simply been stripped of their energy and faith in life by exploitative, inhumane oil barons and their local representative on Osage land, the infamous Hale. Traumatic changes lead to spiritual death: "People were turning away from one another, but there were splittings, mind from heart, body from spirit. Some broke quickly, weeping openly and without shame in public spaces" (170). The novel centers around the violent death of Grace Blanket, whose murderers have appropriated oil-filled Native lands through killing and stealing. In the middle of this vortex of violence one powerful female figure arises and restores hope for the Osage people: Nola, Grace's daughter, will use her traumatic experience to become a strong, fierce figure. Along with Belle, Moses, Stace, and others, she will bear witness to the tragedy and move from the state of victim to that of storyteller, the new agent of history.

This novel, though mostly about the destruction of a people and a way of life, does not depict Osage Indians as helpless victims of history. They are victims, yes, but through testimony—whether as narrative voices in Hogan's text or as witnesses, speakers of the truth, in the trials that take place throughout the novel—they become the messianic, powerful voices of trauma. These voices speak against both the murderers of their people and a judicial system that relies on "books filled with words, with rules about how the story can and cannot be spoken. There is no room enough, nor time, to search for the real story that lies beneath the rest" (341).

Bibliography

Anderson, Eric Gary. "States of Being in the Dark: Removal and Survival in Linda Hogan's *Mean Spirit*." *Great Plains Quarterly* 20, no. 1 (winter 2000): 55–67.

Krasneva, Yonka Kronmova. "The Politics of Border in Linda Hogan's *Mean Spirit*." *Studies in American Literatures* 11, no. 4 (winter 1999): 46–60.

Sophie Croisy

Medawar, Mardi Oakley (1945–)

An Eastern Band Cherokee born in Olla, Louisiana, in 1945, Medawar attended San Diego State University and has taught writing at several colleges. Inspired by Stephen King's complex characters, she strove to match his skill within her fiction. Self-described as an "Intertribalist," Medawar has set her historical mysteries within Crow and Kiowa country.

Before discovering her flair for mystery, Medawar constructed a multigenerational saga that followed one family thorough the Indian Wars and their encounters with historical figures. Particularly notable for its incorporation of the Crow oral tradition of the killing of the buffalo and the coming of the white nation, *People of the Whistling Waters* (1994) won the Medicine Pipe Bearer's Award for the Best First Western Novel awarded by the Western Writers of America.

As the first novel in her first mystery series, DEATH AT RAINY MOUNTAIN (1996) provides an alternative to stereotypes of Native American characters. Set in Crow country in the 19th century, the novel portrays Tay-bodal's serious role as a healer

as tempered by his humorous perspective. Lauded for its inclusive depiction of historical Kiowa culture, her writing was honored with the Prose Fiction Writer of the Year Award presented to her by Wordcraft Circle of Native Writers in 1998.

Improvements evident in the second mystery, *Witch of Palo Duro* (1997), are the strength and authenticity of voice, as well as the strong theme of the supernatural. Medawar further develops Tay-bodal's character by contrasting his scientific worldview against that of his mystically oriented brethren and in doing so illustrates intratribal differences. Again the HUMOR is evident, but this time Medawar's skill at description is displayed in sections characterizing the physical landscape.

Strengthened by her attention to Kiowa lore and traditions and further developing Tay-bodal's humor, *Murder at Medicine Lodge* (1999) integrates themes from the period such as the effects of Reconstruction upon the Kiowa and cross-cultural tensions between the Kiowa and African-American cavalry. In 1999 Medawar earned another award, the 1999 Writer of the Year Award from the Woodcraft Circle of Native Writers. *Ft. Larned Incident* (2000) continues the story of Tay-bodal, who struggles to solve murders in addition to dealing with marital problems with his wife.

Taking a break from Tay-bodal, Medawar created a second mystery series in a contemporary setting with *Murder on the Red Cliff Rez* (2002). Though departing from her richly detailed historic settings, Medawar endowed her new characters, a male and female crime-solving team of the tribal chief of police and a ceramicist, with her distinctive sense of humor.

Bibliography

Fogarty, Taylor. "The Mystery and Humor of Mardi Oakley Medawar." Available online. URL: http://www.readthewest.com/interviewMardiOakleyMedawar.html. Accessed on August 15, 2005.

Medawar, Mardi Oakley. *Death at Rainy Mountain.* New York: St. Martin's Press, 1996.

———. *Ft. Larned Incident.* New York: St. Martin's Minotaur, 2000.

———. *Murder at Medicine Lodge: A Tay-bodal Mystery.* New York: St. Martin's Press, 1999.

———. *Murder on the Red Cliff Rez.* New York: St. Martin's Minotaur, 2002.

———. *Witch of the Palo Duro: A Tay-bodal Mystery.* New York: St. Martin's Press, 1997.

Rebecca Tolley-Stokes

Medicine River   Thomas King (1989)

Medicine River, THOMAS KING's first novel, encapsulates the difficulty of a MIXED-BLOOD man's integration into an Indian community on the southern Alberta prairie. Although King grew up and was educated in the United States, his writing often employs a Canadian setting. The protagonist's mother marries a white man, and because the government no longer considers her an Indian, the family is legally prevented from returning to the reserve after her husband's death. Instead, Will, his mother, and his brother, James, move to Standoff, a literal and metaphorical place signifying Will's relationship with the two cultures of his heritage. Will moves to Toronto to be a professional photographer but returns after his mother's death. At the instigation of a man who becomes a close friend, Will settles in the town of Medicine River, near the reserve, and establishes Medicine River Photography. The narrative of the novel recounts the experiences of the nonstatus Indian in this community and incorporates important incidents from his youth and life in Toronto, exploring the power of memory in shaping identity. Using satiric humor, King includes a contemporary version of the TRICKSTER FIGURE in the novel and addresses the negotiation of Indian identity and of intercultural interaction.

Will must come to terms with his dual identity. His last name is never told. He is always referred to as "Rose Horse Capture's boy" (139). The father, a white rodeo cowboy, is absent and the community defines Will according to matrilineal customs: That is, the mother's heritage is favored. His mother's last name wittily evokes the Blackfoot tradition of capturing horses and other prized items from enemies. When Will later dates Louise Heavyman, three people mistakenly define him as Mr. Heavyman, in an ironic extension of the notion of matri-lineal definition. That Will ultimately finds his place within the Indian community is symbolized when he is integrated into a family portrait that quickly transforms into a community picture.

Will's friend, Harlen Bigbear, an individual central to many events in Will's new existence, is evocative of the Indian TRICKSTER FIGURE. He guides Will in his initial return to Medicine River and suggests Will settle there permanently. Harlen is also a pivotal factor in having Will establish a business, join the community's basketball team, and date Louise: "Helping was Harlen's specialty . . . Bertha over at the Friendship Centre called it meddling. Harlen would have thought of it as general maintenance" (31). Harlen, like the trickster, is a central figure of the Indian community. In an ironic inversion the narrator's initial description humorously suggests storklike qualities rather than those of the more traditional coyote or raven.

Harlen's belief in sharing other people's burdens affects Will, and he ultimately enacts a similar philosophy. In becoming a metaphoric Mr. Heavyman, he too takes on the weight of responsibility for caring for others. As the novel progresses, Will illustrates his "will"ingness to help others; he becomes a surrogate father to the daughter he ironically names South Wing (Wilma) Heavyman. He fulfills the promise his own father made to deliver a toy top to his sons; at the close of the narrative he wraps a toy top to give to his pseudoadopted daughter.

Will's own youth and his unwitting love affair in Toronto serve as episodic counterpoints to the present narrative of his life in Medicine River. Will's white lover asks him early in their relationship, "You're Indian, aren't you?" (108). However, his reply is significantly absent. Using HUMOR, the novel contends with versions of the "authentic" Indian. Eddie Weaselhead, also a mixed-blood, dons the recognizable paraphernalia—ribbon shirts and bone chokers—while the full-blood Big John Yellow Rabbit wears suits and ties. Their problematic relationship illustrates a serious issue for many Indian people: Who may define "Indian" and how would they define it?

King explicitly engages with the notion of storytelling, of Indian literature as extension of traditional orality. Lionel, an older Indian who fulfills the vision of how an Indian should appear, travels to Europe to tell traditional stories despite his preference to tell contemporary tales of RESERVATION LIFE. In consciously ironic form Lionel employs a traditional tale of Raven and Coyote with an untraditional ending to provide a commentary on his own experiences. He confides to Will and Harlen that the stories that he tells are ones that he commonly heard his wife tell their children. He expresses his surprise at his audience's reaction when they clap "[l]ike they never heard that story before" (175).

The women in the novel illustrate strength in terms of both individuality and community. The women maintain cultural stories and traditions for their children and underscore the importance of cultural identity. Granny Oldcrow is the reserve's medicine woman, and, as Will discovers to his chagrin, she is also known as the marriage doctor. Louise Heavyman has a child with a Cree, one of the traditional enemies of the Blackfoot, and decides to raise the child herself rather than marry the father, engaging instead in a relationship with Will. The women in the novel ultimately determine and construct the parameters of their relationships.

The novel engages with and questions historical and contemporary discrimination. One of the stereotypes that appear is that of the Indian convict: The star player of the Medicine River Friendship Centre Warriors, ironically named Clyde Whiteman, returns to jail repeatedly. King's novel demonstrates the destructive potential of stereotypes, both within and without the community, and underscores the necessity of communal responsibility. Various narratives of resistance, such as those of WOUNDED KNEE and the AMERICAN INDIAN MOVEMENT (AIM), appear throughout the text, serving to question colonialism and the external shaping of identity.

The novel was adapted to create a television movie, with a cameo appearance by Thomas King.

Bibliography

Davidson, Arnold E., Priscilla L. Walton, and Jennifer Andrews. *Border Crossings: Thomas King's Cultural Inversions.* Toronto: University of Toronto Press, 2002.

King, Thomas. *Medicine River.* Toronto: Penguin Books, 1989.

Schorcht, Blanca. *Storied Voices in Native American Texts: Harry Robinson, Thomas King, James Welch, and Leslie Marmon Silko.* New York: Routledge, 2003.

Joanie Crandall

Men on the Moon: Collected Short Stories   Simon Ortiz (1999)

The only complete collection of short stories by the renowned Acoma poet SIMON ORTIZ, *Men on the Moon* (1999) demonstrates Ortiz's fluency in expressing his people's Aacquemeh (Acoma Pueblo) oral tradition through narrative prose. *Men on the Moon* collects the 19 short stories originally published as *FIGHTIN': NEW AND COLLECTED STORIES* (1983), plus seven stories (most published first in the anthology *The Man to Send Rain Clouds* [1974], edited by Kenneth Rosen, and in Ortiz's 1978 collection, *HOWBAH INDIANS*), in order to acquaint "a younger generation of readers and listeners" (ix) with Ortiz's short fiction. Consistently with Native storytelling traditions, Ortiz has made minor revisions to a few of the stories in *Men on the Moon* because, as he explains in his preface, "Rereading previous writing—just like telling old stories—always involves change" (ix). For the most part the stories remain as originally published.

The landscapes of Ortiz's stories range from the familiar terrain of his Southwest Aacquemeh homeland, to a lonely migrant work camp in rural Idaho ("Woman Singing"), to the urban strangeness of San Francisco, where earnest white hippies play at being "real Indians" ("The San Francisco Indians"). Ortiz's direct, understated, conversational language and quiet tone at once underscore the oral quality of his tales, while amplifying the themes of his more political stories involving the abuse of power by colonial authority against Native peoples, such as an incident with a racist policeman ("The Killing of a State Cop") or a young Pueblo man's flight from one of the federal Indian BOARDING SCHOOLS ("Pennstuwehniyaahtse:Quuti's Story"). Other stories register powerfully in more intimate contexts, as when a Laguna Pueblo couple helps their white Oklahoma neighbors mourn the death of a younger brother, who stepped on an American mine in Vietnam, by giving the Oklahoma couple an ear of white corn and a ceremonial corn husk bundle in traditional Laguna fashion ("To Change Life in a Good Way"). Ortiz also uses humor to highlight kinship and cultural perspectives, as in the title story, "Men on the Moon," in which an Acoma grandfather receives his first television and puzzles over the intentions of the Mericano astronauts he watches blast off in a rocket ship to "look for knowledge" on the Moon. These stories illustrate the small details of life within its epic sweep through interrelationship and attempts at understanding, some of which succeed, some of which fail, and many of which remain unresolved and under negotiation.

Ortiz has stated that from earliest memory he has always existed inside language, and that language has always existed in the form of stories. "Story has its own power," writes Ortiz, "and the language of story is of that power. We are within it, and we are empowered by it" (viii). In a manner as compelling as his poems, Ortiz's short fiction cultivates a similar narrative intimacy between reader and author that reveals the values that shape Ortiz's identity and allows his readers to be moved.

Jane Haladay

Miranda, Deborah   (1961–   )

Deborah Miranda was born on October 22, 1961, in Los Angeles, California, to Alfred Edward Robles Miranda and Madgel Eleanor Gano Miranda. Her father is of Esselen and Chumash ancestry, and her mother is of French and Jewish descent. At the age of five Miranda moved to Washington State, where she developed the desire to reconnect with tribal members. She writes: "I feel that my life mirrors the history of my tribes in many ways: begun in beauty, subjected to trauma and upheaval, and now a slow re-creation of the web of connections that make the world both possible and a celebration" ("Deborah Miranda," official Web site 1). Miranda is an enrolled member of the Esselen Na-

tion. She received a bachelor's degree from Wheelock College in Boston, and an M.A. and Ph.D. from the University of Washington in Seattle. She taught at Pacific Lutheran University in Tacoma, Washington, and has accepted a position as assistant professor of English at Washington and Lee University, in Lexington, Virginia.

Miranda has won many awards for her poetry, including the 49th Parallel Poetry Prize (1993), the poetry prize for the Pacific Northwest Writers Conference (1995), the Diane Decorah Award for Poetry (1997), and Writer of the Year for Poetry (2000) for her book *Indian Cartography* (1999). Her poetry and articles have been included in numerous anthologies and journals, such as *Through the Eye of the Deer* (1999), *The Dirt Is Red Here: Art and Poetry from Native California* (2002), *American Indian Quarterly, Cimarron Review, Sojourner,* and *Callaloo.* Her article "Silver," in *"Bad Girls"/"Good Girls": Women, Sex, and Power in the Nineties* (1996), is autobiographical.

In her work Miranda writes of unpleasant and disturbing situations with both honesty and delicate sensitivity. CARTER REVARD writes that her "poems are truthful without being mean, angry without being nasty" (*Indian Cartography* back cover). Despite the difficult obstacles she and her people have encountered, Miranda maintains a sense of optimism. She states: "Because some of my relatives survived Missions, survived secularization, survived the poverty, prejudice, alcoholism, diabetes, and abuse that followed and still persists, I am here" (*Indian Cartography* xiii). Survival, both physical and psychological, is also an important theme in her writing.

Bibliography

Miranda, Deborah. *Indian Cartography.* Greenfield Center, N.Y.: Greenfield Review Press, 1999.

———. "Silver." *"Bad Girls"/"Good Girls": Women, Sex, and Power in the Nineties,* edited by Nan Bauer Maglin and Donna Perry, 125–133. New Brunswick, N.J.: Rutgers University Press, 1996.

———. "What's Wrong with a Little Fantasy? Storytelling from the (Still) Ivory Tower." *American Indian Quarterly,* 27 (2003): 333–348.

"Deborah Miranda." Available online. URL: http://www.hanksville.org/storytellers/miranda/index.html. Accessed on February 9, 2004.

"Deborah Miranda." Native American Authors Project. Available online. URL: http://www.ipl.org/div/natam/bin/browse.pl/A523. Accessed on January 12, 2004.

Dubin, Margaret, ed. *The Dirt Is Red Here: Art and Poetry from Native California.* Berkeley, Calif.: Heyday, 2002.

Dunn, Carolyn, and Carol Comfort, eds. *Through the Eye of the Deer: An Anthology of Native American Women Writers.* San Francisco: Aunt Lute, 1999.

Deborah Weagel

missionaries

Since the earliest European settlements in the "New World" four centuries ago, Christian missionaries have had a complex, and often tragic, relationship with the original peoples of North America. It is thus unsurprising to find the figure of the missionary recurring throughout Native American literature. In fact, missionaries appear in the earliest writings of Native Americans, and they continue to inform some of the most recent writings of Native authors today.

While their professed goal was to spread the gospels throughout the Americas, missionaries of all denominations deemed it their Christian duty to educate, convert, and thereby "civilize" the tribal peoples of North America. Governed by a Christian theology and a Eurocentric value system, both of which included intolerant racial and paternalistic assumptions about Native peoples' inferiority, early missionaries believed that Native "savagery" could be vanquished by a dual approach of "civilization" (education) and conversion. Accordingly, it is the missionary who first formally schooled Native Americans, believing that literacy would enable them not only to read and accept the gospels as their only faith, but then to spread its Scriptures to other "heathens."

Indeed, the earliest Native American writers were those who had been educated and converted by missionaries, and who often became mission-aries themselves. These Native missionary authors produced salvationist literatures—autobiographies, sermons, and conversion narratives that recount their spiritual journeys from "paganism" to Christianity. Examples of these writers of the mid-1700s and early 1800s include WILLIAM APESS, George Copway, and SAMSON OCCOM. Yet Native missionary writers do not simply tell of their wholehearted ASSIMILATION into Christianity and their abandonment of all things Native. Instead, their texts are more often narratives of acculturation that reveal the authors' balance between two worlds as they embrace Christianity while affirming their Native identities. Moreover, they attest to the innate rationality, intelligence, and humanity of Native peoples, thus proving to European readers that Native Americans have always been capable of "higher" learning. And though these Native writers celebrate their "salvation," they also criticize missionaries at times, highlighting discrepancies between missionaries' words and actions. Occom, for instance, protests in his 1768 *Short Narrative* that missionaries exploited him to procure funds from charitable donors and underpaid him: "[they] have used me thus, because . . . 'I am a poor Indian'" (735).

Other mixed responses to missionaries continue throughout the 1800s and into the early 1900s by Native authors such as CHARLES EASTMAN, LUTHER STANDING BEAR, SARAH WINNEMUCCA, E. PAULINE JOHNSON, and ZITKALA-ŠA. In her 1883 autobiography, *Life among the Paiutes,* Winnemucca censures the missionaries' role in implementing Grant's Peace Policy. Eastman's *The Soul of the Indian* (1911) charges that "[t]he first missionaries, . . . imbued with the narrowness of their age, branded us as pagans and devil-worshipers, and demanded of us that we abjure our false gods," and then notes that they do not themselves abide by Christian tenets. These authors, like Occom, also testify to unfair treatment. As the historian Robert Berkhofer explains, "No matter how pious and exemplary the Indian Christian became, the white population still considered him [*sic*] a savage and an inferior" (123).

This strained relationship between missionaries and Native peoples continued into many Native American texts of the 20th century. In N. SCOTT

MOMADAY's Pulitzer Prize–winning novel *HOUSE MADE OF DAWN* (1968), Fray Nicolás's 1888 letter reveals his frustrations with Native parishioners who continue to practice "their dark custom[s]" (42): "After four centuries of Christianity, they still pray in Tanoan to the old deities" (52). And though the newer priest, Father Olguin, prays that he will "become a figure, an example . . . of industry and repose" (48), he goes about his mission with an impaired spiritual vision: "He closed his good eye; the other was . . . hard and opaque, like a lump of frozen marrow" (48). Thus, Momaday reveals the darker aspects of the missionaries' lives; the priests are, at times, paranoid, impatient, weak, lonely, overwhelmed, and even marked by sin: "It seemed as tho' I had done some evil—," confesses Fray Nicolás, and "I am by myself & tired" (43, 44).

Native authors also represent missionaries as sympathetic and helpful, functioning as intermediaries between the dominant culture and Native peoples. Hence, Momaday depicts Father Olguin aiding Abel at his trial, testifying that Abel acted according to his culture's beliefs. Likewise, D'ARCY MCNICKLE's *The Surrounded* (1936) portrays a devoted Father Grepilloux trying to help the Flathead adapt to the white world. Disillusioned with the mission's assimilation efforts (but not with Christianity), the older priest notes how the Flathead "have lost a way of life, and with it their pride, their dignity, their strength" (42). In LOUISE ERDRICH's *TRACKS* (1988) Father Damien tries to assist with the Anishinabe struggle for their lands; acting as an ally, he counsels the Jesuit-educated Nanapush to deal with the government. In fact, missionaries frequently functioned as government agents, mediators, and translators, particularly during TREATY negotiations, and they did sometimes side with Native tribes when the government's economic interests were not compatible with their interests in "saving souls."

Several other Native writers explore the missionary's impact on Native peoples, as well as the Native peoples' impact on the missionary. MAURICE KENNY's Pulitzer Prize–nominated *Blackrobe: Isaac Jogues* (1982) imagines the life of a 17th-century Jesuit priest among the Mohawk people from several perspectives. LINDA HOGAN's *MEAN SPIRIT* (1990) shows Father Dunne adopting Native practices in his own life. And while the band in SHERMAN ALEXIE's *RESERVATION BLUES* (1995) sings about the abuses of "the black robes . . . in the name of Jesus," Father Arnold—who first vows "to save them all" but falls in love instead—forms a partnership with the Native community through Big Mom: "You cover all the Christian stuff; I'll do the traditional Indian stuff. We'll make a great team" (80).

Recently the outpouring of testimonies concerning abusive conditions at BOARDING SCHOOLS (United States) and residential schools (Canada) have again reshaped our understanding of missionaries and their involvement with the forced Assimilation, conversion, education, and often mistreatment of Native Americans. Breaking the silence, Native authors are now writing about this aspect of Christian missions in all genres. As a character in Eden Robinson's novel *Monkey Beach* (1999) shouts: "[The missionaries] were after numbers! That's all they wanted! How many converts they could say they had" (109). TOMSON HIGHWAY's semiautobiographical novel *KISS OF THE FUR QUEEN* (1998) paints an equally harsh view of priests' treatment of Native students, while other texts, such as BASIL JOHNSTON's memoir *INDIAN SCHOOL DAYS* (1988), try to find value in the missionaries' education, despite the harsh conditions.

Given the extensive relationship to Native Americans, missionaries have thus long informed, and continue to inform, Native American literature in important ways, revealing the often uneasy coexistence of Native Americans and evangelicals as they struggle through the intricacies of cultural exchange.

Bibliography

Berkhofer, Robert F., Jr. *Salvation and the Savage: An Analysis of Protestant Missions and American Indian Response, 1787–1862.* Lexington: University of Kentucky Press, 1965.

Stevens, Laura M. *The Poor Indians: British Missionaries, Native Americans, and Colonial Sensibility.* Philadelphia: University of Pennsylvania Press, 2004.

Karen M. Clark

mixed-blood

The understanding of racial blending, among both Indian and white writers, has changed dramatically during the last two centuries. Formerly an object of scorn and suspicion in the American imagination, the mixed-blood has more recently become a central figure in Native American literature, embodying both the conflict and the reconciliation between traditional and modern ways of life.

Throughout the 18th and 19th centuries white writers, scientists, and legislators suggested that intermarriage between Indians and whites might serve as a form of biological ASSIMILATION, a peaceful alternative to war and removal, facilitating the transition from savagery to civilization. Some progressive thinkers viewed the mixed-blood as the personification of the new, vigorous, heterogeneous United States taking shape on the western frontier. More frequently, however, American culture regarded racial blending with suspicion. The "half-breed" seemed to embody the worst characteristics of both races, possessing both the cruelty of the Indian renegade and the greed of the white outlaw. Popular writing often reflects the mixed-blood's perceived moral degeneracy in grotesque physical form: a somber brow, a fanged sneer, or a hunched stature. In *The Oregon Trail* (1849) Francis Parkman famously describes the mixed-blood as "a race of rather extraordinary composition, being, according to the common saying, half Indian, half white man, and half devil" (362). Perhaps the most memorable example of this 19th-century image of the "half devil" appears in Mark Twain's *The Adventures of Tom Sawyer* (1876). In the novel the "murderin' half-breed," Injun Joe, robs graves, murders his accomplices, and plots revenge on Widow Douglas, whose late husband had him horsewhipped for vagrancy. Joe demonstrates his cruelty as he anticipates his revenge: "When you want to get revenge on a woman you don't kill her—bosh! You go for her looks. You slit her nostrils—you notch her ears like a sow! . . . I'll tie her to the bed. If she bleeds to death, is that my fault? I'll not cry, if she does" (254–255).

Nineteenth-century Indian writers, most of whom claimed mixed descent, were forced to react to these negative stereotypes. In his poem "The Stolen White Girl," for example, JOHN ROLLIN RIDGE recasts the half-breed outlaw as a romantic hero, whose white captive swoons in his grasp:

> The prairies are broad, and the woodlands
> are wide
> And proud on his steed the wild half-breed
> may ride,
> With the belt round his waist and the knife
> at his side,
> And no white man may claim his beautiful
> bride. (1–4)

For most early Indian writers, however, racial blending occasioned deeper self-scrutiny. In his autobiography, *A Son of the Forest* (1829), WILLIAM APESS first describes the conflict of identity that becomes a dominant theme in 20th-century Native American writing. He relates a childhood encounter with several Indian women while picking berries in the forest, when he becomes frightened and runs home to his white foster parents: "The many stories I had heard of their [Indians'] cruelty toward the whites—how they were in the habit of killing and scalping men, women, and children" (11). As an adult Apess realizes that he has been torn between two cultures, taught to fear his own people and to hate himself.

This sense of internal division and alienation predominates in 20th-century Native writing. MOURNING DOVE's *COGEWEA: The Half-Blood* (1927) portrays a plucky mixed-blood cowgirl who enters a segregated horse race, competing as both a "lady" and a "squaw." She wins both races but draws derision from both sides. A white rider protests, "Why is this *squaw* permitted to ride? This is a *ladies* race!" (63). Likewise, one of the Indian riders tells her, "You have no right to be here! You are half white! This race is for Indians and not for *breeds!*" (66). Mourning Dove generally laments the "maligned outcast half-blood" for whom "there seemed no welcome on the face of God's creation" (65).

JOHN JOSEPH MATHEWS's novel *SUNDOWN* (1934) dramatizes the conflict between the mixed-bloods who promote the commercial development of the oil-rich Osage reservation and the full-bloods who fight to maintain tribal control of the land. Mathews places little faith in assimilation but at the same time reveals the difficulty of returning to the old ways of life. On the reservation the young mixed-blood Chal Windzer, as Cogewea does, feels the rejection of traditional full-bloods, who jibe him for his effeminate looks and view him as a collaborator with greedy, dishonest whites. At college Chal feels equally awkward, joining a fraternity and the football team, but often fleeing to the open range beyond campus to chant traditional Osage songs. Chal's experiences generate his conflict—comforted by the brief reconnection with his tribal childhood but also ashamed of his inability to adjust to civilized life.

Contemporary Indian writers continue to represent the racial and cultural uncertainty embodied by the mixed-blood as a sometimes fatal severance from tradition. JAMES WELCH's *The DEATH OF JIM LONEY* (1979) portrays a mixed-blood who wanders the Blackfeet reservation in an alcoholic daze. Rhea, his white girlfriend, tells him, "Oh, you're so lucky to have two sets of ancestors. Just think, you can be Indian one day and white the next. Whichever suits you" (102). Loney reflects that he "had no family and he wasn't Indian or white.... [Rhea] had said he was lucky to have two sets of ancestors. In truth he had none" (102). SHERMAN ALEXIE expresses similar unease with the idea of simply choosing one's racial identity. In his novel *INDIAN KILLER* (1996) Alexie mocks "those pretend Indians" who "called themselves mixed-bloods and wrote books about the pain of living in both the Indian and white worlds" (232). Speaking for "real Indians" like Marie Polatkin, a college student and Indian activist in the novel, Alexie continues, "Those mixed-blood Indians never admitted their pale skin was a luxury. After all, Marie couldn't dress up like a white woman when she went on job interviews. But a mixed-blood writer could put on a buckskin jacket, a few turquoise rings, braid his hair, and he'd suddenly be an Indian" (232).

For many Native writers the erosion of tribal identity exacerbated by racial blending necessitates a reinforcement of ethnic identity. In *Sending My Heart Back across the Years* (1992) Hertha Dawn Wong reflects on her discovery of her own mixed ancestry and the uncertainty it provokes: "I felt that I could write only as dimly related to, but outside of, the indigenous communities of the United States. But over the years, I have met other displaced mixed-blood people, all of us wrestling with the various labels" (v). Like many mixed-blood characters in Native American fiction, Wong is uncertain of her place, her "label." Some of these characters, such as Abel in N. SCOTT MOMADAY's *HOUSE MADE OF DAWN* (1968) and Archilde Leon in D'ARCY MCNICKLE's *The SURROUNDED* (1936), find some solace in a return to tribal tradition, though their retreat sometimes reflects a tragic incapacity to cope with the realities of the modern world.

Other writers represent mixed descent not as a condition of irreconcilable conflict and disorientation but rather as an expanded consciousness, a means of containing, understanding, and reconciling conflicts of culture and identity. In *EARTHDIVERS* (1990) GERALD VIZENOR writes that "crossblood culture heroes" undermine racist stereotypes and "create a new consciousness of coexistence" (ix). LOUISE ERDRICH explores this hybrid consciousness in *The ANTELOPE WIFE* (1998), a novel that opens with a skirmish between a cavalry troop and a band of Ojibwe. After the raid a young soldier rescues a lost Indian child and raises her as his own in order to atone for the atrocities he has committed. More than a century later in present-day Minneapolis Cally Roy, a descendant of both the young soldier and the Indian families he had massacred, sees herself as a living reconciliation of racial conflict, a mender of what history has rendered, in Ojibwe, *daashkikaa,* or "cracked apart." She says, "Some bloods they go together like water—the French and Ojibwas: You mix those up and it is all one person. Like me" (110).

LESLIE MARMON SILKO's *CEREMONY* (1977) expresses a similar "consciousness of coexistence," portraying a mixed-blood army veteran, Tayo, who returns to the Pueblo reservation in sickness and confusion. His aunt makes him feel worse by reminding him that he is a bastard born to a woman who prostituted herself to white men and eventually killed herself with drink. Other men on the reservation deride Tayo, viewing his hazel eyes and pale skin as signs of collusion with the white dispossessors. A Mexican prostitute, however, advises him, "They are afraid, Tayo. They feel something happening, they can see something happening around them, and it scares them. . . . They think that if their children have the same color of skin, the same color of eyes, that nothing is changing. . . . They are fools. They blame us, the ones who look different. That way they don't have to think about what has happened inside themselves" (99–100). The mixed-blood medicine man Betonie, who has hazel eyes like Tayo's, also represents such change, using both traditional and modern talismans in his healing ceremonies. Betonie tells Tayo, "At one time, the ceremonies as they had been performed were enough for the way the world was then. But after the white people came, elements in the world began to shift; and it became necessary to create new ceremonies. I have made changes in the rituals. The people mistrust this greatly, but only this growth keeps the ceremonies strong" (126). As Betonie's ceremonies do, mixed-bloods in contemporary Native writing represent the future of a people who must live in a world that has changed and continues to change, a living reminder of the destruction of Native cultures but also of their survival and growth.

Bibliography

Alexie, Sherman. *Indian Killer.* New York: Warner Books, 1996.

Apess, William. *On Our Own Ground: The Complete Writings of William Apess, a Pequot,* edited by Barry O'Connell. Amherst: University of Massachusetts Press, 1992.

Brown, Harry J. *Injun Joe's Ghost: The Indian Mixed-Blood in American Writing.* Columbia: University of Missouri Press, 2004.

Erdrich, Louise. *The Antelope Wife.* New York: HarperCollins, 1998.

Mathews, John Joseph. *Sundown,* edited by Virginia H. Mathews. 1934. Reprint, Norman: University of Oklahoma Press, 1988.

McNickle, D'Arcy. *The Surrounded.* 1936. Reprint, Albuquerque: University of New Mexico Press, 1994.

Momaday, N. Scott. *House Made of Dawn.* 1968. Reprint, New York: Perennial Classics, 1999.

Mourning Dove. *Cogewea, the Half-Blood: A Depiction of the Great Montana Cattle Range,* edited by Lucullus Virgil McWhorter. 1927. Reprint, Lincoln: University of Nebraska Press, 1981.

Parkman, Francis, Jr. *The Oregon Trail,* edited by David Levin. 1849. Reprint, New York: Penguin, 1985.

Scheick, William J. *The Half-Blood: A Cultural Symbol in Nineteenth-Century American Fiction.* Lexington: University Press of Kentucky, 1979.

Silko, Leslie Marmon. *Ceremony.* New York: Penguin, 1977.

Twain, Mark. *The Adventures of Tom Sawyer.* 1876. Reprint, Mahwah, N.J.: Watermill, 1980.

Vizenor, Gerald. *Earthdivers: Tribal Narratives on Mixed Descent.* Minneapolis: University of Minnesota Press, 1981.

Welch, James. *The Death of Jim Loney.* 1979. Reprint, New York: Penguin, 1987.

Wong, Hertha Dawn. *Sending My Heart Back across the Years: Tradition and Innovation in Native American Autobiography.* New York: Oxford University Press, 1992.

Harry Brown

Mohawk Trail   Beth Brant (1985)

Mohawk Trail, BETH BRANT's first published book, gathers stories and poems most notable for addressing Native and lesbian themes simultaneously. This innovation has made Brant's work difficult to categorize and may have limited the critical attention it has received. Yet Brant's mandate remains to write with pride and compassion about characters who often inhabit the margins of both mainstream and Native societies.

Mohawk Trail consists of three parts: "Native Origin," "Detroit Songs," and "Long Stories." In the six independent pieces that constitute part one Brant lovingly (and sometimes humorously) pays tribute to her Mohawk heritage, the comic element being most pronounced in "Coyote Learns a New Trick." This tale features a cross-dressing female Coyote whose plans to seduce, shock, and disappoint a female Fox are foiled by Fox's greater wiliness and her unexpected willingness. Such bold interweaving of Native mythology and lesbian eroticism distinguishes Brant's work.

Generally more somber than the stories in part 1, the as-told-to testimonials in "Detroit Songs" concern labor and urban hardship. Using the speaker's name as a title for each monologue, Brant eloquently captures the rhythms and diction of speech, giving a vivid and authentic voice to each character, whether he or she works in a salt mine, a car factory, a women's bar, or a day care center. Part 2 concludes with "Her Name Is Helen," a poem that powerfully depicts the suffering of a "gay Indian girl" and imaginatively restores to her beauty, sensuality, and love.

Part 3 of *Mohawk Trail* contains a trio of longer stories that explore and draw parallels among oppressions based on gender, race, and sexuality. In the first story, "The Fifth Floor, 1967," the narrator's husband has committed her to a mental ward, where she uses autoeroticism to heal herself. This creative resistance to institutional authority typifies Brant's characters, as the two alternating narratives that make up "A Long Story" also reveal. In the first, set in 1890, government agents have seized the children from a Native community, leaving the adults to grieve, search, and rage. In the second, set in 1978, a lesbian mother has lost her daughter in a custody battle because of her sexual orientation. Brant's pairing of these stories parallels (and implicitly condemns) the two forms of injustice. The final story, "A Simple Act," similarly juxtaposes two narratives of loss: an adolescent lesbian couple must part when their families discover their love, and Mohawk family treasures disappear in a basement fire. In response to these losses Brant declares her faith in the regenerative capacity of language.

Equally inspired by the political fight for justice and the ethical imperative to love, Brant both indicts oppression and embraces beauty as she writes of trauma and resilience.

Bibliography

Brant, Beth. *Mohawk Trail.* Toronto: Women's Press and Ithaca, N.Y.: Firebrand Books, 1985.
———. *Writing as Witness: Essay and Talk.* Toronto: Women's Press, 1994.
Cullum, Linda. "Survival's Song: Beth Brant and the Power of the Word." *MELUS* 24, no. 3 (fall 1999): 129–141.

Jodi Lundgren

Momaday, N. Scott (1934–)

Novelist, poet, playwright, painter, and man of letters, N. Scott Momaday is the grand old man of Indian literature. Momaday's HOUSE MADE OF DAWN (1968) not only won the Pulitzer Prize in 1969, but ushered in the AMERICAN INDIAN LITERARY RENAISSANCE. Momaday's list of honors also includes the Academy of American Poets Prize in 1962 for "The Bear"; the Western Heritage Award in 1974 for *Colorado: Summer, Fall, Winter, Spring* (1973); the Premio Litterario Internazionale Mondelo, Italy's highest literary prize, in 1979; the Distinguished Service Award from the Western Literature Association in 1983; the Native American Literature Prize in 1989; and the Returning the Gift Lifetime Achievement Award in 1992. His paintings and drawings have been exhibited widely throughout the West.

Momaday was born on February 27, 1934, in the Kiowa and Comanche Indian Hospital in Lawton, Oklahoma. Born Navarro Scott Mammedatty, he is the son of Al Mammedatty and Natachee Scott. The family changed their surname to *Momaday* shortly after his birth. On his father's side the family is primarily Kiowa with traces of French-Canadian and Mexican ancestry, apparently reflecting descent from Kiowa captives. Momaday's mother's Indian heritage is limited to a Cherokee great-grandmother; however at an early age Natachee identified herself as Indian. Immediately after high school she enrolled in an Indian school, Haskell Institute, in Lawrence, Kansas, where she met Al Mammedatty. They married in 1933. After a brief period in Oklahoma they moved to the Southwest, where they eventually settled in New Mexico, at Jemez Pueblo, teaching in the local day school until their retirement.

In 1958 Momaday received a B.A. in political science from the University of New Mexico. He minored in English and speech, reflecting his love of literature and explaining in part his impressive oratorical abilities. After graduation he taught at the Dulce School on the Jicarilla Apache reservation. There he married Gaye Mangold, with whom he had three daughters, Cael, Jill, and Brit. The poet and critic Yvor Winters read Momaday's poetry and arranged a scholarship to Stanford University. Winters persuaded Momaday to stay on for his Ph.D., which he completed in 1963.

After graduation Momaday taught at the University of California (UC), Santa Barbara. He later moved to UC Berkeley, Stanford, and finally the University of Arizona, where he has been Regents Professor of the Humanities since 1981.

Momaday published *House Made of Dawn,* a novel set in Jemez, in 1968 and rapidly followed it with a memoir, *The Way to Rainy Mountain,* a lyrical description of his family and tribal history. *House Made of Dawn* is the novel of an Indian veteran, Abel, who returns to a fictionalized Jemez Pueblo (Momaday calls it *Walatowa,* the old Tanoan name for Jemez) after World War II. He has a very hard time adjusting to life in peacetime and is something of an outcast in his tribe since his father was illegitimate. When humiliated by a mysterious albino at a tribal ritual Abel murders his tormentor, and after serving eight years in jail, he takes part in a government relocation program and gets a job in Los Angeles. There his hard times continue, and after humiliation at the hands of a Kiowa peyote cult leader and a beating by a Chicano policeman, he heads back to Jemez. As the novel ends he is participating in a ritual race that his grandfather had won decades before.

Abel, as his name suggests, is the archetypal victim, but despite what many critics have suggested, Cain is not white society: it is Abel's brother Indians. Ironically the Kiowa peyote cult preacher, John Tosamah, who bothers Abel in LA, is a caricature of Momaday himself. They are both Kiowa, have the same physical characteristics, and when the preacher tells his life story, it is Momaday's story he tells: He recites a passage out of *The Way to Rainy Mountain.*

Although any synopsis of the book sounds dismal, actually the ending is hopeful. As Abel runs in the race for good hunting and harvests, he sings a Navajo creation song, "House Made of Dawn." He had learned in LA that his father was Navajo, and in singing a sacred Navajo song while taking part in a Walatowa ceremony, Abel is reestablishing a link to both his maternal and his paternal heritage.

The Way to Rainy Mountain, illustrated by Momaday's father, Al, is a memoir in the form of a literary collage, composed of essays, poems, myths, historical notes, and personal anecdotes. The theme is the rise and fall of the Kiowa tribe, which moved from the Rockies onto the Great Plains and developed, in Momaday's words, "the last culture to evolve in North America." Momaday intertwines memories of his family with Kiowa myth and history, telling of his grandmother, Aho, who was born when "the Kiowas were living the last great moment of their history."

In 1974 Momaday published his first book of poetry, *Angle of Geese.* In 1976 he published two more collections, *The Gourd Dancer* and *The Colors of Night.* In 1977 Momaday returned to autobiography, publishing *The Names,* a memoir of his childhood.

Momaday's poetry has two distinct styles: His earliest poems are written in the manner his mentor Yvor Winters called "post-symbolist"; later Momaday incorporated the rhythms of traditional Indian song in his verse. Postsymbolist verse incorporates very clear, sharp details, the symbolic meaning of which is clear to the reader, despite the fact that this meaning is not explicit in the text. A good example of this sort of verse is one of Momaday's best and best-known poems, "Angle of Geese."

The poem describes two events: the death of one of Momaday's friends' children, and the death of a goose that someone shot on a hunting trip. The first part of the poem deals with the difficulty of making an adequate verbal response to a shattering event. The second part employs the postsymbolic image; that is, it uses the description of an object, the goose, to make a metaphysical point. The dying goose, "huge" and "eternal," transcends the limits of time for eternity. To make his point Momaday strains the limits of language in using the trope of catachresis: The formation of geese is like the "angle of time / and eternity," (7–8) and the dying goose has moved to a state "wide of time" (9).

The second type of poetry incorporates the rhythms and repetitions of traditional Indian song. "Plainview: 2" is a good example. The refrain explores variations of a single phrase: "Remember my horse running / Remember my horse . . . / Remember my horse wheeling" (1–3).

During the 1970s Momaday became more involved in painting, when he was not writing, teaching, and lecturing. His first exhibition, held at the University of North Dakota Art Galleries in 1979, contained a series of paintings of Indian war shields. While on a lecture series in Germany he met Reina Heitzer, whom he married in 1978. They have a daughter, Lore.

Momaday published his second novel, *The Ancient Child*, in 1989. The highly autobiographical work depicts a Kiowa painter, Locke Setman, raised by a white father, who tries to come to grips with his Indian identity. *The Ancient Child*, as does Leslie Marmon Silko's novel *Ceremony*, combines the conventions of the modern novel with Indian myth, in Momaday's case the story of Tsaoi, the boy who changes into a bear and chases his sisters into a tree. The sisters become the stars of the Big Dipper; the tree, Devils Tower.

The use of mythology to add a symbolic dimension is nothing new, but Momaday's use is fundamentally different from that of James Joyce or Bernard Malamud, who are more well known for this technique. Momaday is writing about a different plane of reality. He has said that he feels as though he is the reincarnation of the bear, present in every generation. The name of the protagonist in *The Ancient Child*, Locke Setman, is derived from *Loki*, the Norse shape shifter, and *set*, the Kiowa word for "bear." At the climax of the novel, at the end of his quest to find out who he really is, Setman turns into a bear.

Momaday published a series of short stories *In the Presence of the Sun* (1992) to accompany his illustrations of war shields. He has also completed a series of paintings of shamanistic fetishes and an impressive series of watercolors on Billy the Kid. His latest work is *In the Bear's House* (1999), a collection of drawings, poems, and dialogues about Bear,

a figure who, as William Faulkner's does, embodies the spirit of the wilderness. Momaday currently lives with his wife Barbara Glenn Momaday, in Tucson.

Bibliography

Lincoln, Kenneth. *Native American Renaissance*. Berkeley: University of California Press, 1983.

Momaday, N. Scott. *The Ancient Child*. New York: HarperPerennial, 1990.

———. *Angle of Geese and Other Poems*. Boston: D. R. Godine, 1974.

———. *House Made of Dawn*. Tucson: University of Arizona Press, 1996.

———. *The Way to Rainy Mountain*. Tucson: University of Arizona Press, 1996.

Trimble, Martha Scott. *N. Scott Momaday*. Boise, Idaho: Boise State University Press, 1973.

Moose Meat and Wild Rice   Basil Johnston (1978)

Basil Johnston's collection of 23 fablelike tales, all of which are based on real people and real events and set on the Moose Meat Point Indian Reserve, in Ontario, Canada, relates the realities and ironies of reserve life with gentle humor. Originally published in Canada, the book was republished in the United States as *Ojibway Tales* (1993).

In one story the priest forgets about a wedding, and the couple waits all day, holding the reception anyway because the food is ready, and when the remorseful priest arrives, the groom extracts a promise from him to drive the couple to their honeymoon destination because they missed their bus. In another, in order to get their stories straight, a group of friends arrested for disturbing the peace and drunkenness take advantage of the unilingual police. The friends claim the right to have a Sunday worship service, and the guard naïvely believes that what he hears from the pulpit is prayer but really is instruction regarding interrogation. The stories have characters named Almighty, Mrs. Pine Cone, Big Flossie, and Low Down, people known by nicknames more often than not.

In these stories the Indian agent and the priest are integral to community life and often are pitted against the Native people. They are ready-made for a part in the conflict every engaging story needs and frequently are duped and frustrated. Johnston's preface to the stories is less gentle in its description of how conditions did not improve and the people did not "get ahead," in spite of "Better English, service in war, correct deportment, . . . social graces" (8). The stories focus on all of these matters, demonstrating fundamental differences and the unchanging nature of whites and aboriginals.

Johnston is especially concerned with the survival of languages, most particularly of Ojibwe. He understands that retention of the language is critical, and one story, "A Sign of the Times," explores the problems of language by dramatizing a meeting where locals provide abbreviated translations of long-winded speeches, ask for definitions of such words as *unilaterally* and *emasculated,* and confuse the pronouns *he* and *she.* Big Flossie complains to the visitors that "white peoples come 'ere tells us poor Indians what to do, ast us questions. An' when us Indians ast questions, youse neber answer" (175). By the time she finishes her questions, the community learns that the woman in charge of teaching family planning is unmarried and has no children, and the woman who teaches Cree and Ojibway cannot speak either language. In the end in spite of these and other revelations, the Moose Meat Point Ojibway have a banquet and feed their guests moose meat and wild rice. To some extent this book and its title are a metaphor for returning help for harm.

Bibliography

Johnston, Basil. *Moose Meat and Wild Rice.* Toronto: McClelland & Stewart, 1978.

Van Eck, Lani J. Review of *Ojibway Tales. American Indian Quarterly* 19, no. 4 (fall 1995): 593–594.

Whitson, Kathy J. Review of *Ojibway Tales. Studies in Short Fiction* 33, no. 1 (winter 1996): 138.

A. Mary Murphy

Morning Girl   Michael Dorris (1992)

Morning Girl, a young adult novel, tells the story of a Taino family on a Bahamian island in 1492. Through the alternating first-person narrative of Morning Girl and her younger brother, Star Boy,

their lives are presented in such a way as to show the complexity of their culture before the invasion of Columbus. As Jim Charles says, "Michael Dorris' young adult fiction does much to humanize American Indians and eradicate the deeply ingrained and popularly sanctioned mythic image of the American Indian" (6). Through this depiction a face and identity are given to the peoples who will eventually be incorrectly labeled as savage.

Morning Girl, named because she rises early and learns from the quiet of the dawn, lives with her brother, Star Boy, and her mother and father. Star Boy, named because he listens to the night and learns from it, battles with his sister in a friendly rivalry meant to provoke understanding and eventual maturity. Through the events of their daily lives we discover philosophical conversations between family members within a gently joking framework that teaches through a form of what we now refer to as the Socratic method, hardly the activities of savages.

The loss of a child not yet born teaches all the family to see the love they feel for each other. Star Boy learns through losing his father's canoe that he means more to his parents than mere possessions, even important ones. Morning Girl learns that though she cannot see herself, her image is not all that she is to others. Star Boy survives a hurricane and has a mystical experience with his departed grandfather. Morning Girl, and her entire family, stand behind Star Boy as he sheds his childhood name of *Hungry* and earns the name *The One Who Stands Beside* from him. All of these lessons prepare the reader for the final chapters, as Morning Girl goes swimming one day and sees a boat filled with strangers. She calls to the strangers and offers to befriend them. The final chapter is a letter from the captain of the vessel, Christopher Columbus, describing the gentleness and intelligence of the people and his plan to kidnap six of them as an offering to his king. The preceding chapters leave no doubt in the mind of the reader who the true savages are.

*Morning Girl'*s lessons of humanity and understanding have led to well-deserved awards. Winner of the 1993 Scott O'Dell Award for historical fiction, *Morning Girl* has also been a *Horn Book* Fan Fare book, a *Booklist* Editor's Choice, a *New York Times*

Notable Book of 1992, and an *American Bookseller* Pick of the Lists.

Bibliography

Charles, Jim. "The Young Adult Novels of Michael Dorris." *The Alan Review.* 25, no. 3 (January 16, 2005). Available online. URL: http://scholar.lib. vt.edu/ejournals/ALAN/spring98/charles.html. Accessed on August 15, 2005.

Chavkin, Allen, and Nancy Feyl Chavkin, eds. *Conversations with Louise Erdrich and Michael Dorris.* Jackson: University Press of Mississippi, 1994.

Dorris, Michael. *Morning Girl.* New York: Hyperion, 1992.

Slapin, Beverly, and Doris Seale, eds. *Through Indian Eyes: The Native Experience in Books for Children.* Berkeley, Calif.: Oyate, 2003.

Solomon Davidoff

Mourning Dove   (Christal, Christine Quintasket, Humishuma)   (1888–1936)

Mourning Dove was a Salishan writer, lecturer, and politician whose best-known work, Cogewea, the Half-Blood: *A Depiction of the Great Montana Cattle Ranch* (1927), is one of the earliest novels written by an American Indian woman. In her posthumously published memoir, *Mourning Dove: A Salishan Autobiography* (1990), Mourning Dove describes how she, the child of Joseph Quintasket (Okanogan) and Lucy Stukin (Colville), adopted the name *Morning Dove* initially in 1912 as she planned to write *Cogewea* and later changed the spelling to *Mourning Dove* in 1921 after seeing a bird with that name in a Spokane museum. With only three years of formal education and one business school course, Mourning Dove wrote while employed as an itinerant worker, typing late into the night after picking fruits and vegetables during the day.

In 1914 at a Frontier Days celebration in Walla Walla, Washington, Mourning Dove met Lucullus V. McWhorter, who became both her ardent supporter and her literary collaborator. Founder of the *American Archaeologist* and an activist dedicated to preserving Native culture and history,

McWhorter not only encouraged Mourning Dove to write but also edited, annotated, and rewrote her work and inserted his own. This partnership helps explain *Cogewea*'s uneven style, one that blends Native storytelling and western romance with lectures about injustice done to Native Americans, anthropological research, and 15 pages of scholarly annotations at the book's end. Published over 15 years after Mourning Dove completed her initial manuscript, *Cogewea* is the story of three sisters: Mary, a Native woman faithful to the tradition; Julia, who is assimilated into white culture; and Cogewea, the half-blood who seeks the middle path. After a troubled marriage to the despicable Densmore, Cogewea returns to Native customs with the help of Stemteema, who teaches Cogewea tribal traditions and the art of storytelling.

Mourning Dove's final work, *Coyote Stories* (1933), is a collection of folkloric tales she compiled while listening to elderly tribal members. For this work McWhorter introduced her to Heister Dean Guie, a journalist who helped her edit, encouraged her to sculpt the tales for a white audience, and created illustrations to accompany the published collection. An enlarged version of these stories called *Tales of the Okanogans* was published in 1976. This edition, compiled by Donald M. Hines, attempts to restore Mourning Dove's original manuscript before Guie's revisions.

See also Mourning Dove's Stories.

Bibliography

Mourning Dove. *Cogewea, the Half-Blood: A Depiction of the Great Montana Cattle Range.* 1927. Reprint, Lincoln: University of Nebraska Press, 1991.

———. *Coyote Stories,* edited and illustrated by Heister Dean Guie. 1933. Reprint, Lincoln: University of Nebraska Press, 1981.

———. *Mourning Dove—a Salishan Autobiography,* edited by Jay Miller. Lincoln: University of Nebraska Press, 1990.

———. *Tales of the Okanogans,* edited by Donald M. Hines. Fairfield, Wash.: Ye Galleon Press, 1976.

Blake G. Hobby

Mourning Dove's Stories   Mourning Dove (1991)

Issues of authority and identity have always played major roles in MOURNING DOVE's/Humishuma's work. Perhaps the most critically celebrated area involves her novel *Cogewea, the Half-Blood* (1927). *Cogewea* is celebrated as the first novel by a Native American woman author, but this accolade is always qualified because this novel is not exclusively the product of its author, as are, for example, LESLIE MARMON SILKO's novels. Instead, much of her original novel was edited and rewritten by Lucullus V. McWhorter. Similar editing and revision by McWhorter and Dean Guie occurred with her next major work, *Coyote Stories* (1933). The extent of such revision and editing illustrates the dramatic difference between these earlier periods of Native American literature and those more recent times in which authors such as Silko, LOUISE ERDRICH, and SHERMAN ALEXIE command complete autonomy and a great deal of respect.

Despite the overwhelming obstacles that Mourning Dove faced as an author, she persevered with her recording of traditional tales until her death. When not working all day in apple orchards or performing other sorts of hard labor, Mourning Dove actively sought out and collected oral stories from storytellers among the northern Washington and southern British Columbian tribes. Her adult ambition to preserve such stories and communicate them with nontribal peoples was a natural outgrowth of her childhood. Then she had seen how highly valued stories and storytellers were and had come to love those traditions. However, prejudice during her lifetime prevented her from voicing her own and her people's stories.

To correct this injustice, the editors of the volume, Clifford E. Trafer and Richard D. Scheuerman, have allowed her to speak through her collected traditional stories in a way that she had not previously had. They sought to preserve as much as possible of her original manuscripts. The result is a minimally edited collection of her stories. There we glimpse the complexities and vitality of traditional storytelling. For example, we witness the TRICKSTER FIGURE Coyote in his full range of identity from traditional agent of mischief (as in "Coyote the Medicine Man," 54–57, and "Coyote and Fox," 69–73) to his role as father (in "Wooing Grizzly Bear," 82–91). We learn traditional explanations for the distribution of salmon through "Coyote Brings the Salmon" (104–111) as well as the origins of disease in "How Disease Came to the People" (51–53) and of ants ("The Ant," 15–17). We hear traditional stories like "The Legend of Omak Lake" (18–20), which recounts the consequences of the love triangle popular among many Plains and coastal tribes. We also hear tales that are more unique, though no less traditional, to northern tribes, such as "Lynx and Wife" (29–34) and "Lynx the Hunter" (35–43), which celebrate a supernatural protagonist. Because Trafzer and Scheuerman did not edit these tales to reflect nontraditional values, we can also see the ways in which qualities such as sexuality and violence functioned within traditional contexts. By leaving such aspects in these tales, the editors preserve characteristics central to these tribal people's identities. Moreover, they honor Mourning Dove's love for these stories.

Bibliography

Mourning Dove. *Mourning Dove's Stories,* edited by Clifford E. Trafzer and Richard D. Scheuerman. San Diego: San Diego University Press, 1991.

Clay Smith

My People, the Sioux   Luther Standing Bear (1928)

LUTHER STANDING BEAR's account of his childhood, adolescence, and life as a young man offers an invaluable resource for readers to appreciate the richness of Sioux life prior to reservations, the difficult transition toward ASSIMILATION, the experiences of students in BOARDING SCHOOLS, and the tense return to Indian life. *My People, the Sioux,* perhaps more than any other early Indian text, vividly portrays the changes that took place in the traditional ways of life as the U.S. government encroached deeper and deeper into the lives and the territories of American Indians.

Standing Bear, who was known as Ota Kte (*Plenty Kill* in English), narrates his early childhood and adolescence in great detail. He describes the way they lived, making frequent comparisons to white, or European customs. In describing the family tipi, for instance, he compares the structure and its accessories to the kinds of structures and furniture that would be found in white homes. He does not make judgments, favorable or unfavorable, but his comparisons serve as an excellent point of reference for non-Indian readers of his time, as well as for all contemporary readers. This section of the text, as well as the section in which he discusses the games played by Indian youth, are quite detailed and accompanied by Standing Bear's illustrations.

In chapter 5, Standing Bear describes his first buffalo kill, an important rite of passage. In addition to this scene's being quite effective in an autobiographical sense, because it illuminates his relationship with his father and his desire to please him, it is also important in that it gives the reader a vivid picture of what the killing of a buffalo must have been like. One of the elements that make this text so important is its meticulous recording of detail. Unfortunately this abundance also prevents the text from being truly sophisticated, but when he details the killing, skinning, butchering, and preserving of the magnificent creature around which much of Plains Indian culture was structured, this information is invaluable.

Shortly after Standing Bear's first buffalo kill, the buffalo begin to die out, contributing to the erosion of the traditional Sioux way of life. Young Plenty Kill offers to leave his home to be a member of the first class of the Carlisle Indian Industrial School in Carlisle, Pennsylvania. This school, the first and most infamous of the Indian boarding schools, was established to "educate" and "civilize" Indians, in other words, to make them into whites.

As CHARLES EASTMAN, did, Plenty Kill viewed his entering the white world as a demonstration of his bravery. He says, "My idea was that I was leaving the reservation and going to stay away long enough to do some brave deed, and then come home again alive" (128). Once at the school he has difficulty adjusting to the white ways, but as ZITKALA-ŠA does, not only does he learn, he excels. He takes the name *Luther* (his father's name was Standing Bear) and is chosen to represent the school by being given a job at a department store in Philadelphia. As it is for many others, his return to the reservation is somewhat difficult, but he gets a job teaching on the reservation, making him one of the lucky few who adjusted well to life after the boarding school experience.

My People, the Sioux was published when Standing Bear was 50 years old and considering that he is writing about his boyhood, understandably contains a few factual errors most likely caused by faulty memories. For instance, it is unlikely that his father played as important a role in the life of the Sioux tribe as Standing Bear claims he did. He also calls himself Oglala, whereas it is much more likely that he was of the Brulé clan. Despite these problems, this is an extremely valuable text for understanding this period in Indian history from the perspective of someone who lived it.

Bibliography

Hale, Frederick. "Acceptance and Rejection of Assimilation in the Works of Luther Standing Bear." *Studies in American Indian Literatures: The Journal of the Association for the Study of American Indian Literatures* 5, no. 4 (winter 1993): 25–41.

Jennifer McClinton-Temple

Nanook of the North (1922)

Nanook of the North: A Story of Life and Love in the Actual Arctic was the first film of the American documentary pioneer Robert Flaherty (1884–1951). Appearing as it did less than a decade after the overtly racist silent film milestone *Birth of a Nation* (D. W. Griffith, 1915), Flaherty's film, funded by the French fur company Revillon Frères and distributed by Pathé, presented a stark contrast: a humanistic, poignant, dramatic, starkly beautiful, and sympathetic look at an Inuit hunter's struggle to survive in an inhospitable environment. *Nanook* was made for $50,000 and was a box-office success.

Flaherty knew a great deal about his subject from long service in the Far North as a business-man and engineer, but *Nanook,* as are many of the great documentaries, was anything but an exact record. Nanook's family in the film, for example, is a fictional construct. The dramatic capture of a seal, killed by Nanook through a breathing hole in the ice, was, in fact, staged for the camera. The suspenseful ending, in which Nanook struggles to find lifesaving shelter, was completely staged. (In reality, Nanook would indeed die of starvation two years after the film's completion.) A natural storyteller but a not-so-authentic anthropologist, Flaherty was determined to craft his tale of a noble savage even if he had to lie to tell the truth as he perceived it.

Nanook nevertheless captures, with admiration and without condescension, a multitude of valid and engaging ethnographic moments in the lives of his subjects: Nanook's "son," suffering from a stomachache, actually enjoying the taste of castor oil; Nanook's rapid construction of an igloo, complete with an ice window, before our very eyes (though one wall of the bigger-than-life-size enclosure was left unfinished to allow for proper lighting and camera access); the collective vanquishing of a two-ton walrus; the "family" settling down for a night's sleep, wrapped in furs. *Nanook* is full of faces: the rich countenance of Nanook himself, the extraordinary muzzles of his team of huskies, the face of nature itself.

The Library of Congress has designated *Nanook* a "culturally significant" work worthy of preservation in the National Film Registry.

Bibliography

Barsam, Richard Meran. *The Vision of Robert Flaherty: The Artist as Myth and Filmmaker.* Bloomington: Indiana University Press, 1988.

Flaherty, Robert J. "How I Filmed *Nanook of the North:* Adventures with the Eskimos to Get Pictures of Their Home Life and Their Battles with Nature to Get Food: The Walrus Fight." Available online. URL: http://www.cinemaweb.com/silent-film/bookshelf/23_rf1_2.htm. Accessed on August 15, 2005.

David Lavery

Native Alaskan tribal literature

A substantial portion of the literature written by Native Alaskans reflects the mythologies, oral traditions, histories, and folkways of often bitter survival conditions in this arctic region. The coastal and inland areas of Alaska have been home to the Inuit, Tlingit, Kwakiutl, Klamath, and Yurok. Given the tribes' dependence on the region's natural resources, the most popular characters found in the folktales of the Native Alaskan peoples are killer whale (or Keet), raven (Yethl), crane, otter, salmon, seal, sea lion, caribou, and grizzly bear. These animals were a very visible part of the ecological environment upon which these tribes depended and therefore were accorded privileged status.

Perhaps more than many other Native American folk legacies, many of the tales and mythologies of Alaskan tribal peoples have been lost to the decimation of these tribes through disease, the breakdown of tribal systems, and modernization. Almost equally disturbingly, other stories were "preserved" with questionable authenticity by non-Native scholars, such as the *Tsimshian Texts,* a collection of 13 Tsimshian stories "collected" by Franz Boas in the Nass River dialect in late 1894 (published by the Bureau of American Ethnology in 1902). In the early 1970s attempts to record Native stories by more respectful and reputable means began in earnest. Native ethnographers such as William A. Oquilluk, who collected legends of the northern Native people in 1973; James K. Wells, who collected tales of the Ipani Inuit in 1974; and Emma and Frank Williams, who worked with the Tongass in 1978, began to record the tales and mythologies.

Recently numerous books, research papers, articles, and essays written about Alaska Natives have given way to a growing body of works by Native Alaskan people themselves. These works challenge the stereotypes about traditional life and honor the knowledge and skills of the region's tribal peoples. New works concerning the region and its peoples detail historically significant struggles for the survival of indigenous folkways. Many authors have written of the "Great Disasters," the name given the decimation of tribal populations by concurrent flu and tuberculosis epidemics of the 19th and 20th centuries. New writers, such as Herb and Andy Hope, have begun to renew interest in the region's unique heritage. Herb Hope's work on the Battle of 1804 between the Russians and Kik.sádi details the survival march of the Kiks.ádi from Indian River to Point Craven. Andy Hope's poetry offers a lyrical sense of what it is to be of Native Alaskan ancestry in today's Alaskan territory.

Bibliography

Andrews, Susan B., and John Creed, eds. *Authentic Alaska: Voices of Its Native Writers.* Lincoln: University of Nebraska Press, 1998.

Association on American Indian Affairs. *American Indian and Eskimo Authors: A Comprehensive Bibliography,* edited by Arlene Hirschfield. New York: Interbook, 1900.

Bruchac, Joseph, ed. *Raven Tells Stories: An Anthology of Alaskan Native Writing.* Greenfield, N.Y.: Greenfield Review Press, 1991.

Spatz, Ronald, and James Jacob Liszka, eds. *Alaska Native Writers, Storytellers and Orators.* Anchorage: University of Alaska, 1986.

Michelle LaFrance

Native American Literature: A Brief Introduction and Anthology Gerald Vizenor (1995)

This anthology, which includes works by William Apess, Luther Standing Bear, Wendy Rose, Mary TallMountain, Jim Barnes, and Hanay Geiogamah, among other, more frequently anthologized authors, is part of the HarperCollins Literary Mosaic Series, a series of volumes anthologizing ethnic American literature. In addition to a few idiosyncratic selections, such as Gerald Vizenor's own play *Ishi and the Wood Ducks,* the element that makes this text stand out among others is the brilliant introduction by Vizenor himself. It is rare in anthologies of this nature, which so often are used as classroom texts, to have such a detailed examination of the subject by such a well-respected and honored practitioner of the art.

In this introduction Vizenor explains that Native American literature cannot be reduced to one, homogeneous item. It is complex and complicated, has various sources, and spans a long period. Understanding those facts at the outset is an important key to studying the literature.

Vizenor then launches into a history lesson, from contact to the present day, explaining how historical events influence writers and the texts they produce. Along the way he makes comparisons between Native American texts of importance and corresponding texts by white authors. For instance, he compares D'ARCY McNICKLE's *The Surrounded* (1936), which tells the story of Archilde Leon, displaced by the "burden of his identities," and the depression, with F. Scott Fitzgerald's *Tender Is the Night* (1934). Few white people, even today, have heard of McNickle or his novel, while Fitzgerald and all his novels are widely read and studied. However, Vizenor points out, to believe the period in which both are set was merely hedonistic and full of "tragic dissolution," as Fitzgerald's work would suggest, is to ignore an important counterbalance. Comparisons such as this are crucial because they create bridges across texts and because they are rarely made in print. From a writer of Vizenor's fame and caliber, they make the "Brief Introduction" portion of this anthology invaluable.

Jennifer McClinton-Temple

Native "chic"

A trend whereby real and imagined American Indian identities are appropriated, promoted, or idealized by non-Indians, "going Indian" offered artists, activists, and those involved in countercultures a means through which to challenge American ideologies, especially consumerism and conformity, as well as the ecological and spiritual crisis that characterized the 1950s and 1960s. During the 1960s and 1970s many people went "ethnic," claiming a tribal identity, an Indian heritage, or aligning themselves with Indian activism. For instance, "A Gathering of Tribes" drew together non-Indian "longhairs," including countercultural icons such as Timothy Leary, Jerry Rubin, and Allen Ginsberg, for an artistic POW wow in the Golden Gate Park in San Francisco in early 1967.

Paralleling the African-American and Chicano rights movements, ethnicity became a hip signifier providing non-Natives with an opportunity to express individuality and subversive politics.

The artistic appropriation and representation of Indians have been well documented throughout the history of American and British letters. In the 18th century J. Hector St. John Crevecoeur used Indians to confront the emerging question of "What, then is the American, this new man?" In the 19th century Henry William Wadsworth Longfellow, James Fenimore Cooper, Walt Whitman, and others variously developed what Philip J. Deloria calls a form of "symbolic Indianness" (159) that utilizes Native American characters as a lens through which to understand mainstream culture better. In the 20th century Ken Kesey's *One Flew Over the Cuckoo's Nest* featured an Indian narrator, the author admitted, to allow him to articulate the paranoia and repression felt by many in America under the technological and authoritarian forces of the early 1960s.

Many non-Native radical activists in the 1960s also transformed themselves into Indians for political causes, living in communes, donning headbands, and promoting earth-based lifestyles. The "Indians of All Tribes" movement occupied Alcatraz in 1969 and consisted of many non-Natives from San Francisco's counterculture. The AMERICAN INDIAN MOVEMENT (AIM) similarly consisted of Indians and non-Indians alike; AIM occupied WOUNDED KNEE in 1973, drawing mainstream attention to Indian activism, aligning it with other civil rights movements.

A variety of celebrities claimed Indian ancestry during this period, including Burt Reynolds and Johnny Cash, while others, such as Jonathan Winters, Jane Fonda, and Sammy Davis, Jr., donated money to various Indian activist groups. Most famously, on March 27, 1973, Marlon Brando rejected an Oscar awarded him for his role in *The Godfather*. In his place Sasheen Little Feather was sent to read a 15-page statement describing the effects of colonization on indigenous peoples, the media's continued stereotypical representation of Indians, and the current struggle at Wounded Knee. In her comments Sasheen Little Feather also identified how non-Indian involvement in Native American activism had become so popular that she described Brando as "a friend of the American Indian long before it was fashionable to pile on the turquoise and the feathers" (DeLoria 163).

By the 1980s and 1990s larger social and political goals had been replaced by New Age spirituality and the rise of self-help philosophies only loosely connected to Indian beliefs. Popular books among non-Indian readers continue to include John Neihardt's BLACK ELK SPEAKS; John Fire Lame Deer's *Lame Deer, Seeker of Visions;* and HYEMEYOHSTS STORM's *Seven Arrows.* Responding to a call for multiculturalism in the 1980s and 1990s, television shows like *Northern Exposure; Dr. Quinn, Medicine Woman;* and *Walker, Texas Ranger* often featured Indian or MIXED-BLOOD characters within their predominately white casts.

Bibliography

Deloria, Philip J. *Playing Indian.* New Haven, Conn.: Yale University Press, 1998.

Brian Gempp

Neekna and Chemai Jeannette C. Armstrong (1984)

This book, a shorter and slightly different version of its predecessor, ENWHISTEETKWA—WALK IN WATER, was published in the Kou-Skelowh/We Are the People series and won the Canadian Children's Book Centre "Our Choice" Award. It is divided into four chapters, each corresponding to one of the four seasons, starting with winter, which is the beginning of the year and "preparation time" for spring, summer, and fall—when people go gathering berries, hunting, and collecting what is necessary for life.

Neekna, the narrator, and her best friend, Chemai, are two little Okanagan girls who live happily, playing; listening to stories and songs by Tupa, their great-grandmother; and taking part in everyday activities. They have a "play-tipi" that they share with other girls; their education is gained through imitation of their mothers and the traditional stories they love to be told, some of which are embedded in the main story. In this manner they are taught to beware of the North Wind, who chastises "disrespectful" behavior, such as not wearing the proper clothes to go out in the cold, and to honor the Great One, "Chief Bitterroot," "Chief Salmon," and Rock Woman. Ways of speaking, customs, dances, objects, foods, meals, underground lodges, summer tipis, in short, all elements of the tribe's life, are carefully explained and made understandable thanks to the young narrator's reactions and explanations.

The girls weave mats and baskets, dig bitterroot, and pick berries, sharing in the work to become competent women. Boys' tasks and girls' tasks are clearly defined as different: Young boys track rabbits, make snares; older boys make spears and arrow tips; all of them take meat and fish to the family. Such ways are accepted as balanced and self-evident. There is no revolt in this enchanted context, simply the wish to go on forever. In Tupa's words, "So it has been for all time, since we were formed as people of this land. . . . Everything will die and diseases eat up all living things if we do not live according to the plan of the Great Spirit. You must remember that always. You must carry these things I tell you to your great-grandchildren."

The emphasis is on the beauty and generosity of nature, on the pleasure of seeing each season go by with its particular harshness but also its rewards. There are explanations for every aspect of life. Also, the link between the visible and the invisible worlds is made explicit. Throughout the story a network of dependencies on plants and animals is stressed so as to make the fictitious children and the readers aware that to maintain universal balance they must express gratefulness to nature and various spirits. In this educational yet lively story, life is hard work, but very exciting.

Bibliography

Armstrong, Jeannette C. *Enwhisteetkwa—Walk in Water.* Penticton, Canada: Okanagan Indian Curriculum Project, 1982.

Simone Pellerin

Neon Powwow: New Native American Voices of the Southwest   Anna Lee Walters (1993)

The significance of this anthology lies primarily in its attempt to represent Native writers of the Southwest portion of the United States as a coherent whole, without overlooking the differences that make these individuals and their tribes unique. ANNA LEE WALTERS presents *Neon Powwow* as related to the prophecies common to a number of tribal people in the Southwest, which offer a way to resist oppression in today's world: Whatever the changes in lifestyles and despite any odds, survival of Native people is possible through "honoring age-old tribal values and teachings," especially through storytelling. In her own words, "[t]his modern collection of work very much reflects this old and new tribal consciousness" (1).

The collection includes a wide variety of poems, short fiction, autobiographical pieces, variations on traditional stories, and experimental pieces, such as Lorenzo Baca's "Ten Rounds" (10 visual poems) and Melissa A. Pope's "The Coffee Maker," which plays with blanks on the page and avoids punctuation throughout.

The 34 texts are by Native authors who either were originally from the Southwest or lived there for some time. Among the 23 writers in all, 10 are Navajo or of Navajo descent. Their poems and stories often include Navajo words. Some writers contribute only one piece, while many contribute two or even four pieces (Irvin Morris); half of them have never been published; and a few present here their first written text, as Rachael Arviso does her striking "The Crows." Many of these writers are also visual artists, photographers, actors, teachers, or dancers.

As in the title story, "Neon Powwow" by Dan L. Crank, ALCOHOLISM is an overwhelming theme in the collection: Descriptions of drunkards and the denunciation of the total dehumanization entailed by alcohol on Saturday night bouts in Gallup, New Mexico, which serves as the epitome of the border town, are powerfully predominant here. Also recurrent are the themes and forms of traditional beliefs and views on life, which are portrayed as helpful, even healing, for Native people in today's incoherent world—a world vividly described by Carlson Vicenti in "Hitching" and "Oh, Saint Michael." Recollections of historical facts also make up a number of narratological elements, as in Irvin Morris's "The Hyatt, the Maori and the Yanoama," when the narrator's grandmother tells him what she remembers her own grandmother told her about the Long March. An alternative logic from the Euro-American one is the backbone of some of the texts, most convincingly in Patroclus Eugene Savino's "A World before the Bilagàana." Equally interesting are Esther G. Belin's poem "Blues-ing on the Brown Vibe," about relocation, and Karen and Wally Strong's play *The Turkey Tender,* a revision of the Cinderella tale. Lorenzo Baca's "San Lorenzo Day in Laguna" pleasantly makes fun of tourists caught in the traditional "throwing away" of "Grab Day" in the pueblo.

Of course, HUMOR runs right through many texts, and if Vee Browne's pieces are odes to the Southwest, she nevertheless keeps an ironical distance: As her coyote character puts it in "Southwest Navajo Moonlight." "This is the most beautiful Coyote's den on the whole Mother Earth. The Butte Gods reign over our desert site. The clouds are only for picture taking—never giving enough rain, except when the Pueblo people request it" (117).

See also SOUTHWESTERN TRIBAL LITERATURE.

Bibliography

Beck, Peggy V., Anna Lee Walters, and Nia Francisco, eds. *The Sacred: Ways of Knowledge, Sources of Life.* Flagstaff: Northland, 1992.

Simone Pellerin

New Voices from the Longhouse: An Anthology of Contemporary Iroquois Poetry   Joseph Bruchac (1989)

As its title indicates, *New Voices from the Longhouse* presents the works of contemporary Iroquois poets. In doing so, it also presents the widely divergent range of styles and subjects produced by these poets. This diversity defies those arguments that would have all members of a tribal community speak with a single or similar voice. Instead, it represents the Iroquois community as composed of sometimes radically different voices—each as unique as its owner. Moreover, this anthology enacts the same sorts of democracy that have distinguished the Iroquois Nation for centuries. As such, *New Voices from the Longhouse* articulates essential aspects of Iroquois culture and tradition.

These elements are immediately visible on each page of the anthology. There one may find works by members from all the tribes constituting the Iroquois Nation: Cayuga (Germaine General-Myke), Mohawk (PETER BLUE CLOUD and BETH BRANT), Onondaga (Audrey Shenandoah and Gail Tremblay), Oneida (Melanie M. Ellis and ROBERT HILL WHITEMAN), Seneca (Dwayne Lesley Bowen and Tom Huff), and Tuscarora (Richard Hill and Ted C. Williams). This anthology further underscores the individuality of its poets by including a verbal and visual image of each before her or his works. In keeping with the traditional Iroquois values of democracy, these images range from autobiographical and hand-drawn self-representations to formal biographies and photographs. Again these images defy categories that would reduce identity to a single standard.

This diversity of identity is equally matched by a diversity in poetic form and content. Poems range from celebrations and explorations of traditional values and views (like those of Ray Fadden's rearticulation of wampum traditions and Carol Snow's invocation of natural imagery) to postmodern experiments (like Blue Cloud's "A Gentle Earthquake" [19–24] and Rokwaho's "Passenger Pigeon Poem" [268]). This anthology also includes wide-ranging examples of prose by its poets, such as David McDonald's "Life on the Farm" (210–214), John Mohawk's "Origins of Iroquois Political Thought" (218–228), and Williams's "The Trailers" (284–292). As these examples show, this anthology defies convention for the sake of individuality.

In addition to its emphasis on individual expression, this anthology represents a time of transition for Iroquois and Native American poetry. Not only does it chronicle those poets who had already achieved a high degree of national and international acclaim (such as MAURICE KENNY and RO-BERTA HILL WHITEMAN), but it also includes poets who were at the beginning of their wider fame as poets (such as David Back and Pam Colorado). In collecting these poets JOSEPH BRUCHAC again provided a venue for poets who otherwise would not be accessible to the general public. In addition, Bruchac enhanced the reputation of Greenfield Press Review as one of the preeminent publishers of Native American literature. Finally, through this anthology he furthered the renewed interest in Native American literature that he had helped generate in 1983 with his poetry anthology *SONGS FROM THIS EARTH ON TURTLE'S BACK*. As these qualities indicate, *New Voices from the Longhouse* embodies essential aspects specific to Iroquois identity and in general to Native American identity.

Bibliography

Bruchac, Joseph, ed. *New Voices from the Longhouse: An Anthology of Contemporary Iroquois Poetry.* Greenfield Center, N.Y.: Greenfield Review Press, 1989.

———, ed. *Songs from This Earth on Turtle's Back: Contemporary American Indian Poetry.* Greenfield Center, N.Y.: Greenfield Review Press, 1983.

Clay Smith

Niatum, Duane (1938–)

The Klallam poet and editor Duane Niatum was born to Dorothy Patsy in Seattle, Washington, on February 13, 1938. His father, an Italian-American merchant seaman, was not a presence in his son's life, and the name with which he grew into adulthood was that of his stepfather, Howard McGinnis, whom his mother married when Niatum was young. After a difficult adolescence, involving some time in reform school, he enlisted in the navy. His troubles did not end then, however, and he subsequently spent a month in a navy brig. Upon his discharge from the navy in 1959, he married and had a child, Marc. Staying in and around the Seattle area for the next few years, he ultimately enrolled in the University of Washington, from which he earned a B.A. in English in 1970. His first book of poetry, *After the Death of an Elder Klallam,* was published that same year under the name *Duane McGinnis.* Shortly afterward, his great-aunt, Anna Patsy Duncan, "gave" him the name of his great-great-grandfather, *Niatum.* The poet has stated that he believes this name, which he made legal, may have been what ultimately changed the character of his life.

After receiving an M.A. in creative writing from Johns Hopkins University in 1972, Niatum went on to teach high school in the Seattle area for a few years. He has also had short teaching appointments at, among other places, Evergreen State College in Olympia, Washington; the University of Washington; and Northwest Indian College. He is the winner of the 1982 American Book Award from the Before Columbus Foundation for his 1981 book *Songs from the Harvester of Dreams.* Niatum also holds a Ph.D. in American studies from the University of Michigan.

In his poems, Niatum's difficulty accepting his status as a MIXED-BLOOD is evident. As do many mixed-blood authors, he frequently navigates between the urban world and the traditional world, but he does so in a way that rejects easy sentimentality. For instance, in his poem "Chief Leschi of the Nisqually" he writes of a historical figure quite important to the Indians of the Pacific Northwest. Chief Leschi was a leader of the Nisqually tribe hanged for murder by the U.S. government in 1858. However, since the killing occurred during wartime and the man was armed, such an act does not constitute murder under U.S. law. Niatum refuses to sentimentalize this miscarriage of justice, saying, "He burned in the forest like a red cedar / his branches flaming blue flames toward / the white men" (5–7). He also says that the white men "laugh at his fate, frozen as a bat / against his throat" (14–15). Instead of valorizing the hero, Niatum insists on calling attention to the bad, unjust way in which this good man, helpless to save his physical self, died.

In other poems Niatum keeps up his honest, clear-eyed portrayal of the life of a modern mixed-blood. In "Digging Out the Roots" the roots are of his own life, not the lives of all Indians or even of all the members of his tribe. The poem resists universalization and is instead quite particular to

Niatum's own life. He does not ignore tradition, however, noting that when he joined the navy as a young man, he "chained most of the voices of fear to coyote" (20–21).

Although quite well known as a poet, Niatum has made one of his most valuable contributions to the field of literature as an editor. He has been the editor of Harper and Row's Native American Authors Program, which has published works by such important writers as N. SCOTT MOMADAY, RAY A. YOUNG BEAR, JAMES WELCH, and SIMON ORTIZ.

Bibliography
Bruchac, Joseph. "Closing the Circle: An Interview with Duane Niatum." In *Survival This Way: Interviews with American Indian Poets.* Tucson: University of Arizona Press, 1987.

Jennifer McClinton-Temple

Nickel Eclipse: Iroquois Moon   Eric Gansworth (2000)

Nickel Eclipse: Iroquois Moon, Eric Gansworth's second published volume, suggests his origins as a visual artist, for the work is not just a collection of poetry but of narrative paintings as well. As Gansworth himself notes in his statement at the beginning of the work, *Nickel Eclipse* utilizes two contrasting metaphors: the *Haudenosaunee* or Iroquois cycle of moons and the buffalo nickel, with a Native American profile on one side and the image of a buffalo on its reverse.

Both the poems and paintings of *Nickel Eclipse* are highly imagistic and frequently depend upon symbols and metaphors, as the volume's title indicates. The title poem, "Nickel Eclipse," announces the book's central theme—the gradual effacing of Native Americans, in both history and current perception, and an eventual reclamation of Native American identity. At the end of the poem Gansworth emphasizes the Native American side of the buffalo nickel, seeing that image emerge "from the buffalo's shadow, while we flip / coins relentlessly into the night, watching and waiting / for the tides to shift again under his influence"

(3). As this poem indicates, in the rest of the volume Gansworth is not interested in modern reactions to or evaluations of Native Americans, but, instead, the realities of modern Native American life and culture. "Nickel Eclipse" prefaces the rest of the book's poems and paintings, for it does not belong to any section or "moon" of the volume, but instead acts as an introductory poem to both narrative forms—poetry and painting. The poem is highly dependent upon a visual image, that of the buffalo nickel, for its meaning and thus combines both verbal and visual art forms.

Gansworth's poems are often highly personal and frequently both poignant and ironic. They contain a lifetime's cast of characters and examine a wide variety of perspectives, from that of a "reservation woman" to a graduate student cutting his hair in order to conform. The poems also frequently experiment with narrative form, combining prose with poetry or, as in "Spanish Lessons," using a question and answer format.

The last poem in the volume, "It Goes Something Like This," confirms the book's initial intention to explore and reclaim a vision of Native American history and identity. This final poem tells the story—a story the speaker himself has heard over and over—of the meeting and marriage of the speaker's grandparents. It is a story "repeated / in the best oral tradition" (184), a tradition that Gansworth's own poetic and visual styles have attempted to reflect and renew. The poem ends with an acceptance of the inconsistencies in the story and a realization that the truth is not so important as the mere fact of the story's telling itself. The poem and the book end with the observation "Sometimes the story is / enough to bring me home" (185).

Bibliography

Gansworth, Eric. *Nickel Eclipse: Iroquois Moon.* East Lansing: Michigan State University Press, 2000.

Strom, Karen M. Eric Gansworth. "Storytellers: Native American Authors Online." Available online. URL: http://www.hanksville.org/storytellers/ericg/. Accessed on August 15, 2005.

Winter Elliott

Nightland Louis Owens (1996)

Louis Owens's fourth novel, *Nightland,* begins appropriately on a day of threatening thunderclouds. The Cherokee half-blood boyhood friends Billy Keene and Will Striker are on a hunting trip near the "dried-up one-horse town of Corona, New Mexico" (49). They see a man fall from the sky to his death followed by a parachuted suitcase containing nearly $1 million in drug money. The murder mystery that follows continues a common theme in Owens's work, that of the frustrations and complications of MIXED-BLOOD heritage and the tragedy of undervalued cultural identity in American society.

The Keene and Striker families represent the complexities and losses of the Indian community that resulted from the government-forced TRAIL OF TEARS in the early 1800s. Ironically the displaced Keenes and Strikers find themselves occupying the lands of another tribe, and as the Mescalero Apache Odessa Whitchawk tells Will, "You and Billy aren't supposed to be here. You're no better than the whites. You let them push you off your own land in the east and march you into the homes of other Indian people in that so-called Territory, and you became just like them. . . . You live on top of my people's bones now" (301–302). The bones of those dead ancestors and the Cherokee story of the Thunder Twins collide and/or collude to free the land of its curse of occupation and bloodshed.

In the Cherokee story the Thunder Twins are sons of Kana'ti (First Man, Lucky Hunter) and Selu (Corn Mother). One son is the Wild Boy and the other is the follower; they live together in the west, in the darkening land, and can be heard talking to each other through the thunder from the west. In *Nightland* Billy is the wild schemer, the faded rodeo star living with his grandfather, Siquani Kaneequayokee, on land that no longer supports cattle or corn. It is Billy who insists the fallen money is a "gift from the Great Spirit" (7), which will help them rebuild their drought-worn ranches. Will's family life is as sparse as the few stalks of corn he still grows, as his wife has left him because of boredom after the children were grown and gone. Will, the follower, fears the money is "corpse money" (8). He says it will only cause trouble, and it does—along with the opportunity for both men to find their way between their two cultures.

Many of *Nightland*'s ensemble of characters are also struggling between the differing cultures they represent, some getting lost along the way in the Cherokee darkening land, Nightland, land of spirits: "You got to be careful about things that come from over there," says Siquani (59). The southwestern drug lord Paco Ortega uses the knowledge of his Pueblo history and traditions to create a new story in which he is the vengeful reaper of white death: "Remember those smallpox blankets they passed out to the Indians? . . . I'm giving those blankets back. . . . Drugs will destroy this country" (246). And ironically his heir and nephew, Arturo Cruz, whom in Ortega's story "the white world would help educate . . . to destroy it" (203), becomes instead the man falling from the sky and then a ghost whose job it is, as in traditional Pueblo storytelling, to give the lifegiving rain. Odessa Whitehawk views her white world education as a "Ph.D. in genocide" (302) and surrenders her dreams of pursuing Indian SOVEREIGNTY: "When I was young and innocent," she says, "I thought I could get a white education and fight back. But I was stupid. Now . . . I'm going to have the American dream" (302).

But watching over Billy and Will is grandfather Siquani, a man who keeps the path of their Cherokee culture open for both Billy and Will to find. It is Siquani, the traditional storyteller, the elder beyond time who sees the troubling storm about to break over Will and especially Billy. And it is Billy who loses himself just when he thinks life is going to get better. As Odessa tells him, "Love is like money; it makes people careless" (278). Billy's carelessness leads Odessa to him, to the money he keeps too close, and to his death. It is Will who will be able to resist the money's temptation, who will give it back to the land, to the bones of the land, the bones who will once again let the rains fall, the water flow, and his family flourish.

Bibliography

Kilpatrick, Jacquelyn. ed. *Louis Owens: Literary Reflections on His Life and Work.* American Indian Literature and Critical Studies series, vol. 46. Norman: University of Oklahoma Press, 2004.

LaLonde, Chris. *Grave Concerns, Trickster Turns: The Novels of Louis Owens.* American Indian Literature and Critical Studies series, vol. 43. Norman: University of Oklahoma Press, 2002.

Lee Karalis

Night Sky, Morning Star   Evelina Zuni Lucero   (2000)

The Isleta/San Juan Pueblo writer Evelina Zuni Lucero's first novel, *Night Sky, Morning Star,* won the First Book Award in 1999 from the Native Writers' Circle of the Americas. This novel, set in the Southwest, is the story of the artist Cecelia Bluespruce and her lost lover, Julian Morning Star.

The novel opens with Julian's heading to his parole hearing, cynically sure that he will again be turned down. As a youngster Julian was a basketball star. He struggled with the attention that the game gave him and the way it separated him from his fellow Indian students. He became a puppet for the white establishment in a lot of ways and once Julian goes to college his life changes drastically. Julian's relationship with Viola, an AMERICAN INDIAN MOVEMENT (AIM) radical, leads him to change his last name to *Morning Star* and become involved in drugs and political activism. Although Viola leaves him and moves to California, Julian decides to attend an AIM rally, where he is arrested and charged with illegal interstate transport of weapons, possession of an illegal substance, possession of an unregistered firearm, and murder. The arresting officers recognize Julian's limited contact with whoever might have been the real killers, but his reluctance to identify them angers the officers, and before he realizes what has happened, he comments, "I was charged, tried, and found guilty in such a rapid succession it stunned my parents and my lawyer" (157).

In prison Julian discovers the healing power of his Native traditions and ceremonies and fights for religious freedom for him and his fellow Native prisoners. His stay behind bars is given a glimmer of hope when he recognizes his long lost love, Cecelia, in an advertisement for an art school in Albuquerque. His attachment to the picture and subsequent injury on his way to the parole hearing merge in his mind and lead him to want to contact Cecelia.

Cecelia's life changes when, as a young girl just out of high school, she finds out she is pregnant just after Julian leaves for college. Keeping the secret from him meant struggling on her own, but with the help of her family and friends, Cecelia became a prominent artist and raised her son, Jude. It is only through struggles with her past feelings and present loneliness and telling the truth to Jude that she finally realizes that she has loved no one else but Julian.

Night Sky, Morning Star is a story of survival and healing. Lucero details many of the harsh realities of the legacy of the BOARDING SCHOOLS, the joys of POW wow life, the American Indian Movement, wrongful imprisonment, but she does not wallow in the mire of these issues. Rather, she shows how reconciliation, redemption, and love can help heal some of the wounds in Native American life and provide a strong foundation for the future. Lucero, through Cecelia, Julian, and Jude, provides a story of the healing power love and tradition can have over time and pain.

John D. Miles

No Parole Today Laura Tohe (1999)

In the same vein as "The School Days of an Indian Girl" by ZITKALA-ŠA, LAURA TOHE's *No Parole Today* chronicles the tragic experience of life in an Indian BOARDING SCHOOL. The book reflects Tohe's own experience (as well as that of her community) as a Dine student in a government boarding school in 1950s Albuquerque, New Mexico. Composed of poems and prose vignettes, *No Parole Today* gives voice to Native people whom the U.S. government attempted to silence through forced ASSIMILATION.

The introduction and prologue tell the stories, respectively, of Tohe's and her grandmother's boarding school experiences. Despite taking place decades apart, their stories reveal the shared damage inflicted upon tribal cultures. Tohe's introduction is an open letter to General Richard Henry Pratt, known both for saying, "Kill the Indian, Save

the Man" and for founding the infamous Carlisle Indian School, which became a model for all Indian boarding schools. Because Pratt's legacy continues to inflict damage, Tohe argues that Native people must "decolonize" themselves: "The land, the Dine, the Dine culture is how I define myself and my writing. That part of my identity was never drowned; it was never a hindrance but a strength. To have no stories is to be an empty person. Writing is a way for me to claim my voice, my heritage, my stories, my culture, my people, my history" (xii).

The title poem continues the theme of surviving forced assimilation. Upon hearing the news of a prison riot, the speaker is reminded of her own "incarceration" as a student in a government boarding school. She recalls her own scars and is consequently reminded that her "life / was separated by walls / and roll calls" (23–25). The poem ends with the image of rioting prisoners taking their hats off behind barbed wire and smoke" (27). This image hints at the possibility that the speaker too might find a moment of control within the confines of her colonial imprisonment.

Even under the colonial threat Tohe manages to capture moments of lighthearted fun. We are reminded that the people who populate Tohe's landscape are more than mere victims. For example, "Sometimes Those Pueblo Men Can Sure Be Coyotes" tells the story of two Dine girls who take a liking to their driver, who happens to be Pueblo. They "were making all kinds of comments about him in Dine" (22), their "enthusiasm running away" (23) with them, leaving the girls to whisper "those things adolescent girls say" (24) only to discover in the end that he speaks their language and the joke is on them.

No Parole Today is a testament to the survival of all Native people and serves as a reminder to General Pratt that these people are human beings with their own likes and dislikes, their own strengths and flaws, joys and sorrows.

Bibliography
Tohe, Laura. *No Parole Today.* Albuquerque, N. Mex.: West End Press, 1999.

Brad Gambill

Northeastern tribal literature

Northeastern tribal literature is inextricably tied to the land of customs of the upper Eastern Woodlands of the United States. In addition, and perhaps in contrast to other regional tribal literatures, it reflects a complex system of government that existed long before contact with Europeans.

The tribes whose ancestral homes lie in the northeastern part of the United States were the first affected and perhaps the hardest hit (in terms of the effect on their culture) by the colonization of North America. Tribes in this region include Algonquian-speaking tribes such as the Narragansett, Pequot, and Mohegan and those in the famed Six Nations Iroquois Confederacy (also known as the Iroquois League), composed of the Mohawk, Seneca, Oneida, Onondaga, Cayuga, and, from the 18th century on, Tuscarora tribes. The Iroquois Confederacy, primarily because of its unique, complex political system, is often cited as the most influential and important Native American group in North American history. Although widely overlooked by history and seldom cited, the Iroquois "Great Law of Peace," the founding constitution of the union of the Six Nations, was arguably a source of inspiration for the Constitution of the United States. This document stressed righteousness, unity, health, and power, as unified whole, not as individual entities. Linked with the "Great Law" is the "Epic of Dekanawida," an oral epic (set down and approved by the Council of Chiefs in 1900) that spread a unifying philosophy and sought to create a binding sense of identity in the people. This epic was told before readings of the "Great Law."

Although the Iroquois were politically dominant in the region, Algonquian-speaking tribes carried much influence as well. A Mohegan, SAMSON OCCOM, has been referred to as "the father of American Indian Literature." His sermon, "A Sermon Preached at the Execution of Moses Paul, An Indian Who Was Executed at New Haven on the 2nd of September 1772 for the Murder of Mr. Moses Cook, late of Waterbury, on the 7th of December 1771," was delivered and published in 1772 and became the first work of American Indian literature to be widely read, so widely read in fact that it went through at least 19 editions and was translated into Welsh.

Another Algonquian, the Pequot author WILLIAM APESS, in his autobiography *A Son of the Forest,* vigorously challenged racism and the historical oppression of Native Americans. In observations that are still pertinent today, he questions the use of terms such as *savage* and *Indian* and notes that the behavior of whites is often lacking in the "civilization" they so worship.

In the contemporary era two Mohawk authors have made an impact on the field of literature. BETH BRANT, with her focus on the roles of women in Indian communities and in each other's lives, calls to mind the traditional matrilineal systems of the Iroquois. Theirs was a society that engendered equality and shared responsibility of men and women and Brant's work seeks to restore that balance.

MAURICE KENNY, one of the most honored Native American poets, works to detail the predicaments of Native Americans caught between two worlds, especially the difficulties of forging Indian identity while inhabiting an urban environment, a special concern for contemporary Indians who live in the densely populated Northeast. It is in Kenny's work as well that we may see significant Mohawk historical figures discussed. In *TEKONWATONTI* Kenny draws inspiration from the military leader Molly Brant, illuminating her life in a way not seen in any history text.

Bibliography

Bruchac, Joseph. *The Boy Who Lived with the Bears and Other Iroquois Stories.* New York: Parabola Books, 2003.

Feest, C. F. *Indians of Northeastern North America.* New York: E. J. Brill, 1986.

Tooker, Elizabeth. *Native North American Spirituality of the Eastern Woodlands: Sacred Myths, Dreams, Visions, Speeches, Healing Formulas, and Ceremonies.* Mahwah, N.J.: Paulist Press, 1980.

Northrup, Jim (1943–)

The second of 11 children, Jim Northrup was born on April 28, 1943, in the "government hospital" in Cloquet, Minnesota, on the Fond du Lac Reservation. Located about 20 miles west of Duluth, the reservation was originally about five times its current size. As was the upbringing of most Native Americans of his generation, Northrup's formative years were governed by the policies of the Bureau of Indian Affairs, rather than being shaped by tribal tradition and custom. When he was six years old, he was required to attend one of the government-run BOARDING SCHOOLS, in Pipestone, Minnesota, some distance removed from his family home, and for his secondary education, he was sent first to the Brainerd Indian Training School in Hot Springs, South Dakota, and later to the public high school in Carlton, Minnesota, where he graduated in 1961. He enlisted at 18 in the Marine Corps and served for just over five years, from 1961 to 1966. A 13-month tour of duty in Vietnam has left him with his grim share of memories of that war's horrific events.

After his honorable discharge from the military, Northrup spent the next decade working in law enforcement, culminating in his position as the chief investigator for the public defender's office in Racine, Wisconsin. Ultimately he made his way back to the Fond du Lac Reservation, where he has established his home in the town of Sawyer. From that base he has made a determined effort to live a "traditional" life and to preserve the language, customs, crafts, and storytelling traditions of his tribe. His birch-bark baskets are part of the permanent collection at the Smithsonian Institution in Washington, D.C. A natural performer, Northrup has given a very public face to his causes. He has performed the one-man stage show *Jim Northrup: Stories and Lies* (2004), has appeared in the award-winning film *The United States of Poetry* (1996), and is the subject of the PBS program *Jim Northrup: With Reservations* (2004). Beside his books he is the author of a popular and highly regarded newspaper column, *The Fond du Lac Follies,* which has appeared for over 15 years in several newspapers. In 1999 it received the "Best Column" award from the Native American Journalists Association.

WALKING THE REZ ROAD (1993) is a collection of consistently engaging short stories with diverse tones and themes. Although the stories convey their characters' gradual reengagement with the rhythms and practices of traditional Native American life, they do so against a backdrop of very different experiences on battlefields and in cities far removed from the reservation. Likewise Northrup's ear for the perfectly pitched anecdote is balanced by his poignant awareness of the most crippling aspects of reservation life. For this collection Northrup received the Minnesota Book Award in 1994. In his work Northrup takes great pains in attempting to foster an appreciation for the sense and sound of Native American languages; at the same time he cautions against the "rent-a-shaman" marketing of Native American history and culture. A person of diverse interests and an author of diverse talents, Northrup has contributed his very individual voice to Native American causes and to Native American literature.

In introducing himself to audiences, Northrup often offers this self-estimate: "Born on the Rez, lives on the Rez, will probably die on the Rez. 'Twas a lot that happened in between but it was just details. From those details I make my stories."

See also RESERVATION LIFE.

Bibliography

Hoefel, Roseanne. "Walking with Jim Northrup and Sharing His 'Rez'ervations." *Studies in American Indian Literatures* 9, no. 2 (summer 1997): 11–21.

LaLonde, Chris. "Stories, Humor, and Survival in Jim Northrup's *Walking the Rez Road.*" *Studies in American Indian Literatures* 9, no. 2 (summer 1997): 23–40.

Northrup, Jim. *The Rez Road Follies: Canoes, Casinos, Computers, and Birch Bark Baskets.* New York: Kodansha America, 1997.

———. *Walking the Rez Road.* Stillwater, Minn.: Voyageur, 1993.

Martin Kich

northSun, nila   (1951–)

Born in Schurze, Nevada, in 1951, northSun is of Shoshone and Anishinabe descent. Growing up in the San Francisco Bay area, she witnessed and participated in the Native American activism that began in the 1960s. She also maintained her connections to traditional practices by serving as pow-wow princess in California and Nevada. Currently northSun lives on the Fallon Paiute-Shoshone Reservation in Fallon, Nevada, where she directs a teen crisis center and continues to write poetry.

As this brief biography shows, northSun's commitment to activism informs all aspects of her life. For her poetry can carry as loud a message for reform as a protest sign. northSun began to develop her literary activism while she was a student at the University of Montana, where she received her B.A. While there she also coedited *Scree,* a literary magazine devoted to avant-grade poetry, and ran Duck Down Press, a small, nontraditional publishing company, which also published several of her works, including her first collection of poetry, *diet pepsi & nacho cheese* (1977), and two other chapbooks, *coffee, dust devils, & old rodeo bulls* (1979) and *small bones, little eyes* (1981).

In addition to these works northSun's poetry appears in most anthologies of Native American literature and in many anthologies of contemporary poetry. Most recently she has collected her work into an anthology, *A SNAKE IN HER MOUTH: POEMS 1974–1996* (1997). This collection marks her return to poetry. Her resumption of writing, she explains, was the result of the inspiration that she found as a participant in the Returning the Gift Festival of Native American authors held at the University of Oklahoma in 1992 (Bruchac 357).

Virtually every aspect of northSun's poetry manifests her unconventionality, from its consistent use of lowercase letters to her subjects. Moreover she often reveals the devastation inflicted on Native peoples by POVERTY, ALCOHOLISM, and violence. For example, poems like "99 things to do before you die" indict racist and classist assumptions in mass media conventions like *Cosmopolitan* questionnaires: "stupid questions" explicitly articulates this protest. Elsewhere her works present the complexities of Native American identity, as in "future generation," which argues that reservation life holds treasures unappreciated until they are gone. As these works illustrate, northSun remains committed to activism and art.

Bibliography

Bruchac, Joseph, ed. *Returning the Gift: Poetry and Prose from the First North American Native Writers' Festival.* Tucson and London: University of Arizona Press, 1994.

Fitzgerald, Stephanie. "Myth, Memory and Narrative: The Poetry of nila northSun." Available online. URL: http://grad.cgu.edu/~fitzgers/webpage/mainpage.htm/. Accessed on August 15, 2005.

Harjo, Joy, and Gloria Bird, eds. *Contemporary Native Women's Writings of North America,* 394–397. New York and London: W. W. Norton, 1997.

northSun, nila. COFFEE, DUST DEVILS, & OLD RODEO BULLS. 1979. Fallon, Nev.: Duck Down Press, 1979.

———. DIET PEPSI & NACHO CHEESE. 1977. Fallon, Nev.: Duck Down Press, 1977.

———. SMALL BONES, LITTLE EYES. 1981. Fallon, Nev.: Duck Down Press, 1981.

———. A SNAKE IN HER MOUTH: POEMS 1974–1996. 1997. New York: West End Press.

Clay Smith

Not Vanishing   Chrystos (1988)

Not Vanishing, a collection of poetry arranged in chronological order and illustrated by the poet, includes elegies, statements of anger and hurt, erotic love poems, nature poems, social and political protest, and meditations on the author's life as a Native American lesbian. CHRYSTOS, a Menominee, writes free verse poetry from a Native American woman's viewpoint, "to be a voice for all of us who aren't supposed to speak" (103). Nonetheless her voice remains that of an individual. She refuses to be considered the Voice of Native women, nor representative of Native women in general. The poetry, usually in narrative form, is highly personal, focusing on Chrystos's emotional and spiritual life.

She writes from a place of "fury" (as she calls it in the preface) caused by white Americans' inhumane treatment of the American Indian. The narratives of *Not Vanishing* contain strong images of racial, sexual, and domestic violence. The white government and white individuals have perpetrated acts of violence against American Indians. Within the context of Chrystos's world her fury is justified, even necessary. The persona of "I Walk in the History of My People" carries the memory of the great pain of her people in her marrow. She is crippled by the war between the white government and the American Indian: "My knee is wounded so badly that I limp constantly / Anger is my crutch" (7). Her anger is directed at superficial and thoughtless "liberal" whites, particularly in "Today Was a Bad Day like TB," "I Am Not Your Princess," "Table Manners," and "White Girl Don't."

Much of *Not Vanishing* is set in a dangerous world of great violence and pain. The longer poem "For Eli" is the center of *Not Vanishing,* both literally and thematically. The child Eli is a character who cannot speak for himself; he has been beaten to death by his Cherokee father. The persona of the poem is haunted by Eli and his family, a father who could kill his own son and a mother who would allow the violence and torture. She is frightened of the violence and apathy, but she is also frightened by her own potential for violence: "Am I most afraid of this rage in myself / reflected like a splinter / buried deep in the palm /" (58).

Although much of *Not Vanishing* is concerned with harsh realities, Chrystos also writes of the softer aspects of human life. Her love poems, especially "O Honeysuckle Woman," "Your Tongue Sparkles," "Let Me Touch," and "Double Phoenix," are tender and serene. Her optimism does not extend only to her women friends and lovers. "For Chrystal Rebecca" and "Three" celebrate the beauty and joy of childhood. Thus, Chrystos writes of the complexities of modern Native American life in a genuine and compelling voice.

Bibliography

Chrystos. *Dream On.* Vancouver: Press Gang, 1991.
———. *Fire Power.* Vancouver: Press Gang, 1995.
———. *In Her I Am.* Vancouver: Press Gang, 1993.
Roscoe, Will, ed. *Living the Spirit: A Gay American Indian Anthology.* New York: St. Martin's Press, 1988.

Kelvin Beliele

Now Poof She Is Gone　Wendy Rose (1994)

In the preface of *Now Poof She Is Gone* WENDY ROSE rebukes critics who attack confessional poetry. In a 1992 epiphany, Rose realized that male poets who related personal expression held sacred places in literary society while female poets who wrote to share their feminine experiences were looked down upon. In addition the epiphany revealed that the poetry Rose most enjoyed and remembered was poetry that shared intimate, female expressions. Armed with this new perspective, Rose unveiled (in this celebratory publication) over 20 years of poems that she had kept "safely tucked away so that no one would see them" so that we readers may not only learn to "value the universality of specific episodes" but also "empower ourselves through the ritual of sharing burdens."

The first section of the book is entitled "Ayata," which Rose reveals means "to cry for help" in the Hopi language (18). These poems are stark revelations of the delicate nature of the human mind. Recalling fragile personal moments, Rose reveals life experiences that leave her battered and emotionally exhausted. By admitting her own human frailty and turning to others in a time of need, Rose breaks through the barriers of alienation inhibiting her healing process.

Section two, "Memoir of the Alien," and section three, "Murder of the Girl," disclose the painful experiences that have alienated Rose. "Urban Breed, Go Get Your Gun" shows the cultural alienation she feels having a MIXED-BLOOD heritage: "As for love, you are too white / for the red, too red for the white" (28). Her poem "On Receiving a Letter from Hotevilla" highlights her quest for her father's love. Absence of parental love is also highlighted in "Naming Power" as she repeats, "there has to be someone to name you" four times, a number sacred to Native cultures. The poem ends claiming, "A thirty-year-old woman is waiting for her name" (36). Parental alienation is highlighted again in the poem "Mom, Dad" as Rose ends with the plaintive plea "Was there anything about me / you could call your own?" (53). Rejected by her parents and accepted into neither white nor Native culture, Rose finds solace in her connections to nature, who would welcome her death as a return "home."

The final section, "Now Poof She Is Gone," focuses on women who are, as Norma C. Wilson notes of the poem "Is It Crazy to Want to Unravel," "dissolving, evaporating, and disappearing" yet also "have tremendous, invisible power" (106). Rose submits her poems in this collection as a tribute to, as she says in the preface, "the spirit of women's voices lying along the ground like a magic mist."

Bibliography

Rose, Wendy. *Now Poof She Is Gone.* Ithaca, N.Y.: Firebrand Books, 1994.

Wilson, Norma C. *The Nature of Native American Poetry.* Albuquerque: University of New Mexico Press, 2001.

Patti Diamond

Occom, Samson (Occum) (1723–1792)

Samson Occom was by his own account "born in a wigwam" in New London, Connecticut, in 1723. His parents were Joshua Occom and Sarah Uncas. He was a member of the Mohegan nation and boasted an impressive heritage: He was the great great-great-grandson of Uncas, the Grand Sachem of the Mohegan. An English-educated Christian leader, Occom served as a Calvinist missionary to Native Americans. He was the first Native American writer to publish in English and is often referred to as "The Father of American Indian Literature." He has also been called "the first Native American published composer" (Brooks 67). His original hymn texts also establish him as the first Native American to publish poetry in English. His famous execution sermon, "A Sermon Preached at the Execution of Moses Paul, An Indian Who Was Executed at New Haven on the 2nd of September 1772 for the Murder of Mr. Moses Cook, late of Waterbury, on the 7th of December 1771," was delivered and published in 1772 and became the first Native American best-seller. It subsequently went through at least 19 editions and was translated into Welsh. His two short autobiographies, written in about 1765 and 1768, were not written for publication and were not published during his lifetime. He also compiled, edited, and published a hymnbook entitled *A Choice Collection of Hymns and Spiritual Songs, Intended for the Edification of Sincere Christians of All Denominations* (1774), journals, a tribal history of the Montauk, a booklet of Indian remedies, and many letters and original manuscripts. Occom is remembered and celebrated by the Brothertown Indian Nation, the Mohegan Nation, the Montauk, and the Shinnecock, who celebrated Samson Occom Day in June 1970 (Peyer 5).

At the age of 17 Occom converted to Christianity. He taught himself to read and write so that he could learn Protestant philosophy. Occom described seeing his own people "perishing for a lack of Vision." Christianity provided an alternative for many Native Americans, who converted for a chance at a better life. At the age of 19 he was elected to the Mohegan community's 12-person governing council. In 1743 at the age of 20 Occom entered Eleazar Wheelock's college preparatory school in Lebanon, Connecticut. In four years he advanced from his status as a self-taught man to fluency in English and proficiency in Latin, Greek, and Hebrew. In 1749 Occom visited Montauk territory in Long Island, New York, for a fishing trip. The Montauk invited him to stay and serve them as their schoolmaster. It was there that Occom married Mary Fowler, the daughter of a leading Montauk family. The couple had 10 children together. While among the Montauk he served the community as schoolmaster, minister, scribe, adviser, healer, and judge. Occom received little pay for his work, either from the Montauk, who were unable to pay, or from the Society for the Propagation of the Gospel in Foreign Parts, who seemed unwilling to pay much to a Native American, even one in their employ. In 1759 the poorly paid minister was officially ordained by the Presbytery of Suffolk. Later (1765–68) Occom traveled extensively to England to raise money for a Native American charity school that became Dartmouth College—and soon afterward ceased to serve Native American students.

Wheelock promised to care for Occom's family while the minister traveled in England. But upon his return Occom found Wheelock had broken his promise. Impoverished and bereft of protection from the white community, Occom wrote a 10-page autobiography. The text entitled "A Short Narrative of My Life" is one of the earliest written pieces of Native American literature in English. It remained unpublished until 1982. In it Occom recounts details of his day-to-day life and remarks on the prejudice he faces as a Native American. In particular he describes how he was paid 180 pounds for 12 years of service as a missionary, where, as he writes, "I was my own Interpreter. I was both a School master and Minister to the Indians" (1768). At the same time a European-American missionary was paid 180 pounds for one year of service, including the cost of his interpreter and other assistance.

Occom's best-known work is "A SERMON PREACHED AT THE EXECUTION OF MOSES PAUL" (1772). This sermon was delivered in September 1772. Moses Paul was a Mohegan who had converted to Christianity who was executed for murder. Execution sermons were popular in colonial America and constituted a genre. Rationality is a crucial theme in this sermon. While it is influenced by the Great Awakening, sparked in the 1730s by the repeated delivery of Jonathan Edwards's sermon "Sinners in the Hands of an Angry God," it is also strongly influenced by many American thinkers' growing interest in reason. Although this is a Christian sermon that calls for conversion and repentance, it is also a declaration of the inherent reason of human beings and, in particular, of American Indians. In the sermon Occom tells the audience members, both listeners and readers, both Native American and European American, to behave themselves "as

becomes rational creatures." His Native American listeners, he implies, can behave as rationally as his European-American listeners. Additionally, though Occom blames the Native Americans in this sermon for their drunkenness, it is painfully obvious, though Occom never states it directly, how the Native Americans acquired their alcohol. Occom also includes in this sermon a ministry to people whom we would today describe as suffering from low self-esteem. Occom claimed that a people who "don't regard themselves" will not themselves be regarded. Much of his sermon, then, is a call to Native Americans to see themselves as worthy of esteem: that is, to see themselves as "reasonable creatures."

Occom spent his life as a minister, doctor, and activist. He died in 1792. The coalition of Christian Indians he created now considers itself to be a Native American nation called the Brotherhood Indian Nation. This nation is currently seeking federal recognition.

Bibliography

Brooks, Joanna, "Six Hymns by Samson Occom." *Early American Literature* 38, no. 1 (March 2003): 1–19.

Murray, David. *Forked Tongues: Speech, Writing, and Representation in North American Indian Texts.* Bloomington: Indiana University Press, 1991.

Occom, Samson. "A Sermon Preached at the Execution of Moses Paul." In *The Elders Wrote: An Anthology of Early Prose by North American Indians, 1768–1931,* edited by Bernd Peyer, 19–22. Berlin: Dietrich Reiner, 1982.

———. "A Short Narrative of My Life." In *The Elders Wrote: An Anthology of Early Prose by North American Indians, 1768–1931,* edited by Bernd Peyer, 3–18. Berlin: Dietrich Reiner, 1982.

Peyer, Bernd. "The Betrayal of Samson Occom." Waterville Public Library Web Site. Available online. URL: http://www.borg.com/~wpl/Samson.htm. Accessed on August 15, 2005.

Tamara Powell

Offering Diane Glancy (1988)

PAULA GUNN ALLEN argues that whereas Anglo literature is mostly secular, Native American literature cannot be properly understood separately from its spiritual underpinnings. The world of myths and dreams, the sacralization of the everyday, and the strong relations with ancestors are at the heart of the Native American psyche and the basis of DIANE GLANCY's poetry in *Offering*. Experimenting with poetry and prose effects, Glancy attempts to reconcile her Cherokee and German/English heritage and her Christian and Native American beliefs.

In section I Glancy's concern with reconciling her Christian beliefs with Native American spiritualism is evident. "Two Animals, One Flood" integrates images of reservation life with the story of Noah and the Ark. Images of the natural world succumbing to the intrusion of the suburbs mingle with the personification of animals that is common in Native American poetry and the image of Christ walking on the water in "There Won't Be Another."

The dream world is important to Glancy as well. In an interview she suggests that poets carry images from the dream world into the conscious world, a process that completes the poet. In "Indian Girl Bored with Ceremonies" a young girl is more in tune with the daytime world, reading a book and paying little attention to the ceremonies unfolding before her. However, the next morning she awakens "clutching a small rock in her hand" (8). She has taken something tangible back from the dream world, implying that the boundary between worlds is brittle and capable of being pierced.

At the heart of *Offering* is the power of language. Anne Bromley suggests that for the Native American poet the English language must serve as a bridge between both her and the Native experience. The poems in section II of *Offering* explore how language explains and shapes experience and helps to provide this bridge.

Glancy writes in "To See Sequoyah's Cabin," "He made a Cherokee alphabet / so you could reach another / from that place within a place" (4–6). Here language is a bridge from one experience to another. In "Reservation School for Girls" a teacher attempts to teach the girls English, but the "letters will not stay on the page / but fall like crows" (5–6). The words of many Native American languages are akin to Chinese pictographs in that one word carries a meaning that would be translated by a sentence in English. To understand the word, the stories behind it need to

be understood as well. The dream lives of the girls are filled with vision quests, with wandering buffalo and crows calling their names. The teacher cannot reach them through written language, which is for his students "letters on the wind" (11). The poem concludes with the line "He reads crow-marks on the page but does not know / crow" (12–13). Language is a barrier not only to communication, but to integration of cultures, a phenomenon with which Glancy is familiar.

Many of the poems focus on the difficulties of being part of two worlds—the Anglo and the Native American. The poem sequence that concludes the volume is an experimental poetry/prose section entitled "Photo Frames #1–11, Kansas City Stockyards (Or How to Be Indian)." The anger of dislocation, of both individual and Native experience, is recorded as the speaker addresses her father. The difficulties of maintaining a connection to a heritage that is represented by a "great- / grandfather [who] was the last full-blooded Cherokee relative / I have" (2–4) are explored in the poem and throughout *Offering*.

See also SPIRITUALITY.

Bibliography

Andrews, Jennifer. "A Conversation with Diane Glancy." *The American Indian Quarterly* 26, no. 4 (fall 2002): 645–659.

Bromley, Anne. "Renegade Wants the Word: Contemporary Native American Poetry." *The Literary Review* 23 (1980): 413–421.

Turner, Sarah E. "Spider Woman's Granddaughter": Autobiographical Writings by Native American Women." *MELUS* 22, no. 4 (winter 1997): 109–132.

P. K. Bostian

Oklahoma tribal literature

With oral history and storytelling traditions of 38 federally recognized tribes in the state, as well as the now-centuries-old interactions between tribal people and mainstream American life, Oklahoma is home to a wide variety of both traditional and contemporary American Indian literature. While Native writers from Oklahoma, such as N. SCOTT MOMADAY (Kiowa), JOY HARJO (Muscogee), LINDA HOGAN (Choctaw), ANNA LEE WALTERS (Pawnee/Otoe), and CARTER REVARD (Osage), have succeeded at literature's highest levels, such storytellers as Will Hill (Muscogee), Leon Hawzipta (Kiowa), Tim Tingle (Choctaw), and Ralph Williston (Choctaw) actively maintain the oral traditions of their tribes in the 21st century. Both groups explore identity issues of what being a tribal person means and address the conflict between traditional and contemporary life for American Indian people. Additionally Native writers and storytellers from Oklahoma preserve tribal memory through the symbolic use of stories and literary symbols that represent values and important traditional concepts of their respective tribal backgrounds. Finally, many authors who have MIXED-BLOOD backgrounds discuss the subject of belonging to two different cultures that do not necessarily understand each other, as well as the personal dynamics of being "caught in the middle" between two traditions and not being totally accepted by either group.

Given the relatively longer history of interaction between the Southeastern tribes and mainstream American society, compared to that of tribes from the Great Plains or farther west, one should not be surprised that the largest number of significant American Indian writers from Oklahoma are connected to the tribes of the southeastern United States who were forcibly removed to Indian Territory from the 1820s.

Popularly known as the "FIVE CIVILIZED TRIBES," specifically because of the tribal institutions related to government, businesses, schools, and newspapers, these tribal nations (Cherokee, Muscogee [Creek], Choctaw, Chickasaw, and Seminole) are discussed in the entry SOUTHEASTERN TRIBAL LITERATURE. One of the best recent collections of southeastern folktales is *Totkv Mocvse—New Fire: Creek Folktales by Earnest Gouge* (2004). Published with Muscogee (Creek) and English side by side on the page, *Totkv Mocvse* is a modern edition of traditional Muscogee (Creek) stories written in the Muscogee language in 1915 by a tribal member, Earnest Gouge (1865–1955). Non-Indian anthro-

pologists of the late 19th and early 20th centuries, James Mooney and John R. Swanton, also contributed massive amounts of documentation related to the oral traditions and history of tribes who originated in the Southeast, such as Mooney's *Myths of the Cherokee* (1900) and Swanton's *Myths and Tales of the Southeastern Indians* (1929).

As Native people began the transition into modern life and were encouraged to leave behind their traditional ways, many Native children were removed again, this time from their homes. Placed into government BOARDING SCHOOLS far away from their families, these generations began to learn trades, but also to read, write, and express themselves using the English language. Graduates of government boarding schools usually did not teach their children Native languages, for fear of the children's being punished at school as the parents had been, and slowly the Native languages began passing out of common use by the majority of tribal people in Oklahoma. Today almost all of Oklahoma tribal literature is in English. Although some fluent speakers over 50 years old still tell stories in Cherokee, Kiowa, and Muscogee (Creek), the number of people who can understand a fluent speaker is dwindling.

While Native Americans wrote many plays, poems, and novels throughout the 19th and 20th centuries, the modern period of American Indian literature is often cited as beginning with a Kiowa from Oklahoma, N. Scott Momaday (born 1934 in Lawton, Oklahoma). Momaday's first novel, *HOUSE MADE OF DAWN*, won the Pulitzer Prize in fiction in 1969 and led to new acceptance of the artistic and academic validity of literature by American Indians, perhaps best exemplified by GERALD VIZENOR's *NATIVE AMERICAN LITERATURE: A BRIEF INTRODUCTION AND ANTHOLOGY* (1995). Indicating the contemporary prominence of tribal authors, poets, and playwrights who have ties to tribes in Oklahoma, Vizenor's anthology incorporates Momaday, as well as LOUIS OWENS (Choctaw/Cherokee, born 1948), JOHN JOSEPH MATHEWS (Osage, 1894–1979), THOMAS KING (Cherokee, born 1943), Betty Louise Bell (Cherokee, born 1949), LEANNE HOWE (Choctaw, born 1951), JIM BARNES (Choctaw, born 1933), DIANE GLANCY (Cherokee, born 1941), LINDA HOGAN (Chickasaw, born 1947), JOY HARJO (Muscogee [Creek], born 1951), and HANAY GEIOGAMAH (Kiowa, born 1945).

Two other important writers who have achieved significant status in Native American literature circles and are members of Oklahoma tribes are CARTER REVARD (Osage, born 1931), whose elegant and humorous style is on full display in *Family Matters, Tribal Affairs* (1998), and ANNA LEE WALTERS (Pawnee/Otoe). Waters's GHOST SINGER (1988) is a dark and spooky story about the moral and spiritual issues surrounding sacred tribal objects in non-Indian museums. Other authors who have contributed strongly to the literary traditions of their tribe are the poet ROXY GORDON (Choctaw, 1945–2000); the novelist RON QUERRY (Choctaw, born 1943); the novelist and historian ROBERT J. CONLEY (Cherokee, born 1940); the novelist, essayist, and storyteller W. S. PENN (Osage, born 1949); the poet CAROLYN DUNN (Muscogee [Creek]/Seminole, born 1965); the author, poet, short story writer, and essayist GEARY HOBSON (Cherokee/Chickasaw/Quapaw, born 1941); and the children's author Jack Wooldridge (Potawatomi, born 1929).

Finally, while not an enrolled member of any tribe, in the poet Todd Fuller's (born 1965) *60 Feet Six Inches and Other Distances from Home: The (Baseball) Life of Mose Yellowhorse* (2002) he furthers the important discussion of what can be considered tribal literature as a writer working with tribal people to tell stories about the people of a given tribe. In a multigenre work in the postmodern tradition Fuller combines his own poems with box scores, tribal oral history, *Dick Tracy* comics, and newspaper reports to provide an important literary portrait of this historic figure of American sports. By doing so, Fuller adds a third element to the active 21st-century Native American literary traditions in a form that might be termed "collaborative," as it is neither traditional storytelling nor literature by an enrolled or unenrolled tribal author, but literature with a Native focus by an Oklahoma creative writer working with the approval and assistance of tribal people.

Bibliography

Trout, Lawana. *Native American Literature: An Anthology.* NTC/Contemporary, 1999.

Vizenor, Gerald. *Native American Literature: A Brief Introduction and Anthology.* Watson-Guptill, 1995.

Hugh W. Foley, Jr.

Old Shirts and New Skins Sherman Alexie (1993)

Old Shirts and New Skins (1993) is SHERMAN ALEXIE's third collection of poems and the ninth book in the Native American series sponsored by the American Indian Studies Center at the University of California at Los Angeles. This collection received more attention than any of Alexie's previous volumes. Its publication marks the beginning of the perception of him as a Native American poet, short story writer, novelist, and screenwriter of national stature.

Old Shirts and New Skins consists of 50 poems divided into three almost perfectly balanced sections: "Indian Education," 17 poems; "Songs from the Film," 16 poems; and "Drought," 17 poems.

The poems in the first section typically treat the poet's personal and family history and aspects of everyday life on the reservation. One of the most powerful of these poems is "Learning to Drown." With a straightforwardness that permits moments of both startling dark humor and great poignancy, Alexie recounts, in the second and fourth of the five stanzas, what he has heard about his own crisis as an infant with hydrocephalus. In the second stanza he dryly recounts how a cousin's accidentally dropping him from a swing actually led to his doctors' diagnosis of the condition, but he immediately juxtaposes that surprise with his mother's desperate charting of daily measurements that she had begun taking of his head. In the first, third, and fifth stanzas of the poem Alexie links his "drowning" in his own cranial fluid with other drownings: prisoners of war being marched to a river in which they were drowned by their captors, a 300-pound woman who has Down's syndrome who falls face down in a puddle and drowns because no one around her is strong enough to lift her face out of several inches of water, and Alexie's brother and some friends' repeatedly attempting to swim the Spokane River.

Most of the poems in the second section ironically present the distorted stereotypes of Native Americans and the so-called Indian wars in mainstream American histories and in American popular culture. The second and the last poems of the section are, respectively, "Custer Speaks" and "Crazy Horse Speaks." Each poem is a seven-part monologue delivered from beyond the grave. Although Custer is clearly rationalizing some of his actions against the Plains tribes and most specifically the disaster at the Little Bighorn, he is more sympathetic—or at least more human—than in many other characterizations of him by Native American writers. But in the last stanza Alexie explicitly links the devastation wrought against the Plains tribes and embodied in Custer with many of the other rationalized calamities in American history and culture: the atomic bombings, the enslavement and postemancipation segregation of African Americans, the exploitation of immigrant labor, the military adventurism of the last half-century, and the gross distortions of history in Hollywood films. While echoing Custer's strong sense of connection with his Native American foe, "Crazy Horse Speaks" offers a striking contrast between Custer's relentless, self-aggrandizing quest for fame and political power against Crazy Horse's desire for anonymity and his fear of being reduced to the equivalent of a museum exhibit. In contrast to Custer, who was so hungry for glory that he recklessly provoked a battle against a much larger Native American force, Crazy Horse was fighting out of a sense of necessity, in a desperate attempt to prevent the destruction of the Plains tribes' whole way of life. In the last two lines of the poem Alexie suggests that Crazy Horse's spirit still resides with his descendants, waiting to reassert itself, whereas Custer's "Last Stand" has become an increasingly tarnished catch-phrase.

In the poems of the third section Alexie returns to the details of reservation life, but with a more pointed emphasis on the salient issues facing Native American society and culture than in the first section. In the title poem of this section, "Drought," he presents the thirst for water in an arid landscape as both an ironic corollary of and counterpoint to the high incidence of alcoholism among Native Americans. Satisfying thirst has too often been a self-destructive confirmation of the hard realities of reservation life, but Alexie seems to reinvest it with the possibilities of transcending those difficulties, of tasting real satisfaction.

Bibliography

"About Sherman Alexie." *Ploughshares* 26 (winter 2000–2001): 197–202.

Berner, Robert L. Review of *Summer of the Black Widows, World Literature Today* 71 (spring 1997): 430–431.

Evans, Stephen F. "'Open Containers': Sherman Alexie's Drunken Indians." *American Indian Quarterly* 25 (winter 2001): 46–72.

McFarland, Ron. "'Another Kind of Violence': Sherman Alexie's Poems." *American Indian Quarterly* 21 (spring 1997): 251–264.

Martin Kich

One Good Story, That One Thomas King (1993)

One Good Story, That One is a collection of 10 short stories, previously published in a number of different sources between 1985 and 1992. Critics have seen a sustained theme in the way stories examine borders, in both the literal and metaphorical senses (Davidson). This theme is most obvious in the story "Borders," in which the narrator's mother refuses to identify herself as either American or Canadian, instead insisting her citizenship is "Blackfoot." Since neither border would recognize such citizenship, this traps the mother and her son in the zone between the American and Canadian borders, until they are finally allowed to cross under their own identification.

Also part of KING's "border crossing" is his consistent and extremely effective use of HUMOR: One of the first critics to approach these stories before their collection was Margaret Atwood, who explored King's use of "subversive laughter." King certainly makes fantastic use of irony and wit in stories like "Joe the Painter," in which the title character—a non-Native—stages a pageant about the founding of his town. The pageant's title, "Matthew Larson and the Deer Island Massacre," is set up to evoke the idea of an Indian raid, but to Joe the simple reality is that "you can't muck around with history" (108). This statement does not mean he can look past the problem that the "Indians don't look like Indians" (112), forcing them to put on long-haired wigs, but it does mean that the massacre is actually committed by the whites while they scream, "Death to the heathens!" (118).

There is another sort of exploration taking place in King's stories: that of interrogating notions of identity. As King stated in an interview, "That whole idea of 'Indian' becomes, in part, a construct. It's fluid. We make it up as we go along" (Canton 90–91). *One Good Story, That One* describes different aspects of being Native, without seeking to contain itself by actually defining any aspect as correct. In the title story, for example, we have a narrator who is an oral storyteller, giving a group of "whitemen"- presumably anthropologists, since they carry recorders and cameras—a retelling of the Judeo-Christian creation story. He is forced into this because his friend insists that they would prefer a "good Indian story" of the creation as opposed to something more contemporary.

The reader, though, is later given an example of a "good Indian story" with "Trap Lines," the tale of a father and son who attempt to negotiate what should be passed down from generation to generation in a world where the father ironically observes, "Nobody runs a trap line anymore" (35). To contemplate the implications of the modern world, complete with television, pizza, and chainsaws, the father spends a great deal of time on the toilet, in the "true" tradition passed down from his father.

Bibliography

Davidson, Arnold E., Priscilla L. Walton, and Jennifer Andrews. *Border Crossings: Thomas King's Cultural Inversions.* Toronto: University of Toronto Press, 2003.

King, Thomas. *One Good Story, That One.* Toronto: Harper, 1993.

———. *The Truth about Stories: A Native Narrative.* Toronto: Anansi, 2003.

Derek Irwin

One More Shiprock Night   Luci Tapahonso (1981)

LUCI TAPAHONSO's *One More Shiprock Night* is characterized by themes of heritage, Navajo storytelling, family, and the Dinetah land. Many of the poems address Tapahonso's family and her desire to be close to them, such as "The Dust Will Settle" and "My Parents." "A Good Time to Wash Hair" describes how a mother is able to convince her daughter of the necessity of personal hygiene. "Cracker Crumbs," "Child's Play," and "Misty Dawn at Feeding Time" all speak of motherhood and maternal revelations. "The Hardness in Me" describes how a mother survives by counting expenses and telling stories to her child. Other poems discuss the female strength of the Dine women, particularly in their relationships with men, such as "Ending," "Too Navajo," and "I Couldn't Do Anything." "The Jilters" tells of Joe, a man who breaks women's hearts easily. Many poems discuss Dinetah land directly, as do "Shiprock" and "A Summer Poem." "It Was a Special Treat" describes a family trip to Farmington and how the father would sing on the return to Shiprock. In another poem on singing, "I'm Safe," a young child is lulled to sleep by her family's melodies. Some poems describe continuing racist perceptions, for example, "From the Looks of Me" recounts an incident in which a woman who has forgotten her identification is held at the border because she is a person of color.

Bibliography

Bataille, Gretchen M. "Luci Tapahonso: A Navajo Voice in the Midwest." In *Native American Women in Literature and Culture,* edited by Susan Castillo and Victor M. P. Da Rosa, 25–31. Porto, Portugal: Fernando Pessoa University Press, 1997.

Brill, Susan. "Critical Boundaries and Luci Tapahonso's 'What I Am.'" In *Wittgenstein and Critical Theory: Beyond Postmodern Criticism and toward*

Descriptive Investigations. Athens: Ohio University Press, 1995.

Dunaway, David King, and Sara L. Spurgeon, eds. *Writing the Southwest.* Albuquerque: University of New Mexico Press, 2003.

Smith, Patricia Clark, and Paula Gunn Allen. "Earthly Relations, Carnal Knowledge: Southwestern American Indian Women Writers and Landscape." In *The Desert Is No Lady: Southwestern Landscapes in Women's Writing and Art,* edited by Vera Norwood and Janice Monk. New Haven, Conn.: Yale University Press, 1987.

Tapahonso, Luci. *One More Shiprock Night.* San Antonio: Tejas Art Press, 1981.

Laura Madeline Wiseman

One Stick Song   Sherman Alexie   (2000)

One Stick Song is SHERMAN ALEXIE's fifth poetry collection and continues many of the same themes he worked with in previous collections. His poetry revolves around the struggle for identity and understanding in a society filled with endless complication, whether by ethnicity, history, economics, or memory. Alexie's poetry often comments on the misperception of Native Americans and their history, the sadness that governs many aspects of all life, and the human need to seek out and nurture love, even in the most unlikely places.

Metaphor is a powerful form of expression in many of Alexie's poems. Poems such as "The Unauthorized Biography of Me," "Open Books," and "A Poem Written in Replication of My Father's Unfinished Novel" celebrate storytelling and writing using the concepts of "books" or "novels" to convey larger ideas while alluding to the complexity of human identity and experience wrapped up in the stories being told. "Water" looks at the concept of water both literally and figuratively. It is something that people physically interact with but is also something that carries the connotation of larger issues such as fear, lost love, and memories of the past.

Love is another powerful theme expressed through many of the poems in *One Stick Song.* One of the longest, the prose poem "The War-

riors," narrates childhood memories of baseball, listing the ideal players who made up fantasy teams while using the baseball stories as an opportunity to examine love and relationships between friends and brothers, men and women, American Indians and whites. The title poem of the collection, "One Stick Song," describes a need to reclaim loved and lost family members through the invocation of not only their tragedies but also vibrant colors and song. "Why Indian Men Fall in Love with White Women" speaks of loving the deep, yet vulnerable, simplicity of a woman working in a doughnut shop and how the life and sadness that she embodies bridge ethnic differences in favor of shared human struggles. Love is also an intrinsic part of "Sugar Town," as Alexie bridges three generations, speaking of his father, himself, and his son, while discussing the complications of lineage and inheritance. In this poem Alexie feels the burden of being his father's son and at the same time feels the sense of responsibility in what he willingly or unwillingly passes to his own son.

Alexie's poems comment on current and past struggles, in individual terms and as part of a larger society, but still embody a degree of hope and optimism for the future. While he shows that the world is indeed not perfect and is complicated by multiple degrees of complication and sadness, there is hope in what Alexie conveys about humanity. Fundamentally people are looking for love and understanding, and those common desires transcend many of the obstacles one confronts in life.

Sara Kosiba

orality

Prior to contact with Europeans Native North American cultures were primarily oral. Most ideas were circulated through the spoken word, and verbal art assumed such forms as speech, chant, or song. Ability to speak effectively often contributed to one's status, and individuals might assume leadership roles at least partially because of their oratorical ability. The art of the spoken word involved not only what was said but also how it was said: changes in volume, tempo, and voice quality; use of gestures and other body language; manipulation of physical objects; and direct and indirect interactions with the audience. This meant that each "performance"—telling a story, singing a song—was unique, because it responded to particular circumstances and because no written version "froze" what was said into a permanent text.

Attempts to assign some permanence to orally performed verbal art have produced variable results. One of the pioneers in this endeavor was the Indian agent Henry Rowe Schoolcraft, who recast the stories he heard from the Ojibwe relatives of his wife in the florid literary prose of the mid-19th century. Schoolcraft also expurgated matter from the stories that he deemed unsuitable for publication. The texts that he published in *Algic Researches* in 1839 have the virtue, though, of emphasizing that the material should be considered literature. In the late 19th century anthropologists working for the Smithsonian Institution's Bureau of Ethnology as well as Franz Boas and his students in anthropology at Columbia University began to record stories from Native American performers, especially in the Southwest and on the Northwest coast. They were able to preserve scrupulously what the storytellers said, but the circumstances of recording—which involved dictation in languages that the anthropologists might not understand—deleted many of the artistic features that would have characterized more natural performance situations. Attempts to capture in print other forms of orally performed verbal art such as songs and oratory met with similar fates: Either the texts were accurate linguistically but preserved little of their artistic value or they sacrificed accuracy for literary qualities, which often reflected the aesthetics of the transcribers and translators more than indigenous artistic standards.

The ethnopoetics movement, which emerged in the 1960s, attempted to redress the failings of previous attempts to translate and textualize American Indian oral art. Most successful and influential has been the work of Dennis Tedlock and Dell Hymes. Tedlock, who worked with taped performances by storytellers at Zuni Pueblo, devised an approach called "pause phrasing," which captured the tempo of oral performance by organizing it into lines whose lengths were determined by pauses made by the storytellers. Tedlock used typographic manipulation to reflect other features of the performance such as changes in pitch or volume. The reader can use the typographic cues to apprehend the resulting texts, which appear as poetry on the printed page, in a way that approximates the ways the storytellers performed them. Hymes has returned to some of the dictated texts recorded in the late 19th and early 20th centuries. Working from the Native language originals, he has identified recurrent structuring devices that allow him to organize the stories into lines and larger units that represent verbal style more effectively than the previous renderings. Although he has no tape recordings to work from and consequently cannot identify stylistic features such as changes in volume and pitch, Hymes has demonstrated that the artistry available in orality can survive the aesthetically stifling effects of the dictation situation.

The evanescent quality of orality has drawbacks. Stories and songs depend upon the memories of their performers for survival, and the vagaries of those memories as well as intentional emendations may produce accounts that do not mesh with the events that they purport to represent. But orality also has positive features: particularly the immediacy and sense of community that oral performance produces. In many societies the spoken word is perceived as having efficacy; to say something sets events in motion. Furthermore the process of tradition does not necessarily produce errors. Historians and archaeologists have demonstrated that orally disseminated accounts of past events often correspond with what they have found by using the conventional resources of Western scholarship.

Some students of communicative media have argued that a "great divide" separates what Walter Ong calls "primary oral cultures" such as those of Native North America from the literate cultures of Europe. Because of the way they communicate ideas, the argument goes, people enculturated in these two categories of culture think differently. The difficulty in effectively converting oral performance into print lends support to this perspective. Contrarily, others suggest that a more appropriate image is that of a continuum from oral to written. The work of many American Indian authors supports the latter view.

Even the earliest American Indian writers drew upon the oral traditions of their heritages. George Copway's *Indian Life and History,* published in 1860, incorporates a set of myths and other narratives from his Ojibwe culture. William Warren, another Ojibwe, who wrote a history of his people in 1852 (published in 1880), drew extensively upon orally circulated stories for his account. CHARLES ALEXANDER EASTMAN celebrated the Dakota storyteller Smokey Day in a number of his works, including his first autobiography, *Indian Boyhood,* published in 1902.

In the late 20th century two of the most prominent Native American authors saw their work as a continuation of oral tradition. In *The WAY TO RAINY MOUNTAIN* N. SCOTT MOMADAY perceives his role as the ultimate preserver of an oral heritage that he received through his grandmother. The Pulitzer Prize–winning novelist places himself in the ongoing oral process that generated the myths and other narratives that compose the first section of each of the chapters in his memoir of the spiritual and physical pilgrimage that his grandmother's death inspired him to take to the homeland of his Kiowa ancestors. The novel *HOUSE MADE OF DAWN* also emphasizes an oral-literate continuum. A central character in the book, the peyote priest Tosamah, celebrates the Kiowa heritage and the power of the spoken word through sermons that recall the importance of oratory in many American Indian cultures, including the Kiowa. The Kiowa etiological myth dealing with the origins of the landmark Tsoai (Devil Tower) informs another Momaday novel, *The ANCIENT CHILD,* in which the protagonist embodies the continuing relevance of the orally disseminated literary tradition in his life in the 20th century.

Similarly Tayo, the protagonist of LESLIE MARMON SILKO's novel *CEREMONY,* lives out a recurrent story from the oral tradition of Laguna Pueblo as he searches for healing after his experiences in World War II. Myth provides a model for his restoration to wholeness. Silko's book *STORYTELLER* forcefully demonstrates the author's perception of herself as heir to Laguna oral performers. The book contains short stories, poems, autobiographical vignettes, and photographs that connect Laguna past and present. The short story "Storyteller," which—unlike most of Silko's work—is set outside her native Laguna (in this case, in Alaska), shows how the power of the orally performed story shapes reality in a way that allows the narrator to enjoy some triumph over the exploitative Euro-Americans who are despoiling the environment and the indigenous cultures of the region.

Momaday and Silko are only two of the many contemporary Native American writers who have drawn upon oral tradition and who see themselves as perpetuators of that tradition. Other writers of fiction have updated themes, characters, and images from myths, legends, and folktales; poets have adopted and adapted the rhythms and imagery of songs to the print medium; and essayists have celebrated the centuries-old literary heritages of which they perceive themselves a part.

The dichotomy between orality and literacy has been exaggerated, if it exists at all. In fact, most primary oral cultures in Native North America have had ways of visually preserving ideas: petroglyphs and pictographs throughout the continent, winter counts among many Plains groups, and glyphic representations of song texts on bark among the Ojibwe. The ability to interpret images in these media may not constitute literacy in an alphabetic sense, but it does represent a response to a kind of preliterate writing. Moreover, once cultures become literate, they do not eschew orality, which remains a principal way of communicating ideas and a principal medium for much verbal art. In the 21st century even the electronic media have not supplanted orality in many respects.

Bibliography

Copway, George. *Indian Life and Indian History, by an Indian Author; Embracing the Traditions of the North American Indians Regarding Themselves, Particularly of That Most Important of All Tribes, the Ojibways.* Boston: Albert Colby.

Finnegan, Ruth. *Oral Poetry: Its Nature, Significance, and Social Context.* Cambridge: Cambridge University Press, 1977.

Hymes, Dell. *"In Vain I Tried to Tell You": Studies in Native American Ethnopoetics.* Philadelphia: University of Pennsylvania Press, 1981.

Momaday, N. Scott. *The Ancient Child.* New York: HarperPerennial, 1990.

———. *House Made of Dawn.* New York: Harper & Row, 1968.

———. *The Way to Rainy Mountain.* Albuquerque: University of New Mexico Press, 1969.

Ong, Walter J. *Orality and Literacy: Technologizing the World.* London: Methuen, 1982.

Schoolcraft, Henry Rowe. *Algic Researches: Comprising Inquiries Respecting the Mental Characteristics of the North American Indians. First Series. Indian Tales and Legends.* 2 volumes. New York: Harper & Brothers.

Silko, Leslie Marmon. *Ceremony.* New York: Penguin, 1977.

———. *Storyteller.* New York: Seaver Books, 1981.

Tedlock, Dennis. *The Spoken Word and the Work of Interpretation.* Philadelphia: University of Pennsylvania Press, 1983.

Warren, William W. *History of the Ojibways, Based upon Tradition and Oral Statements* 1880. Reprint. St. Paul: Minnesota Historical Society Press, 1984.

William M. Clements

Ortiz, Simon   (1941–)

Simon Ortiz, an Acoma Pueblo poet, fiction writer, and editor, was born in Albuquerque, New Mexico, on May 27, 1941. He grew up in the Dyaamih hanoh (Eagle Clan) in the Aacqumeh honoh (Acoma community) of Deetseyamah (McCartys), on the Acoma Pueblo Indian Reservation about 60 miles west of Albuquerque. As Ortiz writes in the introduction to *Woven Stone* (1992), he grew up speaking "a language that was specifically Acoma, mostly, with a scattering of English words and phrases and even Spanish that had been 'Acomized' and incorporated into the Native tongue" (3). From his earliest day, he was an avid reader, a boy who had fun reading because he loved language and stories. When he attended McCartys Day School as a child, however, he was forced to speak and read only English, a language he did not speak at home. Since then, the tension between the Acoma language and English has been at the center of Ortiz's writing life. His challenge has been to "demystify" the English language.

He has struggled with the compromise that writing in English represents and wonders whether translation between the two languages is even possible.

Starting in the 1960s, Ortiz served in the army, then attended Ft. Lewis College (Colorado), the University of New Mexico, and the University of Iowa. He has taught Native American literature and creative writing at many different colleges, including San Diego State University, Navajo Community College, and the University of New Mexico, and is currently at the University of Toronto. He has served as lieutenant governor of the Pueblo of Acoma and consulting editor of the Pueblo of Acoma Press.

Ortiz writes about travel, family life, and a connectedness to the natural world. A focus on what is important in life—family, language, spiritual growth, and home—is at the heart of his poetry. A major theme of Ortiz's poetry are the various definitions of *home* and our ability to lose and find it. By returning home, a person can return also to his or her true self with the knowledge gained in the journey. He further expands the journey metaphor in the introduction to the collection *GOING FOR THE RAIN*:

> The man has brought back the rain. It falls, and it is nourishing. The man returns to the strength that his selfhood is, his home, people, his language, the knowledge of who he is. The cycle has been traveled; life has beauty and meaning, and it will continue because life has no end. (4)

In his introduction to *Woven Stone* (1992) Ortiz states that his early poetry "expresses a closeness to a specific Native American way of life and its philosophy, and it is structured in the narrative form of an actual journey on the *heeyaanih*, the road of life, and its experience" (5).

To take the immediacy and intimacy of the oral form and evoke it as closely as possible in writing is a further challenge in poetry. In the preface to *GOOD JOURNEY* (1977), Ortiz articulates this process:

> This book tries to achieve the direct impact that spoken narrative has. . . . For me, poetry and

most prose stories should be read aloud because the voice and other movements of the general body language are critical to what is shared by speaker and listener. . . . I try to show that the listener-reader has as much responsibility and commitment to poetic effect as the poet. When this effect is achieved the compelling power of language is set in motion towards vision and knowledge. (ix)

Ortiz, first and foremost, participates in the Native American oral tradition. He states: "Indians always tell a story. The only way to continue is to tell a story" (x). The theme of connectedness to the natural world is central in his work. For example, the poem "How to Make a Good Chili Stew" from the collection *A Good Journey* (1977) is an actual chili recipe with some significant idiosyncrasies. For example, it insists that it is important to have a dog with you while you cook. The poem further instructs readers to make their chili in the right setting: Outdoors in an inspiring place will make it taste best. Connection with the landscape while cooking is also vital to bring out the flavor.

As a writer of fiction Ortiz returns to the themes of home, language, and memory. He made his debut with *Howbah Indians* (1975), a collection that was rereleased as a part of the larger *Men on the Moon* (1999). The title story of the earlier collection is a fine example of how memory and storytelling combine to form a seamless whole. The story remembers a deceased old friend named Eagle, a veteran, wild and unique, who opened a gas station with the eponymous name and then died/was killed in a ditch:

When the guys talk about Eagle now, they always spread their arms and hands full out, describing and seeing that bright yellow and red sign on the horizon—WELCOME HOWBAH INDIANS—and they laugh and laugh for the important memory and the fact that it is. (4)

"Home Country" is an experiment in voice, in capturing the cadence and speech, as a woman contemplates her relationship to her family. "Men on the Moon" tells the story of the first moon landing from the perspective of an old man watching television for the first time. He wonders why the "Mericanos" need to go all the way to the Moon to search for knowledge. "Something's Going On" tells the story of a nine-year-old boy's literal and metaphorical search for his father, a fugitive murder suspect. Ortiz's children's book *The People Shall Continue* (1988) tells the story of the creation of the Earth in a colorful and lively form.

Ortiz's work continues to reinterpret history through the eyes of the Acoma. For example, Roxanne Dunbar-Ortiz, in the preface to *Fight Back: For the Sake of the People, For the Sake of the Land* (1980), describes what follows as

a tribute to the struggles of the Indian people, Indian workers and to the Revolt. The book was written for the tricentennial celebration of the 1680 Revolt, and reminds us that the revolt left a legacy of resistance that continues in the mines, in the fields, and in the factories. The real heroes of Indian resistance are portrayed here . . . workers fighting for freedom, for liberation and for decent, healthy lives. (v)

This collection is filled with poems about uranium mining, poor pay, and abusive conditions on reservations. It ends with the poem "A New Story," wherein a man is asked to be a prop for a Frontier Day Parade by a woman who needs authentic Indians for her float. The man says yes. Later, when the woman calls back with another request, he declines. He will no longer participate in the merchandizing of cartoon Indians.

Ortiz also works as an essayist and editor, a leader in the burgeoning field of Native American literature. Ortiz introduces the anthology *Speaking for the Generations: Native Writers on Writing* (1998) by saying:

Since the 1960s, contemporary Native written expression has gained a wide and large audience. It has received serious critical attention . . . and has earned considerable recognition, but it still needs to be heard in every corner of the Americas and beyond. About this there is no doubt. (4)

Speaking for the people is inextricably linked to speaking for the land; we exist because our ancestors found a way to live in harmony with the land. He continues to be among the most well-known and prolific Native writers.

With his former wife, Marlene, Ortiz has three daughters, Raho Nez, Rainy Dawn, and Sara Marie. He lives in his hometown of Deetseyamah.

Bibliography

Fitz, Brewster E. "Undermining Narrative Stereotypes in Simon Ortiz's 'The Killing of a State Cop.'" *MELUS: The Journal of the Society for the Study of the Multi-Ethnic Literature of the United States* 28, no. 2 (2003): 105–120.

Ortiz, Simon. *Fight Back: For the Sake of the People For the Sake of the Land.* Albuquerque, N. Mex.: Institute for Native American Development, 1980.

———. *Going for the Rain.* New York: Harper & Row, 1976.

———. *A Good Journey.* Tucson: University of Arizona Press, 1977.

———. *Howbah Indians.* Tucson, Ariz.: Blue Moon, 1978.

———. *Men on the Moon.* Tucson: University of Arizona Press, 1999.

———. *The People Shall Continue.* San Francisco: Children's Book Press, 1988.

———, ed. *Speaking for the Generations: Native Writers on Writing.* Tucson: University of Arizona Press, 1998.

———. *Woven Stone.* Tucson: University of Arizona Press, 1992.

Smith, Patricia C. "Coyote Ortiz: *Canis latrans latrans* in the Poetry of Simon Ortiz." In *Studies in American Indian Literature: Critical Essays and Course Designs,* edited by Paula G. Allen, 192–210. New York: Modern Language Association of America, 1983.

William Gillard

Owens, Louis   (1948–2002)

Louis D. Owens was born in Lompoc, California, on July 18, 1948. Of Choctaw, Cherokee, and Irish descent, he spent his childhood moving between Mississippi and California, picking beans and working on a mushroom farm in the Salinas Valley and in a bracero camp on the outskirts of Merced. Of the nine brothers and sisters in the Owens family, Louis and his brother Gene were the only two who completed high school, and Louis was the only one who attended college. He earned his bachelor's and master's degrees in English from the University of California, Santa Barbara (1971, 1974) and his Ph.D. from the University of California, Davis (1981). While in graduate school Owens worked seasonally for the U.S. Forest Service, as a wilderness ranger in the North Cascades and a firefighter in Washington, Arizona, and California. He remembered each of those jobs and lifestyles as a most wonderful experience: "In my dreams I seek out wildfire and search for eagles that soar over granite and glacier. In my next life I will do it over again, every single thing" (*Train* 63). He defined himself as a "reluctant graduate student the whole way, dropping out several times to return to working for the Forest Service" ("Outside Shadow" 41). Throughout his career Owens held teaching appointments at California State University, Northridge; the University of New Mexico; and the University of California (UC), campuses at Santa Cruz and Davis. Between 1980 and 1981 he also taught, as a Fulbright Fellow, at the University of Pisa, Italy. At the time of his tragic death in July 2002 Owens was looking forward to being a distinguished scholar-in-residence at Harvard University, in 2004.

Owens began his writing career as a Steinbeck scholar. His doctoral dissertation, *John Steinbeck's Revision of America,* published in 1985, was followed by *The Grapes of Wrath: Trouble in the Promised Land* (1989). Besides a deeply literary interest in the American writer, Owens's fascination with Steinbeck also has significant personal motifs. According to Professor Emeritus James Woodress, Owens's mentor and dissertation director at UC Davis, Owens was first drawn to the work of John Steinbeck because he knew intimately the landscape of Steinbeck's fiction and because his own life resembled a Steinbeck novel, with migration and tenant farming as prominent themes. Even though issues of MIXED-BLOOD/Native American identity occupied a central role in Owens's subsequent writing, Steinbeck's influence remained visible throughout his entire professional life. At the time of his death Owens was working on an additional major critical study of John Steinbeck.

Of his own novels Owens said: "Though each of my novels begins and ends with place itself, the mysteries of mixed identity and conflicted stories, both the stories we tell ourselves and the stories others tell about us and to us, are what haunt my fiction" (*Mixedblood Messages* 181). Set among a Salish community in the North Cascades, Owens's first novel, WOLFSONG (1991), is about a search for identity and the crucial importance of place in shaping such an identity. As various critics have pointed out, Owens in the novel strives to convey a Native land ethic according to which humans are highly responsible for the environment they inhabit. In his second novel, *The* SHARPEST SIGHT (1992), Owens explores his Choctaw ancestry while drawing on family experiences between Mississippi and California. Critically acclaimed as a murder mystery deeply grounded in Native traditions (translated into French, the novel was awarded the 1995 Roman Noir prize, a distinctively French award for the outstanding mystery novel published in French), *The Sharpest Sight* weaves layers of Choctaw mythology within a distinctively Indo-European mythic frame. The result is a sophisticated hybrid narrative of healing through love and violence.

Owens's academic reputation in Native American literature began in 1985 with an article,

"The Map of the Mind: D'ARCY McNICKLE and the American Indian Novel," published in *Western American Literature*. But it was not until his seminal *Other Destinies: Understanding the American Indian Novel* (1992), which won the Josephine Miles, PEN Oakland Award in 1993, that his public acknowledgment as a leading critic in the field officially occurred. Mixing fiction and criticism would become a regular pattern in Owens's extraordinarily prolific career. *BONE GAME* (1994), the most experimental of all of Owens's novels, further delves into his Choctaw ancestry while exploring "the enormous sense of loss that the indigenous people of the Santa Cruz area, the Ohlone, experienced . . . as the result of the coming of Europeans" ("Clear Waters" 10). And *Nightland* (1996), winner of the 1997 American Book Award, is Owens's tribute to his Cherokee heritage.

In *Mixedblood Messages: Literature, Film, Family, Place,* Owens continued to explore his mixed heritage while suggesting new critical paths for Native American Indian criticism. Blending autobiography, film commentary, literary criticism, and environmental reflections, Owens proposes a creative theoretical model that significantly challenges conventional Western critical modes of communication and thought. With this collection Owens received the Writer of the Year Award from the Wordcraft Circle of Native Writers and Storytellers. *Dark River* (1999), Owens's last novel and a further search for a centered self in place, was followed by his last mixed-genre collection of critical essays, *I Hear the Train: Reflections: Inventions, Refractions* (2001). Similar to the previous collection in range and scope, *I Hear the Train* can be considered the *summa* of Owens's ongoing exploration of the intricate patterns and labyrinths in his complex existence. In his own terms, "We make stories in order to find ourselves at home in a chaos made familiar and comforting through the stories we make, searching frantically for patterns in the flux of randomly recorded events, a world in which endings stalk us and we can only keep inventing ways to both explain and forestall closure" (*Train* xiii).

Indeed, stories defined Owens's life and career. That seemingly universal impulse to make sense of the world we inhabit helped him "to fill in empty places in memory and received history" (*Train* xi) while attempting to get at the core of mixed-blood experience. Whether or not he succeeded, he taught all of us to believe that telling stories is surviving.

Bibliography

Kilpatrick, Jacquelyn. ed., *Louis Owens: Literary Reflections on His Life and Work.* Norman: University of Oklahoma Press, 2004.

Lalonde, Chris. *Grave Concerns, Trickster Turns: The Novels of Louis Owens.* Norman: University of Oklahoma Press, 2002.

———, ed. "Louis Owens." *Studies in American Indian Literatures* 10, no. 2 (1998): 1–127.

Lee, Robert A. "Outside Shadow: A Conversation with Louis Owens." *Louis Owens: Literary Reflections on his Life and Work,* edited by Jacquelyn Kilpatrick, 20–52. Norman: University of Oklahoma Press, 2004.

Owens, Louis. *I Hear the Train: Reflections, Inventions, Refractions.* Norman: University of Oklahoma Press, 2001.

———. *Bone Game: A Novel.* Norman: University of Oklahoma Press, 1994.

———. *The Sharpest Sight: A Novel.* Norman: University of Oklahoma Press, 1992.

———. *Mixedblood Messages: Literature, Film, Family, Place.* Norman: University of Oklahoma Press, 1998.

Purdy, John. "Clear Waters: A Conversation with Louis Owens." *Studies in American Indian Literatures* 10, no. 2 (1998): 6–22.

Elvira Pulitano

Owl's Song, The Janet Campbell Hale (1974)

The Owl's Song, perhaps JANET CAMPBELL HALE's most renowned work, was published in the 1970s. That it remains in print today testifies to its contribution to the field of American Indian literature. The work follows the teenager Billy White Hawk, who leaves the Coeur d'Alene, Idaho, reservation in hopes of finding a more rewarding future; however, his journey to the city and return home function as White Hawk's own vision quest as he discovers the importance of self-definition. Interspersing the dreams and visions of father and son throughout the novel, Hale highlights an important cultural sanctuary that proves invaluable to Billy on his journey to manhood.

After graduation from elementary school Billy faces a bleak future on the reservation. Raised by his widowed elderly father, who constantly struggles with irregular bouts of employment and heavy drinking binges, Billy finds few role models. Even Billy's hero, his cousin Tom, returns from Vietnam dishonorably discharged. Later, after accidentally burning down the White Hawks' home and unable to deal with his failures, Tom shoots himself; Billy is witness to the suicide. Now stripped of his role model, Billy decides to leave the reservation.

Billy goes to live with his older stepsister, Alice Fay, who has tried to reject her heritage completely. She pressures Billy to go to the Bureau of Indian Affairs (BIA) school and constantly pushes him to assimilate. But Billy does not share Alice Fay's shame about his heritage; nor does he try to conceal it. At school he finds himself in a predominantly African-American facility, where he is the target of racial prejudice. At the school talent show Billy ascends the stage amid racial slurs and calls for him to "'Do a Rain Dance'" (117). After delivering a bitter version of American history from the indigenous perspective that results in his exclusion from an upcoming art exhibition, Billy decides to return home.

Soon after Billy's return his father dies. Yet Billy has attained a more global perspective and a spiritual balance. He realizes "he'd been sent his vision. He was a man like Sah-hult-sum had been, like White Hawk had been and he would always be" (152). Accepting of himself and secure in his own identity, Billy now has the spiritual and emotional protection to face the world, knowing that "all this would remain with him when he went away and would not change. He was the son of Sah-hult-sum, the grandson of White Hawk, the tribe's last shaman" (152).

See also ASSIMILATION; VIETNAM WAR.

Bibliography

Hale, Frederick. "Dreams and Vision Quests in Janet Campbell Hale's *The Owl's Song.*" *Studies in American Indian Literatures: Newsletter of the Association for the Study of American Indian Literatures* 12, no. 1 (1980): 69–82.

———. *Janet Campbell Hale.* Boise State University Western Writers Series 125 Boise, Idaho: Boise State University Press, 1996.

Hale, Janet Campbell. *The Owl's Song.* Albuquerque: University of New Mexico Press, 1997.

Patti Dimond

P

Pacific Northwestern tribal literature

The tribes of the Pacific Northwest lived and thrived in communities that were intimately tied to the water and the life that surround it. Their mythology abounds with animals unfamiliar to most of the rest of the country, such as whales, seals, sharks, and salmon. For the most part tribes were rooted to small areas and were not nomadic. Because their primary source of food was the sea, they lived along the coastline and did not generally travel far inland. They were largely peaceful and are known for their sophisticated woodworking, including totem poles and seafaring vessels far more complicated than they might have appeared to an observer. Tribes located in this region include the Tlingit, Haida, Kwakiutl, Salish, Nootka, Chinook, Tillamook, and Spokane.

One of the earliest and most influential American Indian novelists, D'ARCY MCNICKLE, hails from this region. A member of the Salish tribe, McNickle in his work critically examines the difficulty of communicating across racial and cultural barriers, the devastating effects of government policies on tribal societies, and the return of the native to the tribal community—all themes that remain crucial to Native literature. His most famous work, *The Surrounded,* is the story of a young MIXED-BLOOD, Archilde Leon. Archilde, who has been earning his living in the white world by playing the fiddle, arrives home intimidated by his white father but scornful of his Indian relatives and what he believes to be their backward way of life. During the course of the novel, however, Archilde begins to appreciate and identify with his Indian heritage and finds it increasingly difficult to leave.

At the other end of the contemporary spectrum from McNickle, SHERMAN ALEXIE, one of the most well-known Indian writers, also writes from a northwestern perspective. A member of both the Idaho Coeur d'Alene and the Spokane, Alexie resists misconceptions and stereotypes about modern Indians. In his work, although he does espouse a pantribal view of the contemporary world, he is careful to note his origin. For instance, in *The Lone Ranger and Tonto Fistfight in Heaven* Thomas Builds-the-Fire, poking fun at his friend Victor's insistence on adopting the stereotypical "tough Indian" persona, notes that Americans think every Indian is a Plains Indian, and quips that his people's movie would be "Dances with Salmon." In general, the salmon as a symbol plays an important role in Alexie's work, demonstrating that one may be pantribal and tribally specific at the same time.

Other writers from tribes located in this area include GLORIA BIRD (Spokane), who has been influential as a promoter, as well as a producer, of Indian women's writing. She coedited with JOY HARJO the groundbreaking anthology of Native women's writing *Reinventing the Enemy's Lan-*

GUAGE and is one of the founding members of the Northwest Native American Writers Association. Another influential feminist writer from this area is the Coeur d'Alene writer JANET CAMPBELL HALE. Her novel *The JAILING OF CECELIA CAPTURE* was nominated for a Pulitzer Prize in 1985. Hale is well known for addressing issues faced by urban Indians who feel displaced in that setting.

Bibliography

Ruby, Robert H. *Indians of the Pacific Northwest: A History.* Norman: University of Oklahoma Press, 1988.

Jennifer McClinton-Temple

Penn, W. S.   (William Swain) (1949–   )

W. S. Penn is a critically acclaimed novelist and essay writer. Of mixed Nez Perce, Osage, and Anglo ancestry, he was born in Los Angelos, California, to William and Elizabeth (Hall) Penn. He married Jennifer Siani in 1983. They have two children, Rachel Antonia and William Anthony Charles. As his father did, Penn pursued academics, graduating from University of California, Davis, in 1970 and completing his doctorate of arts at Syracuse University in 1979.

Penn's fiction and nonfiction rely on themes of cultural identity and the simultaneous messiness and necessity of family relations. He often humorously meditates on the complications of MIXED-BLOOD Indian identity and maintaining of family traditions in the face of an unsympathetic white and materialistic culture, employing overlapping fictional realms of magic and mundane reality to illustrate the difficulty of spanning cultural divides. He is drawn toward characters on the fringes, whether these characters are Indian or not. In his acclaimed *THIS IS THE WORLD,* for instance, fewer than half of the stories involve characters who are identified as Indian, yet all of the stories involve characters who are trying to create identities outside the mainstream.

The willingness to write about non-Native characters does not also signify a lack of engagement with Native issues. In his first novel, *The ABSENCE OF ANGELS,* the protagonist must grow to understand his mixed heritage and find his own sense of place. In *All My Sins Are Relatives,* an amalgamation of memoir, history, and storytelling, he deeply investigate, what it means to be of mixed race, specifically to be of mixed race and to be Indian.

Penn's awards and honors are numerous. He was the two-time recipient of the Stephen Crane Prize for Fiction (1977 and 1979). Financial support for his projects has been granted by the Yaddo Writer's Colony, Ludwig Vogelstein Foundation, Inc. (1985), a New York Foundation for the Arts Prize (1988), and the Michigan Council on the Arts (1990). He was the resident writer at the Banff Center for the Arts in 1991. Penn has also received the North American Indian Prose Award (1994). Wordcraft Circle of Native Writers and Storytellers twice named him writer of the year (1997 and 2002). In 2003 Penn received the Distinguished Faculty Award from Michigan State University and in 2005 the Critic's Choice Award for Most Acclaimed Books. *The Telling of the World: Native American Stories and Art* appeared on the list of Best University Press Books (2000); *This Is the World* was awarded the Choice Magazine Outstanding Academic Book Award (2000), and *Killing Time with Strangers* was awarded the American Book Award for Literary Merit (2000).

A member of the National Advisory Council on Native American Writing and the Native Writers Circle, he is a professor of English at Michigan State University, where he directs the Creative Writing Program. He currently lives in East Lansing, Michigan.

Bibliography

Conner, David. "Native American Author Speaks to Students." *California Aggie,* 18 February 1998, 1.
Penn, W. S. *The Absence of Angels.* Norman: University of Oklahoma Press, 1995.
———. *Killing Time with Strangers.* Tucson: University of Arizona Press, 2000.
———. *The Telling of the World: Native American Stories and Art.* New York: Stewart, Tabori & Chang, 1996.
———. *This Is the World.* East Lansing: Michigan State University Press, 2000.

Sherwin, Elisabeth. "William Penn Is Not an Imagined Native American Stereotype." *Printed Matter*, 8 March 1998, 3.

Michelle LaFrance

Pipe for February, A   Charles H. Red Corn (2002)

Charles H. RED CORN's premier work, *A Pipe for February,* is a perfect example of an AMERICAN INDIAN NOVEL that cuts against the grain of what many readers would consider the "typical" Indian novel. Red Corn is a member of the Osage tribe and grew up in Indian country in Oklahoma. The Osage occupied three main villages under the 1906 Allotment: Pawhuska, Hominy, and Gray Horse. These towns are still the center of their culture; Pawhuska remains the tribal capital. In the late 1800s oil was discovered under the land the Osage tribes occupied, and by 1923 the Osage Indian tribe was the richest population group in the world. In that year alone the tribe received some $27 million from drilling rights sold. This newfound wealth meant that the clans of the Osage tribe could greatly improve their lifestyle by owning houses, land, and businesses in Oklahoma Indian country.

Red Corn begins his story during this opulent time of Osage history. But he also tackles a most disturbing part of this same era, known as the "Osage Reign of Terror." At the center of this reign was William Hale, a devious and manipulative man who lived on the Osage Reservation and did his best to swindle money and oil rights from Osage families. Red Corn weaves a tale that incorporates all these complicating elements into one beautiful story. The story is told from the point of view of John Grayeagle, an Osage who experiences this exciting and frightening time in Osage history firsthand. John's life as an Osage is full of parties and trips, shopping and wonderful meals. His grandfather has taught him the ways of the tribe, and he has grown into a man and faithful friend. John's peaceful existence in the midst of the small town of Pawhuska is changed as his relatives and friends become the targets of scam artists and deceivers who are trying to acquire portions of the Osage wealth.

Red Corn not only narrates the daily activity of the lives in Pawhuska during this era, he also transmits the important tribal rituals and ideas that were passed down to John by his grandfather and other clan leaders. The uses of the pipe, the ceremonies, the traditional activities and rites of the Osage are an integral part of Red Corn's story. John is something of an intercessor, between the ancient era of his grandfather and the immensely shifting times of the 1920s. Red Corn shows this mediation best as he explains the importance of the pipe (the symbol of the communication with the Osage ancient ceremonies and rituals) and the significance of the month of February (the Osage word for the month can be interpreted as "don't let it fool you"). John's mediation is essential as he strives to find a place for his people's ancient traditions in the unexpected and inexplicable times in which they are embroiled. "I am grateful the Old People did not bury all of our teachings and all of our rituals. I will search for those qualities within Indian People and in those teachings the Old People did leave us" (268).

Rhonda Kyncl

Plains tribes literature

Native American literature from the Great Plains region of the United States holds a rich history firmly rooted in the oral traditions of the various tribes making up this unique cultural treasure. Although the most familiar tribes associated with the Great Plains include the Sioux (Lakota, Dakota, and Nakota), the Cheyenne, the Blackfeet, the Crow, and the Comanche, many others once flourished in the vast grasslands, valleys, streams, and hills that stretched from south Texas to Canada. Over time these ancestral territories diminished as the United States continued to expand its borders westward, leaving behind a legacy of literary works that compel readers to explore tribal identities and histories through masterful incorporation of traditional themes and narrative elements. While given the task of documenting the cultural and spiritual value of the Native American past, these literary texts illuminate the modern world for both contemporary Native and non-Native Americans.

Early examples of Plains tribes literature emerged with the transcription of tribal history and folklore. One vital link between the oral cultures of the Plains tribes and the literate culture of contemporary Native Americans can be found in the work of Gertrude Simmons Bonnin, also known as ZITKALA-ŠA (her tribal name, which means "red bird"). Born in 1876 on a Sioux reservation in South Dakota, Zitkala-Ša was educated at Earlham College and the Boston Conservatory. Her collection *Old Indian Legends* (1901) aimed to transplant the Native spirit of her tribal folklore into the English language. Her words were the first among American Indian women to be written without the aid of an editor or interpreter, providing the reader with a pure glimpse into the vast spiritual wealth housed within each legend. "The School Days of an Indian Girl" (1900) (see *AMERICAN INDIAN STORIES*) opened a window into the assimilationist schooling Native Americans endured, an education that formed the foundation of cultural alienation she would have to overcome. Through her work Bonnin not only voiced her tribe's struggle with cultural dislocation and injustice, but used language as a tool to forge an identity of a Native American that bridged the two cultures. Two decades later her book *American Indian Stories* (1921) built upon Zitkala-Ša's contribution to Plains tribes literature by revealing such multicultural dilemmas as gendered family role expectations and mother-daughter conflict. Her themes touched the potential of merging literary art and protest without losing the universality of womanhood, of motherhood, of the human dignity Anglo America did not understand belonged in equal measure to the Native American.

The autobiography served as another tool in introducing Plains tribes history into the literary realm. The autobiography genre can be divided into two categories: those written by literate Native American writers and those dictated by a formally uneducated Native American to a literate person who actually wrote the text. BLACK ELK SPEAKS, *Being the Life Story of a Holy Man of the Oglada Sioux,*

as told through John G. Neihardt (1932) became a classic of the "as-told-to" autobiography. Neihardt shapes a narrative around BLACK ELK's self-described failure to live up to the vision that had been entrusted to him to lead his nation through four difficult periods until he found a four-colored herb that would revitalize his people. The bicultural authorship found in *Black Elk Speaks,* however, creates certain difficulties. Although the language of the text is clearly Neihardt's, the tone and the content are credited to Black Elk, leaving critics and scholars with grounds for argument; however, the story within the argument that relates the frustration, the struggle, the injustice, and the beauty surrounding the vision received by Black Elk provides the true legacy for Plains tribes literature. In this volume the killing of Crazy Horse, the last of the great Sioux war chiefs, finds an audience and chronicles, from the Native American perspective, the determination of the U.S. Army to place all Indians on reservations or destroy them.

CHARLES EASTMAN, a Santee Sioux, provides a powerful example of the self-written Native American autobiography. In the volume *From the Deep Woods to Civilization* (1916) Eastman documents his years of formal education and professional participation in Anglo-American culture and reveals ambivalence toward both cultures making up his life. Eastman's father, convinced of the wonders of civilization, had his family renounce their tribal ties in order to become "citizen Indians," to allow them to homestead in South Dakota. Eastman's struggle does not result directly from the U.S. government's forcing the rejection of his tribal identity experienced by Black Elk, but from a cultural betrayal set up by a foreign government and instituted by his own father. This unique view into the problem of detribalization had great literary success. Two additional volumes, *Indian Boyhood* (1902) and *The Soul of the Indian* (1911), complete Eastman's chronicle of Native American life under Anglo-American domination and are still in print today. His works generated a popular audience among Anglo youth and had a large impact on Boy Scouting, as well as the Indian-hobbyist movement. Eastman's format, a combination of autobiography and commentary, ushered in similar works, most notably by LUTHER STANDING BEAR and James Paytiamo.

The move of Plains tribes writers into fiction was a gradual evolution in literary history. Various changes had to take place in American writing before Native American thought and culture could become reasonably accessible to non-Native readers. Fundamental differences in these areas exist, forming an ideological abyss between tribal consciousness and that of industrial or urbanized cultures. Put simply, there is a gap between New World and Old World thought. One system promotes wholeness, while the other is based on division and separation. Tribal narratives reflect a sense of events occurring in a circular, unified field of interaction. This approach differs from established Anglo plotting techniques that tie significance to conflict resolution—a feature that is merely incidental in tribal narratives. For the Native American writer of fiction developments are dependent on ritual rules of ordering for their meaning. These rules have more relation to the interaction of spirits, thoughts, arcane forces, and tradition than to the more external European-American elements such as personality and politics. It took time for American fiction to accommodate the Native American tribal narrative, to open to the absence of redeemed situations, unchanged forces of alienation, the dark reality of colonization, and the genocide and hopelessness that thematically thread through Plains Tribes fiction.

The novels of JAMES WELCH (Blackfeet) contribute immensely to the complex nature of Native American fiction. Using a fragmented set of numbered vignettes to organize various portions of his multiple narratives, Welch combines European and traditional Native American structures in WINTER IN THE BLOOD (1974) and The DEATH OF JIM LONEY (1979). This device allows Welch to appeal to non-Native audiences while reflecting an accurate Native American view of human experience. The paranormal and mystical experience in Native American life form an integral part of Welch's story without becoming the blatant focus. Intertwined with the paranormal world of spirits, visions, and mystical forces impinging on the world of human beings are stories about loneliness, alienation, loss, and grief. Welch creates stories expressing the interrelationships among the human soul, the spirits, and the physical realm of seasons, plants, and animals. In *The Death of Jim Loney* Welch probes the consequences of Assimilation along with its accompanying loss of tribe and personal history. Loney has nothing, no ancestors, no close relatives, to accept and nurture him, and no tribe, but Welch also paints a portrait of a man destroyed not only by loneliness and alcohol, but by the dreams and visions of his tribal heritage. Without a tribal matrix by which he can discern dreams and visions, Loney's fate is sealed. There will be no resolution, no reintegration of Loney with his tribe, no last-minute intervention to lead Loney into happier times—only death.

This survey must include ELIZABETH COOK-LYNN, who gave an experimental narrative structuring to readers in *Then Badger Said This* (1983). Using essay techniques combined with traditional Sioux narratives paired with poems allows each style to enhance and illuminate the other. Her multiple-genre technique creates a forum through which her personal voice sounds through the voices of the Sioux. Through her words the Sioux experience is shared, their history documented, their insight revealed. Through her words the reader understands how the writer is both herself and her people. Cook-Lynn manages to join portions of oral history, tribal custom and culture, and contemporary narrative into one unified story. Her work, as does that of other Plains tribes authors, provides a glimpse of the spiritual and cultural complexities of Native American life, past and present.

Bibliography

Momaday, Natachee Scott. *American Indian Authors.* Boston: Houghton Mifflin College, 1972.

Rosen, Kenneth, ed. *The Man to Send Rain Clouds.* New York: Penguin, 1974.

Sherzer, Joel, ed. *Native American Discourse: Poetics and Rhetoric.* Cambridge: Cambridge University Press, 1987.

Susag, Dorothea M. *Roots and Branches: A Resource of Native American Literatures—Themes, Lessons, and Bibliographies.* Urbana, Ill.: National Council of Teachers of English, 1998.

Wiget, Andrew. *Handbook of Native American Literature.* New York: Garland, 1996.

Christine Marie Hilger

Posey, Alexander   (1873–1908)

Alexander Posey, Creek educator, journalist, and political leader, is best known today as a poet and the author of the Fus Fixico letters, a series of satirical letters giving the Native viewpoint on politics and life in the Indian Territory.

Posey was born on August 3, 1873, to Lewis Hence (Henderson) Posey, a Scotch-Irish farmer, and Nancy Harjo Phillips, who had a distinguished Creek family and was of the Wind Clan. Creek was Posey's first language, and he did not learn to speak English until he was 14. He attended Creek national school at Eufaula and then enrolled at Bacone Indian University, where he spent three years. He worked at a number of jobs, including as superintendent of public instruction, owner and editor of the *Indian Journal,* and field worker for the Dawes Commission. While at Bacone he fell in love with literature, began writing poetry, and became a noted orator speaking on subjects pertaining to the Native community. Much of his poetry is derivative and is informed by a heavy reliance on the English romantics, such as William Wordsworth and Percy Bysshe Shelley; however, there are moments, even this early in his writing career, when Posey introduces themes, images, subjects, and figures from his Creek childhood in dialogue with the romantic models he follows. After graduation from Bacone in 1895 he worked for the Creek nation and was elected to the nation's House of Warriors. In 1902 he became the owner and editor of the *Indian Journal.*

It was at the *Journal* that he wrote the Fus Fixio letters and his genius as a writer came to fruition. Over the next six years Posey wrote 73 letters in the series. The letters were written in dialect and focused on the conversations of four Creek men who are representative of different aspects of Creek culture. Deeply satirical, the letters depict the political and social life of the Natives in the Indian Territory as the DAWES ACT and statehood for Oklahoma began. Posey's Native characters allow the reader to see this new political and social landscape as it develops and, when judged through the perspective of traditional ways, understand why it is so often found wanting. As he shows the reader what the antics of Dawes commissioners, U.S. presidents, and federal bureaucrats looked like from the perspective of the Creek, Posey's satire is hard-hitting, full of irony, but consistently informed by deep insight and buffered by humor. In 1904 Posey took a position as an agent and interpreter for the Dawes Commission. He returned to the editorship of the *Indian Journal* in 1907 and, in addition, became a real estate broker for the lands allotted to fellow Indians in the commission's controversial work. Tragically his career was cut short when he drowned on May 2, 1908, while crossing a river.

Bibliography

Womack, Craig. "Alexander Posey's Nature Journals: A Further Argument for Tribally-Specific Aesthetics." *Studies in American Indian Literatures: The Journal for the Association of American Indian Literatures* (summer–fall 2001): 49–66.

Steve Brandon

poverty

Before the establishment of reservations, Native Americans used an economic system primarily based on bartering goods, such as horses, beads, pelts, women, and children, in order to acquire items beyond what the land could provide. Contact with European colonists violently disrupted this system, leading to a cycle of poverty among Native Americans that continues today. Although at first trade between tribes and Europeans supplied Native Americans with trinkets and novelties, eventually the tribes began to barter for more substantial goods as land encroachment increased. This barter was rarely, if ever, fair.

As a result of their reliance upon the land Native Americans suffered devastating consequences when natural disasters occurred. Traditionally such disasters caused tribes to migrate to safer and more fertile, plentiful areas—but white settlements made this migration nearly impossible. All tribes possessed rituals, chants, and prayers to counteract these hunger catastrophes. These concerns are reflected in the literature. RAY A. YOUNG BEAR's *WAITING TO BE FED* (1975) approaches hunger literally and metaphorically. Frank Applegate's *The Hopi Famine* (1929) and Cromwell Galpin's "The Corn People: A Story of Zuni" (1901) present two examples of how tribes and their members responded to calamities.

Even after Native Americans relocated, the discovery of gold and oil led to many instances of swindling by individual prospectors, as well as by state and federal governments. These issues appear in Fred Grove's *The Years of Fear: A Western Story* (2002), CHARLES H. RED CORN's *A PIPE FOR FEBRUARY* (2002), and Margaret Coel's *The Eagle Catcher* (1995).

Loss of land also occurred when tribes' need for money to buy food for their people escalated. In Frank LaPointe's "Millie's Gift" (1971) an old woman sells her land in order to live with her son and provide some money for her grandson's education. Those Native Americans who were able to retain their land suffered in other ways. One of the most well known results of white encroachment was the extinction of the buffalo. The hope that the buffalo would return led to the GHOST DANCE movement, which is referred to in Earl Murray's *Song of Wovoka* (1992).

In the modern era restrictions on fishing, hunting, and construction of dams have had some negative impact on Native Americans who rely on the land and water to provide sustenance and to obtain a surplus that can be sold for profit. Elizabeth COOK-LYNN's trilogy *AURELIA: A CROW CREEK TRILOGY* (1999), John Hockenberry's *A River Out of Eden* (2001), LINDA HOGAN's *SOLAR STORMS* (1995), and *A Ritual Death* (1997) by Father Brad Reynolds, S.J., all include conflicts over water and fishing rights. The award-winning crime writer Dana Stabenow's series of novels also examines issues regarding natural resources on Aleut lands. Issues of illegal mining and deforestation of Native American lands in order for whites to profit from the valuable resources on reservations appear in Wayne Johnson's *Six Crooked Highways* (2000), MARDI OAKLEY MEDAWAR's *Murder on the Red Cliff Rez* (2002), Naomi M. Stokes's *The Tree People* (1995), and *Whiskey Jack* (1993) by J. F. Trainor.

Once Native Americans were forced to accept government policies, the accumulation of monetary wealth became much more necessary to economic viability for the tribe than bartering. In fact, Hamlin Garland's "Big Moggasen" (1923) depicts an Indian chief confronted with the problem of feeding his people. Because the tribe can neither purchase food nor obtain it through farming, the government attempts to take advantage of their vulnerability, insisting that they assimilate in exchange for food. Similarly *Reservations* (1999) by Harold Burton Meyers discusses in great length the negative effects of the federal government's financial crisis during the Great Depression on the Navajo reservation.

The harsh realities of many Native Americans' dependence on government programs and the importance of these programs to these individuals' survival are presented in Byrd Baylor's "The Winner" (1972) and "A Faint Glow under the Ashes" (1973) for *Redbook*. David Treuer's *The Hiawatha* (1999) follows the life of a woman who participates in the 1950s Urban Relocation program for Native Americans. In *Madchild Running* (1999) Keith Egawa includes the Urban Native Support Services program as an integral part of the plot.

Unemployment on reservations also contributes to the impoverishment of Native Americans. When they attempt to find work off the reservation, Native Americans often encounter racism. Elizabeth Shepley Sergeant's "Good-by to the Superintendent" (1937), George A. Boyce's "Enough for Two" (1974), and Craig Kee Strete's *Paint Your Face on a Drowning in the River* (1978) portray these problems. The poverty on the reservation is also a focal point of ADRIAN C. LOUIS's *SKINS* (1995). Furthermore, Native American addictions to alcohol often pose obstacles to the realization of economic independence. Byrd Baylor's *Yes Is Better Than No* (1977) and SHERMAN ALEXIE's *The LONE RANGER AND TONTO FISTFIGHT IN HEAVEN* present the ways alcoholism, the stress of assimilation, and poverty relate to each other.

Whereas pre-1970 stories, such as Grace Coolidge's "The Indian of the Reservation" (1919), Frank Applegate's "The Mystery of Manzano" (1932), and Applegate's "Tricks in All Trades" (1932), often depicted Native Americans being duped out of their land and money, the period after the 1970s introduced works advocating Indian rights. Frank Bonham's 1970 novel *Chief* shows how Native Americans have been able to recover their land through attracting legislative, judicial, social activists devoted to helping them reclaim their rightful property. Similarly Clair Huffaker's novel *Nobody Loves a Drunken Indian* (1967) focuses on Indian advocacy. In this case the National Association for the Advancement of Colored People (NAACP) works to raise public awareness of the blight of poverty on the reservation.

Joseph Bruchac's apocalyptic novel *The Dreams of Jesse Brown* (1978) provides an idiosyncratic treatment of Native American poverty. In this work Native Americans are the only survivors of a nuclear holocaust. The key combination of their poverty and a wise man of the tribe leads to their salvation. An innovative, albeit more traditional theme surfaces in Louis Owens's novel *Nightland* (1996). This work seeks to redefine riches as not related to cash, but rather to the earth's natural resources.

Since the Native American Gaming Regulatory Act was passed in 1988, many tribes have elected to participate in the New Buffalo movement (i.e., gaming industry) as a means to alleviate poverty. Because casinos and bingo palaces often yield speedy and large profits, gaming has become a quick fix for funding reservation improvements, including welfare programs and educational scholarships. While this movement has had positive results in the short term, many Native Americans fear that this "cure" may result in yet another disappointment for these peoples if the state governments elect to legalize gambling. The ease with which the government could devastate tribal casinos alarms many tribal members, who fear that they will realize wealth only to return to a state of abject poverty.

See also ALCOHOLISM; RESERVATION LIFE.

Bibliography

Barrington, Linda. *The Other Side of the Frontier: Economic Explorations into Native American History.* Boulder, Colo.: Westview Press, 1999.

Bierhorst, John. *The Sacred Path: Spells, Prayers, and Power Songs of the American Indians.* New York: William Morrow, 1983.

Frantz, Klaus. *Indian Reservations in the United States: Territory, Sovereignty, and Socioeconomic Change.* Chicago: University of Chicago Press, 1999.

Hosmer, Brian, and Colleen O'Neill, eds. *Native Pathways: American Indian Culture and Economic Development in the Twentieth Century.* Boulder: University Press of Colorado, 2004.

Louis, Adrian C. *Skins.* New York: Crown, 1995.

Owens, Louis. *Nightland.* Norman: University of Oklahoma Press, 1996.

Young Bear, Ray. *Waiting to Be Fed.* St. Paul, Minn.: Graywolf Press, 1975.

Amy C. Branam

Power   Linda Hogan   (1998)

By reexamining the Western concept of power (which is usually hierarchical, masculine, and human centered), Linda Hogan's third novel, *Power* (1998), reinforces the tribal concept of power (which tends to be nonhierarchical, feminine, and earth centered) by using the voice and transformation of a 16-year-old Taiga tribal daughter named Omishto (the One Who Watches). Set in Florida, this deeply inspiring novel begins as Omishto witnesses Aunt Ama Eaton's killing an endangered Florida panther, Sisa (the Taiga name), on a stormy night. Along with Ama, Omishto goes through two trials—a white court and a tribal court. Nevertheless *Power* is not about law and order or right and wrong. It is about what is absent and what is present, what is seen and unseen, and how these categories work together.

Furthermore, *Power* articulates the process of becoming a tribal daughter. Omishto, the narrator, is faced with two irreconcilable lives, one her Americanized mother's life in the complex modern world and the other that of her spiritual mentor, Aunt Ama, in the simple natural world. In the eyes of white people her mother is a beautiful and decent Christian woman, and her aunt is an ugly, dark, and fearless outsider called "a human ruin" (9). However, Omishto, the watcher, sees the pure beauty in Ama, who accepts who she is, and the endless fear in her mother, who attempts to pass for white. Ultimately Omishto, the younger tribal generation, is aware of continual conflicts between the diminished Taiga world and the larger Euro-American world and intensified tensions between resistance and assimilation: "Two worlds exist. Maybe it's always been this way, but I enter them both like I am two people" (97). In the end of the novel Omishto is going home (her tribe) and dancing: "the world will go on living" (235).

Indeed, this beautifully written novel portrays the American Indian dilemma: that American Indian people cannot ignore the impact of the white encounter upon their lives or completely abandon their tribal tradition, but they are forced to choose either the white world's modern ways or the tribal world's ancient ways. By challenging "Indianness" created and perpetuated in the dominant historical and fictional accounts and showing two different ways of thinking and seeing the world, Hogan's *Power* advocates traditional ways of life and tribal heritage in the complex relationships of myth, nature, and human beings.

Bibliography

Anderson, Eric Gary. "Native American Literature, Ecocriticism, and the South: The Inaccessible Worlds of Linda Hogan's Power." In *South to a New Place: Region, Literature, Culture,* edited by Suzanne W. Jones and Sharon Monteith, 165–183. Baton Rouge: Louisiana State University Press, 2002.

Bowen-Mercer, Carrie. "Dancing the Chronotopes of Power: The Road to Survival in Linda Hogan's Power." In *From the Center of Tradition: Critical Perspectives on Linda Hogan,* edited by Barbara J. Cook, 157–177. Boulder: University Press of Colorado, 2003.

Hogan, Linda. *Power.* New York: W. W. Norton, 1998.

Heejung Cha

Power of Horses and Other Stories, The   Elizabeth Cook-Lynn (1990)

The Power of Horses is the only collection of stories by the academic, novelist, poet, and teacher ELIZABETH COOK-LYNN. Even more than Cook-Lynn's other works, it is a clear, accessible English language appropriation of the oral storytelling tradition that, for Cook-Lynn, partially defines the diverse Sioux peoples. The themes of the stories are similar to those in other works by Cook-Lynn: continuing marginalization of the Sioux Indian; dilution of Dakota/Lakhot culture, bafflement caused by alien, uncomprehending Christian missionaries; familial discord caused by domestic abuses in the past; threats to the traditional Sioux connection of the land of South Dakota; and large-scale environmental changes effected by white activities.

Representations of horses feature in many of the stories, indicating the Sioux connection to the past. When the tradition of horse management is lost, links to the past are broken. In the story "Loss of the Sky" Joseph Shields, a middle-aged Sioux, owns 200 head of horses. He proudly passes on his lifestyle to his children. He observes his son, Leo, on horseback and stresses the excellence of his son's riding skills to others. Joseph had refused an Indian commissioner's offer of American citizenship, so Leo's decision to fight for America in the Great War upsets his father. Leo dies in the 1917 campaign in France. Distraught, Leo neglects his horses and the herd declines. Involvement in white affairs has led, ultimately, to a family's demise, one symbolized through the destruction of their horse-raising abilities.

The link to horses is essential to Sioux identity: In one story Jack La Deaux becomes isolated, partly because he shows no interest in the horses in which Sioux men have traditionally taken pride. In "Last Days of a Squaw Man," a story about a damaged MIXED-BLOOD family, a little girl flees her white father's brutality by hiding in a horse stall, underlining her affiliation with the animals. The title story describes the pressures put on a Sioux man to sell his horses to a white businessman. The story is seen through the eyes of a child, whose connection to the land is based on her use of her horse, Shōta. At the story's end the girl decides not to sell the horses, but to retain them in the traditional Indian way. It is a rare moment of joy in a collection that is as angry and bitter about Sioux Indians' acceptance of white men's patronage as it is about historical cruelties by white settlers.

Bibliography

"Guide to Sioux Culture, Heritage, History and Present." Available online. URL: www.lakhota.com. Accessed on February 1, 2004.

Strom, Karen. "Elizabeth Cook-Lynn." Available online. URL: www.hanksville.org/storytellers/cooklyn. Accessed on August 15, 2005.

Wilson, Norma C. "Elizabeth Cook-Lynn." In *Dictionary of Literary Biography.* Vol. 175, *Native American Writers,* edited by Kenneth M. Roemer. Washington, D.C.: Gale Research, 1997.

Kevin DeOrnellas

pow wow

A pow wow is a celebration of American Indian life, centered on dance, drums, and regalia. The main goal of the event is to gather people. Families and friends, often scattered between distant reservations and urban centers, reunite on this occasion. Organized by a tribe, an association, a family, or even a casino, a pow wow can last from one to several days and celebrate a special event or a seasonal anniversary. Most of the time non-Indians are welcome and have the opportunity to discover and learn about Native American values.

The contemporary pow wow was formalized in the 1950s, combining traditional elements from various regions. As a result very few references to pow wows can be found except in the work of the most recent generation of Native writers. The festival described in D'ARCY MCNICKLE's *The SURROUNDED* is a good example of the pre–pow wow time, when the older generation was struggling to maintain some of the traditional ways. On the other hand, authors such as SHERMAN ALEXIE, SUSAN POWER, Dan Crank, and Allison Adelle Hedge Coke, born and raised with the pow wow as a genuine part of their lifestyle, frequently refer to it in their poems and novels.

In Sherman Alexie's writing a pow wow is an event that conveys two major aspects of contemporary Native life. It is a celebration of a time and a place where Indians can rejoice, party, love, show off, be completely alive and visible. But it is also a place where tradition and modernity collide. For instance, urban Indians can stay in touch with a part of their family values and express their belonging to an Indian community. Alexie often uses stereotypes from pop culture and Hollywood to show how Indians themselves integrate these ideas and play with them. Aware of the way white people sometimes view the pow wow as a re-created fake ritual and a show, Alexie creates humor and derision in his writing: "The fancy dancers wear bells, you know, so they can't sneak up on white tourists" (51).

Comparing the glittering dancers' regalia to the city lights, Allison Adelle Hedge Coke in her poem "Sequinned" depicts a Native life deeply rooted in modern time and urban life. Here the intertwined ornaments of a dress are like the freeways and the bridges of New York; the feathers are erected as skyscrapers. The city, at first so distant from the traditional lifestyle, is now a component of contemporary Indian life.

Intertribal relations, a crucial element of the modern pow wow, are in the center of Dan Crank's short story "Neon Powwow." Telling the tale of Indian students, several Navajo and a Hopi, spending some time in a bar, Crank uses the metaphor of the pow wow as a gathering to express the reality of these intertribal ties. These two tribes share an old troubled history not only of conflicts, but also of intermarriages. These relations, maintained today, are now given light by the fake brightness of neon, embedded in modern life.

D'Arcy McNickle's *The Surrounded* also deals with conflict between two cultures, but here the main character, Archilde Leon, is half-Spanish and half-Flathead. Taking place in the 1930s, an episode of the novel describes a gathering of Indian dances and drums as a part of the Fourth of July celebration. Archilde, trained as a classical violinist, experiences the struggle of a half-blood, torn between his European knowledge of music and the Indian drumming that he first perceives as a relic from the past. He will finally understand how important this event is to his mother in defining a little of who she is as an Indian and will help him to take the same path.

Eventually a pow wow may very well be a place of revelation, of reassurance, of comfort, or as in the example of Harley Wind Soldier in the *Grass Dancer* by Susan Power, a place of redemption. During a pow wow he dances drunk with the sacred design of his ancestors on the face. His mother, who had made with great care a beautiful dress for this special event, feels so ashamed that she publicly slaps him on the face. To put him on the right side of the track, she asks their relatives on a North Dakota reservation to look after him. There he will find the way to accept his lineage and to embrace his identity, understanding that what he was looking for was in his family and especially in himself. That revelation occurs when he realizes that while he was singing with his relatives, "what he heard was the music of his own voice, rising above the rest" (300).

See also *Neon Pow Wow*; reservation life.

Bibliography

Alexie, Sherman. *The Business of Fancy Dancing.* Brooklyn, N.Y.: Hanging Loose Press, 1992.

———. *The Lone Ranger and Tonto Fistfight in Heaven.* New York: Harper Perennial, 1994.

———. *Old Shirts and New Skin.* Los Angeles: University of California Press, 1996.

Coke, Allison Adelle Hedge. *Dog Road Woman.* Minneapolis: Coffee House Press, 1997.

Crank, Dan. *Neon Powwow.* In *Neon Powwow: New Native Voices of the Southwest,* edited by Anna L. Walter. Flagstaff, Ariz.: Northland, 1993.

McNickle, D'Arcy. *The Surrounded.* Albuquerque: University of New Mexico Press, 1978.

Power, Susan. *The Grass Dancer.* New York: G. P. Putnam's Sons, 1994.

Matthieu Charle

Powwow Highway   (1989)

Bankrolled by George Harrison's Hand-Made Films and based on the 1979 novel of the same name by David Seals, *Powwow Highway* was one of the first movies to attempt to present Indian people other than as historical nemeses, noble savages, or mystical touchstones for white America. Directed by Jonathan Wacks, the basic story follows the militant Buddy Red Bow (A. Martinez) and gentle giant Philbert Bono (Gary Farmer) along the contemporary Powwow Highway on a political and spiritual quest. The two travel in Philbert's "war pony"—a worn-out Buick that Philbert names "Protector"—from the Cheyenne reservation at Lame Deer, Montana, to Sante Fe, New Mexico, with significant stops at Pine Ridge, South Dakota, and Denver, Colorado. Buddy and Philbert have a twofold goal: to purchase new bulls for the Cheyenne tribe's herd and to rescue Buddy's sister, Bonnie, who has been framed by local authorities and jailed in an elaborate ruse to draw Buddy off the reservation before a crucial vote concerning the tribe's mineral wealth.

The movie is often approached as an inversion of the old Hollywood "cowboys and Indians" archetype, in which the virginal white woman is captured by Indians, and the white-hat-wearing cowboys must rescue the fair maiden. In this version the roles are reversed, culminating in Bonnie's dramatic rescue as Philbert uses Protector to pull the bars from the jailhouse window. Bonnie's purity is emphasized by her Madonna-like garb as she languishes in the prison and exaggerated by a licentious white girlfriend, given the sexually suggestive name "Rabbit."

Thematically the movie presents a new avenue for contemporary cinematic treatment of Indian people. Philbert and Buddy are neither romanticized nor stigmatized, and each is presented as a complex individual with his own issues. Buddy, who early in the film ridicules a pow wow, saying, "You'd think that a few lousy beads and some feathers was a culture," begins to temper his role as a contemporary warrior even as Philbert navigates the difficult terrain of discovering valid ways to integrate traditional spirituality into contemporary Indian life. The critic T. V. Reed cites Philbert's act of leaving a candy bar as an offering to his ancestors as a suggestion that contemporary Indians will survive into the future by blending the past with the often impure present (78).

Bibliography

Gerster, Carol, and Toman, Marshall. "*Powwow Highway* in an Ethnic Film and Literature Course." *SAIL: Studies in American Indian Literatures,* 2nd series 3, no. 3 (1991): 19–23. Available online. URL: oncampus.richmond.edu/faculty/ASAIL/search.html. Accessed on August 15, 2005.

Johnson, Brian D. "*Powwow Highway:* Highway of Dreams." *Macleans* 102, no. 17 (1989): 62–63.

Reed, T. V. "Old Cowboys, New Indians: Hollywood Frames the American Indian." *Wicazo Sa Review* 16, no. 2 (2001): 75–96.

Justin Blessinger

Pushing the Bear: A Novel of the Trail of Tears   Diane Glancy (1996)

Pushing the Bear, DIANE GLANCY's first novel, published in 1996, is an excellent example of the interaction of postmodern ideas of art and Native American ethnicity. The narrative is divided into short sections told from the points of view of a dozen or more characters. It tells the story of one woman's losses in the course of the forced march from Georgia and the Carolinas to Oklahoma in the winter of 1838. Glancy's narrative strategy, which flows from both Cherokee traditions of storytelling and postmodern distrust of the single point of view, allows the reader to see the TRAIL OF TEARS experience with a wide perspective. The narrators range from Maritole, a young wife and mother who suffers the loss of her home, her parents, and her child and seeks comfort in the arms of one of the white soldiers who accompany the Cherokee travelers; to her husband, Knobowtee, a proud man completely undone by the loss of masculine power, property, and control of his family; through a range of their relatives, friends, and neighbors, including a philosophical Basket Maker and a sardonic old man, War Club, who provides a measure of comic relief. A few voices of white soldiers, suppliers, and preachers are also heard, but Glancy's work imagines the broad range of human response to dispossession, misery, and death from distinctly Cherokee points of view. Her text also presents some material in the Cherokee language, in its alphabet, as well as maps of the route taken.

Glancy's work is a historical novel with mostly invented characters. But it does contain quotations from and discussions of historical documents such as treaties, speeches, and newspaper articles that provide more perspectives on the events. The reader learns about the politics of Indian removal through the conversations of the Cherokee and their discussions of key figures such as Andrew Jackson and Chief John Ross and important events that preceded the Trail of Tears. A good deal of ironic richness is developed as the reader considers the optimism and naiveté of these documents alongside the crushingly miserable reality of the Cherokee experience.

With its focus on Maritole, *Pushing the Bear* is a decidedly feminist text. Maritole is a young woman with conventional expectations who is thrust into an unconventional experience. She develops her understanding of Cherokee myth into a personalized spiritual resistance that sustains her in the midst of her maddening losses, her husband's seeming indifference, and her own emotional confusion. She moves from being pushed by the bear, which as a constantly changing symbol represents fate, adversity, and persecution, as well as Maritole's own self-destructive anger and personal and cultural self-doubt, to pushing back. While she complains of Knobowtee's emotional absence and lack of loving support along the way, she does not ultimately depend upon him or upon Sergeant Williams to define who she is. When they arrive in Oklahoma, Maritole and Knobowtee reconnect and seem at the end of the novel to be on the way to genuine reconciliation. Maritole's experience, like that of a tragic hero, seems more than any one person should be able to survive, but she does survive it, becoming stronger and wiser as a result.

Joe Skerrett

Querry, Ron (1943–)

Ron Querry, a descendant of the Sixtown Clan of the Choctaw Nation, was born in Washington, D.C., in 1943. He has taken on many roles in his life, most notably as rancher, author, and professor. He earned his Ph.D. at the University of New Mexico and has taught at the University of Oklahoma. He is also a member of the Native Writers Circle of the Americas. His novels offer the reader mystery, science, and a new outlook for those not familiar with Native American traditions.

Querry has won the Mountains and Plains Booksellers Award and the Border Regional Library Association Southwest Book Award for his first novel, The DEATH OF BERNADETTE LEFTHAND (1993). He has often been compared to Tony Hillerman, a non-Native author who is known for his novels about RESERVATION LIFE.

The Death of Bernadette Lefthand and BAD MEDICINE (1998) show how Native American traditions and modern ideas combine and sometimes clash in today's world. For example, Querry uses excerpts from various Navajo resources to explain occurrences that result in the death of Bernadette Lefthand. These excerpts are then explained so that those not familiar with these beliefs can understand. One belief system is not chosen as better than the other. Querry merely presents an alternate way of looking at the world.

Both novels deal with the characters' sense of identity. In The Death of Bernadette Lefthand the young girl is left with her sister's baby and no idea of what went wrong in her sister's life. With no one to talk to, she uses her own cultural knowledge to try to discover where events went bad. In Bad Medicine the characters deal with their own personal journeys toward self-identification. Some of the characters have been raised without a clear sense of cultural identity and struggle to obtain a balance of both cultures. Although there are various tribes represented in Querry's novels, the message is constant: "All things are related."

For those familiar with Native American tradition The Death of Bernadette Lefthand and Bad Medicine provide refreshing and accurate depictions of Native American life, particularly for those who live on the reservation. Even though the beliefs among the different tribes vary, many of their customs are similar.

In a world where technology and science are changing every day, Ron Querry offers readers a glimpse into the lives of a people whose daily events still echo those of their ancestors. His novels show how Old World meets New World.

Bibliography

Querry, Ron. Bad Medicine. New York: Bantam Books, 1998.

————. *The Death of Bernadette Lefthand.* Santa Fe, N. Mex.: Red Crane Books, 1993.

Rikki Noel Williams

Quick Brush of Wings, A   Mary Tall-Mountain (1991)

MARY TALLMOUNTAIN portrays the life of a people who meet terrible hardship with courage and laughter because they cherish each other and the life that surrounds them. This volume affords a glimpse into an Athabascan/Koyukon village at mid-20th century and is an important example of the contributions of MIXED-BLOOD writers to AMERICAN INDIAN POETRY.

Most of the poetry represents the way Tall-Mountain lovingly remembers the world of her early childhood. In the words of one of her poems, "Memories stretch and pull around me— / Bark drying on a new canoe" ("Ts'eekkaayah, Spring Camp" 5). TallMountain's reconstruction of her childhood home is particularly remarkable because she was taken away at the age of six by her adoptive family because her mother had tuberculosis that soon would take her life, and the poet did not return for 40 years.

Nulato, Alaska, 100 miles south of the Arctic Circle, is the setting for most of the poems, along with the three prose pieces that are excerpts from TallMountain's unpublished autobiographical novel *Doyen.* The writing evokes such sights, sounds, smells, and sensations as those of spring camp, the flight to the hills when the river ice breaks up, the preparation for the desperate cold and snow of winter, and the salmon's upriver journey to spawn. Athabascan/Koyukon words (accompanied by brief glossaries) help to transport readers to the Yukon village.

TallMountain is attentive to ways the people's lives are shaped by nature. In a 1989 interview with Joseph Bruchac she explained, "I think there is very little that I write about which doesn't have something in it about nature. Because it is part of us" (Bruchac 17–18).

The title poem introduces the shimmering presence of spirits with stories of a talking beaver, a Christmas tree "shining on river ice" ("A Quick Brush of Wings" 12), a dog that howls with a woman's voice and then goes crazy, a feeling of being touched by icy fingers at the instant an old man dies, and "Something cold [that] feathers my arms" (29). That "quick brush of wings" represents the pervasive penetration of the human world by the spirit world in the life of this village. TallMountain emphasizes the communal quality of the village life by placing the narratives in the voices of the women, who tell the stories during a sewing circle.

A Quick Brush of Wings is the product of Tall-Mountain's struggle "as a writer to make public sense of all the conflicting threads of her life" (Welford 61): her Athabaskan, Russian, and Irish-American heritages, as well as Catholic and pagan influences. It is a portrayal of the value of a tribal perspective that reveres nature and the life of the tribe.

Bibliography

Bruchac, Joseph W. III. "We Are the Inbetweens: An Interview with Mary TallMountain." *Studies in American Indian Literals* 1 no. 1 (summer 1989): 13–21.

TallMountain, Mary. *A Quick Brush of Wings.* San Francisco: Freedom Voices, 1991.

Welford, Gabrielle. "Reflections on Mary TallMountain's Life and Writing: Facing Mirrors." *Studies in American Indian Literals* 9, no. 2 (summer 1997): 61–68.

Susan Bowers

R

Ravensong   Lee Maracle (1993)

Ravensong is the story of Stacey, a Salish teenager attempting to understand her place in the world while her community struggles through an influenza epidemic; through this coming-of-age story, LEE MARACLE presents complex sociological theories of cross-cultural communication, medical anthropology, and sexuality. Stacey lives in a Salish village but attends high school in the "white town" across the river. The bridge over the river symbolizes the possibilities and problems of cultural interchange. It allows Stacey to move between worlds and to take knowledge, food, and medical supplies back to her community; however, it is also a site of possible invasion by white characters, who are unable to recognize the dangers of crossing the boundaries between worlds. Stacey connects the arc of the bridge with the "invisible power" of a young white man who walks her home without asking (74). Movement across the bridge allows characters on both sides of the river to learn from each other, but the river always keeps the communities separate and represents the barriers to real interchange.

These barriers are further demarcated by the diseases that plague both communities. Poverty, close living quarters, and a lack of Western medicine make the Salish people susceptible to influenza and other diseases introduced by the colonizers, who themselves lack spiritual and community health. Stacey's detached observation of her schoolmates uncovers a lack of connection between individuals in white Canadian society. The diseased European patriarchy that denies women power and enforces a double standard of sexual purity leads to the suicide of Stacey's white classmate Polly, after the disclosure that Polly is sexually active. While Western medicine could alleviate the effects of the flu, Salish concepts of health and balance could alleviate "the sickness" rooting the settlers "to their own ugliness" (191). Although each community holds the cure to the other's illness, mutual distrust and prejudice prevent them from helping each other.

Stacey's story is intertwined with that of Raven, the TRICKSTER FIGURE of the Pacific Northwest and an agent of change in Salish mythology. Raven takes the Europeans to North America and inflicts diseases on the Salish community, hoping it will force them into the white world to "fix the mess over there" (14). Throughout the novel Stacey worries that she has "too much Raven" in her, but in the epilogue she realizes that her problem is the opposite: "Not enough Raven" (198). Maracle suggests that in order to negotiate the complex changes that are happening in the world and to overcome the difficulties of establishing an identity in the face of cultural and sexual expectations, people must take on the border-crossing and transformative characteristics of a trickster.

Bibliography

Hoy, Helen. "'Because You Aren't Indian': Lee Mara- cle's *Ravensong*." In *How Should I Read These? Na- tive Women Writers in Canada*, 127–152. Toronto: University of Toronto Press, 2001.

MacFarlane, Karen. "Storying the Borderlands: Liminal Spaces and Narrative Strategies in Lee Maracle's *Ravensong*." In *Creating Community: A Roundtable on Canadian Aboriginal Literature*, ed- ited by Renate Eigenbrod and Jo-Ann Episkenew, 109–124. Penticton, Canada: Theytus, 2002.

Maracle, Lee. *Ravensong*. Vancouver: Press Gang, 1995.

Judith Leggatt

Raven Tells Stories: An Anthology of Alaskan Native Writing   Joseph Bruchac, ed. (1991)

Raven Tells Stories: An Anthology of Alaskan Na- tive Writing documents the "blossoming of the talent and energy" (ix) of Native Alaskan writers during the late 1980s. James Ruppert's introduc- tion emphasizes that this book combines old and new voices of Alaskan Native literature and places them side by side. The Native Alaskan experience is interpreted through the eyes of writers who wit- nessed firsthand the arrival of "schools, transpor- tation, and the cash economy" (ix) from the south and through the eyes of those who grew up as ac- tive participants in both Native culture and the new dominant culture. A distinguishing feature of this collection is that nearly all of the 23 writers represented have contributed a brief introduction to their work and life. These sections are told in the first person and serve as informal pathways into a writer's work. A person interested in biographi- cal details about a specific writer can find useful information even in a space so brief. Many of the entries include photos.

Among the writers represented in this collec- tion, some were already well known before 1991. Fred Bigjim, for example, was already an estab- lished poet and scholar in 1991; he had published two collections of his poetry as well as essays and three books dealing with multicultural issues in

education and law. To this volume Bigjim contrib- uted six poems as well as the article "Developing Alaskan Native Humanistic Themes," a scholarly argument for the use by the academic world of the humanities to understand Native culture in all of its complexity and variety better.

Nora Marks Dauenhauer remains an inter- nationally recognized figure in Native language culture and literature. For decades Dauenhauer has been at the forefront in the emergence of pub- lished Southeast Alaskan Native literature, doing everything from creating textbooks on Tlingit language and literature to recording folktales and songs in the Tlingit language. She continues to be a community leader not only in literature but also in linguistics and history. To this volume Dauen- hauer contributed six poems and "Raven, King Salmon, and the Birds," a short play based upon a traditional folktale.

Mary TallMountain was, by 1991, a well-re- spected and internationally famous writer and teacher. Her nomadic life took her up and down the west coast of North America, yet she returned often through her writing to her Yukon River roots. Her work has been published in works too numerous to count. To this collection she con- tributed eight poems that speak of love and loss and conflict between civilizations, and the short story "Outflight," about going home to the Yukon again.

See also Native Alaskan tribal literature.

William Gillard

recognition

In August 2005 there were 562 tribes recognized by the U.S. government. Established in 1978 and overseen by the Bureau of Indian Affairs (BIA), the process of recognition formalizes a legal rela- tionship between the sovereign tribal "nation" and the U.S. government. This relationship is seen as a government-to-government relationship and is often referred to as the "right" of self-government for indigenous peoples.

Once granted recognition, tribes maintain jurisdiction over their members, lands, and resources. They may define who may and may not be members of the tribe, draft tribal legislation, and enact law enforcement, court systems, and taxes. The U.S. government must consult tribal governments about issues that affect tribal communities and properties.

Criticism of the process holds that it consumes too much of a tribe's resources, takes too long, and is inconsistent. In 2001 BIA officials estimated that it could require up to 15 years for all the completed petitions to be resolved. Recent congressional acts to revise the process have focused on the issues of limited resources and timeliness.

See also SOVEREIGNTY; TERMINATION.

Bibliography

"Amending the Indian Self-Determination and Education Assistance Act to Provide Further Self-Governance by Indian Tribes: Report." Washington, D.C.: U.S. Government Printing Office, 2004.

Bordewich, Fergus M. *Killing the White Man's Indian: Reinventing Native Americans at the End of the Twentieth Century.* New York: Doubleday, 1996.

Deloria, Vine, Jr., and Clifford M. Lytle. *American Indians, American Justice.* Austin: University of Texas Press, 1983.

U.S. Government Accountability Office (GAO). *Indian Issues: Timeliness of the Tribal Recognition Process Has Improved, but It Will Take Years to Clear the Existing Backlog of Petitions.* Testimony of Robin M. Nazzaro before the House of Representatives. Washington, D.C.: U.S. Government Accountability Office, 2005. Available online. URL: http://www.gao.gov/newaitems/d053471.pdf. Accessed on November 14, 2006.

Wunder, John R., ed. *Native American Sovereignty (Contemporary and Historical Perspectives on American Indian Rights, Freedoms, and Sovereignty).* New York: Garland, 1996.

Michelle LaFrance

Red Clay: Poems and Stories   Linda Hogan   (1991)

In *Red Clay: Poems and Stories* (1991) LINDA HOGAN, one of the most influential Native American writers, begins "the journey home" by declaring, "Home is in blood, and I am still on the journey of calling myself home" (1). In these poems and stories, based on personal and tribal histories, Hogan explores the traditional indigenous view of human relationships with the land, animals, and plants; that is what is called home for American Indian people: "We are the earth" (6). Through the journey home and telling the story about her tribal ancestors' uprooted lives and survival, Hogan, a MIXED-BLOOD Chickasaw, reinvents self-identity, harmonized with her tribal heritage and the natural world. Moreover, she seeks to restore the balance of the life cycle in the earth, especially the Oklahoma earth, which she sees as poisoned with white oil and white greed.

Half this collection is poetry, which "live(s) red land and light" (1), and half is prose, which is "to uncover and discover a new truth" (41). In the two poetry sections Hogan uses recurrent images of nature and landscape such as turtles, trees, red clay, crows, insects, and fish. Whereas the poems of the first section, "By the Dry Pond," are spiritual, those of the second section, "Heritage," are political. For example, in "Red Clay" in the first section Hogan thankfully praises a harmony of tribal people and the earth: "We are here, the red earth / passes like light into us / and stays" (7). In turn in "Blessing," in the second section, she satirizes white rich men who steal "the land of red grass" from "red people": "Blessed are the rich / for they eat meat every night / They have already inherited the earth" (30).

The broken tribal life and unspoken truth in the poetry section are sadly and humorously redepicted in the prose section with "That Horse," based on her father and forefathers' (hi)stories. In this section Hogan illustrates "how the oral becomes the written, how life becomes a story" (43). Set in an Oklahoma "stained with oil" (21), "planned poverty" (59), and "38¢ death" (60), the stories are the multilayered history of Hogan's family and Oklahoma tribes, such as the Chickasaw and the Cherokee, who are surrounded by their grief, resistance, strength, and wholeness, as well as their love. In the face of white capitalism in "That House," tribal people disappear during the night without a trace. The historical facts of the story show that white life generates brutal death in exchange for money. In the face of Christianity in "Amen," Hogan demonstrates that tribal people remember who they are through a character named Jack who was born with only one eye and is internally connected to the image of a large fish. In the end through these poems and stories Hogan asks us to listen "when no one is left to speak" (31).

Bibliography

Bonett, Kay, ed. "Linda Hogan." In *Conversations with American Novelists,* 184–200. Columbia: University of Missouri Press, 1997.

Hogan, Linda. *Red Clay: Poems and Stories.* Greenfield Center, N.Y.: Greenfield Review Press, 1991.

Womack, Craig. "A Review of *Red Clay: Poems and Stories.*" *American Indian Quarterly* 17 (1993): 103–104.

Heejung Cha

Red Corn, Charles (1936–)

Whether championing Osage tribal rights as an educator, community leader, or novelist, Charles Red Corn invests a remarkable sense of dedication to honoring his tribe's cultural identity and a commitment to maintaining that heritage. Perhaps best known for his first novel, *A PIPE FOR FEBRUARY* (2002), Red Corn has also had a long and distinguished career as an innovator in educational and economic development programs for Native peoples. He has also distinguished himself by retrieving revenues lost and stolen from Osage tribal members during the times he features in *A Pipe for February.* Red Corn has been married for many years to Jeri Red Corn, celebrated for her work with traditional Caddo pottery; he also holds a master of education degree from Penn State University.

A Pipe for February appeared to much critical claim. In this novel Red Corn fashions a fictional account of the actual turmoil and tragedy that began for the Osage people in the first decades of the 20th century.

Since the publication of his first novel Red Corn has received increasing recognition as a major voice in Native American literature. In fall 2004, for example, he was a Rockefeller Fellow at the Newberry Library, where the led a workshop on tradition and innovation in Native American literature. That same fall Red Corn became the first Fellow of the Tribal Scholars Program in Dartmouth's Native American Studies Program. While there, he concentrated on writing his second novel and advancing issues of tribal SOVEREIGNTY. Speaking about his next novel, Red Corn also addressed his role as a Native American author: "In my writing I acknowledge that American Indians have been treated badly, but I also want to communicate those things that have sustained us. I tend to think our ancient teachings are what pull us through" (Walsh). And in "Still Strong after All These Years" (2004) Red Corn makes similar arguments. Given the centrality of these themes in his writing and professional careers, Red Corn will continue as an advocate for the sovereignty of Osage tribal identity, and all Native peoples, whenever he can.

Bibliography

Red Corn, Charles. "American Indians: Still Strong after All These Years." *The American Indian Quarterly* 28, no. 1–2 (winter–spring 2004): 118–120.

———. *A Pipe for February.* Norman: University of Oklahoma Press, 2002.

Walsh, Peter. "Red Corn Is First Tribal Fellows Scholar." *Vox of Dartmouth* (5 November 2004). Available online. URL: http://www.dartmouth.edu/~vox/0405/1108/redcorn.html. Accessed on August 15, 2005.

Clay Smith

Red on Red: Native American Literary Separatism   Craig Womack (1999)

CRAIG WOMACK's *Red on Red* is an essential contribution to scholarship on Native American sovereignty. In his introduction Womack articulates his central argument: "I say that tribal literatures are not some branch waiting to be grafted onto the main trunk [of the Western canonical tree]. Tribal literatures are the *tree,* the oldest literatures in the Americas, the most American of American literatures. We *are* the can. . . . I am saying with all the bias I can muster that *our* American canon, the Native literary canon of the Americas, predates *their* American canon. I see them as two separate canons" (6–7). Womack wants Native peoples to set the criteria and judge the works of their own writers. He argues that they have a responsibility to their community, and this responsibility inflects Native literature with a political component. In *Red on Red* Womack concentrates on politicizing Native literature and using autonomy, self-determination, and sovereignty as tools of analysis (28).

In "The Creek Nation" Womack briefly explains Creek history and some traditional ceremonies. By using *we* or writing in the present tense when describing a ritual (such as stomp dancing), Womack sees writers demonstrating the vital presence of Native culture in the present time (27). In "Reading the Oral Tradition for Nationalist Themes" Womack argues that the "oral tradition has always been a deeply politicized forum for nationalistic literary expression," and that there is a "deep interaction between political, spiritual, and oral stories" (51–52). In his chapter on JOY HARJO Womack argues that "Harjo's work demonstrates that connection to one's tribal nation vitalizes one's writing . . . [and that] contact with other cultures does not cancel out her Muskogean center," but rather such a "grounding strengthens her pan-tribal vision" (225). According to Womack, Harjo's poetry and her poetic vision, centered in tribal culture, is not weakened by exposure to other cultures.

Finally in "Lynn Riggs as Code Talker" Womack argues that ROLLIE LYNN RIGGS's theory of Oklahoma "is better understood as the internal terrain of a closeted gay man than as an actual literal rendering of Oklahoma and its people" (275).

Bibliography

Shoemaker, Nancy, ed. *Clearing a Path: Theorizing the Past in Native American Studies.* New York: Routledge, 2001.

Warrior, Robert Allen. *Tribal Secrets: Recovering American Indian Intellectual Traditions.* Minneapolis: University of Minnesota Press, 1994.

Womack, Craig. *Red on Red: Native American Literary Separatism.* Minneapolis: University of Minnesota Press, 1999.

Ben Carson

Reinventing the Enemy's Language: Contemporary Native Women's Writings of North America   Joy Harjo and Gloria Bird (1997)

At the time of its publication *Reinventing the Enemy's Language* was the most comprehensive collection of contemporary North American indigenous women's writings yet published. This landmark collection was 10 years in the making, and the co-editors JOY HARJO (Muscogee) and GLORIA BIRD (Spokane) "wanted the anthology to be a collective voice from the women of the continual indigenous presence here" in the lands European colonizers named North America. This collective voice of indigenous female continuance is beautifully realized through the inclusion of writing by 87 women from 50 tribal nations, in over 100 stories, poems, and personal narratives. While a number of well-known Native women are published here—such as LESLIE MARMON SILKO, JEANNETTE ARMSTRONG, and LINDA HOGAN—many writers receive first-time publication in *Reinventing*. The literature in this collection is as vast in scope as the ages, experiences, tribes, languages, and geographies of the women producing it and represents urban and rural lifeways, on reservation and off. Topics range from BOARDING SCHOOL, corrupt tribal councilmen, and rape, to relocation, love, healing, and ancestral spirits, with events set in prisons, kitchens, sun-drenched pueblos, pulsing city streets, and the space of dreams. Alongside this diversity of experience and locale, the selections also highlight the "similar concerns based on community" that are shared by Native North American women (23). Harjo and Bird have arranged the women's writings into four thematic sections that underscore the cycle of creative process: genesis, struggle, transformation, and returning (29).

As the volume's title emphasizes, Harjo and Bird chose to highlight the creativity, ingenuity, resilience, and power contemporary Native women demonstrate in transforming a colonial language (English, in this case) historically forced upon them and their ancestors into one of beauty and resistance that reflects indigenous perceptions and oral storytelling patterns. These Native women speak for themselves not only through their poetry and stories, but in the italicized first-person statements that preface the authors' work. Kim Caldwell, Tsalagi-Shawnee, prefaces her poem "Moonlight" by clarifying that "when the invaders came to this continent they did everything within their power to silence the voices of the indigenous women. . . . It is now our responsibility to reach out to the young women and encourage them to not be afraid to lift their voices and be heard" (529–530). Here as elsewhere Harjo and Bird enact in text one of their primary motivations for bringing this collection into being: the creation of a dialogue between many Native American women (and their readers), in their own voices, about their lives within a community of survivors. *Reinventing the Enemy's Language* attests to both the diversity and the commonality of Native North American women's experiences; their continued survival over centuries of colonial efforts to silence, speak for, or eliminate them outright; and the eloquent power with which their stories sing in a language they have reclaimed on their terms.

Jane Haladay

Relief of America, The   Diane Glancy (2000)

DIANE GLANCY is a poet immersed in the power of language. Her manipulation of language is a way to navigate and find balance between two disparate cultures. Through her creative expression Glancy recollects a fragmented and painful past in order to offer restoration on many levels.

The Relief of America opens with a black and white projection of North America. In her epigram Glancy asks the reader to turn the map around and see that the land is actually the outline of an "Indian's head." Through this she is not only underscoring the fact that the Americas are indigenous land, but showing the reader that one must challenge the status quo by shifting one's perspective of the world. Ultimately this stands as a metaphor for what Glancy is doing in her poetry throughout the collection as readers' assumptions and presupposed ideas about history and what con-

stitutes "America" are challenged and ultimately subverted.

In the first poem from the collection, "Christopher," Glancy transforms language in order to rewrite the paradigmatic myth of the "discovery" of America. She does this by flipping the perspective—the Native's voice tells the story, not the newcomer's: "Here come Christopher Columbus comming ober t' wabes. / PUFF PUFF. / He think he come to the segund part of urth" (9). Although this wordplay and the voice of the storyteller could be deemed crude or simply phonetic, it is precisely this voice that has the intelligence to understand that Columbus is not where he thinks he is. Further, each line that follows has a crucial insight into the truth of "contact" mythology: European colonizers sought wealth in the form of gold and other resources and felt divine obligation to missionize the Native inhabitants in order to save the "savages'" souls.

By questioning fundamental suppositions of language, land, and history through a Native perspective, Glancy's text considers what hinders and hurts America: cultural and environmental genocide, historical amnesia, and the suppression of all voices but one—the colonizer's. More importantly, however, Glancy considers what can *heal* America. The final poem, "The Relief of America," is a paraphrase of the words of Oren Lyons of the Onondaga Nation that recount the "great light of peace" (66) that once illuminated the Americas and was shared with the newcomers. But this light "began to die" (66) as the newcomers indoctrinated and conquered the indigenous people, both their way of life and their land. The poem cites the Six Nation Iroquois Confederacy's influence on the United States Constitution but also notes how the U.S. government lacked spirit and balance in creating and executing the law of the land. In the end, however, Glancy states, "The light can come back, what a / relief, if you could have seen America from that distance in time" (66). Glancy, through her poetry, illustrates how all Americans must recognize and honor Native knowledge and ways of being before everything—the earth, humanity, spirit—is sick beyond resuscitation.

Bibliography

Glancy, Diane. *The Relief of America.* Chicago: Tia Chucha Press, 2000.

———. "Two Dresses." *I Tell You Now: Autobiographical Essays by Native American Writers,* edited by Brian Swann and Arnold Krupat 167–184. Lincoln: University of Nebraska Press, 1987.

———. *The West Pole.* Minneapolis: University of Minnesota Press, 1997.

Strom, Karen. "Native American Authors On-Line." Available online URL: http://www.hanksville.org/storytellers/glancy/. Accessed on August 15, 2006.

Molly McGlennan

Remembered Earth, The   Geary Hobson   (1979)

Released by Red Earth Press in 1979, this anthology is widely respected for introducing many Native American poets, fiction writers, scholars, and artists as well as including works by the well-known authors LESLIE M. SILKO and N. SCOTT MOMADAY. Frequently cited by scholars, *The Remembered Earth* was considered one of the most comprehensive collections of Native writing and poetry for many years. This seminal text presents, to name only a few, the writers JOY HARJO, LINDA HOGAN, ROBERT CONLEY, CARROLL ARNETT, ADRIAN LOUIS, PAULA GUNN ALLEN, CARTER REVARD, SIMON ORTIZ, and LUCI TAPAHONSO and the artists Lee Marmon, Emmi Whitehorse, and Juane Quick-to-See Smith. Many now have their own substantial bodies of creative works. In all, 75 contributors are represented by poems, short stories, essays, photographs, excerpts, plays, and drawings. (The second and subsequent editions were published by University of New Mexico Press and include 74 contributors.)

GEARY HOBSON's introduction, "Remembering the Earth," offers an excellent historical review of Native American literature and addresses several issues still relevant today. "Native American literature, like the life and culture of which it is a part, is immeasurable centuries old . . . and its roots are deep in the land—too deep, I would venture to say, for a mere five centuries of European influence to upturn in any lasting, complete and irrevocable way" (2). Emulating this history, the works are organized into four geographical regions.

Concerning identity, Hobson rejects criteria that determine tribal membership based solely on blood quantum as a form of colonization. Instead, he promotes identity based on mutual recognition between an individual and a tribal community. Thus many contributors to this collection are not able to produce a Certificate of Degree of Indian Blood (CDIB) or other official forms of tribal enrollment.

Hobson also emphasizes the importance of Native people's speaking for themselves; "After all, when all is said and done, the writing we leave behind us will be there for the people" (9).

Hobson's influential essay "The Rise of the White Shaman as a New Version of Cultural Imperialism" (1976) is reprinted here. Written as a companion to Leslie Silko's essay "An Old-Time Indian Attack Conducted in Two Parts" (1977), the essays are critical of processes that erase Indian people from America's history even while some poets and other pop culture artists proclaim themselves to be modern-day prophets and "Indian" shamans.

Hobson's inspiration for the book's title is N. Scott Momaday's essay "The Man Made of Words" (1970). "Once in his life a man ought to concentrate his mind upon the remembered earth" (vii). The writers and artists included here have done so, sharing a wide range of emotions, including anger, determination that continues to grow out of 1960s era civil rights movements, and celebration for moments of profound beauty and life.

See also NATIVE "CHIC."

Bibliography

Berry, Brewton. *Almost White.* New York: Macmillan, 1969.

Momaday, N. Scott. *The Man Made of Words: Essays, Stories, Passages.* New York: St. Martin's Griffin, 1998.

Wilson, Norma C. *The Nature of Native American Poetry.* Albuquerque: University of New Mexico Press, 2001.

Barbara K. Robins

Remnants of the First Earth   Ray A. Young Bear (1996)

Told as a series of overlapping and intersecting stories in both first and third person, *Remnants of the First Earth* is RAY A. YOUNG BEAR's second novel and his first told largely in prose. In this work Young Bear revisits many of the characters and stories found in BLACK EAGLE CHILD: *The Facepaint Narratives.* Although the novel also incorporates some of the same themes his previous work explored, including ASSIMILATION, tensions between Native American tradition and modernity, ALCOHOLISM, POVERTY, and violence between Native Americans, Young Bear focuses even more prominently on the emerging literary voice of his chief protagonist and fictional alter ego, Edgar Bearchild, and the corruption—both internal and external—that plagues the members of the settlement.

In "Part One" of the novel Edgar describes the settlement itself and relates the story of its founding in two of the many examples in which history and fiction collide in Young Bear's novel. Edgar's maternal great-great-grandfather, Bear King, facilitated the 1858 purchase of land in Iowa that would become the tribe's settlement. The failure to transfer the chieftainship to his son upon Bear King's death in 1890 would have ripple effects on the tribe for generations. The white politicians of Why Cheer, a town near the settlement, blackmailed Bearchild, Edgar's paternal ancestor, to introduce education to the settlement in exchange for covering up the murder of a young woman committed by Bearchild's father.

The settlement's dark past is complemented by an equally dark present in which teachers at the Weeping Willow Elementary School terrorize the students into learning English, Indians beat each other and fall victim to alcoholism, families struggle with poverty and poor housing, and whites and Indians alike profit from Native American artifacts. For example, thanks to Jake Sacred Hammer, a "paid cultural informant," the "traditional ethic of respect began to diminish" (115; 120). Known for showing paying tourists the settlement despite "no trespassing" signs, Jake also encouraged settlement members to pose for photographs, and Edgar

admits that he, too, posed for a photograph as a child for 75 cents. Yet Jake is not the only one who betrays the settlement. Edgar's schoolmates, Horatio Plain Brown Bear and Kensey and "Grubby" Muscatine, are second generation "cultural informants" who care more about casino profits than the settlement's future.

A significant portion of the text is devoted to the murder of Edgar's close friend, Ted Facepaint, who was attacked by the Hyena brothers and stabbed repeatedly with a screwdriver. White authorities rule his death the result of a car accident and his murderers have solid alibis. While the murderers will never face white justice, their families and those who watched the attack and did nothing will meet with tragedies of their own. Junior Pipestar, an old friend of Edgar's and now a medicine man, tells Ted's friends and family that after four years the murder weapons and clothing worn during the attack will be found; only then will Ted's spirit be free to go to the afterlife.

Young Bear's darker vision of the Black Eagle Child settlement is juxtaposed by Edgar's role as a writer and preserver of his tribe's history—he refers to the latter as "word-collecting"—and his growth in both roles owes much to his ancestors. Edgar himself feels compelled to tell stories, to "be the harbinger of prophecy" and counter the agents of the "Red Pedagogical Army" of which his teachers and the white school system are a part (85). Eventually he will become the keeper of the "Journals of the Six Grandfathers," the journals of his ancestors that trace the history of the people of the settlement. Edgar's daughter with Selene Buffalo Husband (his muse in this novel as well as in *Black Eagle Child*), Maya Mae Bearchild, will follow in her father's footsteps, as well as serve as a "ceremonial" replacement for all of the loved ones her father has lost. In the character of Maya Mae Young Bear instills the text with hope, a hope born out of storytelling and remembering.

Winner of the Ruth Suckow Award for outstanding work of fiction about Iowa in 1997, *Remnants of the First Earth* resonates far beyond its local "roots." The physical, emotional, and cultural betrayals described in the text are not isolated to members of the Black Eagle Child settlement alone. Implicated in the text are not only the white culture responsible for generations of cultural alienation and destruction, but other Native Americans whose detachment from their own history and tradition make texts like *Remnants of the First Earth* vital to healing the wounds of imperialism and time.

Bibliography

Ellefson, Elias. "What It Means to Be a Mesquaki: A 1994 Interview with Ray Young Bear." *Des Moines Register,* 4 September 1994. Available online. URL: http://www.english.uiuc.edu/maps/poets/s_z/youngbear/1994.htm. Accessed on August 15, 2005.

Moore, David, and Michael Wilson. "Staying Afloat in a Chaotic World: A Conversation with Ray Young Bear." *Callaloo* 17, no. 1 (1994): 205–213.

Young Bear, Ray A. *Remnants of the First Earth.* New York: Grove Press, 1996.

Erika Hoagland

Removal

Removal refers to the aspect of the United States Indian policy that resulted in the coerced relocation of virtually all Indian tribes from east of the Mississippi River to the Indian Territory (what are today Kansas and Oklahoma). Pro-Removal advocates saw the policy as being a net benefit to the Indians who were removed. They argued that the Indian nations were being destroyed by contact with Euro-American civilization and, specifically, by the sale and consumption of alcohol. Moreover, they suggested, Indians needed time to move toward civilization at their own pace. Others argued that the "savage" Indian could never coexist with the "civilized" white. Thomas Jefferson saw voluntary removal as the only solution to the "Indian Problem" that would ensure the survival of Indian society. In 1808 the Jefferson administration encouraged a group of Cherokee to exchange their ancestral lands in the East for federally "owned" lands in the West. From 1814 to 1824 President Jackson negotiated nine separate treaties that divested Indian nations of ancestral lands in the East and South in exchange for land west of the Mississippi.

Congress formally adopted Removal as a policy with the passage of the Indian Removal Act in 1830. The act gave the president the right to negotiate and enforce removal treaties. The policy remained the cornerstone of U.S./Indian relations until after 1854, when Indian Commissioner George W. Manypenny called for its end. In so doing, he said, "By alternate persuasion and force, some of these tribes have been removed, step by step from mountains to valley, and from river to plain until they have been pushed half-way across the continent. They can go no further. On the ground they now occupy, the crisis must be met, and their future determined."

Implementation of the Indian Removal Act was rife with corruption and bloodshed. Indian leaders and federal agents were bribed. Goods and food meant to support the Indians—both during Removal and in the West—were diverted and resold. Shoddy goods and spoiled food were often what finally made their way into the hands and mouths of Indians. Moreover, the federal government was not prepared to handle the number of Indians forced into Indian Territory. Letters from Indian agents often contain unanswered requests for addition resources, goods, and personnel.

The most infamous example of Removal was the Cherokees "Trail Where They Cried" or, as it is more popularly known, the TRAIL OF TEARS. For many years prior to Cherokee removal Georgia planters, hungry for additional lands on which to grow cotton, argued that another nation should not exist within the borders of the state. Georgia built much of its case on an 1823 Supreme Court decision that allowed Indians to occupy lands but not hold title to those lands. The Cherokee fought removal through a variety of means, one of which was to prove that the so-called civilization policy, first adopted during the Washington administration, was working. However, when Andrew Jackson ran for the presidency, one of the issues in his platform was a "humane and wise" Indian Removal. The final result was that in May 1838, 7,000 federal troops under the command of General Winfield Scott began rounding up 15,000 to 16,000 of the

Cherokee still living in what had officially become Georgia.

Most of the Cherokee families were forced to leave behind land, which was assigned to Georgia settlers by lottery, and almost all of their belongings. Some Cherokee were able to escape the process, mainly in the mountains of North Carolina, but those who remained were driven into stockades, where they stayed until October, when the forced 800-mile overland march began. Between October and March—during the height of winter—early rains made roads nearly impassable. Disease, inadequate food, and lack of shelter resulted in the deaths of 4,000, a fifth or more of the total Cherokee population. Most of the deaths were among the children and the elderly. A soldier would later write, "I fought through the Civil War and have seen men shot to pieces and slaughtered by thousands, but the Cherokee removal was the cruelest work I ever knew."

However, while that of the Cherokee is the most infamous example of the devastating hardships and deaths suffered by Indian nations because of Removal, one must remember that the Cherokee were only one of many southern, eastern, and northern nations to suffer. Starting in the 1830s and continuing into the 1860s, the Creek, Seminole, Chickasaw, and Choctaw from the Southeast and the Seneca, Potawatomi, Sauk, Wyandot, Delaware, Fox, Miami, and Ottawa from the East and North, along with the remnants of other tribes, suffered their own "Trails of Tears." Alexis de Tocqueville was an eyewitness to the Choctaw removal in the winter of 1831, and he later wrote of what he saw in Memphis: "The wounded, the sick, the newborn babies, and the old men . . . I saw them embark to cross the great river and the sight will never fade from my memory. Neither sob nor complaint rose from that silent assembly. Their afflictions were long standing, and they felt them to be irremediable."

Many authors have addressed issues of removal in their work. One of the most notable examples is Diane Glancy's novel *Pushing the Bear*. This novel successfully conveys both the horrors of forced Removal, including disease, hunger, injury,

death, and displacement, and the resilience of the Native people forced on this journey. The poet Joy Harjo also addresses issues of Removal in her poem "New Orleans." In this poem the speaker searches desperately for evidence of the Creek in their homeland, the Mississippi River valley. Here, too, one experiences both the sadness of a society displaced and the strength demonstrated by that society's ability to survive. The novel *Josanie's War*, by Karl Schlesier, is an interesting example of Removal in literature because it does not focus on the Five Civilized Tribes, but instead on the 1886 Apache Revolt, which was caused by their removal from their ancestral lands.

Bibliography

Foreman, Grant, ed. *Indian Removal: The Emigration of the Five Civilized Tribes of Indians.* New York: Textbook, 2003.

Steve Brandon

Reservation, The   Ted C. Williams (1976)

The Reservation is Williams's only novel. Composed of a series of sketches of reservation life, the novel is affectionate and humorous, as well as poignant and thoughtful, in its depiction of the members of the Tuscarora Indian reservation in western New York. Williams, a member of the Tuscarora, recounts his time living on the reservation over several decades, beginning in his childhood in the 1930s. Also an illustrator, Williams includes illustrations of his family, neighbors, or specific incidents in each chapter. The novel is anchored by the unnamed narrator (who can be viewed as Williams himself), whose observations of the reservation range from stories about his parents, extended family, and eccentric neighbors, to stories dominated by powerful confrontations with the ever-encroaching white world.

Williams blends the traditionally linear narrative of biographical writing with a decidedly episodic frame. When specific "episodes," or chapters, are viewed together, thematic links may be made. For example, "Mrs. Shoe's Gang," in which a neighborhood family is viewed as wild and rather eccentric, and "Bedbug," named after a neighborhood boy who tricks the narrator and his mother into throwing him a 12th-birthday party, both relate the effects of poverty and hunger on members of the reservation. Mrs. Shoe is constantly foraging around the reservation for food and exchanging cleaning services for vegetables from gardens or fresh meat in order to feed her large family. Bedbug's voracious appetite at his birthday dinner prevents him from eating more than two pieces of his birthday cake. The narrator later discovers that Bedbug has tricked another family into giving him a birthday party. The narrator refrains from judging Bedbug, whose mother is an alcoholic, who is frequently in town drinking. When mother and son are tearfully reunited, Bedbug's physical hunger is juxtaposed to his emotional hunger for his mother's presence.

"My Father" and "Thraangkie and You-swee(t)-dad" examine the conflict between Native American tradition and Euro-American culture, a recurrent theme in Native American literature. While the narrator is still a child, his father is approached by white businessmen who wish to strike a partnership with the medicine man. His father tells the men that he can't "betray that medicine for money," a statement the businessmen do not understand (25). Nor can they understand that the success the narrator's father achieves as a medicine man has much to do with his respect for the earth and for balance. This miscommunication is also found in one of the longest chapters in the novel, an encounter between a converted Tuscarora, Thraangkie, and a tribal elder, You-swee(t)-dad. The elderly chief tells the minister that the "Bible carriers" who went to America "did not try to understand the Indians' ways" and judged them as "evil" (132). Thraangkie misses the chief's point and insists that You-swee(t)-dad's words would please the devil. Their exchange further highlights the ways in which white culture has divided Native Americans, a theme Williams revisits in "The Reservoir."

As the title implies, the reservation is itself a prominent "character" in the novel. Both a re-minder of white domination and treachery and a fiercely protected home, the reservation is at the center of the many adventures the narrator experiences. In "The Reservoir" the reservation is threatened by the Federal Power Commission, which in 1958 attempted to condemn Tuscarora lands in order to create a reservoir. "If the state of New York is like a big brother in one big family," Williams writes, "one day big brother wanted a bite of little brother's candy" (181). This intrusion creates a split between those Indians who, out of necessity, take jobs with the surveyors and those who have chosen to resist actively. Despite the many and creative ways in which members of the reservation undermine the reservoir project, including stealing and sabotaging equipment, they are unable to prevent the project from proceeding. The narrator states that he is "pissed off because the pike [cannot] swim up Gill Creek anymore," but he considers the possibility that the Tuscarora lost the fight because they had "forgot[ten] the power of Mother Earth" (204). The strong connection his people once had to the earth has grown increasingly weak, as has their connection to their traditions and past.

Bibliography

Williams, Ted C. *The Reservation.* Syracuse, N.Y.: Syracuse University Press, 1976.

Erika Hoagland

Reservation Blues Sherman Alexie (1995)

SHERMAN ALEXIE's novel *Reservation Blues* follows the characters Thomas Builds-the-Fire, Victor Joseph, and Junior Polatkin, who are central figures in Alexie's first work of fiction, *The LONE RANGER AND TONTO FISTFIGHT IN HEAVEN.* In *Reservation Blues* the three are influenced by the appearance of the blues legend Robert Johnson, who mysteriously arrives on their Wellpinit reservation to seek counsel from the Spokane tribal elder Big Mom. Johnson's presence reinforces the novel's Faustian storyline since according to legend, Johnson sold his soul to the devil in order to play the guitar. Johnson passes on his guitar to Thomas; however, it is Victor who takes the guitar and sells his soul to the devil in exchange for talent. Unaware of Victor's deal and inspired by his conversation with Johnson, Thomas starts an Indian band called Coyote Springs. Thomas's band includes Victor and Thomas as well as two Flathead women they meet during the course of the novel, Chess and Checkers Warm Water.

The band experiences some success as they play various clubs, but their big break occurs when they are offered a recording contract by Cavalry Records. Two of the record executives, Sheridan and Wright, try to change the band's image by making them look more "authentically" Indian. The record company wants the band to act and appear as the stereotypical Indians in Hollywood films, so they can sell the band to an American mainstream audience who knows little about Native people. Unfortunately the band disintegrates while in the New York recording studio as the guitar, which has a mind of its own, rebels, and the band fails. By the end of the novel Junior commits suicide because of Victor's deal with the devil, Victor is overwhelmed with guilt because of Junior's death, and Thomas, Chess, and Checkers persevere in hopes of a brighter future.

Alexie's use of the blues music is significant because the blues is the music of survival. Even though there are bleak moments in the novel, the overall message is the celebration of survival. Alexie's novel is also making a statement about how inauthentic Indian images are bought and sold, and about how damaging these images can be to Native peoples. For example, Alexie names the two record executives Phil Sheridan and George Wright, who bear the names of their ancestors, real historical figures. They were cavalry officers responsible for many injustices against Native peoples. After meeting the band, Wright "saw their Indian faces. He saw the faces of millions of Indians, beaten, scarred by smallpox and frostbite, split open by bayonets and bullets. He looked at his own white hands and saw the blood stains there" (244). Sheridan and Wright wish to make Coyote Springs marketable, and it is their desire for profit that causes the band's dreams of success to crumble. Here we see the damaging effects of the inauthentic Indian images. The damage that the historical Sheridan and Wright had done to Native peoples in the 19th century continues, but in a different form.

The creation of the Reservation Blues conveys the ambivalence of the suffering and the joy of survival. For Coyote Springs the blues are cathartic and provide a way of expressing their culture.

Bibliography

Delicka, Magdalene. "The Dynamics of Contemporary Cultural Politics in Sherman Alexie's *Reservation Blues.*" *American Studies* 18 (1999): 73–80.

Jorgensen, Karen. "White Shadows: The Use of Dopplegangers in Sherman Alexie's *Reservation Blues.*" *Studies in American Indian Literatures* 9, no. 4 (1997): 19–25.

Richardson, Janine. "Magic and Memory in Sherman Alexie's *Reservation Blues.*" *Studies in American Indian Literatures* 9, no. 4 (1997): 39–51.

Meredith James

reservation life

Because Indian reservations are a prominent feature of the modern Native American landscape, many contemporary work of Native American literature offer a representation of reservation life. Reservation life is a central feature of Native American reality. According to figures from the 2000 U.S. Census, approximately 2.5 million Native Americans live in the United States, making up slightly less than 1 percent of the total population. Almost half of Native Americans live on one of the 285 federally administered reservations in the United States, whose total land area is approximately 55.7 million acres—less than 5 percent of the total land area of what was their aboriginal domain.

Reservations range in size from the 32-acre Oneida reservation near Syracuse, New York, to the Navajo Reservation in the Four Corners area of New Mexico, Utah, Colorado, and Arizona, which is 16 million acres (roughly the size of West Virginia). Whereas almost every western state is home to one or more reservations, relatively few states east of the Mississippi contain reservations.

White settlers in North America began to establish reservations for the Native inhabitants within 100 years of their arrival, beginning in 1638 at the New Haven Colony. Because of the U.S. government's well-documented policy of treachery and exploitation in regard to Native peoples, Indian reservations have always endured a tenuous existence, and their present total acreage represents considerable reduction from the originally allotted areas. Reservations have often been dissolved or reduced in order to facilitate white settlement or the private extraction of natural resources. Even today some "neotermination" groups advocate abandoning the reservation system in a renewed attempt to force Indian ASSIMILATION into the dominant culture.

Most U.S. Indian reservations are stigmatized as regions of extreme POVERTY with high rates of ALCOHOLISM and drug abuse. Aside from farming, which is the main economic base on many reservations, most reservations lack any kind of economic development or income source other than natural resource extraction or, more recently, GAMING—both of which tend to be sources of intertribal controversy. Poverty rates on the reservations are double the national average and reflect the fact that Native Americans occupy the lowest economic tier in U.S. society. Indians living on reservations suffer under the dual burden of the highest unemployment rates and the lowest average incomes in the United States. Such difficulties of life on the reservation are frequently compounded by substandard housing, lack of education, and poor health care services.

Many of the problems associated with reservation life are a function of their complicated relationship with the U.S. government and its various jurisdictional agencies. As a result of the DAWES ACT between 1887 and 1934 many parcels of tribal land were purchased by non-Indian owners, especially on the western reservations. According to Bureau of Indian Affairs (BIA) figures, today over half the residents on reservations are non-Indians.

In the 1950s the government renewed its attempts to produce assimilation by eliminating some reservations and actively encouraging Indians to relocate to urban centers. As with other government-sponsored attempts at assimilation, the move failed to integrate Indians into the American "melting pot" and instead helped to reinforce the cultural chasm between the mainstream, urban culture, and life on the reservation.

This divide has perpetuated a crippling double bind for many young Indians: On the one hand, the reservations in most cases fail to offer few educational or economic opportunities; on the other hand, urban relocation poses a whole range of new problems: racial discrimination, cultural dislocation, and alienation.

Though conditions on the reservations appear bleak by white social and cultural standards, it must be pointed out that the reservations also represent a world in which Indians have maintained a cultural and geographical identity. For better or worse, many reservations are regions distinct from mainstream America. The sense of Indian cultural identity that has resisted and withstood all attempts at assimilation is continually reinforced by frequent ceremonies and gatherings on reservation lands, and those practices, tied to the lands themselves, help define a land ethic that emphasizes Native American identity and spiritual stability.

Many reservations have also benefited in recent years from younger Indians who have temporarily left the reservations to seek a college education and returned to provide professional resources on the reservations. Many reservations have thriving tribal colleges, and many tribes are in the process of expanding and improving health care services.

Both the positive and the negative effects of life on the reservations are reflected in Native American literature. This is true of some of the earliest works, most notably D'ARCY MCNICKLE's *The Surrounded* (1936). N. SCOTT MOMADAY's later watershed novel *HOUSE MADE OF DAWN* (1968), which fostered the AMERICAN INDIAN LITERARY RENAISSANCE, also contrasted reservation life with the outside world through the eyes of its main character, Abel, who as many figures in Native American literature do, remains unable to feel at home in either place. LESLIE MARMON SILKO's celebrated novel CEREMONY (1977) describes life on the Laguna Pueblo reservation after World War II, and much of LOUISE ERDRICH's award-winning novel LOVE MEDICINE (1984, 1993) takes place on a fictional Chippewa reservation in North Dakota.

More recently a new wave of young Native American writers has produced a number of books (some of which have been turned into films) that offer an up-to-date and realistic portrait of contemporary reservation life.

JAMES WELCH's *The Death of Jim Loney* (1979) depicts the life of a young man of mixed heritage living in Harlem just off the Fort Belknap Reservation in Montana—his struggles with alcoholism, cultural anxiety, and the lure of the outside world. Loney's sister, who has left the reservation and gained wealth and success in Washington, D.C., offers a contrast to the existential crisis of her brother's character. Though she returns to rescue him from his depression and alcoholism, she respects his autonomy and allegiance to the only world with which he has any emotional familiarity. Welch's first novel, *WINTER IN THE BLOOD* (1974), was also praised for its frank presentation of reservation life. Though some readers criticized the book for its tone of despair, its defenders suggested those critics had failed to appreciate Welch's sense of HUMOR.

David Seals's novel *POWWOW HIGHWAY* (1990) was turned into a film starring the Canadian First Nations actor Gary Farmer and has become a cult classic. The story involves two young men from the Northern Cheyenne reservation near Lame Deer, Montana, who make a journey south to rescue their sister, who has been wrongfully jailed in Santa Fe, New Mexico. They pause along the way to attend a POW WOW on the Pine Ridge Reservation in South Dakota. The story presents a compelling contrast between the patient wisdom and spiritual, traditional worldview of Philbert Bono and the frustrated and angry passion of the activist Buddy Red Bow. The novel also makes indirect reference to the AMERICAN INDIAN MOVEMENT and its impact on reservation politics.

The young Spokane/Coeur d'Alene Indian SHERMAN ALEXIE's novels and stories are rich with descriptions of reservation life, including *RESERVATION BLUES* (1995) about the Spokane Indian Reservation in Washington State. The novel describes the musical odyssey of Thomas Builds-the-Fire, who inherits a guitar from the legendary bluesman Robert Johnson. The novel's comic sensibility is balanced by its passionate dedication to immortalizing the spirit of survival that pervades the reservation in spite of its problems. As Builds-the-Fire and his band Coyote Springs return to the Spokane reservation from a foray to Ellensburg, the narrator surveys the ambiguous cultural landscape and offers a succinct summary of its mixed heritage of despair and hope:

> The reservation was gone itself, just a shell of its former self, just a fragment of the whole. But the reservation still possessed power and rage, magic and loss, joys and jealousy. The reservation tugged at the lives of its Indians, stole from them in the middle of the night, watched impassively as the horses and salmon disappeared. But the reservation forgave, too. (96)

Alexie's work has gathered much praise for its honesty and accuracy in its depictions of reservation life, though it has inspired much controversy as well. Supporters emphasize the critical power of his talent for satire, whereas critics accuse him of reinforcing white stereotypes, especially of "the drunken Indian," a frequent figure in his novels and poetry. Alexie does not shy away from presenting the harsh reality of alcoholism on the reservation, but in *Reservation Blues* he carefully points out that "most Indians never drink. Nobody notices the sober Indians" (152). In addition Alexie's work underscores the sense of close cultural kinship and identity that the reservations foster: He remarks in the novel, for example, that reservation Indians universally refer to each other as "cousin," whether they are blood relatives or not.

On the Rez (2001), written by the self-described "middle-class white guy" and former *New Yorker* staff writer Ian Frazier, is based on his numerous interviews and experiences with his friend Le War Lance on the Pine Ridge Reservation in South Dakota. The book had great critical success for its documentary view of life on the reservation. Many critics praised Frazier for neither glossing Indian culture with typical white sentimentality nor offering political judgment on the squalor readily visible from the road. Others, however, were appalled at the prospect of a white man's writing about the "rez." Sherman Alexie, for example, wrote a scathing review of the book in *The Los Angeles Times* (23 January 2000), though he took offense more at the audacity of the enterprise than the actual content of the book. Though he spoke in awe of Frazier's "transcendent talent," Alexie wondered whether tribal sovereignty is violated when a white man writes a book about Indians without being invited to do so.

Though the reservations are in the view of some critics a breeding ground of entitlement-oriented government dependency, they are in the minds of many others one of the last available places for Native cultures to flourish and for a sense of self-determination to prosper. Native American writings produced in the last few decades clearly illustrate this tension and the often-contradictory reality of reservation life. At one point in James Welch's *Winter in the Blood* the unnamed main character sits in a car and tersely muses at the prospect of returning to the reservation: "I should go home, I thought, turn the key and drive home. It wasn't the ideal place, that was sure, but it was the best choice" (120).

Bibliography

Alexie, Sherman. *Reservation Blues.* New York: Warner, 1995.

———. *The Toughest Indian in the World.* New York: Grove, 2000.

———. *Ten Little Indians.* New York: Grove, 2003.

Bird, Gloria. "The Exaggeration of Despair in Sherman Alexie's *Reservation Blues.*" *Wicazo Sa Review* 11, no. 2 (fall 1995): 47–53.

Davis, Mary B., ed. *Native America in the Twentieth Century: An Encyclopedia.* New York: Garland, 1994.

Evans, Stephen F. "'Open Containers': Sherman Alexie's Drunken Indians." *American Indian Quarterly* 25, no. 1 (winter 2001): 46–72.

Frazier, Ian. *On the Rez.* New York: Picador, 2001.

Lason, Charles R. *American Indian Fiction.* Albuquerque: University of New Mexico Press, 1978.

Seals, David. *Powwow Highway.* New York: Plume, 1990.

Welch, James. *The Death of Jim Loney.* New York: Harper & Row, 1979.

———. *Winter in the Blood.* New York: Harper & Row, 1974.

Aaron Parrett

Returning the Gift: Poetry and Prose from the First North American Native Writers' Festival Joseph Bruchac (1994)

This collection is made up of original works collected at the Returning the Gift Festival, held at the University of Oklahoma in Norman in 1992. Its significance can be brought into relief by comparing it to *Songs from This Earth on Turtle's Back*, an anthology that Joseph Bruchac also edited (1983). In the decade between publications of the two anthologies Native American literary studies had burgeoned with the publication of numerous works by and about Native American authors and the establishment of literary studies programs at colleges and universities around the country. This renaissance also manifested itself in unprecedented events, including the Returning the Gift Festival.

Attended by over 300 writers, the festival remains the largest single gathering of Native American authors in history. The festival also caused an intense rearticulation of what constitutes Native American literature, as Bruchac explains in his introduction. There he details the intricate process that the steering committee undertook to determine who could be invited to the festival. "Provable Native heritage, self-identification as a Native person, and affiliation with the tribal community" became the criteria (xx). These criteria enabled the festival to include the widest possible number of authors, including those from officially unrecognized tribes such as the Wampanoag of Mashpee and the Abenaki of Vermont as well as tribes from outside official U.S. borders such as the Chicmec and the Siberian Yupik. This inclusivity, in turn, allowed the festival to reflect the variety and validity of all existent Native American tribal identities. Notably, NILA NORTHSUN was so inspired by the quality and quantity of Native American voices at this festival that she resumed the poetry that she had given up earlier (356).

This diversity exhibits itself in the anthology's content, which Bruchac defines as a "showcase of Native American literature" (xxvii). These works, by approximately one-third of the festival's attending authors, are previously unpublished. As such they represent the current state of Native American literature. Consequently they are as diverse as the range of authors who produced them. Some authors (JOY HARJO, LINDA HOGAN, Denise Sweet, and LAURA TOHE) contributed pieces articulating traditional voices, while other (like SHERMAN ALEXIE, CARTER REVARD, and Drew Hayden Taylor) contributed postmodern pieces that question all aspects of identity. Still others (including Annette Arkeketa and Barney Bush) contributed tributes to the festival and its participants. Many authors addressed political issues in their works; some (such as Tracey Bonneau, BETH BRANT, and Haunani-Kay Trask) explicitly dedicated their works to such political causes and their leaders.

As these works reveal, their authors' creativity derives from deep commitments to traditional tribal identities and to contemporary political realities. These works also reflect an endurance of spirit reflected in Bruchac's comment "Returning the Gift both demonstrated and validated our literature and our devotion to it, not just to the public, but to ourselves" (xxi). Given this sense of possibility, Native American literature will continue to develop its inherent strengths throughout the 21st century.

Bibliography

Bruchac, Joseph, ed. *Returning the Gift: Poetry and Prose from the First North American Native Writers' Festival.* Tucson and London: University of Arizona Press, 1994.

———, ed. *Songs from This Earth on Turtle's Back: Contemporary American Indian Poetry.* Greenfield Center, N.Y.: Greenfield Review Press, 1983.

Clay Smith

Revard, Carter   (1931–)

Carter Curtis Revard was born to a mother of Osage descent on March 25, 1931, in Pawhuska, Oklahoma, and grew up in the nearby Buck Creek Valley. In 1952 he earned a B.A. from the University of Tulsa and received in a traditional ceremony the Osage name *Nompehwahthe* (literally, fear-inspiring). He attended Merton College, Oxford University, as a Rhodes Scholar and received a Ph.D. in English from Yale University in 1959. Revard taught at Amherst College and in 1961 was appointed professor in the English Department at Washington University in St. Louis, where he remained until retiring in 1997. During that time he also taught as a visiting professor at the University of Tulsa in 1981 and the University of Oklahoma in 1989. Revard was named writer of the year in 2000 by the Wordcraft Circle of Native Writers.

Revard's work includes poetry, memoir, and scholarly essays in medieval studies, linguistics, and Native American literature. Revard's poetry has appeared in numerous anthologies and journals; his collections include *My Right Hand Don't Leave Me No More* (1970); *Nonymosity* (1980); *PONCA WAR DANCERS* (1980); *An EAGLE NATION*, which won the Oklahoma Book Award for poetry in 1994; and *COWBOYS AND INDIANS CHRISTMAS SHOPPING* (1992). Revard's book *Family Matters, Tribal Affairs* (1998), a finalist for the Oklahoma Book Award, consists of personal and scholarly essays on topics ranging from reflections on his childhood experiences and travels in Europe to a meditation on the significance of naming, all of which together form a "community of words on Indian ground" (xi). Revard's autobiography, *WINNING THE DUST BOWL* (2001), comprises his poetry surrounded by a "meadow . . . of history and autobiography," which draws on personal and family experience and opens outward to engage with national and literary history (xiii). Revard's measured and candid prose, punctuated by wry and learned asides and deft character sketches, is a distinguished and distinctive contribution to the rich and varied traditions, from Anglo-Saxon to Osage, on which it draws.

Bibliography

Ballinger, Franchot. "Carter Revard." In *Dictionary of Native American Literature,* edited by Andrew Wiget. New York: Garland, 1994.

Bruchac, Joseph. "Something That Stays Alive: An Interview with Carter Revard." In *Survival This Way: Interviews with American Indian Poets,* 231–248. Tucson: University of Arizona Press, 1987.

Cowboys and Indians Christmas Shopping. Norman, Okla.: Point Riders Press, 1992.

Krupat, Arnold. *I Tell You Now: Autobiographical Essays by Native American Writers,* 67–84. Lincoln: University of Nebraska Press, 1987.

Revard, Carter. *An Eagle Nation.* Tucson: University of Arizona Press, 1993.

———. *Ponca War Dances.* Norman, Okla.: Point Riders Press, 1980.

———. *Winning the Dust Bowl.* Tucson: University of Arizona Press, 2001.

Revard, Carter, and Karen Storm. "Biography of Carter Revard." Available online. URL: http://www.hanksville.org/storytellers/revard. Accessed on August 15, 2005.

Alex Feerst

Rez Sisters, The Tomson Highway (1988)

A two-act play that focuses on the empowerment of seven contemporary Ojibwe women in rural Ontario, *The Rez Sisters* is the precursor and companion piece to DRY LIPS OUGHTA MOVE TO KAPUSKASING (1989). Both are dramatic exposés of reservation life as viewed through a gender-specific lens. The community vision is never fully exclusionary, for the TRICKSTER FIGURE Nanabush acts as a gender stabilizer. Ambiguous and multidimensional, s/he symbolizes the more-than-human world, the ancestral legacy, and a spiritual resilience that demands constant articulation.

TOMSON HIGHWAY infuses such mythic realism into the problems on the Wasaychigan reservation: joblessness, POVERTY, ALCOHOLISM, domestic violence, shady governance, and pervasive demoralization. As *Wasaychigan* denotes "widow" in Ojibway, the play offers a powerful, if subtle, indictment of Native men as failing to provide an adequate complement to the resourcefulness and creative potential of their female counterparts.

The play's guiding metaphor is a massive bingo game in Toronto—the "Biggest Bingo in the World"—that the protagonists seek to (and eventually do) attend. Unlike in the adage, life is not merely a game of chance but a combination of chance and deliberate choice. Oscillating between humor and pathos, Highway calls for confrontation and truth telling. Such honest engagement, whether in the form of argument, everyday banter, or confession, should not be overlooked as a central female bonding ritual. The speakers' voices emerge as the ultimate catalyst for communal healing, with English, Cree, and Ojibway intermingled in formal resistance to any totality of vision, even in the linguistic sense.

Connected through a web of personal affinities (familial, emotional, situational, tribal) and sometimes repulsions (old wounds and petty jealousies), the "rez sisters" are Pelajia Patchnoose, Philomena Moosetail, Marie-Adele Starblanket, Annie Cook, Emily Dictionary, Veronique St. Pierre, and Zhaboonigan Peterson. Winning bingo appears to be the best chance to fulfill their individual and collective fantasies—at least those money can buy. To win is symbolically potent because the experience of loss is so often associated with latter-day Native communities (the myth of "dying off" peoples, for instance). These "sisters" desire emotional comfort, economic stability, and a respite from worry. Perhaps more important than the actual prize, the dream of winning offers a forum for sharing aspirations. In the context of tragedies like Zhaboonigan's past rape and Marie-Adele's cancer, money lingers as a false promise, unable to mitigate racism, poverty of spirit, emotional isolation, or the scars of traumatic experience. The riches of human currency (friendship, advice, even criticism) prove less fallible.

Highway's tragicomedy envisions the organic, day-to-day liberation of Native women from such corrosive stereotypes as the silent squaw and the quaint curio maiden. Among these strong, self-reliant, and capable individual, the spirit of cooperative exchange and nurturance shines forth, an invitation and exhortation for others to follow.

Bibliography

Johnston, Denis W. "Lines and Circles: The 'Rez' Plays of Tomson Highway." *Canadian Literature* 124–125 (1990): 254–264.

Perkins, Lina. "Remembering the Trickster in Tomson Highway's *The Rez Sisters*." *Modern Drama* (2002): 259–269.

Nancy Kang

Ridge, John Rollin   (1827–1867)

John Rollin Ridge was born in the Eastern Cherokee Nation (present-day Rome, Georgia), on March 19, 1827, a time of extreme turmoil for his people. His father, John, and his mother, Sarah Northrup (who was of European descent), met in Connecticut and returned to the Cherokee Nation, where they established a successful plantation. At the time of young John's birth the Cherokee were divided over the question of whether or not they should move west to Indian Territory (present-day Oklahoma) or stay on their ancestral lands in the Southeast and continue to resist the advances of the white settlers and the United States government. Ridge's family was quite prominent within the tribe. His father and his grandfather, Major Ridge, were both chiefs. His uncle, Elias Boudinot, was the publisher of the bilingual newspaper the *Cherokee Phoenix*. Although the Ridge-Boudinot family was initially opposed to relocation, by 1835 they had decided resistance was futile, and Ridge's grandfather, father, and uncle were all signatories to the infamous Treaty of New Echota, which ceded Cherokee lands in the Southeast to the United States in exchange for lands in Oklahoma. This treaty set in motion the events that would ultimately lead to REMOVAL and the devastating TRAIL OF TEARS. The factions opposing the treaty took revenge, and at the age of 12 John Rollin Ridge saw his father murdered out-side their home. His grandfather and uncle were also murdered that night, and for their own safety John's mother fled with her family to Arkansas, where they lived for the next few years.

Ridge was educated in Massachusetts, and as his father had, married a white woman and returned with her to the South. He began his short-lived career as a farmer in Arkansas and Missouri, before ultimately returning to the Cherokee Nation. There a dispute over a horse, involving a man from the faction who had killed Ridge's father, turned violent. Ridge killed the man and fled to the gold mines of California. He never returned to the Cherokee Nation and died in Grass Valley, California, on October 5, 1867.

Most of Ridge's literary fame is due to his being the author of what is considered the first novel written by an Indian, *The LIFE AND ADVENTURES OF JOAQUIN MURIETA, THE CELEBRATED CALIFORNIA BANDIT* (1854). Ironically this novel is not about an Indian, or at least not directly about any Indian concerns, but in the 19th century it became something of a legend, its story told and retold by groups across the country. It is the semifictitious tale of its title character, an infamous bandit who made headlines in mid-19th-century California. Murieta loomed large in the popular imagination and was reported to rob only whites and Asians, never Mexicans or others of Latin descent. In addition, although the accounts are sketchy, he was reported to have been an honest man driven to a life of crime by oppression and racism. He was, it was said, determined to avenge the wrongs that had been done him and his family.

This work is an unusual amalgamation of fact and fiction. In that sense it is perhaps ahead of its time, anticipating the blurry lines of the postmodern fiction of the late 20th century. Ridge, however, probably felt a kinship with Murieta and was drawn to write about him. After witnessing his father's death, Ridge had a lifelong desire to extract revenge from those who had killed him. Murieta's extended revenge spree was probably quite satisfying to him. Ridge also portrayed the plight of Mexicans in California quite sympathetically, perhaps seeing a comparison to his own oppressed people, the Cherokee.

In addition to his novel, Ridge also published a book of poetry, most of it written during his early years in Arkansas. His poetry demonstrates an obvious kinship with the British Romantic poets, especially Percy Bysshe Shelley. Ridge's most famous poem, "Mount Shasta" addresses the concept of eternity and the manner in which the concrete reality of a mountain peak reminds us of our mortality while at the same time seeming endless. At the end of his life, Ridge wrote primarily nonfiction for newspapers such as the *Sacramento Bee* and the *San Francisco Herald*.

Although not prolific, Ridge's importance as an Indian writer cannot be overstated. He was one of the first Indians to earn a living as a writer and he never ceased to be an advocate for the needs and concerns of the Cherokee Nation.

Bibliography

Parins, James W. *John Rollin Ridge: His Life and Works.* Lincoln: University of Nebraska Press, 1991.

Jennifer McClinton-Temple

Riggs, Rollie Lynn   (1899–1954)

The Cherokee dramatist and poet Rollie Lynn Riggs was born on August 31, 1899, in the Verdigris Valley, near the town of Claremore in the Indian Territory, one of the two territories that in 1906 formed the state of Oklahoma. Riggs always held a deep and tormented attachment to his birthplace, which obsessed him, alternately attracting and banishing him, and he considered it his duty to speak for the quiet outsiders, the reserved Oklahomans who lived silently on the outskirts of long-established American civilization, through his plays and poetry.

Riggs was one-sixteenth Cherokee through his beloved mother, Rose Ella Buster, who died when he was only a year old. His father, William Grant Riggs, then married another woman of Cherokee descent, but she was difficult and troubled and was often cruel to Riggs and his three older brothers and his older sister, Mattie. As a boy Riggs fled from an unhappy home and went to live in the boarding house of his aunt, Mary Brice, his father's sister, in

Claremore. Abusive and emotionally distant stepmothers are prominent figures in several of Riggs's plays, notably *The Lonesome West* and *The Cream in the Well*, and he translated Aunt Mary Brice into the character of Aunt Eller, the lovable and curmudgeonly matriarch of his best-known work, Green Grow the Lilacs, which later served as the template for Rodgers and Hammerstein's groundbreaking 1943 musical *Oklahoma!*

Attending preparatory school, Riggs harbored the desire someday to become an actor and participated in amateur theatricals. After graduation in 1917 he trekked to Chicago, New York City, and Los Angeles, where he worked as an extra in the silent cinema, but health problems forced him to return home, and in 1920 he enrolled in the University of Oklahoma. He wrote his first play, *Cuckoo*, a folk comedy, in 1922, while a student. During his senior year Riggs—wrestling with homosexuality and exhibiting signs of tuberculosis—suffered a nervous breakdown, and he relocated to the drier climate of Santa Fe, New Mexico. After recuperating at Sunmount Sanitarium, Riggs supported himself by working outdoors at the poet Witter Bynner's chicken ranch. He also ingratiated himself with Santa Fe's other literati.

Santa Fe proved to be a major steppingstone in Riggs's career as a dramatist. While there, he met Ida Rauh Eastman, one of the founders of the Provincetown Players, who encouraged him to write more plays. In 1925 the Santa Fe Players produced his one-act play *Knives from Syria* (published in 1927), a precursor to *Green Grow the Lilacs*, about itinerant peddlers in prestatehood Oklahoma.

Riggs returned to New York City with his first full-length play, *Big Lake*, produced at the American Laboratory Theater. The production elicited mixed reviews. Riggs's next plays—*Sumpn Like Wings, A Lantern to See By, The Lonesome West,* and *Rancor*—are representative of the struggles of prestatehood white Oklahomans. *The Lonesome West* and *Rancor* were produced at the prestigious Hedgerow Theater outside Philadelphia; this company would premiere several of Riggs's plays.

In 1928 Riggs became the first Oklahoman to receive a Guggenheim Fellowship, which enabled him to travel to France and to experience firsthand the progressive European theater. It was there that Riggs began work on the play for which he is best known, *Green Grow the Lilacs,* a folk play in which he romanticized the conflicts between white ranchers and farmers at the advent of Oklahoma statehood by saturating the play with folk songs and cowboy ballads. The Theatre Guild produced the play in 1931, and its 64-performance run surely would have been extended had the production not been previously contracted to tour. Rodgers and Hammerstein's adaptation of *Green Grow the Lilacs,* 1943's *Oklahoma!,* innovative through its use of song and dance to support plot and character, remarkably resembles Riggs's play. Indeed Hammerstein confessed that he kept most of the lines of the original play intact because he could not improve upon them, proclaiming that Riggs and his play were the very soul of *Oklahoma!* Sadly, however, *Oklahoma!* has overshadowed Riggs's original works.

Riggs considered himself to be an "absorbed Cherokee," his own term for an Oklahoma Cherokee who had lost his cultural past because of intermarriage and dilution of Native blood. The "absorbed Cherokee" appears most prominently in Riggs's plays *The Cream in the Well* (1940) and the groundbreaking *The Cherokee Night* (1936), his challenging and unconventional play in which he most explicitly deals with American Indian culture and identity. Breaking from Ibsenian realism and the linear structure comfortable to mainstream theatergoers of the 1930s, Riggs wove the connected tragic stories of MIXED-BLOOD Cherokee in scenes that jump seemingly arbitrarily through time. Riggs asserts in *The Cherokee Night* that there is a hierarchy of Indian identity, determined by blood quantum, and that those who have less than full Native blood are exiled to a wasteland of cultural confusion, stripped of their connection to the natural world; entangled in destructive and often violent relationships, abject poverty, lives of crime; and ultimately doomed to extinction. In *The Cherokee Night* Riggs asserts that Indian blood is a precious commodity and its loss is tragic.

Riggs died of stomach cancer on June 30, 1954, in New York City.

Bibliography

Braunlich, Phyllis. *Haunted by Home.* Norman: University of Oklahoma Press, 1988.

Riggs, R. Lynn. *The Cherokee Night and Other Plays.* Foreword by Jace Weaver. Norman: University of Oklahoma Press, 2003.

———. *Green Grow the Lilacs.* New York: Samuel French, 1930.

Womack, Craig S. "Lynn Riggs as Code Talker." In *Red on Red: Native American Literary Separatism.* Minneapolis: University of Minneapolis Press, 1999.

Douglas Powers

Roads of My Relations, The   Devon Mihesuah (2000)

The Roads of My Relations is a collection of stories, loosely based on Devon Mihesuah's own family history, that follows generations of Choctaw characters as they experience life in their Mississippi homelands, face the adversities surrounding government-imposed relocation to southeastern Oklahoma, and contemplate issues of mixed heritage and identity in a changing world. Importantly Mihesuah's characters specifically and accurately reflect the histories and cultures of Choctaw and are not the pantribal or generic Indians who are characters in many popular westerns. Of particular significance are the collection's strong women characters, who reflect the strength, diversity, and persistence of Choctaw people.

All of the characters in the collection are extended family, ancestors, and descendants of Billie Fontaine McKinney, individuals who reflect the cross-cultural realities of Native life in their confrontation and affiliation with other peoples, and throughout, the text contains references to *fulls, half-bloods, whites,* and *negros,* indicating this cultural hybridity. Integral to Mihesuah's portrayal of white-Choctaw contact and the ramifications of colonialism is the theme of religious oppression. Billie's father, as well as the teachers at the BOARDING SCHOOL Billie attends after arriving in Oklahoma, continually attempt to Christianize the young protagonist and her peers, but despite this imposition, Choctaw spiritual beliefs and worldviews endure into the present generation, varying with individual experiences and perspectives. Ultimately when Ariana, the young vegetarian long-distance runner descendant of Billie, whose chapter completes the collection, reconnects with her Oklahoma Choctaw upbringing in order to confront and overcome the *opas*, owl-men emblems of witchery that have plagued the Choctaw for centuries, her genuine belief in and connection to family stories makes her successful in breaking the evil ones' hold on her people.

Mihesuah's only work of fiction, *The Roads of My Relations* is a fictional counterpart to the author's acclaimed scholarly writings on American Indian identity and activism, and more specifically, the challenges and opportunities that American Indians face in the academic realm. One chapter in particular, "Reggie the Anthropologist," highlights the lack of connection that often exists between academics conducting research on tribal communities for their own benefit and the American Indians who have the potential to—but often do not—benefit from the activities of these anthropologists, archaeologists, historians, and others. Mihesuah's *Indigenous American Women: Decolonization, Empowerment, Activism* is an effective companion to the collection, as it provides a framework for better understanding prominent characters such as Billie, Ariana, and others.

See also ANTHROPOLOGY AND NATIVE AMERICANS.

Bibliography

Guillory, Renee. Review of *The Roads of My Relations*, by Devon A. Mihesuah. *American Indian Quarterly* 24, no. 4 (2000): 659–670.

Mihesuah, Devon. *Indigenous American Women: Decolonization, Empowerment, Activism*. Lincoln, Nebr.: Bison Books, 2003.

———, ed. *Native and Academics: Researching and Writing about American Indians*. Lincoln: University of Nebraska Press, 1998.

Mihesuah, Devon A., and Angela Cavender Wilson. *Indigenizing the Academy: Transforming Scholarship and Empowering Communities*. Lincoln, Nebr.: Bison Books, 2004.

Lindsey Smith

Rose, Wendy   (1948–   )

Born Bronwyn Elizabeth Edwards in 1948, in Oakland, California, Rose was raised in San Francisco by a mother of Miwok and European descent, Betty Edwards, and her white husband. Rose's paternity remains uncertain: She might descend either from Dick Edwards or from the Hopi artist Charles Lloloma, with whom she identified, but who never officially acknowledged her. This uncertainty, the matrilineal nature of Hopi tribal membership, and Rose's strained ties to white relatives made her a cultural outsider. After dropping out of high school, she resumed formal studies in the late 1960s and became active in pan-Indian politics. Rose eventually pursued doctoral studies in anthropology at Berkeley, while publishing several books, including *HOPI ROADRUNNER DANCING* (1973) and *LOST COPPER* (1980), before joining the American Indian Studies Program at Fresno City College, which she coordinates. Rose lives in the San Joaquin foothills with Arthur Murata, to whom she has been married since 1976.

Rose's poetic maturation is evident in collections such as *The HALFBREED CHRONICLES* (1985), *GOING TO WAR WITH ALL MY RELATIONS* (1993), and *BONE DANCE: NEW AND SELECTED POEMS, 1965–1992* (1994). Also a visual artist, scholar, and activist, Rose uses her work to explore gaps in cultural identity and relations. She joins her insider/outsider perspective to a broad imagination and empathy, crafting a social vision that is sharply critical and deeply humane. Her poems speak in many voices—from both sides of cultural conflict, as well as from the middle. In poems such as "Academic Squaw" she explores the relationship between the seeker and her object of study. She has also illustrated some of her works, such as *Lost Copper* and *The Halfbreed Chronicles*, with drawings that use negative space to blur the lines between subject and background, center and margin. Colonialism, militarism, and the commodification of Native cultures are related subjects of her scrutiny, as in "Auction" and "Comment on Ethnopoetics and Literacy." Rose also probes connections among places, cultures, and historical moments. So, for instance, *The Halfbreed Chronicles* juxtaposes the genocide of Native Americans with the exterminations at Auschwitz and Hiroshima. A unique blend of lyricism and protest, autobiography and history, Rose's work is important among contemporary American Indian poets and has also influenced feminist poets and readers.

See also MIXED-BLOOD.

Bibliography

Coltelli, Laura. "Interview with Wendy Rose." In *Winged Words: American Indian Writers Speak,* 121–133. Lincoln: University of Nebraska Press, 1990.

Rose, Wendy. *Going to War with All My Relations: New and Selected Poems.* Flagstaff, Ariz.: Entrada Books, 1993.

———. *The Halfbreed Chronicles and Other Poems.* Albuquerque, N. Mex.: West End Press, 1985.

———. *Lost Copper.* Banning, Calif.: Malki Museum Press, 1980.

Rose, Wendy. "Neon Scars." In *I Tell You Now: Autobiographical Essays by Native American Writers,* edited by Brian Swann and Arnold Krupat, 252–261. Lincoln: University of Nebraska Press, 1987.

Sheila Hughes

Runner in the Sun: A Story of Indian Maize D'Arcy McNickle (1954)

Runner in the Sun: A Story of Indian Maize is D'ARCY MCNICKLE's least known novel, largely because it quickly went out of print when originally published. (It was reissued by the University of New Mexico Press in 1978.) Whereas both of McNickle's other novels, *The SURROUNDED* (1936) and *WIND FROM AN ENEMY SKY* (1978), are tragic tales that envision little hope for the survival of Native American culture, *Runner in the Sun* is an optimistic allegory of cultural survival in the face of adverse conditions created by both an environmental crisis and intratribal hostility.

At the center of the story is the young man named Salt, who belongs to the cliff-dwelling tribes of indigenous people (such as the Anasazi) who lived in New Mexico and Arizona before the arrival of the Europeans. Salt is on the verge of becoming an adult member of the community when his clan experiences a crisis that threatens their survival. Their agricultural relationship with the harsh desert environment has always been fragile, but a dwindling water supply and weak genetic strains of corn have especially endangered Salt's people. The clan's holy man therefore dispatches Salt on a long journey southward in search of some unspecified thing that will save them. Salt therefore embarks on a long adventure that takes him deep into the heart of what is now southern Mexico, where local tribes introduce him to the seeds of a new form of maize.

His return journey is fraught with danger, though along the way he falls in love with a young woman named Quail, whom he rescues from certain death at the hands of a culture that practices human sacrifice. More importantly he discovers a lush valley that he will eventually lead his people to in a migration to escape their tenuous existence in the desert cliffs.

Though McNickle wrote *Runner in the Sun* with young adults as the intended audience, the novel clearly transcends the category of "young adult fiction." Though the narrative language is simple and the tone subdued, the themes of the story are rather complex and mature. The novel incorporates many of the distinctive features of pre-Columbian Native American traditions, including the vision quest, the idea of cosmological balance and harmony, and what anthropologists refer to as *reciprocity,* or the integration of oppositional forces. McNickle likely drew inspiration from Joseph Campbell's *The Hero with a Thousand Faces* (1949) to create his own version of the mythological hero quest, though he also built on his own extensive anthropological studies, reflected earlier in his history of Native Americans, *They Came Here First* (1949).

Bibliography

Parker, Dorothy R. *Singing An Indian Song: A Biography of D'Arcy McNickle.* Lincoln: University of Nebraska Press, 1992.

Purdy, John Lloyd, ed. *The Legacy of D'Arcy McNickle: Writer, Historian, Activist.* Norman: University of Oklahoma Press, 1996.

Aaron Parrett

S

Sáanii Dahataał, The Women Are Singing: Poems and Stories Luci Tapahonso (1993)

LUCI TAPAHONSO's *Sáanii Dahataał* is a collection of poems and short fiction that reflects Tapahonso's strong connection to her Navajo heritage. This book is a tribute to her family and her Navajo community, and she feels compelled to reconnect with her homeland, but also to provide a physical and spiritual travelogue as she recounts her personal and ancestral memories. As she writes in the preface, "For many people in my situation, residing away from my homeland, writing is the means of returning, rejuvenation, and for restoring our spirits to the state of 'hozho,' or beauty, which is the basis of Navajo philosophy" (xii). Many of her poems show her love of family, her reverence for Navajo land and history, and her humor and compassion. Often she combines all of these elements as she pieces together her memories to tell the story of a Navajo woman fully realizing her identity.

The collection reflects her love of family as she begins with "Blue Horses Rush In," a poem about the birth of her daughter, and as she ends with "What I Am," a story about the death of her great-grandmother. Both of these events serve to define who she is in relation to the Navajo world. The first poem sets the tone for the rest of the book, which respects the cycle of life and

the joy and celebration of life among family. Some of her other poems that specifically address family resist sentimentality, and she draws upon the smallest nuances of her loved ones to show how she defines herself. In the poem "Hills Brothers Coffee" Tapahonso describes sharing a cup of coffee with her uncle. On the surface it may seem that simple; however, the poem reveals Tapahonso's desire to emulate her uncle, not only by preferring his brand of coffee, but by desiring to have his sense of humor and his ability to tell stories.

Tapahonso's reverence for land and history is present throughout the collection. The poem "In 1864" recounts the horrors of the forced Removal of the Navajo to Bosque Redondo and the horrifying effects of government Assimilation. Tapahonso shows how histories can reveal themselves to people through oral traditions, but most importantly in the poem history is revealed to a Navajo power-line worker when he listens to the landscape and remembers what happened there.

The humor in this collection is not difficult to find with poems and stories about runaway babies and family pets. Yet, it is in poems such as "Raisin Eyes" that she is able to combine these same elements of humor with compassion as she listens to a friend recount her doomed love affair with a cowboy. The woman in the poem tells her story with self-awareness yet also with a sad vulnerability that reflects Tapahonso's ability to conceptualize the depth of human relationships.

Bibliography

Brill, Susan B. "Discovering the Order and Structure of Things: A Conversive Approach to Contemporary Navajo Poetry." *Studies in American Indian Literatures* 7, no. 3 (fall 1995): 51–70.

Tapahonso, Luci. *Sáanii Dahataał, The Women Are Singing: Poems and Stories.* Tucson: University of Arizona Press, 1993.

Meredith James

Sacred Hoop, The: Recovering the Feminine in American Indian Traditions   Paula Gunn Allen (1986)

PAULA GUNN ALLEN's collected essays in *The Sacred Hoop* (1986) offered a new, feminist revolutionary perspective on American Indian literary and cultural studies. Its title pays homage to her mother's teaching that everything has a place in the circle of life, as well as to John G. Neihardt's rendition of the Oglala Lakota holy man Black Elk's famous life story in BLACK ELK SPEAKS. In these essays Allen demands a radical revisioning of folkloric and ethnographic scholarship, contending that such academic work amounts to a meaningless pile of data without woman at the center and as context. By excising female experience and perspective we are, according to Allen, committing deicide and hence are doomed to perceive only part of the human story.

In her introduction Allen lists the themes and issues important to American Indians that appear in her essays, including spirits; sacred cultures; endurance; Indian genocide by whites that has been/is based on white fear; the two stereotypical categorizations of Native Americans, noble savage and howling savage, and the damage wrought by the projection of these fallacies; Native oral traditions and their continuous appearance in contemporary written literature; and the need for all Americans to understand the importance of American Indian literature, since it also informs white American literature.

The book is divided into three sections. In section one, "The Ways of Our Grandmothers," Allen discusses the appreciation of women in Keres (Southwestern Pueblo) thinking, the Christian devaluing of women and children, and feminine knowledge and presence in architecture, customs, laws, oral traditions, and language. In "The Word Warriors" Allen delves into myth and the sacred, self-definition, alienation, and continuance in contemporary American Indian poetry and prose.

In the last section, "Pushing Up the Sky," she addresses American Indian women's historical resistance to sexual abuse and forced sterilization; the movement in Native America from gynocentric cultures accepting of homosexuality to cultures embodying the patriarchal homophobic and misogynist thinking forced upon them through European colonization; and the claim of the blood, intellectual, and spiritual presence of an American Indian female matrix in European-American women's feminism. Also in this last section Allen offers a corrective interpretation of an oral tale that follows Keres, rather than European, discursive patterns and practices. With its insistence on a woman-centered, culturally relevant approach, Allen's *Sacred Hoop* changed the way American Indian literature was being viewed by many non-Native academics and became part of the bedrock of Native American literary criticism.

Elizabeth McNeil

Salisbury, Ralph   (1924–)

Ralph Salisbury was born in 1924 in Arlington, Iowa, to a Cherokee father and an Irish-American mother. Raised on a family farm with no electricity, Salisbury hunted and trapped for meat and pelts in his early years. During World War II, when he was in his late teens, he served as a member of an American bomber squad, a period in which he also obtained six years of university training. In 1951 he received the M.F.A. from the University of Iowa, he then departed for Norway and Germany as a Fulbright Scholar.

From 1951 to 1994 Salisbury held various positions in the English Department at the University of Oregon, where he is now professor emeritus. During this period he was the recipient of many prestigious awards, including a Rockefeller Foundation Creative Writing Residency at the Villa Serbelloni in Bellagio, Italy, and an Amparts lectureship in India. Salisbury has spent stints teaching literature throughout the world which have garnered him international acclaim. His book *Spirit Beast Chant* has been translated into Hindi, Urdu, and Bengali.

In his nine books of prose and poetry Salisbury relays personal experiences as both a member of the Cherokee and an American. By using indigenous depictions of his early life on the vanishing family farm and by vividly portraying his patriotism in military combat, Salisbury has demonstrated an ability to transcend salient limits on conventional identity and has emerged a complex, racially mixed human being. His most recent collection of poems, *Rainbows of Stone,* is a moving illustration of his devotion to Cherokee traditions and enmeshes the two dominant cultures that have most influenced his life, thereby signifying his hybrid character.

Salisbury is the father of three children and resides in Eugene, Oregon, with his poet wife, Ingrid Wendt. In his half-century academic career he has been instrumental in constructing cross-cultural literary dialogue between Native Americans and the rest of the world.

Bibliography

Salisbury, Ralph. *Rainbows of Stone.* Tucson: University of Arizona Press, 2000.
———. *Spirit Beast Chant.* Marvin, S. Dak.: Blue Cloud Quarterly, 1982.

Ajnesh Prasad

Sanchez, Carol Lee (1934–   )

Carol Lee Sanchez was born in Albuquerque, New Mexico, in 1934 and raised in the village of Pagute, which consisted of approximately 20 families. Despite being raised in an isolated village, she has a multicultural and multilinguistic background. Her mother was Laguna and French-Canadian and grew up in a Spanish-speaking community. Her father was a first-generation Lebanese-American, who spoke Spanish, Arabic, and English. Furthermore Sanchez's maternal Laguna grandmother divorced her first husband and married a German Jew, who spoke his native language. Her paternal grandfathers maintained their Arabic traditions. In 1952 she married a first-generation Italian-American, whose family spoke Italian. In short Sanchez was surrounded with differences. Through her writing, painting, and teaching all differences are harmonized in understanding and respect for multicultural heritages.

At age 44 Sanchez received a B.A. in arts administration from San Francisco State University. During the 1970s and 1980s she was actively involved with American Indian Women Painters, Third World Women in the Arts, and National Women's Studies Association. From 1976 to 1986 she taught American Indian studies and women's studies at several universities, including San Francisco State University and the University of Missouri. In 1997 Sanchez was conferred "the Writer of the Year Award for Poetry" by the Wordcraft Circle of Native Authors and Storytellers. Sanchez currently lives in Hughesville, Missouri.

As a MIXED-BLOOD Indian Sanchez belongs nowhere and everywhere. In other words, she is in between: "all the maps are lost or destroyed" (*From Spirit to Matter* 6). However, she realizes a deeply internalized connection with her tribal heritage. In her poems, which celebrate a land-based life and spirituality of all the living things, her voice is the observer and carrier of history for the future. She becomes a "Message Bringer Woman," who sees, feels, chants, writes, and speaks for a healthy and harmonious linkage of daily life and spirituality. In a sense Sanchez's poems convey the message that all tribal and nontribal people are personally and collectively in between the processes of creating and being created.

Bibliography

Rainbow Visions and Earth Ways. A bilingual English/German publication. O.B.E.M.A. Multicultural Series. Osnabrück: Universitätsverlag Rasch, 1998.
Sanchez, Carol Lee. *From Spirit to Matter: New and Selected Poems, 1969–1996.* San Francisco: Taurean Horn, 1997.

———. *Message Bringer Woman.* San Francisco: Taurean Horn, 1977.

———. *(She) Poems.* Goshen, Conn.: Chicory Blue, 1995.

Strom, Karen M. "Carol Lee Sanchez." Available online. URL: Storytellers Native American Authors Online. http://www.hanksville.org/storytellers/cl-sanchez/. Accessed on August 15, 2005.

Heejung Cha

Sarris, Greg   (1952–   )

Greg Sarris was born in Santa Rosa, California, on February 15, 1952, to Emilio Arthur Hilario, a Miwok/Pomo/Filipino, and Jewish-Irish Mary Bernadette Hartmann. His mother died during childbirth, and his father left him and eventually died of ALCOHOLISM. Greg Sarris was adopted shortly after his birth by the white couple Mary and George Sarris. He left his adoptive parents when home life became difficult; consequently, he lived an unsteady young life, poor and running with gangs, never staying for long at one single place, but remaining in Santa Rosa. Meeting the Pomo elder and basket maker Mabel McKay at the age of 12 gave him new purpose and guidance in his life. Because she was largely responsible for his recognizing the importance of Native American traditions and customs in his life and becoming a writer, McKay is the main focus of interest in Sarris's first two books. In 1978 he received a B.A. from the University of California Los Angeles (UCLA), and in 1981, an M.A. from Stanford. He also earned a Ph.D. in modern thought and literature. He teaches in the Native American Studies Department at UCLA.

Sarris often incorporates personal narrative in academic work, as in his study KEEPING SLUG WOMAN ALIVE, in which he mixes storytelling, ethnography, autobiography, and literary criticism. GRAND AVENUE consists of 10 short stories, all of which revolve around one clan of Pomo, covering three generations marred by tribal disagreements and divisions. Each story has a different first-person narrator and each is about cultural survival. The novel WATERMELON NIGHTS concentrates on the lives of one Pomo family, again spanning three generations. Johnny Severe; his mother, Iris; and his grandmother, Elba, respectively narrate the three sections. Despite their family's breakdown what bind them together are tribal tradition, love, and kindness.

Greg Sarris is not only a writer and a professor, but also active in Pomo-Coast Miwok politics. He was chairman of the Federated Coast Miwok Nation during the 1990s.

Bibliography

Burnham, Michelle. "Pomo Basket Weaving, Poison and the Politics of Restoration in Greg Sarris's *Grand Avenue.*" *Studies in American Indian Literatures: The Journal of the Association for the Study of American Indian Literatures* 14, no. 3 (winter 2002): 18–36.

Hardin, Michael. "Greg Sarris's *Grand Avenue:* Variations on Three Themes in Gabriel Garcia Marquez's *One Hundred Years of Solitude.*" *Notes on Contemporary Literature* 29, no. 4 (September 1999): 5–7.

Sarris, Greg. *Grand Avenue.* New York: Hyperion, 1994.

———. *Keeping Slug Woman Alive: A Holistic Approach to American Indian Texts.* Berkeley: University of California Press, 1993.

———. *Watermelon Nights.* New York: Hyperion, 1998.

Slowik, Mary. "'More to the Story': Ethnography and Narrative Form in Greg Sarris's *Keeping Slug Woman Alive* and Keith Basso's 'Stalking with Stories.'" *North Dakota Quarterly* 64, no. 2 (spring 1997): 49–65.

Fabienne Quennet

Secrets from the Center of the World   Joy Harjo   (1989)

In *Secrets from the Center of the World* JOY HARJO continues to give voice to those who have none—in these prose poems, animals, such as birds and rocks. An occasional woman on horseback, sometimes the speaker herself, intrudes on the landscape but vanishes again, leaving no trace of her visit. The reciprocal relationship of traditional Native American culture with the land is seen in both the photographs and the accompanying poems as the earth is honored and the speaker's position in the interconnective web of the natural world is celebrated.

Stephen Strom's photographs of the Southwest close in on details of the landscape instead of offering clichéd panoramas. By doing so, he offers Joy Harjo a venue for unfolding her particular talent of seeing the infinite in the details. In the lines accompanying the photograph of Tuba City's mud hills, Harjo embraces the history of the world and its physical imagery: "Invisible fish swim in this ghost ocean now described by waves of sand. . . . Soon the fish will learn to walk. Then humans will come ashore and paint dreams on the drying stone" (46). The land does not serve as just an excuse for beautifully descriptive writing. For Harjo the words and the landscape they give voice to are part of the same spiritual realm. The Native American tradition of viewing nature as a powerful force, instead of as something to be subdued and exploited, informs Harjo's poetry (Wong 72). The beauty of a landscape populated with bears, horses, and "giant butterflies burrow[ing] and dream[ing]" (38) is evoked against Strom's stark and empty landscapes.

The timelessness of Harjo's poems is another element of Native American writing, where the circularity of time is valued over the chronological view of history: "Anything that matters is here. Anything that will continue to matter in the next several thousand years will continue to be here" (*Secrets* 32). History for Harjo is a combination of tradition, memory, and story—each equally important to the telling of the story of Native Americans in general and Harjo in particular. In an interview with Laura Cotellie Harjo says that her Creek heritage "provides the underlying psychic structure, within which is a wealth of memory" (*Spiral* 61). These memories, collective and personal, inform the core of the poems in *Secrets*. The memories of old men recognizing the morning star, of the dreams of bears, of two women meeting on a rise to exchange gossip, "the memory described by stone and lichen" (48), help the narrator remember who she is and show her the way home.

The sense of movement in the poems, created by Strom's photographs, echoes the forced travels of the Creek and the journeys of Harjo herself (*Spiral* 5). A frequent theme of her poetry is the search for home. In the tradition of Native American writers the narrators in Harjo's poems are often trying to reconnect to their Indian identities and their cultures from whom they are separated by place and time. The closing line of one poem asks, "Did we ever make it home?" (26), a pertinent question for a people that have lost their home again and again.

Bibliography

Harjo, Joy. *Secrets from the Center of the World*. Tucson: Sun Tracks and the University of Arizona Press, 1989.

———. *The Spiral of Memory: Interviews*, edited by Laura Coltelli. Ann Arbor: University of Michigan Press, 1996.

Scarry, John. "Representing Real Worlds: The Evolving Poetry of Joy Harjo." *World Literature Today* 66, no. 2 (spring 1992): 286–291.

Wong, Herta D. "Nature in Native American Literatures." In *American Nature Writers*. Vol. 2, 1,141–1,156. New York: Charles Scribner's Sons, 1996.

P. K. Bostian

"Sermon Preached by Samson Occom, Minister of the Gospel, and Missionary to the Indians; at the Execution of Moses Paul, An Indian"   Samson Occom (1780)

This sermon, considered the first published work in English by an American Indian, was delivered in 1772 to a crowd of several hundred people, both white and Indian, shortly before its subject, Moses Paul, was hanged. It was published by William Watson in 1780. It is a version of the "execution sermon," a popular genre in New England at the time, meant to serve as a deterrent to future criminals and sinners. Paul, who was convicted of the murder of Moses Cook, a well-known white citizen of Waterbury, Connecticut, requested that SAMSON OCCOM preach the sermon. Because Paul was drunk when he committed the murder, most of his audience would have presumed that Occom would address the problem of ALCOHOLISM among Indians.

Occom takes the theme of his sermon from Romans 6.23: "For the wages of sin is death, but the gift of God is eternal life through Jesus Christ our Lord." He stresses the idea that all human beings are sinners, and all sinners may be redeemed through their faith in Jesus Christ. This message works well for his mixed audience. It reminds the whites that they too, not just the people of color in their midst, are sinners. It reminds the Indians that, as all sinners may, that they also may be redeemed and welcomed into the Kingdom of Heaven. Occom argues that the universality of all human beings: "We are all dying creatures, and accountable unto God." Further, all people, regardless of color, "disregard" eternal life, engaging in sin without thought to their souls.

Occom then moves from the subject of sin to the happier topic of redemption. After arguing extensively that sin will give only eternal death, he shows his audience that the way to eternal life is "union of the soul to God," which is available to everyone. He uses the example of St. Paul to demonstrate that even the most wretched can be converted—an especially effective example given the subject at hand.

Occom ends his sermon by addressing Moses Paul himself. The condemned man, whom he calls "flesh of my flesh," he urges to turn to Christ, for only Christ will be his judge. For Paul (and for the larger audience) this would have underscored the point that Christians should not judge one another. Occom reminds the church elders in the audience, that "we are all dying creatures"—they too will die and be judged just as Moses Paul will. It is their job, he says, to fight sin for God. The audience would have known that his implication here is that we should abhor not just the murder, but all sin, including those committed by whites. Finally, he addresses the Indians, his "poor kindred." Here he vividly describes the toll alcoholism takes on the Indian family and urges them to resist this temptation. The way in which Occom ties all humanity together, from the beginning of

the sermon, and then deliberately splits his audience at the end, serves to drive home his point that all will sin, all may be redeemed, and all will be judged after death, a religious point to be sure, and for Occom, a social commentary as well.

Bibliography

Elliot, Michael. "'This Indian Bait' Samson Occom and the Voice of Liminality." *Early American Literature* 29 (1994): 233–253.

Seventh Generation: An Anthology of Native American Plays   Mimi D'Aponte (1999)

Released in the same year as the broader historical anthology *Stories of Our Way,* Mimi D'Aponte's source holds the distinction of being the first major collection of contemporary Native American plays. *Seventh Generation* provided initial exposure to the dramatic work of modern North American indigenous playwrights. Her efforts to galvanize scholarly energy reveal themselves in a multilayered showcase of such playwrights as Drew Hayden Taylor and DIANE GLANCY.

In a brief introduction D'Aponte surveys cultural and dramatic heritage. She summarizes tribal ceremonies (Sioux Sun Dances, Northwest Coast object ceremonies) and Native cultural performances (intertribal meetings, social gatherings), as well as the theatrical manifestations of the "Indian," from the John Augustus Stone melodrama *Metamora* (1829) to the semidocumentary *Trail of Tears* (1966). The historical journey of Native American performance and Native Americans representations in performance enriches D'Aponte's position that each playwright is the product of a "journey," one that shares similarities with those of the others but is also the playwright's own.

A brief statement from the author and a production history precede each play. Each concludes with the playwright's biography. Through the collection D'Aponte's introduction provides an organizing paradigm for each play's unique style. Manipulated stereotypes become visible. In HANAY GEIOGAMAH's *BODY INDIAN* the alcoholic

Bobby becomes the victim of group addiction and social oppression, as much as personal failure. In LEANNE HOWE and ROXY GORDON's *Indian Radio Days* the authors parody a host of social and historical concerns, from the excesses of consumer capitalism to the repeated invasions of North America by white nations. Traditional religion manifests itself in William S. Yellow Rose Jr.'s *The Independence of Eddie Rose*, in which a smoke bath strengthens the protagonist's spirit, that he may break with his dysfunctional family and rescue his younger sister. Storytelling provides foundations for Spiderwoman Theater's *Power Pipes* and Drew Hayden Taylor's *Only Drunks and Children Tell the Truth,* both of which incorporate Native language and social relationships. Diane Glancy's *Woman Who Was a Red Deer Dressed for the Deer Dance* and Victoria Nalani Kneubuhl's *Story of Susanna* mix past and present, the first through a conversation between the community-conscious Grandmother/Deer spirit and her modern, practical granddaughter; the second, through a parable of injustice that has played in both ancient and recent history.

Seventh Generation is a showcase of contemporary Native drama and a call for future activity. Elizabeth Theobald, the Cherokee director of Public Programs at the Mashantucket Pequot Museum and Research Center, concludes the source by noting a need for more productions, not merely of Native American dramas, but of Native American dramas presented by Natives intimately involved in the process, as playwrights and actors obviously, but also as directors, designers, and other collaborators.

Bibliography

D'Aponte, Mimi, ed. *Seventh Generation: An Anthology of Native American Plays.* New York: Theater Communications Group, 1999.

Geiogamah, Hanay, and Jaye T. Darby, eds. *Stories of Our Way: An Anthology of American Indian Plays.* Los Angeles: UCLA American Indian Studies Center, 1999.

Ben Fisler

Shadow Country Paula Gunn Allen (1982)

Shadow Country is a key text in contemporary Native American poetry. In it PAULA GUNN ALLEN reveals how poetry can forge a healing vision for a world in which all peoples can survive. These poems depict Allen's quest for such a vision. The poet first must face the pain and suffering of the past and present—both personal and global. She ultimately must learn to understand the messages of the gods that she heard as a child on the mesas above the Lugana village of Cubrero.

Allen's mixed ancestry—Laguna, Sioux, Lebanese, and Scots—as well as her "affiliations as lesbian [and] feminist" (McDaniel 30) allow her to open new "psychic spaces where alternations of consciousness can occur," in the words of AnaLouise Keating, who sees Allen as a "threshold" figure capable of developing new models of human identity (163).

The title *Shadow Country* is significant. Shadows permit clearer vision than would be possible in bright sunlight, but they are not the "real thing." Thus Kenneth Lincoln declares that Allen "writes in the shadows of visions" (vii). The shadows also allude to the ways these poems are both haunted and nurtured by spirits of those no longer living. Finally the title suggests urgency, as John Lowe explains: "One must take advantage of the dying light to retrieve the usable detritus of the past" (62).

Allen's method reflects her nonlinear tribal perspective. The poems circle around the central themes of coming home, trying to remember, and waiting for the rain. Rain in Allen's poems is "a sign of poetry, generation, spirituality" (Lowe 58). One of the first poems, "Mountain Song," is a revelation of the poet's ceremonial purpose. She begins by asking the reader to allow her to sprinkle pollen on the reader's head (a sacralizing act) and to "tell / the tales that hold the rocks to life" (3–4). She then announces that she "will walk/ nobly to Black Mesa" (6–7). The destination is significant because the mesas (high plateaus) are the residence of the gods. The poem declares that the "treacherous" potholes are "drunk/ with clouds" (10–12), meaning that the way is dangerous, but the promise of a saving rain is there, nonetheless. The poem's final stanza is a parenthetical warning of the trickery possessed by "the enemy" (13–14). The parentheses de-emphasize the threat so that the journey toward vision remains paramount.

The vision reached at the end names the female principle of the universe as the source of healing and "making everything new" ("He Na Tye Woman" 19): "He na tye (woman) that is recognition and remembering" (24). "That rain is you," the poet announces. "How did I wait so long to drink" (55–56).

Bibliography

Allen, Paula Gunn. *Shadow Country,* vii–xiii. Los Angeles: American Indian Studies Center, University of California, Los Angeles, 1982.

Hanson, Elizabeth. "Shadows in Paula Gunn Allen's 'Shadow Country.'" *ARIEL: A Review of International English Literature* 25, no. 2 (April 1994): 49–55.

Jahner, Elaine. "Climbing a Sacred Ladder: Technique in the Poetry of Paula Allen." *Studies in American Indian Literatures* 7, no. 3 (fall 1983): 77–81.

Keating, AnaLouise. "Back to the Mother? Paula Gunn Allen's Origin Myths. In *Women Reading Women's Writing: Self-Invention in Paula Gunn Allen, Gloria Anzaldua, and Audre Lorde,* 93–117. Philadelphia: Temple University Press, 1996.

Lincoln, Kenneth. "Foreword." In *Shadow Country* by Paula Gunn Allen, vii–xii. Los Angeles: American Indian Studies Center, University of California, Los Angeles, 1982.

Lowe, John. "Cantas Encantadas: Paula Gunn Allen's *Shadow Country.*" *Studies in American Indian Literatures* 7, no. 3 (fall 1983): 56–66.

McDaniel, Cynthia. "Paula Gunn Allen: An Annotated Bibliography of Secondary Sources." *Studies in American Indian Literatures* 11, no. 3 (summer 1999): 29–42.

TallMountain, Mary. "Paula Gunn Allen's 'The One Who Skins Cats': An Inquiry into Spiritedness." *Studies in American Indian Literatures* 5, no. 2 (summer 1993): 34–38.

Susan Bowers

Sharpest Sight, The   Louis Owens (1992)

Louis Owens's second novel, *The Sharpest Sight,* develops the complications and importance of discerning MIXED-BLOOD cultural identity in America. The story opens as a murder mystery in the small town of Amarga in California's Salinas Valley. Deputy Sheriff Ramon "Mundo" Morales sees the body of his childhood pal and Vietnam veteran friend floating down the Salinas River. The search for Attis's body and his killer is the catalyst for both Mundo and Attis's brother, Cole, to discover their identities.

Both Mundo and Cole begin to understand the truth of their respective cultural heritage despite a concerted effort by those in power to strip them of that knowledge. Mundo's proud and once powerful Castilian family, land barons by right of the king of Spain, has conspired for generations to bury the "disgraceful" truth of their matriarch, a Chumash slave taken from the mission by their patriarch. But the playful spirit of Mundo's grandfather, Antonio, and the mysterious Mondragon sisters who are so choked by family lies even in death conspire to push the truth from the grave and into life. And although the land grant and family prestige have long ago been lost, it is the duality of Mundo's blood that he must reconcile for himself: descendant of slaveholder and slave, illegitimate heir of the land through the conqueror, legitimate heir to the land through the conquered. In the end Antonio says, "My grandson has become more comfortable with the dead. . . . He knows at last who his is" (262). The dead owe that knowledge to the living.

The conspirators against Cole and his father, Hoey, are even more complex and far-reaching. They are centuries of government policies designed to annihilate whole tribes for their land through slaughter, pestilence, starvation, and cultural eradication. Cole is confused and cynical about his own Mississippi Choctaw roots. He thinks of himself as "more Irish than anything else" (14) and of Hoey as "a California Choctaw living in a made-up world . . . busy creating himself out of books and made-up memories" (15). But the truth of Hoey's cultural memories, the stories, flows from his Mississippi childhood along the unconstrained Yazoo River in traditional Choctaw homelands with his uncle, Luther. Cole's cultural knowledge has been dammed and siphoned as has the Salinas River's natural flow. When Uncle Luther "sees" Attis's death in the Salinas River, he calls his nephew's *shilup,* his outside shadow or ghost, to return home to rest in Mississippi, but because of its violent end, it cannot travel on without its bones. Uncle Luther knows that Cole must be the one to finish Attis's story and begin his own. When Cole returns to the Salinas River, he has begun to dream again, "begun to know who he is" (244), so that later, in the dry season, Cole is able to hear the call of his brother's bones. He follows the river to Attis's body, "cupped in the branches ten feet off the ground . . . as if he had been placed there with loving precision" (251–252), as if on a traditional Choctaw burial scaffold. Over time the river has stripped the bones, but as in stories of the traditional Bone Picker, Cole will clean them, wrap them, and carry them east to their Mississippi homeland.

Further Reading

Kilpatrick, Jacquelyn. ed. *Louis Owens: Literary Reflections on His Life and Work.* American Indian Literature and Critical Studies series, vol. 46. Norman: University of Oklahoma Press, 2004.

LaLonde, Chris. *Grave Concerns, Trickster Turns: The Novels of Louis Owens.* The American Indian Literature and Critical Studies series, vol. 43. Norman: University of Oklahoma Press, 2002.

Owens, Louis. *The Sharpest Sight.* Norman: University of Oklahoma Press, 1992.

Harriet L. Karalis

She Had Some Horses   Joy Harjo (1983)

JOY HARJO's third book of poetry, *She Had Some Horses,* is a powerful description of a woman who is healing, and by extension, a prescription for the healing of all women in despair. As a group these poems are more concentrated on women than Harjo's other collections are. She describes women's pain and confusion at being trapped, metaphorically held prisoner by men and by society. Ultimately, however, the description is optimistic, as it acknowledges and celebrates female power and life.

In the introduction GRAG SARRIS claims that these poems present a "woman unafraid to stand before the ills about us in this world—poverty, the disenfranchised and dispossessed, internalized oppression—and see them, learn their ways, illuminate them so they might lose their hold over us and be cast off" (3). The book is divided into four sections, and when the poems are read in sequence, the progression of which Sarris speaks is clear. The first section, entitled "Survivors," begins with the poem "Call It Fear." In this poem Harjo immediately names what scares us: "There is this edge where shadows / and bones of some of us walk / backwards" (1–3). The poem goes on to speak about this "edge" and how it can take different forms, yet continue to appear throughout life.

Other poems in this section speak of the different ways in which women "survive." In "For Alva Benson, And For Those Who Have Learned to Speak," the emphasis is on continuity. Harjo gives us images of birth and renewal and implies that in childbirth, an act that is simple and complicated at the same time, Native women are engaged in surviving. She says, "[we] keep giving birth and watch / ourselves die, over and over" (33–34), but the earth that talks to us, that speaks to the Navajo woman at the beginning of the poem, "goes on talking" (36).

Harjo also takes pains to relate this sense of continuity to her audience—to allow the reader to feel a part of what is happening in the poems. Critics have often noted that Harjo's poems are not directed only at readers of her tribe, or even at readers of Indian descent. In "The Woman Hanging from the Thirteenth Floor Window" she describes a woman who, in desperation, is contemplating suicide. Harjo gives the reader so many details of the woman's life: She is the mother of Carlos, Margaret, and Jimmy; she has had two husbands; she is loved by her parents. Then, as she looks out on the Chicago skyline, she sees "other women hanging from many-floored windows / counting their lives in the palms of their hands" (25–26). Harjo skillfully engages the reader with the woman and then suggests that she is Everywoman, and that all can relate to her pain.

In section two, entitled "What I Should Have Said," Harjo turns to the personal. All the poems in this section involve intimate pronouns: *I, me, you, we.* Moving through this section, a reader feels the uncertainty and confusion of a woman who feels left behind or separated, even if only metaphorically. In "Motion" she says, "I am next to you / in skin and blood / and I am not" (8–10). She feels "frantic" and unsure, although she feels love as well. In "What I Should Have Said" the speaker explores the intense confusion she feels in her relationship, feeling frustrated and wondering whether her idea of love is just a "cushion" and not real at all. She says, "I feel bloated with what I should say / and what I don't" (9–10) and bemoans the state of limbo in which she and her lover drift. She says, "We are caught between clouds and wet earth . . . no life to speak of" (18, 21).

Although section two explores these tumultuous feelings, it ends with a celebratory feel. As the section moves toward its end, the women in the poems begin to be thankful for their very lives. In "Alive" the speaker triumphantly says, "This woman can cross any line" (33), and in the last poem in this section, "September Moon," we are left with one image: that of strong, powerful womanhood: "Such beauty / Look / We are alive" (16–18).

In section three the horses of the title come thundering in on the heels of this strength. All of the poems in this section speak of horses, and all use the pronoun *she* in a way that feels universal. However, it is the title poem that relays this universality best. All the lines but the last begin with the phrases "She had some horses" or "She had horses." These horses are from the natural world and from the world of human invention. They are positive and negative. They are destructive and they are redemptive. They are, in the end, all aspects of woman and they are all necessary to her life. And in the end, as the last line of the poem says, "These were the same horses" (51).

The final section of the text contains just one poem, "I Give You Back." In it the speaker gives back the fear she named at the beginning and in doing so sets herself free forever. Having moved through the sections of the text, she is now healed, is alive, and can finally put her fear to death.

Shell Shaker   LeAnne Howe (2001)

In her novel *Shell Shaker* LeAnne Howe uses an unconventional mode of storytelling, interweaving multiple storylines to construct a living history of the Choctaw Nation. In a statement that denotes a series of issues at the heart of the novel, Howe writes, "One Indian can't do anything alone, but needs the help of ancestors and young people to build the future" (162). To illustrate this vision, Howe interweaves historical events that occur during the 1738 autumnal equinox with a parallel storyline during the 1991 autumnal equinox, which emphasizes the relationship between past and present generations and the preservation of tribal and communal values in the face of colonization.

Howe constructs a fissure between body and spirit that objectifies the body (most poignantly illustrated by the bone-picking ceremonies) and mobilizes the spirit (in alignment with Choctaw belief in "life everlasting"). She thus obliterates the false barrier that skin and bones create and notes that all Choctaw believe "the spirit is related to the body as perfume is to the rose" (105). Thus the spirit may roam beyond the boundaries of the body during life, and after death the human spirit may survive eternal reincarnation as a shape shifter, or TRICKSTER FIGURE. Shakbatina, who sacrifices her life during the heated political events of the 1738 autumnal equinox, fulfills the role of the shape shifter in the novel as she infiltrates future periods, namely, the 1991 equinox, in order to defend the descendents of her tribe against Osanos, or bloodsuckers, whose greedy acts threaten tribal peace and democracy.

The separation between body and spirit—as it demonstrates the perpetual cycle of spiritual life as characters and events from 1738 reappear in new bodies, or "shells," in 1991—reaffirms the communal and political relationship between the past and present in *Shell Shaker.* As the ancestral spirits are reincarnated in the 1991 generation, the political conflicts reemerge. The equinox signals the time of year when the Sun crosses the Earth's equator and day and night are of equal length; *Itilauichi,* the spirit of the autumnal equinox, symbolizes efforts to create balance and restore order in the Choctaw nation. *Shell Shaker* shows that a fusion of efforts between past and present generations is necessary to the survival of the Choctaw against Osanos within their tribe and against the continuous pressures exerted by mainstream U.S. culture.

Bibliography

McCullough, Ken. "If You See the Buddha at the Stomp Dance, Kill Him! The Bicameral World of LeAnne Howe's *Shell Shaker.*" *Studies in American Indian Literatures* 15, no. 2 (summer 2003): 58–69.

Steeves, Carolyn. "Review of *Shell Shaker,* by LeAnne Howe." *Voices from the Gaps: Women Writers of Color.* Available online. URL: http://voices.cla.umn. edu/newsite/resound/HOWEshellshaker.htm. Accessed on August 15, 2005.

Lee Ann Hunter

Silent Words   Ruby Slipperjack-Farrell (1992)

Silent Words exposes the consequences of cultural alienation and dislocation in a young Anishinabe adolescent's life. Danny Lynx is forced to leave traditional life on his father's trapline and move to an area where he has little contact with his Native community. In this environment Danny undergoes ASSIMILATION and begins to communicate in English, rather than in Ojibwe. The loss of his language and his culture has left Danny without a sense of belonging and makes him an easy target of abuse from his stepmother and racism in the non-Native community. Not until Danny has reconciled with his culture can he overcome the abuse and resist assimilation.

Early in the narrative Danny leaves his abusive home environment to search for his mother. Although he feels quite vulnerable as a runaway, he is in fact much safer away from home. During his trip he encounters many members of the Anishinabe community who take him in, no questions asked. Without realizing it, the boy is part of this Native community all along. In a sense leaving his hometown signifies returning home to his Native culture. Danny, who has no sense of a cultural identity, sees the world he travels with assimilated eyes and is at first unable to communicate without misunderstandings. This changes as he observes the people he meets and learns through experience that observation teaches the skills needed to communicate with people and with nature. Rather than being taught, Danny plays an active role in his own education. Early on he has the fortune to meet an elder named Ol'Jim, who feels a responsibility to hand down his knowledge to Danny in order for tradition to continue. This also means Danny has the responsibility to teach the next generation of young Natives when the time comes. Through Ol'Jim Danny learns about respect and reciprocity as he gains an understanding of the importance of spirituality to the interrelations among humans, animals, and the land.

As the title suggests, silence is a significant element in the novel that takes on different meanings throughout the narrative. Silence goes from being an oppressive force to giving Danny a language he can share with his community. At the outset Danny is silenced as his father chooses to believe his abusive wife rather than his son. With the Native elders he learns one of the most important lessons: to understand an Anishinabe language of silence. At first he misinterprets their silences, but he soon learns to pay attention to their nonverbal language. By observing his elders, he receives clues on how to relate to the world around him without words ("silent words"). In addition Danny reconnects with his language, which, together with his culture, had been silenced when he was forced to move to town. By learning to pay attention, Danny is also able to receive the cultural knowledge handed down to him by Ol'Jim's stories.

See also SLIPPERJACK-FARRELL, RUBY.

Bibliography

Horne, Dee. *Contemporary American Indian Writing: Unsettling Literature.* New York: Peter Lang, 1999.

Slipperjack, Ruby. "Ruby Slipperjack." In *Contemporary Challenges: Conversations with Canadian Native Authors,* 203–215. Saskatoon: Fifth House, 1991.

Joanna M. Daxell

Silko, Leslie Marmon (1948–)

Leslie Marmon Silko was born in Albuquerque, New Mexico, on March 5, 1948. Her mother, Virginia, was originally from Montana. Just out of the army, her father, Lee Marmon, was beginning a career as a professional photographer and managing the Marmon Trading Post in the village of Old Laguna, about 50 miles west of Albuquerque. Along with her younger sisters, Wendy and Gigi, Leslie was raised in a house on the edge of the village, a short distance from Rio San José. Silko attended the Bureau of Indian Affairs' Laguna Day School through fourth grade, then commuted to Manzano Day School, a Catholic institution in Albuquerque. Here in the fifth grade Silko created a story out of assigned spelling words, an event she sees as initiating her literary life.

Relatives who have had a direct impact on Silko's writing include her paternal great-grandmother, Marie Anaya Marmon (Grandma A'mooh), and great-aunt, Susan Reyes Marmon (Aunt Susie). Both attended the infamous Carlisle Indian School, a BOARDING SCHOOL in Pennsylvania; Susan returned to Laguna to teach. They helped raise Silko, relating Laguna history and culture and impressing upon her the role of the storyteller. Laguna, or Ka-waikah, Lake People, is the largest of the seven Keresan-speaking pueblos, consisting of six main villages and nearly 8,000 residents. The 19 agricultural pueblos of New Mexico, which have been occupied since "prehistory," are famous for their unified 1680 revolt, which succeeding in banishing the Spanish colonizers for several years. Silko's identity is closely tied to Laguna, and resistance to colonization is a major theme in her work.

Silko's life and writing have also been shaped by her family's mixed Laguna, Mexican, and Anglo heritage. Silko's Anglo great-grandfather, Robert Marmon, and his brother entered the area in the 1870s as surveyors for the railroad. They married Laguna women and settled there. Though controversial, the Marmon brothers both served as governors of the pueblo and created the first tribal constitution. Later, Silko's father, Lee Marmon, a professional photographer, held the post of Tribal Council treasurer. Though the MIXED-BLOOD Marmon family lived at the physical fringes of Laguna, Silko grew up a witness to Laguna politics, life, and art.

Silko entered the University of New Mexico (UNM) in 1964. A year later she married Richard Chapman and gave birth to their son, Robert. In 1969 she graduated Phi Beta Kappa with a B.A. in English and entered UNM's American Indian Law School Fellowship Program. She also separated from Chapman and published her first short story, "The Man to Send Rain Clouds," in the *New Mexico Quarterly.*

During this period the long legal case for Laguna remuneration from seized lands resulted only in payment at 19th-century prices. Disillusioned, Silko quit law school after three semesters, convinced that injustice was part of the Anglo legal system. Knowing the power of the well-told story to serve as an agent of change, Silko returned briefly to UNM in 1970 to begin the M.A. in creative writing, but she soon left to teach at Navajo Community College in Tsaile, Arizona. There she wrote LAGUNA WOMAN (1974, 1994), a collection of introspective poems suffused with images from nature. Also in 1970, Silko married John Silko, an attorney, and was awarded a National Endowment for the Humanities Discovery Grant. Silko's second son, Cazimir, was born in 1972, and the next year the family moved to Ketchikan, Alaska, where Silko began to write her first novel, CEREMONY (1977).

Silko's fiction and poetry began to appear in publication in earnest during the mid-1970s. Seven stories were published in *The Man to Send Rain Clouds* (1974), now seen as a landmark of the AMERICAN INDIAN LITERARY RENAISSANCE. Her best-known story from the collection, "YELLOW WOMAN," now widely anthologized, is set in Laguna and features a present-day character who is suddenly caught up in a repetition of the ancient pattern of generative Yellow Woman (Kochininako) stories from Laguna myth. Also in 1974, Silko published another often-anthologized story, "Lullaby" (*The Chicago Review*), in which an elderly Navajo woman remembers losing her children, one to war and the others, at a very young age, to U.S. government health officials. Because of the close ties between the Laguna and Navajo, Navajo characters often appear in Silko's work. Silko received *The Chicago Review*'s 1974 Award for Poetry, and the following year "Lullaby" was selected as one of the 20 best short stories of 1975. When Silko returned to Laguna in 1976, her one-act play of "Lullaby," adapted with the playwright Frank Chin, was first performed.

In 1977 Silko had another productive literary year. She won a Pushcart Prize for Poetry and saw *Ceremony* published to critical acclaim, as well as some controversy. The author and scholar PAULA GUNN ALLEN, for example, who, as is Silko, is of mixed ethnic heritage and grew up at Laguna, criticized Silko for violating convention by using a clan story in the novel. Mixing the real and mythic, *Ceremony* tells of the mixed-blood Tayo's return home to Laguna after World War II. Haunted by the war's violence and by his guilt that he had not been able to protect his brother/cousin, who died there, Tayo is spiritually ill. Betonie, a Navajo medicine man, puts into motion a ceremony in which Tayo is ultimately transformed and healed.

Moving to Tucson in 1978, Silko began to teach at the University of Arizona. Also that year she began a correspondence with the poet James Wright. Their remarkable collection of letters became *The Delicacy and Strength of Lace* (1986), edited by Wright's wife, Anne. Showing a mutual love of language, the letters chronicle the friendship from its beginnings, with Wright's praise of *Ceremony*, through Silko's expression of her feelings about the cancer to which Wright finally succumbed in 1980.

STORYTELLER (1981), Silko's next major work, is a collection of poems and stories, some of which had been published earlier, and photographs. The majority of the photos were taken by Silko's father. In this multigenre text Silko explores her family's complex history, results of colonization, the land, love, sex, identity, HUMOR, and power. Further demonstrating an interest in visual images that she shares with her father, Silko completed the film *Estoyehmuut and the Gunnadeyah* (Arrow Boy and the Witches) in 1980 and a video about storytelling from a Laguna perspective, *Running on the Edge of the Rainbow: Laguna Stories and Poems* in 1982, which features Silko sitting on a porch with friends (one of whom is the poet JOY HARJO),

reading from her work. The video effectively demonstrates the seriocomic quality and function of storytelling.

In 1981 Silko also began notes for *ALMANAC OF THE DEAD* (1991), her second novel. Completed with the help of a prestigious MacArthur Fellowship, this apocalyptic almost-800-page story is the most overtly political of Silko's works to date. Though it was published to mixed reviews, Silko reports she is pleased with both the negative and the favorable responses because many of the reviews are, she says, "wildly impassioned" outpourings that show critics' involvement with the text (Coltelli 78). Publication of this darkly comic exposé of ruthless (and ridiculous) hierarchies of violence and exploitation coincided with the 500-year commemoration of the European incursion into the Americas. Set mainly in the Southwest United States in the near future, *Almanac*'s numerous characters embody the moral and spiritual depravity Silko sees in the Americas. The novel defines and presents a choice for readers between destruction, represented by colonialism, and creation, posited as equitable access to land and resources and shared responsibility for human and environmental welfare.

While writing *Almanac*, Silko received the University of New Mexico's Distinguished Alumnus Award (1988). Two years after her controversial second novel's publication, she produced a limited edition of *Sacred Water: Narratives and Pictures* (1993) and a new edition of *Laguna Woman* (1994), both with her own Flood Plain Press. In 1996 she brought out a collection of essays (many published previously), *Yellow Woman and a Beauty of the Spirit: Essays on Native American Life Today*, which focuses on a range of topics, from politics and poverty to intriguing notes on *Almanac of the Dead*.

In Silko's most recent novel, *GARDENS IN THE DUNES* (1999), she weaves indigenous storytelling with the Victorian novel. The GHOST DANCE and Gnostic and Celtic mysteries counteract the destructive powers of colonization. After soldiers raid a local Ghost Dance ceremony, the last of the fictional Sand Lizard people, a family of women who live in dunes near the Arizona-California border, are separated. The grandmother and two granddaughters return home, but the girls are later apprehended by whites. Sister Salt launders in a labor camp, while Indigo is shipped to the historical Sherman Institute, where Silko's Grandpa Hank had received the standard vocational education. When Indigo flees the oppressive boarding school, she finds refuge with a college-educated white woman and her botanist husband. After Edward dies, a victim of his own greed, Hattie travels to England to explore her Celtic spirituality. Ultimately reunited, Indigo and Sister Salt restore their homeland's gardens. In addition to depicting Victorian era imperialism, Silko emphasizes positive possibilities for cultural cross-pollination in this novel, as she does in much of her work.

Bibliography

Allen, Paula Gunn. "Special Problems in Teaching Leslie Marmon Silko's *Ceremony.*" *American Indian Quarterly* 14 (fall 1990): 382–383.

Barnett, Louise K., and James L. Thorson, eds. *Leslie Marmon Silko: A Collection of Critical Essays.* Albuquerque: University of New Mexico Press, 1999.

Coltelli, Laura. "*Almanac of the Dead:* An Interview with Leslie Marmon Silko." *Forum* 4–5 (1992–93): 78.

Fisher, Dexter. "Stories and Their Tellers—A Conversation with Leslie Marmon Silko." In *Third Woman: Minority Women Writers of the United States,* edited by Dexter Fisher (Boston: Houghton Mifflin, 1980), rpt. in *Conversations with Leslie Marmon Silko,* edited by Ellen L. Arnold, 23. Jackson: University Press of Mississippi, 2000.

Jakoski, Helen. *Leslie Marmon Silko: A Study of the Short Fiction.* Twayne's Studies in Short Fiction 71. New York: Twayne and London: Prentice Hall International, 1998.

Salyer, Gregory. *Leslie Marmon Silko.* Twayne's United States Authors Series 692. New York: Twayne and London: Prentice Hall International, 1997.

Silko, Leslie Marmon. *Almanac of the Dead: A Novel.* New York: Penguin, 1992.

———. *Ceremony.* New York: Viking, 1977. New York: NAL and New York: Signet, 1978.

———. *Gardens in the Dunes.* New York: Simon & Schuster, 1999.

———. *Laguna Woman: Poems.* 2nd ed. Tucson, Ariz.: Flood Plain Press, 1994.

———. *Storyteller.* New York: Seaver Books, 1981 and New York: Arcade, 1981.

Velie, Alan R. *Four American Indian Literary Masters: N. Scott Momaday, James Welch, Leslie Marmon Silko, and Gerald Vizenor.* Norman: University of Oklahoma Press, 1982.

Elizabeth McNeil and Laura Jeselnik

Singing Spirit, The   Bernd C. Peyer   (1989)

This collection offers 18 stories by 11 American Indian authors originally published between 1881 (Susette La Flesche) and 1936 (D'Arcy McNickle). More than half "can be said to represent a conscious effort on the part of the authors to educate their readers concerning everyday Indian existence and the problems resulting from cultural contact. As such, they are atypical Indian stories for the times and may openly run counter to current stereotypical expectations" (xii).

Bernd Peyer's expertise in early writings by Native Americans is obvious both in his soundly documented introduction and in the authors' biographies, which include references for further reading and a chronological bibliography of their short stories. All in all the book is an excellent source of pleasure and scholarly information. Some of its assertions about the relative accessibility of early texts are now outdated, but most of the stories are nowhere else to be found, and the collection is a powerful one.

While a few stories read as rather plain autobiographical sketches, most are subtle, well-devised tales, and some even testify to experimental treatment, for example, by not using the conventional codes for reported speech, as in William Jones's "In the Name of His Ancestor"; a number of them evince great sophistication, most of all McNickle's "Hard Riding," a sharply humorous and meditative picture of the efforts of an Indian superintendent to get "his" Natives to establish a court to try cattle thieves.

The eponymous story of the collection is by CHARLES EASTMAN and is composed of two sections of roughly equal length. The first half is mainly seen through the eyes of a party of starving Yankton Indian hunters who think the strange noise they hear in the night is that of the legendary singing spirit, who is said to play weird music that sometimes bewitches lone travelers. Intrigued but bold, they put on their war paint and rush into the log hut where the voice is heard, only to find a hairy fiddle player. The second part of the story focuses on Antoine Michaud, a first-generation Canadian MIXED-BLOOD. While hunting, the man gets caught in the middle of a buffalo herd and is driven away into a wood, where he finds refuge in a tree, as does a bear that was already waiting in like manner for the buffalo to leave. Antoine makes friends with the bear, whom he calls "Ami" (friend in French), and creates a home in the forest, until one night Indian hunters rush into his cabin. As a whole the story is about sharing; it ends with Antoine's helping the starving hunters by telling them where to find the buffalo herd, after which he is thanked by the tribe and given a wife.

Bibliography

Jaskoski, Helen, ed. *Early Native American Writing: New Critical Essays.* Cambridge: Cambridge University Press, 1996.

Peyer, Bernd C. *The Tutor'd Mind: Indian Missionary-Writers in Antebellum America.* Amherst: University of Massachusetts Press, 1997.

Simone Pellerin

Skins Chris Eyre (2002)

Skins (2002), directed by Chris Eyre and based on the novel by ADRIAN C. LOUIS, is the story of two brothers on the Pine Ridge Reservation (Oglala Sioux) in South Dakota. Rudy (Eric Schweig) is a reservation police officer, and his older brother, Mogie (Graham Greene), is an unemployed Vietnam War vet who sports a Madonna T-shirt and a grim sense of humor while committing slow suicide by alcohol. A story of brotherly love, *Skins* examines the possibilities—and limitations—of justice, spirituality, and laughter in a world of continued inequality, violence, and poverty.

With Springsteen's *Born in the U.S.A* on the soundtrack *Skins* opens with a sweeping overview of the Black Hills, sacred land taken from the Sioux by the U.S. government during the 1870s. The panorama then cuts to a collage of documentary and newsreel footage ranging from *Incident at Oglala* to President Clinton's visit to Pine Ridge in 1999. This visual prologue provides a fluid transition from historical and contemporary realities into the fictional story of the film. *Skins* was actually shot on location in and near Pine Ridge (with 80 percent unemployment, it is located in the poorest county in America) without "dressing" (embellishing) its sets and using many local residents as minor characters, further infusing Rudy and Mogie's story with realistic detail. The houses in the film are lived in, the football field belongs to a local high school, and Eyre is careful to include the central meeting places on and around the reservation (the Sioux Shopping Center, Big Bat's convenience store, and the border town of White Clay, Nebraska, the closest place off-reservation to purchase liquor legally). The setting of *Skins* is as important as character and story: It is the historic locale of WOUNDED KNEE (both I and II), inhabited by people whose ancestors include Crazy Horse, Red Cloud, American Horse, and Nicholas Black Elk.

The figure of the TRICKSTER spider of Indian myth, Iktomi, is present throughout: *Iktomi* embodies both foolishness and wisdom, and Rudy takes on Iktomi's identity to mete out vigilante justice when official channels of justice fail. Rudy's vigilantism contains elements of ancient tribal justice as well as echoes of the Old West, both of which accept violence as a natural part of life. But the success of Rudy's vigilantism breaks down over the course of the film, especially as his own actions become threaded into other people's acts of "personal" justice, which include domestic and community violence. In the end Rudy elects a more benign, symbolic (and, importantly, humorous) act of defiance by splattering George Washington's face on Mount Rushmore with red paint in tribute to his brother Mogie. This image is accompanied by a closing voice-over, reminding us that cinema preserves important qualities of oral storytelling. In advance of its theatrical release (and accompanied by the filmmaker himself), *Skins* was screened free of charge at reservations across America using a full-scale, mobile cinema on its first tour in U.S. history, which included a stop at Pine Ridge.

Anne Kern

Skins and Bones   Paula Gunn Allen (1988)

The poetry in *Skins and Bones* represents a significant development in the work of this important Laguna poet, novelist, and critic. It demonstrates how PAULA GUNN ALLEN uses her writing to work through spiritual and social issues confronting American Indians today. The focus is primarily on women, including Allen's retelling of the stories of four famous Indian women: Pocahontas; Molly Brant, an Iroquois woman whose brother, Joseph, sided with the British in the American Revolution; Sacagawea; and Malinal, a slave given to the conquistador Cortez, from their points of view. Sacagawea declares herself to be "Chief Woman" (6), and Pocahontas writes to her English husband that he would have died if she had not taken care of him. "The series is designed to call attention to the spiritedness which guided these and other native women of American history," according to MARY TALLMOUNTAIN (69).

Many of these poems illuminate Native American SPIRITUALITY. For example, Allen uses the Lakota words *Taku Skanskan,* meaning "God's presence," as the title of a poem about God and human life as activity, "whatmovesmoves" (12). She explains, "They [the Lakota] don't call god 'what moves something'" (13), but "GOD / is what happens, is: / movesmoves" (18–20). The poem's final stanza demonstrates God and life as moving events with a narrative about riding a mare: "eventuality" (22), from the moment of taking her out of the corral.

Allen's use of HUMOR in her poetry is particularly evident in this volume. For example, she retells the story of Adam and Eve as a sexy seduction story (Allen's Eve "knew the joy of swivelhips" [8]), and in one poem describes taking a visitor to see the "old Indian ruins" (26) that turn out to be the narrator's mother and grandmother.

The advantages of a tribal perspective are evidenced in several poems, including "Horns of a Dilemma," which contrasts being able to think in more than one way with being "one-brained" (5). Humans who think in only one way are compared to birds that have only one wing and beasts that have only one leg.

Skins and Bones exemplifies Allen's own ability to think and write in many different ways. Thus along with the spiritual and humorous poems are painful reflections about history and modern life. For example, in the long poem "Teaching Poetry at Votech High, Santa Fe, the Week John Lennon Was Shot," the poet contrasts the image of the Beatles' Lennon, who dreamed of peace and a better world, with her students, who have "no future they can bear" (III.17) and are too jaded to dream. Yet, the book begins and ends with hope. Hence, the first poem, "C'koy'u, Old Woman," asks Grandmother Earth whether she dreams of birth—"we are waiting inside you" (10)—and the final poem is "New Birth," which celebrates new beginnings.

TallMountain, who is also a poet, concludes about this volume, "We need to hear the far, threadlike voice of a Sacagawea, and the more timely catalytic tones of a Gunn Allen" (75).

Bibliography

Allen, Paula Gunn. *Skins and Bones.* Albuquerque, N.Mex.: West End, 1988.

TallMountain, Mary. "Paula Gunn Allen's 'The One Who Skins Cats': An Inquiry into Spiritedness." *Studies in American Indian Literatures* 7, no. 3 (summer 1993): 34–38.

Susan Bowers

Slash   Jeannette Armstrong (1985)

Slash figures prominently in the literary canon as the first novel written by an aboriginal woman in Canada. In the dedication at the beginning of *Slash* JEANNETTE ARMSTRONG offers a poem "To

Tony," and in the final lines of this poem she writes: "all the stories you used to make laughter / will be told around the tables of your people / and we will be rich with weapons" (18–19). This line functions as an important clue regarding the story's central technique of exploring political activism within the Native activist movements in the 1960s and 1970s in North America. It highlights the necessity of stories as central to the struggle for self-government, and as equally important to the realization of cultural identity after years of colonial occupation and cultural genocide. Stories are memory, and remembering is one way in which characters ground themselves in their identities and garner the strength needed to pick through the tangled mess of North American aboriginal policies, TREATIES, and laws since colonization. The character of Tommy/Slash offers his story not only as a record of his experience within the movement, but also as a record of his own realization of his identity as an Okanagan man and as a First Nations person.

Despite the novel's historical accuracy in tracing important activist events, the prologue claims that it is fictitious, and that any resemblance of characters to persons living or dead is coincidental. Simultaneously the novel claims to be a retrospective of how Slash changed and what caused the change, and in so doing understood "what changes our people went through during those times and what we are coming up against" (13). Significantly, then, the novel is an attempt to bridge a gap between the formality of colonial discourse and the messiness of history and oral history.

The novel is underscored by violence: violence against Natives in the form of discrimination; colonization; usurpation of rights, land, and self-governance; and racism. This intercultural violence becomes a sustained threat throughout the numerous demonstrations staged by various Native groups against the governments of both the United States and Canada. This violence is inscribed symbolically in both Tommy's scar, sustained in a bar-room knife fight, and his nickname *Slash*. As the title of the novel, the word might act as a verb that enacts a severing of Native experience from colonial historical precedent.

Bibliography
Armstrong, Jeannette. *Slash*. Penticton, Canada: Theytus Books, 1985.

Green, Matthew. "A Hard Day's Knight: A Discursive Analysis of Jeannette Armstrong's *Slash*." *Canadian Journal of Native Studies* 19, no. 1 (1999): 51–67.

Hodne, Barbara, and Helen Hoy. "Reading from the Inside Out: Jeannette Armstrong's *Slash*." *World Literature Written in English* 32, no. 1 (spring 1992): 66–87.

Jolene Armstrong

Slipperjack-Farrell, Ruby   (1952–   )

Ruby Slipperjack-Farrell is a scholar, a visual artist, and a certified First Nations hunter. She was born in Whitewater Lake, Ontario, Canada, and spent her formative years on her father's trapline. She is an Ojibwa from the Fort Hope Indian Band in Ontario and attended Shingwauk Residential School in Sault-Ste. Marie, and later high school in Thunder Bay. Slipperjack-Farrell earned her B.A. (history) in 1988, a B.Ed in 1989, and her M.Ed. in 1993 from Lakehead University. She received the William A. West Education Medal for being the highest-ranking masters of education graduate at Lakehead University. She holds a Ph.D. in education from University of Western Ontario and is the first graduate of the Faculty of Education's Ph.D. program, with a dissertation on aboriginal teachings in Native literature.

Slipperjack-Farrell is currently an assistant professor and chair in the Department of Indigenous Learning at Lakehead University. She has retained much of Ojibwa traditional spirituality and heritage. Her work is informed by her cultural upbringing and focuses on themes related to cultural values and cultural retention, such as the role of SPIRITUALITY, vision quests, hunting, the oral tradition, the importance of harmony in the natural world, healing, and language.

Slipperjack-Farrell believes that her writing comes naturally to her because she is a member of a family of storytellers. Her knowledge of the Ojibwa language and culture has provided her with a strong foundation. She is fluent in Ojibwa and can read and write in Native syllabics. Her novels recount the experiences of children approaching adolescence, detailing the spiritual and cultural growth and development as the characters mature. Recurring themes, such as race, ASSIMILATION, self-awareness, identity, reverence for elders, the importance of nature, imposition of residential schools, and the importance of Native traditions to self-identity and survival, appear in some of her novels.

Her first novel, HONOUR THE SUN (1987), details the life of a young girl growing up in a tiny Ojibwa community in northern Ontario, who faces issues of identity, such as gender and race, as she matures and realizes that her identity and means of survival are dependent on her cultural awareness. Slipperjack-Farrell's other works include SILENT WORDS (1992), which chronicles the life of a young Ojibwa boy who achieves self-knowledge through his vision quest and learns the value of silence and the importance of the credo "Listen, watch, and learn." WEESQUACHAK AND THE LOST ONES (2000) is a story that explores the culture clash between contemporary and traditional Native life; Little Voice (2001), her most recent work, highlights the themes of self-awareness, assimilation through residential school education, and the Ojibwa traditional way of life. All these novels can be said to encompass the importance of community-based living, as well as the role of nature in sustaining harmony and balance and their significance in achieving a holistic life. Slipperjack-Farrell enjoys painting and sewing. She also has written a play called Snuff Chewing Charlie (2001) and is currently working on two more novels.

Bibliography

Johnston, Basil. Ojibway Ceremonies. Toronto: McClelland & Stewart, 1987.
———. Ojibway Heritage. New York: Columbia University Press, 1976.

Sharon Morgan Lewis

Smith, Martin Cruz   (1942–)

Martin William Smith, of the Pueblo and Yaqui tribes, was born in Reading, Pennsylvania, on November 3, 1942. His parents were John Calhoun, a musician, and Louise, a jazz singer and Indian rights leader. He later changed his middle name to Cruz, adopting his grandmother's surname. He earned his B.A. in 1964 from the University of Pennsylvania and worked as a journalist from 1965 until 1969. Throughout the 1970s he wrote a series of westerns under the pen name Jake Logan, and many mysteries as Nick Carter. His 1975 detective novel Gypsy in Amber was made into a TV movie entitled The Art of Crime. He has been nominated for the Edgar Award four times. Smith has written little about Indians, or issues concerning Indians, but is often included in discussion of Indian literature because his career sheds interesting perspective on what it means to be an "Indian writer." His first novel, The Indians Won (1970), does imagine an alternate version of U.S. history, in which Indians have resisted the forces of the U.S. government.

While Smith supported himself by publishing westerns and potboiler mysteries, he began conducting extensive research into what would become his most famous character, Arkady Renko, a homicide detective living in cold war Russia. Published in 1981, Gorky Park features Renko and an American detective working to solve the case of a particularly gruesome multiple homicide in Moscow. In addition to solving the crime and working with an American, Renko must contend with the Communist Party, to which he belongs but of which he does not really feel a part. Gorky Park was awarded the Crime Writers' Association Gold Dagger Award and was also made into a major motion picture. Detective Renko has since appeared in four subsequent novels: Polar Star (1989), Red Square (1992), Havana Bay (1999), and Wolves Eat Dogs (2004). Cruz Smith won the 2000 Hammett Award for Havana Bay. Throughout the series Renko is portrayed as a man who feels like an outsider, whether he is working in his own country, on a ship at sea, or in a foreign land.

Although primarily known for his mysteries, Smith in his novels explores other issues as well, usually in a historical setting. *Stallion Gate* (1986) is set immediately after World War II at the nuclear facility in Los Alamos, New Mexico. The protagonist is Joe Pena, a sergeant in the U.S. Army. Sergeant Pena investigates charges that Robert Oppenheimer, a scientist who helped develop the first atomic bomb, is a spy for Communist Russia. *Rose,* published in 1996, is set in 19th-century Lancashire and features Johnathon Blair, an engineer who worked in Africa. *December 6: A Novel* (2002) features Harry Niles, of American and Japanese heritage, who is living in Tokyo in 1946. Throughout Smith's novels we find protagonists who consistently feel at odds with the societies to which they belong. And yet these alienated characters consistently triumph by solving the crime at hand, overcoming racism, or creating for themselves enough psychological space to maintain their dignity and individuality.

Bibliography

Riggs, Thomas, ed. *Reference Guide to American Literature.* Detroit: St. James Press, 2000.

Smith, Martin Cruz. *Canto for a Gypsy.* New York: Putnam, 1972.

———. *Gorky Park.* New York: Random House, 1981.

———. *Stallion Gate.* New York: Random House, 1986.

———. *Wolves Eat Dogs.* New York: Simon & Schuster, 2004.

Brian Johnson

Smoke Signals   (1998)

Smoke Signals is the most critically and commercially successful feature film made by and starring Native peoples in the world to date. It was shot on a $2 million budget after being developed at a Sundance Institute program for Native American filmmakers; Miramax Films acquired the distribution rights to the film before it premiered at the Sundance Film Festival in 1998. It was distributed in Europe, Japan, Canada, and South America as well as throughout the United States, and it won numerous film festival awards around the world. Between its opening weekend in June and the middle of October 1998, *Smoke Signals* grossed almost $7 million in the United States alone. In turn the filmmakers pledged a portion of their profits to the American Indian College Fund and the Honor the Earth Campaign.

The director, Chris Eyre, is of Cheyenne/Arapaho descent, educated at the prestigious New York University (NYU) film school; *Smoke Signals* was his first feature film. The film's screenwriter, SHERMAN ALEXIE, is a prolific novelist and poet of the Coeur d'Alene/Spokane tribes; he developed the screenplay for *Smoke Signals* from his 1993 short story collection *The LONE RANGER AND TONTO FISTFIGHT IN HEAVEN.* Increasingly film has been used by historically underrepresented cultures throughout the world to continue deep cultural traditions of oral storytelling. It has also been used as a powerful political speech act and as an effort to reclaim and control the way one's own images are used. This is not to suggest that *Smoke Signals* is a film that preaches its message; on the contrary, its tone is bittersweet, sympathetic, and funny.

Smoke Signals relates the journey of two young men as a metaphor for a more universal process of grief and healing. The story involves the friendship of Victor (Adam Beach) and Thomas (Evan Adams), Coeur d'Alene Indians who share a traumatic event in their personal histories. On the night of July 4, 1976—the night their tribe celebrated the "white man's independence"—Thomas's parents were killed in a fire. Victor's father, Arnold Joseph (Gary Farmer), saved his own son and the baby Thomas but was devastated by a secret involving the fire that night. Arnold finally left the reservation when Victor and Thomas were about eight years old, and Victor did not hear from him again until his mother received word that he had died.

Victor and Thomas decide to travel to Phoenix, Arizona, to retrieve Arnold's remains, and it is at this moment that the film's present-day story begins. In keeping with a common strain in Native American stories, the two protagonists represent opposing character types (Thomas as shaman and Victor as "stoic" warrior). We learn about Victor and Thomas's linked histories through their distinctly different forms of remembering: Thomas commemorates Victor's father by spinning fantastic stories that lionize Arnold, amplifying all that was best about him. Victor, in contrast, experiences memories of his father as intrusive flashes of drunkenness and abuse, in which instances of his tenderness are almost always followed by violent outbursts. Victor and Thomas's trip to Arizona is their first venture off the reservation, and as another character reminds the two warriors, off the reservation is "as foreign as you can get"—she recommends they take their passports.

Throughout the film there is a humorous acknowledgment of the way white society imagines American Indians and its effect on the way Thomas and Victor see themselves. But the characters in *Smoke Signals* constantly transform such images for their own use, a process that becomes ever more resonant in the context of a work created by a Native writer, director, and actors for an audience of millions, most of whom are non-Indian. *Smoke Signals* reveals contemporary Native American identities to be a hybrid of traditional and pop cultures. It is ultimately a question of recognition, of recognizing oneself onscreen.

Victor and Thomas travel to Arizona by bus, a humorous downplay of such "road buddy" movies as *Easy Rider* (1969) and *Powwow Highway* (1989). The young men finally arrive at Arnold's trailer in a barren, desolate corner of desert—not entirely unlike the tracts of land that untold numbers of American Indians have been squeezed onto over the last two centuries. There they meet Arnold's neighbor, Suzy Song, an ethereally beautiful young woman (Irene Bedard). She is the keeper of Arnold's secret, as well as the keeper of more complicated memories of him. She remembers him warmly, accepting both his strengths and his weaknesses.

As Victor and Thomas travel back to the reservation in Arnold's old truck, both young men struggle to integrate a more composite picture of Victor's father. When Victor gives a portion of his father's ashes to Thomas, they realize that they have both considered scattering them into the nearby Spokane River. For Thomas it would be the ritualization of a tender vision of man; for Victor, it would be "like throwing things away when they have no more use." We find that their travels have resulted less in personal transformation than in the beginnings of acceptance, forgiveness, and moving on. Indeed, by the time Victor and Thomas have returned to the reservation in Arnold's (now Victor's) truck, the rearview mirror is broken off. No need for an exact reflection of what is behind us, Eyre seems to say, except through the stories we tell in the service of the present and future. Though Thomas's (and Alexie's, and Eyre's) stories transmit a fanciful version of events, they likewise reveal that we must often embellish the real in order to arrive at the truth of an experience—and to make that experience useful. When Thomas returns to his grandmother at the end of the film, she sums up this impulse succinctly, as only grandmothers can: "Tell me what happened, Thomas," she intones. "Tell me what's going to happen."

See also HUMOR; *SKINS*.

Bibliography

Kilpatrick, Jacquelyn. *Celluloid Indians: Native Americans and Film.* Lincoln: University of Nebraska Press, 1999.

Singer, Beverly R. *Wiping the War Paint off the Lens: Native American Film and Video.* Minneapolis: University of Minnesota Press, 2001.

Anne Kern

snake in her mouth, a: poems 1974–1996   nila northSun (1997)

Many of the poems in this volume have appeared in NILA NORTHSUN's earlier collections of poetry. Although the poems represent a 22-year span in northSun's career as a poet, the cadence of the poems, the exacting portrayal of contemporary Indian life, and the use of colloquial reservation English have remained surprisingly consistent and consistently compelling.

northSun began writing poetry and coediting *Scree,* an avant-garde literary magazine, in the

1970s. While avant-garde poets like Charles Bukowski have certainly influenced the way she crafts her poems, northSun also draws on the oral tradition and on the colloquial language of RESERVATION and urban Indians.

Much of northSun's poetry deals with the sense of alienation experienced by those born of relocation. In "moving camp too far" the speaker does not have access to her individual or communal history. She cannot tell of "many moons / moving camp on travois" (2–3). Instead, she searches for images of Indianness in "an eagle / almost extinct / on slurpee plastic cups" (7–9). She eats "buffalo meat / at the tourist burger stand" (9–10). She ultimately implicates herself in the appropriation of her own culture.

northSun suggests that policies of relocation and ASSIMILATION not only complicate an urban Indian's sense of self but also rupture relationships between generations. Living in the city, the speaker finds herself alienated from her grandmother and therefore alienated from her culture and language. She does not know how to speak like an Indian or how to skin a rabbit. She has difficulty bonding with and even communicating with her grandmother. Because of relocation the grandchild has "no gramma there to / teach us the ways" (22–23).

The consequences of relocation, of alienating a people from their families and cultures, figure heavily in northSun's poems. Numerous poems deal with the desperation, alienation, violence, and ALCOHOLISM experienced by urban Indians. They are "in and out of jail," stuck with "a baby at 14 years" (11), "cussing a blue streak" (15). They have swollen faces and black eyes. They run over boyfriends, think "about slitting . . . wrists," and "od . . . on the freon & alcohol" (17–18). Their seemingly self-destructive behavior, northSun suggests, stems from their sense of alienation from their families, histories, cultures, and lands.

northSun's carefully constructed poems provide a gripping depiction of contemporary Indian life. Her stark language and sharp humor create a voice unique to American poetry. Despite the difficult lives of the characters she depicts, northSun suggests that the hope remains that "no matter what / you belong / . . . you fall into place" (20–21).

Bibliography

Allen, Paula Gunn. "A Stranger in My Own Life: Alienation in American Indian Poetry and Prose." In *The Sacred Hoop: Recovering the Feminine in American Indian Tradition*, 127–146. Boston: Beacon Press, 1986.

Smith, Patricia Clark. "Ain't Seen You Since: Dissent among Female Relatives in American Indian Women's Poetry." In *Studies in American Indian Literature*, edited by Paula Gunn Allen, 108–126. New York: MLA, 1983.

Amanda Cagle

Sneve, Virginia Driving Hawk   (1933–   )

A member of the Rosebud Sioux tribe, Sneve (rhymes with "navy") is an author and educator with several books for children and adults to her credit. She is most known for portraying the female perspective of stories from her ancestors' time to the present day. Born on February 21, 1933, Sneve grew up on the Rosebud Agency in South Dakota and was educated at the Bureau of Indian Affairs Day School at Oak Creek and St. Mary's School for Indian Girls at Springfield. She holds a B.S. degree in English and history from South Dakota College (now University), and a master's in education and counseling from South Dakota University.

Though her father was a minister at the local Episcopal church, because of financial strain during the depression, both of Sneve's parents, James Driving Hawk and Rose Ross Posey, often had to find seasonal work off the reservation. While they were gone, they left Sneve and her brother under the care of their two grandmothers on the reservation. From this experience and tribal stories she heard, Virginia became aware of the contributions of the women in her tribe and ancestry and later in her writing career wanted to share their perspective.

Beginning in 1954, Virginia worked as an educator and counselor for many years. She taught English at the White Public High School in White, South Dakota. Throughout her career she taught at both reservation and public schools. By the time she retired in 1995, she had held joint appointments as an associate instructor of English at Oglala-Lakota College and counselor at Rapid City Central High School for several years.

Arguably Sneve's most visible work today is her chronicle of the personal and ancestral history of the women in her family, including her, in *Completing the Circle* (1995). Through this work, which sets the stories of individual women within a well-researched larger cultural context, Sneve succeeds at providing an inside look at women's lives and histories in Sioux culture.

In addition to her books, Sneve is known for her many articles, essays, poems, television scripts and dramatizations, readings, workshops, and presentations. In all of these forms Sneve works to portray her people authentically and accurately. In 1995 she was awarded the Living Indian Treasure Award from Northern Plains Tribal Arts and South Dakotans for the Arts.

Bibliography

Sneve, Virginia Driving Hawk. *Completing the Circle.* Lincoln: University of Nebraska Press, 1995.

Connie Ann Kirk

Sojourner's Truth and Other Stories   Lee Maracle (1990)

Sojourner's Truth and Other Stories is LEE MARA-CLE's first collection of short stories. Maracle wrote these 13 stories for a Native audience, and her attempts to alienate white readers are transparent throughout *Sojourner's Truth and Other Stories.* More important, however, is her desire to continue a tradition of Native oral storytelling, which she does by combining Native and European storytelling in written text.

Sojourner's Truth and Other Stories revolves around issues of writing, ORALITY, and prejudices based on ethnicity, gender, and class discrimination. Maracle directly addresses the process of writing in the preface and in the suggestively autobiographical story "Lee on Spiritual Experience." While the intended audience for her stories is Native, not all of her characters are. Maracle's stories

cross cultural and ethnic divides, but they all concern subjects fighting against oppression. Maracle tells women's stories; often they are in desperate situations, because of their ethnicity and/or class and/or other limiting factors. Sometimes the restrictions are self-imposed, as is the case in "Eunice," the story of an agoraphobe. Some of the female protagonists in the collection are crushed by a lifetime of external oppression and are only able to escape it in death. "Bertha" is a story about the loss of Native language, culture, and dignity at the hands of Christian proselytizers. The European preacher made Bertha's tribeswomen obsolete by usurping their traditional roles as storytellers and educators. This short story is not only about Bertha's death, but also about the symbolic death of a way of life forgotten by the younger generations. Maracle, through the character of Bertha, directly links the loss of women's power with the loss of power by the entire Native community, as the two maintain a symbiotic relationship.

The title story, "Sojourner's Truth," is a journey of discovery for Mike, the recently deceased protagonist, who must face the truths of his life with postmortem insight and without the luxury of guilt. With painful clarity he never had during his lifetime, Mike is witness to atrocities ranging from the pollution of the Frazer River, to deforestation, to human suffering; in South Africa he mourns the racism of apartheid and the many deaths of 1976 riots in the township of Soweto. Mike's story is also his widow, Emma's, story. Her second husband is physically abusing her, just as Mike abused her during their marriage. Sickened that he lived his life comfortable with Emma's suffering, Mike cajoles her into resisting her own subjugation. Emma rises up and stabs her second husband through the heart. At her trial Mike meets several deceased famous historical figures; they remain vigilant "about the possibilities that lay ahead for women and earth should Emma win" her trial (132). In the end Emma is acquitted. *Sojourner's Truth,* the title, alludes to the historical civil rights activist of the same name who appears in the story, but it also references Emma as a sojourner whose truth required empathy beyond the laws of man. Furthermore, the title hints that the truths of every sojourner are best understood outside the confines of the law, predicated on patriarchal value systems that muddy truth.

Each of the 13 stories in this collection addresses issues of gender, class, and/or ethnic discrimination. Maracle is telling women's stories to Native listeners. Her goal is to empower women, thereby empowering Native communities; her logic is based on the wisdom that without strong women and mothers, there cannot be strong communities.

Bibliography

Maracle, Lee. *Sojourner's Truth and Other Stories.* Vancouver: Press Gang, 1990.

Sheena Wilson

Solar Storms   Linda Hogan (1995)

Set on the landscape of the Boundary Waters between Canada and Minnesota, Linda Hogan's rich novel *Solar Storms* focuses on five generations of Native American women caught between traditional and contemporary ways. The prologue, set off in italics to indicate the past, begins with Angela Jensen's memory of her great-grandmother, Agnes Iron, and her storytelling. Agnes relates the story of her son, Harold, and his wife, Bush, who took Angela in when she was a child. Bush placed a high priority on traditional ways and tried hard to protect Angela from her birth mother, Hannah Wing, a troubled woman with many demons.

But Bush's traditional methods do not spare Angela from her childhood with Hannah, at whose hand Angela endures physical abuse. In fact, half of Angela's face has been scarred by her mother—a wound that takes on multiple meanings as Angela finds out more about the circumstances that led to such violence. The action of the story begins when 17-year-old Angela Jensen arrives at Adam's Rib to live with her great-grandmother, Agnes, and her great-great-grandmother Dora-Rouge. Bush resides in nearby Fur Island, where Angela also spends some time. Here among her foremothers Angela reconciles her modern teenage world of Wal Mart, Big Macs, and Mick Jagger with her traditional one of song, story, and ceremony.

In the spring the women travel the treacherous journey to Dora-Rouge's homeland in the north so that she can die among her people, the Fat Eaters, and Angela can reconnect with her mother, Hannah. But in a curious twist of fate Agnes dies en route, leaving the other women, including her elderly mother, to complete the trip without her. While sadness prevails at the loss of Agnes, the women rely on their inner strength and on each other to complete their expedition under severe conditions. Angela's physical journey to her ancestors' native land parallels her emotional journey toward self-awareness and self-reliance.

That Dora-Rouge's homeland is different from her memory of it places the theme of the conflict between the old and new at the fore. As a result of white men's effort to make their hydroelectric project succeed, the region's natural resources are depleted. Much hostility occurs between the Native Americans and the whites who reroute the rivers, desecrate the landscape, and intimidate those who oppose them—such as Angela and her relatives.

After a long, complicated, and hard-fought battle, the story ends with a victory for Angela and her people. She mourns her mother's death; welcomes her half sister, Aurora, into her home; and looks forward to a new beginning with her love interest, Tommy, always acknowledging the memory of her strong female ancestors.

Bibliography

Owens, Louis. *Other Destinies: Understanding the American Indian Novel.* Norman: University of Oklahoma Press, 1994.

Carla L. Verderame

Song of the Turtle: American Indian Literature 1974–1994   Paula Gunn Allen (1996)

Song of the Turtle: American Indian Literature 1974–1994, an anthology edited by Paula Gunn Allen, is the companion volume to *Voice of the Turtle,* the anthology of Native American literature she released in 1994. It stands out among other anthologies for several reasons, including Allen's incisive description of what she terms second- and third-wave Indian literature, her diverse choice of contributors, and the way in which it spans the time from the all-important decade of the 1970s to the time of its publication.

Including short stories and poetry, *Song of the Turtle* contains 33 works by 33 different authors including the well-known LESLIE MARMON SILKO, ALLEN, N. SCOTT MOMADAY, LOUSIE ERDRICH, MICHAEL DORRIS, SHERMAN ALEXIE, and JOY HARJO. She also includes quite recent, as yet unheralded authors such as Debra Earling, SUSAN POWER, and Karen Wallace. These young female authors provide stories of transition and crossing of boundaries that typify the real conditions many Indians faced in the late 20th century. In addition, Allen includes two popular Indian authors who are not frequently represented in "scholarly" anthologies, ROBERT J. CONLEY and MARTIN CRUZ SMITH, helping to expand the conception of what constitutes "Indian Literature."

This second anthology was designed to provide examples of writing from what Allen terms the second and third waves of Native American fiction, which began in the 1960s. Allen lists the "defining characteristics of second wave fiction" as "a sense of renewal and hope; reasserted often deeply angry, Native identity; and incorporation of ritual elements in both structure and content drawn from the ceremonial traditions" (8). Allen describes second-wave Native American literature as writing that exoticizes Native Americans and often portrays Native Americans as victims. Allen sees this state of affairs as "largely a reflection of the Euro-American intellectual's construction of the Indian," or in other words, the legacy of entrenched stereotypes (11).

In her introduction to *Song of the Turtle* Allen points to a third wave of Native American writing. She cites N. Scott Momaday as the premier writer of this new wave, although as in other literary traditions, there is no clear, distinguishing, defining moment that separates one wave from the next. Also, each wave builds to the following one in a recursive progression. Allen writes, "The new narrative was fashioned from a fusion of the west's phonetic alphabet and narrative conventions with tribal modes of inscription and narration. The merger . . . signaled a new era in both native and American litera-

ture" (11). *HOUSE MADE OF DAWN* is the example of this new fusion, and by the late 1980s, Native Americans would have written in every genre of American literature and left a permanent mark upon the field. In Allen's estimation, "[t]he third wave of Native fiction . . . is following the oldest First Nations traditions" (13). Characteristics of the third wave are "inclusion, incorporation, and transformation of alien elements into elements of ceremonial significance" (13). The description of the changing or transformation occurring in Native American literature in *Song of the Turtle* builds on the theme of transformation elaborated upon in the introduction to *Voice of the Turtle*.

As in *Voice of the Turtle* the shorter, individual introductions to each selection provide a brief biography of the writer, information the reader may need to understand the selection such as explanations of myth or context of the excerpt and the relation of the selection to the overall theme of the anthology.

Bibliography

Allen, Paula Gunn. *The Sacred Hoop.* Boston: Beacon Press, 1992.
———. *Spider Woman's Granddaughters.* Boston: Beacon Press, 1986.
———, ed. *Song of the Turtle: American Indian Literature 1974–1994.* New York: Ballantine Books, 1994.
———, ed. *Voice of the Turtle: American Indian Literature 1900–1970.* New York: Ballantine Books, 1994.
Justice, Daniel Heath. "We're Not There Yet, Kemo Sabe: Positing a Future for American Indian Literary Studies." *American Indian Quarterly.* 25, no. 2 (2001): 256–269.

Tamara Powell

Songs from This Earth on Turtle's Back: Contemporary American Indian Poetry   Joseph Bruchac (1983)

The appearance of *Songs from This Earth on Turtle's Back* heralded the flood of Native American literature that would be published in the 1980s and that continues into the present. This collection, however, was not the first such collection of contemporary Native American poetry. For example, *Carrier's of the Dream Wheel* (author DUANE NIATUM, 1975) and *The REMEMBERED EARTH* (GEARY HOBSON, 1980) had appeared within the decade preceding it. For many decades previous various anthologies had included traditional poetry and songs classified as poetry; however, JOSEPH BRUCHAC's anthology focuses exclusively on the contemporary state of Native American poetry. In addition to its primary role this anthology distinguishes itself for the quality and quantity of works that it collected.

Positioned as it was at the beginning of renewed academic and public interest in Native American literature, this anthology helped develop the voice for this literature. Bruchac's introduction speaks to this climate of emerging interest in Native American literature (xv–xvi). There he identifies the struggles that many Native American authors and their works were experiencing at this time. He also carefully distinguishes this volume from the vast majority of its predecessors, which sought to reinscribe Native American literature as historically defined artifacts that supported reductive images of Native American literature as simply another product of noble savagery. Instead, he argues, *Songs from This Earth on Turtle's Back* demonstrates the vitality and variety of contemporary Native American poetry, and by extension all of Native American literature. Moreover, he argues, this collection provides a valuable resource for those who wish to see those qualities by collecting into a single, easily accessible volume the work of 52 poets. For example, this collection contains the works of the then relatively unknown poets BETH BRANT and NILA NORTHSUN as well as the internationally recognized poets N. SCOTT MOMADAY and SIMON J. ORTIZ. By including such a range of talent and experience, this anthology also provides a time capsule of Native American literary development.

Despite the range of subjects and styles collected in this anthology, Bruchac argues that Native American poets and their poetry share several common aspects that inform Native American identity (xvi). For example, he first claims that they share a common respect for the earth and the natural world. They share folk cultures that are the result of traditional upbringings or personal searches. They share a respect for the power and potential of language to articulate or annihilate tribal languages, as well as the ability to alter that language to express all of these shared traits.

Bibliography

Bruchac, Joseph, ed. *Songs from This Earth on Turtle's Back: Contemporary American Indian Poetry.* Greenfield Center, N.Y.: Greenfield Review Press, 1983.

Hobson, Geary, ed. *The Remembered Earth.* Albuquerque: University of New Mexico Press, 1980.

Niatum, Duane, ed. *Carriers of the Dream Wheel.* New York: Harper & Row, 1975.

Clay Smith

Son of the Forest, A   William Apess   (1829)

A Son of the Forest: The Experiences of William Apess, a Native of the Forest. Comprising a Notice of the Pequod Tribe of Indians. Written by Himself is the first autobiography written and published by an American Indian. It has also been referred to as a "conversion narrative" because its primary focus is WILLIAM APESS's discovery of and devotion to Methodism.

Apess begins his tale with a brief description of his childhood, which was a sad one. His parents left him and his siblings with his maternal grandparents when they were very small and they were kept hungry, cold, and wanting for affection. At the age of four he was violently attacked by his grandmother, who would have killed him had it not been for the intervention of an uncle. He and his siblings were consequently bound out to white families as indentured servants; William went to live with the Furmans, a family who had shown them kindness in the past. After a year of convalescence William began what would become six years of formal schooling, the only such schooling he would receive in life. He began to think of the Furmans as his family during this time, especially the kindly Mrs. Furman.

However, he frequently refers to falling in with bad company, other boys who lead him astray. One of these boys convinces him that it is "fashionable" to run away. William devises a plan, all in the spirit of childish fantasy; the other boy informs Mr. Furman of the plan; and suddenly William has been bound out to another family, that of the prominent Judge Hillhouse. At this point, when William realizes that he has been *sold,* that he is a piece of property, his view of life changes. He moves around more, having his indenture transferred more than once and on occasion simply leaving without permission.

However, it is during this time, while he is bound out to the family of William Williams, that he encounters the Methodists for the first time. In contrast to the more established Protestant denominations of Congregationalism and Presbyterianism, Methodism was seen as being a "low" variety of Christian worship, to be suspicious of and to avoid. Apess says he was told "the character of a respectable man would receive a stain, and a deep one, too, by attending one of their meetings" (18). But Apess does attend and is quite taken by them. Their enthusiasm and sincerity, far away in his mind from the memorization and formality of the orthodox, affect him emotionally.

In addition, the Methodists defined themselves as a religion of outsiders and openly promoted understanding and tolerance for all, regardless of race. They were an openly opposed, persecuted group, and Apess saw this as having a connection to his own outsider status as an Indian. After attending their meeting for a period, he has a revelation: "I felt convinced that Christ died for all mankind—that age, sect, color, country, or situation made no difference. I felt assurance that I was included in the plan of redemption with all my brethren" (19). At this point and throughout the rest of the narrative Apess explicitly links his Methodism with his ethnicity, believing that it was the religion that allowed him to truly be who he was.

At 15, he joins the United States Army, despite being too young to do so legally. He fights in the War of 1812, leaves the militia in 1815, and moves around the Northeast and Canada, performing a variety of jobs. In 1817 Apess moves back to Con-

necticut, the place of his birth, and begins to attend Methodist meetings once again, being similarly moved. He marries, has children, and becomes a Methodist preacher.

Throughout *A Son of the Forest* Apess develops a complex argument admonishing whites for the racist oppression of people of color, especially Indians. He based this argument, in large part, on Christianity and its tenets. Apess challenged many different stereotypes with this autobiography. He used writing for Indian causes, instead of against them, as whites so often had. His complex alignment of Christianity and race demonstrated that an Indian could be a true Christian, not just a mimic of Europeans. Finally he demonstrated that ordinary people's lives were worth reading about, an important point that merits discussion still today.

See also NORTHEASTERN TRIBAL LITERATURE; SPIRITUALITY.

Bibliography

O'Connell, Barry, ed. *On Our Own Ground: The Complete Writings of William Apess: A Pequot.* Amherst: University of Massachusetts Press, 1992.

Ruoff, A. LaVonne Brown. "Three Nineteenth-Century American Indian Autobiographies." In *Redefining American Literary History,* edited by Ruoff and Jerry W. Ward, Jr., 60–71. New York: Modern Language Association, 1990.

Jennifer McClinton-Temple

Sound of Rattles and Clappers, The: A Collection of New California Indian Writing　Greg Sarris　(1994)

The Sound of Rattles and Clappers: A Collection of New California Indian Writing, celebrating a sound long regarded as extinct, features regional but multivoiced portraits of particular people in a specific land. Edited by GREG SARRIS, the volume includes essays, short fiction, autobiographical narratives, and, predominantly, poems written by 10 Native Americans of California Indian ancestry. The collection aims to invite reading audiences to listen to the sound and voices that, in fact, have continued without cessation for generations. In an introduction Sarris delivers a call to readers: "From this place called California, . . . you have the voices of many California Indians. They are singing, telling stories, their voices echoing on the pages so you will know. Listen" (xiii).

The collection contains two short stories by Sarris and works by JANICE GOULD, Frank LaPena/Tauhindauli, James Luna, Stephen Meadows, William Oandasan, WENDY ROSE, Georgiana Valoyce-Sanchez, Kathleen Smith, and Darryl Babe Wilson. In these works 10 writers of California Indian descent forge a voice to claim subjectivity. In them they aim to refute the objectification of Native American cultures, depict American Indians' painful experiences in the past and the present, express their anger over political oppression, celebrate their power to withstand hardship, and record a continuing dialectic between the land and people.

In "Notes: 1985 / James Luna / Luiseño Indian," James Luna insists on "existence," declaring, "The truest of Indian artists are not dead—they are, though, ignored, bypassed or placed as archaeological wonder" (39). Janice Gould in "We Exist" expresses an urgent desire in a similar vein: "Our writers try to counteract the history / that says we are dead, a conquered People. / But our words are like a shout in a blizzard" (7). To contest the fact that Native American cultures have been long fossilized in cultural representations, Wendy Rose in "We Live!" pictures the way Native Americans are objectified in Western museums—"our bones exposed / to weep and howl / to clatter helplessly" (60). In addition, James Luna in "The Artifact Piece" critiques the ossified Native American image, offering his own body as an exhibit, dressed in a loincloth and remaining motionlessly on a bed. In adjoining texts Luna explains not only the visible scars on his body but also the less visible "emotional scars" (33).

Besides these themes many poems address the history of the land and invoke an orientation to and assessment of place. For example, Janice Gould's "History Lesson" narrates the forced resettlement of Native people in Northern California and ends by calling attention to their continuous impact of the history of the region. Frank LaPena's

"The Man Who Travels" highlights a primordial experience closely related to place. Darryl Babe Wilson's essay "Diamond Island: Alcatraz" retells the story of "Diamond Island," once the location of America's most famous prison, from a Northern California Native American perspective. These works suggest that as people and places are mutually constitutive, to reactivate meanings of the land is to recarve identity back into the different topography of the region.

See also CALIFORNIA TRIBAL LITERATURE.

Bibliography

Jaskoski, Helen. "Review: California Renaissance." *College English* 56, no. 4 (1994): 461–470.
Lincoln, Kenneth. "Greg Sarris." *Dictionary of Literary Biography* 175 (1997): 267–273.
Sarris, Greg, ed. *The Sound of Rattles and Clappers: A Collection of New California Indian Writing.* Tucson: University of Arizona Press, 1994.

Fu-jen Chen

Southeastern tribal literature

Native American literature from the southeastern United States is deeply rooted in the oral traditions of the various tribes who have historically called that region home. While the tribes most integrally associated with the southeastern United States in the American popular mind—the FIVE CIVILIZED TRIBES (Cherokee, Chickasaw, Choctaw, Creek, and Seminole)—were forcibly relocated to Indian Territory (present-day Oklahoma) from their ancestral territories in the American South, descendents of those tribes have created compelling literary works that have kept alive their tribal identities and histories by incorporating traditional themes and narrative elements. While reflecting profound awareness of the value of the Native American past, these literary works have also revealed knowing perspectives on the meaning of the modern world in the lives of contemporary Native Americans.

Much of the literature written by Native Americans from the southeastern United States draws from traditional tribal myths. Many of these myths have been transcribed and translated into English by various ethnographers and folklorists, and in the case of the Cherokee myths have been collected and published in acclaimed books. The anthropologist James Mooney, an employee of the federal government at the end of the 19th century and the beginning of the 20th century, collected a large number of mythological stories from informants during his years of fieldwork among the Eastern Band of the Cherokee in western North Carolina; Mooney incorporated that material into the important compilation *Myths of the Cherokee* (1900). A century later the folklorist Barbara R. Duncan, a researcher employed by the Museum of the Cherokee Indian in Cherokee, North Carolina, collected from her informants additional traditional myths and legends, as well as family and personal stories, and included those stories in the book *Living Stories of the Cherokee* (1998). Additional books have showcased the storytelling traditions of other tribes, including *Creation Myths and Legends of the Creek Indians,* edited by Bill Grantham (2002); *Nations Remembered: An Oral History of the Cherokees, Chickasaws, Choctaws, Creeks, and Seminoles in Oklahoma, 1865–1907,* edited by Theda Perdue (1993); and *Native American Legends: Southeastern Legends—Tales from the Natchez, Caddo, Biloxi, Chickasaw, and Other Nations,* edited by George E. Lankford and W. K. McNeil (1987).

Members of the Five Civilized Tribes were at the vanguard of Native American literature during the 19th century. The earliest work of fiction in English by an author of native descent is generally thought to be *Poor Sarah, or Religion Exemplified in the Life and Death of an Indian Woman,* an 1823 pamphlet probably written by Elias Boudinot (circa 1804–39). A formally educated member of the Cherokee tribe who was born in Georgia, Boudinot was the editor of the bilingual newspaper *The Cherokee Phoenix,* the first periodical published by Native Americans. *Poor Sarah* was not commercial fiction—it was a propagandistic tract from a religious advocate. The first overtly commercial work of fiction written by a Native American was *The LIFE AND ADVENTURES OF JOAQUIN MURIETA, THE CELEBRATED CALIFORNIA BANDIT* (1854), a best-selling novel set in California during the gold rush; the author of that novel, JOHN ROL-

LIN RIDGE (also known as Yellow Bird, 1827–67), was a Cherokee born in the Cherokee Nation (in present-day Georgia) who later worked as a journalist in California. Later Ridge became the first Native American to produce a published volume of poetry in English—his's posthumous collection *Poems* (1868).

Several authors born in Indian Territory as members of the Five Civilized Tribes eventually attracted a measure of national attention. ALEXANDER POSEY (1873–1908), a Creek, composed poems—collected posthumously in the 1910 book *The Poems of Alexander Lawrence Posey*—that celebrated aspects of his tribe's cultural past; that author was also renowned for his Fus Fixico letters, a series of humorous fictional pieces published in various Indian Territory newspapers regarding the Allotment phase of the Oklahoma statehood process, in which Posey satirized both the Creek tribal leadership and the federal government. The Cherokee author John Milton Oskison (1874–1947) wrote short stories and novels in the popular frontier romance genre. While he wrote numerous editorials for periodicals on various Native American issues, Oskison wrote just one book that explored Native American concerns—his 1938 biography *Tecumseh and His Times: The Story of a Great Indian.* Also born in Indian Territory was the Cherokee playwright ROLLIE LYNN RIGGS (1899–1954), whose best-known play, *GREEN GROW THE LILACS* (1931), was commercially successful when staged on Broadway. The composer Richard Rodgers and the lyricist Oscar Hammerstein later adapted that play in their blockbuster 1943 musical *Oklahoma!*

Distinguished contemporary authors who are descendants of the Five Civilized Tribes and who were born or reared in Oklahoma include JIM BARNES (Choctaw, born 1933), a prolific poet, translator, editor, and critic, whose books include the acclaimed 1982 poetry volume *The American Book of the Dead;* LINDA HOGAN (Chickasaw, born 1947), a poet, fiction writer, playwright, and essayist, whose work reflects her tribe's sense of place and attitude toward the past as well as such contemporary political issues as feminism and environmental issues; and JOY HARJO (Creek, born

1951), a poet and screenplay writer whose work portrays a modern American social landscape from a distinctly Native American perspective.

Two distinguished contemporary Native American authors associated with the southeastern United States are LOUIS OWENS (Choctaw/Cherokee, born 1948), a Native American studies scholar and novelist (especially of mysteries), who grew up in Mississippi; and the lifelong Tennessee resident Marilou Awiakta (Cherokee, born 1936), who is best known for *Selu: Seeking the Corn-Mother's Wisdom.* Combining essays, stories, and poems that celebrated the Corn Mother, a mythic figure present in many Native American cultures, Awiakta's book reinterpreted that myth in order to revitalize contemporary life with traditional Native American wisdom.

Significant books featuring representations of southeastern tribes written by authors without Native American ancestry include three books exploring interactions between Native Americans and settlers on the southern frontier: William Gilmore Simms's classic novel *The Yemassee: A Romance of Carolina* (1835), James Alexander Thoms's historical novel *Follow the River* (1986), and John Ehle's account of the U.S. government's expulsion of the Cherokee from their ancestral territory, *The Trail of Tears: The Rise and Fall of the Cherokee Nation* (1988).

One of the most controversial books to depict Native American life in the southeastern United States was written by a white man pretending to be a Cherokee. Proclaiming on its original cover that it was "a true story" written by a Cherokee author named Forrest Carter, *The Education of Little Tree* (1976) purported to convey the experiences of a Cherokee boy who lived in rural east Tennessee during the Great Depression. In 1991 a dozen years after the death of the book's author, *The Education of Little Tree* became a national best seller and won the American Booksellers Book of the Year (ABBY) Award. That same year several scholars identified that the book's author was in fact Asa Carter (1925–79), a white supremacist who in the 1960s had scripted speeches for the segregationist Alabama governors George and Lurleen Wallace.

Subsequent public doubt about the moral legitimacy of *The Education of Little Tree* was challenged when the African-American scholar Henry Louis Gates, Jr., in a *New York Times* article, asserted that a work of fiction—as *Little Tree* was by then known to be—should be judged separately from the societal reputation of its author.

Bibliography

Crawford, James M. ed. *Studies in Southeastern Indian Languages.* Athens: University of Georgia Press, 1975.

Susag, Dorothea M. *Roots and Branches: A Resource of Native American Literatures—Themes, Lessons, and Bibliographies.* Urbana, Ill.: National Council of Teachers of English, 1998.

Wiget, Andrew. *Native American Literature.* Boston: Twayne Publishers, 1985.

Ted Olsen

Southwestern tribal literature

Native American literature from the southwestern United States is rich in cultural traditions and expresses strong ties to the land and to the people. The Native American communities in this region are spread across Arizona, New Mexico, southern Nevada, southern Utah, and southern Colorado and include the Navajo (Diné, Dineh), Hopi, Yaqui, Apache, Pueblo, Papago (Tohono O'odham), Pima (Akimel O'odham), Mohave (Aha Makav), Ute, Chemeheuvi, and Paiute.

Southwest Native American literature often conveys the unique cultural histories and beliefs of these indigenous communities. For example, Southwest origin stories are specific to the people and their environment and are frequently found in writings from this region. Some of these origin stories involve an emergence from subterranean worlds or a migration from other lands. Other traditional stories involve important cultural figures, such as Changing Woman (Navajo), Thought Woman (Pueblo), and the Twin Hero Brothers (Pueblo). For many Native people of the Southwest the number 4 is sacred: the four directions (Hopi, Navajo, Yaqui), the four sacred winds (Hopi), the four sacred mountains (Navajo), and the four corners of the world (Pueblo). Native American writers from this region often directly or indirectly reference these cultural figures or sacred elements in their writing.

Southwestern Native American literature also exhibits influences of Spanish culture and Catholicism as a result of early contact with Spanish conquistadors and Jesuit missionaries throughout the 1500s–1600s. While the encounters with these other cultures often resulted in disease and threatened traditional ways of life, Native Americans benefited from acquisition of sheep and horses and exposure to various religious customs that they have incorporated into their own spiritual and cultural practices. Even after the Southwest became an official part of the United States in the mid-1800s, Spanish cultural influences remained strong and continued to influence Native American communities and literature of this area.

One of the earliest writers from this region is SARAH WINNEMUCCA (Paiute, 1844–91), who was the first American Indian woman to publish an autobiography, *Life among the Piutes: Their Wrongs and Claims* (1883). In this book Winnemucca chronicles her life experiences and educates non-Native readers about the experiences and beliefs of her people. *Life among the Piutes* also records Winnemucca's frustration with the U.S. government and corrupt reservation agents, which greatly contributed to her activism and her founding of the Peabody Indian School. Hence her early work provides an important perspective in understanding the historical and governmental forces that shaped the lives of later Native writers from this region.

Also of Paiute ancestry, ADRIAN LOUIS (Paiute, born 1946) writes from a very different perspective. In fact, Louis's work has often been met with sharp criticism for its often painful and brutal portrayal of contemporary Native American communities dealing with POVERTY and ALCOHOLISM. In poetry Louis has published numerous volumes including *Ceremonies of the Damned* (1997) and *ANCIENT ACID FLASHES BACK* (2000). Louis also authored the novel *SKINS* (1995), which became a major motion picture in 2002 directed by Chris Eyre. As a whole Louis's work deals with various contemporary issues of

identity that pervade the work of other Southwest Native writers.

Many contemporary Navajo writers share the importance of land and traditional values while merging their family and individual lives in their work. This can be seen in the work of various Navajo writers, such as LAURA TOHE's (born 1958) *NO PAROLE TODAY* (1999) and Irvin Morris's (born 1958) *From the Glittering World: A Navajo Story* (1997). The award-winning poet and professor of American Indian studies and English LUCI TAPAHONSO (born 1953) also writes of the importance of family in her various publications: *ONE MORE SHIPROCK NIGHT: Poems* (1981), *A BREEZE SWEPT THROUGH* (1987), *SÁANI DAHATAAƚ, THE WOMEN ARE SINGING: POEMS AND STORIES* (1993), and *BLUE HORSES RUSH IN* (1997).

Many contemporary Pueblo writers also express the importance of traditional values in their literary work. SIMON ORTIZ (Acoma Pueblo, born 1941) has published numerous collections of poetry and short fiction, such as *WOVEN STONE* (1992), *AFTER AND BEFORE THE LIGHTENING* (1994), and *MEN ON THE MOON: COLLECTED SHORT STORIES* (1999). Ortiz's work blends traditional values with contemporary living and focuses on the importance of the Acoma Pueblo oral tradition. In a similar fashion Nora Naranjo-Morse (Santa Clara Pueblo, born 1953) emphasizes the continued importance pottery holds for Pueblo people in *Mud Woman: Poems from the Clay* (1992) and articulates what it means to be a Pueblo woman in contemporary society.

PAULA GUNN ALLEN (Laguna Pueblo/Sioux, born 1939), a Native American feminist, introduced feminist issues to American Indian literature and communities with the publication of *The SACRED HOOP* in 1986. She has also published other works, such as *LIFE IS A FATAL DISEASE: COLLECTED POEMS 1962–1995* (1997), and edited numerous volumes including *SPIDER WOMAN'S GRANDDAUGHTERS: TRADITIONAL TALES AND CONTEMPORARY WRITING BY NATIVE AMERICAN WOMEN* (1989) and *SONG OF THE TURTLE: AMERICAN INDIAN LITERATURE 1974–1994* (1996).

Another Laguna Pueblo writer, LESLIE MARMON SILKO (born 1948), writes of the importance of land and traditional values in a majority of her works. In her highly acclaimed first novel *CEREMONY* (1988),

Silko weaves together traditional Laguna Pueblo stories with the narrative of Tayo and his reconnection to the land and ancient ceremonies. After *Ceremony* Silko published *STORYTELLER* (1989), a collection of short stories that includes autobiographical material as well as traditional stories of Kochininako and her significance to the Laguna Pueblo people. Her other works include *ALMANAC OF THE DEAD* (1992), *YELLOW WOMAN* (1997), and *GARDENS IN THE DUNES* (1999).

In recent years other Southwest writers have also been active in recording traditional oral stories and ceremonies in both English and tribal languages. Felipe Molina's (Yaqui, born 1952) *Yaqui Deer Songs Maso Bwikam: A Native American Poetry* (1987), co-authored with Larry Evers, is written in Yaqui and English and contains stories and traditions specific to the Yaqui people. The University of Arizona professor of linguistics OFELIA ZEPEDA (Tohono, O'odham, born 1952) also conveys the importance of traditional stories in both English and Tohono O'odham in *Ocean Power: Poems from the Desert* (1995).

Other writers of Southwest heritage write from the urban center. These writers blend contemporary living with traditional values in ways that do not sacrifice their personal identities or tribal heritages. Two writers in particular, WENDY ROSE (Hopi, born 1948), and Esther Belin (Navajo, born 1968), deal with the struggle to maintain traditional ties while living in urban settings. Rose's poetry, including *GOING TO WAR WITH ALL MY RELATIONS* (1993) and *BONE DANCE: NEW AND SELECTED POEMS 1965–1993* (1994), is highly autobiographical and deals with issues surrounding her personal identity as a MIXED-BLOOD Hopi woman. *From the Belly of My Beauty* (1999), Belin's first book of poetry, revolves around urban alienation stemming in part from the Federal Indian Relocation Program of the 1950s and 1960s.

Southwestern Native American literature vibrantly illustrates a range of individual styles and references various traditional and contemporary cultural traditions. Contemporary writers articulate the complexity of maintaining traditional values and relationships to the land while dealing with urban alienation and a changing world.

Bibliography

O'Donnell, Joan K. *Here, Now, and Always: Voices of the First Peoples of the Southwest.* Santa Fe: Museum of New Mexico Press, 2001.

Sheridan, Thomas E., and Nancy J. Parezo, eds. *Paths of Life: American Indians of the Southwest and Northern Mexico.* Tucson: University of Arizona Press, 1996.

Christina Roberts

sovereignty

In recent years no concept within Native American intellectual, literary, and political life has proved more influential than sovereignty—this despite the term's complicated pedigree. On its European side the word *sovereignty* traces roots through several languages back at least to the 14th century. Its meanings, in their various mutations, pertain to the exercise of supreme authority and/or the protection from external control, especially as both relate to a body politic. Specific definitions over time have included supremacy in respect to rank, dominion, or authority; the position, rank, or power of a supreme ruler; absolute and independent authority; and a territory under the rule of a sovereign, or one existing as an independent state. On the one hand, many observers point to the many meanings of the word as proof of sovereignty's incompatibility with indigenous political philosophies, which are the products of non-European histories and worldviews.

On the other hand, others maintain that the concept has Native American origins. These indigenous forms of sovereignty trace their roots through distinct tribal conceptual traditions. The Mohawk political theorist Taiaiake Alfred, for example, points to the Mohawk word *tewatatowie,* or "we help ourselves," which honors group autonomy and self-sufficiency. The parallels here with European notions of self-rule are clear; indeed, *self-determination* and *self-governance* are among the most common synonyms for *tribal sovereignty* today. Indigenous concepts of sovereignty, however, embody an added element, which European concepts of the idea lack: a moral, spiritual, and cultural dimension that emphasizes balance.

Important to this concept is an internal balance within the tribe, with external entities, and with the natural world. In this sense sovereignty has at least as much to do with cultural freedoms as it does with political ones.

Given this broad range of meanings, it is no surprise that the concept of sovereignty has taken hold on so many levels of inquiry and purpose. As an object of inquiry for Native American literary and cultural studies, the concept of sovereignty prompts commentators to revisit questions on the viability of certain institutions, practices, and ideas associated with tribal self-determination. Generally speaking, these reconsiderations take place on two primary fronts: revivalism and revisionism. Revivalism gives credence to the enduring vitality of Native American life and looks to the efficacy, self-sufficiency, and adaptability of tribal traditions. The author and critic ELIZABETH COOK-LYNN introduces the concept of sovereignty to Native American literary criticism by calling for Native writers to focus more closely on tribal histories and tribally specific treaty processes and to reject the tastes, values, and expectations of non-Native, metropolitan reading audiences. Along a similar line, the author and critic CRAIG WOMACK envisions protocols for an "American Indian literary self-determination" that would redefine tribal literary traditions as distinct national literary traditions in their own right rather than as petitioners to the American ethnic literary canon; establish tribally specific measures for analyzing and evaluating literary texts; and reexamine tribal oral traditions with an eye to their role in the creation and perpetuation of a nationalist ethos. One specific literary text that adopts this kind of perspective is LOUISE ERDRICH's historical novel TRACKS (1988).

Revisionist approaches to indigenous sovereignty question some of the time-honored qualities commonly associated with the concept. For example, the author and critic GERALD VIZENOR disapproves of the way indigenous sovereignty has become synonymous with nationalism, which Vizenor sees as a perverted ideology of group belonging based on power and territorial control. Instead, Vizenor argues, traditional indigenous sovereignty is individualistic and postterritorial, an expression of natural reason, personal freedom, and uninhibited mobil-

ity. As Vizenor does, the political theorist Taiaiake Alfred points out the shortcomings of common definitions of *sovereignty*. Alfred maintains that indigenous sovereignty has become too entangled with European notions of hierarchy and domination and that the traditional values of peace, cooperation, and respect should be restored both to its meaning and to its implementation as a traditional form of governance. A prominent Native American literary text that thematizes such issues is SHERMAN ALEXIE's "One Good Man" in the short story collection *The Toughest Indian in the World* (2000).

Fully understanding sovereignty's meanings and significance to Native American literature, however, means examining the concept of sovereignty in its legal and political contexts. The legal history of Native American tribal nations and the U.S. federal government has been a history of complications and contradictions. As the legal scholar David Wilkins points out, the problem stems from confusion over the difference between *inherent* and *delegated* sovereignty. This confusion revolves around the fact that tribal nations never surrendered away their *inherent* sovereignty to their European and American treaty partners. Philosophically speaking, the doctrine of inherent sovereignty holds that a nation's powers of self-determination are inalienable. Inherent sovereignty can thus be regarded as the source of a people's voice, vision, identity, and will. Practically speaking, inherent sovereignty refers to those core powers of self-determination not specifically ceded to another authority. As the history of treaty making shows, tribes did indeed sign away land, resources, rights, and other assets, but they never explicitly relinquished the core sovereignty to govern themselves, practice their cultures, and manage their affairs—both internal and external—as they see fit. *Delegated* sovereignty, on the other hand, refers to those specific powers of self-governance that a ruling authority hands down to a subordinate authority. While the U.S. Supreme Court has upheld the tribes' inherent sovereignty in several key decisions, a chief example of which is *Worcester v. Georgia* (1832), the Court has more frequently denied it, arguing in some instances, as in *Oliphant v. Suquamish* (1978), that what rights the tribes can be said to enjoy have been *delegated* to them expressly by Congress and in no way constitute the basis for autonomous, self-determining polities. How this legal snarl affects the production of Native American literature is a complex matter overdetermined by the many ways legal issues pertaining to tribal sovereignty have impacted different authors and different tribes at different points in the history of Indian-U.S. relations. One prominent text touching on matters tied to the legal status of Native American tribal nations is D'ARCY McNICKLE's novel *WIND FROM AN ENEMY SKY* (1978).

In its political context, indigenous sovereignty follows an equally complicated course, one made difficult to chart by the several levels—international, domestic, and local—on which indigenous politics are conducted. This complexity, however, should not distract one from the fact that the politics of sovereignty powerfully determine Native American life and literature. Issues pertaining to the political status of tribal nations and the nature of their relationships with other polities have shaped tribal cultures, institutions, and identities. For example, federal ASSIMILATION policies in the late 1800s and early 1900s threatened to fracture tribal societies—and by some standards, succeeded—by imposing free-market principles and Western ideologies of individualism to alienate tribal individuals and their land allotments away from collective tribal control. The literature of the period reflects this political climate in the kinds of themes authors developed in their texts and in the kinds of writing authors used to express themselves and their new realities. For example, the Indian autobiography becomes an important literary form during this period. In *From the Deep Woods to Civilization* (1916) CHARLES EASTMAN chronicles events of his own life in an attempt to build bridges of understanding between the white and Indian worlds he simultaneously inhabits. These mediations between political conditions and literary production over the issue of sovereignty are also a defining feature of the AMERICAN INDIAN LITERARY RENAISSANCE, the literary and cultural flowering attending the postwar conjunction of repressive federal termination policies and the resurgence of tribal cultural nationalism. A prominent literary text of this period that deals with the impacts of

termination policies on tribal peoples is N. SCOTT MOMADAY's *HOUSE MADE OF DAWN* (1968).

For those interested in further study of indigenous sovereignty's various aspects, an excellent and accessible overview is VINE DELORIA, JR., and Clifford Lytle's *The Nations Within: The Past and Future of American Indian Sovereignty* (1984).

Bibliography

Alfred, Taiaiake. *Peace, Power, and Righteousness: An Indigenous Manifesto.* Don Mills, Canada: Oxford University Press, 1999.

Cook-Lynn, Elizabeth. *Why I Can't Read Wallace Stegner and Other Essays: A Tribal Voice.* Madison: University of Wisconsin Press, 1996.

Deloria, Vine, Jr., and Clifford Lytle. *The Nations Within: The Past and Future of American Indian Sovereignty.* Austin: University of Texas Press, 1984.

Eastman, Charles. *From the Deep Woods to Civilization: Chapters in the Autobiography of an Indian.* Lincoln: University of Nebraska Press, 1977.

Erdrich, Louise. *Tracks.* New York: Holt, 1988.

Momaday, N. Scott. *House Made of Dawn.* New York: Harper & Row, 1989.

Vizenor, Gerald. *Fugitive Poses: Native American Indian Scenes of Absence and Presence.* Lincoln and London: University of Nebraska Press, 1998.

Wilkins, David, and K. Tsianina Lomawaima. *Uneven Ground: American Indian Sovereignty and Federal Law.* Norman: University of Oklahoma Press, 2001.

Womack, Craig S. *Red on Red: Native American Literary Separatism.* Minneapolis: University of Minnesota Press, 1999.

Matt Herman

Spider Woman's Granddaughters: Traditional Tales and Contemporary Writing by Native American Women   Paula Gunn Allen (1989)

PAULA GUNN ALLEN's *Spider Woman's Granddaughters* is one of the first publications to make Indian women's writing accessible to a wider audience and actively pursue and link the woman-warrior image to the collective of Native American women storytellers. A pioneering work in American Indian scholarship, this collection of 24 stories includes traditional tales and a varied range of contemporary writing by 17 Indian women. Allen's landmark anthology won the Before Columbus Foundation's American Book Award in 1990.

In her comprehensive introduction to the Indian act of storytelling, Allen explains that her collection is named for the "light of intelligence and experience" (1) shed upon the people by Grandmother Spider in the Cherokee tale. The anthology thus serves as an introduction to tribal literatures and the role of women in the shaping of these stories, illuminating especially for the non-Indian reader the significance of such tales in the Indian communities. For Allen and her people a story's literary worth is irrevocably tied to its value in the community.

The traditional stories are selectively placed to lend context to the modern renditions of Indian life, illustrating the dynamic process of how "Native writers write out of tribal traditions, and into them" (4). By giving these tales a context from which they may be read there emerges a sense of community-based tribal aesthetics. As does the constant of change, the tradition-imbued act of storytelling links the mundane with the spiritual power of the sacred.

The volume is subdivided into three sections: "The Warriors," "The Casualties," and "The Resistance." In compiling this collection of what Allen calls "women's war stories or woman-warrior stories" (18), she demonstrates an understanding of war that goes beyond the military. As this potent mix of traditional and contemporary tales establishes, it is as American Indian women that they battle spiritually, economically, emotionally, historically, and culturally from a legacy of domestic, academic, physical, and national abuse.

Some especially noteworthy modern contributions include Vickie L. Sears's "Grace," which deals with the issue of child abuse, and Anna Lee Walters's "The Warriors," which deals with the issue of finding dignity and beauty even in an alcoholic's life. Enforced removal of children from their true communities is a common theme that runs through the traditional Chippewa story "Oshkikwe's Baby," LINDA HOGAN's "American Horse," and EMILY PAULINE JOHNSON's "As It Was in the Beginning." The captivity of the tribes, their enthrallment and enslavement by the TRICKSTER Europeans, is an essential part of the inheritance of loss that Allen wishes to highlight.

This book presents a varied selection of women writers of different tribal affiliations and personal demographics whose stories intersect at the various points of their marginalization to extend the representational range of the collection as a work of the women of the Indian nations. Their stories are a testament to endurance and strength in spite of all forms of oppression.

Bibliography

Allen, Paula Gunn, ed. *Spider Woman's Granddaughters: Traditional Tales and Contemporary Writing by Native American Women.* Boston: Beacon Press, 1989.

P. K. Choo

spirituality

The spirituality of Native Americans, often misunderstood, provides a rich contribution to American literature. Joseph Epes Brown reminds us in *The Spiritual Legacy of the American Indian* that the word *religion* does not exist in any Native American language. In traditional Native American cultures spirituality is not a category or a limited expression of dualities such as good versus evil, spirit versus body, or sacred versus profane, but a belief system in which the world is a sacred place filled with wonder and awe. God's mystery can be found everywhere—the early morning mist, the rising sun, in the dense forests, on the vast plains, under star-filled skies, and beneath the changing phases of the moon. For the Native American peoples, regardless of tribe, spirituality cannot be separated from society or from any aspect of life.

The origins of Native American spirituality in literature can be found in the telling of creation myths. Chewing Black Bones, a respected Blackfeet elder, narrated a creation myth to Ella E. Clark in her book *Indian Legends from the Northern Rockies,* published in 1953. His account mirrors the Christian account of Genesis with references to an "Old Man" who forms a woman and a son out of clay. However, whereas the Genesis story focuses on God first, followed by the creation of a man, the creation of a woman from the rib of the man, and the production of offspring, the Blackfeet story focuses on the centrality of family and community. The "Old Man" did not create a man first, thereby justifying a societal role of domination; nor did he create a father first. Instead, the "Old Man" created a woman, and through the creation of her son, made her a mother. Spirituality is not based on individual or role, but on relationship with the family.

An example can be found in the vision quest ritual found in many tribes. In the vision quest a person goes off to a secluded place for three or four days to communicate with the spirits in order to gain purpose and direction in his or her life. Through enduring the elements, fasting, praying, and experiencing solitude, the person receives an opportunity for direct contact with the supernatural that often results in his or her receiving a dream or a vision from which spiritual knowledge and power that can later be used to help the larger community are gained. Although Christians do not place the name *vision quest* on the 40 days and 40 nights Jesus spent in the wilderness fasting and praying, parallels clearly exist. It was during that period of intense spiritual focus that Jesus overcame the devil's temptations and gained the strength needed to begin his public ministry. The spiritual principle is the same in the Native and non-Native tradition—prayer, fasting, and solitude achieve spiritual enlightenment and strength. Native American literature pursues the vision quest, the physical, mental, and spiritual preparation to receive divine guidance, in a way that focuses not on the vision quest as an obscure ritual of aboriginal peoples but as a vital link of tribal member to the community and to the spiritual realm.

For instance, in *Black Elk Speaks, Being the Life Story of a Holy Man of the Oglala Sioux, as told through John G. Neihardt* (1932), the narrative reveals the intimacy with which God communicates to the individual who is receiving the dream or vision. Black Elk describes his failure to live up to the vision entrusted to him, which resulted in his failure to lead his nation through four difficult periods. The vision is not *his;* rather it has been entrusted to him for the benefit of his tribal community. Likewise, the vision quest is not a sacrifice for him alone, but for the community. A holy man and his assistants typically help prepare the individual for the vision quest, and family members often accompany him or her with prayer throughout the duration of the experience. The vision quest, as does the focus of Native American spirituality as a whole, gives preference to the broader good of the community.

Another fundamental means of communication between humans and the spiritual realm is through animal spirit guides. This common element in biographical and historical narratives reveals another vehicle by which tribal members receive wisdom, healing, and self-identity from God. This element of Native American spirituality posed particular difficulty for authors who attempted to appeal to a larger, non-Native audience. Various changes had to take place in American writing before Native American thought and culture would become reasonably accessible to non-Native readers.

Among many Native American tribes is the central belief that behind all individual spirits and personifications of the divine is a single creative life force. Often called "the Great Mystery," this life force expresses itself throughout the universe in all things, whether human, animal, tree, or grain of wheat. Likewise, every story is a working out of this life force. Although similar to the Christian all-powerful, all-knowing, ever-present God, the Native American conception of the divine is more far-reaching, less restricted to one being, and more accessible to humans. This difference created a substantial divide between tribal consciousness and the consciousness of industrial or urbanized cultures driven by monotheism. One system promotes wholeness, while the other is based on division and separation. One system promotes a circular, unified field of interaction, while the other is linear and sequential. For Native American literature these differences have significant consequences. For instance, established European narrative techniques move in a linear fashion and give great significance to conflict resolution—a feature that is merely incidental in tribal narratives. For the Native American writer of fiction developments are often dependent on the interaction of spirits and arcane forces rather than the more external European-American elements such as personality and politics. It took time for American fiction to accommodate the Native American tribal narrative, to be open to the possibility of the expression of divinity in something other than biblical Scriptures.

One author who had particular success in bridging the gap between Native American spirituality and Western readers is JAMES WELCH, who probes the idea of animal spirit guides in both a contemporary setting in *The DEATH OF JIM LONEY* (1979) and a historical one in *FOOLS CROW* (1987). The protagonist of the first novel, Jim Loney, is a hopeless alcoholic who experiences a recurring vision of a bird. He believes the repeated visitation by the bird is a message from his mother's tribe, but because he is not in community with his Native American relatives, he knows he is incapable of interpreting the message.

Set in the 19th century, *Fools Crow* contrasts with *The Death of Jim Loney,* whose 20th-century protagonist suffers spiritual confusion. Fools Crow, born White Man's Dog, a young Pikuni Blackfeet, has no difficulty identifying his animal spirit guide. Without hesitation he follows a raven who delivers a plea for assistance in freeing a wolverine caught in a trap. Fools Crow frees the wolverine and receives a spiritual gift from the raven: to possess the magic of the wolverine.

The Death of Jim Loney and *Fools Crow* represent opposite ends of the spiritual spectrum. Jim Loney does not comprehend the mystical wisdom of his tribe; White Man's Dog has not been tainted by the spiritual brainwashing of the dominant European culture, which dispels the possibility that ravens or other animals can communicate with humans. Through the two novels Welch demonstrates the spiritual abyss that results from community separation. It is the connection with the tribe that would have given Jim Loney the inter-

pretation he sought, the connection White Man's Dog never lost. Within the course of a century the life force so prevalent among all Native American tribes is silenced. The bird's message intended for Jim Loney, and for him alone, passed through time without interpretation as a testimony to the destruction of Native American spirituality brought about both by Anglo encroachment and by Native American neglect of the treasured center of their spirituality: community.

One of the most outspoken authors on Native American spirituality in nonfiction is VINE DELORIA, JR. Born of a Native American Episcopalian father and himself theologically trained, Deloria in his 1973 *GOD IS RED* gives readers a disturbing account of the condition of modern Christianity. But more than a chastisement, Deloria offers an insightful comparison of Native American spirituality and Christianity. It is experience, says Deloria, not intellectual acceptance of doctrine, that is at the heart of Native American spirituality. One crucial distinction between the two forms of spirituality he identifies is the Native American emphasis on space (place) versus the Christian emphasis on time (history). For Native American spiritual traditions spatial layout takes on a profound importance. Whether structured around a north-south or earth-sky division, the structure for a ceremony, the design of a sweat lodge, or the direction one turns in a pipe ceremony has a tribally specific cosmic representation value that reveals the spiritual relationship of a particular tribe with the spatial world around them.

God Is Red again makes the point that Native American ceremonies and rituals are engaged not primarily for personal benefit but rather for that of the entire community or nation. In the same sense violations of the sacred become threatening to the whole community, not simply to the one who commits the offense. In Christian ideology sin removes the sinner from the presence of divine grace. For the tribal member sin affects the community as a whole, therefore weakening all.

It is truly ironic that alcohol, Christians' most sacred substance in the form of the communion wine used in the Mass to represent the blood of their God, has had such a devastating impact on

Native populations. Additionally the Native Americans' most sacred substance, the tobacco used in ceremonial pipes, has caused chronic health problems for many Christians. The forced evangelization of Native peoples acted for a time as a veil to Native American culture, community, and spirituality; through the writing of Native authors the true strength harnessed within Native American spirituality has now been revealed. The multifaceted nature of Native American spirituality will continue to remove the veil and provide literary circles with wisdom and the echo of a continuous call to nurture community.

Bibliography

Allen, Paula Gunn. *The Sacred Hoop: Recovering the Feminine in American Indian Traditions.* Boston: Beacon Press, 1986.

Black Elk. *Black Elk Speaks: Being the Life Story of a Holy Man of the Oglala Sioux, as Told through John G. Neihardt,* Lincoln: University of Nebraska Press, 1932.

Brown, Joseph Epes. *The Spiritual Legacy of the American Indian.* New York: Crossroad, 1982.

Silko, Leslie Marmon. *Ceremony.* New York: Penguin Books, 1977.

Christine M. Hilger

Standing Bear, Luther   (1868?–1939)

Luther Standing Bear was born in the late 1860s, probably in the year 1868. He was born into the Teton or Western Sioux, but there is a debate over whether he was Oglala or Brulé. Standing Bear himself said that he was Oglala and became chief of the Oglala toward the end of his life, but some historians, notably George Hyde, argue that Standing Bear was Brulé and remembered his tribal affiliations inaccurately.

Standing Bear was born shortly before the treaty of Fort Laramie, the battle of Little Bighorn, and the WOUNDED KNEE massacre, that is, before the Sioux were forced onto reservations and before the buffalo were decimated. One could say he was born into the "traditional" Sioux way of life. His boyhood name was *Ota K'te,* or Plenty Kill,

and he was raised to become a successful warrior and hunter. Though it may seem antithetical, his belief that he should not shrink from the enemy and should act bravely encouraged him to go away to Carlisle Boarding School. It was at Carlisle that Ota K'te was renamed Luther Standing Bear. After attending Carlisle Standing Bear got a job at Wannamaker's department store in Philadelphia. Later he became a teacher at Rosebud, then a clerk; he later joined Buffalo Bill's show. Near the end of his life he moved to California and appeared in several movies. Shortly after being elected president of the American Indian Progressive Association, Standing Bear died in California while he was working on the film *Union Pacific.*

It was in California that Standing Bear wrote his four books, *My People the Sioux* (1928), *My Indian Boyhood* (1931), *Land of the Spotted Eagle* (1933), and *Stories of the Sioux* (1934). His goal in writing these was to show that Natives were not lazy and inept, as many Americans believed, and that both Americans and Native Americans were losing a valuable part of their cultural heritage through the discounting of the histories and cultures of Natives. *My People the Sioux* (1928) is particularly important because it provides one of the first Native accounts of the battles of Little Bighorn and Wounded Knee and because it insists upon Natives' rights. It must be noted that Standing Bear lived what he wrote and that he is probably more famous for the court battles he waged against the U.S. government over such matters as land rights than he is for his writing.

Bibliography

Hyde, George. *A Sioux Chronicle.* Norman: University of Oklahoma Press, 1956.

———. *Spotted Tail's Folk: A History of the Brulé Sioux.* Norman: University of Oklahoma Press, 1961.

Mathes, Valerie Sherer, and Richard Lowitt. *The Standing Bear Controversy: Prelude to Indian Reform.* Urbana: University of Illinois Press, 2003.

Nancy, Shoemaker, ed. *American Indians.* Malden, Mass.: Blackwell, 2001.

Standing Bear, Luther. *Land of the Spotted Eagle.* Boston: Houghton Mifflin, 1933.

———. *My Indian Boyhood.* Lincoln: University of Nebraska Press, 1988.

———. *My People the Sioux.* Lincoln: University of Nebraska Press, 1975.

———. *Stories of the Sioux.* Lincoln: Bison Press, 1988.

Christie Firtha

Storm, Hyemeyohsts   (Charles Storm, Wolf Storm, General Storm) (1931–   )

The facts of Charles Storm's early life are murky. Storm claims he was born on the Northern Cheyenne Reservation to a Cheyenne mother. He also alternately claimed his father was Sioux, Cheyenne, or German. Only the last is true. Storm is German-American and has no Cheyenne ancestry or ties to the tribe. Storm is famous primarily for presenting a faux version of Cheyenne religion, one the actual Cheyenne consider blasphemous, exploitative, and disrespectful. His works and person are immensely popular with New Age audiences and reviled among many Native Americans and their supporters.

In 1972 Charles Storm reinvented himself as "Hyemeyohsts" Storm with *Seven Arrows*. Natives, especially the Cheyenne, angrily protested the book as racist and stereotypical, "desecration," "grossly distortive," "outright lies," even "spiritual genocide." Storm responded by producing a Cheyenne enrollment card, which turned out to be fraudulent. Storm's publisher, Douglas Latimer, avoided a judgment against Harper and Row by paying "reparations" to the tribe and relabeling *Seven Arrows* as fiction. This did not stop Storm and his growing cult from claiming the book was literal truth. Storm's appearances to promote his books or sell faux-Native ceremonies faced Native protests from Cheyenne elders such as Joe Coyote and Bernard Red Cherries and activists from the AMERICAN INDIAN MOVEMENT. Two subsequent books added the Mayan to the list of Natives he offended, this time by falsely claiming the existence of "Zero Chiefs." Virtually the only Native to defend Storm was VINE DELORIA, JR., who later withdrew his support. Storm's association with other alleged imposters posing as Native medicine men, such as Harley Reagan, further diminished his credibility. His story took a bizarre twist when members of the Crow tribe, traditional Cheyenne enemies, claimed he was a distant relative but also confirmed he was not Cheyenne.

Storm next attempted to become a leader of MIXED-BLOOD Natives, founding the National American Metis Association (NAMA) in 2001. NAMA proved a failure, with fewer than 300 members. NAMA fled California to avoid paying back taxes and today rarely meets. Members of Storm's inner circle also tried to remake his image through works in academia, with little success. Storm remains a pariah among the Cheyenne and Native Americans as a whole, one of the most notorious "plastic shamans," even while his books remain popular among non-Natives who are largely unaware of or unconcerned by how they appall many Natives.

Bibliography

Storm, Hyemeyohsts. *Seven Arrows.* New York: Harper & Row, 1972.

Hagen, Helene. "Plastic Medicine People Circle." Available online. URL: http://www.sonomacountyfreepress.com/features/spirg-hagan.html. Accessed on August 15, 2005.

Jaeger, Lowell. "*Seven Arrows* Seven Years After." Available online. URL: http://oncampus.richmond.edu/faculty/ASAIL/SAILns/42.html. Accessed on August 15, 2005.

Al Carroll

Storyteller   Leslie Marmon Silko (1981)

Storyteller is a multilayered and multigenred text that defies classification; above all, it foregrounds the Native American practice of storytelling as a means of transmitting knowledge and values. The book is composed of poems, short stories, mythology, letters, autobiographical narratives, and photographs. Taken as a whole the book speaks primarily—though not exclusively—of Laguna Pueblo culture and traditions. LESLIE MARMON SILKO links her personal history to cultural history by conveying traditional stories in the voices that conveyed them to her, especially those of her grandmother and her aunt, Susie.

The stories are sometimes set in a comparatively contemporary moment; many, however, are set during the legendary past, before events can be placed according to historical time. These legendary stories often feature characters common to Laguna mythology, such as Yellow Woman, Spider Woman, the twin brothers, and coyote—one of the most common incarnations of the TRICKSTER FIGURE. Although many of these stories are intended primarily to entertain, especially those featuring the more vulgar behavior of Coyote, others serve as prophetic interpretations of the modern world.

An extended poem in the center of *Storyteller,* for example, reveals the power of "witchery," Silko's term for the manipulation of evil, disorder, and disharmony. In this poem the witches hold a contest, aiming to impress each other with their frightening abilities to shift shapes and celebrate death. Finally the last witch claims to be most powerful at storytelling, a claim the other witches initially dismiss, for what could be so terrible about a story? But the story this witch tells has the effect of action—as the words are uttered, the events they describe begin to occur. This witch tells of "white skin people / like the belly of a fish" who will arrive to destroy the animals, the water, the earth, and the people. The other witches concede defeat, begging the storytelling witch to revoke the story, but it is too late—the events have already been set in motion. This story demonstrates that modern ethnic tensions cannot be reduced simply to "white" versus "Indian," for the Indians themselves spoke white people into existence.

Several other stories rely on the possibility of supernatural events informing the plots or on conflicts of interpretation between those who accept the supernatural and those who reject it. *Storyteller* concludes, however, with an amusing story, "Coyote Holds a Full House in His Hand," in which a man who is particularly unlucky at love persuades several women that he is a medicine man and that he can cure their ills by rubbing their thighs. According to this story, the trickster prevails even in modern times, even in a world also suffering from witchery.

Bibliography

Arnold, Ellen. *Conversations with Leslie Marmon Silko.* Jackson: University of Mississippi Press, 2000.

Silko, Leslie Marmon. *Yellow Woman,* edited by Melody Graulich. New Brunswick, N.J.: Rutgers University Press, 1993.

———. *Yellow Woman and a Beauty of the Spirit: Essays on Native American Life Today.* New York: Simon & Schuster, 1996.

Lynn Domina

Summer of the Black Widows, The
Sherman Alexie (1996)

In this, SHERMAN ALEXIE's fourth collection of poems, he enhanced the reputation that he had established with his previous collections, in particular *OLD SHIRTS AND NEW SKINS.* Almost single-handedly, Alexie has managed to put Native American poetry in the mainstream of American literature while also extending its range technically, thematically, and tonally as an ethnic literature.

The Summer of the Black Widows includes 47 poems divided into seven sections. The first section, "Why We Play Basketball," consists of nine poems, including the title poem, which is the second of the collection. "The Summer of the Black Widows" takes as its starting place the seemingly coincidental appearance of uncountable black widow spiders after a rainstorm. But, in the sixth and seventh lines the speaker reveals that the tribal elders have asserted that the spiders carry stories. From that point on the word *story* is substituted for *spider* as the speaker chronicles the many places in which the spiders were found and then the many ways in which the members of the tribe tried to reduce their number. The poem closes with the spiders' disappearing as suddenly as they had appeared, in this instance in a lightning storm. Among the speculations about what happened to the spiders, the tribal elders suggest that the white sacs of spider eggs that have been left behind in the high corners of houses are really packets of stories waiting to be opened. Thus the poem reaches for understanding in its combinations of whimsy and irony, of fabulation and directness.

Among the other poems of the first section, "Defending Walt Whitman" is notable for its imaginative insertion of the poet into a reservation game, and in the long, five-part poem "Why We Play Basketball" Alexie seeks to suggest why Native Americans typically approach basketball with great ferocity.

The title poem of the second section, "Father and Farther," is the poet's reminiscence about his father's life, his obsessions and compulsions, but it is also a recognition that those memories, both personal and borrowed, constitute something distinct from the man himself. What remains with the son of the father is the result of the son's own natural obsession with trying in some way to pin down a relationship that remains, paradoxically, as elusive as it is resonant.

The focal event of the third section, "Sister Fire, Brother Smoke," is the trailer fire that took the poet's sister's life. It haunts even the section's most powerful poem, "Elegies," in which the poet memorializes, in a voice full of dark comedy and pathetic irony, a broad spectrum of people who have died by accident, bad luck, and stupidity. With a considerable shift in tone the fourth section, "Grand Entry," presents a lyrical celebration of the poet's relationship with his wife.

In the fifth section, "Tourists," Alexie works through themes related to celebrity and notoriety. In the title poem he imagines James Dean, Janis Joplin, and Marilyn Monroe paying visits to the reservation. In "Capital Punishment" the speaker is a prison cook who expresses his sense of connection with a condemned man through the last meal he prepares for him. The sixth section, "To Find Sasquatch," consists of a single poem in 33 sections (or a series of 33 interrelated poems) entitled "The Sasquatch Poems." Here the poet plays with the possibilities that the legendary creature may be imaginary or real—or transcend such categories.

The closing section of the collection is "Bob's Coney Island," a group of nine poems that treat public issues or, perhaps more precisely, issues that reveal themselves in public situations. In "After the Trial of Hamlet, Chicago, 1994," the poet recounts his attendance at a dinner-theater fund-raiser in which the entertainment was a trial of Hamlet for the killing of Polonius. It juxtaposes his reflections on the issues of the play with his discomfort with his dinner companions, an obnoxious millionaire and a distracted Abigail Van Buren, among others. Through its narration of a visit to the camp "Dachau" hauntingly examines with considerable subtlety the degree to which genocides might be similarly described or directly compared and the functions of memorials to atrocities.

Bibliography

"About Sherman Alexie." *Ploughshares* 26 (winter 2000–2001): 197–202.

Berner, Robert L. Review of *Summer of the Black Widows*. *World Literature Today* 71 (spring 1997): 430–431.

Evans, Stephen F. "'Open Containers': Sherman Alexie's Drunken Indians." *American Indian Quarterly* 25 (winter 2001): 46–72.

McFarland, Ron. "'Another Kind of Violence': Sherman Alexie's Poems." *American Indian Quarterly* 21 (spring 1997): 251–264.

Martin Kich

Sundogs   Lee Maracle   (1992)

The novel *Sundogs* (1992) is LEE MARACLE's first foray into the genre of the novel. *Sundogs* encapsulates the social and political concerns Maracle explores throughout the corpus of her writing, whether it is fiction, nonfiction, or literary theory. She is consistently critical of racism, class prejudice, and patriarchy, which she attributes to contemporary Canadian socioeconomic and political systems founded on European patriarchal values. In this novel the reader is given insight into Maracle's political views through her female characters. For Maracle writing is a political act that allows her to *speak* both *to* and *for* her Native audience; her writing becomes an extension of the oral tradition of Native storytelling.

Sundogs is narrated from the perspective of Marianne, a 20-year-old east Vancouver university student studying sociology. She is in conflict because of the disparity between what academia tells her about her Native culture and what her mother expresses to her and to anyone or anything within earshot, including the evening news broadcast. Initially Marianne finds her mother's ravings about the genocidal conspiracy of white Canada embarrassing. By the end she gains insight into her mother's worldview and her sister, Lacey's, feminism; the once-annoying riddles spoken by the women in her family grow on her (87).

The public and historic tensions of the novel, set during the Canadian summer of 1990 and the Oka crisis, a violent battle between Mohawk protecting their land and burial rights and the Canadian government, parallel the tensions of Marianne's inner world. She feels misunderstood, at best, and invisible, at worst. Marianne is not understood by the white community; neither does she understand or empathize with her mother's point of view, to which all of her much older siblings have an emotional access denied to her. However, the events of the summer of 1990 catalyze Marianne's own introspection (87). As she sits glued to the television watching history unfold, she is able to hear Elija's teachings in a way that she has been unwilling to accept from her mother. Marianne begins to understand that Rudy, her brother, who beat his wife and children, is "a casualty in a war we [aboriginals] wage against ourselves" (82). Marianne is motivated to join other Natives, from many unnamed tribes, in a run across Canada to support the Mohawk at Oka.

While on the run, Marianne begins to understand that her knowledge of white intellectualism is irrelevant to Native Canadian life, her life. Consistent themes in Lee Maracle's writing are the futility and falsity of whites's attempts to define the world, and specifically Native people. In *Sundogs* Maracle emphasizes the ineptitude of sociology. While on the peace run Marianne thinks to herself:

> I feel self-conscious embarrassment coming on. My entire educational framework tells me this is really far-fetched. My body carries me anyway; it trudges on with a will of its own. The hills of the Okanogan breathe all around me a different truth. My sociological structures have no relevance here. (177)

Her body and the world reveal truths to her that contrast with her academic learning. The purpose of the run for Marianne is not the end goal, but the lessons she learns. Recognition of the insignificance of personal pride symbolizes Marianne's trepidation in entering the Native community of her mother's family. She still does not entirely understand the languages her family speaks, both literally and figuratively, but the ending suggests that she will learn.

As much of Lee Maracle's writing does, *Sundogs* advocates female and Native empowerment against the oppression of European patriarchal class systems that deny (exclude) Natives while claiming omniscient expertise about Native peoples and their cultures. Maracle sees academic attempts to name and define Native culture as the contemporary form of colonization of the Indian, and the alienation of that specific audience is certainly one of her agendas. She identifies the impotent frustration of Native women and men disempowered by the system as a root cause for women's apathy and men's violence, which often turns inward on the family and the community; Native complicity in community demise is the destructive legacy of a genocide that perpetuates itself through historical momentum.

Bibliography

Maracle, Lee. *Sojourners and Sundogs First Nations Fiction.* Vancouver: Press Gang, 1999.

Sheena Wilson

Sundown   John Joseph Mathews   (1934)

Sundown, JOHN JOSEPH MATHEWS's highly autobiographical novel, provides an important window on the enactment of the DAWES (General Allotment) ACT of 1887. Under the guise of giving "civilization" to the Indians, the Dawes Act required that Indian lands, which were held communally, be divided into individual plots, which Indians were then to farm as whites did theirs. After 160 acres per family (less for individuals) were allotted, the surplus land was opened to white settlement. Set in Oklahoma in the early years of the 20th century as Osage land becomes allotted, Mathews's simply told story of Challenge Windzer's growth to manhood, his exploits as a World War I pilot, and his eventual return to the RESERVATION illustrates the damaging effects of Dawes.

"He shall be a challenge to the disinheritors of his people," proclaims John Windzer, naming his newborn *Challenge* as *Sundown* opens (4). However, the novel turns out to be the story of how young "Chal" attempts to assimilate. From the time he is a young child, and throughout his years at high school and university, Chal's behavior suggests that he has internalized the powerful argument by which the United States justified the Dawes Act, that of "civilizing the savage."

Although the word *savage* is only mumbled under the breath of Chal's angry teacher, its implication is omnipresent in Chal's self-image (20). An imaginative child, Chal associates his love of nature with a lack of civilization. In high school and at university Chal makes solitary trips to the prairie, where he acts out what he believes are primitive actions, which fill him with shame. While he tries to suppress these feelings and to associate himself with whites, Chal, a MIXED-BLOOD, grows away from his full-blood friends, Running Elk and Sun-on-his Wings, who resist ASSIMILATION.

Chal's fears do seem to abate during his service as a World War I pilot, which makes him feel that "he had been gilded with that desirable thing called civilization" (230). However, when he returns to the reservation, Chal's behavior suggests he is unchanged.

The abyss that develops between Chal and his friends as he tries to assimilate mirrors the divisions among the Osage fueled by Dawes, which issued allotments by quantum of Indian blood (mixed-bloods were issued "patents in fee simple," while lands of full-bloods were held in trust for them). Through his portrait of the naive John Windzer who buys "allotment as civilization," Mathews shows that the mixed-blood people were overly optimistic about Dawes; however, he does not fully endorse the noncooperation of the full-bloods (Warrior 54). Writing at a time when Indians were politically powerless, Mathews must have felt resistance to be futile and this land dispossession to be as inevitable as "sundown."

Bibliography

Cheyfitz, Eric. *The Poetics of Imperialism.* Philadelphia: University of Pennsylvania Press, 1997.

Mathews, John Joseph. *Sundown.* Norman: University of Oklahoma Press, 1988.

Warrior, Robert Allen. *Tribal Secrets: Recovering American Indian Intellectual Traditions.* Minneapolis: University of Minnesota Press, 1996.

Rhona S. Mollard

Sun Is Not Merciful, The   Anna Lee Walters (1985)

Winner of the 1985 Before Columbus Foundation American Book Award, *The Sun Is Not Merciful* is the first book by ANNA LEE WALTERS. A collection of short stories, *The Sun Is Not Merciful* begins with a story about hobos called "The Warriors" and ends with the story of the title. In the middle ranges a collection of stories span the beginning of time in "Mythomania" to a visitation by the devil in modern Oklahoma, while an old man named John Stink is resurrected and a young man named Sonny learns an important lesson about tribal identity.

Walters involves a distinctly Native American sensibility in her writing in relation to spirituality and tribal identity. In each story the issues of religion and tribal identity are raised in order to reaffirm why these are central to Native American culture. In one of her stories, "Sister Lena and the Devil," Sister Lena samples churches at whim and argues with pastors over whether or not her soul has been saved. As each pastor tries to convert her to his church and argues against the rest, Sister Lena responds that despite their differences, they are all the same—they all worship God. To Sister Lena, who was visited by the devil as a child, church denomination matters little compared to true faith.

While this story comments on the forced conversion to Christianity of Native peoples across the country, Walter's condemnation of how religion is viewed by society becomes even more poignant when the devil returns to dance at a POW WOW. Walters's portrait of Native dancing and culture becomes poetic as she describes how the dancers join the dance and what they wear. As the dance progresses, the grandmothers—who traditionally sit on the outside of the circle—become restless and whisper. Finally the dance is shut down and everyone is sent back to camp because the devil has joined them in the circle, in the form of a white man. They scatter, and wake the next morning in peace. This is not a condemnation of all white people; as the granddaughter notes, there are white people among them who have married in and "become one of them."

Similarly to the old storytelling tradition in which each story teaches a lesson, many of the wonderful stories that compose *The Sun Is Not Merciful* contain lessons about identity, faith, and love—lessons that are universal but have a distinctly Native point of view. Almost as if in Walters's voice, Sister Lena remarks at the end of the story to her granddaughter, "Looks to me like you learning, baby."

Bibliography

Walters, Lee Ann. "The Devil and Sister Lena." Available online. URL: http://www.hanksville.org/storytellers/ALWalters/poems/DevilSisterLena.html. Accessed on August 15, 2005.

———. *The Sun Is Not Merciful.* Ithaca, N.Y.: Firebrand Books, 1985.

———. *Talking Indian: Reflections on Survival and Writing.* Ithaca, N.Y.: Firebrand Books, 1992.

Brianna R. Burke

Surrounded, The D'Arcy McNickle (1936)

D'ARCY MCNICKLE's 1936 novel *The Surrounded* is the story of a young MIXED-BLOOD, Archilde Leon, the son of a Spanish father and an Indian mother, who returns to his Salish reservation in Montana for what he intends to be a final visit. Archilde, who has been earning his living in the white world by playing the fiddle, arrives at home intimidated by his white father but scornful of his Indian relatives and what he believes to be their backward way of life. During the course of the novel, however, Archilde begins to appreciate and identify with his Indian heritage and finds leaving increasingly difficult. By failing to resume his path toward ASSIMILATION and continuing his involvement in the Indian world, Archilde is led to his downfall.

In the early 1900s, 20 years after the DAWES General Allotment Act forced the division of Indian land into small plots, allowing whites to pour into the reserved lands and buy up the "surplus," conditions on Indian reservations such as that of the Salish were desperately bad. Through Archilde's story McNickle's many times revised novel may be seen to push for the reform of federal Indian policy, then the project of McNickle's employer, Indian Commisioner John Collier. By educating his white audience in the culture and history of the Salish, McNickle works to refute the justification used by Euro-Americans for their subjection of Native peoples: that Indians are "savages," in need of white "civilization."

In *The Surrounded* McNickle critiques, although deferentially, a whole range of whites who control RESERVATION LIFE and whose own aspirations work to maintain Indian subjection: the church, represented by Father Grepilloux, who sees himself, ironically, as a savior of the Indians; the settler, represented by Archilde's father, Max, who cannot understand his Indian family and compares his Indian sons to dogs; the government agent, represented by Parker, who is busy holding on to his job; the trader and unscrupulous speculator in Indian land, represented by Moser; and law enforcement, represented by the brutal sheriff, Dave Quigley. McNickle steers his white audience to ask themselves the question Max asks of Moser: "Put it to yourself—what did we bring? Railroads, banks, a fine business like yours . . . put it to yourself! . . . People are starving! They're freezing to death in those shacks by the church and they don't know why; they had nothing to do with it. You and me and Father Grepilloux were the ones that brought it on" (146–147).

Archilde's superior behavior toward his Indian relatives on his return is also due to white oppression. The protagonist, like his author, was a student in the Indian BOARDING SCHOOL system, which was set up by the U.S. government to "civilize" Indian children. Taken from their reservations, sometimes forcibly, children were sent to boarding schools far away from the "savage" habits and languages of their parents. The children were deliberately alienated from their parents and severely punished if caught speaking their own languages. Indian ways were held to be dirty and ignorant, and Indian beliefs to be pagan superstition. The effect of such schooling is apparent in Archilde at the Indian feast given in honor of his return. Here Archilde feels "disgusted" and "irritated" by his mother, Faithful Catherine, and her people. He feels that Indians are "not real people" and asks himself, "Why he could not endure them for just a few hours? Why did they make him feel sick?" (62).

Archilde's attitudes begin to change, however, when he, along with McNickle's white readers, gets another kind of education. Through a storytelling, representing the oral tradition, the old chief Modeste tells Archilde the history of his Indian heritage: how the Salish moved from a position of power to one of subjection, brought down by whites' divide-and-conquer method of land dispossession; and how the church gained a foothold in the valley. For Archilde, who "still remained on the outside little better than a professor who had come to study their curious ways of life," Modeste's history was "the first story about his people that he understood" (193–194).

As the plot unfolds, Archilde reconciles with his father but moves steadily closer to Indianness, as when he sits in his mother's tipi and feels his people "move in his blood" (222), and yet his identification with them is always fleeting and momentary. While McNickle praises resistance in characters such as Catherine, Modeste, and Archilde's little nephews, Mike and Narcisse, who turn their backs on white culture and embrace traditional Indian ways, he never allows it in his protagonist, who remains a figure of assimilation.

In spite of McNickle's skillful presentation of Indian culture and history and his implication of whites for the Indians' current conditions, the message of Archilde's eventual downfall seems to be that involvement in the Indian world leads to a blind alley. The impulsive, and one could also read "uncivilized," behavior of, first, Archilde's mother and, later, his Indian girlfriend, Elise, leads to the tragic end of the novel, when the innocent Archilde holds out his hands, without protest, to be shackled. Arrested for complicity in two murders, the Indian who might have assimilated is taken down by those Indians who will not.

Writing at a time when Indians were both physically and politically powerless, what other future could McNickle have envisioned except eventual assimilation or extinction?

Bibliography

Adams, David Wallace. *Education for Extinction: American Indians and the Boarding School Experience 1875–1928.* Lawrence: University of Kansas Press, 1995.

Nickle, D'Arcy. *The Surrounded.* Albuquerque: University of New Mexico Press, 1997.

Owens, Louis. *Other Destinies: Understanding the American Indian Novel.* Norman: University of Oklahoma Press, 1992.

Rhona Mollard

Tales of Burning Love   Louise Erdrich (1996)

Tales of Burning Love, LOUISE ERDRICH's fifth novel involving characters who live on and around the Little No Horse Reservation in North Dakota, takes place almost entirely off the reservation and revolves around the love life of John James Mauser, known as Jack. On his mother's side Jack is a MIXED-BLOOD Chippewa, whose Indianness is "buried deep." He is a successful contractor, although as the novel begins, debts have begun to mount, largely because of the treachery of one of his former wives, and he has been arrested.

Jack has recently married his fifth wife, Dot Adare Nanapush, whose family dominates the action of *The BEET QUEEN* and whose first husband is Gerry Nanapush, a prominent character in *The BINGO PALACE.* Ultimately in order to escape his mounting debts, Jack fakes his death in a fire. After his funeral four of his five former wives find themselves trapped in a car in a snowstorm, and they tell each other stories of their lives with Jack in order to keep everyone awake and alive. This lengthy section of the book pays a tribute to the oral traditions of tribal culture—without the stories they simply would not have lived, and without stories to hand down from generation to generation, tribal culture would have died as well.

One of the most interesting aspects of *Tales of Burning Love* is its opening. Here we get June Morrissey's story, told in the well-known first chapter of *LOVE MEDICINE,* told from the viewpoint of Jack, who we now learn is the man in the truck that June leaves as she walks off to her death. For faithful readers of Erdrich's novels this is a relevatory scene. That they were "married" in a bar before leaving in the truck, that the man was not just some white barfly picking up an Indian woman, and that he was haunted by June for the rest of his life add depth to all the previous novels and give us more insight into June's character than had been possible earlier.

See also FOUR SOULS; TRACKS.

Bibliography

Beidler, Peter G. and Gay Barton. *A Guide to the Novels of Louise Erdrich.* Columbia: University of Missouri Press, 1999.

Jennifer McClinton-Temple

TallMountain, Mary (1918–1994)

Mary Demoski was born in Nulato, Alaska—a village 100 miles south of the Arctic Circle—to a Koyukon-Athabascan-Russian mother, Mary Joe Demoski, and a Scots-Irish father, Clement Stroupe, then serving in the U.S. Army in Alaska. Debilitated by tuberculosis, her mother allowed Mary to be adopted in 1924 by an Anglo couple who could provide education and health care.

When Mary was 18, her adoptive family moved to California. With her mother's encouragement she read Wordsworth, Keats, the Brontës, and other British authors; recited poetry; and kept a diary.

By 1945 her birth mother, brother, and both adoptive parents were dead, and she had lost contact with Stroupe. While supporting herself as a legal secretary, she slid into ALCOHOLISM. She also suffered bouts of severe illness, which she attributed to grief and anger at being uprooted from her homeland and heritage. "She's always dying," PAULA GUNN ALLEN remarked in a 1990 memoir of TallMountain, "and always keeping on" (foreword, *Light on the Tent Wall* 2). She began writing seriously in the mid-1960s. Writing and naming herself *TallMountain* helped her to rework her sense of herself as a misfit (a mortification dramatized in her poem "Indian Blood") into a reason for living: As an "Inbetween" she could provide a bridge between cultures (Bruchac 21). Her poetry, fiction, and essays have appeared in over 100 periodicals and anthologies, and her collection *There Is No Word for Goodbye* (1980) won the Pushcart Prize.

TallMountain returned to Alaska for the first time in 1976. Thereafter committed to the work of reconnection, she sought out her father, then living in Arizona, and took care of him until he died in 1978. For many years she lived primarily in San Francisco's Tenderloin district (a poor, multicultural neighborhood), where in 1987 she was a founder of a workshop-support group for women writers. A disability pension enabled her to devote herself to writing and to teaching in Alaskan schools and prisons.

TallMountain's poetry reflects her dual heritage and varied experiences. Often incorporating Athabascan vocabulary, she passes on tribal beliefs about the universe as well as her own story. Several lyrics depict long-dead relatives whom the poet recovers by dreaming and remembering. "Seeing" her maternal grandmother rooted in the ancient earth, the speaker of "Matmiya" thanks her ancestor—representative of the life force—for perpetual renewal: "Your spirit remains / Nourished, / Nourishing me" (*Light* 14–16). Human life is understood to be intertwined with the worlds of spirit and nonhuman nature. "A Song for My Mother" unsentimen-

tally envisions a woman who is gutting salmon (a vital source of food and income for indigenous Alaskans), her "hands honor[ing] / the holiness of all things" (*Light* 13–14). The speaker affirms that memories of her strong, competent mother sustained her while she "went the alien ways" (26). "Brother Wolverine" gives voice to a mother who is missing her daughter "so far away"—but protected from cold and forgetfulness by a hand-sewn parka framing her face with the gray ruff of the "fearless" Doyon (wolverine) trapped by the woman herself (*Light* 2, 34). "My Wild Birds Flying" portrays a reunion of Mary Joe, Clem, and their adult daughter.

TallMountain's poet self also observes the urban wilderness, sensing her spirit "familiar" in Chinatown, "Eyes ebony-dark / in a weatherbeaten face" ("My Familiar," *Light* 12–13), and recognizing a fierce leather-jacketed man as a coyote ("Coyote in the Mission," *Listen to the Night*). She notices a "Ghetto Cat," "indomitable eyes aglow / in emerald pride" despite its apparently wretched existence ("The Cat Named Janis Joplin," *Listen* 1, 6–7). Survival requires struggle, and TallMountain admires survivors.

TallMountain acknowledges the vastness of time, nature's regenerative but not inexhaustible powers, and the kinship of all forms of life. Her works protest modern civilization's assaults on rivers, animals, and indigenous peoples. "O Dark Sister" addresses a beached blue whale, surrounded by garbage—"Offal of careless creatures / Who so lately found the sands / Of your millennial home" (*Light* 12–14). Visualizing the great whale's bones "[d]aubed in dayglo green" (29) for display in a museum, the speaker recalls similarly desecrated buffalo and Indian bones. Those, "at least," were eventually buried in "kindly" earth, "[t]heir mother / And ours" (42–45). Her ecological consciousness is evident as well in "Once the Striped Quagga" and "Listen to the Night," poems about the extinction of species, tribes, and languages. "The Last Wolf" re-creates "a spiritual experience" she had in a hospital (Bruchac 20). Seated on a bed "looking west," the speaker senses the wolf approaching through the "ruined city" (*Light* 19, 2). When he looks into her eyes, she expresses their bond of sympathy: "Yes . . . / I know what they have done" (27–28). This vision of nuclear destruction warns that humans' lust for domination jeopardizes life itself.

See also MIXED-BLOOD.

Bibliography

Moyers, Bill. *The Language of Life: A Festival of Poets.* New York: Doubleday, 1995.

TallMountain, Mary. *The Light on the Tent Wall: A Bridging.* Los Angeles: UCLA American Indian Studies Center, 1990.

———. *Listen to the Night: Poems for the Animal Spirits of Mother Earth,* edited by Ben Clarke. San Francisco: Freedom Voices, 1995.

———. *A Quick Brush of Wings.* San Francisco: Freedom Voices, 1991.

"TallMountain Circle." Available online. URL: http://www.freedomvoices.org/tmcindex.htm. Accessed on August 15, 2005.

Welford, Gabrielle. "Mary TallMountain." In *Dictionary of Literary Biography.* Vol. 103, *American Poets since World War II,* 345–353. Sixth Series. N.p.: Gale Group, 1998.

Mary De Jong

Tapahonso, Luci   (1953–)

Luci Tapahonso, Diné (Navajo) poet and storyteller, was born on November 8, 1953, in Shiprock, New Mexico, to Lucille Deschenne Tapahonso (Salt Water Clan) and Eugene Tapahonso, Sr. (Bitter Water Clan). Growing up on the largest reservation in the United States, Tapahonso was raised in the traditional ways of the Navajo people; Diné (Navajo) was her first language. As a child she attended Navajo Methodist Mission school, and she later graduated from Shiprock High School. She then attended the University of New Mexico (UNM); she earned a bachelor's degree in English in 1980 and an M.A. in creative writing in 1983. She then began her academic career there, holding the position of assistant professor of English, women's studies, and American Indian studies. A few years later she became an associate professor at the University of Kansas; more recently she is professor of English at the University of Arizona,

Tucson, where she teaches American Indian studies and English.

Tapahonso began writing poetry as a young girl, and her talents received great encouragement when she studied under the influential and renowned Native writer LESLIE MARMON SILKO at UNM. Tapahonso's first volumes of poetry, *ONE MORE SHIPROCK NIGHT* and *SEASONAL WOMAN,* were both published in 1981; later Tapahonso published *A BREEZE SWEPT THROUGH* (1989), *SÁANII DAHATAAŁ, THE WOMEN ARE SINGING* (1993), and *BLUE HORSES RUSH IN* (1997), all of which received critical acclaim. Written simply, and with clarity and beauty, her poems nonetheless address issues of great importance to her people as they depict a realistic portrayal of Navajo life. Her works reveal a deep sense of connection to traditional Navajo culture and spirituality; this emerges through her themes, which include the strength of Diné women, her love for her family, and the importance of passing on a cultural heritage to the next generation. Tapahonso's writing is highly innovative; her mixture of Navajo and Anglo influences is echoed in her style, which combines English and Diné. Likewise her work defies generic conventions as it incorporates both poetry and prose, stories and prayers.

Bibliography

Brill de Ramirez, Susan Berry. *Contemporary American Indian Literatures and the Oral Tradition.* Tucson: University of Arizona Press, 1999.

Radar, Dean. "Luci Tapahonso and Simon Ortiz: Allegory, Symbol, Language, Poetry." *Southwestern American Literature,* 22, no. 2 (1997): 75–92.

Smith, Patricia Clark, and Paula Gunn Allen. "Earthly Relations, Carnal Knowledge: Southwestern American Indian Women Writers and Landscape." In *The Desert Is No Lady: Southwestern Landscapes in Women's Writing and Art,* edited by Vera Norwood and Janice Monk. New Haven, Conn.: Yale University Press, 1987.

Tapahonso, Luci. "For What It Is: An Interview with Luci Tapahonso." In *Survival This Way: Interviews with American Indian Poets,* edited by Joseph Bruchac. Tucson: University of Arizona Press, 1987.

————. *One More Shiprock Night: Poems.* San Antonio, Tex.: Tejas Art Press, 1981.

————. *Seasonal Woman.* Santa Fe, N. Mex.: Tooth of Time Books, 1982.

————. *A Breeze Swept Through.* Albuquerque, N. Mex.: West End Press, 1989.

————. *Sáanii Dahataał: The Women Are Singing.* Tucson: University of Arizona Press, 1993.

————. *Blue Horses Rush In.* Tucson: University of Arizona Press, 1997.

————. *Songs of Shiprock Fair.* Walnut, Calif.: Kiva Publishing, 1999.

Kristen Girard

Tekonwatonti/Molly Brant: Poems of War   Maurice Kenny (1992)

Using poetry to evoke history, MAURICE KENNY reconstructs the struggle for continental domination in 18th-century North America. Mainly through dramatic monologues, Kenny depicts a two-stage war, first between the French and English, then between colonists and the English Crown. Missing from textbook histories of this era are the voices and perspectives of Indians, an omission Kenny corrects in these *Poems of War.* His entree into this crucible of history is his Mohawk ancestress, Tekonwatonti (She Who Is Outnumbered), known to the English as Molly Brant, a woman as important to her century as Pocahontas and Sacagewea were to theirs. Natives of the continent, caught in the middle of a European war, were recruited by French, British, and colonists alike. Gambling on an English victory against the colonists encroaching on Mohawk territory, Molly Brant led Mohawk warriors against the revolutionaries. In truth, Kenny has Molly assert, she "didn't give a damn for the British nor the French" (168). She fought because she loved "this earth and [her] kin" more than she hated "battles and bravery." Who would not, she asks, "defend her mother's womb?" (145).

Molly is not only Kenny's proud ancestress, but also the requital for a Native woman wronged a century before. In an early poem in the volume, "New Amsterdam, 1652," an Indian woman, whose hunger "demanded retribution," reaches for a peach and is shot dead by a Dutch farmer. Though the Dutch "chose not to record" her name, Kenny records the act that triggered decades of war between groups claiming rights to the continent (30). In one of the later sections of the work Kenny lets this woman speak. Largely because Molly Brant has defended their heritage, this woman can proclaim, "I have come a long way . . . call me woman" (175).

Amid the cross-currents of racial and political strife, Kenny's history spotlights a peaceful alternative: intermarriage. Molly and her British husband, Sir William Johnson, along with their eight children, are dedicated to a future together. Though whites deem Molly a witch and Johnson mad and vile for loving her, the two successfully blend cultures. Molly, repulsed by "fat" whites, swampy streets of mud, and "bearded men with pinched noses," nonetheless moves into her husband's village (66). William, "an adopted Iroquois, a true Mohawk," not only "speaks the language as fluently . . . as any chief," but has no qualms about "dancing / naked near a blazing fire" (82–83). When Johnson dies, Molly fights for him and their children, as well as for her Mohawk kin. When the British lose, she is forced to flee her native New York for Canada, reduced to a political refugee, and until now, merely a footnote in history. Through Kenny's poetic evocation, Molly and her era pulse with life.

Bibliography

Barron, Patrick. "Maurice Kenny's Tekonwatonti, Molly Brant: Poetic Memory and History." *MELUS* 25, no. 3–4 (2000): 31–64.

Womack, Craig S. "The Spirit of Independence: Maurice Kenny's *Tekonwatonti/Molly Brant: Poems of War.*" *American Indian Culture and Research Journal* 18, no. 1 (winter 1994): 95–118.

Margaret O'Shaughnessey

Ten Little Indians   Sherman Alexie (2003)

All of SHERMAN ALEXIE's works push insistently against stereotypes about Native North Americans, and his third short story collection, *Ten Little Indians,* breaks new ground in this area. Most of the characters are Indians who long ago left the reservation or who never lived there, and all insist in one way or another that "Indians are every bit as relentlessly boring, selfish, and smelly as" white people (11).

Alexie's universalization of Indian experience does not, however, contradict the humor with which he challenges stereotypes, either positive or negative. One character contemplates what it is "about Indians that turns otherwise intelligent, interesting, and capable people into blithering idiots" (139), while another concludes that cultural ignorance and laziness are to blame for continuing racism against Indians. William, the main character in "Flight Patterns," relates how after the September 11, 2001, attacks on the United States someone yelled at him, "Go back to your own country!" William asserts that this verbal attack "wasn't so much a hate crime as it was a crime of irony, right? And I was laughing so hard, the truck was halfway down the block before I could get breath enough to yell back, 'You first!'" (117).

While Alexie humorously addresses Indian stereotypes and racism, he never minimizes the seriousness of their persistence. Discussing the terrible irony of Indians' and other minorities' joining the military, in which "brown people are killing other brown people so white people will remain free" (179), Alexie highlights how Indians only become visible to whites when they appear to be stoics "who rarely spoke" (11) or "shamanic geniuses" (139). Characters like Corliss and Estelle use white people's notions about Indians to their advantage; others, like the Spokane poet Harlan Atwater, sadly note that while being Indian is "easy to fake" (40), what being Indian really means remains ambiguous.

Alexie uses Indians' identity confusion to highlight their complicated positions in North America. Yet, he also uses it to point out that the stereotypes that contribute to such misunderstanding arise in part from white people's own identity crises. *Ten Little Indians* challenges stereotypes about American Indians without reinforcing stereotypes about white North Americans, arguing that regardless of race or class, everyone is in this together. While this is a politically complex work, it is also Alexie's

most hopeful. In spite of the roadblocks 21st-century Indians face, he portrays the homeless man Jackson Jackson unironically exclaiming, "Do you know how many good men live in this world? Too many to count!" (194).

Bibliography

Alexie, Sherman. *Ten Little Indians.* New York: Grove Press, 2003.

"Alexie's Ordinary Indians." Available online. URL: http://www.ammsa.com/bookreviews/rareintellect-july- 2003.html#anchor6082053. Accessed on August 15, 2005.

Wyrick, Katherine H. "Crossing Cultures: Sherman Alexie Explores the Sacred and the Profane." Available online. URL: http://www.bookpage.com/0306bp/sherman_alexie.html. Accessed on August 15, 2005.

Colleen Shea

Termination

Termination is the word used to describe the driving force of U.S. federal policy toward Native Americans in the 1950s. Conservative U.S. congressmen wanted to "emancipate the Indians" by ending all federal ties with the tribes. A bill adopted in 1953 led to the effective termination of several tribes, such as the Klamath and the Menominee. The bill called for removal of federal protected trust status of Indian lands, the dissolution of tribal governments, and the distribution of tribal assets among the members. The goal was to transform Indians into "good citizens" through ASSIMILATION.

Termination, in fact, proved to be a disaster for these tribes and accelerated the decline of traditional practices by destroying the very notions of tribal territory and thus of Indian community. Schools and hospitals had to be closed because of the disappearance of federal funds. Realizing that it meant the end of reservations, many tribes fought back and lobbied Congress to stop this policy. Termination was finally abandoned in the 1960s. While some tribes did manage to reverse the process and reclaim their lands, some remain unrecognized by the federal government.

Literary sources concerning the Termination policy are relatively scarce. One of the most meaningful is *Autumn's Bounty* by Chief George Pierre. The story takes place in the Cascade Mountains of Washington State. The main character, Alphonse, an Okanogan in his 80s, chief of his people for the last 50 years, was once a great hunter. But his influence is declining at a crucial time. The termination of the reservation is discussed by the tribal people and divides the community. Because he opposed Termination, Alphonse is seen by the younger generation as well as by his own family as an old man stuck in the past and challenged in his chieftainship and hunting abilities. He finally decides to track down a cougar in the mountains to prove his people wrong and regain confidence in himself.

This highly metaphorical expedition, ultimately successful, highlights the difficulty of the path Alphonse is on to keep the tradition alive. As a tradition deeply attached to the territory, his successful journey through these lands magnifies the old ways and the memory of his people. Meanwhile the tribe is deciding whether to accept the Termination money and abandon the land or not. The arguments of the elders will finally prevail and, as the hunt is a success, the termination is pushed back.

A clear but subtle antitermination message is present throughout JAMES WELCH's *WINTER IN THE BLOOD*. Although the author was himself a teenager during this period, Charles Larson's analysis of the text reveals the trauma caused by the fear of termination. While in the off-reservation town of Havre, the narrator/main character of the novel feels lost, out of place, in a location where no Indian life could comfort him. Yet every time he goes back from this town to the reservation he rediscovers a place of comfort, of fulfillment, where he will ultimately find a little more of himself. But if the reservation had been terminated the narrator would not have been able to look back at his past (the death of his brother), accept it, and thus gain maturity. The special sense of belonging he is looking for is found in the land of his people.

For the younger generation of Indian writers, who never experienced the Termination era, the reservation is a given. SHERMAN ALEXIE's writing, for example, is very often centered around the reservation life. On one hand, it reveals a contemporary Native life that bears harsh memories of violence, ALCOHOLISM, poverty, or racism. But at the same time it provides a poignant image of the reservation community for every generation. There is no idealization here, just a powerful description: There is a life off the reservation, but there is no real life without it.

If all Indian reservations had been terminated, how would the Indian writers define themselves as Indians today?

Bibliography

Alexie, Sherman. *The Lone Ranger and Tonto Fistfight in Heaven.* New York: Harper Perennial, 1994.

———. *Old Shirts and New Skins.* Los Angeles: University of California Press, 1996.

———. *Reservation Blues.* New York: Warner Books, 1996.

Larson, Charles S. *American Indian Fiction.* Albuquerque: University of New Mexico Press, 1978.

Pierre, Chief George. *Autumn's Bounty.* San Antonio, Tex.: Naylor, 1972.

Welch, James. *Winter in the Blood.* New York: Harper & Row, 1974.

Matthieu Charle

There Is No Word for Goodbye   Mary TallMountain (1980)

There Is No Word for Goodbye was first published as a special issue of *Blue Cloud Quarterly* in 1980. Most of the poems in this chapbook appear in *The Light on the Tent Wall,* published in 1990. The collection works to reconcile the many voices in MARY TALLMOUNTAIN's psyche: Anglo/Native American; Indian spiritualist/Franciscan; citizen of the Yukon/inhabitant of the Tenderloin district of San Francisco. In many of her poems TallMountain is searching for who she is and her place in the world.

One poem from the chapbook, "Indian Blood," was awarded a Pushcart Prize in 1981. In the poem TallMountain presents the image of a small child dressed in her Native costume, placed on display at a school assembly. The other children are rudely curious. TallMountain has said in interviews that she is the child in the poem. The vast alienation she felt being removed from her tribal village in Nulato, Alaska, on the banks of the Yukon River created a deep and scarring chasm that she attempts to bridge in her poetry.

TallMountain incorporates words from the Koyukon dialect as they help her translate her mixture of Native American and Anglo experiences for the reader. Her aim is to offer non-Native Americans a glimpse into the world of her Native experience, to combat the often objectifying relationship Anglos have to anything Indian. In "Good Grease," one of her best-known poems, TallMountain relays the joys of good cooked caribou that has been taken home to hungry villagers. The stereotype of Indians circling around a fire feasting on what the hunters have taken home is undercut by the universal humanity of people gathering to eat good food. The grease "was beautiful— / oozing, / dripping and running down our chins" (5–7).

Mary TallMountain was a fighter and her poetry reflects her refusal to give up on herself or those around her. Returning to Alaska after a decades-long absence, she reunites with her ancestors and the spirits of those who have gone before. "Figure in Clay" is dedicated to her grandmother and to all the women who ride her "platelets / like plasma" (4–5). She receives the strength of those women who preceded her and sees her place in the chain that joins past to present to future: from the spiritual world to the everyday one. As she found herself, TallMountain found her creativity. She may have left Nulato without saying good-bye, but she never forgot her early years among the Athabascan people, and in her poetry she keeps those early years alive and turns them into poetry.

Bibliography

Welford, Gabrielle. "Reflections on Mary TallMountain's Life and Writing: Facing Mirrors." *SAIL: Studies in American Indian Literature* 9 (summer 1997): 61–68.

P. K. Bostian

Thirteen Moons on Turtle's Back
Joseph Bruchac (1992)

Thirteen Moons on Turtle's Back (1992) represents yet another of JOSEPH BRUCHAC's prodigious creations for children. In fact, he dedicates this book to "the children of Turtle Island"—an inclusive gesture that also redefines children in terms of a Native American cosmology. This cosmology also defines this collection of poems as it embraces numerous distinct tribal perspectives and emphasizes their shared spaces within Native American worlds. This structure also manifests itself in the 13 featured poems, which in turn correspond to the 13 months that constitute the lunar calendar traditional among most Native American tribes, as he explains in his endnote. Drawing on this cosmology, Bruchac also invokes several themes central to Native American culture as he crafts this collection of poems.

To begin this task, he introduces readers to an Abenaki grandfather and grandson. While the grandfather is carving the turtle that will serve as the explanatory vehicle within the plot and for readers, he is also observing his grandson's patience. His compliments on the boy's virtue highlight traditional Native values as well as signal contemporary readers that they too should be as patient and observant as the grandson. The grandfather then explains the significance of the turtle that he is carving: The 13 scales on Old Turtle's back correspond to the 13 lunar months. The grandfather also contrasts the Abenaki, who remember this correspondence, with those "people who do not know this." He also explains how this knowledge is a legacy of traditional oral practice within Abenaki culture. When asked whether other tribes share this perspective, the grandfather then begins to recount the 13 moons, each representative of a different tribe.

Having established this structuring device, Bruchac then introduces each month's poem and ends by identifying the tribal origin of his poem. Through each poem readers learn about core values shared by Native American tribes. For example, "Baby Bear Moon" reinforces the commonality of human and nonhuman animals; in the process readers learn about Potawatomi culture. Similarly, he introduces Cherokee myth and the shared values of commonality in "Moon of Falling Leaves" when he ends the poem with the image of leaves and people on a journey that is "part of that great circle / which holds us all close to the earth." (7) Other poems reinforce similar perspectives profiled in "Moon When Wolves Run Together," which ends by claiming that "our lives / and songs are stronger / when we are together" (13–14).

Bruchac ends his collection with two significant gestures. First, he ends his poem cycle with "Big Moon," a poem that returns readers to Abenaki culture and the initial structuring device of the grandfather-narrator. Next, he includes an endnote that explains the rationale behind his collection's agenda and reinforces the idea that while Native American tribes traditionally had a variety of temporal schemes, they all shared the values that he has promoted in this collection. His final sentence informs this purpose as well as Bruchac's larger agenda, to celebrate "the beautiful world around us," which "must be listened to and respected."

Bibliography

Bruchac, Joseph. *Thirteen Moons on Turtle's Back: A Native American Year of Moons.* New York: Philomel Books, 1992.

Clay Smith

This Is the World   W. S. Penn (2000)

Feelings of estrangement pervade W. S. PENN's short-story collection *This Is the World.* Penn gravitates toward characters who are at odds with mainstream American culture yet insistent upon forging their own path. These characters may be self-aware, but that self-awareness does not always provide them the means of avoiding disaster.

Fewer than half of the collection's 15 stories explicitly involve characters of American Indian ancestry. Sometimes that ancestry is central, as in the title piece, in which the revelation of the protagonist's ethnicity puts an end to his friendships with white coworkers. But in other instances, such as in "Fog," the fact that the lead character's grandparents are buried in the Nez Perce reservation in Lapwai is of only minor importance compared to his tortured romantic preoccupations.

Penn describes himself as "an urban mixblood Nez Perce," and his stories often reflect the perspective of characters whose identity is less than assured as they straddle different class and ethnic positions. The struggle to find a place of belonging animates much of this collection.

The most successful stories present characters who are easy to sympathize with when their lives spin out of control. In "Tarantulas" the protagonist is a postal employee who becomes obsessed with an exchange of postcards he is supposed to be sorting. Over time he begins to copy and even revise letters. When he is caught, his world begins to unravel. "As I look out the window and wonder how guilty I am, and of what, really, I can see against the faraway sky the dark lines which tell me that what they call my crime is delicate and dark and can only be judged—judged truly in detail—against a yellow New Mexico moon" (20). His inability to stop (or to feel guilty when caught) speaks in many ways to the state of a writer fictionalizing the world around him.

"Early Age and Late Disorder" features Merrill, an Onondaga who works as an accountant and is married to a white woman. From the outside he would appear to be successful and wholly assimilated. Yet, Merrill is on the edge of a nervous breakdown. At work he is reluctant to cook the books for an important client. At home his marriage is collapsing under the weight of mutual infidelity. But what haunts Merrill is the image of his Onondaga mother's decline into insanity, a fate he has desperately tried to avoid. When Merrill decides at the end of the story to try to save both his job and his marriage, readers are sympathetic if not quite hopeful for him.

When Penn's stories are not as successful it is because his characters' introspection has turned into self-absorption. When the personal life of the protagonist in "Star Lake, Long Ago" begins to collapse, it is hard not to feel his fate has been deserved, as he has proved to be a selfish and unsympathetic character.

Penn's reputation is built more upon his work as an essayist than as a short story writer, but this collection remains an intriguing investigation into questions of identity in an unstable world.

Bibliography

Penn, W. S. *This Is the World.* East Lansing: Michigan State University Press, 2000.

Jim O'Loughlin

Through the Eye of the Deer: An Anthology of Native American Women Writers   Carolyn Dunn and Carol Comfort (1999)

Unlike many Native American anthologies that are limited to contemporary writers, *Through the Eye of the Deer* acknowledges the long tradition of Native women's voices by including the early authors ELLA CARA DELORIA and MOURNING DOVE. The collection also offers such well-known writers as LESLIE MARMON SILKO, LOUISE ERDRICH, BETH BRANT, and PAULA GUNN ALLEN as well as up-and-coming authors such as Deborah Miranda and KATERI AKIWENZIE-DAMM. The collection is divided into four sections: Stories of Birth and Creation, Women's Rites of Passage, Women's Rituals, and Women's Mysteries.

Whether retelling origin stories of Coyote and Spider Woman or reimagining such stories in the context of a bar, a national park, or a car accident, this anthology places the traditional in a modern setting. In Suzanne Rancourt's poem "From the Sacred Stones of Coyote," the image of "cobwebby fibers of agelessness, / inked with blueberry, scented with sage" conjures up past and present, the abstract and the material (11–12). In the usual Coyote way this wily figure slips out of any one category: Coyote "needs no tickets" and indeed occupies his (or her) own stanza (16). Through Coyote's eyes we momentarily escape.

> Hold tight the ticket stubs, your proof of entrance,
> your only way back to the place you belong.
> Hold tight (lines 30–32)

Even the assumed confines of death are regularly challenged in this anthology; Lela Northcross Wakely describes it as nothing more than change (13). In turn birth is not an altogether new state but an awakening.

As the title suggests, deer—"the ancestors who never left" (Harjo 31)—figure prominently. A young buck disappears after encountering the narrator's fender, leaving the driver to think of her own son "passing / through this world's happenstance" (Hill 42–43). The snake also assumes multiple forms; in perhaps the most powerful incarnation, it is the tiny dart that escapes the stomach of a dying predator: "It leaves a winding, thin path in the road dust. Maybe it is writing a story of survival there on the road" (Hogan 236). This image of survival, followed by Paula Gunn Allen's testament to the "real Hollywood Indian" leaves the reader with a sense of rebirth—or awakening.

Through the Eye of the Deer is published by Aunt Lute, a feminist nonprofit publisher. Aunt Lute's mission corresponds well with the editors' wish to "redress the silence" (xiii). The book's influence on the field of Native American literature is evident in its appearance on a number of course syllabi.

Bibliography

Moore, MariJo. "*Outfoxing Coyote*, by Carolyn Dunn." *SAIL Studies in American Indian Literatures* 14, no. 4 (2002): 72–75.

Steinberg, Sybil. "*Through the Eye of the Deer: An Anthology of Native American Women Writers.*" *Publishers Weekly* 246, no. 51 (December 1999): 56.

Cari Carpenter

Tohe, Laura (1952–)

Laura Tohe was born in Fort Defiance, Arizona, in 1952 to Laura Florence and Benson Tohe. She is a member of the Navajo (Diné) tribe and was raised on the Navajo reservation in Arizona and New Mexico. While living on the reservation, she learned how to read and write in her native Navajo language, Dine. After attending Indian BOARDING SCHOOLS and public schools, Tohe attended the University of New Mexico, where she obtained a

B.A. in psychology in 1975. While enrolled in the university she took a fiction writing class with the author Rudolpho Anaya and discovered her interest in writing. Tohe then turned to writing of her experiences of living on the Navajo reservation and the oral storytelling tradition she learned from her grandmother, a former Navajo teacher on the reservation, and her father, a member of the celebrated Code Talkers, Navajo soldiers who used Dine words in codes to help the U.S. military send messages in World War II.

While developing her creative writing, Tohe earned her M.A. in English at the University of Nebraska in 1985. In the following year her first collection of poems, *Making Friends with Water: Poems,* was published. She received critical praise for her portrayal of Navajo women and community and several of her poems were published in notable journals, such as *Calyx* and *Callaloo.* Tohe then went on to earn a Ph.D. in English at the University of Nebraska in 1993 and work at Arizona State University, where she is employed as an associate professor in the English Department.

Tohe's second compilation of work, *No Parole Today,* is composed of prose and poetry and takes its title from her doctoral dissertation. Critics took notice of Tohe's lucid style and the incorporation of the significance of her Native language in the poem "Our Tongues Slapped in Silence," in which she describes her boarding school experience of not being allowed to speak Dine. This authentic depiction of the issues facing Native Americans helped garner Tohe the Poetry of the Year Award from the Wordcraft Circle of Native Writers and Storytellers in 2000 and a nomination for a [Push Cart] Award in 2003.

Tohe has engaged in several literary projects, such as coediting *Sister Nations: Native American Women Writers on Community* with Heidi E. Erdich and completing another collection of poetry and prose titled *Tseyi': The Birth of Red in Canyon de Chelly.* She continues to read at numerous literary events and write reflections of Navajo life in poetry, short stories, and essays.

Bibliography

Harjo, Joy, and Gloria Bird, eds. *Reinventing the Enemy's Language: Contemporary Native Women's Writing of North America.* New York: Norton, 1997.

Ray, Matthew. "Clearing Paths: An Interview with Laura Tohe." *Thin Air* 6, no. 2 (2001): 42–52.

Tohe, Laura. *Making Friends with Water: Poems.* Omaha, Nebr.: Nosila Press, 1986.

———. *No Parole Today.* Albuquerque, N. Mex.: West End Press, 1999.

———. *Sister Nations: Native American Women Writers on Community.* St. Paul, Minn.: Historical Society Press, 2002.

———. *Tseyi: The Birth of Red in Canyon de Chelly.* Tucson: University of Arizona Press, 2005.

Dorsia Smith

Tortured Skins   Maurice Kenny   (2000)

Although most of the critical acclaim he has received is for his poetry, Maurice Kenny is also an accomplished writer of fiction, generally shorter pieces. *Tortured Skins* is a collection of 14 such works—12 narratives and two brief dramatic scenes—most of which date from the 1990s. The stories illustrate Kenny's diverse authorial tones as well as his wide range of fictionalizing techniques. The formal and stylistic variety of the tales does not, however, prevent this volume from being thematically united, and ultimately it is a meditation on the uneasy and often forcible mixture of traditional Indian values with those of white America.

The volume opens with an impressionistic historical fiction (Kenny subtitles it as a "documentary fiction") entitled "Black Kettle: Fear and Recourse," which recounts the last days of the Cheyenne chief Black Kettle, including his unsuccessful journey to Fort Cobb, Kansas, seeking protection prior to the battle of Washita, in which he died. Kenny returns to the figure of Black Kettle again in the dramatic piece "Forked Tongues," which closes the collection. Kenny sets the time for "Forked Tongues" as the "[l]ate 1860s, or any time" (208), but the Sand Creek Massacre of 1864 is clearly the historical context for a surrealistic tribunal involving Black Kettle, Colonel John Chivington, a dead "half-breed" named Jack Smith who speaks the opening lines of the drama, and a "Man in White" who functions both as a judge and as an intrusive stage director.

Many of the other works in the collection are set in a more contemporary time and place, most often upstate New York, which is both Kenny's ancestral Mohawk home and his residence at the time these stories were written. "Blue Jacket" and "Visitation" each involve seemingly supernatural incursions of Indian characters into the everyday world, a trope Kenny also employs in the story "The Girl on the Beach," which is set at a Pacific coast resort. These stories are contrasted by the probing and often disturbing psychological realism of "Ohkwa: Ri," "Tortured Skins," and "One More," all of which use the interrelationships among bears, whites, and Indians as their central theme. A fourth story, "Bacon," depicts these relationships from the narrative perspective of the bears themselves. Finally "Salmon," "She-Who-Speaks-With-Bear," and "What's in a Song?" intentionally leave the reader with an ambiguous impression as to the relation between the physical and metaphysical realms of nature, albeit with comic, tragic, and lyrical overtones, respectively.

Bibliography

Bruchac, Joseph. "Our Own Pasts: An Interview with Maurice Kenny." In *Survival This Way: Interviews with American Indian Poets,* edited by Joseph Bruchac, 22–30. Tucson: University of Arizona Press, 1987.

Kenny, Maurice. "Introduction: A Memoir." In *On Second Thought: A Compilation of Work*, 2–15. Norman: University of Oklahoma Press, 1995.

———. *Tortured Skins and Other Fictions.* East Lansing: Michigan State University Press, 2000.

Wilson, Michael D. "Maurice Kenny." In *The Dictionary of Literary Biography.* Vol. 175, *Native American Writers of the United States,* edited by Kenneth M. Roemer, 137–142. Detroit: Gale, 1997.

Derek Maus

Touchwood: A Collection of Ojibway Prose Gerald Vizenor (1987)

Touchwood: A Collection of Ojibway Prose is an anthology of works by Ojibway (alternately called Chippewa or Anishinabe) authors edited by the critic, novelist, and poet GERALD VIZENOR. The purpose of the collection, as Vizenor writes in the introduction, is "to report the humor and solemn experience of the Ojibway," a people who claim "more published writers than any other tribe on this continent" (v). The authors and works included span the last two centuries and represent various genres: the 19th-century historians William Warren and George Copway, the memoirist John Rogers, and the contemporary authors LOUISE ERDRICH, VIZENOR, JIM NORTHRUP, and Bonnie Wallace. The artwork used in the collection is taken from Ojibway sacred scrolls and the Ojibway painter David Bradley. Since Ojibway did not become a written language until the 20th century, all of the excerpts included in the collection were originally written in English.

Warren's excerpt is from his *History of the Ojibway Nation* written in the 1850s but first published in 1885. A MIXED-BLOOD Ojibway born on Madeline Island, Wisconsin, Warren based his work on the oral tradition of the tribe's migration from the Atlantic coast westward to the south shore of Lake Superior, first contact with European traders and missionaries, and conflicts with other tribes in Wisconsin and Minnesota. The two excerpts from Copway, an Ojibway from Ontario, Canada, are from his memoir *The Life, History, and Travels of Kahgegabahbowh* (1847) and his history *The Traditional History and Characteristic Sketches of the Ojibway Nation* (1850). The former concentrates on Copway's conversion to Christianity as an adolescent; the latter describes the way of life, customs, language, and legends of the Ojibway.

The excerpt from Rogers serves as a "transition between the first published tribal historians and modern prose writers" (vi). Born on the White Earth Reservation in Minnesota in 1890, Rogers attended federal BOARDING SCHOOLS as a child, and these memories serve as the basis of his memoir

Red World and White (written 1957; published 1973). The excerpt recounts his first visit home from the Flanreau school, giving details of the life of Ojibway Indians on his reservation.

Erdrich, a member of the Turtle Mountain Band of Chippewa in North Dakota, is a novelist and the most famous Ojibway writer. Her excerpt, "Lipsha Morrissey," is from her debut novel, *Love Medicine* (1984). Vizenor, a member of the White Earth band of Ojibway, includes two of his historical essays: The first, "Shadow at La Pointe," tells of life in 19th-century Madeline Island; the second, "Laurel Hole in the Day," recounts the experience of one contemporary urban family. The excerpts from Northrup are a series of humorous short stories recounting the experiences of the fictional character Luke Warmwater—as Northrup does, Luke lives on the Fond du Lac reservation in Minnesota and served in Vietnam. Last Wallace, also a member of the Fond du Lac reservation, is represented by the humorous short story "M.A.Y.B.E."

Bibliography

Vizenor, Gerald, ed. *Touchwood: A Collection of Ojibway Prose.* Minneapolis: New Rivers Press, 1987.

Troy Bassett

Toughest Indian in the World, The
Sherman Alexie (2000)

The Toughest Indian in the World continues Sherman Alexie's tradition of offering readers an unabashedly honest look at contemporary Native American culture. What sets this collection apart is that these stories are dominated by protagonists who have found some amount of success. Most have graduated from college and work at respectable jobs. Instead of dealing with alcohol abuse, as in Alexie's previous collection, these characters grapple with relationship and identity issues. In nearly every story characters have doubts about their romantic relationships and question the meaning and feasibility of love, most notably in "South by Southwest." Some characters are unfaithful to their partners, others cross sexual boundaries, and many are unfulfilled in their re-

lationships. Only in "Saint Junior" does Alexie tell the story of an Indian couple who have a healthy and loving relationship.

Simultaneously Alexie's characters struggle to define what it means to be Indian, the theme of the final story, "One Good Man." This question often manifests itself in numerous interracial relationships, effectively linking the themes of identity and love. The main characters in both "Assimilation" and "Class" seek out sexual encounters with other Indians after previously having sex only with white partners. Similarly many of these characters try to fulfill expectations about what it means to be Indian by littering their dialogue with Indian language or colloquialisms and by going to places that they perceive as Indian, all the while admitting that these actions are merely superficial attempts to belong. At times this question leads to confrontation: In "Indian Country" Indian parents disapprove of their daughter's homosexual relationship with a white woman, while in "Class," an upwardly mobile Indian lawyer starts a fight with someone he sees as a regular Indian, something he is not. This question is also addressed through the actions of the characters, one of whom only picks up Indian hitchhikers and another who accepts his son's white stepfather despite continuing to love his former wife.

Complicating this question about Indian identity is Alexie's use of characters who do not usually engage in stereotypical behavior but rather demonstrate an awareness about such stereotypes as well as a desire to avoid them. Some stories challenge the notion that Indians are not smart or successful by featuring Indian characters who have perfect Scholastic Aptitude Test (SAT) scores or write best sellers; other stories show Indian characters desperate to embrace their stereotypical inner warrior. "Dear John Wayne" makes light of anthropologists who lack a real understanding of their subject, thus demonstrating the pervasiveness of ethnic stereotypes. In contrast, "The Sin Eaters," an apocalyptic story that imagines a contemporary incarceration of all tribal people, asserts a grave correlation between Native American identity and the government's brutal treatment of the American Indian.

Bibliography

"Special Issue: Sherman Alexie." *Studies in American Indian Literatures: The Journal of the Association for the Study of American Indian.* 9, no. 4 (winter 1997).

Whittemore, Katharine. "*The Toughest Indian in the World.*" Salon. Available online. URL: http://dir.salon.com/books/review/2000/06/05/alexie/index.html. Accessed on August 15, 2005.

Molly McCaffrey

Tracks   Louise Erdrich (1988)

LOUISE ERDRICH's third novel, *Tracks,* is a sort of prequel to her first novel, LOVE MEDICINE. It concerns the Kashpaw/Pillager family from 1912 to 1924. Although the events portrayed take place before the events in *Love Medicine, Tracks* is one of Erdrich's earliest works in terms of initial composition; she began working on it as a graduate student at Johns Hopkins University.

Tracks depicts the reservation as the first changes wrought by the incursions of the whites are taking place. A tuberculosis epidemic is decimating the Chippewa, and the DAWES ACT is costing many tribal members their land. The novel never mentions Dawes by name, but the act is the root cause of many of the difficulties that characters face in *Tracks.* Indians were often unable to pay taxes on their allotments and had to forfeit their land to the government, which sold it to whites. That is the case with Fleur Pillager, the primary female character, who loses her land at the end of the novel.

Not all of the Indians in *Tracks* suffer because of Dawes; MIXED-BLOODS such as the Morrisseys and the Lazarres benefit from the difficulties that full-bloods such as Nector Kashpaw and Fleur Pillager have with tax laws and acquire enough land to have prosperous farms; eventually the Morrisseys themselves fall on hard times, decline into paupers, and are considered white trash by the full-bloods.

The reservation as Erdrich depicts it is the site of a battle between those who wish to preserve their culture and those who wish to assimilate with white culture. The old man Nanapush is clearly one of the full-bloods, as are Margaret Rushes Bear and her sons, Eli and Nector Kashpaw, and Fleur Pil-

lager and her daughter, Lulu. Pauline Puyat, who will become Sister Leopolda in *Love Medicine,* is mixed-blood, as are the Morrisseys and Lazarres.

The narrators of *Tracks* are Nanapush, who tells the story to Lulu Pillager, and Pauline Puyat, who is addressing the reader directly. In a highly perceptive article about *Tracks* Susan Stanford Friedman talks about the war between Nanapush and Pauline based on their conflicting values.

> As an expression of identity politics, the novel overtly sets up a contrast between Nanapush as the reliable narrator who retains his Anishinabe religion and the unreliable narrator, the convert Pauline whose selfhatred takes the form of a denial of her Indian heritage and the adoption of a self destructive Catholicism. (108)

Even the old man's name, *Nanapush,* is reminiscent of the Anishinabe TRICKSTER FIGURE Nanabozho, while Pauline's name suggests the biblical Paul of Tarsus. As Friedman says, "Like Paul her conversion involves a repudiation of her prior identity—his as Saul, the Jew; hers, as Chippewa." (114) The most surprising thing we learn about Pauline, however, is that she is the mother of Marie Lazarre, the girl with whom she has a brutal battle in the "Saint Marie" episode of *Love Medicine.* Before taking her vows Pauline has an affair with Napoleon Morrissey. She tries to abort the fetus, but, failing, gives birth to Marie, whom she leaves with the Lazarre family. Pauline later kills Napoleon, apparently thinking he is the devil.

As Erdrich fills in Pauline/Leopolda's early life, it is clear that the sadism the nun displays in *Love Medicine* is an outgrowth of the masochism she reveals in *Tracks.* Enamored of martyr saints like Cecelia, who was beheaded, and St. John of the Cross, "half-devoured by his own lice" (152), Leopolda puts burrs in the armpits of her dress and nettles in her neckband. She wears her shoes on the wrong feet and lets her toenails grow until walking hurts and postpones urination for hours.

Erdrich has constructed the novel so that the reader is far more sympathetic to the droll trickster Nanapush than to the forbidding Pauline, whose masochistic practices offend even her mother superior. Nanapush the full-blood may be far more sympathetic than the mixed-blood Pauline, but Erdrich herself is mixed-blood, and it is far too simplistic to read *Tracks* solely in essentialist terms by which full-blood Indian is good and mixed-blood or white is evil.

See also ASSIMILATION; *The Beet Queen; The Bingo Palace; Four Souls; The Last Report of the Miracles at Little No Horse;* SPIRITUALITY; *Tales of Burning Love.*

Bibliography

Friedman, Susan Stanford. "Identity Politics, Syncretism, Catholicism, and Anishinabe Religion in Louise Erdrich's *Tracks." Religion and Literature* 26, no. 1 (1994): 107–134.

Jennifer McClinton-Temple

Trail of Tears

While many Native American groups experienced forced relocation, the term *Trail of Tears* most often refers to the U.S. government's relocation of the Cherokee Indians. Ratification of the first treaty between the U.S. government and the Cherokee that provided for provisional relocation took place in 1817. This treaty allowed the Cherokee to exchange their land in the Southeast for land in the territories west of the Mississippi and promised assistance in relocation efforts, but few Cherokee participated in the plan. In 1836 the Treaty of New Echota was ratified, giving the Cherokee two years to migrate to lands west of the Mississippi. The treaty stated that if the Cherokee had not moved in the two years, they would face forced REMOVAL. At the end of the two years only 2,000 of the 16,000 Cherokee had moved. In 1838 the government sent militia and volunteers to remove the remaining Cherokee. Soldiers forced them away at gunpoint, giving them no time to pack their belongings.

The actual journey to the West visited more horrors upon the Native Americans who faced removal. Although there is no official record of the number of deaths during the Trail of Tears, four of the FIVE CIVILIZED TRIBES sustained staggering losses. The Choctaw lost approximately 15 percent of their population. The Chickasaw saw relatively few deaths, while the mortality rate among both the Creek and the Seminole was roughly 50 percent. Recent scholars have accepted the estimate of 4,000 to 5,000 deaths, or 25 percent of the population, among Cherokee. These deaths occurred in roundup, in stockades prior to removal, during the journey itself, and in the first year in Indian Territory. The casualties were the result of illnesses and diseases such as colds, influenza, measles, diarrhea, fevers, dysentery, whooping cough, and cholera and accidents, exposure, starvation, and soldiers' gunfire.

Treatment of the Trail of Tears in Native American literature, as well as American literature as a whole, is pervasive. Numerous novels, including Barbara Kingsolver's *The Bean Trees* (1988), incorporate characters descended from those forced along the trail, while others like ROBERT J. CONLEY's *Mountain Windsong* (1992) and DIANE GLANCY's *Pushing the Bear* (1996) center on the Trail of Tears. Still more essays, poems, and short stories treat the subject.

Taylor Greer, the main protagonist of Kingsolver's *The Bean Trees,* is descended from a man too old to be forced on the trail. While this is not a major factor in the novel's action, it helps to shape Taylor's character. An earlier writer, Jeremiah Evarts, wrote and spoke against the government's desire to remove the Cherokee. His "William Penn" essays, included in *Cherokee Removal: The "William Penn" Essays and Other Writings* (1981), sympathize with the Cherokee and side with them against the government.

Conley's *Mountain Windsong* and Glancy's *Pushing the Bear* carry the subtitle *A Novel of the Trail of Tears.* Conley's novel purposefully features mixed cultural messages, illustrating the confusion of the trail. It features Oconeechee, the daughter of an Oconeechee mother, and thus not considered a traditional member of the Cherokee; Waguli from the most traditional part of the Cherokee Nation; and Gun Rod, an ally who endures a quest to save Waguli. These three characters provide the system of patterns through which the reader views community. Juxtaposing Cherokee and Oconeechee patterns of thought with the Western European sense of cause and effect forces the reader to question truth and reality and to confront the complexity and horror the Cherokee experienced. Told by its large cast of characters, Glancy's *Pushing the Bear* is a historical novel that focuses on a single family along the trail. The main protagonist, Maritole, becomes alienated from her husband and attaches herself momentarily to a soldier in their armed escort. The reader sympathizes with Maritole as she faces the deaths of her parents and her child and cheers her as her strength and courage develop under the harshest of conditions.

Works of recent nonfiction frequently take a personal approach to the Trail of Tears. Jerry Ellis's *Walking the Trail: One Man's Journey along the Cherokee Trial of Tears* (1991) treats the subject from the viewpoint of the author. Ellis's memoir recounts his travel along the trail from Oklahoma back to Georgia, combining aspects of a travel diary with historical facts and details. Wilma Mankiller's autobiography, *Mankiller: A Chief and Her People* (1993), tells not only the author's life story, but also the story of her people. For her the Trail of Tears is not just about suffering; it is about survival. By intertwining historical information with her memoir, Mankiller demonstrates the enduring strength of the Cherokee. She tells how the tales she heard about the Trail of Tears as a child shaped her perception of the world around her and made her determined to help her people thrive in the conditions they had been given. Mankiller's autobiography, as do all of the major works that deal with the Trail of Tears, invokes the reader's sympathies and reveals the determination of her people.

Bibliography

Anderson, William L. *Cherokee Removal: Before and After.* Athens: University of Georgia Press, 1991.

Carter, Samuel. *Cherokee Sunset, a Nation Betrayed: A Narrative of Travail and Triumph, Persecution and Exile.* Garden City, N.Y.: Doubleday, 1976.

Ehle, John. *Trail of Tears: The Rise and Fall of the Cherokee Nation.* New York: Doubleday, 1988.

Perdue, Theda, and Michael D. Green. *The Cherokee Removal: A Brief History with Documents.* The Bedford Series in History and Culture. Boston: Bedford Books of St. Martin's Press, 1995.

Rozema, Vicki. *Voices from the Trail of Tears.* Winston-Salem, N.C.: John F. Blair, 2003.

Robin Gray Nicks

treaties

Beginning with the 1778 treaty signed between the Delaware nation and ending with the 1868 treaty with the Nez Perce, 373 treaties were signed by Native American tribes and the U.S. government. In addition to this, 73 covenants (agreements similar to treaties) were promulgated from 1872 to 1911, raising the total to 446, of which only 245 were ratified by the U.S. Senate.

Of the 373, more than 100 were peace treaties; the others were land cessions. Many treaties have been litigated for years. Even though none was observed for long, they still provide the legal and moral bases for Native claims against the federal government. The existence of treaties always differentiated Native American claims from those of other indigenous peoples, such as Australian aborigines and Native Hawaiians, who signed no treaties with European settlers. Most contemporary issues, from sacred sites to land rights, are rooted in laws deriving their substance from such agreements. Treaties are, therefore, the central focus of current Native American struggles.

Starting in 1701, the British Crown signed several treaties to encourage peaceful relations between Canada's aboriginal peoples and white settlers. Over the next two centuries treaties were signed to define, among other things, the respective rights of aboriginal peoples and governments to use and enjoy lands the former traditionally occupied. Canadian treaties include historic treaties that were signed between 1701 and 1923 and modern-day treaties known as comprehensive land claim settlements. Treaty rights already in existence in 1982 and those that arose afterward are recognized and affirmed by Canada's Constitution. The 1960s marked the beginning of a new wave of Indian activism. Respect of treaties was a central point of their claims. The first organized structure to adopt such stance was the AMERICAN

INDIAN MOVEMENT, which was founded in Minneapolis in 1968 by a group of Natives including Russell Means and Dennis Banks. The following years saw many spectacular actions such as the occupation of Alcatraz Island (1969–71); the march on Washington, D.C., to protest violations, known as Trail of Broken Treaties; and the 1973 occupation of WOUNDED KNEE, South Dakota.

A major step forward occurred in 1974, when the International Indian Treaty Council (IITC) saw the light. The council, the first Native American organization with an international scope, was founded in June 1974 at a gathering by the American Indian Movement in Standing Rock, South Dakota, attended by some 5,000 representatives of 98 indigenous peoples. The document released at the end of the conference, known as "Declaration of Continuing Independence," openly refers to treaties:

> We, the sovereign Native Peoples recognize that all lands belonging to the various Native Nations now situated within the boundaries of the U.S. are clearly defined by the sacred treaties solemnly entered into between the Native Nations and the government of the United States of America.

From 1977 to 1978 the U.S. Congress passed approximately 50 laws helping redefine tribal issues concerning land acquisition, fishing rights, and water rights. Some land was returned to the tribes, and issues of self-governance were better clarified.

In the 1990s the most significant litigation concerning treaty rights was the one regarding the Western Shoshone territory. This territory was officially defined in the Treaty of Ruby Valley, which was concluded with the U.S. government in 1863. According to the treaty, the territory includes two-thirds of the state of Nevada and small portions of California, Idaho, and Utah. This treaty is not a treaty of cession but of peace and friendship, granting the United States safe passage through Shoshone land, allowing the establishment of mining and agricultural settlements, railway construction, and the safe operation of mail and telegraph services within Western Shoshone territory. The Shoshone furthermore agreed eventually to abandon their life as hunters and gatherers in order to become farmers and herdsmen on their lands. Western Shoshone territory today consists of reservations, communities without reservation status, and ranches scattered over their vast territory.

More treaty litigations occurred throughout the decade. On March 22, 1999, Sioux people established the Oceti Sakowin spiritual camp on La Framboise Island in the Missouri River near Pierre, South Dakota, in protest of the treaty-breaking Danklow Acts (Terrestrial Wildlife Habitat Restoration Act and Water Resources Development Authorization), which gave 200,000 acres of tribal lands to South Dakota. On April 19, 2005, Senator Sam Brownback introduced a joint resolution (S. J. RES. 15) offering an apology to Native peoples on behalf of the United States. The document clearly refers to treaty issues:

> Whereas the United States Government violated many of the treaties ratified by Congress and other diplomatic agreements with Indian tribes; whereas this Nation should address the broken treaties and many of the more ill-conceived Federal policies that followed, such as extermination, termination, forced removal and relocation, the outlawing of traditional religions, and the destruction of sacred places.

In Native American literature THOMAS KING explores the effect of a long history of broken treaties on Native culture in GREEN GRASS, RUNNING WATER. The title of that text is a reference to the language used in many of the treaties, that they would be valid as long as the rivers ran. In LAST STANDING WOMAN WINONA LADUKE dramatizes the 19th-century resistance to the process of treaty making and its effect on tribal culture.

Bibliography

"The Avalon Project: Treaties between the United States and Native Americans." Available online. URL ttp://www.yale.edu/lawweb/avalon/ntreaty/ntreaty.htm. Accessed on August 15, 2005.

"The Alcatraz Proclamation." Available online. URL: http://www.cwis.org/fwdp/Americas/alcatraz. htm. Accessed on August 15, 2005.

"Declaration of Continuing Independence." International Indian Treaty Council. Available online. URL: http://www.treatycouncil.org. Accessed on August 15, 2005.

Deloria, Jr., Vine. *Behind the Trail of Broken Treaties: An Indian Declaration of Independence.* Austin: University of Texas Press, 1983.

———, and Clifford M. Lytle. *American Indians, American Justice.* Austin: University of Texas Press, 1983.

———, and David E. Wilkins. *Tribes, Treaties, and Constitutional Tribulations.* Austin: University of Texas Press, 2000.

Johansen, Bruce E., ed. *Enduring Legacies: Native American Treaties and Contemporary Controversies.* Westport, Conn.: Praeger, 2004.

"Native American Treaties." Available online. URL: http://www.thecre.com/fedlaw/legal22x/native. htm. Accessed on August 15, 2005.

"Treaty of Ruby Valley." Available online. URL: http:// www.nativeweb.org/pages/legal/shoshone/ruby_ valley.html. Accessed on August 15, 2005.

Alessandro Michelucci

Tribal Secrets: Recovering American Indian Intellectual Traditions
Robert Allen Warrior (1995)

Tribal Secrets presents a history of American Indian writers since 1890 and argues the "intellectual sovereignty" promoted by such Native thinkers as JOHN JOSEPH MATHEWS (Osage) and VINE DELORIA, JR. (Standing Rock Sioux) should be privileged over contemporary critical discourses that stress identity, authenticity, and worldview. Native American literary criticism, ROBERT ALLEN WARRIOR (Osage) argues, should move beyond these parochial and essentialist themes. This book presents a new framework for Indian critical studies that recovers American Indian intellectual history, engages the issues of tribal sovereignty and community, and offers suggestions for the work that lies ahead.

Chapter one analyzes "American Indian Intellectual Traditions." Warrior splits the past century into four periods that alternate between solidarity and a lack of cohesion. "Assimilationism and Apocalypticism" characterize the intellectual production of CHARLES ALEXANDER EASTMAN (Santee Sioux), ZITKALA-ŠA (Yankton Sioux), Carlos Montezuma (Yavapai), and other authors in the Society of American Indians from 1890 to 1916. Warrior describes the next period, 1925–60, as "a Generation of Free Agents" that included Mathews, D'ARCY MCNICKLE (Cree, Salish, and Kootenai), MOURNING DOVE (Salish), and ELLA DELORIA (Yankton Sioux). "The Battle to Define 'Red Power'" (1960–73) drew together Indian individuals such as Mel Thom (Walker River Paiute), Clyde Warrior (Ponca), and Deloria, as well as several national Indian organizations: the National Congress of American Indians, the National Indian Youth Council, and the American Indian Movement. The chapter concludes by describing the period since 1973 as "Diversity, Party Lines, and the Need for Generational Perspective."

The second and third chapters of *Tribal Secrets* provide a new reading of works by Mathews and Deloria and discuss the need for "intellectual sovereignty." Warrior analyzes how "sovereign land and community" are important and underappreciated themes in *CUSTER DIED FOR YOUR SINS* (1969), *GOD IS RED* (1973), *SUNDOWN* (1934), and *Talking to the Moon* (1945). These topics are significant, he explains, because they demonstrate a commitment to and concern for the future of tribal communities. Warrior therefore argues that American Indian critical discourse needs to ground itself in these kinds of issues and build upon the models of earlier Native intellectuals. Underscoring the need for critical reflection, he reminds us that a generation ago Red Power militants used their rhetoric of self-determination to capture media attention, yet began to forget that sovereignty would require constructive group action. *Tribal Secrets* concludes with the message that American Indian critical studies must break free of their dependence on contemporary critical discourses, embrace and engage their own intellectual tradition, and provide thoughtful and critical assistance to Indian nations.

Bibliography

Donohue, Betty Booth. "Review of *Tribal Secrets: Recovering American Indian Intellectual Traditions,* by Robert Allen Warrior." *American Indian Culture and Research Journal* 21, no. 4 (1997): 350–354.

Kelly, Jennifer. Review of *Tribal Secrets: Recovering American Indian Intellectual Traditions,* by Robert Allen Warrior. *Canadian Review of American Studies* 25 (fall 1995): 162–166.

Krupat, Arnold. *The Turn to the Native: Studies in Criticism and Culture.* Lincoln: University of Nebraska Press, 1996.

Sterling Fluharty

trickster figures

Tricksters figures are mythological beings who take many different forms. They are central in the oral stories of many nations and tribes: Raven or Blue Jay in the Pacific Northwest, Old Man on the plains, Nanabozho or Nanabush among the Anishinabe, Gluskabe or Glooscap among the eastern Algonkins and Micmacs, Wisakedjak among the Cree and Saulteaux, Iktomi the Spider on the Northern Plains, Hare in the southeastern United States, and Coyote among many nations throughout North America. Transcriptions of oral trickster stories can be found in Paul Radin's *The Trickster* (1955; introduction added 1972), Barry Lopez's *Giving Birth to Thunder, Sleeping with His Daughter* (1977), *A Coyote Reader* edited by William Bright (1993), *American Indian Trickster Tales* edited by Richard Erdoes and Alfonso Ortiz (1998), and numerous other collections. Trickster figures are also central in contemporary Native written literature, in which they always represent a continuation of traditions but are often updated to reflect the realities of contemporary Native life and culture.

Tricksters are not easy to define. One can only point to characteristics shared by many trickster figures, and to ways in which these figures tend to function in their respective societies. Tricksters' main characteristics can be seen in terms of contradiction, ambiguity, and indeterminacy. They are incredibly intelligent in some instances, and incredibly stupid in others. They adopt disguises and are able to change shape in order to trick their opponents. Tricksters can shape shift from human to animal forms and back again, or occupy both forms simultaneously. They are also divine beings with magical powers who can operate independently of the boundaries of time and space that limit human existence. At the same time they are lecherous, gluttonous, and filthy.

Tricksters are liars, thieves, and cheats who disobey the rules of their societies; for this reason they are often outcasts. Because tricksters are breakers of taboos and profaners of sacred beliefs—moral characteristics that can be signaled by mental or physical abnormalities—they tend to move outside the social order and are cut off from "normal" social exchange. They either inhabit the liminal fringes of societies or wander aimlessly, unbounded by any societal constraints. These fluctuating positions in relation to their own cultures allow tricksters to cross the boundaries that separate cultures. Despite the complexities of cross-cultural encounters, tricksters' traditional ability to move between the realms of humanity and of divinity gives them the experience necessary to cross societal boundaries with relative impunity. Such boundary crossings allow tricksters to transport both tools—such as fire—and knowledge from one group to another, and thus to benefit humans.

Because they join different worlds, or move the world from one state to another, trickster figures are often depicted in both oral and written stories as responsible for the existence of Europeans, or for their entry in North America. In a Pima legend Europeans are created when Coyote convinces Man Maker to take people out of the oven too soon. In Thomas King's *A Coyote Columbus Story* (1997) Coyote invents Columbus so that she has someone with whom to play baseball. In Lee Maracle's *Ravensong* (1993) Raven takes Europeans to North America in the hope that Native people will teach them how to live on the planet without destroying it. In all three of these stories the existence of Europeans, or their colonization of North America, is a trickster's mistake. In this way Europeans are reconfigured so that their existence makes sense in terms of Native mythology.

Some contemporary writers construct tricksters as a sign of Native culture and opposed to European culture. JEANNETTE ARMSTRONG uses the different cultural conceptions of Coyote to establish the differences that exist between Native and non-Native North Americans: "When I say 'coyote' to you and in your mind you see some four-legged creature running around, usually pretty rag-tag looking, you know that that coyote has a whole different meaning for you than it does for me" (27). As well as using individual tricksters, many Native writers evoke a pan-Native "Trickster" who stands as a unified representative of indigenous culture and an opposition to non-Native belief systems. For example, Lenore Keeshig-Tobias, TOMSON HIGHWAY, Daniel David Moses, and John McLeod formed a Native writers group called the Committee to Re-Establish the Trickster, which aimed to establish Native voices and argued that writing trickster stories is an important strategy in the resurgence of Native culture seven generations after initial colonization.

Highway, in particular, always defines tricksters in opposition to Christianity; he sees Christ as male, repressed, and tragic and Nanabush as gender ambiguous, scatological, and comic. In Highway's play *DRY LIPS OUGHTA MOVE TO KAPUSKASING* (1989) the rape of Nanabush with a crucifix exemplifies the metaphorical rape of Native culture by colonization. Other writers criticize Christianity by creating trickster-priests, who question or mock the European-based religion that they are supposed to represent. Tosamah in N. SCOTT MOMADAY's *HOUSE MADE OF DAWN* (1968) is both priest and trickster, and his ribald humor adds life to Christianity, even as it mocks it. More recently Father Damien in LOUISE ERDRICH's *The LAST REPORT OF THE MIRACLES* (2001), a woman whose disguise marks her as a trickster figure, is ostensibly Christian but claims to minister for Nanabijou rather than the Christian God.

The Chippewa writer GERALD VIZENOR uses a more secular approach to tricksters in order to make connections between cultures. He sees the tribal trickster not only as a figure in mythology, but also as a narrative strategy. His theory of "trickster discourse," which has influenced much writing about Native American literature involving tricksters, combines the traditional trickster tales with the equally shifty—and, at their best, playful—methods of poststructuralism, deconstruction, and postmodernism. In articles such as "Trickster Discourse: Comic Holotropes and Language Games" Vizenor explains trickster discourse in terms of such Western philosophers as Bakhtin, Lacan, Lyotard, and Foucault. He furthers the idea of tricksters' crossing cultural boundaries by arguing that "crossblood" tricksters "are the new metaphors between communal tribal cultures and the cultures that oppose traditional connections" (*EARTHDIVERS* xix). Vizenor opposes academic and anthropological emphasis on the tragic aspects of colonization and emphasizes instead the comic and communal aspects of both trickster figures and the stories that are told about them.

The shifting and ambiguous narrative structure of Vizenor's fiction illustrates his ideas of trickster discourse better than does his theoretical writing, and his tricksterish Browne family embodies the cultural survival and communal values that he associates with tricksters. Vizenor emphasizes that trickster figures have their roots in the past but exist very much in the present; their stories likewise combine traditional tribal forms with postmodernism. THOMAS KING in *GREEN GRASS, RUNNING WATER* (1993) depicts tricksters who transform mythical landscapes of First Nations and European origin through postmodern parody and who exist in an apparently realistic narrative set in the present day. Similarly, Coyote runs through a contemporary world in the poetry of SIMON ORTIZ and Marie Annharte Baker, both of whom use poetic structures that could be identified as trickster discourse.

Although they have mythological status in most cultures, tricksters are not always considered to be gods; more often they are mediating figures between humanity and a higher god. The ambiguity of tricksters' divinity means that many human characters take on tricksterlike characteristics in contemporary Native literature. In Erdrich's *LOVE*

MEDICINE (1984; expanded 1993), TRACKS (1988), *The BINGO PALACE* (1994), and *The Last Report on the Miracles at Little No Horse* the Nanapush family is, with the possible exception of Nanapush himself, fully human, but their refusal to accept social norms, their rampant sexuality, and their trick playing ability, all link them with Nanabozho, the trickster from whom the patriarch of the family takes his name. Similarly Harlen Bigbear in King's MEDICINE RIVER (1989) behaves in ways reminiscent of the way Coyote functions in King's more overtly tricksterish narratives. Alfred Densmore in MOURNING DOVE's *COGEWEA* (1981) likewise shares many characteristics with traditional trickster figures, especially in his greed and egocentrism.

As does their divine status, tricksters' physical characteristics, such as age and gender, can shift at unexpected times and in unexpected ways. In many Native North American stories tricksters can change their gender at will. The Winnebago trickster, for example, carries his penis in a box on his back; when he removes it and makes himself breasts and a vulva, he is able to bear children. Despite such ambiguities in gender, most anthropologically collected trickster tales portray tricksters as male. Tricksters are often characterized by an enormous phallus and by sexual desire for females.

Despite the male bias of many traditional tales, recent literature often employs female tricksters. Thomas King's Coyote is often female; Erdrich's Lulu Lamartine is as tricksterish as are the male members of the Nanapush clan, as is Agnes/Father Damien. The latter's cross-dressing points to the association of Native tricksters with "two spirits," people who occupy alternate gender roles. BETH BRANT's story "Coyote Learns a New Trick," from *MOHAWK TRAIL* (1985), is perhaps the best contemporary example of a two-spirited trickster tale. In it Coyote, a female, cross-dresses as a male to trick a female fox but ends up discovering the pleasures of lesbian love. With this story Brant successfully reverses the homophobia that is evident in many anthropologically collected narratives of cross-dressing tricksters, or of tricksters who engage in homosexual activity.

Most of the contemporary thinking on tricksters emphasizes their positive characteristics, including their creativity and survival. However, trickster figures can also be destructive and antisocial, and the destructive consequences of tricksters' behavior can serve as a warning for those who hear the stories. Weesquachak in RUBY SLIPPERJACK-FARRELL's *WEESQUACHAK AND THE LOST ONES* (2000) is one of the more sinister tricksters in contemporary Native literature; he possesses some characters and kills others in order to gain his ends.

Even when tricksters create havoc with the lives of those who surround them, their antisocial behavior can be excused because they mean well, or because they are so entertaining. Tricksters' destructive behavior can, as can their boundary crossing, lead to cultural change. From destruction arises new creation, creation that can be either beneficial or detrimental to their societies. Because tricksters can survive the most punishing defeats, the most permanent-seeming deaths, they point the way to cultural survival in the wake of societal disasters. The ubiquity of trickster figures in contemporary Native literature in an indication not only of their own survival, but also of the continued strength of the cultures from which they spring.

Bibliography

Armstrong, Jeannette C. "Words." In *Telling It: Women and Language across Culture,* edited by The Telling It Book Collective, 23–29. Vancouver: Press Gang, 1990.

Hynes, William J., and William G. Doty, eds. *Mythical Trickster Figures: Contours, Contexts and Criticisms.* Tuscaloosa: University of Alabama Press, 1993.

Ryan, Alan J. *The Trickster Shift: Humour and Irony in Contemporary Native Art.* Vancouver: UBC Press, 1999.

Smith, Jeanne Rosier. *Writing Tricksters: Mythic Gambols in American Ethnic Literature.* Berkeley: University of California Press, 1997.

Vizenor, Gerald. *Earthdivers: Tribal Narratives on Mixed Descent.* Minneapolis: University of Minnesota Press, 1981.

———. "Trickster Discourse: Comic Holotropes and Language Games." *Narrative Chance: Postmodern Discourse on Native American Indian Literatures,* edited by Gerald Vizenor, 187–211. Albuquerque: University of New Mexico Press, 1989.

Judith Leggatt

Trudell, John (1946–)

John Trudell (Santee Sioux) is a poet, musician, and actor who has released many albums and appeared in several films, perhaps most notably as a medicine man/trickster in *Thunderheart* (1992), but his most important work might be characterized as that of a Native rhetorician.

Extemporaneous public speaking was at the time of first contact perhaps one of the most highly developed Native art forms. Trudell has not followed traditional forms in a self-conscious way, but his efficacy at public speaking and performance was at one point so profound that many people believe that his entire family was burned to death in retaliation.

Federal Bureau of Investigation (FBI) memos described Trudell as an "eloquent speaker" and "extremely effective agitator" (364). He first achieved prominence in connection with the occupation of Alcatraz from 1969 through 1971 by an ad hoc organization known as the Indians of All Tribes. He was the radio announcer for the "Radio Free Alcatraz" broadcasts from the island aired on Pacifica radio stations during that time.

In 1973 he published with his wife, Tina Manning, a folio document entitled *The James Gang Rides Again: A People's Report of the Misuse of Federal Funds for Indian Education in Oklahoma,* which included material related to broken treaties and failed promises of the Bureau of Indian Affairs.

Throughout most of the 1970s he was the leading public spokesperson for the AMERICAN INDIAN MOVEMENT leadership. In 1979 Trudell burned a flag on the steps of the Bureau of Indian Affairs building in Washington, D.C., at a vigil for Leonard Peltier, an Anishinabe and Lakota activist who was convicted, many believe quite wrongly, of the murder of two FBI agents. Twelve hours later an arsonist set fire to a house on the Duck Valley Reservation in Nevada (Paiute-Shoshone), killing Trudell's wife, mother-in-law, and three children.

Two of Trudell's speeches, one from the Black Hills Survival Gathering in 1980 and another given at American Indian Community House in New York in 1992, appear in Paola Igliori's compilation *Stickman/John Trudell: Poems, Lyrics, Talks, and Conversation* (1994). The 1980 Survival Gathering speech closes with the following:

> No matter what they ever do to us, we must always act for the love of our people and the earth. We must not react out of hatred against those who have no sense. Thank you for your time. (15)

His introduction to the second edition of Serle Chapman's *Of Earth and Elders: Visions and Voices from Native America* (2002) similarly articulates his fusion of spirituality and political awareness as a means of maintaining cultural identity through living it.

Trudell's numerous sound recordings with various collaborators include *AKA Graffiti Man* (1986, 1992), *Johnny Damas and Me* (1994), *Blue Indians* (1999), *Decendant Now Ancestor* (2001), and *Bone Days* (2001).

Bibliography

Churchill, Ward, and Jim Vander Wall. *Agents of Repression: The FBI's Secret Wars against the Black Panther Party and the American Indian Movement.* Boston: South End Press, 1990.

Matthiessen, Peter. *In the Spirit of Crazy Horse.* 2nd ed. New York: Viking, 1991.

Sandra Baringer

Truth & Bright Water Thomas King (1999)

Thomas King's third novel, *Truth & Bright Water,* unfolds through the recollections and observations of its 15-year-old Blackfoot narrator, Tecumseh. Set in an American railroad town, Truth, and the Bright Water reserve in Canada, the bildungsroman, or coming-of-age tale, takes place in both Montana and Alberta, Canada. The presence of the national border underscores the prominence of literal and figurative divisions in the novel, as a variety of characters wrestle with the realities of ruin and loss: Tecumseh's listless father, Elvin, leaves his family; his nomadic aunt, Cassie, returns to the river valley mourning her lost daughter; his mother tries to reconcile her lost love affair with Monroe Swimmer; and his best friend, Lum, abused by his father and generally neglected by the Blackfoot community, commits suicide. Insofar as these characters work from loss toward recovery, they emphasize the balance King strikes in the novel between comedy and tragedy, magic and realism, and joy and sorrow.

At the center of King's narrative is Monroe Swimmer, the self-proclaimed "famous Indian artist" (45) who returns to the town of Truth after establishing his reputation in the East. He makes a name for himself by restoring American landscape paintings: That is, he paints Indians and Indian villages into the wilderness scenes. He returns to Truth to begin another massive restoration project: He purchases an abandoned church that overlooks the town and paints it out of the landscape. After returning the high plains to its preconquest state, he enlists Tecumseh to help him fill the "restored" prairies with hundreds of iron buffalo that are nailed to the ground with huge railroad spikes.

In using the church as a canvas for his restored prairies and the railroad spikes as the tool to restore the buffalo, Monroe engages in an act of cultural and physical repossession that utilizes the tools of Euro-American colonization symbolically to reverse the damage done and the losses inflicted by this colonization. In doing so, Monroe embodies a paradigm of recovery and restoration. In this manner he offers Tecumseh a vital alternative to the cynical, defeatist attitude of Tecumseh's father, who bitterly proclaims that the Indians should have "left" with the buffalo during the 19th century (91), and the unscrupulous maneuverings of Franklin, the tribal chief of the Bright Water reserve in Alberta, who, among other questionable money-making ventures, buys a herd of buffalo so he can charge white tourists to shoot at them with paintballs.

Monroe's reconstructed landscape functions as a site for two important ceremonies of healing: a giveaway of the trickster-artist's possessions around a ceremonial bonfire, which draws the Truth and Bright Water communities together, and a bone repatriation ceremony, in which the bones of Indian children Monroe has rescued from museums all over North America are ceremoniously cast into the Shield River by him and Tecumseh. While these ceremonies cannot fully reverse the damage done by colonization, nor prevent further tragedy, as Lum's suicide does, they impart to Tecumseh the value of community and the importance of taking a longer view of history. That is, they help him to place personal and cultural loss within the context of nature's cycles, as embodied in the restored prairie and the returning buffalo.

Bibliography

Davidson, Arnold E., Priscilla L. Walton, and Jennifer Andrews. *Border Crossings: Thomas King's Cultural Inversions.* Toronto: University of Toronto Press, 2003.

King, Thomas. *Truth & Bright Water.* New York: Atlantic Monthly, 1999.

Ridington, Robin. "Happy Trails to You: Contexted Discourse and Indian Removals in Thomas King's *Truth & Bright Water.*" *Canadian Literature* 167 (2000): 89–107.

Matthew Cella

Two-Rivers, E. Donald (1945–   )

E. Donald Two-Rivers is an Ojibwe Indian from the Seine River Reserve in northwestern Ontario. He left Canada for Chicago in the 1960s before moving to Green Bay, Wisconsin, in 2003. Two-Rivers's body of work crosses generic boundaries. It includes the award-winning *Survivor's Medicine* (1998), a collection of short stories that garnered the prestigious American Book Award in 1999; *A Dozen Cold Ones* (1992) and *Pow Wows, Fat Cats, and Other Indian Tales* (2003) chapbooks of poetry; *Briefcase Warriors: Stories for the Stage* (2000); and *I'm Not Tonto* (1993), a short video based on Two-Rivers's early poem of the same name.

In addition the author is artistic director of Chicago's Red Path Native Theater Company, and a performance artist sought after for dynamic poetry readings that are calibrated by his trademark gritty wit. He is also an energetic activist committed to equal rights for Native Americans and the environment, and he takes a public stand against gang violence and the death penalty. This dedication to community and internationally minded service earned Two-Rivers the Iron-Eyes Cody Award for Peace in 1992.

Two-Rivers's prose, plays, and poetry address broad social and political issues that face contemporary urban Indians—POVERTY, violence, drugs, and alcohol—while also presenting an intimate portrait of the indomitable Native spirit. *Survivor's Medicine* depicts street-savvy, hard-living characters who not only struggle to survive in a hostile environment but fight to remain visible in a society that subscribes to the myth of the "Vanishing Indian." *Briefcase Warriors,* six plays that range from one-act vignettes to extended dramatizations, presents resistance by workers and Native Americans in the now familiar rhetoric of environmentalism. Yet Two-Rivers also uses humor to smash stereotypes. The poems of *A Dozen Cold Ones* and *Pow Wows, Fat Cats, and Other Indian Tales* are a potent blend of pathos and satire that sheds a comedic but nevertheless disquieting light on Native culture. And *I'm Not Tonto,* the video coproduced with the Native filmmaker Beverly Moeser, critiques the stereotype of the Hollywood Indian sidekick made famous by the character "Tonto" in the 1950s avenger television series *The Lone Ranger.* As such, Two-Rivers's collective work offers a critique of Native culture from within.

Bibliography

Adamson, Joni. *American Indian Literature, Environmental Justice, and Ecocriticism: The Middle Place.* Tucson: University of Arizona Press, 2001.

Fast, Robin Riley. *The Heart as a Drum: Continuance and Resistance in American Indian Poetry.* Ann Arbor: University of Michigan Press, 1999.

Geiogamah, Hanay, and Jaye T. Darby, eds. *American Indian Theater in Performance: A Reader.* Los Angeles: UCLA American Indian Studies Center, 2000.

Gidley, Mick. "The Repeated Return of the Vanishing Indian." *American Studies: Essays in Honor of Marcus Cunliffe,* edited by Brian Holden Reid and John White, 189–209. New York: St. Martin's Press, 1991.

Two Rivers, Donald E. *Briefcase Warriors: Stories for the Stage.* Norman: University of Oklahoma Press, 2000.

———. *A Dozen Cold Ones.* Chicago: MARCH/Abrazo Press, 1992.

———. *Pow Wows, Fat Cats, and Other Indian Tales.* Lawrence, Kans.: Mammoth, 2003.

———. *Survivor's Medicine: Short Stories.* Norman: University of Oklahoma Press, 1998.

Tracey Wymand Marchand

Vietnam War

During the Vietnam War American Indians had the largest number of soldiers as a ratio of their population of any ethnic group. Understandably then, this war features prominently in contemporary American Indian literature. In both fiction and nonfiction Indian writers, some of whom are Vietnam War veterans, have described the emotion and physicality of the hardships that were faced before, during, and after a war that many have deemed misguided.

Works such as *Son of Two Bloods* (1996), by Vincent Medoza (Creek), and *Year in Nam* (1999) by Leroy TeCube (Jicarilla Apache) are personal accounts of Native American soldiers' involvement during the war and return to civilian life afterward. Both of these texts contribute to the already substantial body of literature on the Vietnam War, but they do it from the perspective of outsiders, people who have risked their lives in war, yet feel they are second-class citizens at home.

In fiction and poetry notable references to the Vietnam War can be found in LOUISE ERDRICH's *LOVE MEDICINE,* in which the veteran Lyman Lamartine ultimately commits suicide; LOUIS OWENS's *Dark River* and *The Sharpest Sight;* and the poetry of SIMON ORTIZ. and RAY A. YOUNG BEAR. Literature that deals with the Vietnam War firsthand is often purging of the inner turmoil that the author faced after returning home. For some In-

dian authors, the traditional beliefs that they took into battle helped them to return.

Bibliography

Holm, Tom. *Strong Hearts Wounded Souls: Native American Veterans of the Vietnam War.* Austin: University of Texas Press, 1996.

Mendoza, Vincent L. *Son of Two Bloods.* Lincoln: University of Nebraska Press, 1996.

Tecube, Leroy. *Year in Nam: A Native American Soldier's Story.* Lincoln: University of Nebraska Press, 1999.

Rikki Noel Williams

Vizenor, Gerald (1934–)

Gerald Vizenor, one of the most prolific and controversial writers of the AMERICAN INDIAN LITERARY RENAISSANCE, was born in 1934 in Minneapolis, Minnesota. To date he has written nine books of poetry, eight books of nonfiction, six novels, a play, and a film. His awards include the Film in the Cities Prize from the Sundance Institute for *Harold of Orange,* which also won the best film award in the category of American Indian Films at the San Francisco Film Festival in 1984; the New York Fiction Collective Award (1986) and the American Book Award (1988) for *GRIEVER: AN AMERICAN MONKEY KING IN CHINA* (1986); and the Josephine Miles Award for Excellence in Literature from

PEN for *INTERIOR LANDSCAPES: AUTOBIOGRAPHICAL MYTHS AND METAPHORS* (1990).

Vizenor's paternal ancestors were MIXED-BLOOD Anishinabe and French-Canadian. His father, Clement William Vizenor, was born on White Earth Reservation and moved as an adult to Minneapolis, where he worked as a house painter. Vizenor's mother, LaVerne ("Lovey"), was white. Clement Vizenor was murdered when Gerald was two.

Gerald spent much of his childhood in foster homes or with his paternal grandmother, who lived on the reservation. When his mother remarried, Gerald did develop a strong attachment for his stepfather, Elmer Petesch, with whom he lived for a few months when his mother moved to California. The relationship ended abruptly with Petesch's accidental death.

At 16, Vizenor lied about his age and joined the national guard and then the army. During his tour he was stationed in Japan. In 1955 he was honorably discharged and enrolled at New York University, where he studied creative writing. In 1959 Vizenor married Judith Horns, an elementary school teacher. The couple had a son together, Robert. They divorced in 1969.

After graduating from the University of Minnesota, Vizenor began work with the Minnesota Department of Corrections as a social worker and corrections agent. In his spare time he wrote, principally poetry. Although Vizenor's reputation is based primarily on his novels and nonfiction, his earliest books were collections of poetry, many of them based on the principles of haiku. Vizenor was fascinated with the resemblance of haiku to Anishinabe song. Song is very important in Anishanabe culture, and as in haiku songs are often concise, depict scenes from nature, and are often tied to a specific season. He began publishing his poetry in 1960, 15 years before his first novel appeared.

From 1964 to 1968 Vizenor served as a community organizer for Indians in Minneapolis including a two-year term as director of the American Indian Employment and Guidance Center. He organized demonstrations to call attention to "racism and failure in the BIA (Bureau of Indian Affairs)" and began writing magazine articles critical of government efforts to aid urban Indians. In 1968 Vizenor joined the *Minneapolis Tribune* as a staff writer. Many of his articles and editorials from this period have been collected in *Tribal Scenes and Ceremonies* (1976).

In 1970 Vizenor began his career as a professor of English. His first position, at Lake Forest College, Illinois, was followed by brief periods at several schools ending with the University of California at Berkeley, where he currently teaches in the Department of American Studies. While at Berkeley he met and married Laura Hall, an ethnic studies scholar from London.

In 1978 Vizenor published his first novel, *Darkness in Saint Louis Bearheart* (he revised it slightly and reissued it as *BEARHEART: THE HEIRSHIP CHRONICLES* in 1990). *Bearheart* is the wildly fantastic saga of a TRICKSTER FIGURE, Proude Cedarfair, who leads a band of misfits, clowns, and tricksters on a journey across America after the country has literally run out of gas. Many cultures have a "trickster" figure, a kind of spirit often depicted as an animal, that makes mischief and creates obstacles, but whose actions usually teach as much as they trouble. The book is a pastiche of wildly comic horrors, as when an itinerant group of cripples pull apart limb by limb a beautiful dwarf named Little Big Mouse when she excites them by dancing for them. Vizenor calls his version of magical realism—it has more magic and less realism than the South American sort typified by the works of Gabriel Garcia Marquez—"mythic verism." At the climax of the novel Proude turns into a bear and leaves this, the third world, for the fourth, in another dimension.

Vizenor is one of the first writers of the American Indian literary renaissance to introduce a trickster figure into a contemporary novel. Throughout Indian country readers, writers, and critics recognize Vizenor as trickster incarnate. *Bearheart* is a novel by a trickster, about tricksters, in which the author tries to manipulate his readers into being tricksters who will take up the fight against the many villains of the world, using their wit as their weapon.

In 1983 Vizenor published two books, EARTH-DIVERS: TRIBAL NARRATIVES ON MIXED DESCENT, a collection of essays and short stories, and *The PEOPLE NAMED THE CHIPPEWA: NARRATIVE HISTORIES*, a series of historical essays about his tribe. *Earthdivers* focuses on the theme of being a MIXED-BLOOD, or to use one of Vizenor's terms, a "crossblood." Since more than half of America's Indians are married to whites, the number of full-bloods is rapidly diminishing. Vizenor is one of the first to explore in depth the ramifications of biracial identity among Indians.

The title of *The People Named the Chippewa* may seem straightforward, but it is also a trick: *Named* is a verb, the implicit subject of which are Europeans and European Americans. Vizenor points out that his tribe called themselves Anishinabe until white settlers began calling them "Chippewa" and "Ojibway."

In 1985 Vizenor introduced his most interesting trickster hero, Griever de Hocus, in his short story "*Luminous Thighs.*" He followed that with a novel in which Griever is the main character, *Griever: An American Monkey King in China* (1987). A year later Vizenor published *The Trickster of Liberty: Tribal Heirs to a Wild Baronage,* which fills in Greiver's earlier history, and that of his companions on the reservation. The Baronage is a fictionalized version of White Earth, the reservation of Vizenor's family.

In 1991 just before the 500th anniversary of the European discovery of America, Vizenor published *The HEIRS OF COLUMBUS*, a postmodern historical novel. Resisting the temptation to demonize Columbus, Vizenor depicts him favorably, if oddly. Vizenor's Columbus is an Indian who traces his ancestors to the Mayan by way of Sephardic Jews.

In 1994 Vizenor published *MANIFEST MANNERS: POSTINDIAN WARRIORS OF SURVIVANCE*, a volume of essays in which Vizenor applies poststructuralist ideas to questions of Indian identity and culture. The same year A. Robert Lee issued a Vizenor reader, *Shadow Distance,* which caused an uproar that almost destroyed the Native American Studies (NAS) Department at Berkeley. The cover of the book, displayed in a case in front of the NAS office, showed a picture of Vizenor superimposed on a scene that included a naked figure dancing in front of a bear. A graduate assistant complained that the picture looked as if it depicted a woman committing sodomy with the bear. Vizenor countered that the figure was not a woman; it was the androgynous trickster, and the sex act was strictly in the eye of the beholder. Vizenor's latest works are *HOTLINE HEALERS: AN ALMOST BROWNE NOVEL* (1997) which picks up the stories of the Browne family of the Baronage; *Fugitive Poses: Native American Indian Scenes of Absence and Presence* (1998), a book of essays; and *Chancers* (2000), another exercise in autobiography, a novel about Solar Dancers who sacrifice faculty and administrators at Berkeley who oversee the collections of Indian remains.

Bibliography

Coltelli, Laura. *Winged Words: American Indian Writers Speak.* Lincoln: University of Nebraska Press, 1992.

Lee, A. Robert, ed. *Loosening the Seams: Interpretations of Gerald Vizenor.* Bowling Green, Ohio: Bowling Green University Press, 2000.

Roemer, Kenneth, ed. *Native American Authors of the United States: Dictionary of Literary Biography.* Vol. 175. Detroit: Gale Group, 1997.

Vizenor, Gerald. *Bearheart: The Heirship Chronicles.* Minneapolis: University of Minnesota Press, 1990.

———. *Chancers.* Norman: University of Oklahoma Press, 2000.

———. *Earthdivers: Tribal Narratives on Mixed Descent.* Minneapolis: University of Minnesota Press, 1981.

———. *Griever: An American Monkey King in China.* Minneapolis: University of Minnesota Press, 1990.

———. *The Heirs of Columbus.* Hanover, N.H.: Wesleyan University Press/University Press of New England, 1991.

———. *Hotline Healers: An Almost Browne Novel.* Hanover, N.H.: Wesleyan University Press, 1997.

———. *Interior Landscapes: Autobiographical Myths and Metaphors.* Minneapolis: University of Minnesota Press, 1990.

———. *Touchwood: A Collection of Ojibway Prose.* St. Paul, Minn.: New Rivers Press, 1987.

Voice of the Turtle: American Indian Literature 1900–1970   Paula Gunn Allen (1994)

PAULA GUNN ALLEN is one of the most respected, prolific, and important contributors to Native American literature and literary criticism. *Voice of the Turtle* (1994), published two years before its companion SONG OF THE TURTLE (1996), was hailed at publication as a landmark contribution to the field of Native American literature. *Voice of the Turtle* contains 23 narratives, some excerpted from longer narratives, by 19 writers. Most of the contributors are Native Americans, but two are European Americans who translated or related narratives by Native Americans. Contributors include EMILY PAULINE JOHNSON, D'ARCY MC-NICKLE, N. SCOTT MOMADAY, BLACK ELK, CHARLES ALEXANDER EASTMAN, Simon Ortiz, ZITKALA-ŠA, and Pretty-shield. Allen desired that the two volumes would "provide a kind of a map, a template of that complex, vast, and myriad chronicle" (4) that is Native American writing in the past 100 years. *Voice of the Turtle* was designed to contain examples of the first wave of American Indian writing, generally held to have occurred from 1900 to 1970. Most reviewers received the work with high praise.

Allen's introduction to this edition presents an important perspective on Native American literature in English, looking at the tradition as heavily influenced by "over five hundred years of multicultural encounters of the devastating kind" for Native Americans (3). This introduction is in sharp contrast to most of the introductions to the few existing Native American literature anthologies. More often editors use the introduction, first, to justify the creation of a Native American literature anthology at all and, second, in the anthology *Native American Writing in the Southeast: An Anthology, 1875–1935,* edited by Daniel F. Littlefield, Jr., and James W. Parins, to characterize Native American literature by using criteria from European-American literary analyses. In contrast, Allen describes Native American literature from the perspective of Mayan and Aztec prophecies dealing with a period of 500 years. This description is valuable for its details regarding Native and European-American efforts to document personal narratives from Native Americans, its description of Native American writing of 1900–40, the "long silence that occurred between the mid-thirties and the late sixties" (4), and the AMERICAN INDIAN LITERARY RENAISSANCE of the 1960s to the present.

Allen states that the theme of her anthology is "transformation" as it "informs Native life and thought" (6). In choosing the theme of transformation, she endeavors to demonstrate through her choices for the anthology that there is a wholeness to Native American literature illustrated by shared history and worldview of the first people in what is now the United States. Defining transformation in *opposition* to its common meaning, which is change and progress, Allen states that "Native people see change as the fundamental sacred process, as Transformation, as Ritual, as intrinsic to all of existence whenever and wherever, in whatever form or style it takes. Transformation: to change someone or something from one state or condition to another. Magic" (7). This theme is repeated in later introductions, most notably in Allen's book *Loose Canons.* The introduction to *Voice of the Turtle* is also valuable to students of Native American literature because it describes the complexity of categorizing Native American literature and the Native narrative tradition in relation to the literatures of other groups of Americans.

The introduction to the volume also includes a rationale for the choices Allen made in including each author. Each narrative included is preceded by a short biography of each author, a short note on the importance of the narrative, and the narrative's relation to the overall theme of the anthology or the larger field of Native American tradition and literature. The excerpt from BLACK ELK SPEAKS contains Black Elk's vision of his destiny. This point in the narrative is pivotal and transformative.

The best known writer included in this anthology is N. Scott Momaday. Allen chooses an excerpt from *HOUSE MADE OF DAWN* and entitles it "Feast Day." Her choice of excerpt is understandable in that this portion she has chosen encapsulates all of the key issues of the larger text: Abel's loss of identity, the contrast between his adoption of white ways and his grandfather's traditional ways, and the murder of Juan Reyes. However, the larger text, *House Made of Dawn,* is difficult to interpret in its entirety. Allen's introductory note to this selection could never provide the mass of detail a reader would need to understand the excerpt fully. Only by reading the entire novel could one make sense of the section of the novel that Allen has chosen to include. Momaday is a writer who is difficult to excerpt. Allen validates her choice in the preface, writing that "any given narrative arises out of a vast constellation of stories. . . . In short, every story is an excerpt" (xi).

Bibliography

Allen, Paula Gunn. "A Funny Thing Happened on My Way to Press." *Frontiers: A Journal of Women's Studies.* Special Issue: Indigenous Women 23, no. 2 (2002): 3–6.

———. *Off the Reservation.* Boston: Beacon Press, 1998.

———, ed. *Song of the Turtle: American Indian Literature 1974–1994.* New York: Ballantine Books, 1996.

———, ed. *Voice of the Turtle: American Indian Literature 1900–1970.* New York: Ballantine Books, 1994.

Gourly, Beth. "Review of *Voice of the Turtle,* by Paula Gunn Allen." *School Library Journal* (May 1995): 136.

"Review of *Voice of the Turtle* by Paula Gunn Allen." *Publishers Weekly.* 13 August 2004. Available online. URL: http://www.amazon.com/exec/obidos/tg/stores/detail/-/books/0345395050/reviews/102<0x2013>6026758–9456930#03453950507298. Accessed on August 15, 2005.

Tamara Powell

Voice That Was in Travel, The   Diane Glancy (1999)

DIANE GLANCY published *The Voice That Was in Travel* as her 20th book and third short story collection. Although Glancy's voluminous work establishes her as a major contemporary Native American author, very little academic scholarship has been devoted to her writings thus far.

In the 20 stories in *The Voice That Was in Travel,* ranging from one-page sketches ("Blast," "The Birds with the Breeze of Their Wings," "Jupiter") to the 20-page novella "America's First Parade" (an allusion to the TRAIL OF TEARS), Glancy creates characters who are peculiar and edgy and struggle with cultural dislocations of the past and present. In Glancy's narrative universe travel as the creation of a sense of place is a powerful means to relocate her characters, to root them within themselves. In "America's First Parade," for example, the narrator concludes the novella by stating that the protagonist "felt a place within her as long as she was on the move" (116).

The Christian faith works as another force that offers consolation by providing a spiritual refuge. Her positive depiction of Christianity is somewhat unusual in contemporary Native American literature, yet Glancy perceives its healing power mostly in combination with tribal traditions and spirits, such as in "The Bird Who Reached Heaven," a story about a pastor and his wife, or in "Sumac," which retells a traditional story of a girl in search of a vision.

Variations on the quest narrative, as part of both Judeo-Christian and Native American cultures, inform most of the stories in *The Voice That Was in Travel.* The women warriors in "Badlands" proclaim that their "voice will be in travel," (5) and "The Man Whose Voice Was in Travel," the title of another story, refers to Jesus Christ. For the main character in "Road" her life on the move is an assertion of independence that erodes traditional concepts of womanhood, and in "America's First Parade" the protagonist feels "the long trail of her ancestors . . . a small, hard part of her that had to keep moving because it relieved her brokenness, her separateness" (109).

Glancy writes in the preface that words are "firesticks," traveling between genres and places as a unifying force in a world that is characterized by ethnic diversity. The view that words create, rather than reflect, social and cultural realities is deeply embedded in Glancy's Native American heritage. In *The Voice That Was in Travel* the conflicting voices in the stories articulate a sense of displacement shared by all of Glancy's Native American travelers, and the disrupted narratives reflect the broken context of contemporary Native American life. Whether Glancy's characters are traveling on business or vacationing, in Oklahoma, Arkansas, Australia, or Europe, their journeys are always filled with memories of tribal migrations, and it is always words that help them survive.

Bibliography

Glancy, Diane. *The Voice That Was in Travel: Stories.* Norman: University of Oklahoma Press, 1999.

Alexandra Ganser

Walking the Rez Road   Jim Northrup (1993)

A collection of 21 poems and 21 stories, Jim Northrup's *Walking the Rez Road* presents Anishinabe (Chippewa/Ojibwe) life in the 1990s on the Fond du Lac reservation in northern Minnesota. Northrup's main character, Luke Warmwater, both endures and celebrates times of lean and plenty, and trauma and celebration. The stories vacillate between brutal examinations of individual complicity and scathing indictments of what Northrup calls the "manifest destiny dominant society." The poems have been less than warmly received by critics, one of whom insists that while his stories reflect a voice that is "very funny, gutsy, and immediate," his poetry lacks "the technique or subtlety of . . . Joy Harjo or Leslie Marmon Silko" (Melvin), to whom he is sometimes compared. Other critics focus instead on the subject matter of his poetry, such as the annual rice harvest. Chris LaLond asserts that such poetry "indicates how taking part in an aspect of the traditional lifeways of the Anishinaabe reaffirms the essential connection with place and family" (LaLond 25). Taken in sum, while traditional activities are certainly "specific glimpses into traditional Fond du Lac lifeways, largely the selections are about being human" (Hoefel 5).

Issues dealt with in the stories and poems include posttraumatic stress disorder, addiction, treatment, unemployment, courtship, gambling, marriage and family, tribal politics, and harvest. Permeating the stories is a very wry and punning sense of humor—character names include Harry Pitts, Tuna Charlie, and a lawyer named Juris Mc-Brief—that Northrup only barely prevents from clouding his message. It is his method that makes the difference.

Central to Northrup's method are reversals that seek to subvert stereotypes and demonstrate a greater complexity to characters' motives even when stereotypes seem to be affirmed. In one story of reversal, a character seeks counseling for his posttraumatic stress disorder, only to feel guilty when the psychiatrist commits suicide. In another, more subversive tale Warmwater unapologetically estimates that he and his friends have been drunk for "about three weeks, I think"; when they have the unlikely and dubious fortune that a full beer truck arrives at their party, they take only a few 12-packs, leave an IOU pinned to the passed-out-drunk white driver, and lock the truck. In such moments Northrup deploys both his strategic technique and humor, openly mocking stereotypes even as he allows his characters the humanity sometimes to indulge in stereotypical behavior.

Bibliography

Hoefel, Roseanne. "Walking with Jim Northrup and Sharing His 'Rez'ervations." *SAIL: Studies in American Indian Literatures* 2nd ser. 9, no. 2 (1997):

11–21. Available online. URL: http://oncampus.richmond.edu/faculty/ASAIL/search.html. Accessed on August 15, 2005.

LaLond, Chris. "Stories, Humor, and Survival in Jim Northrup's *Walking the Rez Road.*" *SAIL: Studies in American Indian Literatures* 2nd ser. 9, no. 2 (1997): 23–40. Available online. URL: http://on-campus.richmond.edu/faculty/ASAIL/search.html. Accessed on August 15, 2005.

Melvin, Jackie. "Review of *Walking the Rez Road,* by Jim Northrup." *Magill Book Reviews,* 1 March 1994. *Academic Search Premier* EBSCOhost. Karl E. Mundt Lib, Madison, SD. 29 Available online. URL: http://search.epnet.com. Accessed on August 29, 2005.

Justin Blessinger

Walters, Anna Lee   (1946–   )

Anna Lee Walters was born in Pawnee, Oklahoma, on September 9, 1946. She is the daughter of Luther and Juanita McGlaslin and is a member of the Pawnee and Otoe tribes. She married Harry Walters, a museum curator, in 1965, and they have two sons, Anthony and Daniel. Walters has spent most of her adult life working as a writer or as a teacher of writing. She has had a long career as a technical writer, at the Institute of American Indian Arts in Santa Fe and at Diné College in Tsaile, Arizona. She is an accomplished writer of fiction for children and adults and currently teaches at Diné College. She holds a B.A. and an M.F.A. from Goddard College in Plainfield, Vermont.

Her first book, *The Sun Is Not Merciful,* received the 1985 American Book Award from the Before Columbus Foundation. It is a collection of short stories that highlights issues of tribal identity and Native spirituality. Her second book, and first novel, *Ghost Singer,* is a very interesting take on the horror novel, involving supernatural activities surrounding Indian artifacts at the Smithsonian Institution. She has also published several children s books, including *The Two-Legged Creature, An Otoe Story Retold,* and *The Pawnee Nation.*

See also *Neon Powwow: New Native Voices of the American Southwest.*

Jennifer McClinton-Temple

Warrior, Robert Allen   (1963–   )

Born in rural Kansas and raised in Kansas, Missouri, Michigan, and California, Warrior is the author of *Tribal Secrets: Recovering American Indian Intellectual Traditions* (1995) and, with Paul Chaat Smith, *Like a Hurricane: The Indian Movement from Alcatraz to Wounded Knee* (1996). Subsequent to receiving his B.A. in speech communication from Pepperdine University in 1985, Warrior studied religion at Yale University Divinity School and earned his M.A. in 1988. He went on to receive his M.Phil. in 1991 and doctorate in 1992 from the Union Theological Seminary in New York City.

Warrior has had a distinguished career as a writer and as a journalist. He served as the New York correspondent for the *Lakota Times.* He has also played a substantive role in the Children's Television Workshop in New York. In 1993 he was a contributing editor for *Wicazo Sa Review.* Warrior's articles on Native American literature and politics have appeared in *Media Studies Journal, Genre, Wicazo Sa Review,* and others. In 1991–93, he held a place on the board of governors for the Native American International Prize in Literature. Warrior has won many accolades. In 1995, he was a member of the advisory board for academic systems and helped develop a multimedia-writing curriculum. Warrior is now an associate professor at the University of Oklahoma, where his undergraduate and graduate teaching focus on American and Native American writing.

Warrior's books continue to gain critical acclaim in their attempt to establish the processes of Native American resistance and identity formation as one of perpetual struggle. The ability of Warrior's texts to draw on existing narratives of Native American and American history along with his own subjectivity as a member of the Osage nation corresponds well with the subjects of displacement, resistance, and activism addressed in his work. The application of various theoretical and methodological approaches in his work has enabled Warrior to analyze the processes and aftermath of the incursion and cultural deracination that Native peoples have been subjected to in order to formulate structures of political and cultural critique. In his work Warrior recognizes the centrality of indigenous epistemologies that have been dismissed as "marginal" by the dominant discourse and by doing so underlines the political and historical location of the Native American subject.

By deploying this discourse he seeks to negate the malignant inheritance of colonialism and to reconstruct Native American histories that compose cultural memory and myth. Such narratives enable Native peoples to take charge of their social and political destinies. By articulating the political, social, and historical practices of the indigenous population, Warrior creates a site on which indigenous thought patterns, structures, and rhythms are accompanied by the delineation of an alternative social reality. This approach emphasizes the human interests in the act of telling a story as political intervention. Warrior's work is a crucial component of the blossoming field of Native American theory and criticism.

Bibliography

Smith, Paul Chaat, and Robert Allen Warrior. *Like a Hurricane: The Indian Movement from Alcatraz to Wounded Knee.* New York: New Press, 1996.

Warrior, Robert Allen. *Tribal Secrets: Recovering American Indian Intellectual Traditions.* Minneapolis: University of Minnesota Press, 1995.

Nyla Ali Khan

Waterlily   Ella Cara Deloria (1988)

In the 1930s and 1940s, under the direction of the anthropologists Frank Boas and Ruth Benedict, ELLA CARA DELORIA collected data about the social life of the Sioux. This research provided the foundation for her novel *Waterlily,* which she began writing in 1942 and completed in 1948, though it was not published in her lifetime. As Raymond J. DeMaille explains in the afterword, the novel "represents a blurring of categories: in conception it is fundamentally a work of ethnographic description, but in its method it is narrative fiction" (241). As an ethnographic novel *Waterlily* provides an in-depth study of the cultural life-ways and kinship rules of the Sioux at a time when the encroachment of white civilization was imminent. Rather than focus on the changes wrought by this encroachment, however, Deloria dramatizes the everyday activities of the *tiyospaye,* a group of households within the Sioux camp circle related by both blood and marriage.

Waterlily is essentially a bildungsroman: It traces the growth of the title character from her birth in the first chapter to her second marriage at the end of the book. In following the course of Waterlily's life Deloria's novel presents a chronological and interconnected series of vignettes that detail various aspects of Sioux society: her *hunka* ceremony when she is honored as a "child-beloved" by her stepfather and takes on an elevated position in the tribe (73); her stepfather's induction into the Kit Fox Society, an "old and time-honored" military order charged with guarding the camp (96); the elaborate Sun Dance ceremony, in which she meets her future second husband; her unmarried cousin's participation in the ritual of the Virgin's Fire, held to protect her reputation from "unfounded rumors" lodged against her (139); and this same cousin's responsibility as a ghostkeeper, "caretaker" for the departed spirit of her grandmother (141–143). Taken together, these ceremonies and rituals demarcate the importance of maintaining ties to the community.

With its focus on Waterlily's growth, Deloria's portrait of Sioux life is particularly valuable for its presentation of women's roles and habits within the camp circle, providing an important female perspective on Sioux culture. As her mother had, Waterlily must continually adjust to changing social circumstances as her kinship ties shift through marriage. For example, when Waterlily marries Sacred Horse, she moves to a new camp circle and must adjust to her husband's *tiyospaye.* This initially proves difficult for Waterlily as she is overwhelmed by homesickness and feelings of being an outsider among her husband's family. This adjustment becomes easier after she makes contact with some blood relatives within her husband's camp who become her auxiliary parents. In establishing ties with these relatives and in creating closer relationships with her husband's *tiyospaye,* Waterlily develops a deep appreciation for the extended community of the two "halves" of kinship: "the family of birth and the family of marriage" (178).

Tragically, the close-knit nature of this extended community exacerbates the damage done when Waterlily's *tiyospaye* is inflicted with smallpox, forcing her to adapt to camp life as a pregnant widow. Kinship ties prevail once again, however, as her inlaws and auxiliary parents watch over her and pair her with her second husband, Lowanla, Sacred Horse's cousin. This second marriage is much easier for Waterlily, since through her past trials and through the "cumulative wisdom of Dakota women" (226) she has accepted her role as a wife within the camp circle. With this acceptance the central aspect of Sioux cultural identity is made manifest: The endurance of their community demands that all respect kinship rules and fulfill their role within the framework of these rules. In delineating this framework, Deloria's narrative ultimately preserves the heritage and traditions of the Plains Indians and provides a fictionalized rendering of what life was like in the time before the whites.

Bibliography

Deloria, Ella Cara. *Waterlily.* Lincoln: University of Nebraska Press, 1988.

DeMaille, Raymond J. Afterword. In Ella Cara Deloria, *Waterlily,* 233–244. Lincoln: University of Nebraska Press, 1988.

Hoefel, Roseanne. "'Splendid Discipline': American Indian Women's Ethnographic Literature." In *Between Anthropology and Literature: Interdisciplinary Discourses,* edited by Rose De Angelis, 23–42. London: Routledge, 2002.

Matthew Cella

Watermelon Nights Greg Sarris (1998)

When exploring GREG SARRIS's work, scholars most often celebrate how he redefined ethnobiography in his representation of his grandmother and their shared Miwok culture in KEEPING SLUG WOMAN ALIVE (1993). However, Sarris has also produced a variety of compelling fiction, including a collection of short fiction, GRAND AVENUE (1994), and the novel *Watermelon Nights* (1998). In doing so, Sarris has created works comparable to those of other Native American authors (such as LOUISE ERDRICH and SHERMAN ALEXIE) in the emphasis on redemption through forgiveness. *Watermelon Nights* demonstrates this ability through Sarris's complex and startling representation of three generations of a Pomo family and their struggles to find and maintain their identity despite innumerable forces that would erase them.

In this chronicle Sarris explores the impact on tribal and individual identity of a range of competing forces. For example, he details the effects of physical and psychological abuse on the tribe and its members when he presents Elba's sexual abuse and Felix's assault on Johnny. Other topics that Sarris interweaves include the extermination of the original tribal members by Hispanic colonizers and the consequential enslavement of Carmelita and subsequent enslavements of her descendents to Anglo colonizers over the following centuries. He also interjects the revival of traditional cultural values and identity as a counter to such depredation as well as the growing tribal activism that opens the book. He presents in often excruciating detail the effects of such factors on the lives of the individual characters in this novel.

In representing these forces and their effects, Sarris reveals how the fundamental principle of forgiveness allows tribal members to regain and retain their proper place within the tribal identity. Such reparation takes a variety of forms, from Old Uncle's intentional return and empowerment of Elba to Johnny's unintentional inspiration of community through sharing watermelons. By so characterizing the range of forgiveness possible, Sarris sensitizes his characters and readers to the possibility of mercy and love. This agenda also informs the apparent structure and division of the novel into three parts named for the three main characters, Johnny, Elba, and Iris. Sarris complicates this apparently neat division by emphasizing the characters' commonalties and their need for forgiveness: As characters endure similar situations and react in similar ways, Sarris underscores how central mutual support and love are to their abilities to function. He also demonstrates how acts of love and forgiveness can, if only momentarily, heal wounds. To underscore his thesis, he entitles this novel *Watermelon Nights*, emphasizing the numerous acts of reconciliation that occur amid the chaos and despair that would otherwise destroy the tribe and its members. By doing so, Sarris adds another emphatic statement to the body of works by Native American authors who stress the centrality of forgiveness and tolerance as defining qualities of Native American identity.

Bibliography

Sarris, Greg. *Grand Avenue.* New York: Penguin, 1995.
———. *Keeping Slug Woman Alive.* Berkeley: University of California Press, 1993.
———. *Watermelon Nights.* New York: Hyperion, 1998.

Clay Smith

Waters Between, The   Joseph Bruchac (1998)

The Waters Between is the final book of JOSEPH BRUCHAC's Dawn Land trilogy, a series of novels for young adults set in the Lake Champlain region of New York and Vermont. It continues the stories of Young Hunter and his community begun in the first two books, *DAWN LAND* (1993) and *Long River* (1995), but, as Bruchac insists in the introduction, a reader need not be familiar with the earlier novels to appreciate *Waters.* This trilogy is of special interest for the way that Bruchac re-creates the precontact lifeways of the Abenaki people. He combines ethnographic detail and magic realism to provide an imaginative narrative that presents a Native-centered perspective in which the "world of the spirit is as everyday as eating and sleeping" (xv). Bruchac explains in the introduction how the events narrated in *Waters* are "based on Abenaki traditions, Algonquin material culture" and are "also deeply informed by the stories that I have been told are our oldest Abenaki stories and by the living Abenaki language" (xiii). These materials

join in an adventure tale that intersperses ancient stories and folklore to deepen the context of the action. In this manner Bruchac's Dawn Land trilogy follows in the tradition of other Native American historical romances such as JAMES WELCH's *FOOLS CROW* (1986) and ELLA CARA DELORIA's *WATERLILY* (1988).

Waters traces Young Hunter's continued growth as a "deep seer" and leader of the Abenaki people. The action centers on two threats against Young Hunter's village: Padoskoks, a large snakelike creature who haunts the shores of the Waters Between (Lake Champlain), and Watches Darkness, an evil shaman who wants to destroy the 13 villages of the Abenaki people as revenge for his own rejection by his grandmother. By working together as a community and through the efforts of their "deep seers" the Abenaki are ultimately able to tame Padoskoks and enlist its help to capture Watches Darkness.

The Abenaki success is due to the power of "deep seeing," a shamanic practice that underscores the interconnectedness of all things and that highlights the value of cultivating a reciprocal relationship with the natural world. Young Hunter, of course, recognizes the source of "real power": "There were reasons for everything in the world. Everything was caused by something else. Everything was connected by thin strands like those of a spider's web. Sometimes Young Hunter could see those strands of power and connection, floating in the air, touched by the light" (36). He draws on this power of interconnectivity to defeat Watches Darkness, whose "mind is so twisted that he sees nothing but darkness" (99). Watches Darkness's monomaniacal pursuit of absolute control over the Abenakis stands in stark contrast to the paradigm of cooperation implicit in the practice of deep seeing.

The Abenaki also benefit from a profound respect for their cultural heritage. This heritage is passed on through storytelling, as stories impart valuable lessons about their origins as the "Only People" and about how the Abenaki ought to live. The stories Bruchac weaves within the main narrative provide context for the actions of the community and guide them as they defend themselves against the forces that threaten them. Ultimately the Abenaki victory over the selfish and power-hungry Watches Darkness highlights the main values of the community: cooperation, forgiveness, respect for the nonhuman community, and faith in the vitality of storytelling and ritual.

Bibliography

Bruchac, Joseph. *The Waters Between.* Hanover, N.H.: University Press of New England, 1998.

Ricker, Meredith. "A *MELUS* Interview: Joseph Bruchac." *MELUS* 21, no. 3 (1996): 159–176.

Matthew Cella

Way to Rainy Mountain, The N. Scott Momaday (1969)

N. SCOTT MOMADAY's *The Way to Rainy Mountain* (1969) is a nonfiction book that features a textured portrayal of the Kiowa tribe's cultural history. In the late 17th century the Kiowa people migrated from their former tribal territory in present-day Montana to a section of present-day Oklahoma, where they adapted to living on the southern Great Plains. Momaday's book metaphorically compares the tribe's difficult historic trek to Rainy Mountain (a knoll in Oklahoma that the Kiowa have deemed as sacred) with the imaginative journey the contemporary reader must embark upon to attain heightened spiritual awareness and increased interconnectedness with the natural world and with the past.

Ostensibly a collection of Kiowa folk narratives, *The Way to Rainy Mountain* also features Momaday's subjective interpretations of that tribe's heritage. The work is noted for its graceful and detailed writing style as well as for its keen insights into the values and meanings of Kiowa culture. *The Way to Rainy Mountain*—along with its author's commercially and artistically successful novel *HOUSE MADE OF DAWN*, published in 1968—drew considerable national attention to Momaday, who by the early 1970s was widely lauded as a major new figure in American literature and as a leading voice in the AMERICAN INDIAN LITERARY RENAISSANCE.

Published by the University of New Mexico Press in 1969, *The Way to Rainy Mountain* was Momaday's revision of his first book, the limited-edition Kiowa folk narrative collection *The Journey of Tai-me* (1967); the earlier work had featured Momaday's English translations of Kiowa myths transcribed from oral tradition, which tribal elders had told the author during his childhood. In 1968 a major publisher, Harper & Row, issued Momaday's second book, *House Made of Dawn,* which received the Pulitzer Prize. For his third book the author—encouraged by the poet and critic Yvor Winters, Momaday's former professor at Stanford University—crafted an experimental revision of *The Journey of Tai-me.* The new work, *The Way to Rainy Mountain,* juxtaposed Momaday's translations of Kiowa myths with the author's impressionistic prose commentaries on aspects of Kiowa cultural history along with his evocation of his experience growing up in modern America as a tradition bearer from an indigenous New World culture. The latter book also featured two of Momaday's best-known poems

In interpreting Kiowa history from traditional and modernist perspectives, *The Way to Rainy Mountain* affirmed the importance of contemporary Kiowa people's maintaining meaningful connections to their tribal traditions. That work reflected Momaday's recognition that modern Native Americans were leading lives profoundly shaped by the same historical forces that affected the lives of their tribal ancestors.

Significantly *The Way to Rainy Mountain* explored only part of Momaday's ancestry—that of his father's side of the family (his mother was one-eighth Cherokee, with the rest of her bloodlines traceable to various white ethnicities). To be sure, Momaday was born within the historic territory of the Kiowa, yet he grew up among people of other tribal affiliations (specifically, Navajo and San Carlos Apache) and lived in various communities across the southwestern United States. Momaday claimed the motivation for writing the book was his psychic need to assess Kiowa identity in modern America after the recent death of his paternal grandmother, which made him realize that she had "belonged to the last culture to evolve in North America." Momaday's identification with his father's cultural heritage is underscored by the fact that his father—Al Momaday, a skilled visual artist—illustrated the original edition of *The Way to Rainy Mountain.* Yet critics have asserted that the book, while focused on Kiowa culture, reflects the universal predicament of all Native Americans today—the need to reclaim a usable tribal past to help contemporary Natives better cope with life in mainstream America.

Ted Olson

Bibliography

Prampolini, Gaetano. "'Many Journeys into One': *The Way to Rainy Mountain* and N. Scott Momaday's Literary Work." In *Native American Literature,* edited by Laura Coltelli, 3–30. Pisa: SEU, 1994.

Roemer, Kenneth, ed. *Approaches to Teaching Momaday's* The Way to Rainy Mountain. New York: Modern Language Association of America, 1988.

We Are the Dreamers: Recent and Early Poetry   Rita Joe (1999)

We Are the Dreamers, which republishes RITA JOE's inaugural collection, *Poems of Rita Joe* (1978), alongside 53 more recent, previously unpublished poems, embodies in both form and content the poet's conciliatory philosophy. Beyond linking distinct periods in Joe's poetic life, *We Are the Dreamers* unites traditional SPIRITUALITY with Christianity, Mi'kmaq with the English language, philosophical commentary with the mundane, and the intensely personal with universal insights. Through the vehicle of concise, autobiographically charged poetry Joe wages what she calls a "gentle war" (26) against racism and sexism—modes of thought that divide and oppress—promoting positive engagements with the colonial legacy. At a time when indigenous resistance literature is dominated by confrontational voices, Joe's poetry endorses forgiveness and unity.

In poems like "Weji-uli-Niskam (Holy Spirit)," which is at once a prayer to the apparently Christian God and a celebration of the way the divine can be engaged through traditional Native means, Joe envisions a form of religious syncretism, or the combination of two separate belief systems into one, born Mi'kmaq heritage. Although the Mi'kmaq were among the first tribes broadly to adopt Christianity in the 1600s, they have maintained many aspects of their traditional culture, including their language. "Weji-uli-Niskam" unites the Christian concept of the Holy Spirit with a Mi'kmaq worldview first by articulating God in Mi'kmaq—*Niskam*—and second by developing a method of praising that mobilizes indigenous heritage materials: "My tobacco is there, the sweetgrass ready, / The peace pipe is in my family. / O Holy Spirit I thank you" (17).

Joe's unifying vision in *Dreamers* extends beyond the spiritual realm to the interactions among (often disparately empowered) individuals and cultures. In "Poor Man, Poor World" Joe addresses the denigration of Native cultures by non-Natives, but in a way that actively bridges the schism of misunderstanding and promotes reconciliation. Joe's speaker, an indigenous writer and cultural spokesperson, is confronted by a non-Native, who asks, "Will you come to our school to speak? / I would appreciate it. / Whatever it is you speak about, basket weaving or what" (14). Although disheartened by the reduction of her artistry and heritage to "basket weaving," the speaker determines to "speak to his schoolchildren" nonetheless and thereby combat and eclipse the teacher's ignorance. She declares, "I love his children, I am a determined Indian / I love his children and I have a heart" (14). Rather than allow herself to be immobilized by the weight of racism, Joe's speaker is inspired to act: "The crooked world will never change. / *I will though,* / Putting a badge on my heart" (14).

Joe's poetry enacts a unique type of resistance that is exercised in sympathy for and transcendence of ignorance, racism, and sexism, a poetic stance more forgiving than condemning, but never naively so. As Joe writes at the beginning of both halves of *We Are the Dreamers,* "I am the Indian, / And the burden / Lies yet with me" (1, 57).

Bibliography

Joe, Rita. *We Are the Dreamers: Recent and Early Poetry.* Sydney, Australia: Breton Books, 1999.

Sam McKegney

Weesquachak and the Lost Ones   Ruby Slipperjack-Farrell (2000)

Weesquachak and the Lost Ones narrates the struggles and triumphs of two characters from an Ojibwe trapping settlement in northern Ontario. Of importance to understanding this novel is the presence of Weesquachak, or the TRICKSTER FIGURE, and his interference and interaction with the characters. This is the story of "the lost ones," Janine and Fred, and their struggles to negotiate landscape, relationship, identity, and culture. While Janine is searching to find independence and self-sufficiency in urban centers and attempting to leave behind her rural roots, she finds herself continuously returning to those roots on the trapline of northern Ontario, and to Fred, a hunter and trapper whose own struggle to find his way is complicated by the clash of aboriginal and nonaboriginal worlds.

Weesquachak, as a trickster, possesses the ability to shape shift as needed, but not always for reasons and in ways that are necessarily helpful to the humans that are affected by Weesquachak's meddling. At the beginning of the novel Weesquachak states his irritation that he has been forgotten about by the latest generation; this is evidenced by his comment that Janine "seems lost" (7). The motive for his appearance in the lives of Fred and Janine is to take them back to their culture. His purpose is to effect change; hence Janine and Fred are forced by Weesquachak's meddling to confront the various issues in their lives and make changes; otherwise they would certainly not survive the challenges of balancing tradition with modernity, urban and rural, aboriginal with nonaboriginal culture. The trickster creates disorder so that the humans must work together to restore order and in the process grow as individuals and as members of their community. Weesquachak's presence should be understood as a symbol of cultural rebirth.

Janine was educated in a residential school and has returned to her settlement only to find herself frustrated with the limited options. Desiring more, she leaves for the city in search of employment, a sojourn that will take her farther from her roots but will afford her the independence that she seeks; however, while she is successful in her pursuit of career, she is drawn to Fred and all that he represents to her of her traditions and roots. Her transition from city life to trapline is less than smooth and it becomes imperative that Janine face her own limitations and take responsibility for herself in the bush.

Fred is a traditional hunter and trapper. Janine has been promised as his wife, a deal brokered in order to ease a debt from Janine's father to Fred's, and so Fred views her as property. Fred must lose Janine's faith and trust, along with their baby, before he is willing or able to live in an equal relationship, based on love instead of ownership. Fred must also reconcile his isolated existence with the demands of community and cohabitation and learn to trust himself in order to trust Janine and break the cycle of alcohol abuse and physical abuse into which he has entered.

Bibliography

Bowerbank, Sylvia."Wild Lessons: Native Ecological Wisdom in Ruby Slipperjack's Fiction." In *Homemaking: Women Writers and the Politics and Poetics of Home,* edited by Catherine Wiley and Fiona R. Barnes, 223–238. New York: Garland, 1996.

Slipperjack, Ruby. *Weesquachak and the Lost Ones.* Penticton, Canada: Theytus Books, 2000.

Jolene Armstrong

Welch, James   (1940–2003)

James Philip Welch, Jr., an enrolled member of the Blackfeet tribe, was born on November 18, 1940, in Browning, Montana, headquarters of the Blackfeet Indian Nation. His father was Blackfeet and Irish, and his mother was Gros Ventre and Irish. Welch attended schools on the Blackfeet and Fort Belknap reservations, finishing high school in Minneapolis. He attended the University of Minnesota and Northern Montana College and graduated from the University of Montana in 1965 with a B.A. in liberal arts. That fall he enrolled in the creative writing program at Montana, where he studied with Richard Hugo and Madeline DeFrees. Hugo was especially influential to the young poet and encouraged him to write about what he knew: life on the reservation and the plains and being Indian in a predominantly white world. With Hugo's encouragement Welch considered making writing a career.

In 1968 Welch married Lois Monk, then professor of comparative literature and English at the University of Montana in Missoula, where they made their home. Welch published his first (and only) volume of poems, RIDING THE EARTHBOY 40, in 1971, followed by WINTER IN THE BLOOD (1974), *The DEATH OF JIM LONEY* (1979), *FOOLS CROW* (1986), *The INDIAN LAWYER* (1990), *Killing Custer* (1994), and *The HEARTSONG OF CHARGING ELK* (2000). Welch occasionally accepted invitations to teach creative writing and Native American literature at the University of Washington and Cornell University, led workshops and short writing seminars, and gave readings all over the country and abroad. From 1979 to 1990 Welch served on the Montana State Board of Pardons, work that inspired *The Indian Lawyer.* He died in August 2003 after a year-long battle with cancer.

Welch was highly praised for his work and received public recognition for his contributions to literature and wider understanding of Native Americans. Among his many awards are the Indian Council Fire National Achievement Award, the American Book Award, and the Pacific Northwest Book Award. He received honorary doctorates from the University of Montana, Montana State University, and Rocky Mountain College. Especially praised in France, Welch was "knighted" by the French government when they named him Chevalier de l'Ordre des Arts et des Lettres of France in 1995.

Welch, along with N. SCOTT MOMADAY and LESLIE MARMON SILKO, launched the so-called AMERICAN INDIAN LITERARY RENAISSANCE, a rebirth of Native American literature marked by Momaday's Pulitzer Prize–winning *HOUSE MADE OF DAWN* (1968), followed closely by Welch's first novel, *Winter in the Blood.* Most distinct about Welch's work are the care he takes with language and the precision with which he imagines ordinary as well as extraordinary lives. Welch's unsentimental gaze strips away romanticized notions of

Native peoples that still fill American mainstream imaginations. His early work concerns itself with questions of what it means to be an American Indian in a predominantly white world and focuses on the search for identity through the excavation of a meaningful past in the face of the devastating effects of colonialism on tribal cultures. His later projects increase in historical and geographical scope in order to examine and critique major narratives of American history—such as the myths surrounding the battle at the Little Bighorn. Welch deconstructs historical representations of American Indians and instead reimagines U.S. history from the "other side" in order to celebrate the perseverance of Native American peoples.

Applauding the 2004 rerelease of *Riding the Earthboy 40,* his fellow Native American writer and poet SHERMAN ALEXIE proclaimed the book to be the most important volume of poems in the Native American literary canon. Welch's poetry—abstract, surreal, and ironic—is admired for its imagery, precision, and measured rhythms. Many of his poems express desperation, but they also voice an urgent longing for belief and hope, evident in poems such as "In My Lifetime," in which the speaker says that even if he is "desperate in my song" (5), he also is "rhythm to strong medicine" (6). Welch stopped writing poetry after *Earthboy* because he felt he needed fiction's wider canvas to explore his subjects; however, many readers still detect the sound of poetry in his fiction.

Welch's *Winter in the Blood* established him as one of the leading voices in Native American literature. The unnamed 32-year-old protagonist of the novel lives on the Fort Belknap Reservation in Montana and gradually comes to terms with the haunting memory of his brother's death, learning to put together fragments of stories into a cohesive understanding not only of the past but also of his identity in relation to that past. The novel received national attention with a front-cover review in the *New York Times Book Review,* in which Reynolds Price described it as "an almost flawless novel." The novel's humor, sometimes not noted upon a first reading, is seen by some critics as its distinguishing characteristic. Welch himself reads the novel's humor as countering "that vision of alienation and purposelessness, aimlessness" often associated with Native American novels (McFarland 9).

Welch's much bleaker second novel, *The Death of Jim Loney,* features a protagonist who is haunted by the past and disconnected from both his Indian and his white heritage. Unlike the narrator of *Winter,* Loney is unable to interpret the signs that disrupt his life because he lacks the necessary cultural references. Some readers find hope in the fact that Loney actively orchestrates his own death, after rejecting the lure of white ASSIMILATION (always already doomed by failure) and moving onto the reservation.

Welch's third novel explores the mystery genre while portraying a more contemporary and successful model of American Indian. *The Indian Lawyer,* which is more conventional in structure and style than his other novels, features a successful attorney who becomes caught up in a blackmail scheme while serving on the Montana State Board of Pardons. Indian identity is much less important to Sylvester Yellow Calf than to Welch's earlier protagonists. Primarily focused on what it means to be a successful American Indian in white America, *Indian Lawyer* also portrays the increasing distance felt by the successful Indian from his native community.

Fools Crow marks a departure for Welch not only because it is a historical novel, but also because the language he created for the novel can be read as a translation of verbal Blackfeet into written English. Imagining what life must have been like for the Blackfeet on the plains of the late 1860s, Welch uses a mix of straightforwardness and surrealism, creating a text that approximates the way the Blackfeet perceived the particular western landscape around and within them. For non-Indian readers, the novel produces an initial sense of alienation, forcing them to readjust their expectations and to occupy, if only for a while, an experience altogether "other" from a mainstream American perspective. Much of the novel is informed by the stories that Welch's great-grandmother told his father—who then passed them on to him. She survived the Marias River Massacre of 1870 with which the novel ends. Despite the well-known history lying in wait for the Plains tribes,

the novel has an optimistic ending, reinforcing an argument underlying much of Welch's work: Despite conquest, ALCOHOLISM, suicide, and unemployment ravaging reservations today, Native Americans are resilient and will persevere.

Killing Custer, Welch's only nonfiction work, developed from his collaboration with the filmmaker Paul Stekler on the documentary *Last Stand at Little Bighorn.* In this book Welch explores from an Indian perspective the history and mythology surrounding the battle at the Little Bighorn, where Sioux and Cheyenne defeated Custer and the Seventh Cavalry. Welch found this project nothing short of intimidating, considering that the battle "may be the most depicted event in our nation's history" (*Killing* 22). His book makes no claims to be a historical textbook but instead is meant to provide an alternative understanding of American Indians through a mix of personal reflection and reinterpretation of historical documents. The book is Welch's most overt criticism of the U.S. government and the military's treatment of the indigenous population, a legacy still felt today.

The Heartsong of Charging Elk is about a young Lakota who travels to France as a performer in Buffalo Bill's Wild West Show in 1889. His story of being stranded in Marseilles where no one speaks his language, is based on historical incidents that Welch researched on trips to France in the 1990s. Welch here explores what happens to someone in a radically foreign environment and how someone finds his way in such circumstances against great odds. Thematically the novel complicates questions of home and national belonging. Also, it challenges romanticized images of the vanishing Indian produced by Buffalo Bill's Wild West Show during the late 19th century. Welch was working on a sequel to *Heartsong* at the time of his death. In this novel, to be set in 1916, he intended to have Charging Elk take his young son back to America. Thus he would explore both the joy and the difficulty of returning to a culture as changed for the Indians as Europe had just been by World War I.

Bibliography
McFarland, Ron. "Interview with James Welch." In *James Welch.* Lewiston, Idaho: Confluence, 1986.

———. *Understanding James Welch.* Columbia: University of South Carolina Press, 2000.

Owens, Louis. "Earthboy's Return: James Welch's Acts of Recovery." In *Other Destinies: Understanding the American Indian Novel,* 128 166. Norman: University of Oklahoma Press, 1992.

Price, Reynolds. Review of *Winter in the Blood. New York Times Book Review* 10 November 1974, p. 1.

Shanley, Kathryn. *"Only an Indian": Reading James Welch.* Norman: University of Oklahoma Press, 2005.

Welch, James. *The Death of Jim Loney.* New York: Harper & Row, 1979.

———. *Fools Crow.* New York: Viking, 1986.

———. *The Heartsong of Charging Elk.* New York: Doubleday, 2000.

———. *The Indian Lawyer.* New York: Norton, 1990.

———, with Paul Stekler. *Killing Custer: The Battle of the Little Big Horn and the Fate of the Plains Indians.* New York: Norton, 1994.

Winter in the Blood. New York: Harper & Row, 1974.

Andrea Opitz

West Pole, The   Diane Glancy (1997)

Published by the University of Minnesota Press, this is a collection of DIANE GLANCY's commentaries, observations, literary criticism, and speeches. It is organized into nine sections. Every odd-numbered section is entitled "Now," with the other sections focusing on writing, language, stories, history, and reviews. The "Now" sections contain between three and 11 short pieces each. Some are just a few lines of observation, others are full-length essays on culture. In the prefacelike first section, called "Diffusionism," Glancy explains a bit of her life, especially the way her desire to tell stories and connect with her Cherokee and white heritages awoke. This is her "West Pole." The term returns often, including in a short essay called "The West Pole" about halfway through the volume.

The speeches were originally given to different audiences, such as at a college or a scholarly conference, but they are not written for just one group of listeners. "Culture and the Environment: Voices in the Wind" is built on the premise that the land itself is also a storyteller. Glancy refers to an ancient belief that the Great Spirit spoke, or told, the world into existence. "Their Eyes Have Seen the Buffalo" is a commentary on Native American literature, as she sees it. She says she writes at a distance from her traditions because of the path of her life but that all current Indian writers are also living at a distance from their people's culture.

Her history section is both profound and playful. One piece is the essay "Columbus Meets Thelma and Louise and the Ocean Is Still Bigger Than Any of Us Thought." She discusses the cultural conflicts of both Columbus's crashing into a very different society in the New World and her thoughts after seeing the 1991 movie about two women searching for a sense of freedom in a male-dominated world. She also presents a more personal history with a family photo album that covers a few generations.

The reviews are of books by her fellow Native American writer LESLIE MARMON SILKO, the author Charles Fergus, and on what she calls "Emergent Literatures That Challenge the Standard." Silko, whose book CEREMONY (1977) Glancy calls the Great American Indian Novel, had just published ALMANAC OF THE DEAD (1992). Glancy's reaction to the book is visceral. She finds it shocking and challenging to her idea of self and her culture. Fergus, who is not a Native American, is being praised for having written *Shadow Catcher* not only about the Indian conflicts with the settlers but in a way that reflects the true Native American state of mind. Her final review is about not only contemporary theater but also the struggle of new voices to enter the literary discussion. Through these three, including the very impressionist last essay, we are able to gain a sense of Glancy's definition of what Native American literature might be.

Michael Young

What Moon Drove Me to This? Joy Harjo (1979)

In JOY HARJO's *What Moon Drove Me to This?* the Native American philosophy of the cyclical nature of time marries the past and present seamlessly. Harjo, of Creek descent and an enrolled member of the Creek Nation, mines the mythology, legends, and history of her ancestors. Poems solidly anchored with the mundane details of everyday life take on a cosmic significance as past and present dissolve.

Technology is seen as a tool of Anglo oppression rather than one that provides freedom and makes life easier. In "3 AM" the speaker and her companion are stranded in an airport terminal trying to make their way to Third Mesa, the Hopi spiritual home. Having taken away their homeland, the technology controlled by the white man refuses to help them reach their spiritual home. The "guncatcher machine" is a technology set in another airport that fails to detect the gun in the speaker's head ("I Am a Dangerous Woman").

Personal relationships are also negatively affected by technology. The telephone in "Are You Still There?" fails to make the speaker closer to her estranged lover. Her voice "stumbles" and "is caught / shredded on a barbed wire fence" (52). Frustration with the limitations of telephone communication is explored in "Half-Light" as well. The speaker's old lover calls her in the middle of the night but leaves her "waiting someplace on the wire / where my words left home / years ago" (63). The phone does not have the power to bridge the gap yawning between the two, and the sound of her lover's voice only serves to "twist" her.

Cars and trucks offer a way to use technology to good advantage in *What Moon?* Along with Noni Daylight, the poet's alter ego (SHE HAD SOME HORSES, 1983), the speaker of "Evidence" tells us about a night ride to escape a small apartment and sleeping children. In "Looking Back" the full moon is excuse enough to ride 90 miles per hour. Harjo's characters are continually traveling. In "Origins" Noni Daylight thinks "she must still be traveling from [the Grand Canyon]," site of the Hopi birthplace, "but not very far at all" (33). Her characters are wanderers seeking the home from which they were forcibly removed, yet never wind up too far away from where they began. They encounter fellow travelers, often in bars, exchanging stories and maps. By sharing the same pantribal memories and histories, they learn that a physical home is not as important as the spiritual one they carry with them.

Bibliography

Harjo, Joy. *The Spiral of Memory: Interviews,* edited by Laura Coltelli. Ann Arbor: University of Michigan Press, 1996.

———. *What Moon Drove Me to This?* New York: Reed Books, 1979.

Scarry, John. "Representing Real Worlds: The Evolving Poetry of Joy Harjo." *World Literature Today* 66, no. 2 (spring 1992): 286–291.

P. K. Bostian

Whispering in Shadows Jeanette Armstrong (2000)

In this novel JEANETTE ARMSTRONG explores one woman's spiritual and psychological journey, beginning with a separation from herself to a complete embrace of her Native American identity. Penny Jackson finds herself straddling two worlds: the white culture that stigmatizes her because of her racial identity, and the Native American culture that teaches her to embrace its traditions to maintain her identity.

In her life so far Penny has only been able to survive by working odd jobs while taking care of her children. This situation is a recurrent theme throughout Native American literature, and as an author Armstrong consider it her duty to show that Native Americans are not "savage, not dirty and ugly, and not less because [they] have brown skin, or a Native philosophy" ("Voices from the Gaps 2").

Penny enrolls in college and finds that interactions with her young white peers help her begin to transform from an embittered woman unsure of her place to a stronger mother and artist. Returning to school allows Penny to begin realizing her full potential as a Native American artist and to carve out her identity as a Native American woman.

Eventually Penny realizes she must take her children back to the place of her birth, to her extended family. Once she has returned home, her identity continues to develop as she and family try to heal the wounds of the past while she battles cancer. While she has always turned to childhood memories in times of great struggle to give herself a strong identity, Penny now recognizes that her family and her culture have always been the backbone of her struggle to give herself and her children a better life. Now that she has done so for her children by returning them to their community, Penny turns to her sister, Lena, to aid her in overcoming her past. As Penny battles cancer and Lena tries to overcome her drug addiction, both women find healing strength in each other and their community.

Penny, Lena, and their children find healing in the land they had rejected in their youth, allowing them to travel full circle. Both sisters recognize that their rejection of their home is what caused them to feel splintered from their true selves. Returning to their community has allowed the sisters to reunite as a family and find inner peace, especially Penny, whose cancer will eventually take her life. As Penny prepares for death, she discovers that she could go home again and that her identity is the greatest lesson she has learned during her long journey. All of the intricately connected patterns of her life have created a whole human being; someone whose greatest gift to her family, her land, and her causes has been the discovery of self.

Bibliography

Armstrong, Jeanette. *Whispering in Shadows*. Penticton, Canada: Theytus Books, 2000.

"Voices from the Gaps: Women Writers of Color: Jeanette Armstrong." University of Minnesota. Available online. URL: http://voices.cla.umn.edu/newsite/authors/Armstrong. Accessed on August 15, 2005.

Sumeeta Patnaik

Wild Harvest   **John Milton Oskison** (1925)
Wild Harvest: A Novel of Transition Days in Oklahoma is Oskison's first novel. The action takes place just before statehood in the Indian Territory, "the long grass country," near Walnut Creek, with Big Grove as its trading center and metropolis, "a world in the making, and even a child caught the stir and splendid promise of it" (3).

It is the story of Nancy Forest, a "hayseed," between the age 15 and the time of her marriage to Tom Winger, a cowboy with the prospects of a rancher. Nan is an enterprising, honest young woman, whose good looks attract three suitors in turn: Tom Winger, Jack Hayes (who will prove to be a bank robber), and Harvey Stokes, whose jealous and bullying nature will estrange the heroine from him. In spite of her mother's death of tuberculosis three years earlier, when the novel opens, Nan is living happily with her unreliable father, Chester—a reader of romances—, whom she cherishes and protects, and her childless Aunt Susan and Uncle Bill Dines.

A perfect example of popular literature, the novel is replete with stock characters, such as the religious and visionary Sam Davis; the coarse, narrow-minded Harvey Stokes; the generous cattleman Gabe Horner; Cherokee and other Indians, full-bloods and MIXED-BLOODS, at times "placid," at times "drunken"—and, all in all, good and bad "gals" and "guys." Among them is the seductress, the foul-mouthed Ruby Engel, the opposite of fair Nan, who will instigate a number of catastrophes. The situations are similarly predictable: it is also a story of guns, and moonshine; for all her strength of will even Nan can faint, and men kiss girls "furiously"; one chapter is tellingly entitled "Living a Melodrama"; there are fights and killings, but conveniently only bad characters die a violent death.

Along with those stereotypes the story presents an idealized view of life on the "friendly" prairie, where whites, Indians, blacks, cowmen, haymen, farmers, "storekeepers, traders, lawyers, and jus' town folks" (53), can happily enjoy a dance together; where "the new square three-story brick Academy testif[ies] to the alertness of Indians and whites alike in the matter of education" (55); or even where a white man (Vergil Stokes, "a visible, practical link between the two races") (27) can be lawfully elected chair of the local tribal council.

In its careful description of everyday life and chores on a farm throughout the year, its faithful rendering of dialect, the novel is undeniably local color, while the plot itself—love story and foreseeable turns of events—is extremely sentimental.

Above all *Wild Harvest* is a homage to the prairie itself, with lyrical descriptions of its flowers, wild animals, musical birds, and open, exhilarating landscape: "[Nan's] eyes had widened and sparkled at the sight of miles and miles of undulating seas of shining, dew-wet spider webs spun from grasstop to grass-top" (123). In this beautiful country where "there's enough for all," the novel repeatedly asks, "Why can't we all be friends?"

Bibliography

Ruoff, A. LaVonne Brown. *American Indian Literatures: An Introduction, Bibliographic Review, and Selected Bibliography.* New York: MLA, 1990.

Simone Pellerin

Wild Indians and Other Creatures   Adrian C. Louis (1996)

In *Wild Indians and Other Creatures,* a collection of loosely related short stories, ADRIAN C. LOUIS introduces the traditional TRICKSTER FIGURE into modern-day South Dakota. Coyote, Raven, and Old Bear, all protagonists of the short stories, regularly interact with humans and one another, as Louis simultaneously addresses contemporary Indian culture and his own anger with it. As do most trickster figures, these characters are unpredictable and politically incorrect, and, when placed in Budweiser era America, they respond accordingly.

The first story, "How Coyote Got Killed and Resurrected," sets the tone for much of the collection. Coyote, a trickster in his prime, is arrested by two dog catchers, shot by a female prison guard he offends on many levels, only to be resurrected three days later, on Easter Sunday. In a subsequent story nearer the bottom of Coyote's downward spiral, he sees a monster's face inside a glass of "psychedelic gin" (4) and only after several tries to remove this terror does he realizes the "monster" is his own shabby reflection. Most of the characters in the stories are dynamic in that, no matter what direction they are headed, they are undoubtedly headed *somewhere*. Among Coyote's cohorts are Raven, the cynical bird who is skeptical of the writings of BLACK ELK and is addicted to the television program *Cuisine Rapide,* and Old Bear, who has a love for casseroles and an eye for two blonde schoolteachers at the local Indian school.

Equally irreverent is Louis's treatment of Native Americans within the work. Mariana Two Knives, an alcoholic-teen-mother-turned-harlot, is a central figure in many of the stories, which chronicle her journey from teenage pregnancy to untimely death. She, along with Coyote, is testimony to Louis's frustration with modern-day Indian culture. Mariana is an extreme example of an all too typical situation. She started drinking and bearing children before she was old enough to drive, and her drinking never ceased, even when she was pregnant. The result was her baby, Sherman, a victim of fetal alcohol syndrome and the symbol of purity and unadulterated love in the book. Sherman is perhaps the only unaffected creature in the text, but he too meets an untimely end, though Mariana never knows that.

Louis, in equal parts, shows us POVERTY, ALCOHOLISM, and the depths to which one can sink, but he also shows us love, tenderness, and heartfelt grace. Stories that start out sardonically on more than one occasion end with awkward warmth, or in self-revelation and human compassion, which is itself a kind of grace, especially when unexpected.

Jordan Racavich

Wind from an Enemy Sky   D'Arcy McNickle (1978)

Wind from an Enemy Sky is, as is D'ARCY McNICKLE's earlier novel *The SURROUNDED*, a depressing tale that ends in profound tragedy. Nevertheless McNickle is adept at capturing the cultural worldviews of two distinct cultures in a way that exposes the spiritual gulf that lies between them. As a MIXED-BLOOD person born of two cultures (McNickle's mother was Métis, his father the son of Irish immigrants), McNickle was in a privileged position to understand and convey the differences between the Native American traditions and white cultural practices.

The novel weaves together two distinct storylines: One involves the effort of the Indian leader Bull to recover a sacred medicine bundle that his brother, Henry Jim, had many years earlier renounced and turned over to the whites. The other involves the murder of a engineer at a dam recently constructed on the reservation—the suspected perpetrator of which is Bull's nephew, Pock-face. The sympathetic Indian agent Rafferty does his best to track down and recover the Feather Boy medicine bundle even as he is forced to assist the federal marshals in prosecuting Bull's nephew for the murder.

The fundamental theme of the novel is the incommensurability between white culture and Native American culture; the central tragedy originates from the basic inability of the whites to understand the world from the Native American point of view, and vice versa. Though many of the characters mean well, their actions backfire or wreak greater havoc than they intend. One example is Pock-face's murder of the innocent engineer at the dam as vengeance for the white man's having "killed the waters." Another is the white character Adam Pell's attempt to replace the sacred Feather Boy medicine bundle with a Peruvian gold statue as a way of atoning for building the dam. Both gestures result from the inability of both the whites and the Native Americans to communicate beyond their own cultural boundaries.

The novel not only is an exploration of the profound cultural divide between the whites and the Indians, but may be seen as an environmentalist work as well: The Indians remain tragically unable to overcome the loss of a cultural icon after the destruction of the medicine bundle, and they are unable to prevent "the killing of the waters" after the industrialist Adam Pell constructs his huge dam on the reservation.

Many critics have noted that whereas much of McNickle's other work expresses a hope and optimism for the continuity of Indian culture, *Wind from an Enemy Sky* ends on a note of abject despair and pessimism. Parker writes that the overall tone of the tale is one of "overwhelming futility" (234). In this sense McNickle's final novel is much more akin to *The Surrounded* (1936) than to Runner in the Sun (1954).

D'Arcy McNickle worked on his last novel for 30 years. It was published in 1978, just after he died.

Bibliography

Parker, Dorothy R. *Singing an Indian Song: A Biography of D'Arcy McNickle.* Lincoln: University of Nebraska Press, 1992.

Purdy, John Lloyd, ed. *The Legacy of D'Arcy McNickle: Writer, Historian, Activist.* Norman: University of Oklahoma Press, 1996.

Aaron Parrett

Winnemucca, Sarah   (circa 1844–1891)

Sarah Winnemucca was a leader and spokesperson for the Northern Paiute during the turmoil of white expansion in the West. She is remembered today primarily for *Life among the Piutes* (1883), the first full-length autobiography by a Native American woman, in which she explains her people's customs, traces her tribe's history of friendship with whites, and condemns the government's treatment of her people.

Winnemucca was the granddaughter of Chief Winnemucca, leader of a band who traditionally lived in northwestern Nevada. Sarah was a little girl when her tribe first encountered whites, and she begins her autobiography by describing her grandfather's enormous goodwill. He aided the U.S. Army during the Mexican-American War and afterward took members of his family, including the six-year-old Sarah, to California to live for a year with white settlers. Yet with the ravages of disease and the steady encroachment of settlers on Paiute land, the rich culture Winnemucca describes in her autobiography—the strong familial bonds, the courtship ceremonies, the democratic social structure (including the high status of women), and the peaceful religion centered on a strong belief in a spirit land—was threatened.

Conflict with settlers led to the brief Pyramid Lake War in 1860, after which many Paiute settled on a Nevada reservation. Winnemucca briefly attended boarding school in California, then returned to the reservation, where she worked as an interpreter and began appearing with her family on stage to present her culture. Aggressive settlers and corrupt Indian agents, however, continued to plague her tribe, and Winnemucca struggled to maintain her close ties to the U.S. Army as her people were forced to different reservations, often under brutal conditions. She proved a valuable U.S. ally during the Bannock War of 1878 but continued poor treatment by the government provoked her to lecture across the country in order to win support for her people. She appeared some 300 times, winning an especially receptive audience in the Northeast, where the reformer Elizabeth Peabody became an influential advocate and Mary Mann prompted her to write her story. With their support Winnemucca started a school in 1884 that educated Paiute children in both English and their native language; after four successful years, it ran out of funds. Exhausted and in poor health, Winnemucca went to live with her sister in Idaho, where she died in 1891.

Winnemucca was—and remains—a controversial figure. She fiercely defended her reputation against accusations of drinking, gambling, and "loose morals." She was married at least twice, in both cases to former army officers who drank and gambled away her money. In her own time a number of Paiute protested her close ties to the U.S. government and her claim to speak for the entire nation. Her embrace of European-American culture has earned her critics to this day. Others, however, point to her as a bicultural figure, struggling to find a middle ground between white and Indian society. Her autobiography is noted not only for its strong feminism and strident critique of injustice, but also for its ability to adapt Paiute traditions—communal identity, formal speech patterns, and the coup tale—to autobiographical and sentimental conventions. Whatever the exact nature of her legacy, Sarah Winnemucca remains a critical figure in the history of Native and European-American contact.

Bibliography

Canfield, Gae Whitney. *Sarah Winnemucca of the Northern Paiutes.* Norman: University of Oklahoma Press, 1983.

Sanjani, Sally. *Sarah Winnemucca.* Lincoln: University of Nebraska Press, 2001.

Seiner, Siobhan. *Voices of American Indian Assimilation and Resistance: Helen Hunt Jackson, Sarah Winnemucca and Victoria Howard.* Norman: University of Oklahoma Press, 2001.

John J. Kucich

Winning the Dust Bowl   Carter Revard (2001)

Carter Revard's memoir, a finalist for the Oklahoma Book Award in 2001 and described in X. J. Kennedy's cover blurb as "one of the great American autobiographies," chronicles a remarkable life lived in the intersections of multiple cultures and histories. Revard grew up on the Osage Reservation in Oklahoma during dust bowl times amid an extended family of Osage, Ponca, and Scots-Irish relations, attending a one-room school where he worked as a janitor to help support his family. After winning a radio quiz show scholarship to the University of Tulsa, he went on to Oxford and Yale and a brilliant career as a poet and scholar of mediaeval English and American Indian literatures. On a parallel path he participated in the activism of the American Indian Movement (AIM) years and became a gourd dancer and community organizer in St. Louis, where he taught at Washington University until his retirement.

Winning the Dust Bowl is above all, however, the autobiography of a poet. Arranged not chronologically but associatively, it layers previously published poems with new poems, family stories, history, and photographs, to provide a "home" for poems of "transformation and awakening" that mark Revard's development as a poet (xiii) and enable him to make the forms of English verse his own. The book opens with Revard's best-known poem, "Coyote Tells Why He Sings," an unrhymed sonnet that describes the poet's discovery of his poetic voice. "Walking with Friends down Lorigill and Dibadal, on the Isle of Skye" marks Revard's transition from blank verse to free verse, reflecting "a change in my way of seeing the world" (29) that enters his poems in the rhythms of home—the stories, songs, and dances that tell "how Indian people survive as Indians" (184).

The memoir's title poem, "Winning the Dust Bowl," is a tribute to Revard's cousin, Roy, who left the dust bowl for years of migrant labor and "made a way / to put good food on many tables" (74), and a reminder that the wealth of our nation was built on the labor of Native people as well as immigrants (71). By the final chapter the poet's voice has become a communal voice celebrating the rich and dynamic survival of Native people in America. "A Song That We Still Sing" refers to a victory song sung by Ponca warriors in the face of death. Hearing its echoes in the ruins of an old fort, Revard and his Ponca cousins "recognized that song. It's one / that we still sing" (203).

Bibliography

Arnold, Ellen L., ed. "Special Issue in Honor of Carter Revard." *Studies in American Indian Literatures* 15, no. 1 (2001).

Jaskoski, Helen. Review of *Winning the Dust Bowl*. *Studies in American Indian Literatures* 21, no. 1 (2002): 129.

McAdams, Janet. "Carter Revard's Angled Mirrors." In *Speak to Me Words: Essays on Contemporary American Indian Poetry,* edited by Dean Rader and Janice Gould, 193–206. Tucson: University of Arizona Press, 2004.

Revard, Carter. *Winning the Dust Bowl.* Tucson: University of Arizona Press, 2001.

Ellen L. Arnold

Winter in the Blood James Welch (1974)

Winter in the Blood, JAMES WELCH's first and most critically acclaimed novel, was the second great novel (after N. SCOTT MOMADAY's *HOUSE MADE OF DAWN*) of the AMERICAN INDIAN LITERARY RENAISSANCE. Although non-Indians may find the novel depressing, Indian readers recognize it as a classic of comic literature. The main character, a nameless hero (Welch's ironic comment on his aimlessness and lack of certainty), drifts back and forth from his mother's prosperous farm on the Blackfeet reservation to the seedy bars of nearby Havre, Montana, afflicted by emotional frostbite (the source of the title) caused largely by the indifferent attitude of his mother and the death of his father and brother. Although he is in his 30s, the protagonist cannot keep a job or establish a stable relationship with a woman. Welch underscores the protagonist's immaturity by linking him symbolically to a calf on the ranch who will not be weaned.

Much of the action of *Winter* depicts the protagonist's search for Agnes, a Cree woman whom he has told his family he had married. He took her home from a bar one night, but after living with her a short time he decamps, leaving her with his family, who hate her because the Cree are traditional enemies of the Blackfeet. Soon she leaves as well, and the hero hunts for her in the bars of Havre.

At the climax of the book the hero discovers the identity of his grandfather and learns the sad story of his grandmother, who almost starves to death during a winter of famine. The revelation is an epiphany to the hero. The recognition of important relationships is an important motif in literature, but Welch chooses to depict it comically:

> I thought for a moment.
> Bird [his horse] farted.
> And it came to me, as though it were riding one moment of the gusting wind, as though Bird had had it in him all the time and had passed it to me in that one instant of corruption. (158)

Welch's Montana is a wasteland: "It never rains anymore" (4), the soil crumbles into powder, and the fish have all disappeared from the river. Welch consciously incorporates the Holy Grail myth, with the main character serving as a kind of errant, ineffective knight in search of a treasure that will give meaning to his life. In doing this, Welch echoes modernist writers such as T. S. Eliot, Bernard Malamud, and Saul Bellow. In fact, Welch pays homage to Bellow's *Henderson the Rain King* with a reference to a *Sports Afield* story illustrated with a picture of a hunter named Henderson posing with a dead lion. As do Henderson and Roy Hobbs of Malamud's *The Natural,* the hero of

Winter in the Blood frees the waters and ends the drought. In the penultimate scene of the book, the hero fails at his task, freeing a drowning cow, but nonetheless his efforts magically cause the rain, and the action of the book ends with the hero's sitting in the rain musing: "'Some people', I thought, 'will never know how pleasant it is to be distant in a clean rain.'" (172).

Welch passes on the chance to end the book on a positive note and appends an epilogue depicting the funeral of the hero's grandmother. Momaday's *House Made of Dawn* also ends with the burial of a grandparent, but whereas Momaday treats this seriously—Abel's performance of the traditional Pueblo burial ceremonies signals an integration into tribal life—Welch chooses to play it for laughs: "The old lady wore a shiny orange coffin," says the narrator. The eulogy is a farce: "Here lies a simple woman . . . who devoted herself to rocking . . . who never gave anybody any crap" (183), says Lame Bull, the hero's stepfather. The hero hears little of the eulogy: He is daydreaming of finding "the girl who had stolen my gun and electric razor" (symbols of his manhood), getting a few drinks into her, and "marrying her on the spot." The book ends at this point, but there is no reason to think that the hero will succeed in marrying Agnes, or in doing anything else, for that matter.

Welch has a marvelous knack for depicting humorous scenes: the one in which an unknown man dies face down in a bowl of oatmeal, or at the funeral where Lame Bull has made the grave too narrow and has to jump up and down on the coffin to get it to fit in the hole. Humor has always been a crucial part of Indian culture: Most of the traditional tales of tribal culture heroes are tales of the TRICKSTER FIGURE and his frequently comic adventures. In *Winter in the Blood* Welch introduces the tradition of the trickster into the contemporary Indian novel, where it has been a fixture ever since.

See also HUMOR.

Bibliography

Davis, Jack. "Restoration of Indian Identity in *Winter in the Blood*." In *James Welch*, edited by Ron McFarland, 29–43. Lewiston, N.Y.: Confluence, 1986.

Eisenstein, Paul. "Finding Lost Generations: Recovering Omitted History in Winter in the Blood." *MELUS* (fall 1994): 3–18.

Velie, Alan R. "*Winter in the Blood* as Comic Novel." In *Critical Perspectives on Native American Fiction*, edited by Richard Fleck, 189–194. Washington, D.C.: Three Continents, 1993.

Welch, James. *Winter in the Blood*. New York: Penguin, 1974.

Jennifer McClinton-Temple

Winter of the Salamander Ray A. Young Bear (1980)

Winter of the Salamander is RAY A. YOUNG BEAR's first major collection of poems. Young Bear draws from a diverse array of influences, his grandmother, the most significant, taught him the Mesquakie language and cultural traditions. She is honored with the first poem, "Grandmother," in which he recalls her hands on his heel. The poem also acknowledges the speaker's spiritual "grandmother," the earth, claiming that "her words / would flow inside me" (15–21).

Young Bear's active linkage of the present with the past is exemplified in "Winter of the Salamander," thus illustrating an ever-dynamic personal and collective molding of identity. He draws upon his dreams, culture, oral traditions, and the historical and contemporary issues facing the Mesquakie people. Young Bear, often writing from numerous perspectives, generates a point of view that often abruptly shifts, engaging the reader in a dynamic experience that resists strict notions of identity. The "real" and the "imagined" play alongside each other, as do his provocative and often unexpected perceptual shifts.

Several poems in *Winter of the Salamander* express Young Bear's experiences, his frustrations, and the disappointing reality of Indian-white relations. For example, the people of Tama, a town near the Mesquakie settlement, appear: "undaunted, they gladly take our money / into their stores and banks, arrest / at whim our people" (58–61). He disparages individuals who think they know what Mesquakie life is like and who probably "/ sat through the whole two-day ride / back to chicago thinking he was / truly indian" (83–86). Within the same poem Young Bear imagines retribution for a police officer who denies the truth behind a racially motivated fight.

Even within the most graphic or uncomfortable representations Young Bear presents a unique and compelling splendor that suggests repeated readings and reflection. Not all of Young Bear's allusions are of disequilibrium, alienation, or painfully charged expressions of inequality. A beautiful notion of hope emerges: "that we shall one day / meet and talk in mutual good health / and i explain to him my incredible joy" (15–19).

Bibliography

Young Bear, Ray A. *The Invisible Musician.* Duluth, Minn.: Holy Cow! Press, 1990.

———. *The Rock Island Hiking Club.* Iowa City: University of Iowa Press, 2001.

———. *Winter of the Salamander: The Keeper of Importance.* San Francisco: Harper & Row, 1980.

Aaron Denham

Wolfsong   Louis Owens (1991)

Louis Owens's *Wolfsong* tells the story of a young Native American who confronts crises of selfhood and the environment after returning home from college to attend the burial of his uncle. Part coming-of-age narrative and part environmental thriller, *Wolfsong* celebrates the intimate connection between identity and geography fostered by many Native Americans.

Set in northern Washington, *Wolfsong* begins with the efforts of Jim Joseph, an elderly Native American (the tribe is unnamed), to protect a forest from local developers. Working in the shadows of the wilderness, Jim shoots holes in bulldozers and gravel trucks used to build roads and open an unexploited copper mine. Before his death Jim wills his mystical helper, a wolf spirit, to Tom Joseph, his nephew. Tom returns home to attend his uncle's burial, then decides to stay in his native valley and live closer to his familial and cultural origins. But fitting in proves difficult: As he learns about and internalizes his deceased uncle's tribal values and respect for nature, those around him lend support to the environmentally destructive mining project. Tom sympathizes with his childhood friends and neighbors, most of whom envision the copper mine as an opportunity for much needed labor in an economically depressed logging town. However, he also values the land ethic of his Indian ancestors and feels compelled to protect the wilderness. Ultimately Tom accepts the calling of the wolf spirit and becomes an ecowarrior as his uncle was. Sacrificing all ties to his hometown, Tom blows up a water tank at the mine site and retreats to Canada in hopes of finding refuge with a small intertribal community he visited earlier in the story.

Wolfsong effectively dramatizes the struggle of many Native Americans to understand their tribal origins better in an increasingly non-Indian national culture. As the elder descendants of Tom's tribe die of old age, younger ones are assimilated by the dominant culture. His brother, for instance, spends much of his time watching television and drinking beer and implores Tom to "forget about wolf spirits . . . and learn about chainsaws and carburetors" (35). Furthermore, the novel challenges imperialistic views of nature that perpetuate the plunder of natural resources. Whereas profit-oriented businessmen and out-of-work townspeople equate the wilderness with employment opportunities, Tom sees the natural world as a vital part of his personal and tribal identity. He fosters a communal relationship with the land and spends much of his time hiking and learning about his natural surroundings. He argues that the long-term environmental costs of a mining project outweigh the short-term gains. "Nobody seems to realize," he exclaims, "that a mine won't last forever. Twenty, even fifty years, and it'll be dead, and then there'll be nothing here except a bunch of junk and a road to a hole in the middle of what used to be wilderness" (112).

In short *Wolfsong* depicts the tragic cultural and environmental consequences of European colonization for Native Americans and argues, through the words and actions of its protagonist, for the preservation of indigenous cultures and the environment.

Bibliography

Owens, Louis. *Mixedblood Messages.* Norman: University of Oklahoma Press, 1998.

Purdy, John. "Clear Waters: A Conversation with Louis Owens." *Studies in American Indian Literatures* 10, no. 2 (1998): 6–22.

Schweninger, Lee. "Landscape and Cultural Identity in Louis Owens's *Wolfsong.*" *Studies in American Indian Literatures* 10, no. 2 (1998): 94–110.

Neal Bukeavich

Womack, Craig S. (1965–)

Craig S. Womack, Muskogee Creek (a member of the Tallahassee Creek ceremonial grounds) and Cherokee, is a novelist and literary theorist, and currently an associate professor of English at the University of Oklahoma specializing in 19th- and early 20th-century Native American literature, as well as gay and lesbian literature. Womack is the author of the groundbreaking RED ON RED: *Native American Literary Separatism* (1999)—the first Muskogee Creek literary history—in which he advocates a reclamation of Native identity by American Indian writers and the creation of Native literary theories that emerge from nations' specific cultural histories. He is also the author of *DROWNING IN FIRE* (2001), a novel about a young Creek man's homosexual awakening and journey to love. All of Womack's writings are personal, displaying deep pride in his Creek culture, as well as his sexual orientation. He is a member of the Wordcraft Circle of Native Writers and Storytellers' National Caucus, and in 1997 he received that organization's award for Storyteller of the Year. In 2000 he received Wordcraft Circle's Writer of the Year award, for *Red on Red.*

Of particular note in *Red on Red* is Womack's convincing queer reading of the gay Cherokee ROLLIE LYNN RIGGS's play *The Cherokee Night* in "Lynn Riggs as Code Talker." Womack suggests that Riggs's closeted homosexuality not only inspired his anguished relationship with his home state, but also defined his perception of himself as an Oklahoman and as an Indian. In all his work Womack has consistently called for a tribal-specific form of literary criticism, that does not treat all Native American literature as though it were drawn from the same source. This has been one of Womack's most important contributions to the field of Native American literature.

Bibliography

Henry, Michelle. "Canonizing Craig Womack: Finding Native Literature's Place in Indian Country." *American Indian Quarterly* 28, nos. 1–2 (winter–spring 2004): 30–51.

Jennifer McClinton-Temple

Woman Who Fell from the Sky, The
Joy Harjo (1994)

The Woman Who Fell from the Sky won the Oklahoma Book Award in 1995. The volume of prose poems returns to many of JOY HARJO's early themes of alienation, transformation, and mythology of not only the Muskogee tribe, to which she belongs, but of Native Americans in general. *The Woman Who Fell* comprises poems that are followed by Harjo's notes explaining the inspiration for the almost mythical stories she tells. The poems are peopled with alcoholics, VIETNAM WAR veterans, murdered immigrant taxi drivers, and other displaced people.

Violence hovers at the boundaries of many poems, a result of the sense of alienation Harjo sees in both the rural and urban worlds of her characters. In "The Naming" Harjo remembers her grandmother's warnings against the sudden death caused by storms. She describes her grandmother as a woman "who never had any peace" (12). In the notes following the poem she recounts the tale of her grandfather's being forced to work on the railroad—a job that took him away from his wife for extended periods. Returning to find her pregnant with another man's child, he beats her until she goes into labor and gives birth to a stillborn child. The two then attempt a double suicide standing on train tracks awaiting the oncoming train in full view of their children. The domestic violence of the story is echoed in the grandmother's unhappiness in the poem, and the eventual renewal at the poem's end: "The earth is wet with happiness" (12).

Renewal, regeneration, and reconciliation are common endings to Harjo's sometimes dark poems. In the final lines of "A Postcolonial Tale," a poem full of rage at the abandonment of Native American traditions in the face of white oppression, the speaker says, "No story or song will translate the full impact of falling, or the inverse power of rising up" (18). There is always hope in Harjo's poems, no matter how slim.

The violence of the Vietnam War follows its veterans home and regeneration of the spirit is harder to accomplish. The character Johnny, renamed St. Coincidence in the title poem, lost his mind in the war but remembered a girl he had once loved. He catches Lila as she falls from the sky, and the implication at the poem's end is that they renew each other and the healing begins for them both. Whirling Soldier becomes "an acrobat to pain" ("Northern Lights" 23), pawning his war medals for a quart of liquor. After his final act of violence, punching a man who "looked like his brother," the dawn found him "talking to a spirit who had never been a stranger" (24). Harjo tells this story of an Ojibwe writer she met. The poem ends with her return to the theme of renewal and the end of violence.

Even the random violence of everyday life is cause for reflection. The spirit of a murdered Nigerian immigrant searches for his murderer and forgives the man his crime ("Letter from the End of the Twentieth Century"). The story sticks with the poem's narrator: "It sustains me through these tough distances" (37). Even in murder there is room for promise.

"Perhaps the World Ends Here" is the final poem in *The Woman Who Fell*. "The world begins at a kitchen table. No matter what, we must eat to live" (68). The table has been central in sustaining life and easing its passage to the next world: "We have given birth on this table, and have prepared our parents for burial here" (69). The earth con-tinues to spin and home will always offer hope, comfort, and renewal.

Bibliography

Harjo, Joy. *The Woman Who Fell from the Sky.* New York: W. W. Norton, 1994.

Monroe, Jonathon: "Untranslatable Communities, Productive Translation, and Public Transport: Rosmarie Waldrop's *A Key into the Language of America* and Joy Harjo's *The Woman Who Fell from the Sky.*" In *We Who Love to Be Astonished: Experimental Women's Writing and Performance Poetics,* edited by Laura Hinton and Cynthia Hogue, 90–102. Tuscaloosa: University of Alabama Press, 2002.

P. K. Bostian

Woman Who Owned the Shadows, The   Paula Gunn Allen (1983)

Illustrating the belief that stories give meaning to life, PAULA GUNN ALLEN recovers a woman-centered narrative tradition by combining Western novelistic and autobiographic conventions with Native myth, rewriting both as dynamic and nonlinear.

Two related images sustain this idea throughout the novel: the shadows and the spider. The shadows are the conflicting space the protagonist, Ephanie Atencio, inhabits, for she has been displaced to a darkness of silence and invisibility by the patriarchal colonizer. Because of her MIXED-BLOOD nature, she is a fragmented individual: She is at odds with her name, "a split name, a name half of this and half of that" (3). She feels that her traditions were stolen from her. Instead of Guadalupe she speaks "a stranger's tongue" (70). She is also alienated from the Western world, which sees her not as a real person but as "an artifact, quaint, curious, fragile, wronged" (136).

The Christian education she receives makes her believe her female body is sinful and dirty. Her ability to connect to women has been denied: Her childhood friendship with Elena, a "twining [and] twining" (22) that made her complete, is condemned as unnatural. She cannot find companionship from men either: Her first husband leaves her with two children, and both her Native friend, Stephen, and her Nisei second husband, Thomas, put her in a subordinated position, making her the victim of their pain. Ephanie is oppressed, devastated. She cannot find the story that will give meaning to her life, and she lives in a state of desperation that leads her to the brink of suicide.

It is at this moment that Ephanie renews her relationship to the Spider, the original female creator in Laguna Pueblo tradition, which is also associated with shadows. Ephanie analyzes her pain and its sources and uses the Spider's power to weave oppositions into relations. She recovers her twinning companionship with Teresa and achieves wholeness by vindicating her mixed-blood nature. With the Spider's power to remember Ephanie finally learns to "own the shadows," accept ambiguity as a creative force that allows her to find a place in the stories and to pass them on, asserting transformation and continuance as the only means to survive.

Bibliography

Allen, Paula Gunn. *The Woman Who Owned the Shadows.* San Francisco: Spinsters Ink, 1983.

Holford, Vanessa. "Re-Membering Ephanie: A Woman's Re-creation of Self in Paula Gunn Allen's *The Woman Who Owned the Shadows.*" *Studies in American Indian Literatures* 6, no. 1 (1994): 99–113.

Prince-Hughes, Tara. "Contemporary Two-Spirit Identity in the Fiction of Paula Gunn Allen and Beth Brant." *Studies in American Indian Literatures* 10, no. 4 (1998): 9–31.

Silvia Martínez Falquina

Women on the Run   Janet Campbell Hale (1999)

Women on the Run is JANET CAMPBELL HALE's first collection of short stories, all of which are concerned with various forms of captivity and isolation, themes Hale explored in her novel *THE JAILING OF CECELIA CAPTURE* (1988). Hale continues to use realism in these stories to describe the lives of Na-

tive women away from their homelands, though, as the reviewer Ron McFarland has pointed out, the narratives are "not despairing" (157). The six stories take place on the West Coast, from California to the Pacific Northwest and Canada.

The first and most lengthy story, "Claire," describes an elderly woman's experience in a nursing home, where her son, Ozzie, has abandoned her. Claire feels imprisoned and isolated, a feeling that reminds her of mission school, and she devises a plan to escape. Wearing men's clothing, she climbs out a window and finds her way to the bus station. Upon arriving at the Coeur d'Alene Reservation, she recognizes the difficulties of going "home" again: Her house has been rented to a non-Native family and her friends are all gone. Claire decides that she will live with her nephew, Joe Whitehawk, a widower with a young son. She will tell the boy "Indian stories" and help Joe recover from alcoholism (45).

The title story recounts the tales of several "women on the run," the first, a writer named Lena Bowman, and the second, a fugitive, Roberta Trumaine (or Bobbi T), charged with racketeering and murder, who has been captured in Canada (a story Hale connects to the capture of Leonard Peltier, a political prisoner convicted of killing two Federal Bureau of Investigation [FBI] agents on the Pine Ridge Reservation in 1975). Even the protagonist of Lena's novel in progress, Helen, is a woman on the run after her third divorce. As do the couple who turn Bobbi T over to the police, Lena sees financial profit in her connection with the fugitive and decides that she will be the subject of her next book, which she writes as a murder mystery.

The title character of the story "Alice Fay" is held captive by her mother, Norma, an invalid who requires constant care. Norma, a white woman ashamed of Alice Fay's Indian blood, had sent her away to mission school at age six. When Norma dies, Alice Fay meets her father, Joe Whitehawk (Claire's nephew in the first story), at the funeral, and the two stay in contact. In a letter Alice Fay tells him that she feels empty without her mother. "Is this how the slaves felt when they were emancipated at last?" she asks (140). As are the other women in these stories, Alice Fay is accustomed to captivity and must learn how to re-create herself anew.

Bibliography

Hale, Janet Campbell. *Women on the Run.* Moscow: University of Idaho Press, 1999.

McFarland, Ron. Review of *The Toughest Indian in the World* by Sherman Alexie and *Women on the Run* by Janet Campbell Hale. *Wicaso Sa Review* 16, no. 2 (2001): 154–158.

Laura Szanto

Woody, Elizabeth   (1959–   )

Elizabeth Woody was born on December 26, 1959, in Ganado, Arizona, and grew up in Madras, Oregon, which is close to the Warm Springs Reservation. Of Navajo, Warm Springs, Wasco, and Yakama heritage, she is an enrolled member of the Confederated Tribes of Warm Springs in Oregon. She studied at the Institute of American Indian Arts in New Mexico and received a bachelor's degree in English from Evergreen State College in Washington. Woody has been engaged as a teacher, lecturer, and activist, and is a cofounder of the Northwest Native American Writers' Association. She has received numerous awards for her work, including the William Stafford Memorial Award for Poetry in 1995. She is currently employed as the director of the indigenous leadership program at Ecotrust in Oregon and is also working on a master's degree in public administration, with an emphasis in environmental policy and nonprofit management.

Woody is recognized as a poet, writer, and visual artist. Her first book of poetry, *Hand into Stone* (1988), received an American Book Award in 1990 from the Before Columbus Foundation. *Luminaries of the Humble* (1994) was published the same year as *Seven Hands, Seven Hearts* (1994). The latter text comprises her entire first book, *Hand into Stone,* as well as additional poems, essays, and stories. In her work Woody presents themes that deal with preserving the environment and is also concerned with problems involving fishing rights for indigenous peoples. In the introduction to *Seven Hands, Seven Hearts* she writes: "Through my awareness of my history, tradition is alive. I can see my place as a responsible link in a dynamic process" (16). In addition, her visual art has been exhibited nationally.

Woody's work has been included in numerous collections, anthologies, and other texts. Norma C. Wilson states that "Woody utilizes a high level of abstract diction in her poetry," and that "she writes insightfully of human insignificance" (*Nature of Native American Poetry* 125). Richard Dauenhauer says that her poetry helps us "gain a sense of right direction for the future, for physical, spiritual, and political survival, as individuals, as family, as community" (review of *Luminaries* 411).

Bibliography

Cadwell, E. K. "Earth Is Richer for This Voice: Elizabeth Woody." *Dreaming the Dawn: Conversations with Native Artists and Activists,* ix–xiii, 14–22. Lincoln: University of Nebraska Press, 1999.

Dauenhauer, Richard. Review of *Luminaries of the Humble,* by Elizabeth Woody. *World Literature Today* 69, no. 2 (spring 1995): 411.

"Elizabeth Woody." Available online. URL: http://www.hanksville.org/storytellers/ewoody/. Accessed on August 15, 2005.

Rooney, Terrie M., and Gariepy, Jennifer. eds. "Woody, Elizabeth." *Contemporary Authors.* Vol. 152, 476–478. Detroit: Gale, 1997.

Wilson, Norma C. *The Nature of Native American Poetry.* Albuquerque: University of New Mexico Press, 2001.

Woody, Elizabeth. *Hand into Stone.* New York: Contact II, 1988.

———. *Luminaries of the Humble.* Tucson: University of Arizona Press, 1994.

———. *Seven Hands, Seven Hearts.* Portland, Oreg.: Eighth Mountain, 1994.

Deborah Weagel

Wounded Knee

The Wounded Knee Massacre occurred on the Pine Ridge Reservation in southwestern South Dakota (then known as the Dakota Territory) on December 29, 1890. There, close to 300 Lakota (Sioux) men, women, and children were killed in a violent encounter with the Seventh Cavalry of the U.S. Army. The army originally referred to the incident as the battle of Wounded Knee, a fact that helps to demonstrate why evoking the name of Wounded Knee still generates an emotional response among contemporary Native Americans.

Historically Wounded Knee signaled the end of what were known then as the Indian Wars, the armed conflicts that had taken place between European colonizers, later the U.S. Army, and the indigenous people they encountered on their drive toward total domination of the U.S. frontier. Psychologically Wounded Knee symbolizes the long history of brutal treatment of Indians at the hands of the government and the failure of official policies regarding Indian welfare.

The men, women, and children killed at Wounded Knee were members of two different tribes, the Miniconjou Lakota, led by Chief Big Foot, and the Hunkpapa Lakota, who had joined Big Foot's group after the death of their leader, Big Foot's half brother, Sitting Bull. Sitting Bull's followers had gathered two weeks earlier to engage in a GHOST DANCE, during which their leader was slain. The popularity of the Ghost Dance religion had previously put the government on alert, for they saw its potential to unify and strengthen the resolve of the Indians. Big Foot's arrest had been called for, and his group was pursued to Pine Ridge. The cavalry caught up with the Indians on the banks of Wounded Knee Creek and forced them to make camp. In the attempt to disarm the Indians on December 29, shots were fired and the massacre had begun. The cavalry numbered 500 at this point, while the Indians were only 350, all but 120 of whom were women and children. Many eyewitness accounts of the massacre indicate that women and children, some of whom were infants, were deliberately shot at by the U.S. Cavalry. This was clearly not a battle, but rather a brutal slaughtering of innocents, for which no army officer has ever been brought to justice. (Col. James W. Forsyth was taken before a military tribunal on charges of killing innocent noncombatants, but he was exonerated.)

More than 80 years after this tragedy, on February 27, 1973, approximately 200 Indians seized control of a church, a trading post, and a museum near the mass gravesite of those killed during the Wounded Knee massacre. This siege, led by the AMERICAN INDIAN MOVEMENT (AIM), was in immediate response to events that had recently taken place on the Pine Ridge Reservation. Two men, Wesley Bad Heart Bull and Raymond Yellow Thunder, had recently been murdered in separate incidents and their white assailants charged with only second-degree manslaughter. For the Lakota living on Pine Ridge these incidents were only two more in a long series of blatantly racist miscarriages of justice. After this incident a local civil rights organization met with the leaders of AIM, and they decided that a stand, at the highly charged location of Wounded Knee, was the answer.

Approximately 200 armed agents of the federal government quickly surrounded the camp. The many obvious parallels between this Wounded Knee and the original Wounded Knee attracted the attention of the international media. The federal agents were, of course, well armed and well supplied, while the Indians were poorly armed and sporadically supplied and, as at Wounded Knee, included within their ranks many women and children. Despite this, their knowledge of the terrain allowed the Indians to hold the agents off for 71 days. Two of the Indian activists, Buddy Lamonte and Frank Clearwater, were killed during the siege, and one child was born inside the occupied territory. To end the standoff, the leaders entered into an agreement with the U.S. government that stressed fair treatment for the activists as well as a fair review of existing treaties and an investigation of the state of Indian welfare in the country. These agreements have never been fully honored by the U.S. government.

Not surprisingly, Wounded Knee, in both its incarnations, figures prominently in Native American literature. For example, WENDY ROSE in her poem "Wounded Knee 1890–1973" memorializes both the sufferings of the victims of the massacre as well as the bravery of the activists of the siege. Hanay GEIOGAMAH's play FOGHORN plays with our notions of history in order to readdress the injustices such as Wounded Knee (I and II). Sophia Alice Callahan addresses the massacre in *Wynema: A Child of the Forest*, while Elizabeth Cook-Lynn and Sherman Alexie both make frequent references to both the standoff and the massacre throughout their works.

See also *Half-Breed Chronicles and Other Poems*.

Bibliography

Coleman, William S. E. *Voices of Wounded Knee.* Lincoln: University of Nebraska Press, 2000.

Smith, Paul Chaat, and Robert Alan Warrior. *Like a Hurricane: The Indian Movement from Alcatraz to Wounded Knee.* New York: New Press, 1996.

Jennifer McClinton-Temple

Wounds beneath the Flesh   Maurice Kenny   (1983)

Edited and introduced by Maurice Kenny, this anthology of 43 poems by 15 Native American poets pays tribute to "the many wounds, scars that have shaped the flesh, the brain and the spirit"(vi). In his introduction Kenny asserts that poems created by a person indigenous to the land are different from those of an immigrant. Although there is no such thing as an Indian poetry, says Kenny, there is "an Indian sensibility," which is aware of "the oneness in all things" and holds "respect for that oneness" (vii). All too often, Kenny warns, we "forget that the earth, Mother Earth, is the flesh of our flesh, the flesh of all creatures great and small, and when her flesh is wounded our flesh is wounded" (vii).

All the poets speak eloquently of these wounds. In "Rings" Joseph Bruchac writes of passing a logging truck on an Oregon road. Even the smallest log "has more than a hundred / scars around / the wrists of seasons" (7). Watching men strut around a drill site, Linda Hogan in "Oil" knows that because of their work, the "earth is wounded / and bleeds" (27). Other poets commemorate species whose disappearance haunts our memories. Lance Henson in "Flock" sees the snow move "like an ancient herd" (23). "Slim Man Canyon" takes

Leslie Marmon Silko back 700 years as she rides on horseback "past cliffs with stories and songs / painted on rock" by long-ago peoples (43). Some wounds are more psychic. In Simon Ortiz's "The Mind Is Stunned Stark," "Africa, Saigon, Sand Creek" haunt the basement of the Veterans Hospital. "Ice Horses" is Joy Harjo's metaphor for the sharp, overwhelming emotions that "escape / after the last hurt is turned inward" (20).

Many of the poems celebrate survival beyond the scars. In "Taking a Visitor to See the Ruins" Paula Gunn Allen wryly drives her guest to visit not "pueblo ruins carved and built into tall / sandstone cliffs," but rather her mother and grandmother. On the fifth floor of a "tall / high security apartment building" they are "still living pueblo style / up high where the enemy can't reach them" (1). In his "Reflections on Milkweed" Peter Blue Cloud finds that "a great peace descends" as he contemplates their pods. Milkweed seeds, like those "within us," are part of an "an ancient breath" (4). Duane Niatum's "Street Kid," behind bars at age 13, can nonetheless "step / From the window into the darkness" and reach his soul "building a nest against the wall" (28). For Diane Burns late April revives not only the maple trees "On Lac Courte Oreilles" but also the ailing army veterans in Washington Square Park.

Poems by Gladys Cardiff, Elizabeth Cook-Lynn, Wendy Rose and Roberta Hill Whiteman complete the volume. Originally published by Blue Cloud Quarterly Press, the collection was reissued by White Pines Press in 1987.

Margaret O'Shaughnessey

Woven Stone   Simon Ortiz   (1992)

Woven Stone unites Simon Ortiz's first two poetry collections, *Going for the Rain* (1976) and *A Good Journey* (1977), with an updated, previously published collection, *Fight Back: For the Sake of the People, For the Sake of the Land* (1980). This tripartite collection allows Ortiz's readers to trace his movement toward writing more overtly political poetry. Ortiz's travels, which he writes about in his first two collections, made him cognizant of

Native Americans' omnipresence, although denial through history and popular culture has belied their continued existence by fixing them in the past. Therefore *Woven Stone,* when examined as a whole, explores the contemporary social, cultural, and political issues affecting people living in Indian country, which includes non-Indians. This combined collection of poems demonstrates his commitment to uncovering the contemporary lives of Native Americans. Many of the poems express the sorrow felt by Native Americans when examining the past 500 years, but many also articulate the strength of peoples whose heritage and identities have emerged from the foundations of this land.

Ortiz begins *Woven Stone* with an introduction that traces the important events of his life. Despite ominous predictions of cultural loss among Native Americans, Ortiz finds hope for the future in language and through the language that he uses in his writing. Although Native languages are spoken fluently by fewer and fewer people, many Native nations have made language revitalization a goal. Additionally many Native writers, including Ortiz, assert that they have "Indianized" English in order to make it more closely adhere to a Native American philosophy and worldview. At the same time writing in English allows Ortiz's critical assessment of the U.S. government's treatment of Indian lands and Indian peoples in *Fight Back* to reaches a broader audience.

The uranium industry's exploitation of land and labor forms the context of the poems in *Fight Back.* They also contain Ortiz's most explicit critique of industrialized America based on his personal experience working in the uranium mines of northwestern New Mexico near his childhood home. His poems recall the poor surrounding Native American communities and working-class whites from other states who became a cheap labor source. Despite the grim portrait Ortiz paints in *Fight Back,* he remains hopeful, beginning with positive visions of the future: "The land will endure. / There will be victory. / The People shall go on" (8–10). Similarly he ends with a poem that calls for rain to cleanse the earth.

As do the Paiute whose sacred springs were surrounded by a military weapons testing center in "That's the Place Indians Talk About," Ortiz refuses to surrender his land to outsiders. He reminds corporate America that much of their wealth was built on Indian land and by Indian and enslaved hands. Yet life for these people has endured, as "It Will Come, It Will Come" signals through a thundering sound that resembles the earth's heart's beating: "Thundering, the People working. / Thundering, the People's voices. / Thundering, the movement of the struggle" (5–7).

Bibliography

Ortiz, Simon. "Towards a National Indian Literature: Cultural Authenticity in Nationalism." *MELUS* 8 (summer 1981): 7–12.

———. *Woven Stone.* Tucson: University of Arizona Press, 1992.

Ruppert, James. "Ortiz's *A Story of How a Wall Stands.*" *Explicator* 55, no. 2 (winter 1997): 117–119.

Elizabeth Archuleta

Wynema: A Child of the Forest   Sophia Alice Callahan (1891)

The Muscogee author S. Alice Callahan's *Wynema: A Child of the Forest,* believed to be the first novel written by an American Indian woman, was only recently republished (1997) after it was lost from the public eye for more than 100 years. Callahan's *Wynema* spans approximately 20 years, from the 1870s to the early 1890s, as it follows the title character, Wynema, a young Muskogee girl, from early childhood to the first years of her marriage. In many ways Wynema presents a case study in assimilation: When readers first encounter her, she lives in an unnamed Native community 16 miles from the nearest mission. When the novel closes, she has become a teacher at Hope Seminary, a Christian mission school. During this time Wynema becomes fluent in English, embraces dominant dress and attitudes, adopts Christianity, and marries a white husband. Throughout *Wynema* Callahan tends to idealize dominant norms such as that of Western education, which she portrays as inherently tied to Christianity. Wynema is, in the end, a Native heroine made in Callahan's own image, since Callahan herself was a teacher in Muskogee, Oklahoma, at the Harrell International Institute, a private Methodist high school for both Indian and white children, where she taught classes and edited Harrell's journal.

Though Wynema's story serves as the text's title and narrative frame, she is arguably not the novel's central character, an honor that goes instead to Genevieve Weir, a young white Methodist teacher who sets up a school on Wynema's reservation. Genevieve—a Christian feminist who touts the assimilationist platform of the period—arrives in Indian Territory at some point in the 1870s. After founding a school in Wynema's village, Genevieve becomes not only Wynema's teacher, but also her role model and confidant. The ensuing events follow a conventionally romantic plot, leading Genevieve into the arms of the superintendent of a nearby Methodist mission, Gerald Keithly, and Wynema into the arms of Genevieve's brother, Robin Weir. Romantic entanglements do not, however, preclude social involvement in Callahan's text. And so the author laces her love stories with the ongoing debates of the day, including the issues of allotment, suffrage, temperance, and, by the end of the text, the 1890 WOUNDED KNEE Massacre, in which several hundred Lakota were killed by U.S. troops.

Born in 1868, Callahan grew up in what has been called the Muscogee aristocracy, a contingent of MIXED-BLOOD Muscogee families with wealth and political power. In February 1891, just a few months after papers filled with accounts of the Wounded Knee massacre, Callahan took a position at Harrell. *Wynema* was published that same year. Callahan died on January 7, 1894, at the age of only 26.

Bibliography

Senier, Siobhan. "Allotment Protest and Tribal Discourse: Reading *Wynema*'s Successes and Shortcomings." *AIQ* 24, no. 3 (summer 2000): 420–440.

Womack, Craig S. *Red on Red: Native American Literary Separatism.* Minneapolis: University of Minnesota Press, 1999.

Lisa Tatonetti

Y

Yellow Raft in Blue Water, A Michael Dorris (1987)

MICHAEL DORRIS's *A Yellow Raft in Blue Water* holds a prominent place in American Indian literature because of its representation not only of the American Indian experience, but also of the significance of that experience within the larger context of a multicultural America. The novel achieves this confluence of cultures through its protagonist, Rayona Taylor, an African-American, American Indian, and white adolescent who struggles to fit in her non-specific Indian reservation in the Northwest and the white world that surrounds it. With her uncontrollable hair and dark skin, Rayona is ostracized by the more "purely" Indian inhabitants of her native area as well as by white inhabitants of the nearby state park to which she runs away.

Additionally Rayona struggles to be accepted by and to accommodate her Indian mother and grandmother, Christine and Ida, as well as her African-American father, Elgin. Through the novel's three-section framework, which provides first-person narrative voice for Rayona, Christine, and Ida, Dorris presents each character's difficulties and motivations and highlights the intergenerational conflict that pervades their relationships with one another. This narrative technique also reveals a family secret that is crucial to this intergenerational conflict: Ida insists on being called "Aunt Ida" because she is actually Christine's half sister and cousin rather than her mother, thereby making her Rayona's aunt instead of her grandmother. This multinarrative journey into family history marks the way in which, despite their individual pain, the three women are able to reconcile their differences and become a family, an interweaving of lives that LOUIS OWENS and David Cowart have called a braid, an image of particular importance to American Indians.

A Yellow Raft in Blue Water is not the end of the story of Rayona; Dorris pursues more fully her varied genealogical lineage and entry into adulthood in his later novel *CLOUD CHAMBER*, which includes multiple narration from her Irish ancestors. Through both works Dorris offers a contemporary view of multiraciality in America that is somewhat personal; the empathy with which he portrays Rayona may perhaps be explained by his own Irish, Modoc, and Coeur d'Alene ancestry and his raising by his mother, grandmother, and aunts. Yet Dorris's personal connection to his narratives nonetheless has universal implications, suggesting that individuals cannot always be labeled and relegated to neatly assigned roles. As a result Rayona's integration of ostensibly opposing cultures is a story not only about American Indians, but also about America.

See also MIXED-BLOODS.

Bibliography

Cowart, David. "'The Rhythm of Three Strands': Cultural Braiding in Dorris's *A Yellow Raft in Blue*

Water." *Studies in American Indian Literatures* 8, no. 1 (spring 1996): 1–12.

Dorris, Michael. *Cloud Chamber.* New York: Simon & Schuster, 1997.

Owens, Louis. *Other Destinies: Understanding the American Indian Novel.* Norman: University of Oklahoma Press, 1992.

Lindsey Smith

"Yellow Woman" Leslie Marmon Silko (1974)

LESLIE MARMON SILKO's "Yellow Woman" first appeared in Kenneth Rosen's anthology *The Man to Send Rain Clouds.* The story stems from an oral tradition of Yellow Woman stories popular among the Indians of the Laguna and Acoma Pueblos in New Mexico. Although the details vary, the basic plot of the stories remains the same. A young woman, alone, encounters a young man and is abducted—sometimes by force, but sometimes with her cooperation. The man is not an ordinary man, but a kachina, a mountain spirit. The two have a sexual relationship, but eventually Yellow Woman returns home. In some versions she is killed upon her return for her transgressions, but usually she is welcomed back into her village. The recurring theme of these stories is renewal. In each telling the woman gives something new to the pueblo upon her return—new babies, buffalo meat, or in the case of Silko's Yellow Woman, a new version of the story itself.

Silko's "Yellow Woman" begins with a woman who is waking up beside a river. She left her home the day before to walk by the river, hoping for an adventure. She met a man, Silva, who claimed to be a kachina and slept with him. When Silva awakens, he calls her Yellow Woman. The woman protests and says she is not the legendary Yellow Woman.

The woman and Silva head deeper into the mountains. When the woman again denies that she is Yellow Woman, Silva confuses her sense of time by saying people in the future will speak of them as living long ago. The woman's sense of space also becomes confused. She tries to see her pueblo from the mountain but cannot find it. The

confusion of time and space indicates the woman has become Yellow Woman and thereby has lost her connections to the ordinary world.

The woman decides to live the legend and not return home. However, Silva turns out to be a cattle rustler. A rancher accuses Silva of stealing a cow, and as violence arises, the woman leaves and heads for home. Again by the river she thinks wistfully of Silva and hopes she will meet him again some day. As in many Yellow Woman tales, the woman decides to tell her husband she was captured by a Navajo.

The landscape gives a visual picture of the woman's state of mind as she journeys into the legend and back out again. The river represents her desire for an adventure, the mountains her sensual awakening, and the features of the ordinary world, such as the paved road she walks on, draw her back to her family. Although the woman returns to ordinary life at the end, she has been renewed through her journey and has a new tale to contribute.

Bibliography

Graulich, Melody, ed. *"Yellow Woman": Leslie Marmon Silko.* New Brunswick, N.J.: Rutgers University Press, 1993.

Rosen, Kenneth, comp. *The Man to Send Rain Clouds: Contemporary Stories by American Indians.* New York: Viking, 1974.

Holly E. Martin

Young Bear, Ray A. (1950–)

Ray A. Young Bear, Meskwaki, son of Leonard and Chloe Young Bear, was born on November 12, 1950, in Marshalltown, Iowa, and was raised on the Meskwaki Tribal Settlement near Tama, Iowa. He lives there today with his wife, Stella, whom he married in 1973. With her, Young Bear cofounded the Woodland Song and Dance Troupe, a cultural performance group that frequently performs on lecture circuits and at POW wows. His wife, Stella, has enormous influence on his work. He often uses *we* when discussing his work, indicating her crucial role. Stella's beadwork also adorns the covers of two of his books. Young Bear studied creative writing at Pomona College in Claremont, California, and at the University of Iowa. Young Bear has taught both creative writing and Native American literature at the Institute of American Indian Art, Eastern Washington University, Meskwaki Indian Elementary School, the University of Iowa, and Iowa State University.

Young Bear's unique voice has received much critical acclaim, and his dynamic, semiautobiographical narrative BLACK EAGLE CHILD: THE FACEPAINT NARRATIVES (1992) is as singular in voice as it is in structure. *Black Eagle Child,* often billed as a novel athough it works outside the boundaries of that genre, is written in both English and Meskwakie and is also structured in both verse and prose forms. Part prose and part poetry, this text centers on Edgar Bearchild, the narrator, and his struggle to live both in the traditional world and in the white world.

His book of poetry *The* INVISIBLE MUSICIAN also deals with struggle of those who are "between worlds." In this text the way in which he juxtaposes Meskwaki with English symbolizes a bridge between the traditional and the modern. Young Bear seems to want here to emphasize the manner in which life is full of contradictions. One of the many ways he does this is by joining disparate descriptions of dreams and reality, implying that they are more alike than they might seem on the surface.

Young Bear's most substantial book of poetry, WINTER OF THE SALAMANDER, is, as his other works, bilingual. In these poems he comes at the reader from many different perspectives, with a point of view that often shifts abruptly. The effect, however, is not to create merely fragments for the reader, but rather a complex whole, made up of contradictions and complications.

Young Bear's singularity of voice seems innately linked with his bilingual and bicultural experiences.

His first language is Meskwakie, and he began writing poems in English in his teens. His initial method was to think in Meskwaki and then translate into English. Though he has since changed this method, the unique challenges of composing words across languages and cultures remain with him. In an afterword to *Black Eagle Child,* he explains, "Because of the differences of the bilingual/bicultural worlds I live in, it sometimes seems as if what is actually published turns out to be a minute and insignificant fraction of one's perpetual metamorphosis" (257). This notion, that Young Bear's words are capable of scratching only the surface of a dynamic process, also resonates with the philosophy of cosmic insignificance that informs his work—his belief "that humans are but a minute part of world order" (257).

Bibliography

Bruchac, Joseph, ed. "Connected to the Past." In *Survival This Way: Interviews with American Indian Poets,* 337–348. Tucson: University of Arizona Press, 1987.

Nelson, Cary, ed. "Ray A. Young Bear." Modern American Poetry: An Online Journal and Multimedia Companion to Anthology of Modern American Poetry. Available online. URL: http://www.english. uiuc.edu/maps/poets/s_z/youngbear/youngbear. htm. Accessed on August 15, 2005.

Young Bear, Ray A. *Black Eagle Child: The Facepaint Narratives.* 1992. Reprint, New York: Grove Press, 1997.

———. *Winter of the Salamander: The Keeper of Importance.* San Francisco: Harper & Row, 1980.

———. *The Invisible Musician.* Duluth, Minn.: Holy Cow! Press, 1990.

Tracey Watts

Z

Zepeda, Ofelia (1952–)

Born on March 24, 1952, as a member of the To-
hono O'odham (Desert People) nation, Ofelia
Zepeda was raised in Stanfield, Arizona, a rural
farming community near the Tohono O'odham
and Pima reservations in southwestern Arizona.
Her ancestors were migrant workers and farm la-
borers originally from Sonora, Mexico, who settled
in what is now called Arizona. After receiving an
A.A. degree from Central Arizona College in 1974,
Zepeda continued her academic career and earned
B.A., M.A., and Ph.D. degrees at the University of
Arizona, where she now is a professor of linguis-
tics.

As a scholar, consultant, and oral historian to
the Papago and Pima Indian tribes, Zepeda is actively involved in the preservation of the Tohono
O'odham language. In fact, she is the foremost
authority in the scholarship of her native tongue.
She cofounded the American Indian Language
Development Institute and, in 1998, published
the first grammar book on the Tohono O'odham
language, *A Papago Grammar.* For her exceptional
work in her community and insatiable desire to
preserve and revitalize the language and culture of
her people, the John D. and Catherine MacArthur
Foundation awarded Zepeda a prestigious MacArthur Fellowship in 1999. However, the fellowship
she received was not based only on her accomplishments as an educator and community leader;
the foundation also honored her prolific work as
a poet.

Ofelia Zepeda, the poet, has published two collections of poetry, *Ocean Power: Poems from the
Desert* (1995) and *Jewed 'I-Hoi/Earth Movements*
(1997), both of which contain works written in
English and O'odham. Zepeda's poetry addresses
the connection she and her people have to the
natural manifestations, rhythms, and patterns
inherent in the desert landscape that surrounds
them. Rain, for example, is a most important natural phenomenon, for it is intrinsically linked to
her tribe's survival, history, and consciousness. In
"Pulling Down the Clouds" Zepeda writes, "It is
rain. / Rain somewhere in the desert. / Comforted
in this knowledge he turns over / and continues his
sleep, / dreams of women with harvesting sticks"
(*Ocean Power* 9–10). Zepeda's imagery captures
the essence of life found in the Sonoran desert,
a landscape where every cloud, every drop of
water, every tumbleweed, has its proper place in
the scheme of existence. And through her words
Zepeda offers her readers a portrait of an organic
union between nature and human, between the
sound of thunder and the voices of a people.

Bibliography

Krupat, Arnold, and Brian Swann, eds. *Here First: Au-
tobiographical Essays by Native American Writers.*
New York: Modern Library, 2000.
Sonneborn, Liz, ed. *A to Z of Native American Women.*
New York: Facts On File, 1998.
Zepeda, Ofelia. *Jewed 'I-Hoi / Earth Movements:
O'odham Poems.* Tucson, Ariz.: Kore Press, 1997.

————. *A Papago Grammar.* Tucson: University of Arizona Press, 1983.

————. *When It Rains: Papago and Pima Poetry.* Tucson: University of Arizona Press, 1982.

Daniele Pantano

Zitkala-Ša (Gertrude Simmons Bonnin) 1876–1938

Gertrude Simmons (who later renamed herself Zitkala-Ša) was born on the Pine Ridge Reservation in South Dakota, the daughter of Ellen Tate Iyohiwin Simmons, a Lakota, and a white man whose identity remains unknown. For eight years, a time of "wild freedom and overflowing spirits" (8), as she later recalls, Simmons lived as a traditional Lakota girl, learning the arts of beadwork and storytelling from her mother and tribal elders. When Quaker MISSIONARIES entered the reservation, however, she was lured by their promise of a wondrous land to the east. Ignoring her mother's warnings about the whites' empty promises, she boarded the train and enrolled in a missionary school in Wabash, Indiana.

As she writes in her autobiographical essays, "Impressions of an Indian Childhood" (1900) and "The School Days of an Indian Girl" (1900) (which were later published in *AMERICAN INDIAN STORIES*) leaving Pine Ridge marked the traumatic transition between Simmons's traditional childhood and her frustrating struggle to adapt to white culture. She quickly became disenchanted with school, as the missionaries cropped her long hair, fitted her in uncomfortable clothing, and meted out strict discipline. On returning to her mother after three years, she felt deeply estranged from both the traditional Lakota and the younger assimilated Indians, describing herself as "neither a wild Indian nor a tame one" (69).

These early experiences taught Zitkala-Ša to question the value of ASSIMILATION. She returned to the missionary school but secretly carried with her a contraband pouch of "magic roots" prepared by a Lakota medicine man, and, though she distinguished herself academically, she continued to feel deep resentment toward the "palefaces." As a student at Earlham College in Indiana, she won a state oratory competition, but what should have been a moment of triumph was ruined by hecklers in the audience, other college students who jeered her speech and hoisted a large sign bearing the word *squaw*. The incident, remembered at the conclusion of "The School Days of an Indian Girl," represents the bitter culmination of her educational experience.

From this point Simmons would never forget that she was Indian, but rather than silencing her, incidents such as the oratory competition molded her into a more outspoken public advocate for Indian political rights and cultural values. After becoming an accomplished violinist at the Boston Conservatory and teaching at the Carlisle Indian School, she formally began her writing career in 1900, publishing short autobiographical pieces in *The Atlantic Monthly* and *Harper's*. Her first collection, *Old Indian Legends* (1901), conveys the significance of traditional Indian stories for an English-speaking public; her second book, *American Indian Stories* (1921), compiles autobiographical essays, tribal legends, and later political writings. Her most controversial essays, such as "The Soft-Hearted Sioux" (1901) and "Why I Am a Pagan" (1902), directly challenge the white Christian values she herself taught at Carlisle and, consequently, earned the disapproval of some who had previously regarded her as a paragon of the civilized, Christianized Indian.

Around the time she began to publish her work, Gertrude Simmons renamed herself Zitkala-Ša (Red Bird) both to disown her absent father and to affirm her Lakota identity. During the long interval between the publications of her two collections she committed herself to political activism on the Standing Rock Reservation in South Dakota, where she met and married Raymond T. Bonnin, a Lakota. When she was elected as secretary of the Society of American Indians in 1916, she and her husband moved to Washington, D.C., where she edited *American Indian Magazine* and lobbied effectively for the Indian Citizenship Act of 1924. She died there and now lies buried in Arlington National Cemetery.

Although an influential political figure during her lifetime and one of the first Indian writers to transcribe tribal legends in English, Zitkala-Ša is remembered mostly for her early autobiographical writing. Her plainspoken account of her departure from the reservation and her alienation at white BOARDING SCHOOLS gives voice to thousands of Indian youths of her generation who shared these experiences. In "An Indian Teacher among Indians" (1900) she reflects, "Many have passed idly through the Indian schools during the last decade, afterward to boast of their charity to the North American Indian. But few there are who have paused to question whether real life or long-lasting death lies beneath this semblance of civilization" (98–99).

Often she conveys her own questions through simple observations that assume more complex metaphorical significance. At the close of "Impressions of an Indian Childhood," for example, she hears of "The Big Red Apples," mythical symbols of the promise of civilization, and responds with astonishment: "I had never seen apple trees. I had never tasted more than a dozen red apples in my life; and when I heard of the orchards of the East, I was eager to roam among them. The missionaries smiled into my eyes and patted me on the head. . . . 'Yes, little girl, the nice red apples are for those who pick them'" (42). The anecdote recalls the biblical creation story, in which the fruit represents false promise, the destruction of innocence, and the loss of paradise. Here Zitkala-Ša levels the same charges against the "paleface," inverting the Judeo-Christian story by casting the pagan Indians as the innocents, the Christian missionary as the deceitful tempter, and the departure to boarding school as the exile from Eden.

Such subtle critiques of assimilation and her affirmation of Indian traditions and beliefs in a time when many educational and political authorities asserted their degeneracy have led readers today to recognize Zitkala-Ša as an early voice of Indian cultural independence.

Bibliography

Cutter, Martha J. "Zitkala-Ša's Autobiographical Writings: The Problems of a Canonical Search for Language and Identity." *MELUS* 19 (spring 1994): 31–44.

Fisher, Dexter, ed. *Old Indian Legends.* Lincoln: University of Nebraska Press, 1985.

———. "Zitkala-Ša: The Evolution of a Writer." *American Indian Quarterly* 5 (August 1979): 229–238.

Hafen, Jane P., ed. *Dreams and Thunder: Stories, Poems, and* The Sun Dance Opera. Lincoln: University of Nebraska Press, 2001.

López, Tiffany Ana. "A Second Tongue: The Trickster's Voice in the Works of Zitkala-Ša." *Tricksterism in Turn-of-the-Century American Literature: A Multicultural Perspective,* edited by Elizabeth Ammons. Hanover, N.H.: University Press of New England, 1994.

Susag, Dorothea M. "Zitkala-Ša (Gertrude Simmons Bonnin): A Power(full) Literary Voice." *Studies in American Indian Literatures* 5 (winter 1993): 3–24.

Zitkala-Ša. *American Indian Stories.* 1921. Reprint, Lincoln: University of Nebraska Press, 1985.

Harry Brown

APPENDIXES

SELECTED BIBLIOGRAPHY OF WORKS BY AMERICAN INDIAN AUTHORS

The following is a list of major American Indian writers and their publications.

Adams, Howard.

The Education of Canadians; 1800–1867: The Roots of Separatism. Montreal: Harvest House, 1968.

Prison of Grass: Canada from a Native Perspective. Saskatoon: Fifth House, 1975.

Tortured People: The Politics of Colonization. Penticton, Canada: Theytus, 1995.

Akiwenzie-Damm, Kateri.

My Heart Is a Stray Bullet. Wiarton, Canada: Kegedonce, 1993.

Skins: Contemporary Indigenous Writing (editor). Wiarton, Canada: Kegedonce Press, 2002.

Without Reservation: Indigenous Erotica. Wiarton, Canada: Kegedonce, 2003.

Alexie, Sherman.

The Business of Fancydancing. Brooklyn, N.Y.: Hanging Loose Press, 1992.

The Business of Fancydancing (screenplay). Brooklyn, N.Y.: Hanging Loose Press, 2003.

First Indian on the Moon. Brooklyn, N.Y.: Hanging Loose Press, 1993.

Indian Killer. New York: Atlantic Monthly Press, 1996.

I Would Steal Horses. Niagara Falls, N.Y.: Slipstream Press, 1992.

The Lone Ranger and Tonto Fistfight in Heaven. New York: Atlantic Monthly Press, 1993.

The Man Who Loves Salmon. Boise, Idaho: Limberlost Press, 1998.

Old Shirts and New Skins. Los Angeles: American Indian Studies Center, 1993.

One Stick Song. Brooklyn, N.Y.: Hanging Loose Press, 2000.

Reservation Blues. New York: Atlantic Monthly Press, 1995.

Smoke Signals: A Screenplay. New York: Hyperion Press, 1998.

The Summer of Black Widows. Brooklyn, N.Y.: Hanging Loose Press, 1996.

Ten Little Indians. New York: Atlantic Monthly Press, 2003.

The Toughest Indian in the World. New York: Atlantic Monthly Press, 2000.

Water Flowing Home. New York: Atlantic Monthly Press, 1996.

Allen, Paula Gunn.

As Long As the Rivers Flow: The Stories of Nine Native Americans. New York: Scholastic, 1996.

The Blind Lion: Poems. Berkeley, Calif.: Thorp Springs Press, 1974.

A Cannon between Mv Knees. New York: Strawberry Hill Press, 1981.

Coyote's Daylight Trip. Albuquerque, N.Mex.: La Confluencia, 1978.

Grandmothers of the Light: A Medicine Women's Source-book. Boston: Beacon Press, 1991.

Hozho: Walking in Beauty: Short Stories by American Indian Writers (editor with Carolyn Dunn). Los Angeles: Lowell House, 2001.

Life Is a Fatal Disease: Collected Poems 1962–1995. Albuquerque, N.Mex.: West End Press, 1997.

Off the Reservation: Reflections on Boundary-Busting, Border-Crossing Loose Cannons. Boston: Beacon Press, 1998.

Pocahontas: Medicine Woman, Spy, Entrepreneur, Diplomat. San Francisco: Harper, 2003.

The Sacred Hoop: Recovering the Feminine in American Indian Traditions. Boston: Beacon Press, 1986.

Shadow Country. Los Angeles: University of California Indian Studies Center, 1982.

Skin and Bones. Albuquerque, N.Mex.: West End, 1988.

Song of the Turtle: American Indian Literature, 1974–1994. New York: Ballantine Books, 1996.

Spider Woman's Granddaughters: Traditional Tales and Contemporary Writing by Native American Women. Boston: Beacon Press, 1989.

Star Child. Marvin, S.Dak.: Blue Cloud Quarterly, 1981.

Voice of the Turtle: American Indian Literature 1900–1970. New York: Ballantine, 1994.

The Woman Who Owned the Shadows. San Francisco: Spinsters/Aunt Lute Books, 1983.

Wyrds. San Francisco: Taurean Horn, 1987.

Apess, William.

Eulogy on King Philip: As Pronounced at the Odeon, in Federal Street, Boston. Boston: Author, 1836.

The Increase of the Kingdom of Christ. New York: Author, 1831.

A Son of the Forest and Other Writings. Amherst: University of Massachusetts Press, 1997.

Armstrong, Jeannette C.

Breath Tracks. Stratford, Canada: Williams-Wallace, 1991.

Enwhisteekwa: Walk in Water. Penticton, Canada: Okanagan Indian Curriculum Project, 1982.

Looking at the Words of Our People: First Nations Analysis of Literature, edited by Jeannette C. Armstrong. Penticton, Canada: Theytus Books, 1993.

The Native Creative Process: A Collaborative Discourse between Douglas Cardinal and Jeannette Armstrong. Penticton, Canada: Theytus Books, 1991.

Native Poetry in Canada: A Contemporary Anthology, edited by Jeannette C. Armstrong and Lally Grauer. Peterborough, Canada: Broadview Press, 2001.

Neekna and Chemai. Penticton, Canada: Theytus Books, 1984.

Slash. Penticton, Canada: Theytus Books, 1985.

Whispering in Shadows: A Novel. Penticton, Canada: Theytus Books, 2000.

Arnett, Carroll (Gogisgi).

Come. New Rochelle, N.Y.: Elizabeth Press, 1973.

Coyote's Journal. Berkeley, Calif.: Wingbow Press, 1982.

Earlier. New Rochelle, N.Y.: Elizabeth Press, 1972.

Engine. Norman, Okla.: Point Riders Press, 1988.

Like a Wall. New Rochelle, N.Y.: Elizabeth Press, 1969.

Night Perimeter: New and Selected Poems 1958–1990. Greenfield Center, N.Y.: Greenfield Review Press, 1991.

Not Only That. New Rochelle, N.Y.: Elizabeth Press, 1967.

Rounds. Merrick, N.Y.: Cross-Cultural Communications, 1982.

Spells. Blue Creek, Ohio: Bloody Twin Press, 1995.

South Line: Poems. New Rochelle, N.Y.: Elizabeth Press, 1979.

Then: Poems. New Rochelle, N.Y.: Elizabeth Press, 1965.

Through the Woods. New Rochelle, N.Y.: Elizabeth Press, 1971.

Tsalagi: Poems. New Rochelle, N.Y.: Elizabeth Press, 1976.

Barnes, Jim.

The American Book of the Dead: Poems. Urbana: University of Illinois Press, 1982.

La Plata Cantata: Poems. West Lafayette, Ind.: Purdue University Press, 1989.

On a Wing of the Sun. Urbana: University of Illinois Press, 2001.

On Native Ground: Memoirs and Impressions. Norman: University of Oklahoma Press, 1997.

Paris: Poems. Urbana: University of Illinois Press, 1998.

A Season of Loss: Poems. West Lafayette, Ind.: Purdue University Press, 1985.

The Sawdust War. Urbana: University of Illinois Press, 1992.

Summons and Sign: Poems. Kirksville, Mo.: Chariton Review Press, 1980.

Bernard, Gertrude (Anahareo).

Devil in Deerskins: My Life with Grey Owl. Toronto: New Press, 1972.

Grey Owl and I: A New Autobiography. London: P. Davies, 1972.

Bird, Gloria.

Full Moon on the Reservation. Greenfield Center, N.Y.: Greenfield Review Press, 1993.

Reinventing the Enemy's Language. New York: W. W. Norton, 1997.

The River of History. Portland, Oreg.: Trask House Books, 1997.

Black Elk.

Black Elk Speaks: Being the Life Story of a Holy Man of the Oglala Sioux (as told by John G. Neihardt, ed.). Lincoln: University of Nebraska Press, 1961.

The Sacred Pipe: Black Elk's Account of the Seven Rites of the Oglala Sioux. Norman: University of Oklahoma Press, 1953.

The Sixth Grandfather: Black Elk's Teachings Given to John G. Neihardt. Lincoln: University of Nebraska Press, 1984.

Blaeser, Kimberly.

Absentee Indians and Other Poems (Native American Series). East Lansing: Michigan State University Press, 2002.

Gerald Vizenor: Writing in the Oral Tradition. Norman: University of Oklahoma Press, 1996.

Traces in Blood, Bone and Stone: Contemporary Ojibwe Poetry (editor) Bemidji, Minn.: Loonfeather Press, 2006.

Trailing You: Poems. Greenfield Center, N.Y.: Greenfield Review Press, 1994.

Blue Cloud, Peter.

Alcatraz Is Not an Island. Berkeley, Calif.: Wingbow Press, 1972.

Back Then Tomorrow. Brunswick, Maine: Blackberry Press, 1978.

Clans of Many Nations: Selected Poems, 1969–1994. Fredonia, N.Y.: White Pine Press, 1995.

Elderberry Flute Song: Contemporary Coyote Tales. Buffalo, N.Y.: White Pine Press, 1989.

The Other Side of Nowhere: Contemporary Coyote Tales. Fredonia, N.Y.: White Pine Press, 1990.

Sketches in Winter; with Crows. New York: Strawberry Press, 1984.

White Corn Sister. New York: Strawberry Press, 1979.

Brant, Beth.

Food & Spirits: Stories. Ithaca, N.Y.: Firebrand Books, 1991.

A Gathering of Spirit: A Collection by North American Indian Women (editor). Ithaca, N.Y.: Firebrand Books, 1988.

I'll Sing 'Til the Day I Die: Conversations with Tyendinaga Elders. Toronto: McGilligan Books, 1995.

Mohawk Trail. Ithaca, N.Y.: Firebrand Books, 1985.

Writing as Witness: Essay and Talk. Toronto: Women's Press, 1994.

Bruchac, Joseph.

Aftermath: An Anthology of Poems in English from Africa, Asia, and the Caribbean. Greenfield Center, N.Y.: Greenfield Review Press, 1977.

Aniyunwiya/Real Human Beings: An Anthology of Contemporary Cherokee Prose. Greenfield Center, N.Y.: Greenfield Review Press, 1995.

The Arrow over the Door. New York: Dial Books for Young Readers, 1998.

Between Earth & Sky: Legends of Native American Sacred Places. Orlando: Harcourt Children's Books, 1999.

Bowman's Store: A Journey to Myself. New York: Dial Books, 1997.

A Boy Called Slow: The True Story of Sitting Bull. New York: Philomel Books, 1994.

The Boy Who Lived with the Bears: And Other Iroquois Stories. New York: HarperCollins, 1995.

Breaking Silence: An Anthology of Contemporary Asian American Poets. Greenfield Center, N.Y.: Greenfield Review Press, 1983.

Code Talker: A Novel about the Navajo Marines of World War Two. New York: Dial, 2005.

Crazy Horse's Vision. New York: Lee & Low Books, 2000.

Dawn Land. Golden, Colo.: Fulcrum, 1993.

Dog People: Native Dog Stories. Golden, Colo.: Fulcrum, 1995.

Eagle Song. New York: Dial Books for Young Readers, 1997.

The Earth under Sky Bear's Feet: Native American Poems of the Land. New York: Philomel Books, 1995.

The Faithful Hunter: Abenaki Stories. Greenfield Center, N.Y.: Greenfield Review Press, 1988.

The First Strawberries. New York: Dial Books for Young Readers, 1993.

Flow. Austin, Tex.: Cold Mountain, 1975.

Flying with Eagle, Racing the Bear: Stories from Native North America. Mahwah, N.J.: BridgeWater Books, 1993.

Fox Song. Toronto: Oxford University Press, 1993.

The Girl Who Married the Moon. Mahwah, N.J.: BridgeWater Books, 1994.

Gluskabe and the Four Wishes. New York: Cobblehill Books/Dutton, 1995.

The Good Message of Handsome Lake. Greensboro, N.C.: Univorn Press, 1979.

The Great Ball Game. New York: Dial Books for Young Readers, 1994.

The Heart of a Chief: A Novel. New York: Dial Books for Young Readers, 1998.

Iroquois Stories: Heroes and Heroines, Monsters and Magic. Trumansburg, N.Y.: Crossing Press, 1985.

Keepers of the Night: Native Stories and Nocturnal Activities for Children. Saskatoon: Fifth House, 1994.

Lasting Echoes: An Oral History of Native American People. San Diego, Calif.: Silver Whistle, 1997.

Last Stop: Writings from Comstock Prison. Greenfield Center, N.Y.: Greenfield Review Press, 1974.

Makiawisug: The Gift of the Little People. Uncasville, Conn.: Little People, 1997.

Near the Mountains. Fredonia, N.Y.: White Pine Press, 1987.

New Voices from the Longhouse: Anthology of Contemporary Iroquois Writing. Greenfield Center, N.Y.: Greenfield Review Press, 1989.

The Next World. Trumansburg, N.Y.: Crossing Press, 1978.

No Borders: New Poems. Duluth, Minn.: Holy Cow! Press, 1999.

Nuke Chronicles. New York: Contract II, 1980.

Raven Tells Stories: An Anthology of Contemporary Alaskan Native Writing. Greenfield Center, N.Y.: Greenfield Review Press, 1991.

Returning the Gift: Poetry and Prose from the First North American Native Writers' Festival. Tucson: University of Arizona Press, 1994.

Return of the Sun: Native American Tales from the Northeast Woodlands. Freedom, Calif.: Crossing Press, 1989.

Seeing the Circle. Katonah, N.Y.: R. C. Owen, 1999.

Skeleton Man. New York: HarperCollins, 2003.

Smoke Rising: The Native North American Literary Companion. Detroit: Visible Ink Press, 1995.

Songs from This Earth on Turtle's Back: Contemporary American Indian Poetry. Greenfield Center, N.Y.: Greenfield Review Press, 1983.

The Story of the Milky Way: A Cherokee Tale. New York: Dial Books for Young Readers, 1995.

Survival This Way: Interviews with American Indian Poets. Tucson: University of Arizona Press, 1987.

Tell Me a Tale: A Book about Storytelling. San Diego, Calif.: Harcourt Brace, 1997.

Thirteen Moons on Turtle's Back. New York: Philomel Books, 1992.

The Trail of Tears. New York: Random House, 1999.

Trails of Tears, Paths of Beauty. Washington, D.C.: National Geographic Society, 2000.

Translator's Son. Merrick, N.Y.: Cross-Cultural Communications, 1980.

Turtle Meat and Other Stories. Duluth, Minn.: Holy Cow! Press, 1992.

The Waters Between: A Novel of the Dawn Land. Hanover, N.H.: University Press of New England, 1998.

The Warriors. Plain City, Ohio: Darby Creek, 2004.

When the Chenoo Howls: Native American Tales of Terror. New York: Walker, 1998.

The Wind Eagle and Other Abenaki Stories. Greenfield Center, N.Y.: Bowman Books, 1985.

Words from the House of the Dead: Prison Writings from Soledad. Trumansburg, N.Y.: Crossing Press, 1974.

Campbell, Maria.

Achimoona. Saskatoon: Fifth House, 1985.

The Book of Jessica: A Theatrical Transformation. Toronto: Coach House Press, 1989.

Halfbreed. New York: Saturday Review Press, 1973.

Little Badger and the Fire Spirit. Toronto: McClelland & Stewart, 1977.

People of the Buffalo: How the Plains Indians Lived. Vancouver: J. J. Douglas, 1976.

Stories of the Road Allowance People. Penticton, Canada: Theytus Books, 1995.

Tales from the Cloud Walking Country. Athens: University of Georgia Press, 2002.

Chrystos.

Dream On. Vancouver: Press Gang, 1991.

Fire Power. Vancouver: Press Gang, 1995.

Fugitive Colors. Vancouver: Press Gang, 1995.

In Her I Am. Vancouver: Press Gang, 1993.

Not Vanishing. Vancouver: Press Gang, 1988.

Clements, Susan.

The Broken Hoop. Marvin, S.Dak.: Blue Cloud Quarterly, 1988.

In the Moon When Deer Lose Their Horns. Midland Park, N.J.: Chantry Press, 1993.

Conley, Robert J.

The Actor. New York: Doubleday, 1987.

Back to Malachi. New York: Doubleday, 1986.

Barjack. New York: Leisure Books, 2000.

Border Line. New York: Pocket Books, 1993.

Brass. New York: Leisure Books, 1999.

Broke Loose. New York: Leisure Books, 2000.

Captain Dutch. New York: Pocket Books, 1995.

Cherokee. Portland, Oreg.: Graphic Arts Center, 2002.

Cherokee Dragon: A Novel of the Real People. New York: St. Martin's Press, 2000.

Cherokee Medicine Man: The Life and Work of a Modern-Day Healer. Norman: University of Oklahoma Press, 2005.

The Cherokee Nation: A History. Albuquerque: University of New Mexico Press, 2005.

Cold Hard Trail. Farmington Hills, Mich.: Thomson Gale, 2002.

Colfax. New York: M. Evans, 1989.

Crazy Snake. New York: Pocket Books, 1994.

Dark Island. Thorndike, Maine: Center Point Large Print, 2003.

The Dark Island. New York: Doubleday, 1995.

Dark Way. New York: Doubleday, 1993.

Fugitive's Trail. New York: St. Martin's Press, 2000.

Geronimo: An American Legend. New York: Pocket Books, 1993.

Go-Ahead Rider. New York: M. Evans, 1990.

The Gunfighter. New York: Leisure Books, 2001.

Incident at Buffalo Crossing. New York: Leisure Books, 1998.

Killing Time. New York: M. Evans, 1988.

The Long Trail North. New York: Pocket Books, 1993.

The Long Way Home. New York: Doubleday, 1994.

The Meade Solution. Niwot: University Press of Colorado, 1998.

Ned Christie's War. New York: M. Evans, 1990.

Nickajack. New York: Doubleday, 1992.

Outside the Law. New York: Pocket Books, 1995.

The Peace Chief: A Novel of the Real People. New York: St. Martin's Press, 1998.

Quitting Time. New York: M. Evans, 1989.

Rattlesnake Band and Other Poems. Bloomington: Indiana University Press, 1984.

The Saga of Henry Starr. New York: Doubleday, 1989.

Strange Company. New York: Pocket Books, 1991.

To Make a Killing. New York: Pocket Books, 1994.

The War Trail North. New York: Doubleday, 1995.

War Woman: A Novel of the Real People. New York: St. Martin's Press, 1997.

The Way of the Priests. New York: Doubleday, 1992.

The Way South. New York: Doubleday, 1993.

The White Path. New York: Doubleday, 1993.

Wilder and Wilder. New York: Pageant Books, 1988.

The Witch of Goingsnake and Other Stories. Norman: University of Oklahoma Press, 1988.

Zeke Proctor: Cherokee Outlaw. New York: Pocket Books, 1994.

Cook-Lynn, Elizabeth.

Anti-Indianism in Modern America: A Voice from Tatekeya's Earth. Urbana: University of Illinois Press, 2001.

Aurelia: A Crow Creek Trilogy. Niwot: University Press of Colorado, 1999.

From the River's Edge. New York: Arcade, 1991.

I Remember the Fallen Trees: New and Selected Poems. Cheney: Eastern Washington University Press, 1998.

The Politics of Hallowed Ground: Wounded Knee and the Struggle for Indian Sovereignty (with Mario Gonzalez). Urbana: University of Illinois Press, 1999.

The Power of Horses and Other Stories. New York: Arcade-Little, Brown, 1990.

Seek the House of Relatives. Marvin, S.Dak.: Blue Cloud Quarterly, 1983.

Then the Badger Said This. New York: Vantage, 1977.

Why I Can't Read Wallace Stegner and Other Essays: A Tribal Voice. Madison: University of Wisconsin Press, 1996.

Cuthand, Beth.

The Little Duck/Sikihpsis. Penticton, Canada: Theytus, 1999.

Horse Dance to Emerald Mountain. Vancouver: Lazara, 1987.

Voices in the Waterfall. Penticton, Canada: Theytus, 1992.

Dauenhauer, Nora Marks.

Because We Cherish You: Sealaska Elders Speak to the Future. Juneau, Ala.: Sealaska Heritage Foundation Press, 1981.

Beginning Tlingit. Sitka, Ala.: Tlingit Readers, 1976.

Droning Shaman: Poems. Haines, Ala.: Black Current Press, 1988.

Haa Kusteeyí, Our Culture: Tlingit Life Stories. Seattle: University of Washington Press, 1994.

Haa Shuká, Our Ancestors: Tlingit Oral Narratives. Seattle: University of Washington Press, 1987.

Haa Tuwunáagu Yís; For Healing Our Spirit: Tlingit Oratory. Seattle: University of Washington Press, 1990.

Life Woven with Song. Tucson: University of Arizona Press, 2000.

Deloria, Ella Cara.

Buffalo People. Albuquerque: University of New Mexico Press, 1994.

Dakota Grammar. Sioux Falls, S.Dak.: Dakota Press, 1979.

Dakota Texts. New York: G. E. Stechert, 1932.

Deer Women and Elk Men: The Lakota Narratives of Ella Deloria. Albuquerque: University of New Mexico Press, 1992.

Iron Hawk. Albuquerque: University of New Mexico Press, 1993.

Speaking of Indians. Vermillion, S.Dak.: Dakota Press, 1979.

Waterlily. Lincoln: University of Nebraska Press, 1988.

Dorris, Michael.

The Broken Cord: A Family's Ongoing Struggle with Fetal Alcohol Syndrome. New York: Harper, 1989.

Cloud Chamber. New York: Simon & Schuster, 1998.

The Crown of Columbus (with Louise Erdrich). New York: HarperCollins, 1991.

Guests. New York: Hyperion Books for Children, 1994.

Morning Girl. New York: Hyperion Books for Children, 1992.

Paper Trail. New York: HarperCollins, 1994.

Rooms in the House of Stone. Minneapolis: Milkweed Editions, 1993.

Sees Behind Trees. New York: Hyperion Books for Children, 1999.

Working Men. New York: Henry Holt, 1993.

A Yellow Raft in Blue Water. New York: Henry Holt, 1987.

Eastman, Charles Alexander (Ohiyesa).

From the Deep Woods to Civilization: Chapters in the Autobiography of an Indian. 1916. Reprint, Lincoln: University of Nebraska Press, 1977.

Indian Boyhood. 1902. Reprint, Lincoln: University of Nebraska Press, 1992.

Indian Heroes and Great Chieftains. 1918. Reprint, Lincoln: University of Nebraska Press, 1991.

Indian Scout Talks: A Guide for Boy Scouts and Camp Fire Girls. Boston: Little, Brown, 1914.

The Indian Today: The Past and Future of the First American. Garden City, N.Y.: Doubleday, Page, 1915.

Old Indian Days. 1907. Reprint, Lincoln: University of Nebraska Press, 1991.

Red Hunters and the Animal People. New York: Harper & Brothers, 1904.

The Soul of the Indian: An Interpretation. 1911. Reprint, Lincoln: University of Nebraska Press, 1980.

Wigwam Evenings: Sioux Folk Tales Retold. Boston: Little, Brown, 1916.

Erdrich, Karen Louise.

The Antelope Wife. New York: Harper Flamingo, 1998.

Baptism of Desire: Poems. New York: Harper & Row, 1989.

The Beet Queen. New York: Henry Holt, 1986.

The Bingo Palace. New York: HarperCollins, 1994.

The Birchbark House. New York: Hyperion Books for Children, 1999.

The Blue Jay's Dance: A Birth Year. New York: Harper-Collins, 1995.

The Crown of Columbus (with Michael Dorris). New York: HarperCollins, 1991.

Four Souls. New York: HarperCollins, 2004.

Grandmother's Pigeon. New York: Hyperion Books for Children, 1996.

Jacklight. New York: Henry Holt, 1984.

The Last Report on the Miracles at Little No Horse. New York: HarperCollins, 2001.

Love Medicine. New York: Harper Perennial, 1993.

The Master Butchers' Singing Club. New York: Harper-Collins, 2003.

The Painted Drum. New York: HarperCollins, 2005.

Tales of Burning Love. New York: HarperCollins, 1996.

Tracks. New York: Henry Holt, 1998.

Gansworth, Eric.

Indian Summers. East Lansing: Michigan State University Press, 1998.

Mending Skins (Native Stories Series). Lincoln: University of Nebraska Press, 2005.

Nickel Eclipse: Iroquois Moon. East Lansing: Michigan State University Press, 2000.

Smoke Dancing. East Lansing: Michigan State University Press, 2004.

Geiogamah, Hanay.

American Indian Theater in Performance: A Reader (editor with Jaye T. Darby). Los Angeles: University of California, American Indian Studies Center, 2000.

New Native American Drama: Three Plays, edited by with introduction by Jeffrey Huntsman. Norman: University of Oklahoma Press, 1980.

Stories of Our Way: An Anthology of Native American Indian Plays [contains *Coon Cons Coyote, Foghorn, 49, Grandma,* and *Grandpa*], edited by Hanay Geiogamah and Jaye Darby. Los Angeles: University of California, American Indian Studies Center, 1999.

Teatro. Rome: Castelvecchi, 1994.

Glancy, Diane.

(Ado)ration. Tucson, Ariz.: Chax Press, 1999.

American Gypsy: Six Native American Plays. Norman: University of Oklahoma Press, 2002.

Boomtown. Goodhue, Minn.: Black Hat Press, 1997.

Claiming Breath. Lincoln and London: University of Nebraska Press, 1992.

The Closets of Heaven. Tucson, Ariz.: Chax Press, 1999.

The Cold-and-Hunger Dance. Lincoln: University of Nebraska Press, 1998.

The Dance Partner. East Lansing: Michigan State University Press, 2005.

Designs of the Night Sky. Lincoln: University of Nebraska Press, 2002.

Drystalks of the Moon. Tulsa, Okla.: Hadassah Press, 1981.

Firesticks: A Collection of Stories. Norman: University of Oklahoma Press, 1993.

Flutie. Wakefield, R.I.: Moyer Bell, 1998.

Fuller Man: A Novel. Wakefield, R.I.: Moyer Bell, 1999.

In-Between Places. Tucson: University of Arizona Press, 2005.

Iron Woman. Minneapolis: New Rivers Press, 1990.

Lone Dog's Winter Count. Albuquerque, N.Mex.: West End Press, 1991.

Man Who Heard the Land. St. Paul: Minnesota Historical Society Press, 2001.

The Mask Maker. Norman: University of Oklahoma Press, 2002.

Monkey Secret. Evanston, Ill.: TriQuarterly Books, 1995.

Offering: Poetry & Prose. Duluth, Minn.: Holy Cow! Press, 1988.

One Age in a Dream. Minneapolis: Milkweed Editions, 1986.

The Only Piece of Furniture in the House: A Novel. Wakefield, R.I.: Moyer Bell, 1996.

Primer of the Obsolete. Amherst: University of Massachusetts Press, 2004.

Pushing the Bear: A Novel of the Trail of Tears. San Diego and New York: Harvest, 1996.

The Relief of America. Chicago: Tia Chucha, 2000.

Rooms: Selected Poems. Cambridge, England: Salt, 2005.

The Shadow's Horse. Tucson: University of Arizona Press, 2003.

Stone Heart: A Novel of Sacajawea. New York: Overlook Hardcover, 2003.

Trigger Dance. Boulder, Colo.: Fiction Collective Two, 1990.

Two Worlds Walking: Short Stories, Essay, and Poetry by Writers with Mixed Heritages, edited by Diane Glancy and C. W. Truesdale. New York: New Rivers, 1994.

The Voice That Was in Travel: Stories. Norman: University of Oklahoma Press, 1999.

War Cries. Duluth, Minn.: Holy Cow! Press, 1997.

The West Pole. Minneapolis and London: University of Minnesota Press, 1997.

Gordon, Roxy.

At Play in the Lord's Fields. Big Timber, Mont.: Seven Buffaloes Press, 1986.

Breeds. Austin: Place of Herons, 1984.

Crazy Horse Never Died. Paperbacks Plus Press, 1989.

Gods and Indians. Dallas: Wowapi, 1989.

Revolution in the Air. Dallas: Wowapi, 1994.

Some Things Did P. New York: Simon & Schuster Adult Publishing Group, 1972.

Some Things I Did. Austin: Encino Press, 1971.

Unfinished Business. Dallas: Wowapi, 1985.

West Texas Mid-Century. Dallas: Wowapi, 1988.

Gould, Janice.

Beneath My Heart: Poetry. Ithaca, N.Y.: Firebrand Books, 1990.

Earthquake Weather: Poems. Tucson: University of Arizona Press., 1996.

Grieves, Catron.

Moonrising. Oklahoma City, Okla.: Red Dirt Press, 1987.

A Terrible Foe This Bear. Edmond, Okla.: Broncho Press.

Hale, Janet Campbell.

Bloodlines: Odyssey of a Native Daughter. New York: Random House, 1993.

The Jailing of Cecelia Capture. Albuquerque: University of New Mexico Press, 1985.

The Owl's Song. Garden City, N.Y.: Doubleday, 1974.

Women on the Run. Moscow: University of Idaho Press, 1999.

Harjo, Joy.

The Good Luck Cat. San Diego, Calif.: Harcourt Brace, 2000.

How We Became Human: New and Selected Poems. New York: Norton, 2002.

In Mad Love and War. Hanover, N.H.: Wesleyan University Press, 1990.

The Last Song. Las Cruces, N.Mex.: Puerto del Sol Press, 1975.

A Map to the Next World. New York: Norton, 2000.

Native Joy for Real. San Antonio, Tex.: Wings Press, 2005.

Reinventing the Enemy's Language (with Gloria Bird). New York: W. W. Norton, 1997.

Secrets from the Center of the World (with Stephen Strom). Tucson: University of Arizona Press, 1989.

She Had Some Horses. New York and Chicago: Thunder's Mouth Press, 1983.

The Spiral of Memory: Interviews. Ann Arbor: University of Michigan Press, 1996.

What Moon Drove Me to This? Berkeley, Calif.: Reed, Cannon, Johnson, 1979.

The Woman Who Fell from the Sky. New York: Norton, 1994.

Heat-Moon, William Least.

Blue Highways: A Journey into America. Boston: Little, Brown, 1982.

Columbus in the Americas. Indianapolis: John Wiley & Sons, 2002.

PrairyErth. Boston: Houghton Mifflin, 1991.

River Horse: Across America by Boat. New York: Penguin, 2001.

River Horse: The Logbook of a Boat across America. Boston: Houghton Mifflin, 1999.

Henson, Lance.

Another Distance. Norman, Okla.: Point Riders Press, 1991.

Another Song for America. Norman, Okla.: Point Riders Press, 1987.

A Cheyenne Sketchbook. Greenfield Center, N.Y.: Greenfield Review Press, 1985.

In a Dark Mist. Merrick, N.Y.: Cross-Cultural Communications, 1992.

Strong Heart Song: Lines from a Revolutionary Text: Poetry. Albuquerque, N.Mex.: West End Press, 1997.

Highway, Tomson.

Comparing Mythologies. Ottawa: University of Ottawa Press, 2003.

Dry Lips Oughta Move to Kapuskasing. Vancouver: Talonbooks, 1994.

Ernestine Shuswap Gets Her Trout: A String Quartet for Four Female Actors. Burnaby, Canada: Talonbooks, 2005.

Johnny National, Super Hero. Ottawa: Health Canada, 2001.

Kiss of the Fur Queen. Toronto: Doubleday Canada, 1998.

The Rez Sisters: A Play in Two Acts. Saskatoon: Fifth House, 1988.

Rose. Burnaby, Canada: Talonbooks, 2003.

Hill, Roberta (Roberta Hill Whiteman).

Philadelphia Flowers. Duluth, Minn.: Holy Cow! Press, 1996.

Star Quilt: Poems. Duluth, Minn.: Holy Cow! Press, 1984, 2001.

Hobson, Geary.

Deer Hunting and Other Poems. New York: Strawberry Press with Points Riders Press, 1990.

The Last of the Ofos. Tucson: University of Arizona Press, 2000.

The Remembered Earth: An Anthology of Contemporary Native American Literature. Albuquerque: University of New Mexico Press, 1979.

Returning the Gift: Poetry and Prose from the First North American Native Writer's Festival, edited by Joseph Bruchac. Tucson: University of Arizona Press, 1994.

Hogan, Linda.

The Book of Medicines. Minneapolis: Coffee House Press, 1993.

Calling Myself Home. Greenfield Center, N.Y.: Greenfield Review Press, 1978.

Dwellings: A Spiritual History of the Living World. New York: W. W. Norton, 1995.

Eclipse. Los Angeles: University of California, American Indian Studies Center, 1983.

Mean Spirit. New York: Atheneum, 1990.

Power. New York: W. W. Norton, 1998.

Red Clay: Poems and Stories. Greenfield Center, N.Y.: Greenfield Review Press, 1994.

Savings. Minneapolis: Coffee House, 1988.

Seeing through the Sun. Amherst: University of Massachusetts Press, 1985.

Solar Storms: A Novel. New York: Scribner, 1995.

Woman Who Watches Over the World: A Native Memoir. New York: W. W. Norton, 2001.

Howe, LeAnne.

Coyote Papers. Dallas: Wowapi, 1985.

Evidence of Red. Cambridge, England: Salt, 2005.

Miko Kings: An Indian Baseball Story. San Francisco: Aunt Lute Books, 2006.

Shell Shaker. San Francisco: Aunt Lute Books, 2001.

A Stand Up Reader. Dallas: Into View Press, 1987.

Joe, Rita.

Lnu and Indians We're Called. Charlottetown, Canada: Ragweed Press, 1991.

Songs of Rita Joe: Autobiography of a Mi'kmaq Poet. Lincoln: University of Nebraska Press, 1996.

We Are Dreamers: Recent and Early Poetry. Wreck Cove, Canada: Breton Books, 1999.

Johnson, Emily Pauline.

Canadian Born. Toronto: Morang, 1903.

Flint and Feather. Toronto: The Musson Book Company, 1917.

Legends of Vancouver. Toronto: McClelland, Goodchild & Stewart, 1911.

The Moccasin Maker. Tucson: Arizona of University Press, 1987.

The Shagganappi. Vancouver: Briggs, 1913.

The White Wampum. London: John Lane, 1895.

Johnston, Basil.

Anishinaubae Thesaurus. East Lansing: Michigan State University Press, 2006.

The Bear-Walker and Other Stories. Toronto: Royal Ontario Museum, 1995.

Crazy Dave. Toronto: Key Porter Books, 1999.

How the Birds Got Their Colours. Toronto: Kids Can Press, 1978.

Indian School Days. Toronto: Key Porter Books, 1988.

The Manitous: The Spiritual World of the Ojibway.
New York: HarperCollins, 1995.
*Mermaids and Medicine Women: Native Myths and
Legends.* Toronto: Royal Ontario Museum, 1998.
Moosemeat and Wild Rice. Toronto: McClelland &
Stewart, 1978.
Ojibway Ceremonies. Toronto: McClelland & Stewart,
1987.
Ojibway Heritage. New York: Columbia University
Press, 1976.
The Star Man and Other Tales. Toronto: Royal Ontario
Museum, 1997.
Tales of the Anishinaubaek. Toronto: Royal Ontario Mu-
seum, 1993.
Tales the Elders Told: Ojibway Legends. Toronto: Royal
Ontario Museum, 1981.

Kenny, Maurice.

Backward to Forward: Prose Pieces. Fredonia, N.Y.:
White Pine Press, 1997.
Blackrobe: Isaac Jogues. Saranac Lake, N.Y.: Chauncey
Press, 1987.
Between Two Rivers: Selected Poems. Fredonia, N.Y.:
White Pine Press, 1987.
Carving Hawk. Vol. 1. Buffalo, N.Y.: White Pine Press,
2002.
Dead Letters Sent, and Other Poems. New York: Trouba-
dor Press, 1958.
Greyhounding This America: Poems and Dialog. Chico,
Calif.: Heidelberg Graphics, 1988.
I Am the Sun. Buffalo, N.Y.: White Pine Press, 1979.
In the Time of the Present: New Poems. East Lansing:
Michigan State University Press, 2000.
Is Summer This Bear. Saranac Lake, N.Y.: Chauncey
Press, 1985.
Kneading the Blood. New York: Strawberry Press, 1981.
Lewandowski, Stephen: Poacher. Fredonia, N.Y.: White
Pine Press, 1986.
The Mama Poems. Buffalo, N.Y: White Pine Press,
1984.
North: Poems of Home. Marvin, S.Dak.: Blue Cloud
Quarterly Press, 1977.
On Second Thought: A Compilation of Work. Norman:
University of Oklahoma Press, 1995.
Rain and Other Fictions. Expanded ed. Fredonia, N.Y.:
White Pine Press, 1990.
The Smell of Slaughter. Marvin, S.Dak.: Blue Cloud
Quarterly Press, 1982.

Tekonwatonti: Molly Brant (1735–1795): Poems of War.
Fredonia, N.Y.: White Pine Press, 1992.
Tortured Skins, and Other Fictions. East Lansing:
Michigan State University Press, 1999.
Wounds beneath the Flesh (editor). Fredonia, N.Y.:
White Pine Press, 1987.

King, Thomas.

*All My Relations: An Anthology of Contemporary Ca-
nadian Native Fiction* (editor). Toronto: McClel-
land & Stewart, 1990.
A Coyote Columbus Story. Toronto: Groundwood
Books, 1992.
Coyote Sings to the Moon. Portland, Oreg.: West
Winds Press, 2001.
Coyote's New Suit. Toronto: Key Porter Books, 2004.
Green Grass, Running Water. Boston: Houghton Mif-
flin, 1993.
Medicine River. Markham, Canada, and New York:
Viking, 1990.
One Good Story, That One: Stories by Thomas King.
Toronto: Harper Perennial, 1993.
The Truth about Stories: A Native Narrative. Toronto:
House of Anansi Press, 2003.
Truth and Bright Water. New York: Atlantic Monthly
Press, 1999.

LaDuke, Winona.

All Our Relations: Native Struggles for Land and Life.
Cambridge, Mass.: South End Press, 1999.
Last Standing Woman. Stillwater, Minn.: Voyageur
Press, 1997.
*Recovering the Sacred: The Power of Naming and
Claiming.* Cambridge, Mass.: South End Press,
2005.
Strangers Devour the Land (with Boyce Richardson).
White River Junction, Vt.: Chelsea Green, 1991.
*The Winona LaDuke Reader: A Collection of Essential
Writings.* Stillwater, Minn.: Voyageur Press, 2002.

Louis, Adrian C.

Among the Dog Eaters. Albuquerque, N.Mex.: West
End, 1992.
Ancient Acid Flashes Back. Reno: University of Ne-
vada Press, 2000.
Blood Thirsty Savages. St. Louis: Time Being, 1994.
Bone and Juice. Evanston, Ill.: Northwestern Univer-
sity Press, 2001.

Ceremonies of the Damned. Reno: University of Nevada Press, 1997.

Days of Obsidian, Days of Grace (with Jim Northrup, Al Hunter, and Denise Sweet). Duluth, Minn.: Poetry Harbor, 1994.

Evil Corn. Granite Falls, Minn.: Ellis, 2004.

Fire Water World. Albuquerque, N.Mex.: West End, 1989.

The Indian Cheap Wine Seance. Providence, R.I.: Gray Flannel, 1974.

Skins. New York: Crown/Random House, 1995.

Skull Dance. Jamaica, Vt.: Bull Thistle, 1998.

Sweets for the Dancing Bears. Marvin, S.Dak.: Blue Cloud Abbey, 1979.

Vortex of Indian Fevers. Evanston, Ill.: TriQuarterly Books, 1995.

Wild Indians and Other Creatures. Reno: University of Nevada Press, 1996.

Maracle, Lee.

Bent Box. Penticton, Canada: Theytus Books, 2000.

Bobbie Lee: Indian Rebel. London: The Woman's Press Limited, 1990.

Daughters Are Forever. Vancouver: Raincoast Books, 2002.

I Am Woman: A Native Perspective on Sociology and Feminism. Vancouver: Press Gang, 1996.

Ravensong. Vancouver: Press Gang, 1995.

Sojourner's Truth & Other Stories. Vancouver: Press Gang, 1990.

Sundogs: A Novel. Penticton, Canada: Theytus Books, 1992.

Will's Garden. Penticton, Canada: Theytus Books, 2002.

Mathews, John Joseph.

Life and Death of an Oilman: The Career of E. W. Marland. Norman: University of Oklahoma Press, 2003.

The Osages: Children of the Middle Waters. Norman: University of Oklahoma Press, 1961.

Sundown. Norman: University of Oklahoma Press, 1988.

Talking to the Moon. Chicago: University of Chicago Press, 1945.

Wah'Kan-Tah: The Osage and the White Man's Road. Norman: University of Oklahoma Press, 1932.

McNickle, D'Arcy.

The Hawk Is Hungry and Other Stories. Tucson: University of Arizona Press, 1992.

Indian Man: A Life of Oliver La Farge. Bloomington: Indiana University Press, 1971.

Indians and Other Americans: Two Ways of Life Meet (with Harold E. Fey). Rev. ed. New York: Harper, 1970.

The Indian Tribes of the United States: Ethnic and Cultural Survival. New York: Oxford University Press, 1962 (revised edition, *Native American Tribalism: Indian Survivals and Renewals,* 1973).

Native American Tribalism: Indian Survivals and Renewals. New York: Oxford University Press, 1973.

Runner in the Sun: A Story of Indian Maize. New York: Hold, Rinehart & Winston, 1954.

The Surrounded. New York: Dodd, Mead, 1936.

They Came Here First: The Epic of the American Indian. Rev ed. Philadelphia: Lippincott, 1975.

Wind from an Enemy Sky. San Francisco: Harper & Row, 1978.

Medawar, Mardi Oakley.

Death at Rainy Mountain. New York: St. Martin's Press, 1996.

Fort Larned Incident. New York: St. Martin's Minotaur, 2000.

The Misty Hills of Home. New York: Penguin Group, 1998.

Murder at Medicine Lodge: A Tay-Bodal Mystery. New York: St. Martin's Press, 1999.

Murder on the Red Cliff Rez. New York: St. Martin's Minotaur, 2002.

People of the Whistling Waters: A Novel. Encampment, Wyo.: Affiliated Writers of America, 1993.

Remembering the Osage Kid. New York: Bantam, 1999.

Witch of the Palo Duro: A Tay-Bodal Mystery. New York: St. Martin's Press, 1997.

Miranda, Deborah.

Zen of La Llorona. Cambridge, England: Salt, 2005.

Momaday, N. Scott.

The Ancient Child. New York: HarperPerennial, 1990.

Angle of Geese and Other Poems. Boston: D. R. Godine, 1974.

Before an Old Painting of the Crucifixion, Caramel Mission, June 1960. San Francisco: Valenti Angeleo, 1975.

Circle of Wonder: A Native American Christmas Story. Santa Fe, N.Mex.: Clear Light, 1994.

Colorado: Summer/Fall/Winter/Spring. Chicago: Rand McNally, 1973.

The Complete Poems of Frederick Goddard Tuckerman. New York: Oxford University Press, 1965.

The Gourd Dancer. Jackson: University Press of Mississippi, 1997.

House Made of Dawn. Tucson: University of Arizona Press, 1996.

In the Bear's House. New York: St. Martin's Press, 1999.

In the Presence of the Sun: Stories and Poems, 1961–1991. New York: St. Martin's Press, 1992.

Lost Copper (with Rose Wendy). Banning, Calif.: Malki Museum Press, 1980.

The Man Made of Words: Essays; Stories; Passages. New York: St. Martin's Press, 1997.

The Names: A Memoir. Tucson: University of Arizona Press, 1996.

Owl in the Cedar Press. Lincoln: University of Nebraska Press, 1992.

The Way to Rainy Mountain. Tucson: University of Arizona Press, 1996.

Mourning Dove (Christal, Christine Quintasket, Humishuma).

Cogewea, the Half-Blood: A Depiction of the Great Montana Cattle Range. 1927. Reprint, edited by Dexter Fisher. Lincoln: University of Nebraska Press, 1991.

Coyote Stories, edited and illustrated by Heister Dean Guie with notes by Lucullus V. McWhorter and a foreword by Chief Standing Bear. Caldwell, Idaho: Caxton Printers, 1933. Reprint, edited by Jay Miller, Lincoln: University of Nebraska Press.

Mourning Dove—A Salishan Autobiography, edited by Jay Miller. Lincoln: University of Nebraska Press, 1990.

Mourning Dove's Stories. San Diego, Calif.: San Diego State University, 1991.

Tales of the Okanogans, edited by Donald M. Hines. Fairfield, Wash.: Ye Galleon Press, 1976.

Niatum, Duane.

After the Death of an Elder Klallam. Phoenix, Ariz.: Baleen Press, 1970.

Anthology of Twentieth Century Native American Poetry (editor). San Francisco: Harper San Francisco, 1987.

Ascending Red Cedar Moon. New York: Harper & Row, 1973.

Breathless. Seattle: University of Washington Press, 1968.

Carriers of the Dream Wheel: Contemporary Native American Poetry (editor). New York: Harper, 1975.

The Crooked Beak of Love. Albuquerque, N.Mex.: West End Press, 2000.

A Cycle for the Woman, in the Field. Baltimore: Laughing Man Press, 1973.

Digging Out the Roots: Poems. New York: Harper & Row, 1977.

Drawings of the Song Animals: New and Selected Poems. Duluth, Minn.: Holy Cow! Press, 1991.

Harper's Anthology of Twentieth-Century Native American Poetry (editor). San Francisco: Harper & Row, 1988.

Pieces. New York: Strawberry Press, 1981.

Raven and the Fear of Growing White. Amsterdam, Netherlands: Bridge Press, 1983.

Songs for the Harvester of Dreams. Seattle: University of Washington Press, 1981.

Stories from the Land of Red Cedar. Seattle: D. Niatum, 1999.

Stories of the Moons. Marvin, S.Dak.: Blue Cloud Quarterly Press, 1987.

Taos Pueblo and Other Poems. Greenfield Center, N.Y.: Greenfield Review Press, 1973.

To Bridge the Dream. Laguna, N.Mex.: A Press, 1978.

Turning to the Rhythms of Her Song. Seattle: Jawbone Press, 1977.

Northrup, Jim.

The Rez Road Follies: Canoes, Casinos, Computers, and Birch Bark Baskets. New York: Kodansha America, 1997.

Walking the Rez Road. Stillwater, Minn.: Voyageur, 1993.

northSun, nila.

Coffee, Dust Devils, & Old Rodeo Bulls. Fallon, Nev.: Duck Down Press, 1979.

Diet Pepsi & Nacho Cheese. Fallon, Nev.: Duck Down Press, 1977.

Small Bonies, Little Eyes. Fallon, Nev.: Duck Down Press, 1981.

A Snake in Her Mouth: Poems 1974–1996. New York: West End Press, 1997.

Occom, Samson.

A Choice Collection of Hymns and Spiritual Sonts. New London, Conn.: Press of Thomas and Samual Green, 1774.

"A Sermon Preached at the Execution of Moses Paul." In *The Elders Wrote: An Anthology of Early Prose by North American Indians, 1768–1931,* edited by Bernd Peyer, 19–22. Berlin: Dietrich Reiner 1982.

"A Short Narrative of My Life." Unpublished manuscript in archives of Darmouth College Library, 1768.

Ortiz, Simon.

After and Before the Lightning. Tucson: University of Arizona Press, 1994.

Blue and Red. Acomita, N.Mex.: Pueblo of Acoma Press, 1982.

A Ceremony of Brotherhood, 1680–1980. Albuquerque, N.Mex.: Academia, 1981.

Earth Power Coming: Short Fiction in Native American Literature. Tsaile, Ariz.: Navajo Community College Press, 1983.

Fight Back: For the Sake of the People, For the Sake of the Land. Albuquerque, N.Mex.: Institute for Native American Development, 1980.

Fightin': New and Collected Stories. Chicago: Thunder's Mouth Press, 1983.

From Sand Creek: Rising in This Heart Which Is Our America. New York: Thunder's Mouth Press, 1981.

Going for the Rain. New York: Harper & Row, 1976.

Good Journey, A. Tucson: University of Arizona Press, 1977.

Howbah Indians. Tucson, Ariz.: Blue Moon, 1978.

The Importance of Childhood. Acomita, N.Mex.: Pueblo of Acoma Press, 1982.

Men on the Moon. Tucson: University of Arizona Press, 1999.

Naked in the Wind. Pembroke, N.C: Quetzal-Vihio Press, 1971.

Out There Somewhere. Tucson: University of Arizona Press, 2002.

The People Shall Continue. San Francisco: Children's Book Press, 1988.

A Poem Is a Journey. Bourbonnais, Ill.: Pternandon Press, 1981.

Questions and Swords: Folktales of the Zapatista Revolution. El Paso, Tex.: Cinco Puntos Press, 2001.

"Speaking for the Generations." In *Native Writers on Writing,* edited by Simon Ortiz. Tucson: University of Arizona Press, 1998.

Woven Stone. Tucson: University of Arizona Press, 1992.

Owens, Louis.

American Indian Novelists: An Annotated Critical Bibliography New York: Garland, 1985.

Bone Game: A Novel. Norman: University of Oklahoma Press, 1994.

Creative Destruction: Nikos Kazantzakis and the Literature of Responsibility. Macon, Ga.: Mercer University Press, 2003.

Dark River: A Novel. Norman: University of Oklahoma Press, 1999.

The Grapes of Wrath: Trouble in the Promise Land. New York: G. K. Hall, 1989.

I Hear the Train: Reflections, Inventions; Refractions. Norman: University of Oklahoma Press, 2001.

John Steinbeck's Re-vision of America. Athens: University of Georgia Press, 1985.

Mixedblood Messages: Literature, Film, Family, Place. Norman: University of Oklahoma Press, 1998.

Nightland: A Novel. New York: Dutton Signet, 1996.

Other Destinies: Understanding the American Indian Novel. Norman: University of Oklahoma Press, 1992.

The Sharpest Sight: A Novel. Norman: University of Oklahoma Press, 1992.

Wolfsong: A Novel. New York: West End Press, 1991.

Penn, W. S. (William Swain).

The Absence of Angels. Norman: University of Oklahoma Press, 1995.

All My Sins Are Relatives. Lincoln: University of Nebraska Press, 1995.

As We Are Now: Mixedblood Essays on Race and Identity. Berkeley: University of California Press, 1997.

Feathering Custer. Lincoln: University of Nebraska Press, 2001.

Killing Time with Strangers. Tucson: University of Arizona Press, 2000.

The Telling of the World: Native American Stories and Art. New York: Stewart, Tabori & Chang, 1996.

This Is the World. East Lansing: Michigan State University Press, 2000.

Posey, Alexander.

Chinnubbie and the Owl: Muscogee (Creek) Stories; Orations, and Oral Traditions. Lincoln: University of Nebraska Press, 2005.

The Fus Fixico Letters. Lincoln: University of Nebraska Press, 1993.

The Poems of Alexander Lawrence Posey. Topeka, Kans.: Crane, 1910.

Poems of Alexander Lawrence Posey, Creek Indian Bard. Muskogee, Okla: Hoffman, 1969.

Querry, Ron.

Bad Medicine. New York: Bantam Books, 1998.

The Death of Bernadette Lefthand. Santa Fe, N.Mex.: Red Crane Books, 1993.

Growing Old at Willie Nelson's Picnic and Other Sketches of Life in the Southwest. College Station: Texas A&M University Press, 1983.

I See by My Get-Up. Albuquerque: University of New Mexico Press, 1987.

Native Americans Struggle for Equality. Vero Beach, Fla.: Rourke, 1992.

Red Corn, Charles.

A Pipe for February. Norman: University of Oklahoma Press, 2002.

Revard, Carter.

An Eagle Nation. Tucson: University of Arizona Press, 1993.

Cowboys and Indians Christmas Shopping. Norman, Okla.: Point Riders Press, 1992.

Family Matters; Tribal Affairs. Tucson: University of Arizona Press, 1998.

How the Songs Come Down. Cambridge, England: Salt, 2005.

Nuke Chronicles (with Joseph Bruchac). New York: Contract II, 1980.

Ponca War Dances. Norman, Okla.: Point Riders Press, 1980.

Winning the Dust Bowl. Tucson: University of Arizona Press, 2001.

Riggs, Rollie Lynn.

The Cherokee Night and Other Plays. Norman: University of Oklahoma Press, 2003.

Four Plays. New York: Samuel French, 1947.

Green Grow the Lilacs. New York: Samuel French, 1930.

The Iron Dish. New York: Doubleday-Doran, 1930.

Rollin Ridge, John.

The Life and Adventures of Joaquin Murieta, the Celebrated California Bandit. Norman: University of Oklahoma Press, 1955.

Rose, Wendy.

Aboriginal Tattooing in California. Berkeley: University of California Press, 1979.

Bone Dance: New and Selected Poems, 1965–1993. Tucson: University of Arizona Press, 1994.

Going to War with All My Relations: New and Selected Poems. Flagstaff, Ariz.: Entrada Books, 1993.

The Halfbreed Chronicles and Other Poems. Albuquerque, N.Mex.: West End Press, 1985.

Hopi Roadrunner Dancing. Greenfield Center, N.Y.: Greenfield Review Press, 1974.

Itch Like Crazy. Tucson: University of Arizona Press, 2002.

Long Division: A Tribal History, Poems. New York: Strawberry Press, 1976.

Lost Copper. Banning, Calif.: Malki Museum Press, 1980.

Now Poof She Is Gone. Ithaca, N.Y.: Firebrand Press, 1994.

Salisbury, Ralph.

Ghost Grapefruit and Other Poems. Ithaca, N.Y.: Ithaca House, 1972.

Going to the Water: Poems of a Cherokee Heritage. Eugene, Oreg.: Pacific House Books, 1983.

The Last Rattlesnake Throw and Other Stories. Norman: University of Oklahoma Press, 1998.

One Indian and Two Chiefs: Short Fiction. Tsaile, Ariz.: Navajo Community College Press, 1993.

Pointing at the Rainbow: Poems from a Cherokee Heritage. Marvin, S.Dak.: Blue Cloud Quarterly Press, 1980.

Rainbows of Stone. Tucson: University of Arizona Press, 2000.

Spirit Beast Chant. Marvin, S.Dak.: Blue Cloud Quarterly Press, 1982.

The Sun, My Father (with Lars Norstrom and Harold Gaski). Seattle: University of Washington Press, 1988.

War in the Genes in Other Poems. Cincinnati: Wordtech Communications, 2006.

A White Rainbow: Poems of a Cherokee Heritage. Marvin, S.Dak.: Blue Cloud Quarterly Press, 1985.

Sanchez, Carol Lee.

Conversations from the Nightmare. San Francisco: Casa Editorial, 1975.

Excerpts From a Mountain Climber's Handbook: Selected Poems; 1971–1984. San Francisco: Taurean Horn, 1985.

From Spirit to Matter: New and Selected Poems; 1969–1996. San Francisco: Taurean Horn, 1997.

Message Bringer Woman. San Francisco: Taurean Horn, 1977.

(She) Poems. Goshen, Conn.: Chicory Blue, 1995.

Sarris, Greg.

Approaches to Teaching the Works of Louise Erdrich (editor). New York: Modern Language Association of America, 2004.

Grand Avenue. New York: Hyperion, 1994.

Keeping Slug Woman Alive: A Holistic Approach to American Indian Texts. Berkeley: University of California Press, 1993.

Mabel McKay: Weaving the Dream. Berkeley: University of California Press, 1994.

The Sound of Rattles and Clappers: A Collection of New California Indian Writing (editor). Tucson: University of Arizona Press, 1994.

Watermelon Nights. New York: Hyperion, 1998.

Silko, Leslie Marmon.

After a Summer Rain in the Upper Sonoran. Madison, Wis.: Black Mesa Press for Woodland Pattern, 1984.

Almanac of the Dead: A Novel. New York: Simon & Schuster, 1991, New York: Penguin, 1992.

Ceremony. New York: Viking, 1977.

The Delicacy and Strength of Lace: Letters between Leslie Marmoni Silko and James Wright. Port Townsend, Wash.: Graywolf Press, 1986.

Gardens in the Dunes. New York: Simon & Schuster, 1999.

Laguna Woman: Poems. 2nd ed. Tucson, Ariz.: Flood Plain Press, 1994.

Leslie Silko. Trumansburg, N.Y.: Crossing Press, 1974.

Rain (with Lee Marmon). Artists and Writers Series. American Journals Series 4. New York: Library Fellows of the Whitney Museum of American Art, 1996.

Sacred Water: Narratives and Pictures. Tucson, Ariz.: Flood Plain Press, 1993.

Storyteller. New York: Seaver Books, 1981, New York: Arcade, 1981.

Yellow Woman. New Brunswick, N.J.: Rutgers University Press, 1993.

Yellow Woman and a Beauty of the Spirit: Essays on Native American Life Today. New York: Simon & Schuster, 1996.

Slipperjack-Farrell, Ruby.

Honour the Sun. Winnipeg: Pemmican, 1987.

Little Voice (In the Same Boat). Regina, Calif.: Coteau Books, 2002.

Silent Words. Saskatoon: Fifth House, 1992.

Weesquachak and the Lost Ones. Penticton, Canada: Theytus Books, 2000.

Smith, Martin Cruz.

The Analog Bullet. New York: Dorchester, 1981.

Canto for a Gypsy. New York: Putnam, 1972.

December 6. New York: Simon & Schuster Adult Publishing Group, 1992.

Gorky Park. New York: Random House, 1981.

Havana Bay: A Novel. New York: Random House, 1999.

Nightwing. New York: Norton, 1977.

Polar Star. New York: Random House, 1990.

Red Square. New York: Random House, 1992.

Rose. New York: Random House, 1996.

Stallion Gate. New York: Random House, 1986.

St. James Guide to Horror, Ghost, and Gothic Writers. Detroit: St. James Press, 1998.

Wolves Eat Dogs. New York: Simon & Schuster, 2004.

Sneve, Virginia Driving Hawk.

The Apaches. New York: Holiday House, 1997.

The Cherokees. New York: Holiday House, 1996.

The ChiChi HooHoo Bogeyman. Lincoln: University of Nebraska Press, 1993.

Completing the Circle (editor). Lincoln: University of of Nebraska Press, 1995.

Dancing Teepees: Poems of American Indian Youth. New York: Holiday House, 1989.

Grandpa Was a Cowboy and an Indian and Other Stories. Lincoln: University of Nebraska Press, 2000.

Jimmy Yellow Hawk. New York: Holiday House, 1972.

They Led a Nation. Sioux Falls, S.Dak.: Brevet Press, 1975.

The Trickster and the Troll. Lincoln: University of Nebraska Press, 1997.

When Thunders Spoke. Lincoln: University of Nebraska Press, 1993.

Standing Bear, Luther.

American Indians, edited by Nancy Shoemaker. Maiden, Mass.: Blackwell, 2001.

Land of the Spotted Eagle. Boston: Houghton Mifflin, 1933.

My Indian, Boyhood. Lincoln: University of Nebraska Press, 1988.

My People the Sioux. Lincoln: University of Nebraska Press, 1975.

Stories of the Sioux. Lincoln, Nebr.: Bison Press, 1988.

Storm, Hyemeyohsts (Charles Storm, Wolf Storm, General Storm).

Lighteningbolt. New York: Ballantine Books, 1994.

Seven Arrows. New York: Harper & Row, 1972.

Song of Heyoehkah. San Francisco: Harper & Row, 1981.

TallMountain, Mary.

Green March Moons. Berkeley, Calif.: New Seed Press, 1987.

The Light on the Tent Wall: A Bridging. Los Angeles: University of California, American Indian Studies Center, 1990.

Matrilineal Cycle. Oakland, Calif.: Red Star Black Rose Printing, 1990.

A Quick Brush of Wings. San Francisco: Freedom Voices, 1991.

There Is No Word for Goodbye. Marvin, S.Dak.: Blue Cloud Quarterly Press.

Tapahonso, Luci.

Blue Horses Rush In. Tucson: University of Arizona Press, 1997.

A Breeze Swept Through. Albuquerque, N.Mex.: West End Press, 1989.

Navajo ABC: A Dine Alphabet Book. New York: Macmillan Books for Young Readers, 1995.

One More Shiprock Night: Poems. San Antonio, Tex.: Tejas Art Press, 1981.

Saanii Dahataal: The Women Are Singing. Tucson: University of Arizona Press, 1993.

Seasonal Woman. Santa Fe, N.Mex.: Tooth of Time Books, 1982.

Songs of Shiprock Fair. Walnut, Calif.: Kiva, 1999.

Tohe, Laura.

Making Friends with Water: Poems. Omaha, Nebr.: Nosila Press, 1986.

No Parole Today. Albuquerque, N.Mex.: West End Press, 1999.

Sister Nations: Native American Women Writers on Community. St. Paul, Minn.: Historical Society Press, 2002.

Tseyi: The Birth of Red in Canyon de Chelly. Tucson: University of Arizona Press, 2005.

Trudell, John.

Songs Called Poems. Minneapolis: North American Water Office, 1982.

Two-Rivers, E. Donald.

Briefcase Warriors: Stories for the Stage. Norman: University of Oklahoma Press, 2000.

A Dozen, Cold Ones. Chicago: MARCH/Abrazo Press, 1992.

Pow Wows, Fat Cats, and Other Indian Tales. Boston: Mammoth, 2003.

Survivor's Medicine: Short Stories. Norman: University of Oklahoma Press, 1998.

Vizenor, Gerald.

Bearheart: The Heirship Chronicles. Minneapolis: University of Minnesota Press, 1990.

Bear Island: The War at Sugar Point. Minneapolis: University of Minnesota Press, 2006.

Chancers. Norman: University of Oklahoma Press, 2000.

Crossbloods: Bone Courts, Bingo, and Other Reports. Minneapolis: University of Minnesota Press, 1990.

Darkness in Saint Louis Bearheart. Minneapolis: University of Minnesota Press, 1990.

Dead Voices: Natural Agonies in the New World. Norman: University of Oklahoma Press, 1992.

Earthdivers: Tribal Narratives on Mixed Descent. Minneapolis: University of Minnesota Press, 1981.

Fugitive Poses: Native American Indian Scenes of Absence and Presence. Lincoln: University of Nebraska Press, 1998.

Griever: An American Monkey King in China. Minneapolis: University of Minnesota Press, 1990.

The Heirs of Columbus. Hanover, N.H.: Wesleyan University Press/University Press of New England, 1991.

Hotline Healers: An Almost Browne Novel. Hanover, N.H.: Wesleyan University Press, 1997.

Interior Landscapes: Autobiographical Myths and Metaphors. Minneapolis: University of Minnesota Press, 1990.

Landfill Meditation: Crossblood Stories. Hanover, N.H.: Wesleyan University Press, 1991.

Manifest Mariners: Postindian Warriors of Survivance. Hanover, N.H.: University Press of New England, 1994.

Narrative Chance: Postmodern Discourse on Native American Indian Literatures. Albuquerque: University of New Mexico Press, 1989.

Native American, Literature: A Brief introduction and Anthology. Upper Saddle River, N.J.: Pearson Education, 1997.

The People Named the Chippewa: Narrative Histories. Minneapolis: University of Minnesota Press, 1984.

Postindian Conversations. Lincoln: University of Nebraska Press, 1999.

Shadow Distance: A Gerald Vizenor Reader. Hanover, N.H.: Wesleyan University Press, 1994.

Summer in the Spring: Anishinaabe Lyric Poems and Stories. Norman: University of Oklahoma Press, 1993.

Touchwood: A Collection of Ojibway Prose. St. Paul, Minn.: New Rivers Press, 1987.

Walters, Anna Lee.

Ghost Singer. Flagstaff, Ariz.: Northland, 1988.

Neon Pow Wow: New Native American Voices of the Southwest (editor). Flagstaff, Ariz.: Northland, 2003.

The Pawnee Nation. Mankato, Minn.: Bridgestone Books, 2000.

The Spirit of Native America: Beauty and Mysticism in American Indian Art. San Francisco: Chronicle Books, 1989.

The Sun Is Not Merciful. Ithaca, N.Y.: Firebrand Books, 1985.

Talking Indian: Reflections on Survival and Writing. Ithaca, N.Y.: Firebrand Books, 1992.

The Two-Legged Creature: An Otoe Story. Flagstaff, Ariz.: Northland, 1993.

Warrior, Robert Allen.

Like a Hurricane: The Indian Movement from Alcatraz to Wounded Knee (with Paul Chaat Smith). New York: New Press, 1996.

Tribal Secrets: Recovering American Indian Intellectual Traditions. Minneapolis: University of Minnesota Press, 1995.

Welch, James.

The Death of Jim Loney. New York: Harper & Row, 1979.

Fools Crow. New York: Viking, 1986.

The Heartsong of Charging Elk. New York: Doubleday, 2000.

The Indian Lawyer. New York: Norton, 1990.

Killing Custer: The Battle of the Little Big Horn and the Fate of the Plains Indians (with Paul Stekier). New York: Norton, 1994.

Riding the Earthboy 40: Poems. Rev. ed. New York: Harper & Row, 1976.

Winter in the Blood. New York: Harper & Row, 1974.

Winnemucca, Sarah.

Life among the Piutes: Their Wrongs and Claims. Reno: University of Nevada Press, 1994.

Womack, Craig S.

Drowning in Fire. Tucson: University of Arizona Press, 2001.

Red on Red: Native American Literary Separatism. Minneapolis: University of Minnesota Press, 1999.

Woody, Elizabeth.

Hand into Stone. New York: Contact II, 1988.

Luminaries of the Humble. Tucson: University of Arizona Press, 1994.

Pocket Cookbook. New York: Simon & Schuster Adult Publishing Group, 1984.

Salmon Nation: People and the Fish at the Edge. Portland, Oreg.: Ecotrust, 1999.

Seven Hands, Seven Hearts. Portland, Oreg.: Eighth Mountain, 1994.

Young Bear, Ray A.

Black Eagle Child: The Facepaint Narratives (foreword Albert E. Stone). 1992. Reprint, New York: Grove Press, 1997.

The Invisible Musician. Duluth, Minn.: Holy Cow! Press, 1990.

Remnants of the First Earth. New York: Grove Press, 1996.

The Rock Island Hiking Club. Iowa City: University of Iowa Press, 2001.

Waiting to Be Fed. Port Townsend, Wash.: Graywolf Press, 1975.

Winter of the Salamander: The Keeper of Importance. San Francisco: Harper & Row, 1980.

Zepeda, Ofelia.

Bone Dance: New and Selected Poems, 1965–1993. Tucson: University of Arizona Press, 1994.

Home Places: Contemporary Native American Writing from Sun Tracks. Tucson: University of Arizona Press, 1995.

Jewed 'i-Hoi/Earth Movements: O'odham Poems. Tucson, Ariz.: Kore Press, 1997.

Ocean Power: Poems from the Desert. Tucson: University of Arizona Press, 1995.

A Papago Grammar. Tucson: University of Arizona Press, 1983.

When It Rains: Papago and Pima Poetry. Tucson: University of Arizona Press, 1982.

Zitkala-Ša (Gertrude Simmons Bonnin).

American Indian Stories, edited by Dexter Fisher. 1921. Reprint, Lincoln: University of Nebraska Press, 1985.

Dreams and Thunder: Stories, Poems, and The Sun Dance Opera, edited by P. Jane Hafen. Lincoln: University of Nebraska Press, 2001.

Iktomi and the Ducks and Other Sioux Stories. Lincoln, Nebr.: Bison Books, 2004.

Old Indian Legends. 1901, edited by Dexter Fisher. Lincoln: University of Nebraska Press, 1985.

BIBLIOGRAPHY OF SECONDARY SOURCES

The following is a list of important general sources on American Indian literature. For more secondary sources see individual A–Z entries.

Allen, Paula Gunn. *Studies in American Indian Literature.* New York: Modern Language Association of America, 1983.

Brown, Harry J. *Injun Joe's Ghost: The Indian Mixed-Blood in American Writing.* Columbia: University of Missouri Press, 2004.

Cheyfitz, Eric. *The Columbia Guide to American Literature since 1945.* New York: Columbia University Press, 2006.

Claviez, Thomas. *Mirror Writing: (Re)Constructions of Native American Identity.* Berlin: Galda & Wilch Verlag, 2000.

Donovan, Kathleen M. *Feminist Readings of Native American Literature: Coming to Voice.* Tucson: University of Arizona Press, 1998.

Goebel, Bruce A. *Reading Native American Literature.* Urbana, Ill.: National Council of Teachers of English, 2004.

Hollrah, Patrice. *The Old Lady Trill, the Victory Yell: The Power of Women in Native American Literature.* New York: Routledge, 2003.

Home, Dee. *Contemporary American Indian Writing: Unsettling Literature.* New York: Peter Lang, 2004.

Isernhagen, Hartwig. *Momaday, Vizenor, Armstrong: Conversations on American Indian Writing.* Norman: University of Oklahoma Press, 2001.

Kilcup, Karen. *Native American Women's Writing: An Anthology c. 1800–1924.* Boston: Blackwell, 2000.

Krupat, Arnold. *Red Matters: Native American Studies.* University Park: Pennsylvania State University Press, 2002.

———. *The Voice in the Margin: Native American Literature and the Canon.* Berkeley: University of California Press, 1989.

Larson, Sidner J. *Captured in the Middle: Tradition and the Experience in Contemporary Native American Writing.* Seattle: University of Washington Press, 2001.

Lincoln, Kenneth. *Native American Renaissance.* Berkeley and Los Angeles: Regents of the University of California, 1983.

Lundquist, Suzanne. *Native American Fiction.* New York: Continuum International, 2004.

———. *Native American Literatures: An Introduction.* New York: Continuum International, 2004.

Nelson, Elizabeth Hoffman. *Telling the Stories: Essays on American Indian Literatures and Cultures.* New York: Peter Lang, 2001.

Owens, Louis. *Mixedblood Messages: Literature, Film, Family, Place.* Norman: University of Oklahoma Press, 2001.

Parker, Robert Dale. *The Invention of Native American Literature.* Ithaca, N.Y.: Cornell University Press, 2003.

Regier, Willis Goth. *Masterpieces of American Indian Literature*. Lincoln: University of Nebraska Press, 2005.

Roemer, Kenneth M. *The Cambridge Companion to Native American Literature*. Cambridge: Cambridge University Press, 2005.

Ruoff, A. LaVonne Brown. *American Indian Literatures*. New York: Modern Language Association of America, 1990.

Swann, Brian. *Voices from Four Directions: Contemporary Translations of the Native Literatures of North America*. Lincoln: University of Nebraska Press, 2005.

Velie, Alan R. *American Indian Literature: An Anthology*. Norman: University of Oklahoma Press, 1979.

Walker, Cheryl. *Indian Nation,: Native American Literature and Nineteenth-Century Nationalisms*. Durham, N.C.: Duke University Press, 1997.

Weaver, Jace. *Other Words: American Indian, Literature, Law and Culture*. Norman: University of Oklahoma Press, 2001.

———. *That the People Might Live: Native American Literatures and Native American Community*. Oxford: Oxford University Press, 1997.

Wiget, Andrew. *Dictionary of Native American Literature*. New York: Garland, 1994.

———. *Handbook of Native American Literature*. New York: Garland, 1996.

Wilson, Norma C. *The Nature of Native American Poetry*. Las Cruces: University of New Mexico Press, 2001.

CONTRIBUTORS

Elizabeth Archuleta is assistant professor of English at the University of New Mexico.

Jolene Armstrong is assistant professor of comparative literature and English at Athabasca University in Alberta, Canada. She has published on First Nations writing, Canadian literature, postmodern literature, and drama.

Ellen Arnold is assistant director of ethnic studies at Eastern Carolina University.

Sandra Baringer is a lecturer in the College of Humanities, Arts, and Social Sciences at the University of California at Riverside.

Sue Barker is a reference librarian at Northwestern University in Evanston Illinois. She has written a number of articles on American literature for reference publications.

Troy J. Bassett received his Ph.D. in English from the University of Kansas. He has published articles on British literature and publishing and an American Indian literature.

Geraldine Cannon Becker is an instructor of English at the University of Maine at Fort Kent. Primarily a poet, she has also published work on Southern Appalachia and the literature of her ancestors from the hills.

Sharon Morgan Beckford is senior lecturer in the Department of Languages and Letters at Cape Breton University, Sydney, Nova Scotia, Canada. She specializes in multiethnic literatures, black feminist and cultural studies, and African diaspora studies.

Ann Beebe is an assistant professor in the Department of Literature and Languages at the University of Texas at Tyler. She has published articles on Emily Dickinson, Elizabeth Stuart Phelps, and 20th-century American poetry.

Kelvin Beliele is a Ph.D. candidate in American literature at the University of New Mexico, Albuquerque. His areas of specialty are 19th-century literature; travel fiction; and gay, lesbian, bisexual, and transgender (GLBT) literature.

Jeff Berglund is an associate professor of English at Northern Arizona University in Flagstaff, Arizona. He has recently published *Cannibal Fictions: American Explorations of Colonialism, Race, Gender and Sexuality.*

Justin Blessinger is assistant professor of computers and writing at Dakota State University.

Patricia Kennedy Bostian is an instructor in English and humanities at Central Piedmont Community College in Charlotte, North Carolina. She is the editor of *Teaching American Literature: A Journal of Theory and Practice* and *The Wild Goose Poetry Review* and has published on American literature and popular fiction.

Susan R. Bowers is associate professor of English at Susquehanna University in Selinsgrove, Pennsylvania.

Nicholas Bradley is a postdoctoral fellow in the Department of English at the University of British Columbia. He has published essays on Canadian poetry.

Stephen Brandon is assistant professor of English at the University of New Mexico. Amy C. Branam is assistant professor of 19th-century American literature at Frostburg State University. In addition to Native American literature, her research interests include early American drama and transatlantic romanticism.

Harry Brown is an assistant professor of English at DePauw University in Greencastle, Indiana. His book *Injun Joe's Ghost* (2004) discusses the figure of the American Indian mixed-blood in American literature.

Neal Bukeavich teaches courses in 20th-century British literature, science fiction, and environmental literature at King's College in Wilkes-Barre, Pennsylvania.

Brianna Burke is a doctoral candidate at Tufts University in Medford, Massachusetts, currently finishing her dissertation on American Indian literature. She has published on American Indian literature, western films, and race studies.

Stephen Burn is assistant professor of English at the University of Northern Michigan.

Amanda Cagle is a Ph.D. candidate in English at the University of Connecticut.

Jeanetta Calhoun is a Ph.D. candidate in English at the University of Oklahoma.

Cari M. Carpenter is assistant professor of English at West Virginia University (WVU) in Morgantown. At WVU she is also a core member of the Native American studies program, and she has published on 19th- and 20th-century Native American women writers and feminist pedagogy.

Al Carroll teaches for the Alamo Community College District in San Antonio, Texas. He has published on American Indian veterans, Latin American history, and conflict between Natives and the New Age movement.

Benjamin D. Carson is an assistant professor of ethnic American literature at Bridgewater State College in Massachusetts. He has published on Gerald Vizenor, Octavia Butler, Edith Wharton, as well as other American writers.

Matthew Cella is a writer for the *Washington Times.*

Heejung Cha obtained her Ph.D. in literature and criticism from Indiana University of Pennsylvania. Her interests include postcolonial literature, multiethnic literature, transnational and eco-feminism, and women's studies.

Matthieu Charle is a doctoral candidate at the Ecole des Hautes Etudes en Sciences Sociales, Paris. He is working on traditional and contemporary kinship and social organization with the Coeur d'Alene tribe.

Fu-jen Chen is professor in the Department of Foreign Languages and Literature at National Sun Yat-sen University, Taiwan.

Karen M. Clark teaches at the University of Alberta.

William M. Clements is professor of English and folklore at Arkansas State University. He has published several books, chapters, articles, and reviews on American Indian literature, oral and written.

Justin Cober-Lake is an editor and columnist at *PopMatters.* He has published fiction and poetry as well as articles on literature, music, film, and feminism.

Angela Courtney is a research librarian at Indiana University.

Joanie Crandall is a doctoral student at the University of Saskatchewan, Canada.

Paul Craven is associate professor in the Division of Social Science, York University, Canada.

Sophie Croisy teaches at the University of Évry Val d'Essonne (France). She has published in the field of trauma studies and in the fields of technical writing and composition.

Solomon Davidoff is assistant professor of English at Wentworth Institute of Technology in Boston, Massachusetts.

Joanna Daxell is professor of English at the University of Sherbrooke, Canada.

Mary De Jong is associate professor of English and women's studies at Penn State University, Altoona College. Her research interests include 19th-century hymnody, women's poetry, and art novels.

Kevin De Ornellas is a lecturer in English at the University of Ulster, Ireland. He has published widely on English Renaissance drama, 20th-century British prose fiction, and 20th-century American prose fiction.

Aaron Denham is a Ph.D. candidate in anthropology at the University of Alberta. He has conducted research and published on historical trauma, intergenerational identity, and resilience in American Indian communities.

Patricia Dimond is professor of English at the University of South Dakota.

Lynn Domina has published a collection of poetry, *Corporal Works,* as well as reference books on the work of Lorraine Hansberry and Leslie Marmon Silko. She has published articles on N. Scott Momaday, Zora Neale Hurston, Elizabeth Keckley, Mary McCarthy, and Leslie Marmon Silko. She is professor of English at SUNY–Delhi, in the western Catskill region of New York.

James J. Donahue is a doctoral candidate in the English department at the University of Connecticut. He has published articles on James Welch, Henry David Thoreau, and medieval poetry.

Anne Dotter is professor of English at the University of Kansas.

Winter Elliot is assistant professor of English at Glenville State College in West Virginia.

Dina Fachin is a Ph.D. candidate in Native American studies at the University of California–Davis. She is interested in the self-representation of indigenous people from Mexico in literature and video making. She has presented her research at several conferences and published in Italy on Nuorican poetry.

Silvia Martínez Falquina is assistant professor of English at the University of Zaragoza, Spain. She has published on American Indian literature and on gender and ethnicity in contemporary American literature.

Alex Feerst holds a Ph.D. in English from Duke University. He has published on American literature and other topics.

Roland Finger is assistant professor of English at Concordia College in Moorhead, Minnesota. An Americanist who has published articles on ethnicity and gender, he is currently revising his manuscript entitled "Native Americans and Manifest Domesticity" for publication as a book.

Christie Firtha is a Ph.D. candidate in English at the University of California–Riverside.

Ben Fisler is the adviser of the theater program at Harford Community College in Bel Air, Maryland. His publications have appeared in *Theatre Journal, Theatre Survey, The Journal of Dramatic Theory and Criticism, The Puppetry Yearbook,* and *The Encyclopedia of Modern Drama.*

Sterling Fluharty is a Ph.D. candidate in history at the University of Oklahoma.

Hugh Foley, Jr., is assistant professor of communications and fine arts at Rogers State University in Claremore, Oklahoma.

Claire Gallou is visiting assistant professor of modern languages and literatures at the College of the Holy Cross in Worcester, Massachusetts. Her research focuses on 20th century American and French literature; the role of poetry, language, and translation in identity formation; and the European view of American Indian history and cultures.

John Gamber is assistant professor of English and American studies at the College of William and Mary in Williamsburg, Virginia.

Brad Gambill is director of the honors scholars program at John Brown University, Arkansas. A graduate of the Iowa Writers' Workshop, he is currently researching the representation of Christianity by Native American authors, artists, and filmmakers.

Alexandra Ganser is a doctoral fellow at Friedrich-Alexander University, Nuremberg, Germany.

Brian Gempp is a doctoral candidate in English at the University of Tennessee in Knoxville. He is currently at work on a dissertation examining the relationship between the European avant garde and the poetics of William Carlos Williams and the Objectivist poets.

Robert Gibney is doctoral student at the University of Nebraska–Lincoln. He has published on rhetoric and composition and ecocriticism.

William Gillard teaches writing and literature at Fairleigh Dickinson University in New Jersey.

Kristen Girard is Brittain Teaching Fellow in the School of Literature, Communication, and Culture at the Georgia Institute of Technology.

Kathleen Godfrey is an associate professor of English at California State University–Fresno. She has published on women's writing and representations of American Indians.

Julie K. Gonnering is a graduate student at the University of Cincinnati.

Stephanie Gustafson is a Ph.D. candidate in English at the University of New Mexico.

Jane Haladay is assistant professor of English at the University of California–Davis.

Linda Lizut Helstern is an assistant professor of English at North Dakota State University in Fargo and a 2006–07 Larry W. Remele Memorial Fellow of the North Dakota Humanities Council. She is the author of *Louis Owens* (2005) and publishes on Native identity, modernist constructions of race, and globalization/transnational connections.

Matt Herman teaches in the liberal arts program at Stone Child College on the Rocky Boy's Indian Reservation in north-central Montana. He has published articles on Native American literature and politics, composition and rhetoric, and New West literature and culture.

Christine Hilger is a doctoral candidate at Texas Women's University. She has published on visual rhetoric, Latino literature, and German literature.

Erika Hoagland is assistant professor of English at Mercyhurst College in Erie, Pennsylvania.

Blake G. Hobby is a lecturer in the Department of Literature and Language at the University of North Carolina at Asheville. He has published on American Indian literature, multiethnic literature, European modernism, and Booker Prize winners and is currently editing a collection of essays on major American writers, 1945–1970.

Sheila Hughes is assistant professor of English at the University of Dayton, Ohio.

Leeann D. Hunter is a Ph.D. candidate at the University of Florida. She is writing her dissertation on sensation and perception in Victorian literature.

Jami L. Huntsinger is an associate professor of English at the University of New Mexico, Valencia Campus. There, she teaches courses in Native American and American literatures and has published articles on American Indian literature, frontier literature, South Dakota history, and rhetoric/composition.

Derek Irwin is a lecturer at Lakehead University–Orillia Campus, in Ontario, Canada. He has published on Canadian literature and linguistics.

Meredith James is associate professor of English at Eastern Connecticut State University.

Andrea Powell Jenkins is currently a Ph.D. candidate in literature at Ball State University in Muncie, Indiana. She specializes in 20th-century American literature and recently published her first peer-reviewed journal article on Julia Kristeva's "herethics" as represented in the works of modernist writer Evelyn Scott.

Laura Jeselnick is a Ph.D. candidate at Arizona State University.

Brian Johnson is director of the Honors College Writing Center at the University of Oklahoma in Norman. He has published and presented on classical rhetoric, writing program administration, and feminist rhetorics.

Nancy Kang teaches in the Department of English at the University of British Columbia. Her areas of research are ethnic American literatures, literary history, and gender theory.

Lee Karalis (Choctaw-Irish descent) holds an M.A. in creative writing; has taught writing and literature at universities in California, Virginia, and Arizona; and has published poems, short stories, and essays. Currently, she is editor for an international educational environmental nonprofit organization based in Tucson, Arizona.

Amelia Katanski is the Marlene Crandell Francis Assistant Professor of English at Kalamazoo College in Michigan. She is the author of *Learning to Write "Indian": The Boarding School Experience and American Indian Literature* (University of Oklahoma Press, 2005).

Anne Kern is assistant professor of cinema studies at SUNY–Purchase, New York.

Martin Kich is professor of English at Wright State University–Lake Campus, in Dayton, Ohio.

Connie Ann Kirk, of Iroquois-Seneca descent, is the author of a dozen books, including the children's picture book *Sky Dancers* (Lee & Low, 2004), illustrated by Christy Hale, concerning the Mohawks' high-steel construction of the Empire State Building in New York City.

Padraig Kirwan is a lecturer in American literature at Goldsmiths, University of London. He has published on the work of Sherman Alexie and on indigenous narratives in colonial America. He is currently completing a monograph on reexamining the role of place in contemporary Native American fiction.

Sara Kosiba is a doctoral student in English at Kent State University in Ohio. She will be completing her Ph.D. in 2007, and her research interests include modernism, midwestern American writing, and contemporary American literature.

John J. Kucich is assistant professor of English at Bridgewater State College in Massachusetts. He has published on the cross-cultural dynamics of spiritualism, Native American literature, and literature and environment.

Rhonda Dean Kyncl is a graduate teaching and writing across the disciplines assistant at the University of Oklahoma. She has written and presented on Isocrates, pedagogy, and the application of Cornell West's prophetic pragmatism to the composition classroom.

Michelle LaFrance is a graduate student in the Department of English at the University of Washington whose work focuses on reenvisioning graduate studies as "public" intellectualism, vital social criticism, and democratic activism.

David Lavery is chair in film and television at Brunei University, London. His more than 100 published articles and 12 books deal with a wide range of subjects, from poetry to creativity, to film and, especially, television.

Judith Leggatt is an associate professor and chair of English at Lakehead University, in Thunder Bay, Canada. She has published articles on First Nations, postcolonial and speculative literature, and is working on a book-length project on First Nations science fiction.

Wenxin Li is assistant professor of English-language studies at SUNY–Old Westbury, New York.

Jennifer Lightweis is a Ph.D. candidate in English at the University of Rochester, New York.

Rachel Lister lectures on American fiction at Durham University, England. She has published on a range of 20th-century American writers, including Grace Paley and Katherine Anne Porter.

Kim Martin Long is professor of English and Interim Associate Dean of Arts and Sciences at Shippensburg University of Pennsylvania. Her research interests include intersections between literature and the environment, and she is the treasurer of MELUS (Society for the Study of Multi-Ethnic Literatures of the United States).

Jodi Lundgren belongs to the English faculty at Thompson Rivers University (Open Learning Division) in British Columbia, Canada. The author of *Touched: A Novel,* she has published scholarly articles on Métis women writers, feminist subjectivity, and Canadian fiction.

James Mackay teaches at the University of Glasgow, Scotland.

Holly E. Martin is an assistant professor in English at Appalachian State University in Boone, North Carolina. She has published in comparative ethnic literature, ecocriticism, and American literature in languages other than English.

Imelda Martín-Junquera is assistant professor of English at Universidad de León, Spain. Her field of expertise is Chicano/a and Native American literature. She has recently published a book analyzing magical realism in Chicano and Native American writers.

Derek C. Maus is assistant professor of English at the State University of New York at Potsdam. His teaching and scholarship focuses on contemporary fiction in a variety of cultural and national contexts.

Beth Maxfield teaches at Henderson State University, Arkadelphia, Arkansas.

Molly McCaffery is a graduate student in English at the University of Cincinnati.

Jennifer McClinton-Temple is assistant professor of English at King's College in Wilkes-Barre, Pennsylvania. She has published on American Indian literature, rhetoric and composition, and feminism and popular culture.

Molly McGlennen is the Andrew W. Mellon Postdoctoral Fellow in Native American Studies at Vassar College in Poughkeepsie, New York. In addition to publishing her own poetry in a number of creative journals, she has also published scholarly work on Native American Literature, Native American women, and Native American Art.

Sam McKegney teaches indigenous and Canadian literatures at Mount Royal College in Calgary, Alberta. He has published on the residential school system, Rita Joe, Tomson Highway, and the semiotics of indigeneity in Canada.

Elizabeth McNeil is assistant director of undergraduate studies in the English department at Arizona State University in Tempe, Arizona. She has published on indigenous literatures and African-American literature.

Alessandro Michelucci is an Italian journalist and translator living in Florence. He is the editor of the only Italian journal on indigenous affairs.

Laura L. Mielke is assistant professor of English at Iowa State University, in Ames. She has published on American Indian autobiography and representations of American Indians in U.S. literature.

John D. Miles is a Ph.D. candidate in English at the University of New Mexico.

Charles Mitchell teaches in the Department of Fine Arts at Loyola College of Maryland.

Rhona S. Mollard is an adjunct instructor at Kean University in Union, New Jersey.

A. Mary Murphy teaches literature, film, and creative writing at the University of Winnipeg and the University of Calgary. Her primary area of research is life writing, and she also publishes as a poet.

John Nelson is assistant professor of English at Dakota State University.

Rikki Noel-Williams received her M.A. in literature from Northeastern State University in Tahlequah, Oklahoma. She has published and presented essays on female gothic literature and Native American Vietnam veterans.

Robin Gray Nicks is assistant professor of English at the University of Tennessee.

Jim O'Loughlin is assistant professor of English at the University of Northern Iowa.

Ted Olson teaches at East Tennessee State University. He has written or edited several books, including *Blue Ridge Folklife*, a study of traditional Appalachian culture; *Breathing in Darkness*, a collection of poetry; and *CrossRoads: A Southern Culture Annual*.

Andrea Opitz is teaching associate in the Department of Comparative Literature at the University of Washington.

Petra Lina Orloff is a graduate research assistant at Wayne State University in Detroit, Michigan.

Margaret O'Shaughnessey is an English professor at the University of North Carolina at Chapel Hill. She teaches and writes about Native American literature and environmental literature.

Scott Palmer teaches writing and literature courses at New York University in Florence, Italy. He has published on 19th-century American travel writing, race relations, and visual culture.

Daniel Pantano is a Swiss poet, translator, editor, and scholar. He teaches creative writing at the University of South Florida and Florida Southern College.

Aaron Parrett is an associate professor of English at the University of Great Falls in Montana. He publishes short fiction and scholarship in history, literature, and philosophy.

Sumeeta Patnaik is the college transition coordinator at Marshall Community and Technical College in Huntington, West Virginia. She is currently a doctoral student in education at Marshall University's Graduate College in South Charleston, West Virginia.

Anthony Patterson is a lecturer in consumption studies and consumer behavior at the University of Liverpool, England. He has written about postcolonial literature, best-selling books and other curiosities in the marketplace.

Simone Pellerin is professor of American literature at Université Paul Valéry in Montpellier, France.

Jan Pilditch is an associate professor of English at the University of Waikato, New Zealand, and director of the American studies program there. She has published on 19th- and 20th-century American literature. She is the coeditor of the *Australasian Journal of American Studies*.

Veronica Pipestem is a Ph.D. candidate in English at the University of Oklahoma.

Tamara Powell is associate professor of English at Louisiana Tech University in Ruston, Louisiana. She has published in multiethnic literature, literary theory, and technical writing. She is the Charlyne Smith Wyche Endowed Professor of English.

W. Douglas Powers is associate professor and department head of the Department of Theatre at

Susquehanna University in Selinsgrove, Pennsylvania. He has published on Cherokee Indian ritual, Tennessee Williams, and identity and representation in theater performance and dramatic literature.

Ajnesh Prasad is a Ph.D. candidate at York University's Schulich School of Business in Toronto. He has published articles on sexual difference and critical theory.

Elvira Pulitano teaches contemporary anglophone literature at the University of Geneva, Switzerland.

Fabienne Quennet is academic assistant at the Philipps–University of Marburg, Germany. She has published on early American colonial history, Louise Erdrich, and Jewish-Canadian literature.

Jordan Racavich is adjunct faculty at King's College in Wilkes-Barre, Pennsylvania. She received an M.A. in writing, gender, and culture from King's College London.

Cecelia Ragaini is a Ph.D. candidate in English at the University of South Dakota.

Cristina Roberts is a Ph.D. candidate in English at the University of Arizona.

Barbara Robins is associate professor of English at the University of Nebraska at Omaha.

Ellen Rosenberg is a faculty member in humanities at the North Carolina School of the Arts. With an M.A. and Ph.D. in critical history and theory, and an M.F.A. in theater, she specializes in the ethnic and gendered American literatures and performance, history of ideas, creative process in the arts, and creative writing. She developed and is project director of the Kenan Writers' Encounters.

Kelly Rowley teaches at Cayuga Community College in New York.

Lauren Rule is a graduate student at Emory University in Atlanta, Georgia. She is currently writing a dissertation about the tensions between romanticism and empire in contemporary novels of the Americas.

Paul Rüsse is lecturer of American literature in the Department of English at Tallinn University, Estonia. In addition to American Indian literature, his research interests include postmodern, multiethnic, and postcolonial fiction, as well as the history and analysis of English poetry.

Donelle Ruwe is an associate professor of English at Northern Arizona University. She is the editor of *Culturing the Child 1690–1914* and has published extensively in the fields of romanticism, women's writing, children's literature, and poetry.

June Scudeler is a Vancouver-based Métis Ph.D. candidate in English literature at the University of Calgary, Alberta. Her dissertation examines the intersections of Métis, gay, and Jewish selfhoods in Gregory Scofield's poetry.

John Sexton is a graduate student in English at the University of Oklahoma.

Dorsía Smith Silva teaches English literature at the University of Puerto Rico, Río Piedras. She has published articles of ethnic literature, mothering, and migration.

Colleen Shea teaches in the Department of English at Queen's University, Kingston, Ontario.

Joseph T. Skerrett, Jr. is professor of English and director of American studies at the University of Massachusetts–Amherst. He has published on American writers such as Ralph Ellison, Richard Wright and Toni Morrison, Hart Crane and James Purdy.

Gary Sligh is department chair and assistant professor of English and humanities at Lake–Sumter Community College in Leesburg, Florida. He published a book in 2003 on Native American women authors.

Karen Sloan is associate professor of English at the University of Texas at Tyler. She has published several articles on 19th-century American texts. She has also developed a unique critical approach based on principles of human territorialism.

Clay Kinchen Smith is currently an interim assistant professor at Santa Fe Community College in Gainesville, Florida. He has published on children's literature, cultural studies, graphic novels, Native American literature, and world literature.

Lindsey Claire Smith is assistant professor of English at Oklahoma State University. She has published on American Indian literatures and multiethnic literatures and the environment.

David Stirrup is a lecturer in American literature at the University of Kent, England. He has published on contemporary American Indian literature, including writers such as Gordon Henry Jr., Louise Erdrich, and David Treuer.

Cheryl Suzack is an assistant professor of English at the University of Victoria. She has published on indigenous women's writing in relation to feminist and postcolonial issues.

Laura Furlan Szanto is an assistant professor of English at the University of South Dakota, where she teaches American Indian and multicultural literature. Her research focuses on representations of urban Indians in contemporary fiction.

Tereza M. Szeghi is a doctoral candidate at the University of Arizona. In her dissertation she discusses competing visions of just land claims and proper land use in late 19th- and early 20th-century American Indian, Mexican-American, and Anglo-American literature.

Lisa Tatonetti is an assistant professor of English and American ethnic studies at Kansas State University. She has published on American Indian and multiethnic American literatures.

Stella Thompson is assistant professor of English at Prairie View A&M in Prairie View, Texas. She has authored publications in American Indian literature, multiethnic American literature, rhetoric and composition, and popular culture.

Rebecca Tolley-Stokes is associate professor of library administration at East Tennessee University.

Annette Van Dyke is professor of English and interdisciplinary studies at the University of Illinois at Springfield. She is widely published on Native American women authors and women's spirituality.

Andrew Vassar is associate professor of humanities at Northeastern State University in Tahlequah, Oklahoma, where he teaches humanities and leads national and international student tours. He has published on Native American theater and western American literature.

Alan Velie is David Ross Boyd Professor of English at the University of Oklahoma. He teaches Indian literature, Shakespeare, and the Bible.

Carla L. Verderame is associate professor of English at West Chester University of Pennsylvania. She has published on American Indian literature, women writers of the American South, young-adult literature, and writing and literature pedagogy.

Lori Vermaas teaches history at the University of Iowa.

Tracey Watts is a Ph.D. candidate at the University of Texas.

Deborah Weagel received a Ph.D. in English from the University of New Mexico in 2006. Part of her dissertation deals with the metaphor of the quilt in contemporary American Indian literature.

Frederick White is assistant professor of English at Slippery Rock University in Slippery Rock, Pennsylvania. He has published on American Indian literature, linguistics, and is the cowinner of the 2006 Native Writers' Circle of America First Book Award competition for prose.

Malinda Williams is a leturer in the writing program at the University of Denver. She has published in the *African American National Biography* and on the influence of *Don Quixote* on Alejo Carpentier. She is currently finishing her dissertation on colorism and the construction of race in Latino Caribbean literature.

Angela M. Williamson teaches an introductory course to multicultural literature at University of Wisconsin–Fox Valley in Menasha.

Joseph Andrew Park Wilson is currently an adjunct instructor in the humanities at Lander University in Greenwood South Carolina. He has an M.A. in Asian religions and an M.S. in archaeology. In 2007, he will begin work on a Ph.D. in anthropology at the University of Florida.

Sheena Wilson is an assistant professor at Faculté Saint-Jean, University of Alberta, Canada. Her research interests include literary and cinematic representations of human/civil rights abuses as they are represented in literature and film (predominantly Canadian and American) and patterns of exclusion exercised on nondominant communities within the paradigm of state multiculturalism (i.e., ethnicity, nationalism, empire, displacement), and gender politics. She has published on Canadian literature and Canadian documentary film, ethno-cultural literature and film, and Native literature.

Laura Madeline Wiseman is working on a dissertation in creative writing at the University of Nebraska–Lincoln. Her works have appeared in

The Minnesota Review, Red Cedar Review, Tar Wolf Review, and elsewhere. She is an *e4w.org* editor and a *Prairie Schooner* reader.

Tracy Wyman-Marchand is a freelance editor and independent scholar living in Vancouver, British Columbia. Her interests are diverse, and she has published on Ralph Ellison and the blues, the Mexican muralists, and Canadian writers.

Michael W. Young is the director of academic assessment at La Roche College in Pittsburgh, where he also teaches in the English Department. He has published poetry, short stories, and articles on pedagogy and on American, Canadian, and British literature.

INDEX

Boldface numbers indicate major treatment of a topic. *Italic* numbers indicate illustrations.

A

Aacquemeh (Acoma Pueblo) Indians 228–229
Abenaki Indians. *See* Bruchac, Joseph
Aboriginal Achievement Award 194, 196
aboriginal people. *See also* indigenous people
  Howard Adams 4
  Kateri Akiwenzie-Damm 6–7
  Atanarjuat/The Fast Runner 44
  Australian 367
  Bent Box (Maracle) 52
  Crazy Dave (Johnston) 84
  Lee Maracle 220–222
  Joe Rita 194
Absence of Angels, The (Penn) **3–4**, 274
academia 22, 96, 145, 150, 171, 198
Academy of American Poets Prize 146, 235
Acoma Pueblo Indians 114, 141, 143, 267, 268, 338, 410
acquired immunodeficiency syndrome (AIDS) 99, 202, 231
activism. *See also* American Indian Movement; Wounded Knee
  Howard Adams 4
  Alcatraz Island occupation 26, 170, 193, 368, 373
  Paula Gunn Allen 12
  American Indian film 20
  American Indian Movement **26–27**
  American Indian Stories (Zitkala-Ša) 33
  Ancient Acid Flashes Back (Louis) 34
  William Apess 39
  Jeannette C. Armstrong 41
  Carroll Arnett 42

Bent Box (Maracle) 52
Chrystos 76
Elizabeth Cook-Lynn 83
Custer Died for Your Sins (Deloria, Jr.) 86
Dawes Act, The 91
Vine Deloria, Jr. 96
Charles Alexander Eastman 107
From Spirit to Matter (Sanchez) 125
Gathering of Spirit (Brant) 133
Going for the Rain (Ortiz) 140–142
Roxy Gordon 144
government agencies 147
Halfbreed Chronicles and Other Poems, The (Rose) 156
Joy Harjo 157
Linda Hogan 167
Horse Dance to Emerald Mountain (Cuthand) 171
In Mad Love and War (Harjo) 186
Winona LaDuke **203–204**
Native "chic" 244–245
nila northSun 254
poverty 280
Wendy Rose 307
Leslie Marmon Silko 75
Slash 325
Slash (Armstrong) 325
Sojourner's Truth and Other Stories (Maracle) 330
Southwestern tribal literature 338
treaties 367–368
John Trudell 373
E. Donald Two-Rivers 375
Elizabeth Woody 404
Wounded Knee Massacre 405
Zitkala-Ša 413
actors/actresses 194–195, 373
Adams, Howard **4**
(Ado)ration **4–5**

African Americans 30, 55, 86, 148, 157, 186
After and Before the Lightning (Ortiz) **5–6**
AIDS. *See* acquired immunodeficiency syndrome
AIM. *See* American Indian Movement
Akiwenzie-Damm, Kateri **6–7**
Alcatraz Island occupation 26, 170, 193, 368, 373
alcoholism **7–9**
  Sherman Alexie 9
  American Indian Literary Renaissance 24
  American Indian novel 28
  Bent Box (Maracle) 52
  Body Indian (Geoigamah) 62–63
  Beth Brant 66
  Breath Tricks (Armstrong) 68
  Business of Fancydancing, The 70
  Maria Campbell 73
  Earth Song, Sky Spirit (Trafzer) 106
  fetal alcohol syndrome 8, 99
  Four Souls (Erdrich) 123
  from Sand Creek (Ortiz) 124
  Hanay Geiogamah 134
  Good Message of Handsome Lake, The (Bruchac) 144
  Keeping Slug Woman Alive (Sarris) 198
  Adrian C. Louis 215
  Neon Powwow (Walters) 246
  nila northSun 254
  Samson Occom 258
  Remnants of the First Earth (Young Bear) 294
  reservation life 298, 299
  Rez Sisters, The (Highway) 303
  Greg Sarris 312
  "Sermon Preached by Samson Occom" 314
  snake in her mouth, a (northSun) 329
  Southwestern tribal literature 338

spirituality 344–345
Mary TallMountain 354
James Welch 391
Wild Indians and Other Creatures
(Louis) 395
Woman Who Fell from the Sky, The
(Harjo) 401
Alexie, Sherman **9–11.** *See also* Lone Ranger
and Tonto Fistfight in Heaven, The
American Indian film 21
American Indian novel 29
American Indian poetry 32
assimilation 44
Business of Fancydancing, The 9, **70–71**
Dance Me Outside (McDonald, Dir.) 88
First Indian on the Moon 11, 70,
114–115
Ghost Dance 136
humor 176
Indian Killer 29, **179–180,** 233
Adrian C. Louis 214–215
Man Who Loves Salmon, The **219–220**
missionaries 231
mixed-blood 233
Mourning Dove's Stories (Mourning
Dove) 240
Old Shirts and New Skins 11, **261–262,**
347
One Stick Song **264**
Pacific Northwestern tribal literature
273
poverty 279
pow wow 282
Reservation Blues 8, 9, 29, 212, 231,
296–297, 299
reservation life 299, 300
Smoke Signals 212, 327
sovereignty 340
Summer of the Black Widows, The 32,
347–348
Ten Little Indians **356–357**
Termination 358
Toughest Indian in the World, The 8,
340, **364–365**
James Welch 390
Wounded Knee Massacre 406
Alfred, Taiaiake 339, 340
Algonquian Indians 22, 252
Allen, Paula Gunn **11–13**
Hozho 175
Life Is a Fatal Disease **209**
Manifest Manners (Vizenor) 219
Offering (Glancy) 258–259
Sacred Hoop, The 12, 132, 209, 211,
310, 338
Shadow Country 12, **315–316**
Leslie Marmon Silko 321
Skins and Bones **324**
Song of the Turtle 12, **331–332,** 379
Southwestern tribal literature 338
Spider Woman's Granddaughters 12,
341–342

Mary TallMountain 354
Voice of the Turtle 12, 331, **379–380**
Woman Who Owned the Shadows, The
13, **402–403**
Wounds beneath the Flesh (Kenny) 406
All My Relations (King, ed.) **13–14,** 118
allotments 43, 113, 216, 311, 349–350, 365
Almanac of the Dead (Silko) 15, 321, 392
American Academy of Poets Award
192–193
American Book Award
Sherman Alexie 9
Paula Gunn Allen 12, 342
Anna Lee Walters 383
Jim Barnes 50
Joseph Bruchac 69
Diane Glancy 137
Griever (Vizenor) 152
Joy Harjo 157
LeAnne Howe 174
In Mad Love and War (Harjo) 185
Light People, The (Henry) 209
Kenny Maurice 199
Duane Niatum 248
Survivor's Medicine (Two-Rivers) 374
Anna Lee Walters 350, 383
Elizabeth Woody 404
American Book of the Dead, The (Barnes)
50, 336
American Indian children's literature **15–18**
Maria Campbell 74
Beth Cuthand 87
Dawnland (Bruchac) **91–92,** 386
Michael Dorris 99
Enwhisteetkwa—Walk in Water (Arm-
strong) **109–110,** 245
Karen Louise Erdrich 112
Tomson Highway 165
Thirteen Moons on Turtle's Back
(Bruchac) 359–360
Anna Lee Walters 383
American Indian culture and life. *See* culture
and life, American Indian
American Indian drama **18–20**
Body Indian (Geoigamah) 19, **62–63,**
133, 134, 314–315
Maria Campbell 73
Dry Lips Oughta Move to Kapuskasing
(Highway) **101–102**
49 (Geiogamah) **122–123**
Hanay Geiogamah 120, **133–135**
Roxy Gordon **144–145**
Green Grow the Lilacs (Riggs) 19, **151–
152,** 305, 306, 336
Lanson Henson 164
LeAnne Howe 174–175
Rez Sisters, The (Highway) 19, 23, 164,
303–304
Seventh Generation (D'Aponte) 19,
314–315
American Indian film **20–22.** *See also* spe-
cific film

Sherman Alexie 10
Atanarjuat/The Fast Runner **44–45**
Billy Jack **54,** 136
Business of Fancydancing, The **70**
Maria Campbell 73
Dance Me Outside (McDonald, Dir.) 88
Harold of Orange (Vizenor) 376
humor 177
Indian Singing in 20th Century (Trem-
blay) 182
Thomas King 200
Bruce McDonald 88
Smoke Signals 9–10, 21, 88, 175–178,
212, **327–328**
American Indian languages **22–24**
Acoma 267
Algonquian 252
American Indian poetry 32
Anishinabe 209–210
anthropology and Native Americans
37–38
boarding schools 62
Cree 210–211
Creek 278
Dakota 96, 106
Dawes Act, The 91
Eagle Nation, An (Revard) 103
First Nations literature 116, 117
Flutie (Glancy) 119
government agencies 146
Keresan 320
Koyukon 359
Meskwaki 399, 411
Mohawk 14, 195, 252
Navajo (Diné) 23, 69, 355, 361
Northeastern tribal literature 252
Ofo 206
Ojibwe 6, 16, 169, 195, 238, 319, 326
Oklahoma tribal literature 260
Tlingit 288
Tohono O'odham 412
Woven Stone (Ortiz) 407
American Indian Literary Renaissance
24–26
American Indian poetry 30
assimilation 43
Cogewea, the Half-Blood (Mourning
Dove) 80
Ella Cara Deloria 96
Karen Louise Erdrich 110
First Nations literature 117–118
Going for the Rain (Ortiz) 141
Grand Avenue (Sarris) 148
House Made of Dawn (Momaday) 172
N. Scott Momaday 235
reservation life 298
Leslie Marmon Silko 320
sovereignty 341
Gerald Vizenor 376
Voice of the Turtle (Allen) 379
Way to Rainy Mountain, The (Moma-
day) 387

James Welch 390
Winter in the Blood (Welch) 398
written traditions 25
American Indian Literature and Critical
Studies series 196–197
American Indian Movement (AIM) **26–27**
Aurelia (Cook-Lynn) 46
Bearheart (Vizenor) 50
Custer Died for Your Sins (Deloria, Jr.)
86
Vine Deloria, Jr. 97
Roxy Gordon 144
*Halfbreed Chronicles and Other Poems,
The* (Rose) 156
Lanson Henson 164
Storm Hyemeyohsts 346
Jailing of Cecelia Capture, The (Hale)
193
Medicine River (King) 228
Native "chic" 244
Night Sky, Morning Star (Lucero) 250,
251
reservation life 299
treaties 367–368
John Trudell 373
Winning the Dust Bowl (Revard) 397
Wounded Knee 405
American Indian novel **27–29**. *See also* spe-
cific headings, e.g.: House Made of Dawn
(Momaday)
alcoholism **7–8**
Sherman Alexie **9–11**
Paula Gunn Allen **11–13**
American Indian poetry 30–31
Jeannette C. Armstrong 41
assimilation 43
Aurelia (Cook-Lynn) 29, **45–46,** 83
Bearheart (Vizenor) 28–29, **50–51,** 377
Gloria Bird 55
Black Eagle Child (Young Bear) 29,
56–57, 294, 411
Cogewea, the Half-Blood (Mourning
Dove) 27, **79–80,** 239, 240, 372
Robert J. Conley 81
Elizabeth Cook-Lynn 83
Ella Cara Deloria 96
Michael Dorris 99
Karen Louise Erdrich **110–112**
Faces in the Moon (Bell) 29, **113–114**
First Nations literature 117–118
From the River's Edge (Cook-Lynn) 29,
45, 83, **126**
Green Grass, Running Water (King) 29,
149–151, 368, 371, 372
Indian Killer (Alexie) **179–180,** 233
Life and Adventures of Joaquin Murieta
(Ridge) 304, 336
Mean Spirit (Hogan) **225–226,** 231
Pipe for February, A (Red Corn) 29,
275, 290
Power (Hogan) 29, **280–281**
Charles Red Corn 290

Reservation Blues (Alexie) 8, 9, 29, 212,
231, **296–297,** 299
Solar Storms (Hogan) 29, 167–168, **331**
Sundown (Mathews) 27–28, 43, 91, 222,
232–233, **349–350**
Wynema (Callahan) 27, 406, **407–408**
American Indian poetic tradition 187, 188,
192
American Indian poetry **29–32**. *See also* spe-
cific headings, e.g.: Hogan, Linda
Sherman Alexie **9–11**
Paula Gunn Allen 12, 13
Angle of Geese and Other Poems (Moma-
day) **35–36,** 146, 236
Jeannette C. Armstrong 41
Carroll Arnett 42
Gloria Bird 55
Kimberly M.Blaeser **58–59**
Peter Blue Cloud **59–60**
Beth Brant 66–67
Chrystos 76
Susan Clements 78
Robert J. Conley 81
Elizabeth Cook-Lynn 82
Beth Cuthand 87
Nora Marks Dauenhauer 90, 100
Karen Louise Erdrich 112
gaming 129
Good Journey, A (Ortiz) 31, **143,**
267–268, 406
Roxy Gordon 145
Janice Gould 145
Catron Grieves 153–154
Janet Campbell Hale 155
Halfbreed Chronicles, The (Rose) 63,
156, 307–308
Joy Harjo **157–158**
Lanson Henson 163–164
Roberta Hill 165–166
In Mad Love and War (Harjo) 31, 157,
185–186
Thomas King 200
Laguna Woman (Silko) 32, **204–205,**
320
Adrian C. Louis **214–215**
Kenny Maurice 199
mixed-blood 232
N. Scott Momaday 236–237
Duane Niatum **247–248**
nila northSun 254
Simon Ortiz **267–268**
Alexander Posey 278
Carter Revard **302–303**
John Rollin Ridge 305
Rollie Lynn Riggs **305–306**
Joe Rita 194
Carol Lee Sanchez 311
Seeing Through the Sun (Hogan) 31–32,
167
snake in her mouth, a (northSun) 254,
328–329
Southwestern tribal literature 339

Luci Tapahonso 355
Winter of the Salamander (Young Bear)
399–400
Ofelia Zepeda 412
American Indian Stories (Zitkala-Ša) **32–34,**
276, 413
American Indian Studies Center (UCLA)
133, 157
American Mixed Race (prose compilation)
77–78
ancestry 53, 63, 69
Ancient Acid Flashes Back (Louis) **34,** 214,
338
Ancient Child, The (Momaday) **35,** 237, 266
Angle of Geese and Other Poems (Momaday)
35–36, 146, 236
animal/human connections 65, 93, 94, 109,
132, 148, 187
animal spirit guides 343, 344
Anishabe Indians 88, 92, 195
Anishabe language 117, 196
Anishinabe Indians
Kimberly M.Blaeser 58
Winona LaDuke **203–204**
Last Standing Woman (LaDuke)
208–209
missionaries 231
nila northSun 253
Silent Words (Slipperjack-Farrell) 319
Touchwood (Vizenor) 363–364
John Trudell 373
Gerald Vizenor 377
Walking the Rez Road (Northrup) 382
Anishinabe language 209–210
Aniynwiya/Real Human Beings (Bruchac)
36
Antelope Wife, The (Erdrich) **37,** 233
anthropology and Native Americans
37–39
American Indian poetry 30
Franz Boas 243
Bone Game (Owens) 64
Custer Died for Your Sins (Deloria, Jr.)
86
Nora Marks Dauenhauer 90
Ella Cara Deloria 96
Going to War with All My Relatives
(Rose) 142
Heirs of Columbus, The (Vizenor)
162–163
Mourning Dove 80
Native American Literature (Vizenor)
243–244
New Voices from the Longhouse
(Bruchac) 247
orality 265
Simon Ortiz 268–269
*Reinventing the Enemy's
Language*(Harjo) 273–274, **291–292**
Remembered Earth, The (Hobson) 293
Returning the Gift (Bruchac) 301–302
Wendy Rose 307

Seventh Generation (D'Aponte) 314–315
Song of the Turtle (Allen) 331–332
Songs from This Earth on Turtle's Back (Bruchac) 301, 333
Southeastern tribal literature 336
Spider Woman's Granddaughters (Allen) 342
Through the Eye of the Deer (Dunn) 361
Touchwood (Vizenor) 363–364
Voice of the Turtle (Allen) 331, **379–380**
Waterlily (Deloria) 384
Wounds beneath the Flesh (Kenny) 406
Apache Indians 196–197
Apess, William **39–41**, 230, 232, 252, 333–334
Aquash, Anna Mae Pictou 26–27
Arapaho Indians 61, 124, 327
Armstrong, Jeannette C. **41**
     Howard Adams 4
     All My Relations (King) 14
     Breath Tracks 67
     Beth Cuthand 87
     Enwhisteetkwa—Walk in Water **109–110**, 245
     Neekna and Chemai **245**
     Reinventing the Enemy's Language (Harjo) 291
     Slash 4, 41, 67, **324–325**
     trickster figures 371
     Whispering in Shadows **393–394**
Army, U.S. 43, 222, 334
Arnett, Carroll **41–42**
Aroniawenrate. *See* Blue Cloud, Peter
Arrow over the Door, The (Bruchac) **42–43**
artists 41, 76, 125, 144, 155, 157
assimilation **43–44**
     American Indian novel 28
     American Indian poetry 30
     American Indian Stories (Zitkala-Ša) 33
     anthropology and Native Americans 38
     Aztecas del Norte. The Chicanos of Aztlán (Forbes) 46
     Black Eagle Child (Young Bear) 57
     boarding schools 61–62
     Susan Clements 77
     Cogewea, the Half-Blood (Mourning Dove) 79–80
     Charles Alexander Eastman 107–108
     Fight Back (Ortiz) 114
     First Nations literature 116, 117
     government agencies 146–147
     Heartsong of Charging Elk, The (Welch) 161
     In the Time of the Present (Kenny) 188
     Jailing of Cecelia Capture, The (Hale) 193
     Emily Pauline Johnson 195
     Basil Johnston 195
     Kiss of the Fur Queen (Highway) 201
     Adrian C. Louis 215
     Love Medicine (Erdrich) 216

D'Arcy McNickle 224
missionaries 230
mixed-blood 232
Mourning Dove 80
My People, the Sioux (Standing Bear) 240
No Parole Today (Tohe) 251
Plains tribes literature 277
poverty 279
Remnants of the First Earth (Young Bear) 294
Sáanii Dahataal (Tapahonso) 309
Silent Words (Slipperjack-Farrell) 319
Ruby Slipperjack-Farrell 326
snake in her mouth, a (northSun) 329
sovereignty 341
Sundown (Mathews) 350
Surrounded, The (McNickle) 351
Termination 357
James Welch 391
Zitkala-Ša 413, 414
Assimilation (policy). *See* assimilation
associational works 13, 14
Atanarjuat/The Fast Runner (film) **44–45**
Atanarjuat/The Fast Runner (Kunuk) **44–45**
Athabascan Indians 223, 353
Aurelia (Cook-Lynn) 29, **45–46**, 83
autobiographies
     American Indian Stories (Zitkala-Ša) 32–34
     William Apess 40
     assimilation 43
     Jim Barnes 49
     Bent Box (Maracle) 52–53
     Gertrude Bernard 53
     Black Eagle Child (Young Bear) 56
     Black Elk 57–58
     boarding schools 62
     Joseph Bruchac 69
     Maria Campbell 73
     Ceremony (Silko) 74
     Claiming Breath (Glancy) 77
     Completing the Circle (Sneve) 80–81
     Earth Song, Sky Spirit (Trafzer) 106
     Charles Alexander Eastman 107
     First Nations Literature 116
     Roxy Gordon 144
     Halfbreed Chronicles and Other Poems, The (Rose) 156
     House Made of Dawn (Momaday) 173
     Indian School Days (Johnston) 181
     Interior Landscapes (Vizenor) 186
     Emily Pauline Johnson 195
     Keeping Slug Woman Alive (Sarris) 198
     Kiss of the Fur Queen (Highway) 201
     Life among the Paiutes (Winnemucca) 396
     Lone Dog's Winter Count (Glancy) 211
     Adrian C. Louis 215
     Mourning Dove (Mourning Dove) **239**
     Names, The (Momaday) 236
     Samson Occom 257, 258

Plains tribes literature 276
Carter Revard 302
Son of the Forest, A (Apess) 252, 333–334
Southwestern tribal literature 338
Sundown (Mathews) 349–350
Trail of Tears 367
Winning the Dust Bowl (Revard) 397
Zitkala-Ša 414
Awiakta, Marilou 36, 337
Aztecas del Norte. The Chicanos of Aztlán (Forbes) **46–47**

B

Bad Medicine (Querry) **48–49**, 285
Banks, Dennis 26, 368
Bannock War 397
Baptism of Desire (Erdrich) **49**, 112
Barnes, Jim **49–50**, 336
Basho, Matsuo 90, 100
Bear, story of the 35, 55, 187
Bearheart (Vizenor) 28–29, **50–51**, 377
bears 78, 111
Beet Queen, The (Erdrich) **51–52**, 111, 353
beliefs, traditional 246, 352
Bell, Betty Louise 29, 113
Bent Box (Maracle) **52–53**
Bernard, Gertrude **53–54**
BIA. *See* Bureau of Indian Affairs
Bible, the 22, 79, 116
biculturalism 79, 106–108, 411
Big Pow Wow (Gordon) 144, 174
bilingualism 16–17, 90, 168–169, 189, 195, 411
Billy Jack (film) **54**, 136
Billy White Hawk (fictional character) 271–272
Bingo Palace, The (Erdrich) **54–55**, 110–111, 216, 353
Birchbark House, The (Erdrich) 16, 112
Bird, Gloria **55–56**, 157, 273, 291–292
Birth of a Nation (film) 242
Black Eagle Child (Young Bear) 29, **56–57**, 294, 411
Black Elk 18, **57–58**
Black Elk Speaks (Neihardt) 18, 57–58, 276, 310, 343
Blackfoot (Blackfeet) Indians
     American Indian drama 18
     American Indian novel 28
     Fools Crow (Welch) 121
     Green Grass, Running Water (King) 150
     Thomas King 201
     mixed-blood 233
     Plains tribes literature 275, 277
     spirituality 342–343
     Truth & Bright Water 373–374
     James Welch 389, 391
     Winter in the Blood (Welch) 398–399

Black Kettle (Cheyenne chief) 362–363
Blaeser, Kimberly M. **58–59**, 59, 92, 106
blood 36, 65, 98–99
Blue Cloud, Peter **59–60**, 105, 406
Blue Dawn, Red Earth (Trafzer, ed.) **60–61**
Blue Highways (Heat-Moon) 161–162
Blue Horses Rush In (Tapahonso) **61–62**
boarding schools. *See also* Carlisle Indian
   Industrial School
      American Indian languages 23
      American Indian poetry 30
      American Indian Stories (Zitkala-Ša) 33
      Ancient Child, The (Momaday) 35
      assimilation 43
      Bent Box (Maracle) 52
      Earth Song, Sky Spirit (Trafzer) 106
      First Nations literature 117
      Four Souls (Erdrich) 123
      Gardens in the Dunes (Silko) 132
      government agencies 146–147
      humor 177
      Indian Time (Penoi) 184
      In the Time of the Present (Kenny) 188
      Kiss of the Fur Queen (Highway) 201
      Love Medicine (Erdrich) 216
      D'Arcy McNickle 224
      Men on the Moon (Ortiz) **228–229**
      missionaries 231
      My People, the Sioux (Standing Bear)
         240
      Night Sky, Morning Star (Lucero) 251
      No Parole Today (Tohe) 251
      Jim Northrup 253
      Oklahoma tribal literature 260
      Reinventing the Enemy's Language
         (Harjo) 291
      Joe Rita 194
      Leslie Marmon Silko 320
      Surrounded, The (McNickle) 351–352
      Laura Tohe 361
      Touchwood (Vizenor) 363
      Zitkala-Ša 414
Boas, Franz 22, 96, 243, 265, 384
Body Indian (Geoigamah) 19, **62–63**, 133,
   134, 314–315
Bone Dance (Rose) **63–64**
Bone Game (Owens) **64–65**, 270
Bonnin, Gertrude Simmons. *See* Zitkala-Ša
Book of Medicines, The (Hogan) **65**
*Boy Who Lived with the Bears and Other Iro-
quois Stories, The* (Bruchac) **66**
Brando, Marlon 244–245
Brant, Beth **66–67**
      Food and Spirits 67, **120–121**
      Gathering Spirit, A **132–133**
      Thomas King 14
      Michigan Council for the Arts Creative
         Writing Awards 66
      Mohawk Trail 67, **234–235**, 372
      Northeastern tribal literature 252
      Songs from This Earth on Turtle's Back
         (Bruchac) 333

trickster figures 372
Brant, Molly 324, 356
Breath Tricks (Armstrong) **67–68**
Breeze Swept Through, A (Tapahonso)
   68–69
Brieves, Catron **153–154**
Broken Cord, The (Dorris) 8, 99
Brown, Joseph Epes 58, 342
Brownback, Sam 368
Bruchac, Joseph **69**
      Aniyunwiya/Real Human Beings **36**
      Arrow over the Door, The **42–43**
      Boy Who Lived with the Bears, The 66
      Dawnland 91
      Good Message of Handsome Lake, The
         144
      Matrilineal Cycle (TallMountain) **223**
      New Voices from the Longhouse 199,
         246–247
      poverty 280
      Raven Tells Stories **288**
      Returning the Gift **301–302**
      Songs from This Earth on Turtle's Back
         69, 91, 247, 301, **332–333**
      Thirteen Moons on Turtle's Back
         359–360
      Waters Between, The **386–387**
      Wounds beneath the Flesh (Kenny) 406
Buffalo Bill's Wild West Show 20, 43, 57, 58,
   160–161, 345, 391
buffaloes 241, 279, 345
buffalo nickel 248
Bureau of Indian Affairs (BIA)
      Bearheart (Vizenor) 50
      Charles Alexander Eastman 107
      Five Civilized Tribes 118
      Hanay Geiogamah 133
      government agencies 146–148
      Jailing of Cecelia Capture, The (Hale)
         193
      D'Arcy McNickle 224
      recognition 288, 289
      reservation life 298
      Gerald Vizenor 377
Business of Fancydancing, The (Alexie) 9,
   70–71
Business of Fancydancing, The (film) 70

C

California tribal literature **72–73**
Callahan, Sophia Alice 27, 406–408
Campbell, Maria 4, **73**, 117
Canada
      American Indian drama 19
      Atanarjuat/The Fast Runner 44
      Bent Box (Maracle) 52
      Gertrude Bernard 53
      Breath Tricks (Armstrong) 67
      Maria Campbell 73

Dry Lips Oughta Move to Kapuskasing
   (Highway) 101
First Nations literature 115
Harpoon of the Hunter (Markoosie) 159
Tomson Highway 164–165
Honour the Sun (Slipperjack-Farrell)
   170
Indian School Days (Johnston) 181
Inuit Indians 159, 242
Emily Pauline Johnson 194–195
Basil Johnston 195
Thomas King 200
Lee Maracle **220–222**
Sundogs (Maracle) 348, 349
Canadian First Nations 29, 195
Cannon Between My Knees, A (Allen) **73–74**
captivity theme 403–404
Carlisle Indian Industrial School 62, 188,
   241, 251, 320, 345, 413
Carter, Asa 337
Carter, Forrest 16, 337
Carter, Nick. *See* Smith, Martin Cruz
Cash, Johnny 244
casinos. *See* gaming
Catholicism 207, 223, 338
Cavalry, U.S. 405
ceremonies 38, 67, 103–104, 119, 131, 146
Ceremony (Silko) **74–76**, 320, 321
      alcoholism 7, 8
      American Indian novel 28
      government agencies 147
      mixed-blood 233
      N. Scott Momaday 237
      orality 266
      reservation life 298
      Southwestern tribal literature 338–339
      West Pole, The (Glancy) 392
certification policy 77
characterizations (writing) 110–111, 115,
   120, 152, 174
Cheesquatalawny. *See* Ridge, John Rollin
Cherokee Booger Dance 18
Cherokee Indians
      American Indian film 21
      American Indian Literary Renaissance
         25
      American Indian novel 28, 29
      Aniyunwiya/Real Human Beings
         (Bruchac) **36**
      Carroll Arnett 41–42
      Claiming Breath (Glancy) 77
      Robert J. Conley 81
      Five Civilized Tribes 118
      Flutie (Glancy) 119
      Diane Glancy 76, 137
      Joy Harjo 157
      Iron Woman (Glancy) 191
      Thomas King 200
      Lone Dog's Winter Count (Glancy) 211
      N. Scott Momaday 235
      Nightland 249–250
      Offering (Glancy) 259

Louis Owens 269
Pushing the Bear (Glancy) 284
(Ado)ration **4–5**
Red Clay (Hogan) 289
removal 295–296
Rollie Lynn Riggs 305
Ralph Salisbury 310–311
Southeastern tribal literature 336
Thirteen Moons on Turtle's Back
    (Bruchac) 360
Trail of Tears 366–367
West Pole, The (Glancy) 392
Cherokee Nation 21, 118, 153
Cherokee Night, The (Riggs) 18–19, 306
Chewing Black Bones (Blackfeet elder)
    342–343
Cheyenne Indians 38, 61, 124, 163, 275, 327,
    346, 362–363
Chickasaw Indians 29, 118, 167, 289, 336,
    366
child abuse 99, 106, 113
children 108, 117, 141
children's literature. *See* American Indian
    children's literature
China 152–153
Chippewa Indians
    American Indian novel 29
    Antelope Wife, The (Erdrich) **37**
    Baptism of Desire (Erdrich) 49
    Beet Queen, The (Erdrich) 51
    Crown of Columbus, The (Erdrich) 84
    Dawes Act, The 91
    gaming 128
    Love Medicine (Erdrich) 215–216
    Tales of Burning Love (Erdrich) 353
    Touchwood (Vizenor) 362, 363–364
    trickster figures 371
Choctaw Indians
    Bad Medicine (Querry) 48
    Jim Barnes 49
    Bone Game (Owens) 64
    Five Civilized Tribes 118
    government agencies 147
    Roberta Hill 165
    LeAnne Howe 174
    Louis Owens 89, 269, 270
    Ron Querry 285
    removal 296
    Roads of My Relations, The (Mihesuah)
        306–307
    Sharpest Sight, The (Owens) 316–317
    Shell Shaker (Howe) 318–319
    Southeastern tribal literature 336
    Trail of Tears 366
Christal. *See* Mourning Dove
Christianity
    American Indian novel 27
    William Apess 39, 40
    assimilation 43
    Black Elk 58
    Closets of Heaven, The (Glancy) 79
    Vine Deloria, Jr. 96

Dry Lips Oughta Move to Kapuskasing
    (Highway) 102
Charles Alexander Eastman 106–108
First Nations literature 116, 117
Fuller Man (Glancy) 126–127
Gardens in the Dunes (Silko) 132
Ghost Dance 136
God Is Red (Deloria, Jr.) 139–140
Green Grass, Running Water (King)
    149–151
missionaries 230
Samson Occom 257
(Ado)ration 4–5
Red Clay (Hogan) 290
"Sermon Preached by Samson Occom"
    314
Son of the Forest, A (Apess) 334
spirituality 343–345
Sun Is Not Merciful, The (Walters) 350
Touchwood (Vizenor) 363
trickster figures 371
Voice That Was in Travel, The (Glancy)
    380
We Are the Dreamers (Joe) 388
Wynema (Callahan) 407–408
Zitkala-Ša 413
chronological narrative style (writing)
    183–184
Chrystos **76**, 254–255
Chumash Indians 229–230
Circle of Dancers (Cook-Lynn) 45, 83
citizenship 43, 71, 91, 116
civilization policy 118
Civil War, U.S. 94
Claiming Breath (Glancy) **76–77,** 138, 211
Clans of Many Nations (Blue Cloud) 59–60
Clark, Ella E. 342–343
Clements, Susan **77–78**
Clinton, Bill 323
Close to Home (Tremblay) **78–79**
Closets of Heaven, The (Glancy) **79**
Cloud Chamber (Dorris) 99, 409
Code Talkers (World War II) 206, 362
Coeur d'Alene Indians 10, 29, 155, 219, 273,
    274, 403
Cogewea, the Half-Blood (Mourning Dove)
    27, **79–80,** 239, 240, 372
colonialism (colonization)
    Bone Dance (Rose) 63
    Chrystos 76
    Robert J. Conley 82
    Fight Back (Ortiz) 114
    First Nations literature 116, 118
    God Is Red (Deloria, Jr.) 140
    Going to War with All My Relatives
        (Rose) 142
    Lanson Henson 164
    Tomson Highway 164
    Iron Woman (Glancy) 191
    Jacklight (Erdrich) 192
    Northeastern tribal literature 252
    Relief of America (Glancy) 292

Sacred Hoop, The (Allen) 310
Shell Shaker (Howe) 318
Leslie Marmon Silko 320, 321
Slash 325
trickster figures 370, 371
Truth & Bright Water (King) 374
Robert Allen Warrior 384
Wolfsong (Owen) 400
Columbus, Christopher 238, 292, 370, 378
Comanche Indians 61, 275
coming-of-age stories 28, 98, 101, 121, 167,
    169–170
community, tribal
    All My Relations (King) 14
    Aurelia (Cook-Lynn) 45
    Boy Who Lived with the Bears, The
        (Bruchac) 66
    Claiming Breath (Glancy) 77
    Dancing Teepees (Sneve) 89
    Dead Voices (Vizenor) 93
    Drowning in Fire (Womack) 101
    Earth Song, Sky Spirit (Trafzer) 106
    Karen Louise Erdrich 111
    First Nations literature 116
    Hanay Geiogamah 122
    spirituality 343–344
    Luci Tapahonso 68
    Termination 357–358
    Tribal Secrets (Warrior) 369
Completing the Circle (Sneve) **80–81,** 329
Congress, U.S. 368
Conley, Robert J. **81–82,** 332, 366
conservationism 53, 143
Constitution, U. S. 252, 292
Cook-Lynn, Elizabeth **82–83**
    American Indian novel 29
    Aurelia 29, **45–46,** 83
    From the River's Edge 29, 45, 83, **126**
    I Remember the Fallen Trees **190**
    Plains tribes literature 277
    Power of Horse and Other Stories, The
        82, **281–282**
    sovereignty 340
    Wounded Knee Massacre 406
Copway, George 116, 230, 266, 363
Corn Mother (mythic figure) 337
corruption 15, 91, 136
Coyote (trickster figure)
    All My Relations (King) 14
    California tribal literature 72
    Earth Power Coming (Ortiz) 105
    Going for the Rain (Ortiz) 141
    Green Grass, Running Water (King)
        149–151
    Indian Singing in 20th Century (Tremblay) 182
    In Mad Love and War (Harjo) 185
    Thomas King 201
    Storyteller 347
    Through the Eye of the Deer (Dunn)
        361
    trickster figures 370–372

Wild Indians and Other Creatures (Louis) 395
Coyote Stories (Mourning Dove) 239, 240
Crazy Dave (Johnston) **84**
Crazy Horse 262, 276
creation myths 342–345
Cree Indians 22, 23, 87, 164, 210–211, 220, 398–399
Creek Indians
    American Indian children's literature 16
    American Indian novel 27
    American Indian poetry 31
    Conley, Robert J. 82
    Drowning in Fire (Womack) 101
    Five Civilized Tribes 118, 119
    Joy Harjo 157, 158
    Oklahoma tribal literature 260
    Alexander Posey 278
    Red on Red (Womack) 291
    removal 296
    Southeastern tribal literature 336–337
    Trail of Tears 366
    What Moon Drove Me to This? (Harjo) 392–393
critics, literary
    Paula Gunn Allen 12
    Jeannette C. Armstrong 41
    Carroll Arnett 42
    Gloria Bird 55–56
    Kimberly M. Blaeser 59
    Elizabeth Cook-Lynn 83
    Crown of Columbus, The (Erdrich) 85
    Death of Jim Loney, The (Welch) 95
    gender 135
    Sacred Hoop, The (Allen) 310
    Greg Sarris 312
    sovereignty 340
    Tribal Secrets (Warrior) 369
critics, social 83, 135
Crow Creek Agency 82, 126, 190
Crow Indians 226–227, 275, 346
Crown of Columbus, The (Erdrich and Dorris) **84–86,** 99
cultural appropriation 32, 63, 64, 136, 142
cultural identity 290, 307, 316
culture and life, American Indian. *See also* reservation life
    American Indian children's literature 16–17
    American Indian drama 18
    American Indian Literary Renaissance 24
    American Indian novel 28
    American Indian poetry 31
    American Indian Stories (Zitkala-Ša) 33
    Ancient Child, The (Momaday) 35
    anthropology and Native Americans 38
    Jeannette C. Armstrong 41
    Aurelia (Cook-Lynn) **45–46**
    Aztecas del Norte. The Chicanos of Aztlán (Forbes) 46
    Bearheart (Vizenor) 51

Black Eagle Child (Young Bear) 56, 57
Blue Horses Rush In (Tapahonso) 61
boarding schools 62
Boy Who Lived with the Bears, The (Bruchac) 66
Breath Tricks (Armstrong) 68
Breeze Swept Through, A (Tapahonso) 68–69
Maria Campbell 73
Dawnland (Bruchac) 92
Death of Bernadette Lefthand, The (Querry) 94
Ella Cara Deloria 96
Vine Deloria, Jr. 97
Dry Lips Oughta Move to Kapuskasing (Highway) 102
Enwhisteetkwa—Walk in Water (Armstrong) 109
Karen Louise Erdrich 110
First Nations literature 117
Fools Crow (Welch) 121
gaming 130
Ghost Dance 136
Ghost Singer (Walters) 137
government agencies 146
Grand Avenue (Sarris) 148
Griever (Vizenor) 152
Joy Harjo 157
Harpoon of the Hunter (Markoosie) 159
Lanson Henson 163
Roberta Hill 165
Linda Hogan 167
Indian Singing in 20th Century (Tremblay) 182
Invisible Musician, The (Young Bear) 189
I Remember the Fallen Trees (Cook-Lynn) 190
Thomas King 200
Laguna Woman (Silko) **204–205**
Life Is a Fatal Disease (Allen) 209
Light People, The (Henry) 209
Long Division (Rose) 213
Adrian C. Louis **214–215**
Manifest Manners (Vizenor) 218
D'Arcy McNickle 224
Mourning Dove 80
Native Alaskan tribal literature 243
Neekna and Chemai 245
"Nickel Eclipse" (Gansworth) 249
Nickel Eclipse: Iroquois Moon (Gansworth) 249
Jim Northrup 253
Not Vanishing (Chrystos) 255
Oklahoma tribal literature 260
Old Shirts and New Skins (Alexie) 262
orality 265
Pipe for February, A (Red Corn) 275
Plains tribes literature 277
Power (Hogan) 281
In the Presence of the Sun (Momaday) 188

Ron Querry 285
Reservation, The (Williams) 300, 301
Rollie Lynn Riggs 306
Secrets from the Center of the World (Harjo) 312–313
Leslie Marmon Silko 75
Smoke Signals 327
Sound of Rattles and Clappers, The (Sarris) 335
Southeastern tribal literature 337
Southwestern tribal literature 337–339
Spider Woman's Granddaughters (Allen) 342
spirituality 342–345
Storyteller 346
Storyteller (Silko) 346
Surrounded, The (McNickle) 352
Tales of Burning Love (Erdrich) 353
Toughest Indian in the World, The (Alexie) 364–365
trickster figures 370
E. Donald Two-Rivers 375
Voice That Was in Travel, The 381
Way to Rainy Mountain, The (Momaday) 387
Wild Indians and Other Creatures (Louis) 395
Woven Stone (Ortiz) 407
cummings, e. e. 90, 100
Cushing, Frank 38
Custer, George Armstrong 262
Custer Died for Your Sins (Deloria, Jr.) 38, **86,** 97, 176
Cuthand, Beth **87,** 171, 210–211

D

Dakota Indians 149, 211, 266
Dakota language 96, 106
Dakota Sioux Indians 45, 82
Dakota Territory 404–406
dams 126, 190, 279
dance 18, 58, 121, 150, 282, 350–351. *See also* Ghost Dance
Dance Me Outside (film) **88–89**
Dances with Wolves (film) 20
Dancing Teepees (Sneve) **89**
D'Aponte, Mimi 314–315
Darkness in St. Louis Bearheart, The (Vizenor). *See Bearheart* (Vizenor)
Dark River (Owens) **89–90,** 376
Dartmouth College 110, 258, 290
Dauenhauer, Nora Marks 23, **90–91,** 100, 288
Dawes Act, The **91**
    American Indian novel 27
    assimilation 43
    Karen Louise Erdrich 110
    Faces in the Moon (Bell) 113
    Four Souls (Erdrich) 123
    Love Medicine (Erdrich) 216

D'Arcy McNickle 224
Alexander Posey 278
reservation life 298
Sundown 349–350
Surrounded, The 351
Tracks (Erdrich) 365
Dawnland (Bruchac) **91–92,** 386
Dead Voices (Vizenor) **92–93**
death 35–36, 94
Death at Rainy Mountain (Medawar)
   93–94, 226
Death of Bernadette Lefthand, The (Querry)
   94–95, 285
Death of Jim Loney, The (Welch) **95,** 233,
   277, 299, 344, 390, 391
Deloria, Ella Cara **95–96,** 384–386
Deloria, Vine, Jr. 86, **96–98**
   anthropology and Native Americans 38
   God Is Red (Deloria, Jr.) **139–140,** 344
   humor 176
   Storm Hyemeyohsts 346
   spirituality 344
   Tribal Secrets (Warrior) 369
   Wordcraft Circle Writer of the Year
      Award 98
DeMaille, Raymond J. 58, 384
devil 350–351
Devils Tower 36, 187
Diane Decorah Awards 55, 229
Dick Cavett Show (television show) 58, 97
diet pepsi & nacho cheese (northSun) 44,
   254
Diné Indians. *See* Navajo (Diné) Indians
directors 20–21
discrimination 298, 325. *See also* prejudice
disease 48, 68, 122, 366
disenfranchisement 205–206
diversity 210–211
divine beings 370, 371
documentation 22–23
Doe Boy, The (film) 21, **98–99**
domestic violence 52, 66, 155, 194
Dorris, Michael **99–100**
   alcoholism 8
   American Indian children's literature
      16, 17
   Crown of Columbus, The (Erdrich) 84
   Karen Louise Erdrich 110
   Morning Girl **238–239**
   In the Time of the Present (Kenny) 189
   Yellow Raft in Blue Water, A 99,
      409–410
Dream On (Chrystos) 31
dreams 79, 102, 106, 136, 179, 189
drinking. *See* alcoholism
Droning Shaman, The (Dauenhauer) 23,
   90, **100**
Drowning in Fire (Womack) **101,** 401
drug abuse 34, 73, 198, 298
Dry Lips Oughta Move to Kapuskasing
   (Highway) 19, **101–102,** 164, 303, 371

E

Eagle Nation, An (Revard) **103–104,** 302
eagles 103–104
Earthdivers (Vizenor) **104,** 233
Earth Power Coming (Ortiz) **104–105**
Earth Song, Sky Spirit (Trafzer) **105–106**
Eastern Band Cherokee 226–227
Eastman, Charles Alexander **106–108**
   From the Deep Woods to Civilization
      107, 276, 341
   government agencies 147
   missionaries 230
   My People, the Sioux (Standing Bear)
      241
   orality 266
   Plains tribes literature 276
   Singing Spirit, The (Peyer) 323
   Soul of the Indian, The 107–108, 230
   sovereignty 341
Eclipse (Hogan) **108–109**
education 23, 33, 61–62. *See also* boarding
   schools
Education of Little Tree, The (Carter) 16, 337
En'owkin International School of Writing
   41, 221
environmental issues 41, 50, 139, 167, 336,
   400–401, 404
Enwhisteetkwa—Walk in Water (Armstrong)
   109–110, 245
epidemics 243, 365
Erdrich, Karen Louise **110–112.** *See also*
   Dorris, Michael; *Love Medicine*
   alcoholism 7, 8
   American Indian children's literature 16
   American Indian Movement 26
   American Indian novel 28, 29
   Antelope Wife, The **37**
   assimilation 44
   Baptism of Desire **49,** 112
   Beet Queen, The **51–52,** 111, 353
   Bingo Palace, The **54–55,** 110–111, 216,
      353
   Crown of Columbus, The **84–86,** 99
   Dawes Act, The 91
   Four Souls **123**
   gaming 129–130
   government agencies 147
   Jacklight 112, **192–193**
   *Last Report of the Miracles at Little No
      Horse, The* **206–207,** 371
   Little No Horse series 54, 110–111, 123
   missionaries 231
   mixed-blood 233
   Mourning Dove's Stories (Mourning
      Dove) 240
   reservation life 298
   sovereignty 340
   Tales of Burning Love 216, **353–355**
   Touchwood (Vizenor) 363, 364
   Tracks 91, 111, 123, 206, 216, 231, 340,
      365–366

trickster figures 371
Vietnam War 376
erotica 6–7, 49, 76
Esselen Indians 229–230
ethnicity 244, 284, 330, 334, 360
ethnobiography 243, 385
ethnologists 30, 72, 80, 96
Europeans, Pima legend of 370–371
Evers, Larry 168, 339
Eyre, Chris 10, 21, 88, 323–324, 327, 338

F

Faces in the Moon (Bell) 29, **113–114**
Falls-Apart, Lester (fictional character)
   70–71
Family Matters, Tribal Affairs (Revard) 261,
   302
Federal Bureau of Investigation (FBI) 26,
   101–102, 128, 373
feminine sacred 131–133
feminism
   Cannon Between My Knees, A (Allen) 73
   Gathering of Spirit (Brant) 132
   Catron Grieves 154
   Jailing of Cecelia Capture, The (Hale)
      193
   Winona LaDuke **203–204**
   Lee Maracle 222
   Sacred Hoop, The (Allen) **310**
   Shadow Country (Allen) 315
   Southeastern tribal literature 336
   Southwestern tribal literature 338
fetal alcohol syndrome 8, 99
Fight Back (Ortiz) **114,** 268, 406
film. *See* American Indian film
Fire Water World (Louis) 214, 215
First Indian on the Moon (Alexie) 11, 70,
   114–115
First Nations 67, 88, 325
First Nations literature 14, 67, **115–118,** 332
"First People" (Armstrong) 67–68
fishing rights 100, 279, 368, 404
"Five Arrows" (Clements) 77–78
Five Civilized Tribes 82, **118–119,** 260, 296,
   335, 336, 366
Five Civilized Tribes Museum 19, 118
"Fleur" (Erdrich) 129–130
Flutie (Glancy) **119,** 138
Foghorn (Geiogamah) 19, **120,** 133, 134,
   177, 405
folklore 243, 260, 276
Fond du Lac Reservation 253, 364, 382
Food and Spirits (Brant) 67, **120–121**
Fools Crow (Welch) **121–122,** 344, 386,
   390, 391
Forbes, Jack 46–47, 105
forgiveness 385, 386, 388
Fort Belknap Reservation 95, 299, 389, 390
"For Those Who Have Learned to Speak"
   (Harjo) 157–158

49 (Geiogamah) 19, **122–123,** 133, 134
foster care system 118, 194
Four Souls (Erdrich) 111, **123**
Frazier, Ian 299–300
from Sand Creek (Ortiz) **124–125**
From Spirit to Matter (Sanchez) **125–126**
From the Deep Woods to Civilization (Eastman) 107, 276, 341
From the River's Edge (Cook-Lynn) 29, 45, 83, **126**
full-blood 365–366, 394
Fuller Man (Glancy) **126–127**
fur trade 7, 53
Fus Fixico letters (Posey) 278, 336

G

gaming **128–131**
   American Indian film 21
   Bingo Palace, The (Erdrich) 54
   Dark River (Owens) 89
   Karen Louise Erdrich 110
   Heirs of Columbus, The (Vizenor) 162
   Manifest Manners (Vizenor) 219
   poverty 280
   reservation life 298
Gansworth, Eric **131,** 183–184, 248–249
Gardens in the Dunes (Silko) 62, **131–132,** 136, 321
Gathering of Spirit (Brant) **132–133**
Geiogamah, Hanay **133–135**
   American Indian drama 19
   Body Indian 19, **62–63,** 133, 134, 314–315
   Foghorn 19, 120, **120,** 133, 134, 177, 405
   49 19, **122–123,** 133, 134
   humor 177
   Seventh Generation (D'Aponte) 314–315
   Wounded Knee 405
gender **135–136**
   Beth Brant 67
   Chrystos 76
   Dry Lips Oughta Move to Kapuskasing (Highway) 102
   Eclipse (Hogan) 109
   Food and Spirits (Brant) 120
   Grass Dancer, The (Power) 149
   Jailing of Cecelia Capture, The (Hale) 193
   trickster figures 372
General Allotment Act. *See* Dawes Act, The
genetics 163
genocide 31, 76, 179, 310, 325
Ghost Dance **136**
   Billy Jack 54
   Black Elk 57
   Charles Alexander Eastman 107
   Gardens in the Dunes (Silko) 131, 132
   Good Message of Handsome Lake, The (Bruchac) 144

poverty 279
   Leslie Marmon Silko 321
   Wounded Knee 405
Ghost Singer (Walters) **136–137,** 261, 383
Glancy, Diane **137–139**
   (Ado)ration **4–5**
   Claiming Breath **76–77**
   Closets of Heaven, The **79**
   Flutie **119**
   Fuller Man **126–127**
   Iron Woman **191**
   Lone Dog's Winter Count **211–212**
   Offering **258–259**
   Pushing the Bear 138, **284,** 296, 366, 367
   Relief of America **292–293**
   Removal 296
   Seventh Generation (D'Aponte) 314, 315
   Trail of Tears 366
   Voice That Was in Travel, The **379–380**
   West Pole, The 138, **392**
Godfather, The (film) 244
God Is Red (Deloria, Jr.) **137–140,** 344
Gogisgi. *See* Arnett, Carroll
Going for the Rain (Ortiz) **140–142,** 267, 406
Going to War with All My Relations (Rose) 63–64, **142–143**
gold 53, 279
Good Journey, A (Ortiz) 31, **143,** 267–268, 406
Good Message of Handsome Lake, The (Bruchac) **144**
Gordon, Roxy 19, **144–145,** 174, 315
Gould, Janice **145,** 335
Gourd Dancer, The (Momaday) **146,** 236
government, U.S. 288, 289, 338, 345, 367–368
government agencies 119, 136, **146–148.** *See also* specific headings, e.g.: Bureau of Indian Affairs
Grand Avenue (Sarris) **148–149,** 312, 385
Grass Dancer, The (Power) **149,** 283
Great Awakening 258
Great Plains Indians 121, 188
Great Vision 57–58
Green Grass, Running Water (King) 29, **149–151,** 368, 371, 372
Green Grow the Lilacs (Riggs) 19, **151–152,** 305, 306, 336
Grey, Zane 46–47
Gros Ventre Indians 28, 95, 389
Guggenheim Fellowship 112, 151, 222, 305–306
Guie, Heister Dean 239, 240

H

Hale, Janet Campbell **155–156,** 193, 271–272, 274, 403–404
half-breed 4, 34, 54, 95, 117, 232

Halfbreed (Campbell) 4, 73, 117
Halfbreed Chronicles and Other Poems, The (Rose) 63, **156,** 307–308
Hammerstein, Oscar, II 19, 151, 305, 306, 336
Handbook of American Indian Languages (Boas) 22–23
Hans, Birgit 159–160
Harjo, Joy **156–159**
   alcoholism 8
   American Indian Movement 26
   American Indian poetry 31, 32
   Beth Cuthand 87
   Catron Grieves 154
   In Mad Love and War 31, 157, **185–186**
   Last Song, The **207–208**
   Pacific Northwestern tribal literature 273
   Red on Red (Womack) 291
   Reinventing the Enemy's Language 55, 157, 273–274, **291–292**
   Removal 296
   Secrets from the Center of the World 157, **312–313**
   She Had Some Horses **317–318**
   Leslie Marmon Silko 321
   Southeastern tribal literature 336–337
   What Moon Drove Me to This? 208, **392–393**
   Woman Who Fell from the Sky, The 157, **401–402**
Harold of Orange (film) 376
Harper and Row 248, 387
HarperCollins (publisher) Literary Mosaic Series 243–244
Harpoon of the Hunter (Markoosie) **159**
Hawk Is Hungry and Other Stories, The (McNickle) **159–160**
healing
   American Indian novel 28
   Cannon Between My Knees, A (Allen) 74
   Dawnland (Bruchac) 92
   Fools Crow (Welch) 121
   Grand Avenue (Sarris) 148
   Keeping Slug Woman Alive (Sarris) 198
   Light People, The (Henry) 210
   Long Division: A Tribal History 214
   Night Sky, Morning Star (Lucero) 251
   Reinventing the Enemy's Language (Harjo) 291
   Shadow Country (Allen) 315–316
   She Had Some Horses (Harjo) 317–318
   Ruby Slipperjack-Farrell 325
   Voice That Was in Travel, The 380
   Whispering in Shadows (Armstrong) 394
Heartsong of Charging Elk, The (Welch) 95, **160–161,** 391
Heat-Moon, William Least **161–162**
Heirs of Columbus, The (Vizenor) 128–129, **162–163,** 378
hemophilia 21, 98–99

Henry, Gordon 209–210
Henson, Lanson **163–164,** 406
Highway, Tomson **164–165**
    American Indian drama 19
    American Indian languages 23
    Dry Lips Oughta Move to Kapuskasing
        101–102
    Kiss of the Fur Queen 164–165, **201–
        202,** 231
    missionaries 231
    Rez Sisters, The 19, 23, 164, **303–304**
    trickster figures 371
Hill, Roberta **165–166,** 247
historians 39, 46, 80–81, 96, 412
historical novel 29, 147, 162–163, 196–197
history, tribal 243, 276, 309, 313
Hobson, Geary 23, 42, **166–167,** 205–206,
    293, 333
Hogan, Linda **167–168**
    American Indian novel 29
    American Indian poetry 30
    Book of Medicines, The **65**
    Eclipse **108–109**
    Mean Spirit **225–226,** 231
    missionaries 231
    Power 29, **280–281**
    Red Clay **289–290**
    Reinventing the Enemy's Language
        (Harjo) 291
    Seeing Through the Sun 31–32, 167
    Solar Storms 29, 167–168, **331**
    Southeastern tribal literature 336
    Wounds beneath the Flesh (Kenny) 406
Hoka dance 18
Home Places (Zepeda) 23, **168–169**
homosexuality 101, 120, 145, 199, 372, 401.
    See also lesbianism
Honour the Sun (Slipperjack-Farrell)
    169–170, 326
Hopi Indians 18, 48, 307, 339
Hopi Roadrunner Dancing (Rose) 63, **170,**
    307
Horse Dance 18, 58
Horse Dance to Emerald Mountain
    (Cuthand) 87, **171**
horses 281
Hotline Healers (Vizenor) **171–172**
House Made of Dawn (Momaday) **172–173**
    alcoholism 7, 8
    Paula Gunn Allen 12
    American Indian Literary Renaissance
        24
    American Indian novel 28
    American Indian poetry 30
    Angle of Geese and Other Poems (Mo-
        maday) 36
    assimilation 44
    government agencies 147
    missionaries 230–231
    mixed-blood 233
    Scott N. Momaday 235
    Oklahoma tribal literature 260

orality 266
reservation life 298
Song of the Turtle (Allen) 332
sovereignty 341
trickster figures 371
Voice of the Turtle (Allen) 379–380
Way to Rainy Mountain, The (Moma-
    day) 387
James Welch 390
Winter in the Blood (Welch) 398, 399
Howbah Indians (Ortiz) **173–174,** 228, 268
Howe, LeAnne 144, **174–175,** 315, 318–319
Hozho (Allen and Anderson, eds.) **175–176**
Humishuma. See Mourning Dove
humor **176–178**
    Sherman Alexie 9–10
    American Indian film 21
    American Indian novel 28
    Ancient Acid Flashes Back (Louis) 34
    Breeze Swept Through, A (Tapahonso)
        69
    Earth Song, Sky Spirit (Trafzer) 106
    Hanay Geiogamah 134
    God Is Red (Deloria, Jr.) 139–140
    Heirs of Columbus, The (Vizenor) 163
    Hotline Healers (Vizenor) 172
    Hozho (Allen) 175
    Kiss of the Fur Queen (Highway) 202
    Life Is a Fatal Disease (Allen) 209
    Adrian C. Louis 214
    Love Medicine (Erdrich) 216
    Manifest Manners (Vizenor) 218
    Mardi Oakley Medawar 226
    Medicine River (King) 227
    Men on the Moon (Ortiz) 229
    Neon Powwow (Walters) 246
    One Good Story, That One (King)
        262–263
    reservation life 299
    Sáanii Dahataal (Tapahonso) 309
    Skins and Bones (Allen) 324
    Smoke Signals 328
    Clifford E. Trafzer 60
    Winter in the Blood (Welch) 398–399
hunting 78, 95, 98, 106, 166, 185, 279
hybridity 62, 78, 89, 107, 119, 192, 200

I

imperialism 37–38, 41, 46
Indian Act (Canada) 117, 195, 200
Indian Killer (Alexie) 29, **179–180,** 233
Indian Lawyer, The (Welch) 95, **180–181,**
    390, 391
Indian-ness 51, 93, 113, 134, 176, 193
Indian policy, U.S. *See also* Assimilation; Re-
    location; Removal; Termination
    allotments 43, 113, 216, 341, 349–350,
        365
    American Indian novel 27, 29
    American Indian poetry 30

American Indian Stories (Zitkala-Ša) 33
anthropology and Native Americans 38
Aztecas del Norte. The Chicanos of Aztlán
    (Forbes) 46
Susan Clements 77
Completing the Circle (Sneve) 81
Elizabeth Cook-Lynn 83
Dawes Act, The 91
Vine Deloria, Jr. 97
Charles Alexander Eastman 107
From the River's Edge (Cook-Lynn) 126
Gardens in the Dunes (Silko) 131
I Remember the Fallen Trees (Cook-
    Lynn) 190
Josanie's War (Schlesier) 196
Mourning Dove 80
recognition **288–289**
Removal 295
Termination **357–358**
Indian Radio Days (Gordon) 144, 174–175,
    315
Indian Removal Act 295
Indian Reorganization Act (1934) 91, 97,
    224
Indian rights 37, 39, 91, 96, 97, 116, 280
Indian Rights Association 97
Indian School Days (Johnston) **181,** 231
Indian Singing in 20th Century (Tremblay)
    182
Indians of All Tribes 26, 373
Indians' Summer (Nas'naga) **182–183**
Indian Summers (Gansworth) **183–184**
Indian Territory 225, 278, 304, 305, 335,
    336, 366, 394–395. *See also* Oklahoma
Indian Time: A Novel of Western Oklahoma
    (Penoi) **184–185**
indigenous people. *See also* aboriginal
    people
    Almanac of the Dead (Silko) **15**
    anthropology and Native Americans
        37
    Jeannette C. Armstrong 41
    Aurelia (Cook-Lynn) 46
    Aztecas del Norte. The Chicanos of Aztlán
        (Forbes) 46
    Jim Barnes 50
    Bone Game (Owens) 64
    Breath Tricks (Armstrong) 67
    California tribal literature 72
    Beth Cuthand 87
    Fight Back (Ortiz) 114
    First Nations literature 117
    Gardens in the Dunes (Silko) 131
    God Is Red (Deloria, Jr.) 139
    Winona LaDuke 203–204
    sovereignty 339–341
In Mad Love and War (Harjo) 31, 157,
    185–186
Interior Landscapes (Vizenor) **186–187**
In the Bear's House (Momaday) **187,** 237
In the Presence of River Gods (Cook-Lynn)
    45, 83

In the Presence of the Sun (Momaday) 146, **188,** 237
In the Time of the Present (Kenny) **188–189**
Inuit Indians 159, 242
Invisible Musician, The (Young Bear) **189–190,** 411
I Remember the Fallen Trees (Cook-Lynn) **190**
Iron Woman (Glancy) **191**
Iroquois Indians 66, 91, 144, 246–247
isolation theme 403–404

J

Jacklight (Erdrich) 112, **192–193**
Jailing of Cecelia Capture, The (Hale) 155, **193–194,** 274, 403
Jefferson, Thomas 295
Jemez Pueblo Indians 16, 28
Jesus Christ 40, 314, 343, 371, 380
Joe, Rita **194,** 388
Johnson, Emily Pauline **194–195**
Johnson, Robert 296, 299
Johnston, Basil **195–196**
   American Indian languages 23
   Crazy Dave 84
   First Nations literature 117
   Indian School Days **181,** 231
   missionaries 231
   Moose Meat and Wild Rice 84, **237–238**
Josanie's War (Schlesier) **196–197,** 296

K

Keeping Slug Woman Alive (Sarris) **198–199,** 312, 385
Kenny, Maurice **199–200,** 406
   Blackrobe 231
   In the Time of the Present **188–189**
   missionaries 231
   New Voices from the Longhouse (Bruchac) 247
   Northeastern tribal literature 252
   Tekonwatonti/Molly Brant 252, **356**
   Tortured Skins **362–363**
   Wounds beneath the Flesh **406**
Kesey, Ken 244
Killing Custer (Welch) 390, 391
King, Thomas **200–201**
   All My Relations **13–14,** 118
   American Indian novel 29
   Green Grass, Running Water 29, **149– 151,** 368, 371, 372
   Adrian C. Louis 214
   Medicine River 200, **227–228,** 372
   One Good Story, That One **262–263**
   treaties 368
   trickster figures 370–372
   Truth & Bright Water 201, **373–374**
Kingsolver, Barbara 366
Kinsella, W. P. 88

Kiowa Indians
   American Indian Literary Renaissance 24
   American Indian novel 28
   Ancient Child, The (Momaday) **35**
   Angle of Geese and Other Poems (Momaday) 36
   boarding schools 61
   Death at Rainy Mountain (Medawar) 93
   Hanay Geiogamah 133, 134
   Gourd Dancer, The (Momaday) 146
   Indian Time (Penoi) 184
   In the Bear's House (Momaday) 187
   In the Presence of the Sun (Momaday) 188
   Mardi Oakley Medawar **226–227**
   N. Scott Momaday 235
   Oklahoma tribal literature 260
   orality 266
   Way to Rainy Mountain, The (Momaday) **387–388**
Kiss of the Fur Queen (Highway) 164–165, **201–202,** 231
Klallam Indians 247–248
Korean War 174, 201
Koyukon Indians 223, 353, 359
Kunuk, Zacharias 44–45

L

LaDuke, Winona **203–204,** 208–209, 368
Laguna Indians
   Paula Gunn Allen 12
   American Indian novel 28
   reservation life 298
   Carol Lee Sanchez 125, 311
   Leslie Marmon Silko 74, 320
   Southwestern tribal literature 338
   Storyteller **346–347**
   "Yellow Woman" (Silko) 410
Laguna Woman (Silko) 32, **204–205,** 320
Lakota Indians 25, 30, 57–58, 136, 324, 373, 413
Lakota Sioux Indians 5–6
La Mama Experimental Theater Club 19, 133
land encroachment 278–279
Landfill Meditations (Vizenor) **205**
languages. *See* American Indian languages
LaPena, Frank 335
Last of the Ofos (Hobson) 166, **205–206**
Last Report of the Miracles at Little No Horse, The (Erdrich) **206–207,** 371
Last Song, The (Harjo) **207–208**
Last Stand at Little Bighorn (film) 391
Last Standing Woman (LaDuke) **208–209,** 368
Lawrence T. (The One Who Walks) 128–129
leave-us-alone cultural policy 86
legal issues 26, 340, 341
legends. *See also* myths (mythology)

American Indian Literary Renaissance 25
Ancient Child, The (Momaday) 35
Atanarjuat/The Fast Runner 45
Boy Who Lived with the Bears, The (Bruchac) 66
Conley, Robert J. 82
Elizabeth Cook-Lynn 82
gaming 130
In Mad Love and War (Harjo) 185
Basil Johnston 196
lesbianism. *See also* homosexuality
   Paula Gunn Allen 12
   Beth Brant 66–67
   Chrystos 76
   Food and Spirits (Brant) 120
   Janice Gould 145
   Mohawk Trail (Brant) **234–235**
   Not Vanishing (Chrystos) 254
   Shadow Country (Allen) 315
   trickster figures 372
   Craig S. Womack 401
Life among the Paiutes (Winnemucca) 230, 338, 396
Life and Adventures of Joaquin Murieta, the Celebrated California Bandit (Ridge) 304, 336
Life Is a Fatal Disease (Allen) **209**
Lifetime Achievement Award (Native Writers Circle of the Americas) 69, 157, 166
Lifetime Achievement Award for Literature 28, 98
Light People, The (Henry) **209–210**
Lincoln, Kenneth 24, 28, 31, 78–79, 315
linguistics 22, 23, 169
Literary Renaissance, American Indian. *See* American Indian Literary Renaissance
Little Bighorn, Battle of 57, 58, 261, 345
Little Crow's War 208
Little Duck, The/Sikihpis (Cuthand) 23, 87, **210–211**
Little No Horse series (Erdrich) 54, 110–111, 123
Logan, Jake. *See* Smith, Martin Cruz
Lone Dog's Winter Count (Glancy) **211–212**
Lone Ranger and Tonto Fistfight in Heaven, The (Alexie) **212–213**
   alcoholism 8
   Sherman Alexie 9, 11
   American Indian film 21
   humor 176
   Pacific Northwestern tribal literature 273
   poverty 279
   Reservation Blues (Alexie) 296
   Smoke Signals 327
Long Division: A Tribal History (Rose) 63, **213–214**
Longman, Mary 210–211
Lost Copper (Rose) 31, 63, 307
Louis, Adrian C. 34, 147, **214–215,** 279, 323, 338, **395**

love 264, 291, 385, 386
Love Medicine (Erdrich) **215–217**, 353, 365
   alcoholism 7, 8
   American Indian Movement 26
   American Indian novel 28, 29
   assimilation 44
   Karen Louise Erdrich 110, 111
   government agencies 147
   reservation life 298
   Touchwood (Vizenor) 364
   Vietnam War 376
Lucero, Evelina Zuni 250–251
lyricism 142, 173

M

MacArthur Fellowship 321, 412
magical realism 111, 165, 179, 386
Man, the Snake and the Fox, The (film) 196
manifest destiny 124, 131, 140
Manifest Manners (Vizenor) **218–219**, 378
Mankiller, Wilma 36, 367
Man Who Loves Salmon, The (Alexie) **219–220**
Map of Who We Are, The (Smith) **220**
Maracle, Lee **220–222**
   Bent Box **52–53**
   Ravensong **287–288**, 370
   Sojourner's Truth and Other Stories 221, **330–331**
   Sundogs 221, **348–349**, 349
   trickster figures 370
Marias River, Massacre of the 122, 391
Marine Corps, U.S. 253
Mashantucket Pequot Tribal Nation 21
Mashapee Revolt of 1833--1834 40
massacres. *See specific headings, e.g.:*
   Wounded Knee
Mather, Cotton 211
Mathews, John Joseph 27–28, 43, **222**, 232–233, 349–350, 369
matrilineage 12–13
Matrilineal Cycle (TallMountain) **223**
McCurtain, Cole (fictional character) 64–65
McGinnis, Duane. *See* Niatum, Duane
McNickle, D'Arcy **223–225**. *See also Surrounded, The*
   American Indian novel 28
   boarding schools 62
   government agencies 147
   Hawk Is Hungary and Other Stories, The **159–160**
   missionaries 231
   mixed-blood 233
   Native American Literature (Vizenor) 244
   Pacific Northwestern tribal literature 273
   pow wow 282
   reservation life 298
   Runner in the Sun 224, 225, **308**

Singing Spirit, The (Peyer) 322
sovereignty 341
Wind from an Enemy Sky 104–105, 224, 225, 308, 341, **395–396**
McWhorter, Lucullus L. V. 80, 239, 240
Means, Russell 26, 368
Mean Spirit (Hogan) **225–226**, 231
Medawar, Mardi Oakley 93–94, **226–227**
Medicine River (King) 200, **227–228**, 372
memoirs 10, 36, 84, 99, 112, 397–398
memory, selective historical 124, 190
Menominee Indians 76, 149, 254, 357
Meriam Report 62, 91
Meskwaki Indians 29, 189, 410–411
Mestizo Concept, The (Forbes) 46–47
metaphor 138, 141, 144, 172, 179, 186
Methodist Church 39, 333, 334
Métis people 4, 73, 117
Mexican-American identity 46–47
Mexican people 46–47
migrations 46, 73, 77
Mihesuah, Devon 306–307
military veterans 34, 124, 147, 172, 189
Minnesota 80–81
Miranda, Deborah **229–230**
miscegenation 20
missionaries 22, 30, 64, 136, **230–231**, 257, 413
Mississippi Band 203–204
Miwok Indians 72, 307–308, 312
mixed-blood **232–234**. *See also* hybridity
   Absence of Angels, The (Penn) 3
   Kateri Akiwenzie-Damm 6–7
   Almanac of the Dead (Silko) 15
   American Indian drama 18–19
   American Indian film 21
   American Indian novel 27–28
   William Apess 39
   assimilation 43
   Bearheart (Vizenor) 50
   Bone Game (Owens) 64
   California tribal literature 72
   Maria Campbell 73
   Ceremony (Silko) 74
   Chrystos 76
   Claiming Breath (Glancy) 76
   Susan Clements 77
   Cogewea, the Half-Blood (Mourning Dove) 79–80
   Crown of Columbus, The (Erdrich) 85
   Dark River (Owens) 89
   Dead Voices (Vizenor) 92
   Death of Jim Loney, The (Welch) 95
   Doe Boy, The 98–99
   Michael Dorris 99
   Earthdivers (Vizenor) 104
   Karen Louise Erdrich 112
   Faces in the Moon (Bell) 113
   Flutie (Glancy) 119
   Fuller Man (Glancy) 126
   Diane Glancy 137–138

government agencies 147
Griever (Vizenor) 152
Janet Campbell Hale 155
Halfbreed Chronicles and Other Poems, The (Rose) 156
Hawk Is Hungary and Other Stories, The (McNickle) 160
Roberta Hill 165
Linda Hogan 167
Hopi Roadrunner Dancing (Rose) 170
Hotline Healers (Vizenor) 171
Storm Hyemeyohsts 346
Indians' Summer (Nas 'naga) 183
Indian Time (Penoi) 184
Interior Landscapes (Vizenor) 187
Iron Woman (Glancy) 191
Jailing of Cecelia Capture, The (Hale) 193
Emily Pauline Johnson 194, 195
Keeping Slug Woman Alive (Sarris) 198
Thomas King 200
Life Is a Fatal Disease (Allen) 209
Adrian C. Louis 214
Love Medicine (Erdrich) 216
John Joseph Mathews **222**
D'Arcy McNickle 223
Medicine River (King) **227–228**
Native "chic" 245
Duane Niatum 248
Nightland (Owens) 249
Now Poof She Is Gone (Rose) 255
Oklahoma tribal literature 260
Louis Owens 270
Pacific Northwestern tribal literature 273
W. S. Penn 274
Power of Horse and Other Stories, The (Cook-Lynn) 281
Quick Brush of Wings, A (TallMountain) 286
Red Clay (Hogan) 289
Rollie Lynn Riggs 306
Ralph Salisbury 310–311
Carol Lee Sanchez 311
Shadow Country (Allen) 315
Sharpest Sight, The (Owens) 316
Leslie Marmon Silko 320
Singing Spirit, The (Peyer) 323
Southwestern tribal literature 339
Sundown (Mathews) 350
Surrounded, The (McNickle) 351
Tales of Burning Love (Erdrich) 353
Touchwood (Vizenor) 363
Tracks (Erdrich) 365–366
Gerald Vizenor 377, 378
Wild Harvest (Oskison) 394
Wind from an Enemy Sky (McNickle) 395
Yellow Raft in Blue Water, A (Dorris) 409
Modoc Indians 84, 99
Mohawk Indians

Gertrude Bernard 53
Beth Brant 66
First Nations literature 116
Emily Pauline Johnson 194
In the Time of the Present (Kenny) 188
Mohawk Trail (Brant) 234
Northeastern tribal literature 252
sovereignty 339, 340
Sundogs (Maracle) 349
Tekonwatonti/Molly Brant (Kenny) 356
Mohawk language 14, 195, 252
Mohawk Trail (Brant) 67, **234–235,** 372
Mohegan Indians 25, 252, 257–258
Momaday, N. Scott **235–237.** *See also* House
  Made of Dawn
  alcoholism 7, 8
  American Indian children's literature 16
  American Indian Literary Renaissance
    24
  American Indian novel 28
  American Indian poetry 30, 31
  Ancient Child, The **35**
  Angle of Geese and Other Poems **35–36**
  anthropology and Native Americans 39
  assimilation 44
  In the Bear's House **187,** 237
  In the Presence of the Sun 146, **188,** 237
  Going for the Rain (Ortiz) 141
  Gourd Dancer, The **146,** 236
  D'Arcy McNickle 223
  missionaries 230–231
  mixed-blood 233
  Oklahoma tribal literature 260
  orality 266
  Remembered Earth, The (Hobson) 293
  reservation life 298
  Song of the Turtle (Allen) 332
  Songs from This Earth on Turtle's Back
    (Bruchac) 333
  sovereignty 341
  trickster figures 371
  Voice of the Turtle (Allen) 379–380
  Way to Rainy Mountain, The 211, 236,
    266, **387–388**
  James Welch 390
  Winter in the Blood (Welch) 398, 399
Montauk Indians 30, 257
Mooney, James 260, 336
Moose Meat and Wild Rice (Johnston) 84,
  237–238
Moose Meat Point Indian Reserve (Canada)
  237, 238
Morning Girl (Dorris) **238–239**
Mountain Windsong (Conley) 82, 366
Mourning Dove 27, 41, 79–80, 232, **239,**
  240, 372
Mourning Dove (Mourning Dove) **239**
Mourning Dove's Stories (Mourning Dove)
  240
Moyers, Bill 185
multiculturalism
  Paula Gunn Allen 13–14

American Indian children's literature
  16, 17
Robert J. Conley 82
Charles Alexander Eastman 107
From Spirit to Matter (Sanchez) 125
Fuller Man (Glancy) 127
Linda Hogan 167
Keeping Slug Woman Alive (Sarris) 198
Kiss of the Fur Queen (Highway) 201
Map of Who We Are, The (Smith) 220
Carol Lee Sanchez 311
Yellow Raft in Blue Water, A (Dorris)
  409
multilingualism 311
Muskogee (Creek) Indians 185, 207–208,
  260, 401, 407
My People, the Sioux (Standing Bear)
  240–241, 345
mystery novel 180–181
mysticism 35, 277
myths (mythology). *See also* legends
  Ancient Child, The (Momaday) 35
  Antelope Wife, The (Erdrich) 37
  Aurelia (Cook-Lynn) **45–46**
  Bearheart (Vizenor) 51
  Black Elk 58
  Boy Who Lived with the Bears, The
    (Bruchac) 66
  California tribal literature 72
  Ceremony (Silko) 74, 75–76
  Susan Clements 77
  creation myths 342–345
  crisis of myth 75
  Dawnland (Bruchac) 92
  Earthdivers (Vizenor) 104
  Eclipse (Hogan) 109
  Karen Louise Erdrich 112
  First Nations literature 117
  Flutie (Glancy) 119
  Gardens in the Dunes (Silko) 131
  God Is Red (Deloria, Jr.) 140
  Green Grass, Running Water (King)
    149, 150
  Griever (Vizenor) 152
  Horse Dance to Emerald Mountain
    (Cuthand) 171
  Indian Killer (Alexie) 179
  Interior Landscapes (Vizenor) 186
  In Mad Love and War (Harjo) 185
  In the Bear's House (Momaday) 187
  I Remember the Fallen Trees (Cook-
    Lynn) 190
  Jacklight (Erdrich) 192
  Basil Johnston 195
  Thomas King 201
  Mohawk Trail (Brant) 234
  N. Scott Momaday 237
  Native Alaskan tribal literatrue 243
  Pacific Northwestern tribal literature
    273
  Leslie Marmon Silko 75
  Southeastern tribal literature 335–336

trickster figures 370–372
Myths of the Cherokee (Mooney) 260, 336

N

Nanabozo (Anishinabe trickster figure) 210,
  365, 370, 372
Nanook of the North (film) **242**
narrative I (writing) 76–77, 170, 171–172
narrative poems 114–115, 192–193
narrators 111, 148, 169, 183, 198
National Endowment for the Arts 12, 50,
  66–67, 133, 145, 166
nationalism 340, 341
Native Alaskan tribal literature 100, **243**
Native American. *See* American Indian
Native American "chic" 58, 64, **244–245**
Native American Gaming Regulatory Act
  128, 129, 280
Native American Journalists Association
  214, 253
Native American Literature (Vizenor)
  243–244, 260
Native American Renaissance (Lincoln) 24,
  28, 31
Native American scholars 37–39, 46, 82
Native Canadian literature 164–165,
  220–222, 349
Native land 204, 225
Native repatriation movement 137
Native Writers Circle of the Americas 166,
  250, 274, 285
natural environment 114, 128
Naturally Native (film) 21
Navajo (Diné) Indians
  American Indian drama 18
  American Indian languages 23
  American Indian Literary Renaissance
    24, 25
  Angle of Geese and Other Poems (Mo-
    maday) 36
  Bad Medicine (Querry) 48
  Blue Horses Rush In (Tapahonso) 61
  Death of Bernadette Lefthand, The
    (Querry) 94
  Ghost Singer (Walters) 136
  Neon Powwow (Walters) 246
  One More Shiprock Night (Tapahonso)
    263
  reservation life 297
  Sáanii Dahataal (Tapahonso) 309–310
  Leslie Marmon Silko 320–321
  Southwestern tribal literature 338, 339
  Luci Tapahonso 68, 355
  Laura Tohe 361–362
Navajo (Diné) language 23, 69, 355, 361
Navy, U.S. 247
Neekna and Chemai (Armstrong) **245**
Neihardt, John G. 57–58, 276, 310, 343
Neon Powwow (Walters) **246**
New Age 245, 346

New Echota, Treaty of 304, 366
New Voices from the Longhouse (Bruchac) 199, **246–247**
Nez Perce Indians 274, 360, 367
Niatum, Duane **247–248**, 333, 406
Nickel Eclipse (Gansworth) **248–249**
Nightland (Owens) **249–250**, 280
Night Sky, Morning Star (Lucero) **250–251**
nonfiction 161–162, 198, 199, 344, 387–388
No Parole Today (Tohe) **251**, 338, 362
Northeastern tribal literature 144, **252**
Northern Cheyenne reservation 299, 346
Northrup, Jim **252–253**, 363, 364, 382–383
northSun, nila 44, **253–254**, 302, 328–329, 333
Northwest Native American Writers Association 55, 274, 404
Not Vanishing (Chrystos) 76, **254–255**
novels. *See* American Indian novel
Now Poof She Is Gone (Rose) 64, **255–256**

O

O. Henry Award 9, 112
Occom, Samson 25, 230, 252, **257–258**, 313–314
"Occupational Hazards" (Alexie) 114–115
Offering (Glancy) **258–259**
Ogala Sioux Indians 18, 160
oil 29, 225, 275, 279
Ojibwa (Ojibwe, Ojibway) Indians
    American Indian poetry 30
    Antelope Wife, The (Erdrich) 37
    Gertrude Bernard 53
    George Copeway 266
    Karen Louise Erdrich 110
    First Nations literature 116, 117
    Four Souls (Erdrich) 123
    Heirs of Columbus, The (Vizenor) 162
    humor 177
    Last Report of the Miracles at Little No Horse, The (Erdrich) 206–207
    mixed-blood 233
    orality 266
    Rez Sisters, The (Highway) 303
    Ruby Slipperjack-Farrell 325–326
    Touchwood (Vizenor) 363–364
    E. Donald Two-Rivers 374–375
    William Warren 266
Ojibway Tales (Johnston). *See Moose Meat and Wild Rice* (Johnston)
Ojibwe (Ojibwa) language 6, 16, 169, 195, 238, 319, 326
Okanagan Indians 109, 245
Oklahoma. *See also* Indian territory
    American Indian drama 18–19
    American Indian film 21
    Conley, Robert J. 82
    Dawes Act, The 91
    Drowning in Fire (Womack) 101
    Eclipse (Hogan) 108

Five Civilized Tribes 118
Hanay Geiogamah 133
Green Grow the Lilacs (Riggs) 151
Pipe for February, A (Red Corn) 275
Alexander Posey 278
Pushing the Bear (Glancy) **284**
Red Clay (Hogan) 289
Red on Red (Womack) 291
removal 295
John Rollin Ridge 304
Rollie Lynn Riggs 305
Roads of My Relations, The (Mihesuah) 306–307
Southeastern tribal literature 335, 336
Sundown (Mathews) 349
Sun Is Not Merciful, The (Walters) 350
Trail of Tears 367
Way to Rainy Mountain, The (Momaday) 387
Oklahoma! (musical) 19, 151–152, 305, 306, 336
Oklahoma Book Award 50, 103, 157, 302, 397, 401
Oklahoma tribal literature **259–261**
Old Shirts and New Skins (Alexie) 11, **261–262**, 347
One Good Story, That One (King) **262–263**
One More Shiprock Night (Tapahonso) **263–264**
One Stick Song (Alexie) **264**
On the Rez (Frazier) 299–300
opas (owl-men emblems of witchery) 306–307
orality **264–267**. *See also* storytelling
    Paula Gunn Allen 12
    All My Relations (King) 13–14
    American Indian children's literature 17
    American Indian languages 23
    American Indian Literary Renaissance 25
    American Indian novel 29
    American Indian poetry 30
    assimilation 44
    Black Elk 57–58
    Blue Horses Rush In (Tapahonso) 61
    Boy Who Lived with the Bears, The (Bruchac) 66
    Breath Tricks (Armstrong) 67
    California tribal literature 72
    Dark River (Owens) 89
    Nora Marks Dauenhauer 90
    Dawnland (Bruchac) 91
    Earthdivers (Vizenor) 104
    Earth Power Coming (Ortiz) 105
    Fight Back (Ortiz) 114
    First Nations literature 115, 117
    gender 135
    Good Message of Handsome Lake, The (Bruchac) 144
    Green Grass, Running Water (King) 150
    Harpoon of the Hunter (Markoosie) 159
    Home Places (Zepeda) 168

Hozho (Allen) 175
Keeping Slug Woman Alive (Sarris) 198
Thomas King 200–201
Native Alaskan tribal literatrue 243
Oklahoma tribal literature 259–260
Simon Ortiz 268
Plains tribes literature 275–276
Súunii Dahataal (Tapahonso) 309
Sacred Hoop, The (Allen) 310
Ruby Slipperjack-Farrell 325
snake in her mouth, a (northSun) 329
Southeastern tribal literature 335
Southwestern tribal literature 338
sovereignty 340
Sundogs (Maracle) 348
Tales of Burning Love (Erdrich) 353
Clifford E. Trafzer 105
Winter of the Salamander (Young Bear) 399
oratory 39, 40
Order of Canada 53, 165, 194, 200
Ortiz, Simon **267–269**
    After and Before the Lightning **5–6**
    American Indian poetry 31
    Earth Power Coming **104–105**
    Fight Back **114**, 268, 406
    Fightin' 228
    from Sand Creek **124–125**
    Going for the Rain **140–142**, 267, 406
    Good Journey, A 31, **143**, 267–268, 406
    Howbah Indians 173, **173–174**, 228, 268
    Last of the Ofos (Hobson) 206
    Men on the Moon **228–229**, 268
    New Voices from the Longhouse (Bruchac) **246–247**
    Songs from This Earth on Turtle's Back (Bruchac) 333
    Southwestern tribal literature 338
    trickster figures 371
    Vietnam War 376
    Wounds beneath the Flesh (Kenny) 406
    Woven Stone 267, **406–407**
Osage Indians
    American Indian novel 27–29
    Dawes Act, The 91
    Eagle Nation, An (Revard) 103
    John Joseph Mathews **222**
    Mean Spirit (Hogan) **225–226**
    W. S. Penn 274
    Pipe for February, A (Red Corn) **275**
    Charles Red Corn **290**
    Carter Revard **302–303**
    Sundown 349
    Sundown (Mathews) 350
    Tribal Secrets (Warrior) 369
    Robert Allen Warrior 383
    Winning the Dust Bowl (Revard) 397
"Oshkiwiinag" (Vizenor) 60–61
Oskison, John Milton 336, 394–395
Ota Kte (Plenty Kill). *See* Standing Bear, Luther
Owens, Louis **269–271**

Bone Game **64–65,** 270
Dark River **89–90,** 376
government agencies 147
House Made of Dawn (Momaday) 173
*Lone Ranger and Tonto Fistfight in
   Heaven, The* (Alexie) 213
Nightland **249–250,** 280
poverty 280
Sharpest Sight, The 64, 65, 147, **316–
   317,** 376
Southeastern tribal literature 337
Vietnam War 376
Wolfsong 270, **400–401**
Yellow Raft in Blue Water, A (Dorris)
   409
Owl's Song, The (Hale) 155, **271–272**

P

Pacific Northwestern tribal literature 90,
   273–274
Pacific Northwest Indians 219, 248
pacifism 54, 142
Paiute Indians 136, 144, 338, 407
pan-Indian movement 38, 62, 107, 117,
   183, 307
partial assimilation 43–44
patriarchy (European) 287, 348, 349
patriotism 40
Paul, Moses 313–314
Pawnee Indians 18, 383
Peltier, Leonard 26, 373
PEN/Hemingway Award 9, 212
Penn, W. S. (William Swain) 3–4, **274–275,**
   360–361
petroglyphs 25
Peyer, Bernd C. 322–323
photographs 177–178
physicians 106–108
pictographs 211
Pima legend 370–371
Pine Ridge Reservation
   Black Elk 57
   Vine Deloria, Jr. 96
   Charles Alexander Eastman 107
   Adrian C. Louis 214
   reservation life 299
   Skins 323, 324
   Wounded Knee 404–406
   Zitkala-Ša (Gertrude Simmons Bon-
      nin) 413
Pipe for February, A (Red Corn) 29, **275,** 290
Plains tribes literature 110, 160–161, 171,
   241, **275–278**
plays. *See* American Indian drama
Plenty Kill 240, 241
Pocahontas 324
poetry. *See* American Indian poetry
politics
   Ancient Acid Flashes Back (Louis) 34
   Jeannette C. Armstrong 41

Aurelia (Cook-Lynn) **45–46**
Breath Tricks (Armstrong) 67
Elizabeth Cook-Lynn 83
Crazy Dave (Johnston) 84
Death at Rainy Mountain (Medawar) 93
Going for the Rain (Ortiz) 140–141
I Remember the Fallen Trees (Cook-
   Lynn) 190
Mean Spirit (Hogan) **225–226**
Red on Red (Womack) 291
Returning the Gift (Bruchac) 302
Wendy Rose 307
Greg Sarris 312
sovereignty 339–341
Sundogs (Maracle) 348
Pomo Indians 198, 312
Posey, Alexander 119, 214, **278,** 336
postindian 28, 218
poverty **278–280**
   alcoholism 7
   Vine Deloria, Jr. 97
   gaming 128
   Grand Avenue (Sarris) 148
   Howbah Indians (Ortiz) 174
   I Remember the Fallen Trees (Cook-
      Lynn) 190
   Adrian C. Louis 215
   nila northSun 254
   Remnants of the First Earth (Young
      Bear) 294
   reservation life 298
   Rez Sisters, The (Highway) 303
   Southwestern tribal literature 338
   Wild Indians and Other Creatures
      (Louis) 395
Power (Hogan) 29, **280–281**
Power, Susan 149, 283, 332
Power of Horse and Other Stories, The
   (Cook-Lynn) 82, **281–282**
pow wow **282–283**
   Howard Adams 4
   Eagle Nation, An (Revard) 103
   Hanay Geiogamah 134
   Catron Grieves 154
   Native "chic" 244
   Night Sky, Morning Star (Lucero) 251
   reservation life 299
   Sun Is Not Merciful, The (Walters) 350
   Ray A. Young Bear 410
Powwow Highway (film) 147, **283–284,** 328
Pratt, Richard Henry 61–62, 251
prejudice. *See also* discrimination; racism;
   stereotypes
   Aztecas del Norte. The Chicanos of Aztlán
      (Forbes) 46–47
   Cogewea, the Half-Blood (Mourning
      Dove) 79–80
   Elizabeth Cook-Lynn 83
   Dry Lips Oughta Move to Kapuskasing
      (Highway) 101–102
   government agencies 147
   Janet Campbell Hale 155

Howbah Indians (Ortiz) 174
Mourning Dove's Stories (Mourning
   Dove) 240
Sundogs (Maracle) 348
printed word 25–26
prose
   Black Eagle Child (Young Bear) 56
   Claiming Breath (Glancy) 76–77
   Susan Clements 77–78
   Elizabeth Cook-Lynn 83
   from Sand Creek (Ortiz) 124
   Roxy Gordon 145
   Catron Grieves 154
   Joy Harjo 157
   In the Bear's House (Momaday) 187
   Emily Pauline Johnson 194–195
prose poetry 114–115, 171
prostitution 73, 148
publishers 17, 26, 27, 84, 199, 247, 387
Pueblo Indians 38, 94, 326, 338
Pueblo Revolt of 1680 114
Pulitzer Prize. *See also House Made of Dawn*
   American Indian Literary Renaissance
      24
   American Indian novel 28
   American Indian poetry 30
   Blackrobe (Kenny) 231
   Green Grow the Lilacs (Riggs) 151
   Jailing of Cecelia Capture, The (Hale)
      274
   Kenny Maurice 199
   N. Scott Momaday 235
   Oklahoma tribal literature 260
Pushcart Prize 112, 124, 321, 354, 358
Pushing the Bear (Glancy) 138, **284,** 296,
   366, 367
Puyallup fishermen raid 97
Pyramid Lake War 396

Q

Querry, Ron 48, 94–95, **285–286**
Quick Brush of Wings, A (TallMountain)
   286
Quintasket, Christine. *See* Mourning Dove

R

Rabbit (trickster figure) 182, 185
racism. *See also* discrimination; prejudice;
   stereotypes
   Howard Adams 4
   American Indian novel 27
   William Apess 40
   Jeannette C. Armstrong 41
   Aurelia (Cook-Lynn) 46
   Bearheart (Vizenor) 50
   Beth Brant 67
   Chrystos 76
   Dark River (Owens) 89

Drowning in Fire (Womack) 101
Eclipse (Hogan) 109
First Nations literature 117
Green Grass, Running Water (King) 150
Janet Campbell Hale 155
Joy Harjo 157
Storm Hyemeyohsts 346
Indian Killer (Alexie) 179
I Remember the Fallen Trees (Cook-Lynn) 190
Jailing of Cecelia Capture, The (Hale) 193
Life Is a Fatal Disease (Allen) 209
Lone Ranger and Tonto Fistfight in Heaven, The (Alexie) 212–213
Adrian C. Louis 215
Manifest Manners (Vizenor) 218
Lee Maracle 221
Northeastern tribal literature 252
poverty 279
Silent Words (Slipperjack-Farrell) 319
Slash (Armstrong) 325
Sojourner's Truth and Other Stories (Maracle) 330
Son of the Forest, A (Apess) 334
Sundogs (Maracle) 348
Ten Little Indians (Alexie) 357
Gerald Vizenor 377
We Are the Dreamers (Joe) 388
"Raisin Eyes" (Tapahonso) 68–69
Raven (trickster figure) 370, 395
Ravensong (Maracle) **287–288,** 370
Raven Tells Stories (Bruchac, ed.) **288**
recognition **288–289**
Red Clay (Hogan) **289–290**
Red Corn, Charles 29, 275, **290**
redemption 92, 127
Red on Red (Womack) 101, **290–291,** 401
Red Power Movement 26, 140–141
Reinventing the Enemy's Language (Harjo and Bird, ed.) 55, 157, 273–274, **291–292**
Relief of America, The (Glancy) **292–293**
religion 5, 46, 50, 139–140, 342–346, 350. *See also* Christianity; Ghost Dance; spirituality
relocation
    American Indian poetry 30
    Completing the Circle (Sneve) 81
    Robert J. Conley 82
    Crazy Dave (Johnston) 84
    House Made of Dawn (Momaday) 173
    Indian Singing in 20th Century (Tremblay) 182
    Jailing of Cecelia Capture, The (Hale) 193
    Reinventing the Enemy's Language (Harjo) 291
    Removal 295
    snake in her mouth, a (northSun) 329
    Southwestern tribal literature 339
    Trail of Tears **366–367**
Remembered Earth, The (Hobson) 166, **293,** 333

Remnants of the First Earth (Young Bear) **294–295**
Removal **295–296**
    Five Civilized Tribes 118
    Manypenny George W. 295
    Diane Glancy 138
    Joy Harjo 158
    Jacklight (Erdrich) 192–193
    Josanie's War (Schlesier) 196
    Pushing the Bear (Glancy) **284**
    John Rollin Ridge 304
    Sáanii Dahataal (Tapahonso) 309
    Trail of Tears 366–367
renewal 332, 402, 410
Reservation, The (Williams) **300–301**
Reservation Blues (Alexie) 8, 9, 29, 212, 231, **296–297,** 299
reservation life **297–300**
    Sherman Alexie 9
    assimilation 43
    Bad Medicine (Querry) 48
    Kimberly M. Blaeser 59
    Business of Fancydancing, The (Alexie) 70
    Crazy Dave (Johnston) 84
    Death of Jim Loney, The (Welch) 95
    Earth Song, Sky Spirit (Trafzer) 106
    First Nations literature 116–117
    gaming 130
    Hawk Is Hungary and Other Stories, The (McNickle) 160
    Heartsong of Charging Elk, The (Welch) 160
    Indian Summers (Gansworth) 183–184
    Jailing of Cecelia Capture, The (Hale) 193
    Adrian C. Louis 215
    Medicine River (King) 228
    Offering (Glancy) 259
    Old Shirts and New Skins (Alexie) 261, 262
    Ron Querry 285
    Reservation, The (Williams) **300–301**
    Rez Sisters, The (Highway) 303
    Surrounded, The (McNickle) 351
    termination 358
resistance 43, 117, 118, 179, 196, 388
resurrection 79, 136
Returning the Gift (Bruchac) **301–302**
Revard, Carter 103–105, 229, 261, **302–303,** 397–398
revenge 123, 129
Revolutionary War 42, 144
Rez Sisters, The (Highway) 19, 23, 164, **303–304**
Rhodes Scholar 222, 302
Ridge, John Rollin 27, **304–305,** 336
Riggs, Rollie Lynn 18–19, 151–152, 291, **305–306,** 336, 401
rituals 12, 17, 121, 130, 196, 343, 379
Roads of My Relations, The (Mihesuah) **306–307**
Rodgers, Richard 151, 305, 306, 336

Roman Catholic Church 49, 112
Rose, Wendy **307–308**
    American Indian poetry 31
    Bone Dance **63–64**
    Bone Dance (Rose) **63–64**
    Going to War with All My Relations 63–64, **142–143**
    Halfbreed Chronicles, The 63, **156,** 307–308
    Hopi Roadrunner Dancing 63, **170,** 307
    Long Division 63, **213–214**
    Now Poof She Is Gone 64, **255–256**
    Sound of Rattles and Clappers, The (Sarris) 335
    Southwestern tribal literature 339
    Wounded Knee Massacre 405
Runner in the Sun (McNickle) 224, 225, **308**

S

SAA. *See* Society for American Archaeology
Sáanii Dahataal (Tapahonso) **309–310**
Sacred Hoop, The (Allen) 12, 132, 209, 211, **310,** 338
sacred number 337–338
St. Peter Claver's Indian Residential School 181, 195
Salisbury, Ralph **310–311**
Salishan Indians 79, 239
Salish Indians 220, 223, 224, 273, 287, 351, 352
salmon 219, 273
Sanchez, Carol Lee 125–126, **311–312**
Sand Creek Massacre 124, 362–363
Santee Indians 81, 106
Santee Sioux Indians 276, 373
Sarris, Greg 72, 148–149, 198, **312,** 317, 334–335, 385–386
Sasheen Little Feather 244–245
satire 86, 89, 119, 120, 162, 171, 215, 278
Schlesier, Karl H. 196–197
scholars 96, 99, 103, 140, 145
Schoolcraft, Henry Rowe 30, 265
"School Days of an Indian Girl" (Zitkala-Ša) 33, 62, 251
schools. *See* boarding schools
Seals, David 147, 299
Secrets from the Center of the World (Harjo) 157, **312–313**
Seeing Through the Sun (Hogan) 31–32, 167
self-hatred 52, 56, 62–63
self-sufficiency 339, 340, 389
Seminole Indians 118, 128, 366
Seneca Indians 38, 77, 144
"Sermon Preached by Samson Occom" 25, 257, 258, **313–314**
Seventh Generation (D'Aponte) 19, **314–315**
sexism 73, 76, 111, 117, 150, 388
Shadow Country (Allen) 12, **315–316**
shadows 402, 403
shamans 18, 45, 50, 92, 162, 184
shape shifting 370–372, 389

Sharpest Sight, The (Owens) 64, 65, 147, **316–317,** 376

She Had Some Horses (Harjo) **317–318**

Shelley, Percy Bysshe 278, 305

Shell Shaker (Howe) 174, **318–319**

Shoshone Indians 54, 253–254

silence 319, 326

Silent Words (Slipperjack-Farrell) **319,** 326

Silko, Leslie Marmon **320–322.** *See also Ceremony* (Silko)

    alcoholism 7, 8

    Almanac of the Dead **15**

    American Indian novel 28

    American Indian poetry 32

    boarding schools 62

    Gardens in the Dunes 62, **131–132,** 136, 321

    Laguna Woman 32, **204–205,** 320

    D'Arcy McNickle 223

    mixed-blood 233

    N. Scott Momaday 237

    Mourning Dove's Stories (Mourning Dove) 240

    orality 266

    Reinventing the Enemy's Language (Harjo) 291

    Remembered Earth, The (Hobson) 293

    reservation life 298

    Southwestern tribal literature 338–339

    Storyteller 204, **316** 347

    Luci Tapahonso 355

    James Welch 390

    West Pole, The (Glancy) 392

    Wounds beneath the Flesh (Kenny) 406

    "Yellow Woman" 320, **410**

Singing Spirit, The (Peyer) **322–323**

Sioux Indians

    American Indian languages 23

    American Indian Stories (Zitkala-Ša) **32–34**

    Aurelia (Cook-Lynn) 46

    Black Elk 57

    Completing the Circle (Sneve) 81

    Elizabeth Cook-Lynn 82

    From the River's Edge (Cook-Lynn) 126

    My People, the Sioux (Standing Bear) **240–241**

    Plains tribes literature 275, 277

    Power of Horse and Other Stories, The (Cook-Lynn) **281–282**

    Skins 323

    treaties 368

    Waterlily (Deloria) **384–385**

Sitting Bull 136, 405

Six Nations Iroquois Confederacy 252, 292

Skins (film) 147, **323–324**

Skins (Louis) 214, 215, 279, 338

Skins and Bones (Allen) **324**

Slash (Armstrong) 4, 41, 67, **324–325**

Slipperjack-Farrell, Ruby 169–170, 319, **325–326,** 372, 389

small pox 68, 122

Smith, Martin Cruz **326–327,** 332

Smithsonian Institution 38, 136, 137

Smoke Signals (film) 9–10, 21, 88, 175–178, 212, **327–328**

snake in her mouth, a: poems (northSun) 254, **328–329**

Sneve, Virginia Driving Hawk 17, 80, 89, **329–330**

social class 76, 109, 110, 221

social issues 179, 205–206, 324

Society for American Archaeology (SAA) 38–39

Society of American Indians 38, 107, 147

Sojourner's Truth and Other Stories (Maracle) 221, **330–331**

Solar Storms (Hogan) 29, 167–168, **331**

Song of the Turtle (Allen) 12, **331–332,** 379

songs 30, 36, 78, 82, 151–152, 377

Songs from This Earth on Turtle's Back (Bruchac) 69, 91, 247, 301, **332–333**

Son of the Forest, A (Apess) 40, 232, 252, **333–334**

Soul of the Indian, The (Eastman) 107–108, 230

Sound of Rattles and Clappers, The (Sarris) **334–335**

Southeastern tribal literature 119, 158, 260, **335–337**

Southwestern tribal literature 130, 196, **337–339,** 338

sovereignty **339–341**

    Breath Tricks (Armstrong) 68

    Crown of Columbus, The (Erdrich) 85

    Vine Deloria, Jr. 97

    European concepts of 339

    From the River's Edge (Cook-Lynn) 126

    Gardens in the Dunes (Silko) 132

    Heartsong of Charging Elk, The (Welch) 161

    Heirs of Columbus, The (Vizenor) 162–163

    Indians' Summer (Nas 'naga) 183

    Nightland (Owens) 250

    recognition 288

    Charles Red Corn 290

    Red on Red (Womack) 290–291

    Tribal Secrets (Warrior) 369

Speaking for the Generations (Ortiz) 268–269

Spider (Laguna female creator) 402, 403

Spider Woman's Granddaughters (Allen) 12, **341–342**

spirituality **342–345.** *See also* Ghost Dance

    Paula Gunn Allen 12–13

    (Ado)ration **4–5**

    American Indian poetry 31

    Baptism of Desire (Erdrich) 49

    Bone Dance (Rose) 63

    Bone Game (Owens) 64

    Dawnland (Bruchac) 92

    First Nations literature 117

    Food and Spirits (Brant) 120

    49 (Geiogamah) 122

    Fuller Man (Glancy) 127

Gardens in the Dunes (Silko) 131

God Is Red (Deloria, Jr.) 139

Going to War with All My Relatives (Rose) 142

Roberta Hill 165

Indian Killer (Alexie) 179

Indian Time (Penoi) 184

In Mad Love and War (Harjo) 185

I Remember the Fallen Trees (Cook-Lynn) 190

Basil Johnston 195–196

Last Report of the Miracles at Little No Horse, The (Erdrich) 207

Last Song, The (Harjo) **207–208**

Matrilineal Cycle (TallMountain) **223**

Native "chic" 245

Leslie Marmon Silko 75

Skins and Bones (Allen) 324

Ruby Slipperjack-Farrell 325

Sun Is Not Merciful, The (Walters) 350

Anna Lee Walters 383

We Are the Dreamers (Joe) 388

Spokane Indian Reservation 9, 29, 70, 299

Spokane Indians 55, 212–213, 219, 273, 296

Standing Bear, Luther 43, 240–241, 277, **345–346**

Standing Rock Sioux Indians 96, 149, 369

starvation 81, 91, 110

Steinbeck, John 269–270

stereotypes. *See also* prejudice; racism

    Sherman Alexie 10

    All My Relations (King) 14

    American Indian children's literature 15–18

    American Indian film 20, 21

    American Indian poetry 31

    Aniyunwiya/Real Human Beings (Bruchac) 36

    Jeannette C. Armstrong 41

    assimilation 44

    Aztecas del Norte. The Chicanos of Aztlán (Forbes) 46–47

    Bearheart (Vizenor) 50–51

    Gloria Bird 56

    Beth Brant 67

    Ceremony (Silko) 74

    Chrystos 76

    Susan Clements 77

    Dance Me Outside (McDonald, Dir.) 88

    Dark River (Owens) 89

    Dead Voices (Vizenor) 92, 93

    Ella Cara Deloria 96

    Euro-American Indian 332

    Hanay Geiogamah 120

    gender 135

    Going to War with All My Relatives (Rose) 142

    Good Message of Handsome Lake, The (Bruchac) 144

    humor 175–178

    Storm Hyemeyohsts 346

    Interior Landscapes (Vizenor) 186

    Mardi Oakley Medawar 226

Medicine River (King) 228
mixed-blood 232
Mourning Dove 80
Native Alaskan tribal literatrue 243
Native "chic" 244
Old Shirts and New Skins (Alexie) 262
Pacific Northwestern tribal literature
    273
Reservation Blues (Alexie) 297
Rez Sisters, The (Highway) 304
Sacred Hoop, The (Allen) 310
Seventh Generation (D'Aponte)
    314–315
Song of the Turtle (Allen) 332
Son of the Forest, A (Apess) 334
Ten Little Indians (Alexie) 356, 357
Toughest Indian in the World, The
    (Alexie) 364
E. Donald Two-Rivers 375
Walking the Rez Road (Northrup) 382
Wild Harvest (Oskison) 394
Stewart, Michelle Pagni 15–16
Storm, Hyemeyohsts **346**
Storyteller (Silko) 266, 321, 339, **346–347**
storytelling. *See also* orality
    Sherman Alexie 9–10
    American Indian children's literature
        16, 17
    American Indian Literary Renaissance
        25
    Jeannette C. Armstrong 41
    assimilation 44
    Blue Horses Rush In (Tapahonso) 61
    Boy Who Lived with the Bears, The
        (Bruchac) 66
    Breeze Swept Through, A (Tapahonso)
        69
    Joseph Bruchac 69
    California tribal literature 72
    Cogewea, the Half-Blood (Mourning
        Dove) 79
    Crazy Dave (Johnston) 84
    Charles Alexander Eastman 107
    Faces in the Moon (Bell) 113
    Fight Back (Ortiz) 114
    Gardens in the Dunes (Silko) 131
    Going for the Rain (Ortiz) 141
    Good Journey, A (Ortiz) 143
    Catron Grieves 153
    Harpoon of the Hunter (Markoosie) 159
    Lone Dog's Winter Count (Glancy) 211
    *Lone Ranger and Tonto Fistfight in
        Heaven, The* (Alexie) 213
    Lee Maracle 221
    D'Arcy McNickle 225
    Medicine River (King) 227
    Men on the Moon (Ortiz) **228–229**
    Neon Powwow (Walters) 246
    Oklahoma tribal literature 259–260
    One More Shiprock Night (Tapahonso)
        263
    orality 265
    Power of Horse and Other Stories, The
        (Cook-Lynn) 281

Pushing the Bear (Glancy) 284
Reinventing the Enemy's Language
    (Harjo) 291
Shell Shaker (Howe) 318–319
Leslie Marmon Silko 75, 320
Ruby Slipperjack-Farrell 326
Smoke Signals 327
Sojourner's Truth and Other Stories
    (Maracle) 330–331
Spider Woman's Granddaughters (Allen)
    342
Sundogs (Maracle) 348
Surrounded, The (McNickle) 352
Luci Tapahonso 355
"Strange Fruit" (Harjo) 157, 186
Strom, Stephen 157, 313
suicide
    Paula Gunn Allen 12
    Bingo Palace, The (Erdrich) 55
    Susan Clements 77
    Crown of Columbus, The (Erdrich) 86
    Michael Dorris 99
    Karen Louise Erdrich 112
    Harpoon of the Hunter (Markoosie)
        159
    In the Time of the Present (Kenny) 189
    Jailing of Cecelia Capture, The (Hale)
        193
Summer of the Black Widows, The (Alexie)
    32, **347–348**
Sun Dance 121, 150
Sundance Film Festival 99, 327
Sundogs (Maracle) 221, **348–349,** 349
Sundown (Mathews) 27–28, 43, 91, 222,
    232–233, **349–350**
Sun Is Not Merciful, The (Walters) **350–351,**
    383
supernatural 343, 347
Supreme Court, U.S. 46, 340
Surrounded, The (McNickle) **351–352**
    American Indian novel 28
    boarding schools 62
    D'Arcy McNickle 224
    missionaries 231
    mixed-blood 233
    Native American Literature (Vizenor)
        244
    Pacific Northwestern tribal literature
        273
    pow wow 282
    reservation life 298
    Runner in the Sun (McNickle) 308
    Wind from and Enemy Sky (McNickle)
        395
Sutton, Catherine Soneegoh 116–117
Swain, William. *See* Penn, W. S.
symbolism 33, 35, 36, 60, 125, 173, 192

T

Tales of Burning Love (Erdrich) 216, **353**
TallMountain, Mary 223, 286, 288, 324,
    353–355, 358–359

Tapahonso, Luci 23, 68–69, 263, 309–310,
    338, **355–356**
Tekahionwake. *See* Johnson, Emily Pauline
Tekonwatonti/Molly Brant (Kenny) 252, **356**
television 88, 213
Ten Little Indians (Alexie) **356–357**
Termination (policy) **357–358**
Then Badger Said This (Cook-Lynn) 82, 277
There Is No Word for Goodbye (TallMoun-
    tain) 354, **358–359**
Thirteen Moons on Turtle's Back (Bruchac)
    359–360
This Is the World (Penn) 274, 360–361
Thomas Builds-the-Fire (fictional character)
    9–10, 21
Through the Eye of the Deer (Dunn and
    Comfort) **361**
Thunderheart (film) 373
tiyospaye (household group) 384–385
Tlingit Indians 23, 90, 100, 243, 288
Tohe, Laura 23, 251, 338, **361–362**
Tohono O'odham Indians 169, 339,
    412–413
Tortured Skins (Kenny) 362–363
Touchwood (Vizenor, ed.) **363–364**
Toughest Indian in the World, The (Alexie) 8,
    340, **364–365**
Tracks (Erdrich) 91, 111, 123, 216, 231, 340,
    365–366
Trafzer, Clifford E. 105–106, 240
Trail of Tears **366–367**
    Claiming Breath (Glancy) 77
    Robert J. Conley 82
    Faces in the Moon (Bell) 113
    Diane Glancy 138
    Nightland (Owens) 249
    Pushing the Bear (Glancy) **284**
    Removal **295–296**
    John Rollin Ridge 304
treaties **367–369**
    Completing the Circle (Sneve) 81
    Elizabeth Cook-Lynn 83
    Custer Died for Your Sins (Deloria, Jr.)
        86
    Vine Deloria, Jr. 97
    From the River's Edge (Cook-Lynn) 126
    Green Grass, Running Water (King) 150
    Thomas King 201
    Lone Dog's Winter Count (Glancy) 211
    missionaries 231
    Slash (Armstrong) 325
    Trail of Tears 366
Tremblay, Gail 78–79, 182
tribal community. *See* community, tribal
tribalism 43, 86, 224
tribal recognition. *See* recognition
Tribal Secrets (Warrior) **369–370,** 383
tribes. *See specific tribe*
trickster figures **370–373**. *See also* Coyote
    All My Relations (King) 14
    American Indian children's literature 17
    American Indian novel 28–29
    assimilation 44
    Bearheart (Vizenor) 50

Peter Blue Cloud 60
Blue Dawn, Red Earth (Trafzer) 60
Bone Game (Owens) 64
Boy Who Lived with the Bears, The
    (Bruchac) 66
Beth Brant 67
Dark River (Owens) 89
Dead Voices (Vizenor) 92
Dry Lips Oughta Move to Kapuskasing
    (Highway) 102
Earthdivers (Vizenor) 104
Earth Power Coming (Ortiz) 105
Karen Louise Erdrich 111
European 342
Hanay Geiogamah 134
Green Grass, Running Water (King)
    149–151
Griever (Vizenor) 152–153
Hotline Healers (Vizenor) 171
humor 176–177
Indian Singing in 20th Century (Trem-
    blay) 182
In Mad Love and War (Harjo) 185
Landfill Meditations (Vizenor) **205**
Light People, The (Henry) 210
Adrian C. Louis 215
Manifest Manners (Vizenor) 218, 219
Medicine River (King) **227–228**
Mourning Dove's Stories (Mourning
    Dove) 240
Rabbit 182, 185
Raven 370, 395
Ravensong (Maracle) 287
Rez Sisters, The (Highway) 303
Skins 323
Spider Woman's Granddaughters
    (Allen) 342
Storyteller (Silko) 347
Gerald Vizenor 377, 378
Weesquachak and the Lost Ones (Slip-
    perjack-Farrell) **389**
Wild Indians and Other Creatures
    (Louis) 395
Trosdon, William. *See* Heat-Moon, Wil-
    liam Least
Trudell, John **373**
Truth & Bright Water (King) 201,
    373–374
Tsoai-talee (Rock Tree Boy). *See* Moma-
    day, N. Scott
Turtle Mountain Chippewa Indians 29,
    110, 215, 364
Tuscarora Indian reservation 300–301
Twain, Mark 232
Two-Rivers, E. Donald **374–375**
two-spirit characters 120

U

unemployment 77, 279
United States. *See* Dawes Act, The; gov-
    ernment agencies; Indian policy, U.S.;
    treaties

V

Vietnam War **376**
    Ancient Acid Flashes Back (Louis) 34
    Billy Jack 54
    from Sand Creek (Ortiz) 124
    government agencies 147
    Geary Hobson 166
    Invisible Musician, The (Young Bear)
        189
    Love Medicine (Erdrich) 217
    Jim Northrup 253
    Woman Who Fell from the Sky, The
        (Harjo) 401, 402
violence
    American Indian novel 27
    Bent Box (Maracle) 52
    Bone Game (Owens) 64
    Book of Medicines, The (Hogan) 65
    Beth Brant 66
    Gathering of Spirit (Brant) 132–133
    Ghost Singer (Walters) 137
    Keeping Slug Woman Alive (Sarris) 198
    Not Vanishing (Chrystos) 254–255
    Slash (Armstrong) 325
    snake in her mouth, a (northSun)
        329
    Woman Who Fell from the Sky, The
        (Harjo) 401, 402
visions 57–58, 136, 156, 162
Vizenor, Gerald **376–378**
    American Indian Movement 26
    American Indian novel 28
    Bearheart 28–29, **50–51**, 377
    Kimberly M. Blaeser 59
    Blue Dawn, Red Earth (Trafzer) 60
    Bone Game (Owens) 64
    Dead Voices **92–93**, 205
    Earthdivers **104**, 233
    gaming 128
    Griever **152**, 152–153
    Heirs of Columbus, The 128–129,
        162–163, 205, 378
    Hotline Healers **171–172**, 205
    Interior Landscapes **186–187**
    Landfill Meditations **205**
    Light People, The (Henry) 209–210
    Manifest Manners **218–219**, 378
    mixed-blood 233
    Native American Literature **243–244**,
        260
    Oklahoma tribal literature 260
    sovereignty 340
    Touchwood **363–364**
    trickster figure 205, 371
Voice of the Turtle (Allen) 12, 331, **379–380**
Voice That Was in Travel, The (Glancy)
    380–381

W

Wagon Burner Theater Troop 174–175
Walking the Rez Road (Northrup) 253,
    382–383

Walters, Anna Lee 136–137, 246, 261,
    350–351, **383**
wanaki game 92–93
War of 1812 334
Warren, William 266, 363
Warrior, Robert Allen 59, 369–370, **383–384**
Waterlily (Deloria) 96, **384–385**, 386
Watermelon Nights (Sarris) 312, **385–386**
water rights 279, 368
Waters Between, The (Bruchac) **386–387**
Way to Rainy Mountain, The (Momaday)
    211, 236, 266, **387–388**
Weesquachak and the Lost Ones (Slipperjack-
    Farrell) 326, 372, **389**
Welch, James **389–392**. *See also Winter in*
    the Blood
    alcoholism 7, 8
    American Indian novel 28
    Death of Jim Loney, The **95**, 233, 277,
        299, 344, 390, 391
    Fools Crow **121–122**, 344, 386, 390, 391
    Heartsong of Charging Elk, The 95,
        160–161, 391
    Indian Lawyer, The 95, **180–181**, 390,
        391
    mixed-blood 233
    Plains tribes literature 277
    reservation life 299, 300
    spirituality 344
    Termination 358
    Waters Between, The (Bruchac) 386
West Pole, The (Glancy) 138, **392**
Westward expansion 124, 131
What Moon Drove Me to This? (Harjo)
    392–393
Whispering in Shadows (Armstrong)
    393–394
White Earth Reservation 58, 203–205, 208,
    363
Whiteman, Roberta Hill. *See* Hill, Roberta
Wicazo Su Review (journal) 55, 83
Wild Harvest (Oskison) **394–395**
Wild Indians and Other Creatures (Louis)
    214, **395**
William A. West Education Medal 325–326
Williams, Ted C. 300–301
Wind from an Enemy Sky (McNickle) 104–
    105, 224, 225, 308, 341, **395–396**
Winnemucca, Sarah 91, 230, 338, **396–397**
Winning the Dust Bowl (Revard) 302,
    397–398
Winter in the Blood (Welch) 7, 28, 277, 299,
    300, 358, 390, **398–399**
Winter of the Salamander (Young Bear)
    399–400, 411
Winters, Yvor 35, 146, 236
Wolfsong (Owens) 270, **400–401**
Womack, Craig S. 101, 290–291, 340, **401**
Woman Who Fell from the Sky, The (Harjo)
    157, **401–402**
Woman Who Owned the Shadows, The
    (Allen) 13, **402–403**
women. *See also* feminism; gender
    American Indian novel 29

Bone Dance (Rose) 64
Breeze Swept Through, A (Tapahonso) 68
Maria Campbell 73
Cannon between My Knees, A (Allen) 74
Completing the Circle (Sneve) 80–81
Dance Me Outside (McDonald, Dir.) 88
Death of Jim Loney, The (Welch) 95
Dry Lips Oughta Move to Kapuskasing (Highway) 101
Earth Song, Sky Spirit (Trafzer) 106
Karen Louise Erdrich 111
Faces in the Moon (Bell) 113
Food and Spirits (Brant) 120–121
gaming 129
Gathering of Spirit (Brant) 132–133
Diane Glancy 138
Going to War with All My Relatives (Rose) 142
Janice Gould 145
Green Grass, Running Water (King) 150
Joy Harjo 157–158
Linda Hogan 167–168
In Mad Love and War (Harjo) 186
Jacklight (Erdrich) 192
Matrilineal Cycle (TallMountain) 223
Northeastern tribal literature 252
Now Poof She Is Gone (Rose) 255–256
One More Shiprock Night (Tapahonso) 263
Reinventing the Enemy's Language (Harjo) 291–292
Sáanii Dahataal (Tapahonso) 309–310
She Had Some Horses (Harjo) 317–318
Skins and Bones (Allen) 324
Sneve, Virginia Driving Hawk 329
Solar Storms (Hogan) 331

Through the Eye of the Deer (Dunn) 361
Whispering in Shawdows (Armstrong) 393–394
Women on the Run (Hale) **403–404**
Woody, Elizabeth **404**
Wordcraft Circle of Native Writers, Authors and Storytellers 226, 270, 302, 311, 362, 401
World War I 222
World War II
   American Indian novel 28
   assimilation 44
   boarding schools 62
   Crazy Dave (Johnston) 84
   House Made of Dawn (Momaday) 172
   Last of the Ofos (Hobson) 206
   Ralph Salisbury 310
   Laura Tohe 362
Wounded Knee **404–406**
   American Indian Movement 26
   Aurelia (Cook-Lynn) 46
   Black Elk 57, 58
   Vine Deloria, Jr. 97
   Dry Lips Oughta Move to Kapuskasing (Highway) 101–102
   Charles Alexander Eastman 107
   Ghost Dance 136
   Good Message of Handsome Lake, The (Bruchac) 144
   Medicine River (King) 228
   Native "chic" 244
   Skins 323
   Luther Standing Bear 345
   treaties 368
   Wynema (Callahan) 408
Wounds beneath the Flesh (Kenny) **406**
Woven Stone (Ortiz) 267, **406–407**

Wovoka 136, 144
Writer of the Year Award (Wordcraft Circle) 226, 270, 311, 401
written traditions 13–14, 67, 90, 105, 115, 159, 168
Wynema (Callahan) 27, 406, **407–408**

Y

Yankton Indians 95, 323
Yaqui Indians 326, 339
Yellow Bird. *See* Ridge, John Rollin
Yellow Raft in Blue Water, A (Dorris) 99, **409–410**
Yellow Robe, William 18, 19
"Yellow Woman" (Silko) 320, 410
Young Bear, Ray A. **410–411**
   American Indian novel 29
   Black Eagle Child 29, **56–57**, 294, 411
   Invisible Musician, The **189–190**, 411
   poverty 279
   Remnants of the First Earth **294–295**
   Vietnam War 376
   Winter of the Salamander **399–400**, 411

Z

Zepeda, Ofelia 168–169, 339, **412–413**
Zitkala-Ša **413–414**
   American Indian poetry 30
   American Indian Stories **32–34**
   boarding schools 62
   Dawes Act, The 91
   My People, the Sioux (Standing Bear) 241
   No Parole Today (Tohe) 251
   Plains tribes literature 276